TRANSNATIONAL LITIGATION:

A Basic Primer

RICHARD H. KREINDLER

OCEANA PUBLICATIONS, INC.

Library of Congress Cataloging–in–Publication Data

Transnational litigation : a basic primer / by Richard H. Kreindler, general editor

p. cm.

Includes bibliographical references.

1. Civil procedure. 2. Civil procedure (International law)
3. Conflict of laws—Civil procedure. I. Title
K2205.4.T74 1997
347'.05—dc21 98-13248
CIP

9780379213942

Table of Contents

FOREWORD

by

The Right Honourable the Lord Howe of Aberavon, C.H., Q.C.,

Former Foreign Secretary & Deputy Prime Minister of the United Kingdom

Oklahoma, Tiananmen, Chernobyl, Intifada, Glasnost, CNN: Increasingly, we all share the same worldwide satellite-borne vocabulary. Trade, travel, tourism, television, technology—all these are competing with each other in the demolition of time and distance. And the most important of these is trade.

In the half century since World War II, politics and technology alike have been boosting rather than obstructing the growth of transnational business. Sometimes the obstacles for trade have been demolished by conscious political decision: in the European Union or in NAFTA, for example. Elsewhere the process has been triggered by near-revolutionary upheaval: with the displacement of Maoism by Deng Xiaoping's "socialist" marketplace, for example, or with the disintegration of the Soviet Empire. In most of the Asia Pacific region, however, it has been (in Keynes' words) the "animal spirits" of the entrepreneur that have been the main driving force for change. The ASEAN institutions have accompanied rather than promoted this explosion of economic activity.

The process continues to accelerate, with cross-frontier investment now growing even faster than trade. Victor Halberstadt has presented some of the facts about this astonishing change. In 1995 the worldwide flow of foreign direct investment reached a record high: investment inflow increased by 40% to an unprecedented US$315 billion, worldwide. Developed countries were the main dynamos (and beneficiaries) of this explosion, themselves investing US$270 billion and receiving US$200 billion in 1995. But this spectacular growth of foreign direct investment in developed countries was accompanied by a huge rise in flows into developing countries as well, amounting in 1995 to US$100 billion.

So we have grown used to the idea of a single world marketplace, not just for goods but for capital and cash as well—whisked across frontiers invisibly and, literally, at the speed of light. We think less often perhaps of the global market- place of law and legal thinking that must accompany the growth in trade and investment. Yet inevitably there has been a corresponding increase in transitional disputes. So, too, the corresponding need for skill and guidance in avoiding and resolving such disputes has grown.

Multinational trade is inevitably multi-jurisdictional. So the choice of jurisdiction, and the ability to implement that choice, becomes increasingly important. Sometimes one has to create what is in effect a unique jurisdiction, through a tailor-made pattern of alternative dispute resolution. Sometimes even, in truly "adventurous" territories, one has almost literally to take one's own law with one.

Legal practitioners need above all a practical approach to transnational disputes. The business of pursuing, or avoiding, litigation with a foreign component involves indispensable legal and procedural trappings and requirements. And that requires practical and practice-oriented experience of the pursuit or avoidance of such disputes. This present work responds to that practical challenge by bringing together for the first time:

- Both the obvious and the inscrutable aspects of transnational civil procedure in a variety of key trading nations and
- The strategic, tactical and practical choices which accompany such procedures.

This emphasis on "choices" reflects a major concern of practicing lawyers, in-house counsel and non-lawyer managerial staff alike, in knowing and anticipating the different paths which the avoidance or pursuit of an international litigation can take at each step of the process. Richard H. Kreindler, by highlighting this concept of choice, does justice not only to the efficient resolution of disputes that are unavoidable but—equally important—to the cost-effective avoidance or cessation of such disputes (and at an early stage wherever that is possible).

This marriage between legal and practical requirements is the central theme and inspiration of *Transnational Litigation: A Basic Primer*, and of the more extensive country-by-country analysis contained in *Transnational Litigation: A Practitioner's Guide*, the two-volume treatise from which it derives. The totality of Richard Kreindler's background and experience, as the Coordinator of Jones Day's Europe/Middle East Dispute Resolution Practice Group, qualifies him ideally to decide exactly what is needed —and all too often missed—by the transnational practitioner. A lawyer who is American educated and trained, French-admitted and who has resided the last six years in Germany, he has had experience not only of these three key jurisdictions, but also of litigation issues in virtually every other region of the global economy. Along the way he has worked with leading litigation practitioners throughout the world and in many cases with the leading authority on the subject in the country in question.

The Primer is given a tight and regimented focus by Kreindler's imposition of a specific order of issues. This approach, as influenced by Kreindler's emphasis on substance, is not predominantly Anglo-American, continental European, or any other legal or business culture. It has been skilfully designed to bridge real or perceived "divides" in approach between and among Common law, Civil law and other legal traditions. The approach manages at the same time to do justice to the significance of the differences which do arise between one jurisdiction and another.

Kreindler's approach is influenced not simply by his transnational litigation experience, but also by his extensive involvement in international arbitration under various bodies of law and rules and with other forms of "alternative dispute resolution". The Primer does not attempt to address the intricacies of international arbitration in or affecting the countries covered. But its design and implementation is ever mindful of the lawyer's and businessman's need to know in advance what advantages and disadvantages a contractual agreement to litigate disputes, as opposed to arbitration, might have in any given case.

To guide the lawyer's and businessman's strategic decisions, the Primer contains a substantive and practical overview of key distinguishing characteristics of the legal system, the structure of the courts, obtaining jurisdiction and choice of forum and the choice of law. Then, service of process domestically to commence a foreign action and service abroad to commence a domestic action receive particular attention. Commencement of suit, summary judgments and equivalent proceedings, and interim and conservatory relief follow next.

Of particular importance to many practitioners are the sections on the taking of witness and documentary evidence domestically in support of foreign actions as well as abroad in support of domestic actions. Here again the concept of tactical and strategic choice underlies each country discussion. Traditionally, far less attention has been paid to admissibility and presentation at the tribunal of evidence taken domestically or abroad. This Primer makes this problem one of its centrepieces before going on to address appeal and review of transnational judgments. The approach then focuses on damages, recognition and enforcement of foreign civil-commercial judgments, settlement and compromise of proceedings, sovereign immunity, and finally costs and fees.

This first edition of the Primer is an excellent companion to the larger Practitioner's Guide, which in its first edition (December 1997) encompasses some 20 countries, including many of the largest trading nations with the most significant litigation issues and developments. It is contemplated that a second edition will appear in the fullness of time, which will include additional such countries, including major trading nations which are not presently represented, along with updates of the current country chapters. Practitioners around the world welcome this skilfully crafted approach addressing a group of practical legal questions, which ever more frequently arise in the course of multinational trade.

London,
March 1998

ACKNOWLEDGMENTS

Transnational Litigation: A Basic Primer posed the stimulating challenge of achieving a different, more comprehensive and more practically oriented guidebook for cross-border litigation. Yet an equally great challenge was crafting such a work in the midst of the daily and hourly demands of a cross-border litigation practice. In this context, from the initial conception of the Primer, to the coordination of some three dozen leading litigators worldwide as Country chapter authors for the companion treatise *Transnational Litigation: A Practitioner's Guide*— the task proved to be a complex, multifaceted and voluminous effort.

This project was buttressed, motivated and assisted along the way by colleagues, assistants and others at Jones Day throughout the world. Partners, associates and staff in the Frankfurt office of Jones Day, notably my colleague Judith L. Holdsworth, provided assistance. Highly reputed litigation specialists outside of my firm provided advice, thereby lending the legitimacy and soundness of their experience to the work. Needless to say, my wife and son exhibited supreme patience and understanding throughout the conception and realization of the work.

Finally, I am pleased to confirm that future releases of this work are already underway in connection with the forthcoming second edition of the companion treatise which will additionally include, among other countries, Argentina, Belgium, China, Egypt, Hong Kong, Hungary, Kuwait, Mexico, the Netherlands, the Philippines, Saudi Arabia, Turkey, and the United Arab Emirates.

Richard H. Kreindler
Frankfurt, March 1998

AUTHOR BIOGRAPHY

RICHARD H. KREINDLER

Partner, Jones Day Reavis & Pogue, Frankfurt, Germany. Admitted New York; Paris Bar as Avocat; registered Germany as Rechtskundiger. Harvard University (B.A. cum laude); Ludwig-Maximilians University, Munich (Magister); Columbia University (J.D.).

Coordinator of the European/Middle East Disputes Practice of Jones Day. Prior practice in New York and Paris.

Specializes in commercial and construction arbitration before the International Chamber of Commerce, American Arbitration Association, Stockholm Chamber of Commerce and other arbitral institutions, as well as multijurisdictional aspects of U.S., European and Middle Eastern litigation. Languages include English, French, German and Russian.

Recent experience includes responsibility for 1991 Gulf Crisis claims to UN Compensation Commission of the Hashemite Kingdom of Jordan and of various corporate entities in U.S., Europe and Arabian Gulf; commercial and construction arbitrations in U.S., Europe, Middle East and Asia and related challenge and enforcement proceedings; municipal court actions in U.S., Germany, France, Switzerland and elsewhere; and service as arbitrator under ICC, Stockholm Chamber of Commerce and *ad hoc* Rules.

Member of various arbitration institution panels.

Corresponding Member, ICC Institute of International Business Law; Advisory Board, *World Arbitration and Mediation Report*; Editorial Board, *International Commercial Litigation*; International Correspondents Board, *Arbitration and Dispute Resolution Law Journal*; Editorial Board, *Arab Law Quarterly;* Editorial Board, *International Arbitration Law Review;* Conseil scientifique, *Revue de droit des affaires internationales/International Business Law Journal;* Country Correspondents Board, *International Litigation Quarterly*; Editorial Advisory Committee, *International Legal Materials;* Advisory Board, Institute for Transnational Arbitration; Arbitration Practice Subcommittee, Chartered Institute of Arbitrators; Arbitration Committee and Working Group on ICC Rules Revision, U.S. Council for International Business; European Advisory Committee, Center for Public Resources.

General Editor, *Transnational Litigation: A Practitioner's Guide* (2 Vols., 1997). Numerous other publications and lectures on international dispute avoidance and resolution in English, French and German. Adjunct Professor, University of Münster, Germany.

INTRODUCTION

Transnational Litigation: A Basic Primer intends to be a different, more comprehensive, and more practically-oriented concise companion for cross-border litigation. Aware of the increasing need for a work on this subject, Oceana Publications asked me to conceive a practitioner's guide which would satisfy the daily need of the litigator, business person and student for an accessible overview of recurring *practical issues* in dispute resolution based on practical experience in certain principal countries.

In taking up this challenge and trying to fill this vacuum, I have conceived a practitioner's guide which is meant to be equally accessible and useful to the seasoned litigator, the transactional attorney, the in-house lawyer, the nonlawyer merchant and the student alike. It is also meant to be equally approachable for the Anglo-American and the Continental European, the Arab and the Asian, the Latin American and the African working in English. *A Basic Primer* is meant to be consulted in conjunction with the more extensive two-volume country-by-country analysis in *Transnational Litigation: A Practitioner's Guide* (Kreindler with Holdsworth, Oceana 1997), which is to be expanded in a second edition in 1999.

Compromises and limitations of focus, coverage and length must be taken into account in any work of such scope. At the same time, there are two self-imposed goals, among others, used as a consistent compass.

The first was not to compromise on the degree of detail to be devoted to issues of substantive litigation practice and strategy, no matter how abstruse certain such issues might appear at first glance, if they were in fact of practical and recurring relevance. The second goal was not to compromise on seeking a framework and approach which was readily comprehensible to practitioners of vastly different, and sometimes conflicting, legal backgrounds and mentalities. This required self-discipline as to how a reader from one litigation tradition would react to and employ the description of a vastly different litigation tradition. More often than not, the main commonality between two legal traditions may be the mere fact that both the author and the reader can work with relative ease in the English language.

Thus the Japanese practitioner should feel equally at home with the Primer as the American, the Frenchman as the Saudi, the German as the Australian. This is nothing more than an accurate reflection of the increasingly cross-border nature of litigation, whether complex and "high-stakes" or not. It is also a reflection of the fact that practitioners and businessmen need to be aware of concepts and possibilities in litigation procedure and strategy in other countries which may not exist in their own system.

Accordingly, in the context of a practitioner's and student's primer, such matters as long-arm jurisdiction, minimum contacts, document discovery, motions to compel production of documents, punitive and treble damages and court-ordered mediation may exist in a jurisdiction such as the United States but not, or not in the same way, in another jurisdiction such as Japan. In the context of a U.S.-Japanese litigation dispute, the U.S. practitioner and student need to know to what extent such matters can—or cannot—be "translated" to the Japanese environment and back again. And the Japanese practitioner and student must verify what such largely unfamiliar U.S.-linked issues mean for the litigation of the dispute either in the U.S. or at home in Japan. Here, my task, among others, is to ensure completeness, clarity and parallelism of discussion. It would be a disservice to readers from both such divergent backgrounds, no matter how seasoned and experienced each one might be, to assume that they have full knowledge of which characteristics of one system are or are not available in the other one.

Nor does one have to exaggerate the geographical distance to encounter such potential "gulfs" in understanding. Even within the European Union, e.g., in the context of a UK-German litigation dispute, the UK practitioner must make decisions based on choice. Thus, he must be aware of just how useful—or unuseful—such tools as security for costs, Mareva injunctions, Anton Piller orders, Order 14 and Order 29 procedures, etc. might be in a litigation with a German nexus or indeed in front of a German judge. By the same token, the German practitioner has choices. These should be based on an educated understanding of the extent to which his own "tools," even employed in his own court, are useful or optimal where one of the parties is based in England, procedures are pending there, or enforcement of a German order or judgment may be sought in England.

This concept of "choice" is at the heart of my conception of the present primer. Accordingly, the analysis which follows is meant to highlight and elucidate the choices available at various stages of a transnational litigation. These choices may be analogized to "forks in the road" which the practitioner encounters in each and every phase of a litigation. These forks in the road are also encountered in decisions which need to be taken, where applicable, to avoid the commencement of a litigation in the first place. In this regard, the focus of the present work is not solely on dispute resolution, but also on dispute avoidance.

It is thus hoped that the present volume will serve as a useful, practice-oriented guide to the numerous forks in the road encountered when attempting to resolve, or avoid, a transnational dispute—in good faith and with attention to detail, professionalism, and efficiency.

CHAPTER 1

SUBSTANTIVE AND PRACTICAL OVERVIEW OF THE KEY DISTINGUISHING ISSUES OF TRANSNATIONAL LITIGATION

The legal and historical framework is important for understanding litigation procedure and strategy in a particular country, and is crucial to the transnational litigant and student alike. It is meant to make readily understandable—if not necessarily also palatable—the reasons why certain legal institutions which exist in one's own country are present or absent in the same way in a given foreign forum. In this regard, there are certain common denominators of comparison which are relevant to the "choices" confronting the transnational litigator as follows:

i. Federal vs. Regional Bases of Civil Procedure

It is essential to understand whether the law of civil procedure of the country in question is wholly federal or a mixture of federal and regional, cantonal, state or provincial. The interplay between federal and regional, including the manner in which the federal preempts or supersedes the regional level, will differ in important ways from country to country.

The roots and applications of these different levels of legislation must be understood for their substantive and strategic significance. It would be a mistake to assume that the side-by-side existence of federal and cantonal in, *e.g.*, Switzerland can be readily equated or compared with the co-existence of federal and state law and procedure in the United States or of federal and *Land* in Germany. As a general rule, especially in a common-law country with a federal framework, the common law as applied by the courts may vary somewhat from state to state or province to province. Such issues must therefore always be verified by consulting a local practitioner. Likewise, provincial or state statutes which are likely to arise in transnational litigation vary from province to province and state to state, and must similarly be verified locally.

Furthermore, in certain countries with a "federalist" system "federal jurisdiction" extends to a number of areas which may be especially relevant to the international practitioner. These may include foreign affairs, international trade, banking, bankruptcy and insolvency, competition law (anti-trust), copyright, trademarks and patents, and the incorporation and regulation of major corporations. Maritime law may also be dealt with in federal legislation, and on this subject there may also be a body of federal, as opposed to provincial or state, common law, which is applied by the courts of all provinces or states.

Federal Versus Regional or State Jurisdiction

It is likewise important to understand the interrelationship between state-federal law and jurisdictional rules applicable in international disputes. This holds true in particular for recognition and enforcement of foreign judgments. It also applies—although it is intentionally not a subject of discussion here—to international commercial arbitration. Federal law is sometimes deemed to determine certain general procedural issues and the existence and effects of *lis pendens* and *res judicata*, as discussed below. Moreover, certain procedural principles are deemed to flow directly from the federal constitution, where applicable.

Misconceptions about the manner and degree to which state or provincial law or legislation is preempted or superseded by federal law can have serious consequences for the foreign and domestic litigant. Therefore, the practitioner must be wise to areas in which federal courts will be faced with difficult issues concerning the dual application of federal and state laws to particular claims. The practitioner must also understand the manner in which issues will be classified as "procedural" versus "substantive" for the purpose of application of such common-law doctrines as *forum non conveniens*, as also discussed below.

ii. Similarities and Differences in Overarching Procedural Principles

Quite apart from the federal-provincial divide in some jurisdictions are procedural principles which apply to litigation generally, and in transnational litigation in particular. Once again, the practitioner should be wise to the differences, sometimes of a subtle nature, in understanding and implementation of such principles from one country to the next.

Opportunities for Misconception and Misunderstanding

Two or more countries may use the same name for a principle of litigation, and even have common roots regarding such principle. This does not mean that present-day understanding or implementation of that principle is the same in all cases. In the case of countries which are geographical neighbors and/or have common historical roots, practitioners often assume—erroneously, as is meant to be shown here—that they must have highly similar legal systems.

Thus opportunities for misconception lurk in assumptions as to whether the one or the other adversarial or inquisitorial system is thought to have been originally influenced by another country. In the common-law context, because of this historical and conceptual foundation, many of the rules of civil procedure in countries such as Australia, India, Singapore and Canada may appear to be similar to those found in English law and in other British Commonwealth countries. However, English courts' decisions in such countries, although persuasive authority, are not necessarily binding, and may be of small significance depending upon the area of law. Similarly, decisions of other British Commonwealth countries, such as New Zealand or Canada, may frequently be cited and even accorded weight, but they are not necessarily binding. This is quite apart from the fact that just between and among the United Kingdom, Australia and Canada, for example, there are significant differences in procedure and practice depending upon the region involved.

With regard to non-common law countries, the temptation to equate particularly a civil-law system's procedure with that of another civil-law country, especially one which originally influenced it, is just as great and potentially just as misleading. Legal systems such as those of France, Italy, Spain, and Germany have influenced a variety of other countries. However, it seems painfully obvious, but necessary, to affirm that such other countries, including many in West Africa, North Africa, Latin America, and Asia, have each gone their own way. They have done so not only with respect to judicial precedent, but also civil procedure generally, and each one must of course be treated on its own terms. Accordingly, the admonition here against misconceptions and false assumptions applies just as much to the Spaniard working in Argentina or the Frenchman working in Egypt as to the US or UK practitioner confronted with such countries.

In this context, certain overarching principles of procedure and practice can now be identified:

Principle of Contradiction

The principle of "contradiction" (*audiatur et altera pars*) is of paramount importance. It is implemented in different ways in different systems, and is sometimes erroneously equated with the general common-law concept of "adversarial" procedure. This principle of "contradiction" essentially prohibits the court from giving any legal remedy until the other party has had an opportunity to submit its response. The principle requires that the court take into account all parties' interests, giving them the opportunity to present their claims, evidence and cause of action. The parties also have the right to respond to the opponent's claims, evidence and other causes of action as well as to the evidence acquired by the court itself. "Equality of arms" is generally considered to be one aspect of the principle of contradiction. The principles of fair hearing and of fair trial are extensions of this notion, and guarantee that the parties have the right to true equality in court proceedings.

Rule of Free Disposition

The so-called "rule of free disposition" is especially well anchored in such countries as Austria, Germany and Switzerland. It finds varying application in different countries, and holds that the party can freely dispose of the matter in dispute, subject to certain limited exceptions. It also holds that the party is free to withdraw its claim or acknowledge a claim brought against it. By extension, certain countries have enshrined in different ways the concept that a judge may not award more than, or something different from, what a party claims, or less than what the other party recognizes.

Presentation of the Facts and the Law

Another overarching principle which is often encountered is the one to the effect that it is solely for the parties to present and prove those facts and circumstances on which they wish the court to apply the law. This is to be contrasted with the competing principle whereby the judge is under a duty to clarify allegations which are unclear or to consider facts that are in the public domain irrespective of whether they have been alleged. In countries subscribing to the latter approach, there is a common duty of the parties and the court to investigate the facts.

In contrast to the jurisdictional system in common-law countries such as the United States, the civil-law judge in certain countries plays a consistently activist role. He does so notwithstanding the parties' authority to define the scope of the claim and their primary responsibility to establish the necessary factual allegations. In such civil-law systems, the judge need not rely wholly or solely on the evidence which the parties present. Rather, on his own motion he may take all evidence which he considers relevant and informative as to facts alleged by the parties.

In this context, "pleading requirements" will also vary from jurisdiction to jurisdiction and must be verified at the outset. Thus in some common-law systems including the United States, at least until recently, most courts had applied technical and often-times complex pleading rules. In "notice pleading" jurisdictions, parties are not required to plead detailed facts supporting their allegations and are liberally permitted to amend original pleadings to correct deficiencies.

The key distinguishing issues are particularly illustrative in the common law/civil law comparison. This comparison stereotypically assumes a variety of contrasts and areas of incompatibility, only some of which actually hold up on closer scrutiny. Among the important comparisons from the practitioner's point of view include the distinction between the procedural stage, in which the parties make their allegations, and the subsequent stage of taking evidence.

The critical issue here is whether the parties first make their allegations of fact and thereafter the court proceeds to the taking of evidence or the parties first take evidence and thereafter fine-tune their allegations. Particularly from the plaintiff's point of view, verifying this issue is essential. Depending on the jurisdiction, the plaintiff may or may not be able to present evidence or ask for evidence to be produced by the opposing party on matters not previously alleged. Likewise, the defendant may or may not allege a fact before it has achieved knowledge of it through the taking of evidence.

Taking of Evidence and the Trial Process

Another key distinguishing feature which is critical to the range of choice and strategy confronting the international litigant is "pretrial discovery," as it is known in certain common-law jurisdictions including notably the United States. Particularly from the point of view of the U.S. practitioner and the foreign practitioner confronted with a U.S. nexus, certain questions emerge again and again in the context of transnational litigation:

Are pretrial "depositions" as well as broad document discovery proceedings available? Is there an obligation of each party to inform the other, prior to the beginning of the proceedings, of the existence of any document that may be relevant to the outcome of the judgment? To what extent is the taking of evidence under the partial or complete control of the judge? What is the permissible scope, if any, of examination of witnesses by the parties and especially their counsel, including "direct examination" and "cross-examination"? Must evidence generally be presented *viva voce* before the court?

With regard to "discovery," the practitioner must also take care to ascertain the differentiations in approach between and among common-law countries. This also holds true for the differences in approach at the federal and especially state levels within the United States, the foremost exponent of such method of taking evidence. Parties may typically have a broad variety of discovery mechanisms at their disposal to obtain evidence and to narrow the scope of factual and legal issues in dispute. Those discovery tools may include requests for the production of documents, depositions upon oral examination, interrogatories requiring written answers, and requests for written admissions. However, such tools may differ in usefulness—and application—from one jurisdiction to another.

Moreover, the scope of allowable discovery may be broader in one jurisdiction than in another. This difference may also be partially a function of the existence and application of concepts of "attorney-client privilege" and "attorney work-product." In addition, the extent to which courts actively "supervise" discovery will vary. This is quite apart from the question of whether there are rules nominally requiring parties to confer about proposed discovery plans and discovery disputes.

In the United States, for example, recent amendments to the federal civil procedure rules require parties to disclose or produce documents and other information at the outset of the case, without receiving any discovery request by the opposing parties. At the same time, such amendments have not been adopted by certain local courts and are therefore not necessarily applicable depending upon the particular district.

iii. Assessing the Role of the Judge

In an "adversarial" system of adjudication, the judge or, where applicable, the jury may decide solely what the parties in disagreement ask them to decide, and will choose which of the conflicting versions of a dispute should be preferred. However, the practitioner should be careful not to assume that all adversarial systems are alike in this respect. Similarly, he should not assume that in all "inquisitorial" systems, where the role of the judge is meant to be greater and more significant than that of the trial counsel, the role played by the judge is largely comparable.

In some systems, the judiciary do not conduct any separate evidentiary investigation. In such systems, it is uncommon, in a judgment, for a judge to refer to a case that was not cited in court by counsel for either party. By contrast, in other systems the judge does not investigate, but may refer to law not relied upon by counsel themselves.

Stereotypes also break down just within the civil-law family. Within Continental Europe, some civil-law systems are clearly less judge-dominated than others, and some are more akin to the adversarial system of the common-law variety. In addition, some civil-law procedural systems include a mix of adversarial and inquisitorial features depending on whether the issue is amenable to out-of-court settlement (so-called discretionary case) or not (nondiscretionary case).

In this regard, care must be taken to raise and answer a number of questions which impact on the initial shaping and strategy of the litigation, and which may influence the prospects for out-of-court settlement. These include: Will all legally obtained evidence be accepted and have equal importance in the judge's decision? Is there a common-law style "trial" where the parties make oral pleadings? What is the relative importance of written pleadings? Will the court take into consideration only what it hears from the counsel, parties and witnesses in open court?

Judge and Jury

The issue of judge versus jury is also an important one in distinguishing one country from another, including those which in fact offer this choice in certain cases. In some systems which offer the jury trial, it is of declining importance but still readily available. In others, it is frequently used in civil as well as criminal proceedings. In those systems in which the jury system is offered, where a common-law remedy is sought a jury trial may be available as of right or only on application to the court. By contrast, where equitable relief only is claimed, the trial may be by judge alone.

In certain jurisdictions, the plaintiff is permitted to stipulate the mode of trial or the defendant may apply to the court for a jury trial. Moreover, in some instances in which a trial by jury is allowed, the court may exercise its discretion to order trial without a jury. In short, there are numerous permutations between and among jurisdictions which offer a jury trial and even within one and the same system. The practitioner must confront such issues at an early stage and, where a choice is available, assess the advantages, and disadvantages, of a trial by jury.

iv. Accessibility and Use of Legal Precedent

Among the practical, but frequently overlooked, aspects of transnational litigation which should be considered at the beginning of any analysis is the extent to which court decisions are publicly accessible and consistently reported. Different countries have different reporting services, while some have virtually none at all. Even among those which do, not all judgments may be reported.

Various countries have legal index sites on the Internet which may contain some or all federal and provincial cases and legislation, and provide links to other sites specializing in individual areas. Journal indexes and legal digests for commentary on the law can also be accessed through online services in some countries. In any event, the facility of gaining access to legal precedent in various countries, with or without the aid of local corresponding counsel, is a practical factor of potentially enormous significance.

v. Organization of Legal Profession and Strategy

Organization of Judiciary

Judges are chosen in different ways in different countries. In some cases, they are appointed by the executive, in some cases they are chosen by election, and in some cases they are selected by virtue of examination close to the completion of the initial legal education. In some jurisdictions, judges, once appointed, are wholly independent of executive direction and control; in others they are meant to be, but are not. The jurisdictional activity of the State may sometimes be assured by means of a special system of principles and institutional guarantees which, protecting the judicial function, allows judges full exercise of their "public office" (*munus publico*).

There may be constitutional requirements establishing that judges will have a lifetime office, and cannot be removed without justification; that their earnings cannot be reduced; and that they are prohibited from exercising other activities or functions, except as professor, may not receive court fees, and are prevented from political party activity. There may also be requirements that they reside in the district where they exercise their functions and that all hearings and trials shall generally be public, etc. In many countries, the federal court system is structured in part to preserve the independence of the judiciary from the other branches. In both federal and provincial or state courts, as is the case in the United States, there may be rules governing the impartiality of judges. Parties may seek to disqualify judges who have a financial interest or other bias or prejudice in the matter.

These issues are of course critical to an assessment of litigation strategy, procedure and, notably, choice of forum. This is especially the case when a foreign element is involved and predictions of fairness, competence, and speed need to be made at the outset. These issues may also influence a foreign litigant's choice of forum.

Organization of Legal Profession

The legal profession is organized differently from one country to another, and within certain countries from one state or province to another. Just as in the case of the judiciary, so in the case of the bar, it is essential from an outside perspective to understand the way in which lawyers are trained, organized, compensated, certified, and regulated. This is just as important for the assessment of the need and choice of local corresponding counsel as for the evaluation of opposing counsel.

The designations "barristers" and "solicitors" continue to be used in certain countries, whereas in some common-law jurisdictions, such as Canada, the two professions are in fact unified. In jurisdictions where there is a high degree of specialization, notwithstanding the unified profession, an increasing number of practitioners may act exclusively as barristers or "trial lawyers."

Moreover, in some jurisdictions a division of the legal profession between lawyer and "notary" may exist. Notaries may receive at least the same legal training as lawyers and have the same right to give legal advice. In this regard, in countries such as those of Continental Europe "notary" can be an indication of a high degree of experience and seniority among lawyers and does not have the almost clerical meaning attributed to this title in, e.g., the case of "notary public" in the United States. Local law may reserve to notaries the right to draw up certain types of contracts, notably deeds of sale of immoveables, and their practice may tend to be concentrated in this area. Where "notarizations" are required or advisable, such "notaries" are best placed to advise on possible litigation-related issues of notarization.

vi. Rapid Change and, in Some Cases, Harmonization

Finally, for transnational civil and commercial disputes the legal scene in certain countries has recently been changed drastically by major events which, to the greatest extent possible and practical, have been taken into account here. Among these include, e.g., recent accessions to the European Union (e.g., in these pages Austria, Finland and Sweden), ground-breaking amendments to civil procedure legislation (e.g., Austria, England and Wales, Finland, Singapore, United States), accession to multilateral conventions respecting service of process, taking of evidence, mutual recognition and enforcement, etc. with farreaching domestic implications (e.g., Austria, Finland, Sweden, Switzerland), etc.

In this regard, care must also be taken to ascertain the extent to which in certain countries legislation formerly in place under a prior regime has or has not been expressly abrogated or, instead, may still be valid at least in part on the grounds of the *"lex posteriori derogat lex priori"* principle. Cases in point are the Czech Republic, the Russian Federation, and Hong Kong.

For purposes of convenience and accuracy, the descriptions herein are accurate and up-to-date as of **February 1, 1997**. Where appropriate, developments in rapidly changing areas of law have been taken into account up to **August 1, 1997.**

vii. Litigation versus Arbitration in the Transnational Context

As stated above, the focus of this work is intentionally on litigation and not on arbitration. At the same time, the two obviously cannot be divorced completely in either theory or, especially, practice. Where appropriate, reference is occasionally made to issues of arbitration, arbitrability, the arbitration agreement, and challenge and enforcement of foreign arbitral awards. Such references are made without any ambition toward completeness or exhaustiveness. It is appropriate simply to highlight certain issues which arise when considering litigation "versus" arbitration, and therefore in comparison with each other, in the transnational context.

Arbitration has come to be known, and in some circles is still known, as "alternative dispute resolution"—that is, an alternative to resolution by litigation in the municipal courts. Among the reasons for seeking an alternative to the conventional path to the courthouse, the most important in the transnational context have included the hope for simplified commencement of proceedings and service of process, neutrality, and facilitated taking of evidence. They have also included the aspiration of expeditious rendering of a decision, confidentiality, and simplified recognition and enforcement.

For a legal counsel or business person who is faced with the decision of which dispute resolution mechanism to choose, it is crucial not to be lulled into false assumptions about the strengths or weaknesses of the litigation or arbitration "option."

Relative Advantages of Arbitration Versus Litigation

The comparison must begin with the bases for arbitration—the express or implied agreement to arbitrate. Some of the potential advantages of arbitration can be squandered by a poorly drafted arbitration agreement. Some of the potential disadvantages may be counteracted or at least controlled through skilful drafting. It is thus critical to distinguish between those disadvantages which can be circumvented or neutralized by careful drafting and those that may not.

It is important to recall some of the potential advantages of arbitration versus municipal court dispute resolution. As a result of recent developments in various jurisdictions including notably the United States, the practitioner must look at some of these perceived advantages in a new light.

The potential advantages include foremost the ability to limit or even exclude the jurisdiction of the courts over the adjudication of the dispute. Hand in hand with this promise is the prospect of an "equitable playing field." Arbitration, by virtue of an agreement at the beginning of the contractual relationship, can offer a neutral situs and a neutral substantive law. It can also offer consensually agreed-upon procedural rules and input into the selection of a tribunal with a particular background. "Home court" and other perceived advantages may, occasionally, thereby be neutralized or even largely eliminated.

Furthermore, arbitration holds out the possibility, especially when compared to United States civil procedure, of a greater informality in the proceedings and a tailoring of the procedure to the particular parties and dispute. In a relationship between a U.S. and a non-U.S. party, there is indeed ample opportunity in an arbitration for combining civil and common law approaches to evidence and other issues. And where the parties are of different, far-flung nationalities, arbitration may promise simplified mechanisms of commencement and service of process across borders. This can avoid defects in foreign service of process, which in litigation might otherwise be irrevocable.

Compared to court proceedings in certain "congested" jurisdictions, arbitration also holds out the possibility of comparatively expedited proceedings. Once the proceedings conclude, there is the prospect of a greater ability to enforce the result—the award—pursuant to international conventions and bilateral or multilateral treaties. Furthermore, depending on the situs, arbitration may also provide the option of completely excluding any right of appeal against the award. In disputes involving sovereigns, high-tech, intellectual property, trade secrets, and similar sensitive issues, there is either a presumption or an obligation of confidentiality to arbitration proceedings and awards which may be of great importance. While such issue of confidentiality has been a source of recent controversy, and may in any event be lost if and when an arbitral award is challenged or sought to be enforced in the municipal courts, the "promise" of confidentiality is still generally attractive and meaningful.

Moreover, the ability to choose a venue—or situs—with a developed arbitration statute and with local courts experienced in arbitration issues is highly attractive: the "better" the situs, the more likely perhaps that the arbitration will not be bogged down or even sabotaged by dilatory conduct or, occasionally, ill-suited arbitrators. The same applies to the facilitation of taking evidence of foreign-based witnesses and documents, or "discovery" as it is known in the United States. Arbitration may offer formal and also unofficial ways of dealing with such discovery which might not be possible in a municipal litigation setting.

And finally, arbitration sometimes, although not always, holds out a certain promise as to the predictability of costs. Such predictability may be especially desirable in jurisdictions such as the United States where there are no compulsory fee schedules. Such predictability may also be important, again in a country like the United States, where in court litigation the prevailing party cannot assume that it will be awarded its costs or that "costs follow the event."

Relative Disadvantages of Arbitration

A discussion of potential disadvantages of arbitration compared to civil litigation, including involving the United States, is to a certain extent a mirror image of the discussion of potential advantages.

A growing perception holds that the increasing costs of institutional arbitration make it less attractive as an alternative to litigation, even in the United States, than previously. Of course, each dispute has its own dynamic and characteristics which contribute to the level and nature of the costs incurred. However, it is fair to say that certain arbitration proceedings may be as expensive as had they taken place in the courts. By the same token, recent federal litigation reforms in the United States and elsewhere, discussed below, may betoken a greater cost-consciousness and cost-efficiency in the courts than was the case just five or ten years ago.

Another potential disadvantage to arbitration, where the parties' goal is to exclude the courts, is the ability to force judicial intervention in certain jurisdictions. From one party's viewpoint, the courts "assist" the arbitral proceedings, from the other party's perspective they only "disrupt" them. Whatever the motivation, it is clear that agreeing to arbitration is not a guarantee that the courts will be fully removed at any given stage of the arbitration. In this regard, again, recent trends are important to examine, and are discussed where applicable below.

Furthermore, arbitration may appear to be more palatable than litigation in a jurisdiction with a highly-developed arbitration "culture." By the same token, it may be less workable in countries whose courts are inexperienced in or even hostile to arbitration and to the issues which it typically engenders. This must also be considered when deciding between arbitration and litigation. "Blind spots" in a particular country's arbitration statutes or caselaw may have serious consequences for the successful adjudication of a dispute by arbitration or enforcement of the arbitral award. This applies with no less force to "highly developed" jurisdictions such as the United States, France or England, which are also frequently employed as the situs of transnational arbitrations. These and other countries may have not only blind spots, but also a multiplicity of not always reconcilable state statutes and judicial decisions.

A more recent criticism of arbitration is the concern over the rigidity of institutional mechanisms in arbitration: Do the parties want the relatively intensive supervision of an institution such as the International Chamber of Commerce (ICC)? "Terms of reference"? Front-loaded advances on costs? Conversely, do the parties want to leave open the possibility of an award "without reasons" as in some domestic U.S arbitrations? These issues must be weighed against the degree of rigidity which might also be experienced in civil litigation. This is especially so in an "adversarial" environment such as the United States where the role of counsel has historically been proactive and the role of the judge reactive. Again, however, recent liberalizing trends in the United States, and in certain institutional arbitration rules, call for a reexamination of this traditional stereotype.

An arbitral award is ultimately worth only as much as the parties' ability to enforce its terms. Even those with relatively little experience of arbitration sense that the ability to enforce the award pursuant to international conventions and treaties is a powerful promise which argues in favor of arbitration. On the other hand, even under accepted international agreements, enforcement efforts across borders are not without their problems. Whether a given country is a signatory to a multilateral treaty such as the 1958 United Nations ("New York") Convention on Recognition and Enforcement of Arbitral Awards is surely one inquiry. Yet how that country's courts have actually interpreted the grounds for denying enforcement of foreign arbitral awards under Article V of the New York Convention is quite another inquiry, and requires careful and up-to-date scrutiny.

Finally, the parties faced with the choice between arbitration and litigation must consider whether in their particular situation arbitration has any enforcement advantage over court proceedings. This may be the case where the dispute is essentially domestic, or where the assets of the parties are largely in one and the same jurisdiction. It may also be the case where there is an effective treaty or procedural basis for the enforcement of municipal judgments which may be as effective as a convention on enforcement of arbitral awards, if not indeed more effective in a given case.

CHAPTER 2

STRUCTURE OF THE COURTS

The practitioner's range of choice with respect to a transnational litigation is framed first and foremost by the structure of the courts in the jurisdiction in which he contemplates bringing, or is obliged to defend, an action. Accordingly, each country description herein deals first with the general structure of the local court system.

From the choice of a particular court also follow (i) the time horizons for adjudication and (ii) factors which may influence how long an action may take from beginning to end. Finally, the various kinds of judicial and extrajudicial bodies are addressed which may be of relevance in a transnational litigation.

i. General Structure

Most countries have evolved their own court system or systems, in some cases over several centuries and in other cases in a fraction of that time. In each case, one or another form of hierarchical court structure is in place. At the same time, it must be remembered that beyond the structure of the courts there may exist the supremacy of, e.g., European Union law and the European Court of Justice in Strasbourg, as is the case for a number of countries. Thus all of the courts of the Member States of the European Union are subject to the European Court of Justice as to matters within the competence of the European Union. Accordingly, the European Court of Justice is the ultimate appellate court of these countries.

Federal Versus State or Provincial Structure

The most straightforward division between courts is normally between those which deal with the civil law and those which deal with the criminal law. Only the civil-court structure is dealt with in the discussion here. Within the civil structure, the most apparent dividing line is, in countries where a federal system applies, between the federal courts and the regional courts.

At the same time, not all such federal systems have a clear dividing line between federal and state courts. In those countries in which there is no division between a federal system on the one hand and a provincial or state court system on the other, all courts are considered federal courts. In those in which it is necessary to distinguish between the federal and state courts, normally federal jurisdiction is limited *ex ratione materiae* (by reason of the matter) or *ex ratione personae* (by reason of the person).

Common federal courts are often specialized, *ex ratione personae*, in civil suits concerning interests of the federal administration or its legal entities (sometimes referred to as "federal questions") and/or disputes whose amount at stake exceeds a certain threshold level. The jurisdiction of the common federal courts may also include suits involving, on the one side, a foreign State or an international organization and, on the other side, a municipality or individual domiciled in the country; suits based on treaties or contracts entered into by and between the State and a foreign State or international organization; writs of *mandamus* and *habeas data* ("have the information") against acts of federal authority; and enforcement of foreign court judgments.

It is imperative for the practitioner to identify such mandatory or optional areas of federal jurisdiction at the outset. It is also important to determine whether, as is the case in the United States, federal district courts may and often do hear disputes arising under state laws when the case involves a lawsuit by or against a citizen of a foreign

State (so-called "diversity jurisdiction") and where the amount in controversy is in excess of a certain statutorily fixed amount, in this case currently US$ 75,000.

Planning and Strategy Relating to Appellate Instances

Depending on the jurisdiction, there may be a single supreme court of last instance for all civil and constitutional matters, or alternatively there be separate courts of last instance for these two areas. In this regard, while most practitioners are concerned more with commercial matters than constitutional issues, depending on the status of the federal constitution (if any) in a particular jurisdiction, predominantly commercial matters may have, or be shaped to assume, a constitutional element.

This may affect strategy and choices respecting jurisdiction and appeal to the appropriate higher court. Furthermore, some courts of last instance not only have a primary function of protecting the constitutional framework, but also adjudicate litigation between a foreign State or international organization and the State, and between the State and subsidiary territories. By contrast, in other countries (e.g., Finland), constitutional matters are not adjudicated before the courts and there is no special constitutional court. In such countries, legislative or judicial constitutionality, generally speaking, may be of less practical importance in actual legal proceedings. In such cases, the "constitutionality" of legislation may be monitored by the legislative rather than the judicial branch.

Furthermore, the manner in which cases are scrutinized for review by the court of last instance—e.g., the *certiorari* approach in the case of the United States Supreme Court—must be understood before any expectations can be formed as to the prospects of obtaining review before such court. Generally, very few civil appeals actually reach the federal court of last instance. Therefore, for practical purposes the decisions of the various provincial or regional courts of appeal may often be deemed final in commercial litigation unless a point of law of substantial importance is involved.

As is the case in the United States and certain other jurisdictions, access even to the second tier of appellate review, that is the second to last instance, ordinarily is not of right, and such appeals are typically taken at the discretion of those second-tier courts. Thus, ordinarily an adverse ruling on a motion to dismiss or other preliminary motion may not be deemed "final" and therefore not be immediately appealable as of right under the so-called "final judgment rule."

At the same time, there may be exceptions to such rule in the case of, e.g., decisions granting, refusing, dissolving, or modifying injunctions. Also in the case of the United States, and certain other countries under the "collateral order doctrine," a decision may qualify for an immediate appeal if it conclusively determines the disputed question, resolves an important issue completely separate from the merits of the action, and is effectively unreviewable on appeal from a final judgment. This may be particularly relevant to denial of immunity to a defendant that qualifies as a "foreign State" under foreign sovereign immunities legislation.

Where a federal/state distinction is maintained, jurisdiction not pertaining to the federal courts may be submitted, either mandatorily or optionally, to state or provincial courts. These may be organized differently from state to state and province to province, according to respective constitutions, judiciary organization codes and internal court regulations and local rules. In some countries, procedural law may remain federal, as the legislative competence concerning procedural matters is exclusively incumbent on the federal legislator. In others, the state or provincial courts may have their own civil procedure codes and local rules which apply; these may differ in significant respects from state to state and province to province.

Differences in Approach to "Precedent" Value of Decisional Law

The rule of *stare decisis*, under which judgments of a higher court are binding on lower courts, will normally apply in common-law jurisdictions, including those with a federal-state division of court structure. However, this will not always be the case in other legal systems. In the case of Canada, for example, this rule forms part of the common-law system in most of the country but is not part of the civil-law system in Quebec; at the same time, with rare exceptions, it is nevertheless applied by the courts of that province.

Even in countries where *stare decisis* applies, distinctions must be made between binding authority on the one hand and persuasive authority on the other. This is especially the case when a decision in one district or region is sought be used as authority in a court in another district or region. This again applies in countries such as the United Kingdom, Canada, Australia, and the United States. In the U.S., not only are there significant differences in precedent between and among the state courts under respective state law, but also the various federal circuit courts of appeal (the federal courts of second instance) are not necessarily in full harmony on a variety of issues. Only a small number of such state and federal issues become resolved and unified upon *certiorari* to the United States Supreme Court. And while such countries as the United States and, more recently, Canada have a concept of giving "full faith and credit" to final judgments from other provinces or states, the implementation is in reality not always a smooth one.

In this regard, Canada, due to its unusual common law-civil law mix, can be regarded as a vivid laboratory of different precedential influences. Decisions of provincial courts of appeal or the Federal Court of Canada are not binding on courts of appeal or lower courts of other provinces, but are generally treated as persuasive authority. At the same time, in Canada judgments of the English and some other Commonwealth courts are frequently cited as persuasive authority. In the Quebec courts, doctrinal writings and judicial decisions from France are often cited on issues of civil law. Moreover, United States court decisions are increasingly referred to on issues where Canadian and U.S. law are similar. This last situation arises most frequently where modern statutory law is involved.

In the case of non-common-law countries, the doctrine of *stare decisis* does not play as important a role as, for example, in the United States or Canada. The lower courts may not be bound to follow holdings made by the highest court to the same extent as in common-law countries. In addition, the highest court may more easily ignore a precedent if the facts in the case at hand are sufficiently dissimilar from an earlier case. Practitioners concerned with cases at such appellate levels must in any event verify the exact status and role of *stare decisis* in the particular foreign jurisdiction.

ii. Rights of Audience and the Role of Foreign Co-Counsel

A potentially unsettling aspect of transnational litigation, even in the case where highly competent and "known" local counsel is identified, is the feeling that the case is being "abandoned" into a great unknown once local counsel assumes the reins. This need not be the case, and indeed should never occur even in the case of co-counsel with whom one has no prior working experience as long as an understanding of the working relationship and lines of command is established.

Rights of Audience by Foreign Counsel

In some cases, the working relationship with local co-counsel, as in the case of many international arbitrations, can be fundamentally altered for the better by exercising rights of audience in the foreign jurisdiction even without being locally admitted. Generally, rights of audience are restricted to locally admitted attorneys, although there are important exceptions involving certain courts. It is therefore advisable for the practitioner to identify, with local counsel or even before selecting such counsel, what the litigant's scope of activity and representation may be in the faraway locale.

The principle of a public hearing is a major legal maxim in most procedural systems, basically giving citizens the right to obtain information about the rulings of courts and other authorities. Both court hearings and court documents are normally public unless otherwise regulated by the law, and indeed such rights are enshrined in the European Convention on Human Rights and Protocols. A foreign counsel should and can have equal access to such information.

In most jurisdictions, there is no formal recognition of the position of foreign co-counsel. The *jus postulandi* ("right to plead"), except in some cases for labor courts and courts of small claims and for filing the writ of *habeas corpus*, is an exclusive prerogative of attorneys affiliated with the federal or respective state division of the Bar. To appear in a court, the practitioner must be properly admitted in the jurisdiction.

In other cases, the foreign litigant may "accompany" the locally admitted attorney to the court and even plead to the fullest extent, usually subject to linguistic fluency, in the presence of such local attorney. In still other jurisdictions, a foreign legal advisor has no foreseen role in litigation. While he may be present at oral hearings, the right to make motions lies strictly with the party's locally admitted attorney. At the same time, even in such cases, judges may informally grant the foreign lawyer a chance to examine witnesses in addition to the locally admitted colleague and to certify the validity and content of foreign law, through affidavit or legal opinion. Again, the practitioner must carefully ascertain the possibility, and advisability, of his involvement in these and other aspects of the foreign proceedings.

The rights of foreign attorneys from Member States of the European Union are regulated in the Law Implementing the Directive of the Council of the European Union on Facilitation of the Exercise of Free Movement of Services by Attorneys. Foreign attorneys may represent parties in EU Member State courts, acting "in agreement" with an EU attorney admitted to that particular court. The foreign attorney acts as the representative of the party, without the need to reside in the particular Member State or to be a member of an EU bar association. However, he may do so only together with a local attorney admitted to that particular court.

In certain cases, the foreign attorney not only possesses the relevant linguistic skills, but also has a superior factual, technical or other command of the case to that of the local counsel. In such case, pleading by the foreign counsel, if allowed, may be advisable and even appreciated by the court. This may be the case in jurisdictions where a foreign counsel may represent a client in a foreign court under the same conditions as a local colleague. Thus, in Finland for example, which recently acceded to the European Union, there are no differences between counsels from EU and non-EU countries. In other cases, depending on local customs, practices and even prejudices, such a retention of responsibility in the foreign attorney may be inadvisable or even foolhardy.

Foreign Co-Counsel and Attorney Accreditation

In deciding the nature and scope of cooperation with foreign local counsel, the practitioner would do well also to consider how the local counsel "compares" in quality to others in the same jurisdiction. Part of that analysis is an understanding of the selection process to become an attorney in that local jurisdiction. This process may or may not be considered "selective" from the foreign practitioner's point of view. Suffice it to say that the professional standards for qualification as an attorney in one country may be "higher" than in another. In some countries, multi-year practice periods are required, which must include at least a certain period of time at court and also with a single attorney or law firm. In other countries, the formal education is highly practically oriented, and due to a variety of factors the law graduate begins to practice at a comparatively young age, such that after even a short time his level of daily experience may be higher and more significant than his contemporaries in other countries.

In the European Union, Member States such as Austria have implemented relevant EU directives (89/48/EEC regarding the acknowledgement of university diplomas and 77/249/EEC regarding the free exchange of services). These directives regulate the nonpermanent rendering of services by lawyers from other European Economic Area (EEA) states. Thus in the case of Austria, no examination or practice period is required; notification to the local bar is required; the local bar holds disciplinary authority over the foreign attorney; and in activities where Austrian law requires a party's representation by a *Rechtsanwalt* (e.g., in case of obligatory representation by an attorney before the Superior Courts and the courts of second and third instance), the foreign lawyer must be accompanied by a local *Rechtsanwalt.*

With regard to the language or languages of the courts, of course many leading jurisdictions, including certain of the ones addressed herein, are bilingual or multilingual societies. In some such countries, legal proceedings may be conducted in more than one language with equal facility or the language of proceedings may depend on the particular region in that country. To the extent the linguistic elements of a dispute and the linguistic competence of counsel are at issue, these need to be carefully assessed and balanced at the outset.

iii. Time Horizons for Adjudication and Influencing Factors

The time in which cases may be litigated varies widely from jurisdiction to jurisdiction, even within a single country or region in that country. Different courts have substantially different case loads and some courts may be required to give priority to criminal matters which end up occupying a disproportionate amount of their time and resources.

In certain common-law jurisdictions, particularly in the United States, many complex cases become delayed as a result of preliminary "motion practice" devoted to applications by the parties to compel production of testimonial and documentary discovery. Furthermore, different court systems and judges, even within the same country or the same region in that country, may have varying approaches to controlling their case loads, or dockets, and compelling parties to comply with schedules for completing particular stages of the litigation.

Choosing Between Forums Based on Time Factors

In general, depending on the jurisdiction, the plaintiff may or may not have a certain freedom to choose whether to commence an action in more than one court. Where such freedom does exist, there are a number of practical matters which will influence where an action should be brought depending on the circumstances.

The first criterion which will usually influence the appropriate forum is the value of the claim. Thus there is a presumption that any claim valued at under a certain amount should be commenced in the court of lowest jurisdiction. If proceedings are issued for an amount under this value in a court of higher jurisdiction, depending on the rules the action may be struck out by the higher court or be transferred to the lower court of appropriate jurisdiction.

In situations where claims valued between certain threshold amounts may be brought in either of two or more courts, other factors will then ultimately determine which court will try the matter. In such cases, monetary value may not be the sole factor which comes into consideration in allocating cases between the courts. The presumptions as to the appropriate court for commencing proceedings may then be rebutted on the basis of other criteria.

For example, if a case is particularly complex, whether by virtue of the law or of the facts involved or both, a lower court may determine that it is more appropriate for the case to be tried in the higher court even though the claim is worth a relatively small sum. Similarly, a relatively valuable case may be so straightforward as to allow a lower court to deal with it in preference to the higher court. In short, these factors need to be assessed by the practitioner at the start. By doing so, the practitioner can better make the appropriate decision and avoid needless expenditure of time and money initiating the case in a court which is likely to "remove" the case to another court, whether upon its own motion or that of the opposing party.

Time Factors and Cost

With regard to cost, it is important to determine whether there are "rules of thumb" as to whether, both in terms of court fees and legal costs incurred, a lower-court action is likely to be quicker and less expensive than a higher-court action—or perhaps quite the opposite. If a case is not contested and a default judgment is rendered, this may occur in as little as a few months from the time the action was commenced. On the other hand, if the defendant is simply unwilling to pay and its attorney contests the claim, it may be able to avoid final adjudication in the first instance within roughly the first year. This may be possible where not all evidence is taken in one hearing, but rather the hearing is adjourned, and time periods between sessions are long.

Judicial expertise is also a factor which needs to be considered with regard to the court structure and the choice of initial jurisdiction. Invariably, but not always, higher-court judges are more specialized in their understanding of the law, due to the complexity of the cases which they try and the allocation of cases between them. On the other hand, a lower-court judge may try a wider range of disputes but, in general, have a lower level of specific expertise.

Court-Ordered or -Annexed Case Management

In terms of efficiency and speed, it is incumbent on the practitioner to ascertain whether expedited case management systems have been introduced to streamline adjudication and, ultimately, encourage out-of-court settlement. This may take the form of requiring both parties to litigation to adhere to a strict timetable in the preparation of their cases, to agree upon initial methods for taking of evidence or to abide by the edicts of a magistrate. It is not unusual that cases strictly subject to such methods may progress from start to finish in less than one year. Obviously, this will depend on the circumstances and the particular court.

In some jurisdictions, the plaintiff may at its option select a "fast track." Such choice will likely not be rejected by the court unless the complexity of the matter makes the fast-track timetable impractical. Among the considerations which may enter into a decision whether to allow an action to proceed in this manner include (i) the complexity of the issues of fact or law; (ii) the likely expense to the parties; (iii) the importance to the public of the issues of fact or law; (iv) the number of parties or prospective parties; (v) the amount of intervention by the case-management judge that the proceeding is likely to require; and (vi) the time required for proper discovery and preparation for trial or hearing.

In some countries, and not only in the common-law jurisdictions, there is increasing emphasis on settling disputes before trial and even requiring the parties to participate in "alternative dispute resolution" (ADR) or mediation conferences, whether prior to or almost immediately following the close of pleadings. These and related issues are discussed in **Chapter 18** below.

Jurisdiction Versus Venue

In jurisdictions where a case might equally well be brought in two or more different courts, there may be a distinction between "proper jurisdiction" and "proper venue." Particularly in the United States, this distinction is sometimes lost upon foreign parties who are not intimately familiar with U.S. litigation procedure. This difference between the competence of the courts generally and the propriety of a particular court within an otherwise competent district does not arise in the same fashion in many other countries.

Whether in the U.S. or elsewhere, there are particular reasons why venue, whether defined loosely as the general "location" of the court or defined specifically in U.S. terms as the advisable situs, should matter. Particularly in the case of a foreign defendant, there may be an array of differences from location to location including, *inter alia*, (i) characteristics and background of juror pools where applicable; (ii) judicial quality and temperament; (iii) exposure to and experience with foreign defendants and foreign law; and (iv) judicial interpretations as to service of process, substantive issues, and damages. Another factor is the general speed of the suit from complaint to judgment in a particular court, depending in part on its particular case load.

Whether venue is "proper" as to a foreign defendant will depend in large part on statute. For actions in U.S. federal courts, relating to, for example, the Alien Venue Act, 28 United States Code (U.S.C.) § 1391(d) provides that venue is proper in any judicial district in the U.S. For actions in state courts, venue may be proper (i) in any county in which one party resided at the time the action was commenced, (ii) the venue designated by the plaintiff, or (iii) in most real property actions the county in which the real property is located: e.g., New York Civil Practice Law and Rules (CPLR) §§ 503, 507. Thus, in the case of the United States not only must a district court have "personal" and "subject-matter jurisdiction," as discussed in **Chapter 3** below, but also a particular district court must be the proper forum for the action under a set of "venue" statutes designed to ensure that cases are heard in convenient geographical locations.

"Forum shopping" in certain countries' courts is in fact not a major consideration or strategic issue where the law offers several options to file suit only under specific circumstances. Even where such options exist, there may be no general rule as to which courts are better, quicker than others, or populated by more competent judges.

Affecting the Speed of Adjudication

Regarding bureaucratic and procedural means of affecting the speed of the proceedings, the system of appeals in certain countries gives the parties several opportunities to appeal to the higher court (or even to the trial court), either against interlocutory decisions or final judgments. The purpose is in fact to assure the parties the broadest hearing possible under the *due process of law* principle. This may result in multi-instance appeals, the duration of which must probably be estimated at between three and several years, depending on the jurisdiction and the circumstances.

Furthermore, in the European Union context where preliminary questions must be put to the European Court of Justice, the time for adjudication may be considerably prolonged. In recent years, some courts have shown an increasing tendency to make references to the European Court of Justice, although overall the number of referred cases is comparatively small in most EU countries.

iv. Tribunals and Other Judicial Bodies

In some countries, there is no distinction between ordinary courts and administrative courts, and almost all disputes except those relating to, e.g., collective labor agreements will be subject to the jurisdiction of unitary federal district courts. In other countries, a series of tribunals may have been established to deal with civil disputes arising from particular subject areas.

The aim of such tribunals is to produce swift and inexpensive access to justice to ensure that the parties are not adversely affected by their lack of financial means and/or the passage of time. A further aim is to reduce the burden placed upon the traditional court system by the ever-increasing workload of litigation. To further achieve their aims, tribunals often enjoy exclusive jurisdiction in an area of expertise, to the exclusion of the courts normally enjoying original jurisdiction.

Examples of areas of competence sometimes reserved to such tribunals include employment appeals, labor relations, land and water rights, immigration appeals, custom and excise tax, patent and trademark, social insurance, electoral and military matters, and decisions of administrative federal agencies. In the United States, for example, the Court of International Trade reviews a variety of federal administrative agency decisions on customs and other international trade-related matters.

CHAPTER 3

OBTAINING JURISDICTION AND CHOICE OF FORUM

i. Statutory and Other Bases for Acceptance of Subject-Matter and Personal Jurisdiction

Normally, the respective jurisdiction of federal, provincial and state courts is determined by "subject matter" and/or the monetary size of claims brought before them, where such distinction applies. This inquiry is quite apart from whether the particular court has "personal," or *in personam*, jurisdiction over the particular person or entity. The common-law rule, applicable in such jurisdictions, is that a court has jurisdiction over an action where the proceedings were properly issued from that court and were validly served on the defendant within the jurisdiction *(in juris),* or outside the jurisdiction *(ex juris)*, in accordance with the particular rules applicable.

In the United States, the fundamental principles governing personal jurisdiction are largely the same in federal and state courts. Subject-matter jurisdiction, however, differs in a number of respects in the U.S. federal and state court systems. Assuming that the matter has not been committed exclusively to the federal courts by statute, state courts may exercise jurisdiction over any legally cognizable claim if the state legislature has authorized "personal" jurisdiction over the parties and the exercise of jurisdiction is consistent with the state and federal constitution. Federal courts, on the other hand, exercise jurisdiction only to the extent authorized by Congress, and allowable by the Constitution.

Personal Versus In Rem Jurisdiction

Obtaining, and contesting, jurisdiction may revolve around notions of "personal" (*in personam*) and "subject-matter" (*in rem*) jurisdiction, as the concepts are called in the United States. Alternatively, in other countries these notions may be essentially collapsed into one for purposes of determining whether there is jurisdiction.

In the case of subject-matter jurisdiction, the test in those jurisdictions which look at this issue separately or differently from jurisdiction over the person tends to be fairly straightforward. Thus the cause of action must arise under federal law, the amount in controversy must exceed the threshold amount required for federal jurisdiction, and the parties must be of different nationalities or origins.

Depending upon the country, statutory jurisdiction of the federal courts as it relates to "federal questions" may be found in such matters as those in which a writ of *mandamus* or prohibition or injunction is sought against an officer or officers of the State in restrictive trade policies (or anti-trust law) and consumer protection, judicial review of administrative actions, admiralty actions, land claims relating to indigenous populations, etc.

As for "personal" jurisdiction, in many jurisdictions including common-law countries the analysis is less clear and may be in a state of flux from jurisdiction to jurisdiction. The basic common-law rule in certain jurisdictions is often that valid service of initiating process upon the defendant is sufficient to give a court personal jurisdiction and that service within the jurisdiction is valid for these purposes whatever the connection of the defendant or the dispute to the jurisdiction. Furthermore, under local court rules there may be bases upon which jurisdiction may be recognized although service occurs outside the jurisdiction, subject to *forum non conveniens* arguments (discussed below).

"Long-Arm" Bases of Jurisdiction

Among these jurisdictional bases, which find their reflection in part in countries which have "long-arm" statutes, are (i) where the proceedings are founded on a cause of action arising in the State; (ii) where the proceedings are founded on a breach in the State of a contract wherever made; or (iii) where the subject matter of the proceedings is a contract made in the State on behalf of the person to be served by or through an agent carrying on business or residing in the State and is governed by the law of the State.

Further bases include where the proceedings are (iv) founded on a tort committed in the State; (v) for the recovery of damages suffered in the State by a tortious act or omission wherever occurring; (vi) for contribution or indemnity in respect of a liability enforceable by proceedings in the court; (vii) where the person to be served is domiciled or ordinarily resident in the State; (viii) where the proceedings are for an injunction as to anything to be done in the State or against the doing of any act in the State; and (ix) where the proceedings are brought to enforce in the State a judgment wherever rendered.

With regard to jurisdiction based on presence, where there is no single "long-arm" statute that authorizes service of process on nonresidents, some generally applicable principles can be gleaned from common law. For example, where a party was within the jurisdiction at the time of the issue of a writ or summons and has left to evade service, substituted service may be ordered unless the defendant left the jurisdiction before the writ was issued. However, the court will normally refuse to exercise jurisdiction where a defendant is brought within the jurisdiction through the use of physical force or where it has been enticed to come for the sole purpose of serving it with process.

Particularly in a country like the United States, current trends suggest that the kinds of activities which may lead a court to declare competence over a foreign defendant are expanding. In such situations, there may be statutory and constitutional requirements which must be satisfied. In the case of the United States, these requirements relate to (i) long-arm statutes adopted by the state in which the federal or regional court is located and (ii) the "Due Process Clause" of the U.S. Constitution. In other countries, including common-law jurisdictions, the analysis may be quite different. Thus, in Australia, for example, there is no single "long-arm" statute under Australian law authorizing service of process on nonresidents.

In the United States, in a recent trend particularly in the state courts, long-arm statutes have been stretched to assert jurisdiction over foreign manufacturers, particularly in the product-liability context. The 1993 amendment to Rule 4 of the U.S. Federal Rules of Civil Procedure essentially created a "default" federal long-arm statute for all federal question claims and a "national contacts test." Thus the national contacts test may grant jurisdiction if the foreign defendant has substantial U.S. contacts, cumulatively, even if such contacts are spread thinly over a number of individual U.S. states.

"Minimum Contacts" and Constitutional Guarantees

Certain jurisdictions require, for the exercise of personal jurisdiction over domestic or foreign defendants, that (i) there be what in the United States are called "minimum contacts" between the State and the defendant and (ii) it be "reasonable" under such circumstances to assert personal jurisdiction. A benchmark for all parties may be whether the defendant's "purposeful" contacts and connections with the State are such that it could reasonably anticipate being haled into court in that State.

In the United States, "purposeful" contacts have increasingly been interpreted broadly, thereby increasing the likelihood that the net of U.S.-court jurisdiction will be successfully cast over the domestic and the foreign defendant. Such contacts have been interpreted recently to include, e.g., (i) presence of an office, warehouse, etc.; (ii) ownership of property or a bank account; (iii) solicitation of business aimed at state residents; (iv) customizing of products for the state market or a particular purchaser; and (v) shipping products from abroad with invoices on the foreign letterhead.

A recent string of decisions from courts in disparate jurisdictions has fixed on other additional contacts to uphold jurisdiction. These contacts include employment of personnel in the State and direct shipping of products to a State subsidiary or distributor which is used as a "marketing conduit." They have also included presence of a subsidiary, parent, distributor, joint venturer or other entity in the State or with contacts to the State which can be fairly attributed to the defendant on an agent or "alter ego" basis. The last requirement will normally depend on such criteria as (i) common ownership, (ii) financial interdependence, (iii) extent of control, (iv) observance of formal corporate separateness, etc. Other possible bases for exercising jurisdiction may be sending personnel to the State to attend trade shows to demonstrate products or train personnel, and negotiation, signing or performance of part or all of a contract within the State or entering into a contract with a company generally in the State.

"Reasonableness" and Exercise of Jurisdiction

From the foreign defendant's point of view, the jurisdictional reach of the State must normally be subject to a test of "reasonableness." Among the criteria which may be applied are (i) the extent of the foreign defendant's purposeful entry into the State, (ii) the burden on it of defending in that State, (iii) the existence of any conflict with the sovereignty of the defendant's home country, and (iv) the State's interest in adjudicating the dispute. They may also include (v) where the most efficient resolution of the suit is deemed to be, (vi) the importance of the State to the plaintiff's interest in effective and convenient relief, and (vii) the existence of an alternative forum. Here too there has been a recent trend toward expanded application of personal jurisdiction, most particularly in mass tort cases in the United States (e.g., breast implant, asbestos, environmental toxic torts, etc.).

In most jurisdictions other than the United States, neither a single "long-arm" statute nor such concepts as "due process" and "minimum contacts" exist. In such jurisdictions, accordingly, the solicitation of business aimed at a local resident may not create a forum unless the activity takes place in a branch office in the country. The customizing of products for the local market or particular purchase or direct shipping of products to an outlet will not necessarily create a forum by itself. Only if a local subsidiary exists or a permanent distributor is used will this give a basis to a forum based on "assets located" or "permanent representation" or "forum of business establishment."

Some jurisdictions have provisions similar to "long-arm" statutes allowing for the exercise of jurisdiction over physical persons who have no domicile whatsoever (inside or outside of the country at issue). Under such provisions, these persons may be sued at the domestic place of *de facto* stay or, after leaving the country, at their last residence or domicile or stay in that country. However, jurisdiction may not be exercised under such statutes unless the underlying obligation was incurred in that country or is to be fulfilled in that country. The individual laws and statutes must be examined on a case-by-case basis.

Statutory Versus Convention Bases for Jurisdiction

Certain jurisdictions not only have their own codified and case-law bases for exercise of jurisdiction, but also have acceded to bilateral or multilateral conventions which govern, among other matters, jurisdiction between and among Member State courts.

In the case of European Union Member States, the 1968 Convention on Jurisdiction and Enforcement of Judgments in Civil and Commercial Matters ("Brussels Convention") and the 1988 Convention on Jurisdiction and Enforcement of Judgments in Civil and Commercial Matters ("Lugano Convention") may apply. The questions of forum and domestic jurisdiction are dealt with (mostly simultaneously) by such conventions, essentially displacing the rules of local law in cases where the conventions apply.

The texts of most relevant articles of the Brussels and Lugano Conventions are identical. The Lugano Convention essentially applies to Iceland, Norway and Switzerland, as remaining Member States of the European Free Trade Association (EFTA). Former EFTA member states Austria, Finland and Sweden recently joined the European Union, but have not yet ratified the Brussels Convention.

Among the provisions which displace local law for the purposes of the present discussion of jurisdiction are that the main forum shall be the domicile of the defendant (or its seat if it is a company), and that alternatives to the main forum may include, (i) in contract disputes, the place of performance; (ii) in matters related to tort, delict or quasi-delict, the place where the harmful event occurred; and (iii) in disputes which can be combined with an action *in rem* in immovable property, the court where the property is situated.

The Conventions also stipulate certain exclusive forums, regardless of the defendant's domicile. These include (iv) in disputes regarding rights *in rem* in immovable property or tenancies of immovable property, where the property is situated; (v) in disputes related to a company, at the seat of the company; (vi) in disputes concerned with the registration or validity of patents, trade marks, etc., the place of deposit or registration; and (vii) in proceedings concerned with the enforcement of judgments, the court where the judgment has been or is to be enforced.

Brussels/Lugano Conventions Versus Local Law

The dividing line between local procedural law and the Brussels and Lugano Conventions in those countries where they apply is normally clear-cut. In cases which fall within the scope of the Conventions, the Conventions must be applied. Care must be taken, however, to ascertain whether as a general rule, subject to some important exceptions, there is in fact great similarity between the heads of jurisdiction recognized by local civil procedure and by the Conventions. This may differ from jurisdiction to jurisdiction among the Convention States.

This interrelationship is particularly vivid in the case of a country like France. Under Article 15 of the French Civil Code, even if there is no nexus between the transaction and France, so long as the defendant is a French national the French national can demand that French courts have exclusive jurisdiction to hear disputes arising out of the transaction. A foreign judgment rendered against a French national who has asserted an Article 15 defense may be unenforceable in France. A French national can waive its Article 15 defense either contractually or by participating in foreign proceedings without first asserting its Article 15 rights. The Brussels and Lugano Conventions eliminate the Article 15 defense in disputes among domiciliaries of Contracting States. At the same time, under the Brussels and Lugano Conventions a party from a Contracting State that is domiciled in France may assert the Article 15 defense against a party from a noncontracting State.

Among the subjects expressly excluded from the Conventions are status and capacity of natural persons, matrimonial property matters, wills and succession, and bankruptcy. Cases relating to subjects which are not within the scope of the Conventions will in all circumstances be governed by the provisions on jurisdiction in local civil procedure law.

Particular Jurisdictional Issues under the Conventions

The Brussels and Lugano Conventions apply to civil and commercial matters. At the same time, not all signatory states, Denmark being one example, make a legally relevant distinction, France and Germany being the counterexample, between "civil" and "commercial" law. The concept of civil and commercial matters in the Convention is understood as referring to matters of a "private law" nature as opposed to matters of a "public law" nature such as matters of administrative or tax law. With certain exceptions, the Convention rules on jurisdiction apply only to persons and companies which are defendants and domiciled in a Contracting State. Under Article 17, exclusive jurisdiction is conferred upon party agreement and applies regardless of whether it is the plaintiff or defendant who is domiciled in a Contracting State.

The general principle of jurisdiction common to both the Conventions and the local civil procedure law of certain of its contracting states is that a person must be sued in the courts of his home country. All other bases of jurisdiction are regarded as exceptions to this general principle and, therefore, interpreted restrictively. In contrast to the concepts of "minimum contacts" and "due process" which are embedded particularly in United States procedure, under the Conventions a judge has essentially no discretion either to accept or reject jurisdiction on a *forum non conveniens* basis or with reference to due process requirements of minimum contacts as described above. Rather, the important criterion is whether one of the connecting factors specified in the Conventions or in local civil procedure is present or not.

In this regard, the practitioner must be aware of the occasional differences in jurisdictional approach between the Conventions and local procedure in some of the Contracting States. For example, Article 5 no. 1 of the Conventions provides that in matters relating to contract, the courts at the place of performance have jurisdiction. In Denmark, for one, the local civil procedure code has a similar provision, but with a significant difference. The provision of the Conventions includes contractual money-claims, while that is not the case with the corresponding provision of the Danish civil procedure code except where the claim arose during the debtor's presence in the country or locality and the obligation should be performed before departure. Under Danish law, a money-claim, unless otherwise agreed, must be performed at the home of the creditor. That means that the debtor of a money-claim that falls within the scope of the Conventions, and for which Danish law determines the place of performance, may always be sued at the court where the creditor is domiciled, while that is not possible under local civil procedure.

"General" Versus "Exclusive" Jurisdiction

Regarding the local jurisdiction of the courts, some countries distinguish not so much between personal and subject-matter jurisdiction or between federal and state jurisdiction, but rather between "general" and "exclusive" jurisdiction. A primary example is § 12 of the German Code of Civil Procedure (*Zivilprozeßordnung*, ZPO), which distinguishes between a person's general place of jurisdiction (*allgemeiner Gerichtsstand*) and, if applicable, his exclusive place of jurisdiction (*ausschließlicher Gerichtsstand*) for a certain claim. The general place of jurisdiction of an individual is normally determined by the domicile and is supplemented by rules regarding the "special" place of jurisdiction (*besonderer Gerichtsstand*) and, for certain claims, even an "exclusive" place of jurisdiction.

Where local civil procedure provides for a special place of jurisdiction for a certain claim, the plaintiff has an important strategic choice. He can bring his action either in a court at the defendant's general place of jurisdiction or at the applicable special place of jurisdiction. The decision where to bring a suit depends on a variety of strategic questions. These include which of the possible forums is more convenient for the prospective plaintiff and/or the witnesses whom he intends to call. They also include whether the courts in one jurisdiction are known for a particular interpretation of the applicable law, or of the specific issue under that body of law, that could be favorable to the plaintiff's case. Other factors include whether the plaintiff's counsel has a certain reputation at, or a familiarity with, the judges sitting at one particular court and whether proceedings will be faster in one jurisdiction or another.

Where local procedure establishes an exclusive place of jurisdiction, the plaintiff has no strategic choice, but rather must bring his action at such place. Examples of exclusive places of jurisdiction include (i) for claims which assert a right of ownership, encumbrance or possession as to real property, the place where such real property is located and (ii) for claims relating to leased dwellings, the place where such dwelling is located.

ii. Property as a Jurisdictional Basis

The mere fact that a defendant has assets in the jurisdiction may or may not be sufficient for the courts to exercise jurisdiction over a particular dispute. Moreover, it may not be sufficient that the action brought "touches" or "concerns" the land or property if it does not also have a direct effect on the property itself, its possession or title.

In the United States, the existence of real or personal property in a jurisdiction is not sufficient alone, in actions unrelated to the right or ownership of the property, to exercise jurisdiction over a defendant. That is, courts may exercise jurisdiction over a property owner only if the owner has minimum contacts with the applicable forum and the exercise of jurisdiction must be reasonable.

Brussels/Lugano Convention Versus Other Bases of Exorbitant Jurisdiction

In Brussels and Lugano Convention cases, Articles 5 and 16 of the Conventions offer a forum based on the location of the property *(forum rei sitae)*. Under Article 16(1) of the Conventions, the courts where immovable property is situated have exclusive jurisdiction in proceedings which have as their object rights *in rem* in, or tenancies of, such property. This applies regardless of the domicile of the defendant, i.e., also if it is domiciled outside the geographical area of the Conventions. As a result of the latter rule, national law relating to jurisdiction based upon the presence of immovable property loses most of its importance in respect of international jurisdiction in Contracting States.

Outside the Conventions, other optional forums may be available, based partly on property, partly on business activities. These include jurisdiction based on the location of a branch; for contract claims, the place of performance; and the place where the damage was incurred. Of particular note is the "forum based on property situated" (*Vermögensgerichtstand*), e.g., in Austrian and German law. This basis is explicitly excluded by Article 3 of the Conventions for Convention cases. Where applicable, it means that whenever a potential defendant has assets in, e.g., Germany, this forum may present a considerable advantage to the German plaintiff.

The implementation of "property jurisdiction" in German law, it is fair to say, is one of the most controversial German rules regarding local jurisdiction. Under § 23 ZPO, lawsuits concerning financial claims against a person with no domicile or residence in Germany come within the local jurisdiction of the German court within whose district the nondomiciliary's property is located. From the court's local jurisdiction follows its international jurisdiction. Furthermore, it is not necessary that the plaintiff itself be a German resident to be able to assert such international jurisdiction.

Article 3 of the Conventions expressly excludes the application of § 23 ZPO as a jurisdictional basis for municipal court proceedings. However, under the Convention, § 23 ZPO remains applicable for interim measures such as prejudgment attachment of property to secure execution of a later judgment. According to its literal wording, § 23 ZPO contains no minimum requirements as to the value of the prospective defendant's property or any other connection of the dispute to Germany. This leaves the plaintiff with the strategic choice of whether to sue the (foreign) defendant in Germany or, rather, in the defendant's country of domicile. Of course, this decision is subject to a variety of factors. One of the key issues which will tempt the plaintiff is that the judgment rendered by a German court is immediately enforceable in Germany.

After decades of essentially unfettered application, in 1991 the German Federal Court of Justice (*Bundesgerichtshof*) heightened the threshold for § 23 ZPO by holding that for a German court to assert jurisdiction, the subject matter must have a sufficient connection to Germany. In the aftermath, German lower courts have found a "sufficient national connection" when, e.g., the plaintiff was a German resident, where contract negotiations took place in Germany, or where contractual obligations by either party were to be fulfilled in Germany. The situation has continued to be in a state of flux in light of two 1996 decisions of the Federal Court of Justice. While in its recent decisions the Federal Court of Justice has taken an increasingly restrictive approach to § 23 ZPO, it is still a provision with major strategic and substantive consequences for foreign litigants involved in German municipal proceedings.

In sum, in the context of Brussels and Lugano Convention issues, it is apparent that the normal bases for exercising jurisdiction can have a differentially dangerous impact on parties not domiciled in EU or EFTA Member States. All "exorbitant forums" offered by the domestic jurisdictional law of the Contracting States are superseded if both parties are domiciled in a Contracting State. However, these forums are fully available for a plaintiff domiciled in a Contracting State against a defendant not domiciled therein. In such cases, any exorbitant forum provision of a Contracting State's law is available to the plaintiff irrespective of the Contracting State in which it is domiciled, and the judgment resulting from such proceedings is enforceable in all Contracting States of the Convention.

iii. Role of Party Autonomy and Choice-of-Forum Clauses

Providing for the forum or situs, if permissible and practical, may be indispensable, especially in a transnational contractual relationship. The reasons go well beyond the obvious desire to choose a place for proceedings if one has the opportunity to do so. The forum may have a direct and determinative impact upon a number of matters crucial to the litigation. The forum may have a critical influence on the ability to appeal the judgment at that place. It may also help or harm efforts to enforce the judgment at a different location, but in consideration of the laws applicable at the place where the judgment was rendered.

Clauses designating a particular court as the forum for disputes (*forum prorogatum*) will generally be upheld even if the foreign defendant has no presence or contacts with that State. Furthermore, even choice-of-law provisions pointing to that State may also lead to exercise of jurisdiction there. Some courts treat forum-selection clauses as all other contractual provisions, and enforce them unless a valid defense exists under the law applicable to the contract, such as unconscionability or fraud. Some take a slightly more flexible approach but treat forum-selection clauses as presumptively valid, subject to a few additional defenses not typically available under standard contract law. A few jurisdictions treat forum-selection clauses as but one factor in the *forum non conveniens* analysis (addressed below).

In some jurisdictions, a choice of forum (or choice of jurisdiction) does not require that a specific venue be named. This is particularly the case whether, for example, the parties to a contract agree that the courts of a foreign country (e.g., "the courts of France") shall have exclusive jurisdiction, whereupon the courts of another country decide to stay proceedings pending the outcome of the proceedings brought under the choice-of-forum clause.

In other jurisdictions by contrast, choice-of-forum clauses, while generally respected, must specifically provide for "exclusive jurisdiction" over disputes arising from the agreement in question. Absence of the word "exclusive" before "jurisdiction" in the clause may indeed be construed as being a deliberate decision by the parties to refrain from doing anything more than giving "concurrent" jurisdiction to certain courts. The interests of the parties which are considered in determining whether to accept jurisdiction in the face of such a choice-of-forum clause are normally similar to those applied to issues of *forum non conveniens.*

Where the law explicitly regulates domestic jurisdiction (e.g., for status matters), such domestic jurisdiction cannot be created by agreement of the parties. This may extend to contracts of employment where the employee resides in the jurisdiction at issue and to claims arising from consumer contracts where the consumer resides in the jurisdiction at issue. Nor can parties normally agree only on the territorial jurisdiction of a particular court; that is, an agreement is void if it aims to control either the functional competence in relation to the sequence of courts or subject-matter jurisdiction. In other areas, pecuniary disputes in particular, the question whether jurisdiction requires a "minimum connection" of the parties and/or the matter in dispute depends on the applicable statutory or convention basis, as discussed in **Parts i. and ii.** above.

Choice of Forum and Brussels/Lugano Conventions

In the case of the Brussels and Lugano Conventions, Article 17 waives even this minimum "connection" requirement. It construes domestic jurisdiction as an automatic result of a valid choice of a specific forum by the parties. Validity of such an agreement, however, requires that at least one of the parties have its domicile in a Contracting State. Thus the scope of Article 17 may be somewhat broader than other jurisdictional rules in the Conventions, as it applies if either one of the parties is domiciled in a Contracting State. For nonconvention cases, the requirement of "minimum connection" for choice of forum and jurisdiction depends on the particular country, and overlaps with the analysis of *forum non conveniens*, discussed below. Furthermore, while under the Brussels and Lugano Conventions a valid choice of forum between the parties creates exclusive jurisdiction, under local law (i.e., outside the Conventions) this may not be the case. As stated, choice-of-forum clauses, unless they explicitly indicate to the contrary, may merely create an optional forum and not exclude other places of available jurisdiction.

Under the Brussels and Lugano Conventions, also as under most local laws, the parties' autonomy to select the forum is subject to a number of exceptions which provide for either "exclusive" or "mandatory" jurisdiction of courts for specific type of actions. The exceptions relate to actions *in rem* involving real estate, to consumer claims, to selective company law actions, and to proceedings concerned with the registration or validity of patents, trademarks, designs or other similar rights, or generally the validity of entries in public registers. Local law may additionally circumscribe the parties' autonomy in this respect. For example, as under most local laws, under Article 5 para. 2 of the Swiss Private International Law Statute a choice-of-law clause shall be void if a party is thereby abusively denied a forum to which it would otherwise be entitled under Swiss law or an applicable foreign law.

As to formal validity requirements of choice-of-forum clauses, a choice-of-forum clause may be valid if either concluded by the parties to a litigation or by their predecessors. Normally, in litigation the agreement, if contested, must be proven by documentary evidence. Under the Brussels/Lugano Convention (Article 17), a choice-of-forum agreement needs to be in writing or evidenced in writing, or by other documentation in a manner usual between the parties or usual in the particular trade.

iv. Challenges to Jurisdiction: *Forum non conveniens* and Equivalent Notions

The best known manner in which to exercise party autonomy over the imposition of jurisdiction is to seek dismissal of the entire action as to all or some parties for *forum non conveniens*. In many jurisdictions, this notion exists and refers to the situation where the forum is seriously inconvenient for, in this case, the foreign defendant, or a more convenient alternative forum exists elsewhere where the foreign defendant may be properly served. It may be that the alternative forum's law can be more or less favorable, as long as it provides at least a possibility of relief.

Among the matters which have been taken into account in relation to discretion to decline to exercise jurisdiction include (i) the strength or weakness of the claims made, (ii) the policy of exercising restraint before subjecting a nonresident to local jurisdiction, and (iii) whether the jurisdiction is a clearly inappropriate forum. Among the relevant factors in the latter case are whether the objective effect of a continuation of the proceedings is vexatious or oppressive in the sense that it is unfairly burdensome, prejudicial or damaging to the foreign defendant.

Also considered are (iv) the convenience and expense in relation to availability of witnesses, (v) the difficulty of document collection from foreign jurisdictions, (vi) the law governing the relevant transaction, (vii) the places where the parties respectively reside or carry on business, and (viii) whether an appropriate alternative forum for the hearing of the matter is capable of nomination.

Lack of Concept of Forum non conveniens

In certain countries particularly in Continental Europe, a challenge to jurisdiction may not be based on *forum non conveniens* solely. Rather, the basis would be that the connection specified in the relevant provision of either the Conventions, where applicable, or the local civil procedure provisions is nonexistent or that the parties have agreed to exclude local jurisdiction either by a forum clause or an arbitration clause.

Thus the doctrine of *forum non conveniens* is unknown to the Brussels and Lugano Conventions. A court having jurisdiction pursuant to the applicable jurisdictional rules of the Conventions must assume jurisdiction as a matter of law and cannot decline it by reference to considerations of convenience.

In many other jurisdictions, there is likewise no concept of *forum non conveniens*. If the case is foreseen as a basis of local jurisdiction, and local jurisdiction is exclusive, no challenge will be successful. If the jurisdiction of the local and the foreign courts is concurrent and by a valid and acceptable mutual consent the parties elect a foreign forum, the local court may respect such an agreement. If the parties do not waive local jurisdiction by express consent, there are no grounds for challenging jurisdiction. In such a case, even if the cause of action is equally connected to the foreign jurisdiction, and the same suit has been filed abroad, the local judge will examine the litigation.

Agreements to Arbitration

Jurisdiction may also be challenged where the matters in issue are subject to an arbitration clause. The present work intentionally does not address issues of arbitration in any detail. It suffices to say that local law and legislation, as well as applicable bilateral and multilateral conventions, may provide that a party responding to a court proceeding may seek stay or dismissal so that the matter may be referred to arbitration before filing any defense on the substantive matters with the court.

Depending on the law or convention applicable, the court will normally be obliged to stay or dismiss the local court proceeding in the face of an assertion of a prior arbitration agreement unless the arbitration clause is null and void, inoperative, or incapable of being performed. This is the standard foreseen in Article II of the United Nations Convention on the Recognition and Enforcement of Foreign Arbitral Awards of 1958 (hereafter "New York Convention") and the United Nations Commission on International Trade Law Model Law on International Commercial Arbitration of 1985 (hereafter "UNCITRAL Model Law"). Obviously, the caselaw and implementing legislation of the respective jurisdiction concerning these and other bodies of legislation which may apply must be examined closely and in an up-to-date manner in the particular case. National courts have given a variety of interpretations to the standard under Article II of the New York Convention in particular.

Other Grounds for Denying Jurisdiction

Even if all relevant events took place abroad, the local forum may not necessarily be clearly inappropriate if the defendant is resident in the forum, if the plaintiff is resident in the forum and the contract sued upon was entered into in the forum, or if the alternative forum bars or severely restricts recovery of damages or other relief.

The reverse of this principle is that in some jurisdictions the court of first instance or any other instance must deny its own jurisdiction where, even if the defendant has entered an appearance, it becomes apparent that jurisdiction has been lacking from the beginning or disappears. In such case, the court then in charge of the case may annul the proceedings and reject the claim. In Austria, for example, even after the court's decision has become final and unappealable, it must be annulled by the Supreme Court if a lack of domestic jurisdiction at the time the judgment was rendered becomes apparent.

Bilateral treaties contain specific provisions whereby the defendant can limit its exposure by raising the *exceptio incompetentiae internationalis.* This defense does not affect the adjudication of the claim, but may limit recognition and enforcement of the judgment to assets in the state of judgment. This defense may be available only if a foreign defendant, having been sued in a jurisdiction such as Austria, does not enter an appearance, or when entering an appearance makes explicit reservation as to the *exceptio incompetentiae internationalis.* A decision may then not be enforced outside that country. It should be noted that defendants domiciled in a Brussels/Lugano Convention state cannot plead this exception. Defendants domiciled or resident in nonconvention states with a bilateral treaty may make use of it once they are sued in a country, such as Austria, which recognizes the defense.

v. Whether to Object to Jurisdiction *Ab Initio,* and Relevance to Later Efforts to Recognize and Enforce

Pre-Answer Motion Versus Answer

In some jurisdictions, there may be a choice between filing a pre-answer motion and an answer. In the case of a pre-answer motion, the foreign defendant in particular might raise any and all of a number of different defenses. These would include, apart from lack of "subject-matter jurisdiction," a lack of "personal jurisdiction," improper service of process, or improper venue (which in U.S. federal procedure must be raised the first time the foreign defendant files a motion by "special appearance" or its answer, whichever is first). Other grounds might include failure to state a claim upon which relief can be granted or failure to join an "indispensable party" (which can normally be raised at any time prior to trial or at trial).

Alternatively, the local procedure may allow the foreign defendant to choose not to file such a motion, but instead to raise such defenses in its answer. In the case where the foreign defendant makes no appearance whatsoever, or loses on its challenge to jurisdiction through an initial "special" or "limited" appearance, its subsequent failure to make a "general appearance" will normally result in entry of a default judgment. In so doing, the defendant may rely on what it perceives to be an unlikelihood that the plaintiff will be able to execute upon the default judgment against assets of the defendant in either the same jurisdiction or elsewhere.

Such a tactic should be employed only under narrow circumstances and with extreme caution. If the defendant decides to defend the suit on the merits after the first instance has upheld its own jurisdiction, then such appearance will normally constitute a waiver by the defendant of any subsequent ability to challenge the court's jurisdiction.

In short, the tactical advantages for the foreign defendant in appearing only to contest jurisdiction or making a full "appearance" with a reply in substance are to be assessed in view of the law of the country of prospective enforcement, as to whether a full defense is deemed a tacit submission to jurisdiction. If the law of prospective enforcement does not consider a full defense to be a voluntary submission or if the judgment is to be enforced locally, the defendant may wish to adopt the prudent strategy of filing a full defense in a separate petition, in addition to the jurisdictional defense, if possible.

In relation to defendants from signatory states to the Brussels and Lugano Conventions, Article 18 of the Conventions provides that "a court of a Contracting State before whom a defendant enters an appearance shall have jurisdiction." This rule shall not apply where an appearance "was entered solely to contest the jurisdiction." In contrast to, e.g., the Swiss Private International Law Statute, Article 18 of the Brussels and Lugano Conventions requires that the defendant object to jurisdiction *ab initio*, that is, with its very first communication to or appearance before the court, regardless of the reason for such appearance.

Jurisdiction and Service of Process

In addition to the foregoing considerations, the defendant, especially the foreigner, should verify whether service of process on it was proper. While this issue is discussed more extensively in **Chapters 5 and 6** below, it also relates to the initial decisions to be made by the defendant respecting jurisdiction. The foreign defendant may not be obligated to do anything respecting suit until properly served and thereby given adequate notice of suit.

A failure to respond to proper originating process will normally result in a judgment by default which may later be set aside only if the defendant provides a satisfactory explanation for failing to respond and establishes the existence of a meritorious defense. There are similar provisions in the Hague Convention on the Service Abroad of Judicial and Extrajudicial Documents in Civil or Commercial Matters ("Hague Service Convention"), addressed more fully in **Chapters 5 and 6** below.

With regard to jurisdiction based on "submission" or "appearance," the court will have jurisdiction over a defendant who submits to the jurisdiction. In certain jurisdictions, among the factors to be taken to be indicative of submission to jurisdiction by a defendant include (i) entering an unconditional appearance, (ii) making an application for an extension of time for entering an appearance in order to apply for security for costs, (iii) submitting on affidavits and contesting the merits of the case where an appearance has not been entered, and (iv) a choice-of-forum clause.

If the defendant argues the case on the merits, then it is normally taken to have submitted to the jurisdiction of the court. If in such case the service of originating process was faulty and for this reason the court had no jurisdiction prior to the submission, the implication under many court rules and under the common law is that the court obtains jurisdiction at this time.

Although the original service of process was invalid, the defendant by submitting or appearing is precluded from setting up an argument that the invalidity of the service of originating process negates jurisdiction. However, in such cases the plaintiff would be well advised to serve originating process again once the defendant has submitted. Furthermore, the effect of submission or appearance is normally confined to the cure of irregular or invalid service. The submission by a defendant should not confer jurisdiction over a matter that is not otherwise covered by the subject-matter jurisdiction of the court.

Acceding to Jurisdiction and Prospects for Later Enforcement

A significant factor in the decision of the defendant whether to contest the jurisdiction of the court is the location of its own assets. If the defendant does not have assets within the jurisdiction, then it may be indifferent to an adverse judgment in the foreign jurisdiction. At the same time, it should consult the recognition and enforcement rules of the country in which its assets are located as to whether the judgment could be recognized or enforced there.

If the defendant has assets within the foreign jurisdiction, then it would normally be advised to contest the jurisdiction of the court if the court did not appear to have jurisdiction under applicable law. If the defendant proceeds to argue the case on its merits, however, it will normally be taken to have submitted to the jurisdiction of the court and any order that follows will normally be binding upon it and its assets.

The reverse side of the coin is where the original action has been commenced in a foreign country, and the defendant is concerned about recognition of the foreign judgment in his home jurisdiction. This issue is discussed in Chapter Q. below. Suffice it to say here that recognition and enforcement of foreign judgments is normally subject to local statute respecting this issue and/or to bilateral or multilateral conventions or treaties. In terms of the relevance of contesting the jurisdiction of a foreign court, for both recognition and enforcement local statutes and caselaw should be studied for the preconditions to enforcement of the particular foreign judgment.

Convention and Nonconvention Bases

There are cases where there is no treaty or convention basis for recognition and enforcement of judgments between the two countries at issue. In such cases, the defendant may find itself in a situation of needing to do nothing to contest the foreign exercise of jurisdiction if it is absolutely sure that recognition and enforcement could not be achieved anywhere where it has assets or activities.

On the other hand, it may be that the relevant statute or common law provides that a defendant does not submit to the jurisdiction of the foreign court merely by the act of contesting its jurisdiction. In that case, a defendant whose principal assets are located in a country with such law may feel free to participate in the foreign proceedings to an extent necessary to contest jurisdiction or invite the court in its discretion not to exercise its jurisdiction.

Where the Brussels and Lugano Conventions apply, a deficiency in jurisdiction is cured if the defendant first "enters an appearance," unless he does so solely to contest the court's jurisdiction. This, however, does not apply in instances in which exclusive jurisdiction under Article 16 has been disregarded. In such instances, under Article 19 the court on its own motion must declare that it has no jurisdiction.

If the defendant challenges subject-matter and/or *in personam* jurisdiction, and the court considers itself not competent, the action is rejected. Where a different court in the same country may be competent, the plaintiff can "save" its action by a motion to transfer the action to another court which it designates. The new court will initially also examine its competence and the same may happen over and over with the limitation that a "later" court may not deny its competence on the ground that an "earlier" court was competent.

Under the Conventions, it is permissible for the defendant to reply in substance for the event that, contrary to the defendant's objection to its jurisdiction, the court finds that it has jurisdiction. Whether the defendant should also reply to the substance of the complaint depends on an assessment of whether the court will uphold the objection to jurisdiction and on how quickly the defendant desires a decision on the merits.

Under Article 20 of the Conventions, if the defendant does not enter an appearance, the court shall on its own motion examine its jurisdiction. If the court finds that it has jurisdiction, it must ensure that sufficient efforts have been made for the defendant to receive service of process in sufficient time to arrange its defense. This is of importance in connection with the procedure to enforce default judgments under Article 27, no. 2.

Jurisdictional Objections and "Discovery"

Depending on the jurisdiction, there is the distinct possibility that the court may later assert jurisdiction over a foreign defendant if it fails to comply with court-ordered discovery aimed at determining whether jurisdiction exists in the first place. This is an issue particularly in the United States.

In such cases, when the defendant contesting jurisdiction supports the objection with affidavits or other evidence, the plaintiff in the U.S. proceeding must normally make a *prima facie* showing that jurisdiction is proper. Only then will the court order even limited discovery on that issue of jurisdiction. However, the threshold which that plaintiff must meet to overcome the evidence of lack of jurisdiction is normally low. Namely, the party seeking to have jurisdiction upheld must show merely some ambiguity or incompleteness of record as to effective jurisdiction.

At the same time, the foreign defendant can petition the U.S. court to stay U.S. discovery requests going to the merits pending the limited discovery on jurisdiction and the court's ruling on jurisdiction. U.S. courts usually exercise their discretion to grant protective orders against all other discovery until they settle the issue of personal jurisdiction.

A possible ground to limit the scope of discovery even if the court finds it has jurisdiction is then the balancing test favored in Section 442 of the Restatement Third of the Foreign Relations Law of the United States. Section 442(1)(c) lists five factors that a court should consider to determine whether to order production of information from documents located abroad: (i) the importance of the documents in the litigation, (ii) the specificity of the request, (iii) the origin of the information, (iv) alternative means of obtaining the documents, and (v) the extent to which compliance would undermine United States or foreign interests.

vi. Parallel Proceedings

A potential defendant threatened with a lawsuit in a foreign country may actively attempt to "strike first" by opening proceedings outside of that country. The reasons for doing so can include gaining a perceived "home advantage" in the addressed court, the desire by a defendant to retain its regular local attorneys, language considerations, etc. Both local civil procedure law in some cases and the Brussels and Lugano Conventions attempt to prevent parallel proceedings regarding the same subject matter between the same parties in different jurisdictions. From the viewpoint of the judicial system, such proceedings are highly inefficient and also bring about the danger of conflicting judgments.

Lis Pendens and Res Judicata

Depending on the particular procedural rules, "*lis pendens*" normally commences with service of the instituting document (e.g., action, statement of claim, counterclaim on the defendant). If an additional claim is raised during the course of litigation, the relevant date is the first pleading in the court hearing. The *lis pendens* status terminates either by transformation into a valid judgment status or into a definitive refusal (*res judicata*) or definitive withdrawal or settlement. As long as the *lis pendens* status continues, normally no other court in the same jurisdiction may conduct litigation on the same subject matter.

The situation becomes more complex in the case of international *lis pendens*, where a foreign court litigation is pending involving the same parties over the same subject matter. Such a situation can exist only in matters to which a multilateral convention or a bilateral treaty exists. Where no agreement respecting reciprocal recognition and enforcement of judgments exists, the problem of *res judicata* or *lis pendens* does not occur, as the binding effect of a decision does not extend beyond the national borders unless reciprocal recognition and enforcement is guaranteed.

Brussels/Lugano Convention and Nonconvention Bases

In the case of proceedings taking place in a Brussels or Lugano Convention State, under Article 21 the court where the proceedings were later instituted must stay its proceedings (on its own motion) until the first court has ruled on its jurisdiction. If the first court has confirmed its jurisdiction, then the second court must declare itself incompetent; in the event of parallel proceedings when the action is filed, the second court must reject the claim.

An interesting dispute has arisen in Switzerland as to when a court is seized with a claim within the meaning of Article 21 of the Brussels and Lugano Conventions. Is a court seized when conciliation proceedings are initiated or only when an action with the court is subsequently filed?

The Zurich Court of Appeals, confirming a judgment of the Zurich District Court, recently held that the Lugano Convention provides for an independent definition of the substance of the notion "seized," superseding national law. It further held that it was established under the Brussels and Lugano Conventions that a claim must be pending definitively and that merely the initiation of a conciliation proceeding did not suffice if, according to the applicable cantonal procedural law, such a procedural step did not lead to a definitive seizure of the court. The Court of Appeals decision has been appealed, and the case was, as of July 1997, pending before the Federal Supreme Court.

With respect to nonconvention states in cases where a bilateral treaty exists, local law may provide that proceedings pending before foreign courts will create *lis pendens* in relation to local proceedings between the same parties on the same subject if the decision to be rendered is expected to be enforceable in the local courts by virtue of reciprocal enforcement. As the court will hardly get any notice of proceedings pending abroad, it is up to the parties or the defendant to object on the basis of this legal impediment.

Certain courts in nonconvention states will continue to assert jurisdiction over actions properly before them notwithstanding the existence of parallel proceedings in other jurisdictions unless the local proceedings are stayed on grounds of *forum non conveniens* (discussed above). Where no stay is granted and both proceedings continue, it is likely that the local courts will accept the first decision rendered as being conclusive. In Canadian jurisprudence, for example, if the parties chose to litigate in two places rather than settle in one, the judgment of the first court to resolve the matter would be accepted as binding by the second jurisdiction in most cases.

Parallel Proceedings and "Anti-Suit Injunctions"

To avoid the obvious inconvenience which can arise in parallel proceedings and a "rush to judgment," parties before certain courts, Canada again being an example, may request the issuance of an "anti-suit injunction." Such an injunction, where available, may enjoin the opposite party from proceeding further in a foreign court.

It is preferable to apply for such an injunction when proceedings are actually pending in the foreign court and after an attempt to stay those proceedings has failed. As a general rule, the domestic court will not entertain an application for such an injunction if there is no foreign proceeding pending and only if the applicant establishes that some threatened action by the defendant will constitute an actionable civil wrong.

In this respect, the anti-suit injunction is unique in that the applicant does not have to establish that the assumption of jurisdiction by the foreign court will amount to an actionable wrong. Moreover, although where available the application is heard summarily and based on affidavit evidence, the order results in a permanent injunction, which ordinarily is granted only after trial. In order to resort to this special remedy consonant with the principles of comity, it is preferable that the decision of the foreign court not be pre-empted until a proceeding has been launched in that court and the applicant has unsuccessfully sought a stay or other termination of the foreign proceedings from the foreign court.

In the case of the Canadian courts, for example, in determining whether an anti-suit injunction should be issued a court will consider whether or not the foreign court assumed jurisdiction in accordance with *forum non conveniens* principles and could reasonably have concluded that there was no alternative forum that was clearly more appropriate. If the court concludes that the foreign court's assumption of jurisdiction reflects a reasonable conclusion in accordance with *forum non conveniens* principles, the request for an anti-suit injunction will presumably be denied.

On the other hand, if a foreign court assumes jurisdiction on a basis that is inconsistent with local rules of private international law and an injustice results to a litigant or "would-be" litigant in the local courts, the assumption of jurisdiction will probably be deemed inequitable. In that case, the party invoking the foreign jurisdiction can be restrained.

CHAPTER 4

CHOICE OF LAW

i. Statutory and Other Bases for Application of Foreign Substantive Law

Depending on the jurisdiction, either statutory or common-law bases or both will be applied to determine the application of the proper law, which may be a foreign law, to the given dispute.

Application of Common Law Principles

In the case of disputes with an international element, the choice-of-law question must normally be raised by one of the parties to the dispute. No more is necessary to invoke the choice-of-law rules. Where the international character is "insufficient" in a sense made relevant by the applicable choice-of-law rule, then that rule will direct that the forum law is to apply. On the other hand, where it is contended that another forum's law should apply, the court may then be required to refer to its own choice-of-law rules to determine the applicable law.

Invariably, common-law choice-of-law rules with respect to actions on the contract require that if there is no choice of law expressly or impliedly made by the terms of the contract, then the objective proper law is to apply. Such objective proper law is normally the law of the place with which the contract has its "closest and most real connection." This concept is phrased differently in different jurisdictions. Moreover, different weight may be given to different criteria concerning such "connection" depending on the specific local caselaw.

This divergence and variation is apparent in the United States and its several states. The choice of applicable law in U.S. courts is generally a matter of state choice-of-law rules and state statutes, where applicable. When there is no such statute, significantly different rules have been adopted, ranging from traditional territorial or "vested rights" principles such as *lex loci delicti* (the law of the place of wrong governs) to a more complicated multi-factor approach seeking the law of the place that has "the most significant relationship" under the Restatement (Second) of Conflict of Laws (1971). Still other states use a "governmental interest analysis."

Different rules may apply within a given state to claims based on contract as opposed tort. At the same time, under the U.S. Federal Constitution a state may not apply its own law when it has no significant contacts with the transaction or occurrence. A federal court will follow the choice-of-law rules of its home state, even when most of the relevant conduct took place outside the United States, or federal common-law rules in a few contexts involving the Foreign Sovereign Immunities Act and other federal regulatory regimes.

At common law, the tests used in such weighing are a result of caselaw rather than statute. They tend to be applied flexibly to accommodate the particular circumstances of each case. In tort claims, as stated, the general rule is that the law or system of law of the jurisdiction in which the tort occurred will apply (*lex loci delicti*). Should the tort be said to have occurred in more than one jurisdiction, the court will consider the relationship between the plaintiff and the defendant and their expectations as to what law or system of law would apply to their conduct. This test may be particularly relevant in product-liability suits where foreign defendants are accused of having negligently manufactured products that are distributed in the normal course of their business into the local market and are in turn disseminated over a potentially wide-ranging area.

Where the parties to a contractual dispute have not expressly provided for the choice of law or a system of law in their contracts (*lex voluntatis*), common-law courts will attempt to infer a choice on their behalf. In so doing, the court will consider all of the circumstances which surround the transaction at issue to carefully identify the law most substantially connected to the dispute.

Among the factors which may be considered include (i) the form of the documents created and agreed to by the parties, (ii) the currency in which payments between the parties are to be made, (iii) the language used by the parties, (iv) the connection between any preceding transaction and the transaction in issue, (v) the nature and location of the subject matter, (vi) the residence of the parties to the transaction, (vii) the location of the head offices of any of the parties, (viii) whether one party is a government, and (ix) whether the contract would be invalid by one law and valid by another system of law.

Treaties and Conventions Respecting the Choice of Law

Treaties and conventions entered into by the State do not necessarily form part of the local law unless the treaty has been specifically adopted in implementing legislation. Among such treaties figure in particular the 1980 United Nations ("Vienna" or "CISG") Convention on Contracts for the International Sale of Goods. This convention forms a transnational substantive contract law applying exclusively to the international sale of goods (as defined) and superimposed on the relevant national law.

Also of relevance are the 1980 European Community ("Rome") Convention on the Law Applicable to Contractual Obligations, the 1955 Hague Convention on Sale of Goods, the 1961 Hague Convention on the Form of Testamentary Dispositions, and bilateral and multilateral conventions on such matters as family and succession law, e.g., between and among Scandinavian and Nordic countries.

Both the Hague Convention on Sale of Goods and the Rome Convention recognize the right of the parties to a contract to choose the applicable law. The former applies only to international sales and the latter puts certain restrictions on the effect of the choice where no foreign elements are involved. The Rome Convention also restricts the effect of the choice of law by the parties to certain consumer contracts and individual employment contracts.

Otherwise, as a matter of these conventions the parties have an unlimited right to choose the applicable law. The rules of such conventions respecting the choice of the applicable law apply only if the parties have not themselves made a choice of law. For example, failing a choice by the parties the Hague Convention provides for the application of the law of the seller's country, unless the order is received in the country of the buyer. In the latter case, the law of the buyer's country shall apply.

The scope of the Rome Convention is broad, applying to "contractual obligations in any situation involving a choice between the laws of different countries." In signatory countries, therefore, the Rome Convention rules will apply to purely domestic contracts that stipulate a foreign choice of law. It will also apply to agreements between citizens of states not within the European Union or European Free Trade Association (EFTA).

One common-law jurisdiction which has adopted the rules of the Rome Convention is the United Kingdom, with the common-law rules continuing to apply to contracts made before April 1, 1991.

The foregoing conventions, as well as other relevant ones, have been the subject of jurisprudence in various countries. This jurisprudence, which in the case of the CISG is especially extensive in such countries as Germany and the Netherlands, is essential to consult. This is especially so inasmuch as certain of the Convention provisions are spare in the extreme.

In the case of the CISG, the practitioner should pay heed to the fact that some countries have made a reservation and excluded the application of, e.g., Part II of the Convention, which governs the conclusion of a contract. For example, the CISG is not applied between the Nordic countries, as all of them have made reservations in this respect. The basis for these reservations is that the Sales of Goods Acts in the respective Nordic countries are similar.

From a practitioner's point of view, it is important to understand that in international trade a choice-of-law clause resorting to the law of certain such countries may result in the application of the CISG instead of, or superimposed upon, the local law. If the parties prefer to apply exclusively the substantive law of sales of that particular country, the choice-of-law clause should describe the sales of goods act or other applicable legislation and expressly exclude, where applicable, the CISG. Articles 1, 10 and 95 in particular should be reviewed with care.

Foreign Law as a Question of Fact

In certain jurisdictions, foreign law is regarded as a question of fact, not of law. As a result, an earlier decision of a court of the same forum on the content and meaning of a particular foreign law is not binding upon that court when it has to consider the same law on a subsequent occasion. Findings by the court as to the foreign law depend on the evidence of that law placed before that particular court. Thus, it is possible that the court will construe the same law differently on separate occasions. However, an earlier finding by a court of the forum as to the content and meaning of a foreign rule can be relied on subsequently as prima-facie evidence of that law, where direct expert evidence is lacking.

The principle that foreign law is a question of fact may also mean that a decision by a foreign court which purports to construe and explain the foreign law cannot be regarded as conclusively binding on the courts of the forum. However, a decision of the highest appellate tribunal of the foreign country should normally be regarded as presenting a correct view of the law.

The principle that foreign law is a question of fact has another significance. It may be interpreted, depending on the jurisdiction, as meaning that if the law of a foreign State is to be applied in a case, but if no knowledge of it can be obtained, then the law of the court where the action is pending shall apply instead. It is the parties' duty to prove to the court the content of the applicable law, and if they do not do so, the court may apply only its own law. There may be exceptions, such as where the court has a statutory duty to obtain information on the content of applicable foreign law in certain kinds of disputes, such as bills of exchange. Otherwise, even in difficult circumstances, the court shall not resort easily to the substitution of a governing foreign law by local law.

In the case of trial by jury, an issue of foreign law in a case which is being tried by a jury is normally a question of fact to be decided by the judge, and not by the jury. It should also be noted that the appellate court may have a far greater freedom to interfere with the decision of the lower court on the issue of foreign law than with decisions by inferior courts on other issues of fact.

Proving Foreign Law at Common Law

At common law, the forum, when faced with a question governed by foreign law, normally starts with the assumption that the law of that country is the same as that of the forum, unless proven otherwise. Where judicial notice cannot be taken of the foreign law, the onus of proof lies on the party alleging that it is different from the law of the forum. Foreign law must be proved by a person who is an expert in that law. The court can only act upon the evidence of the foreign law which the expert witness places before it.

Sometimes statutes provide for the admission of foreign law upon production of foreign textbooks, statutes or law reports as evidence of the law of that foreign country. If the text of a foreign code or statute is placed in evidence without calling an expert to explain it, the court will probably construe the code or statute according to the rules of statutory construction of the forum. The ultimate decision with respect to the meaning of the foreign law lies with the judge, who may examine for himself the sources of foreign law to which the witnesses have referred in their testimony in order to resolve any ambiguity. Even where the evidence of the witness is uncontradicted, the court is not bound to accept it if it is of the opinion that the evidence of the witness is patently absurd or inconsistent.

In the United States, Rule 44.1 of the Federal Rules of Civil Procedure (binding in federal courts) provides that in determining foreign law, the court may consider "any relevant material or source, including testimony, whether or not submitted by a party or admissible under the Federal Rules of Evidence" and that its determination shall be treated as a ruling on a question of law. Other states retain older common law requirements of pleading and proof of foreign law, including observance of the rules of evidence. Under Rule 44.1, the court may consider any material that the parties wish to present. Discovery may be available to the parties in preparing themselves on issues of foreign law. A state court (or federal court following a state choice-of-law rule) may apply presumptions. These may include that foreign law is similar to local law if there is a failure of proof of the foreign law or if the relevant issue of foreign law is unsettled.

Civil Law Codification of International Private Law

Most civil-law jurisdictions, including in Continental Europe, refer to "conflicts or law" or "choice of law" instead as "international private law" and have specific legislation on the subject. Such legislation is normally applicable to "international matters." Notwithstanding such codification, what degree of "international connection" makes a case an "international matter" is not always clear either in the legislation or in the caselaw.

In cases where such legislation applies, civil law countries normally refer to the "closest contact" or "closest connection." Points of reference will then include (i) the personal statute of the natural person including the law of the State of citizenship, (ii) the personal statute of the legal entity including the law of the State of its seat or headquarters, (iii) in the case of rights *in rem*, the law of the State where the personal or immovable property is located, and (iv) in the case of intellectual property rights, the law of the State where its use or infringement has taken place. With regard to contracts in general where one parties owes money, reference is made to the law of the State of domicile of the other party and to the place of "characteristic performance."

ii. Role of Party Autonomy and Choice-of-Law Clauses

Opportunities to Stipulate the Applicable Law in Contracts

In the case of contractual relationships especially in the transnational context, the parties should decide at the contracting stage which substantive or "material" law they wish to apply to the underlying contract and merits of any disputes. This may appear to be so basic as not to be worth mentioning. However, once again experience dictates, unfortunately, that the choice of law is often lacking or unclear in the agreement.

In international contracts where the counterparties are of different nationalities and perhaps entirely different legal traditions, often a "neutral" third-country law is chosen as a perceived compromise. To the extent possible at this early stage of drafting, the parties should consider a number of issues which impact on which substantive law should be agreed upon.

These include the likelihood that a party might be the plaintiff as opposed to defendant and the likely nature of the claim which would arise. They also include whether the different bodies of law which are being weighed might result in dramatically discrepant outcomes or damages amounts. For example, the availability or nonavailability of "consequential" or "punitive" damages will depend on the jurisdiction and applicable law. Equally crucial is whether the likely subject matter of the dispute might not be considered "justiciable" under the law applicable. Furthermore, it is important to determine whether the conflict-of-law rules of the body of law favored might result, by renvoi, in application of another body of law which was not anticipated.

The choice of substantive law should be clearly expressed in the contract, whether in the choice-of-forum agreement itself or in a "neighboring" article of the contract. Otherwise, once a dispute arises, needless time and money may be expended litigating solely the issue of the applicable law. Some typical but quite harmful drafting problems in this regard include (i) the absence of any choice of law, (ii) two competing indications of the law, (iii) an indication solely on an ancillary document or on general "terms and conditions" on the obverse of the contract, etc.

Such seemingly innocuous or careless drafting matters could result in the addition of months of argument and briefing as to which law applies to the dispute before the merits of a damages claim are even entertained. Moreover, the lack of agreement on a choice of law hinders the parties in their ability to frame their pleadings before the court, which may or may not have particular knowledge or training in a foreign body of law.

Express Selection of the Proper Law

The most obvious way of expressing choice of proper law is by expressly nominating in the contract "the proper law of the contract" or the "law governing the contract." The proper law should be selected at the time of contracting and not left to one of the parties to nominate at a later date. The parties may by agreement subsequently substitute a different legal system to the one originally chosen.

"Explicit" or "tacit" agreement is not necessarily required and under some bodies of law, such as is the case in Austrian law, even the "determination of the parties' joint assumption of a specific law as applicable" will suffice. In the absence of an express choice of substantive law, the inclusion of a clause stipulating that a foreign court or arbitral tribunal sitting in a foreign country shall have exclusive jurisdiction implies a presumption that the parties have chosen the law of that country unless, in the circumstances surrounding the contract, there is an overwhelming connection with another legal system.

Even after commencement of legal proceedings, a choice of law ex post can validly take place and override a prior choice or choices of law. While prior to commencement of legal proceedings a choice-of-law agreement can be made by tacit agreement, it needs to be made explicitly thereafter. Normally, a later choice of law by the parties may not influence the legal position of third parties.

Party autonomy in choosing the law to apply to the contractual relationship is also enshrined in Article 3(1) of the Rome Convention. This provides that the choice must be "expressed or demonstrated with reasonable certainty by the terms of the contract or the circumstances of the case" and that "the parties can select the law applicable to the whole or a part only of the contract." This provision gives contracting parties even greater autonomy than that enjoyed under the common law rules, which suggest the requirement of some connection with the contract.

Incorporation of the Applicable Law by Reference

The selection of a foreign legal system as the proper law of the contract is distinct from the incorporation of specific provisions of foreign law as part of the terms of the contract. It is open for the parties to provide that the provisions of a foreign code or statute shall be read as part of the contract.

While such an incorporation may strongly suggest the selection of that legal system as the proper law, the parties can select another legal system as the proper law. If the latter is the case, the substantive effect of the terms must be determined under the proper law of the contract. An incorporated law is normally ascertained as it existed at the date the contract was made whereas the proper law is applied as it exists from time to time.

Limitations on Party Autonomy and Public Policy

Parties to a contract have, in principle, a wide discretion to choose the law applicable to a contract. Apart from statutory direction, this choice will normally be set aside only if the choice is not *bona fide*, but instead made in order to evade the otherwise applicable law, or if there is no sustainable reason for the choice of a system factually unconnected with the contract or the parties.

A choice of proper law may be justified not merely by physical connection, but by common business practice or where the parties to a contract with connections to several countries choose an unconnected but commercially developed legal system as a "neutral," as is often done in agreements to arbitrate. Accordingly, reliance on the opt-out provision shall be warranted only in exceptional cases and not give the local court an easy excuse not to apply the relevant foreign substantive law.

The choice of proper law can be overridden by the public policy (ordre public) of the forum. A rule of foreign law may not be applied if it would lead to a result incompatible with the basic values of the local legal system. This might include in the areas of human rights, nondiscrimination, shortening of statutes of limitation, exclusion of compensation for pain and suffering, etc. In addition, a statute of the forum may provide that it is to apply notwithstanding the choice of proper law without invalidating that choice with respect to matters to which the statute does not apply. The Civil Code of Quebec, for example, specifically permits the court to apply foreign law contrary to, or in the absence of, a choice-of-law clause, where the issues are closely connected with that foreign law and "where legitimate and manifestly preponderant interests so require" (Art. 3079). This rule is inspired in part by Article 7(1) of the Rome Convention on the Law Applicable to Contractual Obligations.

With respect to certain kinds of claims such as product liability and anti-trust, local law may restrict a plaintiff's right under applicable foreign substantive law to obtain punitive or treble damages. Articles 135 and 137 of the Swiss Private International Law Statute, for example, provide in essence that even if foreign substantive law applies and would allow a plaintiff to be awarded punitive or treble damages, a Swiss court must not award indemnities going beyond those which would be awarded under Swiss law.

Application of Rome Convention

The Rome Convention, where applicable, expressly imposes certain limitations on party autonomy. Article 3(3) provides that a country's mandatory rules will be applied provided that the contract is connected with that country alone. The appropriate time for testing whether the relevant elements are connected with one country only is at the time of the choice. Article 7(2) of the Rome Convention superimposes certain rules on the choice of law made by the parties which have to be applied regardless of the normal rule of conflict of laws. Article 16 of the Rome Convention states that the application of the rule of law may be refused only if such application is "manifestly incompatible" with the public policy of the forum.

Approaches in Different Jurisdictions

In certain common-law jurisdictions, the possibility of rejecting a choice of law by the parties on the ground of public policy, although often mentioned, is seldom if ever carried into effect. Public policy in such jurisdictions is not necessarily offended simply because the foreign law selected leads to a different result than under local law. In other jurisdictions, statute provides that if the proper law of a contract objectively ascertained is different from the subjective choice by the parties, the court may refuse to enforce, avoid in whole or in part, or vary in whole or in part any contract (or provisions thereof) which it finds to have been unjust under the circumstances relating to the contract at the time it was made. This issue is addressed further below.

Among the areas in which party autonomy in the choice of law may be limited include the protection of traditionally weaker contracting parties such as consumers and employees. Choice of law may also not be at the parties' free disposition where "mandatory rules" (known in the German literature as *Eingriffsnormen*) apply. *Eingriffsnormen* are defined as directive measures implemented by the State, in the form of mandatory rules influencing a private legal relationship. Such rules need not be characterized as "public law," and can be "private law" as long as their purpose is essentially to meet public interest. Examples include rules prohibiting performance in the field of foreign exchange or foreign trade law, specific contract limitations in price administration and antitrust law, restrictions on import and export, regulations on working conditions, and public policy.

Civil-law legislation respecting choice of law normally carves out certain other kinds of legal relationships as to which parties are not allowed to designate the applicable law by their own agreement. Such areas may include bills of exchange and checks, contracts on the carriage of goods, legal capacity of a party, matters of family or probate law, matters governed by the law of companies or trusts, and questions as to whether the acts of an agent or organ have resulted in a contract binding the principal. In other instances, a choice of law may be allowed but restricted to include only the parties involved, for instance with respect to the acquisition and the loss of rights *in rem* to movable property.

No Express Choice of the Proper Law

It is generally agreed that the parties to a contract are free to choose the law which governs the construction, legal effect, performance and discharge of an obligation validly and lawfully created. At the same time, in some jurisdictions there is still disagreement on the approach to be taken where the parties have not expressed a discernible choice of law.

Where the parties have not expressed any choice, it is essentially left to the courts to determine the proper law of the contract. In the absence of an express choice of law, and when the terms of the contract do not enable the proper law to be inferred, the proper law of the contract may be determined by ascertaining the law with which the contract has its closest connection. In conducting this inquiry, depending on the jurisdiction the court will be guided by different criteria which tend, even in vastly different systems, to focus on the "center of gravity" and the "characteristic" activity or performance underlying the transaction or the dispute.

Among these factors are (i) the circumstances as they were when the contract was formed, (ii) the system of law with which the contract has its closest connection, as opposed to the country with which the closest connection exists, and (iii) the contract itself as compared to the transaction underlying the contract. In this regard, a distinction may need to be made between the connection between the legal system and the contract and between the legal system and the underlying transaction.

Among the other factors which may be considered are (iv) the nature and subject matter of the contract, (v) any significant differences between the competing legal systems, and (vi) the principle of validation. This latter principle relates to the notion that parties entering into a contract want their agreement to be binding upon them, and the law of conflict of laws should assist them whenever it can in upholding the validity of the agreement.

With regard to notions of "characteristic performance," Article 4(2) of the Rome Convention introduces a rebuttable presumption that "the contract is most closely connected with the country where the party who is to effect the performance which is characteristic of the contract has .... his habitual residence ... or central administration." At the same time, the concept of "characteristic performance" concerns obligations under the contract other than the payment of money—e.g., the supply of goods and services. This concept is somewhat alien to common-law notions of conflicts of law. In Australia, it has nevertheless been recommended for adoption, in the interest of international uniformity, by the Australian Law Reform Commission.

In any event, the relevant factors must be ascertained as of the time the contract was made. Subsequent conduct of the parties after the making of the contract may not be relevant in ascertaining the proper law unless it constitutes an estoppel or the making of a new contract.

Renvoi Doctrine

Certain countries recognize, in statute or in caselaw or both, the nonapplication of the renvoi doctrine. Under this doctrine, a court resorting to foreign law applies foreign conflict-of-law rules, which may in turn refer the court back to the law of the forum. By rejecting the doctrine, the law of the forum cannot be applicable once the law has been opted out. The nonapplication of the doctrine establishes one law as the final applicable law, thus preventing the continuous referral to another country's law.

Article 15 of the Rome Convention, by excluding the conflict of law rules of the law to which it refers, excludes renvoi, including for the United Kingdom as to contracts made before April 1, 1991. Similarly, in the United States contracting parties' choice of law generally will be taken to encompass only the substantive law of the nonforum jurisdiction and not foreign conflicts law or for that matter foreign procedural law.

iii. Relevance to Later Efforts to Recognize and Enforce

This section is meant to consider only the relevance of the law applied by the foreign court and the existence of a choice-of-law clause in a contract that is the subject of a dispute. A more detailed discussion of the enforcement of foreign judgments is contained in **Chapter 17**.

In many countries, generally the law applied by a foreign court is not relevant to the question of recognition and enforcement of the judgment. With one exception this is also true under the Brussels and Lugano Conventions. The exception is in Article 27, no.4 and arises where the foreign court has decided a preliminary question concerning the status or legal capacity of natural persons, rights in property arising out of a matrimonial relationship, wills or succession. Should the foreign court have done so in a way that conflicts with choice-of-law rules in the country where recognition is sought and reached a different result from what would have been reached in the recognizing country, the judgment need not be recognized or enforced.

Under the enforcement law of certain jurisdictions, the law applied by the foreign court is likewise usually not relevant. The existence of a choice-of-law clause in the subject contract and the particular law so named are not relevant to recognition except insofar as the choice of law implies a choice of forum that is not the forum of the foreign court. For enforcement at common law, the law applied by the foreign court will normally not be relevant unless it results in the application of a rule that is contrary to public policy. A foreign judgment may be enforced only if, *inter alia*, the defendant was resident in the foreign country, submitted to the jurisdiction by appearance, or submitted to the jurisdiction by agreement.

The practitioner must verify whether in the particular jurisdiction at issue a choice-of-law clause whereby the parties agree that their contract shall be governed by the law of a certain country does not amount to a submission to the laws of that country. The fact that the choice-of-law clause refers to the law of the country of the foreign court may be insufficient to establish that the foreign court had jurisdiction.

On the other hand, if the choice of law refers to some other law (including the law of the forum), then this will not deny the foreign court jurisdiction if the defendant was resident in the foreign jurisdiction or otherwise submitted to it. The existence of a choice-of-law clause is therefore irrelevant to enforcement at common law.

Under Rule 44.1 of the Federal Rules of Civil Procedure in the United States, a trial court's determination of foreign law is to be treated as a question of law, not fact, so that appellate review likely will be *de novo*. Thus a court of appeals may consider the trial court's findings and the materials introduced by the parties in the lower courts, as well as any information that it discovers itself.

iv. Other Limitations on Party Autonomy

Depending on the jurisdiction, there may be significant limitations to the application of foreign law in that jurisdiction. For example, the forum (i) may not enforce claims based on or related to the exercise of foreign governmental power and (ii) may not give effect to foreign laws and institutions which are contrary to its public policy or to accepted principles of international law or morality.

With respect to the first limitation, the rule may apply to claims enforcing the interests of a foreign sovereign which arise from the exercise of certain powers peculiar to government, including the power to levy taxation, punish, exercise the right to eminent domain, and protect the national heritage, national security and the national economy. Nor will the local courts necessarily give effect to a purported expropriation of assets situated within the forum by a foreign government even though those assets may belong to a national of that government.

With regard to the second limitation, within domestic law there may exist certain policies which prevent the judicial enforcement of certain types of agreement even though they are not prohibited by positive law. These policies include the policy against oppression and undue influence, the policy against private settlement of a criminal offense, the policy against restraint of trade, and the policies against gambling and prostitution. It may also be contrary to public policy to enforce an agreement the performance of which would, to the knowledge of the parties, involve a contravention of the law of another country.

Aside from these aspects of public policy, a foreign contract will not necessarily be unenforceable on the mere basis that it conflicts with a policy underlying a particular local law, unless that law is mandatory. Accordingly, the courts may ignore a choice of foreign law and apply local law designed to protect a certain class of people (for example, employees) only if a proper construction of the specific provision requires it. In the case of the British Commonwealth, there are certain mandatory laws which apply in all Commonwealth jurisdictions.

CHAPTER 5

SERVICE OF PROCESS DOMESTICALLY TO COMMENCE FOREIGN ACTION

The idea of jurisdiction is only conceivable within the scope of delimited territorial space, as judicial powers are confined within the State's territory. For this reason, interjurisdictional cooperation comprises those legal techniques which, by compensating for the lack of a "universal justice," make possible the extraterritorial enforcement of judicial measures.

Most courts are willing to grant legal assistance to foreign courts or authorities in the form of service of process. If under local law the requested activity is within the competence of the civil courts, the local court will normally comply with such a request for assistance. If not, so-called letters of request, sometimes interchangeably called letters rogatory, are transmitted to the competent authorities (e.g., criminal courts, administrative bodies) or otherwise returned. The courts normally provide service of process on all persons domiciled in the respective country. Details are largely regulated in local regulations and, where applicable, in bilateral and multilateral conventions and treaties.

Particularly civil-law countries generally regard service of judicial process to be a sovereign act. Such an act may be performed in their territory only by the country's own officials and in accordance with its own laws. In general, service of process is effected by the court or by specially designated officials (e.g., a "bailiff") subject to the court's authority. As in purely domestic cases, so in international cases, litigants must at a minimum comply with the provisions of local law regarding service. Obviously, a defendant is not obligated to do anything respecting a suit until properly served with adequate notice of suit.

Most of the jurisdictions discussed herein recognize three basic mechanisms for serving process on persons located in the jurisdiction: (i) multilateral and bilateral agreements that provide mechanisms for extraterritorial service of process; (ii) issuance by foreign courts of letters of request or letters rogatory requesting the local courts to assist in service of process; and (iii) in civil cases, allowing service of the notice to be performed by a party itself if justified grounds are found.

i. Conventions

Multilateral Conventions Generally

There are three Hague Conventions—from 1905, 1954 and 1965—on service of documents abroad which are relevant to the discussion. In fact, only the last two Conventions play a significant role in this area of transnational litigation. The latest in time of the three Conventions which has been ratified by both of the countries involved in the service issue will apply in the individual case.

1954 Hague Civil Procedure Convention

With regard to multilateral conventions, many of the countries discussed in this work are contracting states to the Hague Convention of March 1, 1954 on Civil Procedure. Among the contracting states to the 1954 Hague Convention as of July 1, 1997 are Argentina, Austria, Belgium, Croatia, Czech Republic, Denmark, Egypt, Finland, France (plus certain overseas regions), Germany, Hungary, Israel, Italy, Japan, Latvia, Luxembourg, Morocco, Netherlands including Antilles and Aruba, Norway, Poland,

Portugal, Rumania, Slovak Republic, Slovenia, Spain, Suriname, Sweden, Switzerland, Turkey, and the Vatican.

Pursuant to the 1954 Hague Convention, all contracting states are obliged to effect service of process upon the request of the courts of any other Contracting State. There are no provisions in the 1954 Hague Convention on the effect of the actions of service in the requested country. Modified provisions by way of supplemental bilateral agreements between two States are explicitly permissible under the 1954 Hague Convention, as they do not affect third countries.

Article 1 of the 1954 Convention provides that a request for service must be transmitted by a diplomatic representative of the state issuing the request to the State that shall effect service. The respective embassy will hand over the request either directly to the competent court within the country of desired service or to the Ministry of Justice or equivalent central authority. That authority will forward the request to the competent authority at which service will take place. Service of process through so many instances is more time-consuming than under the 1965 Hague Service Convention (discussed below), under which one "Central Authority" may address its request directly to another Central Authority and a detour through diplomatic channels is therefore unnecessary.

The procedure under the 1954 Convention is further complicated by the fact that the request for service itself must be issued in, or translated into, the official language at the place of the authority effecting service. If formal service is required, this also applies to the documents to be served.

1965 Hague Service Convention

Of greater importance for the purpose of service out of jurisdiction is the Hague Convention of November 15, 1965 on the Service Abroad of Judicial and Extrajudicial Documents in Civil or Commercial Matters, to which some, but by no means all, of the countries discussed in this work are Contracting States.

The Contracting States to the 1965 Hague Service Convention as of July 1, 1997 include Anguilla, Antigua, Aruba, Associate States of St. Kitts & Nevis, Barbados, Belgium, Bermuda, Botswana, Canada, Cayman Islands, China, Cyprus (South only), Denmark, Egypt, France, Germany, Gibraltar, Japan, Luxembourg, Malawi, Montserrat, Netherlands, Norway, Pakistan, Portugal, St. Helena and Dependencies, Seychelles, Spain, Sweden, Switzerland, Turkey, Turks and Caicos Islands, United Kingdom (including the Falkland Islands, Channel Islands and Isle of Man), and the United States. Among the countries discussed herein which have not acceded to the 1965 Hague Convention, also known as the Hague Service Convention, are Austria, Australia, Brazil, People's Republic of China, and Singapore.

Among the countries which have only recently acceded to the Hague Service Convention are Switzerland, which did so on January 1, 1995. While Switzerland had previously accepted service based on both comity and bilateral treaties, the Hague Service Convention improved the situation of foreign authorities or foreign parties which needed to serve Swiss residents or Swiss corporations. It did so by allowing each canton to appoint its own central authority to receive procedural documents originating in another Contracting State and to forward the documents for proper service under Article 2.

Furthermore, the Hague Convention of March 18, 1970 on the Taking of Evidence Abroad in Civil and Commercial Matters, also known as the Hague Evidence Convention, is relevant; this Convention is discussed in **Chapters 10, 11, 12,** and **13** below. Practically, the Hague Service and Evidence Conventions supersede the Convention of 1954 and are most relevant in transnational litigation in at least certain countries. Nevertheless, some countries have not ratified all the Conventions and accordingly, the older Convention is still applicable on some occasions.

Scope of the 1965 Hague Service Convention

The Hague Service Convention applies in "all cases in civil or commercial matters, where there is occasion to transmit a judicial or extrajudicial document for service abroad" (Article 1). The concept civil and commercial matters is somewhat unclear and varies from country to country. It is clear that the Convention is not applicable to criminal matters.

The treatment of tax, administrative, "public" law, and family law proceedings remains unsettled under the Hague Service Convention. For example, the United States and the United Kingdom include any legal proceedings, including administrative proceedings, leaving only criminal proceedings outside the Convention. On the other hand, French and Swiss practice includes all matters except criminal and fiscal matters. Japanese practice excludes all administrative matters while German practice excludes all criminal and public law matters. Finland includes family law matters, but excludes administrative and criminal matters and claims based on criminal offense.

The negotiating history of the Hague Service Convention only reveals the phrase "does not comprise only matters which fall within the jurisdiction of civil and commercial tribunals in those States where there exist separate administrative tribunals": III Conférence de la Haye de Droit International Privé, *Actes et Documents de la Dixième Session* 79 (1964).

The Hague Service Convention is not applicable if the address of the person to be served with the document is not known (Article 1 (2)), thus restricting the Convention's applicability. However, even if the address of the person is not precisely known, the Ministry of Justice or other Central Authority may usually accept the documents and on its own initiative try to locate the person as far as possible.

Requests addressed to the Ministry of Justice or other Central Authority should normally contain at least the following information: (i) the authority from which the documents emanate, (ii) the necessary information on the parties, (iii) the address of the receiving party, and (iv) the nature of the documents. If the documents are not in the official language of the place of service, a certified translation into that language must normally be attached, unless the person to be served accepts them or is otherwise sufficiently capable of understanding the language used in the documents (Article 5). If the documents are not translated, or if the person to be served is not able to understand the language, they will be sent back to the requesting authority without any further measures.

Care must be taken in the case of a country which has more than one official language, and especially a different official language depending on the region. Switzerland, for example, is multilingual, and the documents need to be issued in or translated into the official language at the place of residence or registered office of the recipient, which will be either German, French or Italian.

Manner of Service Under 1965 Hague Service Convention

Documents delivered to the Ministry of Justice or Central Authority may be served (i) by a method prescribed by the internal law of the place of service (Article 5(a)); (ii) by a particular method requested by the applicant that is consistent with that local law (Article 5(b)); or (iii) by voluntary acceptance by the defendant if the prescribed method is consistent with local law. Other methods of service allowed under the Convention include (iv) service through diplomatic or consular channels, either directly upon the defendant, unless the destination country has objected, or (v) indirectly by forwarding the documents to the proper authorities (Article 8).

Direct service under the Convention may be possible (i) by direct mail (Article 10(a)); (ii) through "judicial officers, officials or other competent persons" of the originating country directly through the "judicial officers, officials or other competent persons" of the destination country (Article 10(b)); or (iii) through "any person interested in a judicial proceeding" directly through the "judicial officers, officials or other competent persons" of the destination country (Article 10(c)). Other methods of service allowed under the Hague Service Convention include (iv) service pursuant to another treaty between two countries (Article 11) and (v) service by any other method permitted by the destination country (Article 19).

Reservations under 1965 Hague Service Convention

The 1965 Hague Service Convention seemingly makes an ample variety of methods of service of process in a foreign country available. At the same time, it also provides the signatory countries the possibility to object to some of these methods. These reservations relate to, e.g., service of process by foreign diplomats or consuls and sending service of process directly from abroad by ordinary or registered mail.

Thus under Articles 10(b) and 10(c), a Contracting State may reserve its right not to assist in serving documents transmitted by using any of the methods referred to in sub-paragraphs (b) and (c) of Article 10. Such reservation must be examined carefully, however, in tandem with other conventions to which the State in question may have acceded, particularly since 1965, to understand the full scope.

In the case of Finland, for example, a declaration was given under Articles 10(b) and 10(c), but upon recently joining the Lugano Convention Finland did not give a declaration as to the provision which allows judicial and extrajudicial documents to be sent by the appropriate public officers of the originating State to the appropriate public officers of the receiving State. Therefore, the declarations as to Articles 10(b) and 10(c) have lost their original, restrictive meaning, and bailiffs in Finland are obliged to receive the documents directly.

Article 10(a) of the Hague Service Convention allows "the freedom to send judicial documents, by postal channels, directly to persons abroad." There is confusion over whether mail service is allowed at all under the Convention because of the use of the word "send" rather than "serve." In international cases, some foreign courts have ruled that Article 10(a) permits service by mail without resorting to the Central Authority or translation of the documents into the receiving country's official language. Other courts have held that service by mail is not allowed without involving the Central Authority. In those countries which have not objected to Article 10(a), a direct service of process by mail is allowed.

Other Service Conventions

In 1995, the EU Member States entered into negotiations in Brussels with the aim of drafting a Convention on the Transmission and Service of Judicial and Extrajudicial Documents in Civil and Commercial Matters. This convention, if and when finalized and adopted between and among the EU Member States, is meant to establish a uniform system of transnational service of process within the EU.

Two other treaties of a multilateral nature which are significant are the Protocol of Judicial Cooperation and Assistance in Civil, Commercial, Labor and Administrative Matters signed by Brazil, Argentina, Uruguay, and Paraguay (State parties to the Mercosur) signed on June 27, 1992 and the Inter-American Convention on Letters Rogatory signed on January 30, 1975 during the First Specialized Interamerican Conference on Private International Law and its Additional Protocol, signed in Montevideo on May 8, 1979.

ii. Other Means and Absence of Conventions

The regular service of process is a requirement for the exercise of the right to an ample opportunity to defend and is imposed by the due process of law principle. It is a consequence of the fundamental constitutional guarantee that no one may be judged without being heard.

Bilateral Treaties

Numerous supplementary agreements to the 1954 Hague Convention exist in the form of bilateral treaties on mutual assistance in legal proceedings (service of process) in civil and commercial matters or exchanges of diplomatic notes. It appears that where a State is a party to both the 1965 Hague Service Convention and a bilateral treaty, a person seeking to serve documents may choose between the methods for service offered by the different agreements. Such bilateral arrangements may be of great use and importance in the case of countries, such as Austria, which have not acceded to the better known and more widely accepted 1965 Hague Service Convention.

Such bilateral treaties may contain provisions which partly deviate from the rules of the 1954 Hague Convention. They may do so by, e.g., permitting direct communication between the requesting and the requested authorities without a need to use diplomatic or consular channels. By virtue of supplementary agreements to the 1954 Hague Convention, courts in Austria, Germany, Italy, Liechtenstein, Luxembourg, Netherlands, Sweden and Switzerland may transmit documents from court to court. Bilateral treaties also provide for service of process without charges, e.g., between Austria and Denmark, Germany and Finland.

As stated, various important trading countries addressed in this work, such as Australia, Austria, Brazil, People's Republic of China, and Singapore, are not parties to the 1965 Hague Service Convention. In rare cases one or another country may not be a party to any other multi-party or bilateral treaty in relation to the out-of-jurisdiction service of an originating process. Such countries may grant service of process to numerous countries (and vice versa), in spite of the absence of a convention, based on mutual continuous practice. For example, this was the case as of July 1, 1997 between Austria and Ethiopia, Afghanistan, Algeria, Andorra, Brazil, Cameroon, Chile, China, Columbia, Congo, Costa Rica, Indonesia, Iraq, Ireland, Korea, Kuwait, Libya, Mexico, Monaco, Peru, Philippines, Saudi Arabia, South Africa, Syria, USA, Vietnam, Zaire, and Zimbabwe.

The effects of each bilateral arrangement vary greatly. One of the major differences is that some conventions are based on direct rules of jurisdiction and others on "indirect" rules of jurisdiction. Where the rules of jurisdiction are direct, the rules laid down are applicable in the courts of the State in which the judgment was originally given and the courts of the State in which recognition is sought. Where the rules are indirect, they do not affect the courts of the State in which the judgment was originally given, but they are applied by the courts of the State in which recognition or enforcement is sought.

Local Law and Regulations on Service of Process

In addition, again especially in the case of those countries which may not have acceded to any of the major conventions regarding service out of the jurisdiction, the most recent local law and regulations should be studied with great care. In the case of Austria, for example, complex rules and provisions in this field have been laid down to summarize all issues of legal assistance and service of process to be performed at home and abroad in a 1996 act relating to International Legal Relations and Legal Assistance in Civil and Commercial Matters. Normally, a special procedure requested by a foreign court outside of the scope of a multilateral or bilateral arrangement will be followed unless it is contrary to local public policy at the place where service is sought.

Quite apart from multilateral and bilateral treaties, in international litigation there is a long tradition of the courts of one country requesting the courts of another country for assistance in serving process. These requests are commonly referred to as "letters rogatory" or "international judicial assistance." In many civil-law countries, letters of request, which are discussed in **Part iii.** below, are the customary and preferred method for the transnational service of process. They are carried out on the basis of comity, and thus do not require reciprocity. In such cases, the regular procedure in serving of foreign process domestically does not normally require a treaty between the country where service is sought and the requesting country.

iii. Local Procedural Requirements at Place of Action

As a general proposition, the law of the forum governs procedural matters. Thus the service of an originating process to commence a foreign action need normally be done only in accordance with the rules and requirements of the foreign jurisdiction in order to be validly served. Unless the law of the foreign jurisdiction specifically requires some other rules to be complied with, such other rules, not being the law of the forum, have no relevance to the service of an originating process of a foreign jurisdiction.

If the defendant objects to the service of the process in so far as it objects to the jurisdiction of the foreign court to hear the matter, application needs to be made to the foreign court to exercise its discretion not to hear the matter. It is not, at this stage at least, a concern of the courts in which service has been attempted, and there is no central authority with which any request for service need be lodged.

Non-Hague Convention Service

Service of foreign judicial documents in countries which are not signatories to the 1965 Hague Service Convention, in accordance with a letter of request, may be carried out in various ways: First, foreign diplomatic or consular missions transmit the letters of request to the Foreign Ministry or equivalent central authority at the place of service which subsequently transmits it to the Ministry of Justice, which forwards the request to the district court in whose district service is to be effected. Second, the Ministry of Justice of a foreign State transmits the letter of request to the Ministry of Justice at the place of service if bilateral treaties allow this manner of communication. The Ministry of Justice transmits it to the appropriate court of service. Third, direct transmission from the requesting foreign court to the domestic court of service is possible if provided by bilateral treaty.

Such requests should contain at least the following information: (i) the authority from which the documents emanate; (ii) the necessary information on the parties; (iii) the address of the receiving party; and (iv) the nature of the documents. The letter of request must normally be accompanied by original copies of the document to be served and a certified translation into the home language of the place of service. The Hague Conventions and bilateral treaties provide for reimbursement of service fees and expenses only under exceptional circumstances, e.g., when a serving officer must be employed or a special form of service is requested. For nonconvention service, depending on the jurisdiction, there may be a charge for domestic service of process.

Service of judicial documents in nonsignatory countries is performed by the local courts on the basis of local law (*lex fori*). Foreign rules of procedure are normally observed upon explicit request as long as not contrary to domestic law or public policy, which rarely occurs. If the requesting court has, e.g., requested strict personal service (no substitute recipient allowed), the local court will order the equivalent type of service under local law. Judicial documents are generally served by mail and only in specific cases by court agents.

There are two principle kinds of nonconvention service (in both, service is to be recorded by the serving official).. First, in strict personal service, the document may be served only directly on the recipient and not on a substitute recipient unless with formal proxy for such service. This method of service is required for valid service of the statement of claim under Article 27 of the Brussels and Lugano Conventions and under certain bilateral treaties. Second, in personal service, service need not be effected to the recipient personally, but is sufficient if made on a substitute recipient present at the place of service.

If a document to be served is not in the local language at the place of service, the local law may provide, according to the 1954 Hague Convention, that its service may not be effected against the will of the recipient unless a certified translation is added thereto. An addressee in such a country may therefore refuse to be served a judicial document in a foreign language without a certified translation. Depending on the local legislation, if an addressee intends to refuse service from a foreign court or authority due to lack of a translation, then he may be required to sign the certificate of service and explicitly add his refusal to accept. Otherwise, local law may consider service to have been effected.

Service by Direct Mail

Another issue is whether, in the jurisdiction concerned, the transmission of judicial documents by mail with international certification of service is admissible in relation to such jurisdiction. In this regard, Article 10 of the Hague Service Convention provides for service by direct mail to the foreign defendant or by personal service by a local judicial officer or other competent person. However, the UK, Denmark, Germany, Norway and Sweden, to mention just five countries, object to all or portions of Article 10 service. Moreover, the Eighth Circuit Court of Appeal in the U.S. has itself held that Hague service by mail on a foreign defendant is not sufficient: e.g., *Bankston v. Toyota Motor Corp.,* 889 F.2d 172 (8th Cir. 1989). Other Circuits are split on the issue. Other countries which have objected to serve by direct mail generally are Republic of Yugoslavia, Macedonia, Bosnia and Herzegovina, Croatia, Poland, Rumania, Switzerland (inadmissible if personal service is wanted), Spain, Czech Republic, Slovak Republic, Turkey, Hungary and the Russian Federation.

To the extent this is the case under the local law of such jurisdiction applied as *lex fori,* this may be relevant for subsequent enforcement of a default judgment in such jurisdiction (see **Chapter 17** below). Depending on the jurisdiction, however, if the recipient, notwithstanding the defective service, has physically received the document, local law may provide that service has been cured and is effective.

According to Article 6/3 of the 1954 Hague Convention, diplomatic and consular missions abroad may transmit documents in the respective country, provided that the recipient is prepared to accept service. Where bilateral treaties allow such service to their citizens domiciled abroad, diplomatic missions of such countries may effect service only to their citizens domiciled there, although service in this way is not usual in relation to countries with direct communication from court to court.

An originating process may often be served on corporations by leaving a copy of the originating process with an officer, director, agent of the corporation, or other person at the place of business appearing to be in control or management of that business. If the corporation to be served does not carry on business in the jurisdiction of service, service may not necessarily be considered valid on an officer, director or agent of the business who happens to be in that jurisdiction for reasons unrelated to the corporation's business. There may also be specific rules for service on partnerships and sole proprietorships.

If circumstances arise such that it is "impractical to effect prompt service" of any document requiring personal service or service by an alternative means, the courts in some countries may, on a motion, grant an order for substituted service or may, in the interests of justice, dispense with service altogether. To obtain such an order, a party seeking to serve a document should present evidence of a range of reasonable attempts having been made to effect service so that the court will conclude that all reasonable efforts have been made.

Service on Involuntary Agents and Waiver of Service in U.S. Suits

Finally, depending on the jurisdiction, various kinds of service of process may be proper on a foreign defendant. They should be borne in mind before assuming that such an exercise requires gargantuan efforts. In the case of the United States, for example, current trends suggest that under some circumstances it is becoming easier, not harder, to achieve service on foreign defendants in the U.S. courts.

Among the options available are serving the U.S. subsidiary of the foreign defendant as an "involuntary agent." Whether the U.S. subsidiary is such an "involuntary agent" will depend upon the specific facts, including (i) the extent of control of the parent over the subsidiary, (ii) interlocking relationships between the two, and (iii) obligations of the subsidiary to service the parent's product. Recently, even inclusion of the subsidiary's name and address in the parent's advertising was deemed to be a basis for such a relationship in the New York courts: e.g., *Stewart v. Volkswagen of America*, 181 A.D.2d 4, 584 N.Y.S.2d 886 (N.Y. App. Div. 1992).

Furthermore, in the United States the process of service of a written complaint together with a "summons" compelling an answer under Federal Rules of Civil Procedure 3 and 4(a) has been markedly changed by revisions to Rule 4, both for foreign and domestic defendants. The omnibus 1993 amendments to the Federal Rules introduced a mechanism whereby the plaintiff can request the would-be defendant to waive formal service. There are three incentives to accepting informal service: First, that waiver is not deemed to constitute a waiver of defenses against jurisdiction and venue under Federal Rule 4(d)(1). Second, the defendant receives 60 extra days to reply to the complaint if he waives service under Federal Rule 4(d)(3). A further incentive is that if the would-be defendant refuses to waive formal service, that defendant, if located in the U.S., must pay for the costs of formal service under Federal Rule 4(d)(2).

This has interesting implications for foreign defendants who insist, correctly or not, that service must be formal and must be out of the jurisdiction by means of, e.g., the Hague Service Convention. Federal Rule 4(f) provides for service either by "any internationally agreed means reasonably calculated to give notice" and/or "in the manner prescribed by the law of the foreign country," and service by mail is also permitted unless prohibited by local law. As stated above, various countries addressed herein have such a prohibition.

iv. Practical Problems and Time Factors

Once the prerequisites of a request for service are met either under the 1965 Hague Service Convention or under the 1954 Hague Convention or some other basis, there remains little to do for the party or authority having commenced the service proceedings.

Once the Central Authority has received a proper request for service, it depends on the applicable code of civil procedure how the proceedings are continued. In some jurisdictions, the Central Authority, if it is a court, will directly mail the request to the party named in it. In other jurisdictions, the Central Authority, even if it is a court, will forward the request to the district court in which the party named in the request is resident or has its registered office. From here on in, service of documents issued in a litigation abroad does not differ from service of a domestic document: The district court will mail the request to the party named in it.

Depending on the applicability of bilateral or multilateral agreements and on the provisions of local law respecting service, a foreign plaintiff should expect service of process in another country to be effected within a period of several weeks, if not months, and not several days. Experience also indicates that addressees may find ways of avoiding or frustrating proper service and delaying service of process deliberately.

Substitute Service and Other Alternatives

Unless expressly stated otherwise in the letter of request and subject to the relevant treaty or convention basis, a court will not normally order strict personal service, but rather allow service to a substitute. Accordingly, the requesting court should therefore specify in detail any special service request. Special care should also be given to service on corporate bodies.

If direct personal service is required, it is advisable that the letter of request specify natural persons as recipients. Otherwise, substitutes may be personally served and may sign the certificate of service, but such action may in fact render service invalid. Similarly, special care should be taken in spelling correctly the full name of the recipient, as a wrong spelling may give the recipient an opportunity to validly refuse service where his identity as addressee is not beyond doubt.

As a last resort, the requesting court may demand service by publication (public notice, public bulletin) if service otherwise is not likely to be effected within a reasonable period of time. Such service may be effected on a recipient whose residence is unknown or who cannot be reached at a given address and who has not nominated a representative for service of process.

In those jurisdictions which have not acceded to a convention or treaty with the jurisdiction where the action is based, there may be additional impediments. In Brazil, for example, service of process in a litigation within the Brazilian courts' exclusive jurisdiction has occasionally been refused on the grounds that cooperation is not justifiable when Brazilian law does not allow the foreign jurisdiction to settle the dispute. If the parties are bound by an agreement to submit themselves exclusively to the Brazilian jurisdiction, service in Brazil to commence a foreign action will also not be granted.

v. Relevance to Later Efforts to Recognize and Enforce at Place of Service

Lack of proper service under either the Hague Service Convention, the 1954 Hague Convention, or domestic law may provide a defendant with a valid defense against the judgment issued and may prevent the plaintiff from enforcing such judgment.

Compliance with local law is necessary with regard to service of originating process only if the rules of the foreign forum require it. Therefore, once the judgment comes to be recognized in a foreign country, the question as to whether the service of process there was defective under the law of the place of service will be indistinguishable from the question as to whether a service of process wherever else was defective under the law of the foreign forum generally. The relevance of a defective service of process to enforcement is also addressed in **Chapter 17**.

One of the grounds for nonrecognition of foreign judgments is normally that documents instituting the proceedings have not been made properly, i.e., by way of direct personal service on the defendant. This manner of service guarantees the defendant's right of audience and the opportunity to arrange for a defense. The lack of evidence of proper service is not necessarily an impediment if evidence is presented that the defendant participated in the foreign proceedings.

1965 Hague Service Convention

Article 15 and 16 of the Hague Service Convention are also concerned with proper service being a prerequisite for later recognition and enforcement of a judgment. Absent an unconditional appearance of the defendant in foreign proceedings in a Contracting State, the foreign court shall stay any proceedings until proper service has been effected. This also means that service must have been effected in a manner granting the defendant sufficient time to prepare the defense. Article 15 para. 2 of the Hague Service Convention states, however, that any Contracting State may declare that the proceedings may continue and also a judgment may be issued, even if no proof of proper service has been filed. It is obviously the purpose of this provision to prevent a foreign proceeding from being stayed for an indefinite period of time in cases in which service has definitely failed. Nevertheless, the fact that no proper service was effected will later on provide the defendant with a valid defense against a judgment rendered.

Interaction with Brussels and Lugano Conventions

Article 16 of the Hague Service Convention tries to remedy this by granting the defendant the right to appeal. This remedy only partially heals the lack of proper service because it limits the defendant's participation to appellate proceedings. In such proceedings, the defendant's rights of defense may be more restricted than in first-instance proceedings. Further, the foreign court may refuse to grant the remedy at all if it deems the defense to be without merit. Accordingly, where available, a defendant who has not been properly summoned may consider raising the defense of improper service under the Brussels and Lugano Conventions rather than applying for the remedy under Article 16 of the Hague Service Convention, which may be seen as not sufficiently respecting a defendant's right to its day in court.

Criminal Sanctions

Finally, one should be aware that in certain countries no service from party to party is permitted, and instead is left exclusively to the court at which a case is pending. Switzerland has underlined the importance of its position by introducing Article 271 into the Swiss Criminal Code. This provision makes it a crime for a foreign party or authority to serve directly a party resident or having a registered office in Switzerland.

vi. Service of Process and Default Judgments

The Brussels/Lugano Context

Under the Lugano and Brussels Conventions, recognition and enforcement of judgments in default of appearance may be refused according to Article 27 no. 2. This may be done at the request of the person against whom recognition is sought if the defendant was not duly served with the document which instituted proceedings or with an equivalent document in sufficient time to enable arranging for defense. "Document" in this context includes court payment orders and other documents which are rendered without the defendant's appearance before the court. The above rules apply particularly in instances of judgments rendered where the defendant has failed to appear. Proper service and sufficient time must be established in a cumulative way (European Court of Justice, 3 July 1990, C-305/88). The European Court of Justice has held that a court may deny recognition and enforcement based on Article 27 no. 2 of the Brussels and Lugano Conventions even if the court of judgment has ruled that the defendant, based on Article 20 no. 3 of the Brussels and Lugano Conventions in connection with Article 15 of the Hague Service Convention, was served with the instituting document such that he could have arranged for his defense in ample time (European Court of Justice, 15 July 1982, 228/81).

In *Bernardus Hendrikman and Maria Feyen v. Magenta Druck & Verlag GmbH* (Case C-78/95, European Court, preliminary ruling, October 10, 1996), the European Court recently went even further. It held that where proceedings were initiated against the defendant without its knowledge, and a lawyer appeared before the court on the defendant's behalf but without authorization, the defendant must be regarded as being in default of appearance within the meaning Article 27 no. 2.

Accordingly, the State where the enforcement is sought must ensure that service of process was duly served according to the rules of the State where the judgment was rendered. Moreover, the court must check that the time given to the defendant to respond was *in casu* reasonable. If the time-limit is deemed too short, the judgment can neither be recognized nor enforced in another Contracting State of the respective Conventions.

Service, Jurisdiction and Enforcement

All prerequisites of enforceability must be fulfilled. For example, the defendant may still choose not to appear in foreign proceedings if that court is manifestly not competent. In such a case, the default judgment will not be enforceable. However, such defense is not available in relation to countries which are Contracting States of the Brussels/Lugano Conventions.

For a judgment originating from a Contracting State of the Conventions, under Article 28 no. 4 of the Lugano Convention the court in another Contracting State country which is concerned with the enforcement of that judgment may no longer verify whether the issuing court was competent. The defense of incompetence of the issuing court therefore has to be brought forward in the main proceedings abroad. The defendant will have to decide whether it will appear unconditionally or whether it will make a conditional appearance for the purpose of raising the defense only.

Nonconvention Bases

With regard to enforcement of judgments by default originating from countries with mutual recognition on a bilateral basis, specific but mostly uniform conditions on due service of documents must be fulfilled. Certain bilateral treaties require that service abroad be effected in compliance with the applicable conventions or bilateral treaties. For example, where transmission of documents must be communicated from court to court, the defendant may object to improper service and request refusal of recognition and enforcement if service of the instituting documents was made by mail with international certificate of service.

If a judgment was rendered by default, the party seeking enforcement must normally prove to the enforcing court via originals or certified copies that the summons was duly served on the defaulting party. While the judgment creditor has the burden of proof of proper service, the burden of proof for the lack of sufficient time to arrange for a defense normally lies with the defaulting party. Default judgments originating from jurisdictions with which the country of enforcement has no basis of reciprocal recognition and enforcement will normally not be distinguished from other judgments for purposes of enforcement. They may therefore not be enforceable due to a lack of reciprocity.

CHAPTER 6

SERVICE OF PROCESS ABROAD TO COMMENCE DOMESTIC ACTION

Much can be said for the comparative simplicity and ease of commencing a transnational arbitration, at least "on paper" under the respective institutional or procedural rules, as compared with commencing a transnational litigation by serving out of the jurisdiction in relation to a suit in the jurisdiction, or vice versa.

In the arbitration context, depending on the institutional or procedural rules applicable, complicated issues of "service of process," use of international conventions under the Hague regime, employing consular services, etc. may never arise. Indeed launching the arbitration may be a straightforward matter. This may not only be a convenience, but also have substantive import, as there will invariably be statute of limitations considerations for timely commencement of the action.

As for commencement of suit against the foreign defendant in the local courts, the picture has generally been assumed to be much more complicated. However, depending on the circumstances initiating a suit against a foreigner in the local courts may not be as complex and forbidding as might be assumed. This holds true whether service of process abroad to commence such suit is deemed to lie within the competence of the courts on the basis of mutual judicial assistance or instead through multilateral or bilateral treaties, as already discussed in **Chapter 5** above.

i. Conventions

1954 Hague Convention

With regard to multilateral conventions, many of the countries discussed in this work are Contracting States to the 1954 Hague Convention. As stated previously, by virtue of the 1954 Hague Convention all Contracting States are obliged to effect service of process upon the request of the courts of any other Contracting State. Modified provisions by way of supplemental bilateral agreements between two States are explicitly permissible under the 1954 Hague Convention.

1965 Hague Service Convention

Of greater importance for the purpose of service out of jurisdiction is the 1965 Hague Service Convention, to which some, but not all, of the countries discussed in this work are Contracting States. Indeed, some countries have been hesitant to accede to the Hague Service Convention because it is widely considered "outdated" and no longer able to meet the initial expectations for efficient and simplified transmission of (extra)judicial documents by means of modern communication instruments. Thus while Austria joined the European Union in 1995, it did not at that time accede to the Hague Service Convention.

With respect to countries that are signatories to the Hague Service Convention, service may be effected through either the Central Authority in the Contracting State or in another manner permitted by the Convention and by the rules of the jurisdiction out of which the originating process is issued. If service of process is to be delivered to a Contracting State of the Hague Service Convention, or for that matter the 1954 Hague Convention, the request is to be written according to a model annexed to the respective Convention. Whether that service may be effected through the Central Authority in the Contracting State into which service is to be effected, or by other private means, depends on whether the Contracting State is a nonobjecting or objecting Contracting State.

Nonobjecting Contracting States will permit personal service by private means. Private service of process could be beneficial because the party may avoid time-consuming bureaucracy. The foreign State's policy should be consulted to ensure compliance with the State's internal rules.

Objecting Contracting States require personal service through the Central Authority in that State. Other documents relating to a local action which do not require personal service may be served by an appropriate means of alternative personal service permitted by local rules and by the Hague Service Convention. This means that other documents relating to a local action may be served by mail or through judicial officers or other competent persons of the Contracting State into which service is to be effected.

Other Convention Bases

Among those countries which acceded to the 1954 Hague Convention, some declared that court documents relating to service are to be forwarded through diplomatic channels. To the extent such documents must undergo consular legalization, this procedure may be simplified or avoided under the provisions of other multilateral or bilateral treaties, including the 1961 Hague Convention Abolishing the Requirement of Legalization for Foreign Public Documents, which abolishes compulsory legalization of public documents among the Contracting States to that Convention.

Of great potential significance for EU Member States is the new Convention on the Service in the Member States of the European Union of Judicial and Extrajudicial Documents in Civil or Commercial Matters, signed by the Ministers of Justice on May 26, 1997. The EU Service Convention is now being considered for ratification by the national legislatures, so that the Convention is not likely to enter into effect for some time. The intention is to create a uniform system of transnational service on the basis of direct transmission from specific authorities supported by modern means of (tele)communication.

ii. Other Means and Absence of Conventions

As stated, various important trading countries addressed in this work are not parties to the 1965 Hague Service Convention, and in some cases one or another country may not be a party to any other multi-party or bilateral treaty in relation to the out-of-jurisdiction service of an originating process.

The manner by which service outside of the jurisdiction, or *ex juris*, may be effected is to be determined with reference to (i) the rules of the jurisdiction or the individual state, canton or province as applicable, (ii) the Hague Service Convention for Contracting States, and (iii) any applicable bilateral conventions which exist between the local jurisdiction and another State. The Hague Service Convention and the provisions of existing bilateral conventions concerning service of documents have been described above with respect to service of foreign documents within a local jurisdiction.

Recourse to the means of service set out in the Hague Service Convention or bilateral treaties may not necessarily be required under local law. In such cases, however, practitioners instituting proceedings against foreign defendants in that local jurisdiction should be alert to the potential difficulties in enforcing a judgment from that jurisdiction in a foreign court when the procedures set out in the Hague Service Convention or a treaty have not been followed. In this regard, the principle of reciprocity may play an important role.

Bilateral treaties partly modify the 1954 Hague Convention. Some of them, e.g., permit direct communication between the requesting and the requested authorities without using diplomatic or consular channels. For example, transmitting documents from court to court is admissible between Austria, Germany, Italy, Liechtenstein, Luxembourg, Netherlands, Sweden, and Switzerland. Bilateral treaties also provide for service of process without charges or reimbursement of expenses, as is the case between Austria on the one hand and Denmark, Germany, and Finland on the other.

iii. Local Procedural Requirements at the Place of Action

Especially in the case of those countries which may not have acceded to any of the major conventions regarding service out of the jurisdiction, local law and regulations should be studied with great care.

In Austria, for example, the service of judicial documents lies within the responsibility of the court. In Austrian litigation, the judge orders service of judicial documents upon request of the parties or on its own motion, specifying to whom and in which manner service is to be carried out. If due to a mistake by the persons acting on behalf of the court, service is deficient and a party incurs a damage or loss as a result, the State is held liable.

Obtaining Leave of the Court

In some jurisdictions which are not Contracting States to multilateral or bilateral agreements on service out of jurisdiction, prior leave of the court must be obtained in order to serve a defendant overseas. Leave is obtained by *ex parte* application supported by an affidavit in which the basis of the application is described and the deponent states his belief that there is a good cause of action. In other jurisdictions, the initiating process may be served overseas without prior leave of the court. Here, however, leave is required if the plaintiff seeks to proceed after the defendant has failed to enter an appearance.

In jurisdictions which distinguish between service with and without leave, service *ex juris* may normally be made without leave of the local courts provided that the statement of claim alleges facts demonstrating a substantial connection between the jurisdiction and the matters raised in the action. Thus service *ex juris* may be permitted without leave where, e.g., the issues involve (i) real or personal property situated within the jurisdiction, (ii) contracts made in or which are to be executed in the jurisdiction, (iii) contracts in which the jurisdiction is also the choice of law or forum, (iv) torts committed within the jurisdiction, (v) damage sustained within the jurisdiction arising from a tort or breach of contract, or (vi) an injunction requiring a party to do or refrain from doing anything within the jurisdiction or otherwise affecting real or personal property situated within the jurisdiction.

Where prior leave is indeed required, the court generally has discretion as to whether leave will be granted. That is, even where one or another "nexus" provision is satisfied, that will not of itself entitle the plaintiff to leave to serve out of the jurisdiction. Such nexus provisions are intended to show a degree of connection with the jurisdiction and include (i) analyzing where the contract being sued upon was made or breached, (ii) where the tort being sued for was committed, or (iii) whether the foreign defendant is a proper party to a matter already commenced against another defendant in the same jurisdiction. When a plaintiff must seek leave of the court to serve a nonresident party, affidavit evidence may be required to be filed establishing a factual basis for choosing that jurisdiction as a *forum conveniens* and indicating where the person to be served is expected to be found.

Types of Service Under Local Law

Depending on the legal prerequisites, under local law one of the following types of service might be carried out: First, strict personal service, where the postman may leave notification in writing (paper sticker) of the date of the second attempt of service, and a deposit may be made at the post office, indicated by another written message to the recipient. At the post office, the document may be held for the recipient for a certain period, usually at least two weeks. If valid deposit is made, then proper service may be established, even if the documents are not collected and subsequently returned to the court.

Second, any person residing with the recipient or the recipient's employee or employer present at the place of service may be authorized to take service on behalf of the recipient. This type of service is used for judgments and court orders, summons, petitions, and notifications of a party (once the proceeding has been instituted) to the court and opposing party. A substitute recipient needs to accept service voluntarily. If he refuses, this does not constitute service (contrary to refusal by the recipient).

Third, service by publication (public notice, public bulletin) may be possible on recipients of unknown residence or who cannot be reached at a given address and have not authorized a representative for service of process. This procedure may also apply for recipients who remain abroad without a permanent residence and cannot be reached even after serious and diligent investigation of the actual place of residence. This procedure may also apply if the requested authority refuses to perform the act of service and the defendant's domicile is legally deemed to be inaccessible for that reason. Local requirements for service of process by publication must be heeded, including with respect to location, timing, frequency and the content of the publication.

Fourth, service of a document may require legal action in order to safeguard legal interests and need to be made on a recipient whose residence is unknown. In some jurisdictions, the court may, at the applicant's request and cost, appoint and authorize a person to receive service of legal process in such cases on behalf of the unreachable recipient.

Service of process law in some jurisdictions is governed by the "obligation of receipt," namely, that a recipient who refuses to accept documents properly served is treated as if he had actually received the document of service. In Australia, for example, personal service is effected even where the person will not take a copy of the document provided that the contents of the document are explained and it is left as near as possible to that person.

Foreign Service in Relation to Suits in the U.S.

With regard to service of process on foreign defendants in connection with suits pending in the United States, service in the U.S. must typically be completed within 120 days from filing of the complaint; otherwise, the U.S. court may dismiss the defendant without prejudice to refiling. Improper service of process must be raised at the first time the foreign defendant files a motion, by "special appearance," or its answer, whichever is first. Otherwise, the defense is waived.

Where the foreign defendant is a corporation, there are essentially three options for service in connection with the U.S. action. First, a U.S. subsidiary may be served as "involuntary agent" depending on such factors as the extent of control of the parent over the subsidiary, any interlocking relationships, obligations of the subsidiary to service the parent's product, and inclusion of the subsidiary's name and address in the parent's advertising: *Stewart v. Volkswagen of America*, 181 A.D.2d 4, 584 N.Y.S.2d 886 (N.Y. App. Div. 1992).

Second, Federal Rules of Civil Procedure Rule 4 contains provisions as to service on U.S. corporations. These include (i) allowing for personal delivery, (ii) leaving papers with a responsible person at the U.S. subsidiary's place of business, (iii) delivery to an appointed agent, (iv) delivery by registered mail return receipt requested according to the laws of the state in which the federal court is located, or (v) otherwise the best practical means available. The foreign defendant may also be served under Rule 4(i), if there is no involuntary or voluntary agent in the U.S. and as long as Rule 4 procedures have not been limited by international agreements to which the U.S. is signatory, including the Hague Service Convention.

Third, under Rule 4(i) there are additional means of service in the case of a foreign defendant. These may include (i) as prescribed in the foreign court, (ii) as directed by the foreign central authority in response to a letter of request when service is reasonably calculated to give actual notice, (iii) by personal delivery to the foreign defendant's corporate officer or managing or general agent, (iv) by mail return receipt requested, or (v) as directed by the U.S. court where suit was filed. With regard to the Hague Service Convention and the U.S., under *Volkswagenwerk v. Schlunk*, 486 U.S. 694 (1988) if service must be made outside the U.S. and Hague Service is available, it must normally be used.

Service of Letters Rogatory by Foreign Courts

Service of judicial documents by foreign authorities abroad through letters of request or letters rogatory is normally achieved in one of three ways:

First, the requesting court transmits the letter of request to the Ministry of Justice or other Central Authority in that jurisdiction. It then transmits it to the Ministry of Foreign Affairs in that jurisdiction, which in turn transmits it to the Ministry of Foreign Affairs of the requested State (via the first State's diplomatic missions abroad). It must be verified in each individual case whether service of documents may be effected by diplomatic or consular missions.

Second, if bilateral treaties so permit, letters of request may be transmitted from one Central Authority to the other country's Central Authority (which regularly is the

Ministry of Justice or equivalent). This central body transmits letters of requests to the courts where the service is to be effected.

Third, direct transmission from the requesting court in the first State to the court of service abroad may be possible if bilateral treaties so allow. In relation to countries with direct transmission of documents from court to court, the diplomatic or consular mode of transmission is not usual.

Furthermore, depending on the jurisdiction, judicial documents in local proceedings may be validly served on recipients with a known domicile in certain foreign countries, as an exception, through mail with international certificate of service if service of process has been denied or proven difficult or impossible.

Certain jurisdictions provide for specific requirements which must be fulfilled above and beyond the conventional information customarily called for in letters of request or letters rogatory. Such requirements and recommendations may include (i) issuance of a check for each service of process as an advance on costs for each examination of witnesses, (ii) inclusion of original and translated lists of questions to be posed to witnesses, (iii) presentation of the letter to the foreign Central Authority prior to the date appointed for appearance in court and/or filing of the defendant's answer, and (iv) a specified number of originals and copies of a sworn translation of the relevant documents.

iv. Practical Problems and Time Factors

Once the Central Authority has received a proper request for service, it depends on the applicable code of civil procedure how the proceedings are continued. In some jurisdictions, the Central Authority, if it is a court, will directly mail the request to the party named in it. In other jurisdictions, the Central Authority, even if it is a court, will forward the request to the district court in which the party named in the request is resident or has its registered office. From here on in, service of documents issued in a litigation abroad does not differ from service of a domestic document: The district court or equivalent will mail the request to the party named in it.

Timing of Service Abroad

Also as stated above, depending on the applicability of bilateral or multilateral agreements and on the provisions of local law respecting service, a foreign plaintiff should expect service of process in another country to be effected within a period of several weeks, if not months, and not several days. Experience also indicates that addressees may find ways of avoiding or frustrating proper service and delaying service of process deliberately. Some countries execute foreign letters rogatory only on condition that a minimum period for the defendant's answer is granted.

Explicit refusal of service of process is very rare, as most countries are interested in granting service of process. It may however happen that although the state authorities are willing, the court in charge does not perform the request. In this regard, it would therefore be misleading to determine a fixed period of time after which service of process is regarded as impossible. Unless informed by the authorities of the foreign state that execution of the request is impossible, it is advisable for the plaintiff to prod the domestic court with a letter of urgency. In addition, the party interested in the execution should not hesitate to address reminders to the court.

If the political situation in a recipient country is difficult and the authorities seeking to obtain service abroad have already had negative experiences there, such authorities may elect not to continue service efforts in such foreign country. In such a case, in Switzerland for example, the original summons will be published in an official gazette and such publication will be deemed sufficient service for Swiss domestic purposes.

Other Practical Problems of Service Abroad

Service on corporate bodies must be treated with care. If direct personal service is required, it is advisable that the letter of request specify natural persons as recipients. Otherwise it may easily happen that the document is handed over to nonauthorized persons, who then sign the certificate of service, which may render the service invalid.

Merely providing an address for service of process is insufficient in certain jurisdictions. In such cases, the court where the litigation is pending may exercise its discretion to order a foreign party to appoint a domestic representative for service of process if the court considers this more efficient than service abroad. If the party does not follow this order within the prescribed period of time, then the court may order that any further service be made by depositing the documents at the court building. In such cases, however, the court may not normally appoint a representative for a party.

In some cases, a recipient has given proxy to an attorney or other person with full legal capacity and has notified this to the court or authority of procedure. In some jurisdictions, service in such cases may then be made only through the authorized representative. Depending on the local law, service of documents instituting the proceedings (e.g., statements of claim) may not be able to be legally effected on a person who is only generally authorized for receipt of documents on behalf of the addressee but has no special authorization for receipt.

The burden of proof for defective service of process lies with the party claiming it. If a recipient claims that he was permanently absent when service was made, then he must prove this by offering specific evidence to the court.

v. Relevance to Later Efforts to Recognize and Enforce at Place of Service

By using the Central Authority mechanism, where applicable, requests are processed in an official manner, theoretically limiting any problems with subsequent recognition and enforcement. It is therefore advisable to use the Central Authority. The use of other means, such as private measures, should be resorted to only when time factors are extremely short.

Nullity of Judgment

If process is not served, the case cannot proceed. Lack of proper service under either the 1965 Hague Service Convention, the 1954 Hague Convention or domestic law will provide a defendant with a valid defense against any judgment which is nevertheless issued and will prevent the plaintiff from enforcing such judgment. A suspicion of nullity on the basis that a party to the litigation has been unlawfully prevented from being heard or participating in the proceedings due to defective (lack of) service will normally be examined by the court at any time during the proceedings, either on its own motion or on request of the party.

If such nullity affects a judgment, the court where enforcement is sought should refuse its enforcement and withdraw any enforcement orders already issued. Where applicable, local law provides the guarantee of fair trial (due process of law) and the right of a party in civil litigation to be properly heard under Article 6(1) of the European Convention for the Protection of Human Rights and Fundamental Freedoms, Rome, November 4, 1950. If such right has been infringed, a party may appeal to the European Commission of Human Rights after its appeal based on nullity has failed.

As stated previously, one should also be aware that in certain countries no service from party to party is permitted. Instead, service is left exclusively to the court at which a case is pending. It is therefore prudent to approach the relevant local authorities and confirm that personal service in the proposed State is not otherwise prohibited. Some States consider the service of process to be an official act which should be undertaken only by appropriate local authorities. Thus, for example, in Switzerland the parties participating in litigation are not involved in service procedures and, corresponding to this position, service must be effected through the courts.

Enforcement After Service by Publication

As opposed to foreign enforcement proceedings, in domestic enforcement proceedings it will not necessarily help the defendant to argue that publication in an official gazette at the place of enforcement was not proper service under any of the applicable conventions. As long as the local law permits such means, a judgment based upon such service will remain recognizable and enforceable in the place of issuance of the judgment. This is particularly relevant in the case of judgments rendered in jurisdictions solely on the basis of the presence of assets of the defendant, even where the defendant could not be served other than by publication.

In Switzerland, for example, quite often lawsuits are continued although no proper service other than publication could be effected and the plaintiff enforces the judgment against assets attached in Switzerland. The Lugano Convention, to which Switzerland recently acceded, has circumscribed the possibility of such lawsuits by providing in Article 3 no. 2 that the place of attachment is no longer by itself a proper venue.

Moreover, as of January 1, 1997 revised Article 271 of the Swiss Federal Act on Debt Collection and Bankruptcy provides that attachments in Switzerland against foreigners are possible only if the claim on which the requested attachment is based has a sufficient relationship to Switzerland or is based on an enforceable judgment. While the purpose of the revision is to do away with attachments based only on the presence of assets in Switzerland, a sufficient relationship to Switzerland may also be given if the claim on which an attachment is sought is governed by Swiss law.

vi. Service of Process and Default Judgments

Under the Lugano and Brussels Conventions, as stated above, recognition and enforcement of judgments in default of appearance may be refused. This may occur according to Article 27 no. 2 at the request of the person against whom recognition is sought if the defendant was not duly served with the document which instituted proceedings or with an equivalent document in sufficient time to enable arranging for defense. The European Court of Justice has held that lack of service precluded the enforcement of a default judgment even though the defendant had become aware of the judgment and had taken no steps to set aside the judgment.

Accordingly, the State where the enforcement is sought must ensure that service of process was duly served according to the rules of the State where the judgment was rendered. Moreover, the court must check that the time given to the defendant to respond was *in casu* reasonable. If the time limit is deemed too short, the judgment can neither be recognized nor enforced in another Contracting State of the respective conventions.

Brussels and Lugano Convention Bases

The defendant may still chose not to appear in foreign proceedings if that court is not competent. For a judgment originating from a Contracting State of the Brussels and Lugano Conventions, the court in another Contracting State which is concerned with the enforcement of that judgment may no longer verify whether the issuing court was competent. The defense of incompetence has to be brought forward in the main proceedings abroad.

Other Bases

With regard to enforcement of judgments by default originating from countries with mutual recognition on a bilateral basis, specific but mostly uniform conditions on due service of documents must be fulfilled. If a judgment was rendered by default, the party seeking enforcement must normally prove to the enforcing court via originals or certified copies that the summons was duly served on the defaulting party. Default judgments originating from jurisdictions with which the country of enforcement has no basis of reciprocal recognition and enforcement will normally not be distinguished from other judgments for purposes of enforcement.

Whereas documents instituting proceedings normally request the strictest procedure of service provided by local procedural law (direct personal service on the recipient or his proxy), default judgments like any other judgment may also be served on substitute recipients. Where judgment by default has been rendered, depending on the jurisdiction service of that judgment itself is not necessarily a prerequisite to execution.

Furthermore, attachments, seizures and the like of the defendant's property within the local jurisdiction pursuant to a default judgment may or may not necessarily require the service *ex juris* of proceedings in execution. Where, however, the defendant has no known address at the place of enforcement, such service may be effected by leaving a copy of the process at the office of the court.

CHAPTER 7

COMMENCEMENT OF SUIT

Quite apart from issues discussed previously related to the service of judicial or extrajudicial documents, commencement of a suit normally involves the preparation of a summons and/or complaint setting forth the basis for the action. The requirements respecting the form, substance and content of such summons or complaint will obviously differ from jurisdiction to jurisdiction. It is critical that the complaint be prepared and filed properly, since any delay could be irremediable.

For example, the plaintiff may be seeking to toll a statute of limitations by commencement of suit. It might fail to do so if it did not commence the litigation properly before expiration of the limitations period. In some jurisdictions, where expiry of a limitation period is imminent and there is insufficient time to prepare a statement of claim, a more limited notice of action may be issued preliminarily to toll the limitations period temporarily.

Conciliation and Conditions Precedent

In many transnational contracts and especially ones containing an agreement to arbitration but also ones with a choice-of-forum agreement, the parties agree to attempt settlement, conciliation, mediation or some referee procedure as a condition precedent to the right to commence an action. This might also be called a "cooling off" agreement. An example might be that if any dispute is not settled within 30 business days after it has arisen, any party may refer the dispute to a meeting of appropriate higher management of the parties. Such provisions may be a mixed blessing. "Cooling off" periods often motivate the parties to talk before arbitration or litigation. However, just as often, they instead engender jurisdictional disputes as to whether or when a dispute has "arisen" in the first place and whether the condition precedent for suit or arbitration was fulfilled.

In some jurisdictions, such as Switzerland, procedural law requires that prior to filing suit the plaintiff submit its claim to a conciliation official to attempt to settle or to prevent the plaintiff from filing a suit with no prospect of success. In the context of commercial disputes, conciliation proceedings frequently are a mere formality. Although mandatory, they often prove to be unsuccessful in the context of commercial disputes. In other cases, such conciliation procedures may be an effective means of resolving the dispute and even salvaging the relationship, as set forth in greater detail in **Chapter 18** below. In the Swiss case, in some cantons such as Zurich certain types of actions are expressly exempt from the otherwise mandatory conciliation proceeding, including suits involving trademark, patent, copyright, or employment law claims.

Filing of the written request for conciliation under federal substantive law, in the case of Switzerland, may have the effect of interrupting the statute of limitations and, where at least one party is domiciled abroad, render an action pending in Switzerland at the time of filing such conciliation request. Where Article 21 of the Lugano Convention applies, Swiss doctrine is split on whether the mere filing of a conciliation request under local law is sufficient to make the action definitively pending or whether this is the case only at the time the action is submitted to the competent court.

Overarching Principles of Procedural Law

Particularly in civil-law countries, but also to varying degrees in other legal traditions, there are certain fairly consistent principles and maxims which guide civil procedure particularly at the commencement stage of claim and defense in a litigation.

The first of these principles, known in German as the *Dispositionsmaxime*, holds that the plaintiff has the right to determine whether, when and to what extent it wishes to pursue a claim, and the defendant whether and to what extent it wishes to acknowledge or contest a claim brought against it. This maxim also gives the parties the right to determine whether or not to file appeals, to settle pending litigation, or to withdraw a claim or to file only a partial claim. It also prevents the courts from rendering awards exceeding the relief sought by the plaintiff or awarding less than has been acknowledged by the defendant.

Secondly, it is impermissible to force another person to file a claim, under the principle known in German as *Klageprovokation*. However, since it may be possible to file an action for negative declaratory relief if a relevant legal interest may be demonstrated, it is possible to reach the same result, that is, to set an end to a legal uncertainty caused by another person and/or entity.

Thirdly, the *Eventualmaxime* imposes upon the parties the duty to put forward all of their factual allegations, means of evidence, and defenses within a certain time frame of the proceeding. After the lapse of a stipulated time frame, new factual allegations and/or defenses are admissible only if a party can sufficiently demonstrate that it was impossible to submit such allegations, defenses, and means of proof at an earlier stage.

Fourthly, the so-called *Verhandlungsmaxime* imposes upon each party the burden to submit to the court the relevant facts upon which it bases its claim or its defense and the means of evidence by which it wishes to furnish proof. As a consequence, the court subscribing to such principle may, except in some special proceedings, base its judgment exclusively upon facts duly alleged and proved by the parties. It follows that while the court may not on its own motion collect additional facts relating to a certain dispute, it may have the right or even duty to clarify allegations which are unclear and assist inexperienced parties to amend their pleadings.

Fifthly, municipal courts are guided by the principles of *iura novit curia* and due process. According to the first principle, it is solely for the court to apply domestic and foreign law, irrespective of the positions taken by the parties. The second principle requires that the parties be given the right to attend court hearings, be represented by counsel, have access to and review the files, have all relevant means of evidence be considered by the court, and receive reasons from the court for its judgment.

i. The Complaint or Statement of Claim: Form, Substance, Content, Strategic Considerations

Local rules of court provide for different methods of commencement of proceedings. In many jurisdictions, particularly under common law, a distinction between disputes involving contested facts and questions of law is maintained. The originating process can be either a writ, statement of claim or complaint, summons, or notice of motion. In those jurisdictions which maintain this distinction, a summons is used for matters where proceedings raise questions of law or are suitable for summary determination, while where an examination of factual issues is required, commencement is by statement of claim.

Originating Summons or Complaint

To sue a party before a local court, in certain jurisdictions a plaintiff normally cannot validly serve its action directly on the defendant. Rather, it must file it in the court which is presumptively competent. The court examines whether it is competent over the dispute and, if so, serves a copy of the originating document upon each defendant. By contrast, in certain common-law jurisdictions, the various court rules allow for originating process to be "alive" for a period after issue (that is, filed with the court registry) and prior to service. In such cases, service is the responsibility of the plaintiff, not the court, and generally the period allowed between issue and service is 12 months.

The practice of commencing proceedings, but not serving them immediately, is often used in matters where a limitation period is expiring and the plaintiff does not desire, at that time, to serve the proceedings and engage the defendant. The distinction is in any event critical, as is whether the time of commencement of suit is deemed to be the date of submission of the originating summons to the court or rather the date of effective service upon the defendant. In Finland, for example, a case now becomes pending upon the arrival of the application in the court's office, whereas until recently under the former Finnish law a civil case became pending upon the actual service of the summons on the defendant.

Form and Content of the Complaint

The complaint or other document must normally be in writing and, if representation by an attorney is required, signed by the attorney. The complaint must normally contain substantially all factual allegations which, if proved true, form a sufficient basis for a ruling in favor of the claim. The scope of the summons or complaint will obviously also depend on the particular circumstances, nature, and complexity of the case. It will also be a function of the plaintiff's desire and, in particular, its ability at the time of filing the suit to plead with specificity the factual and legal elements of its case. Last but not least, its drafting will reflect the customs, style, and thinking of the plaintiff and/or its counsel.

Thus, the form and content of the complaint should not be and cannot possibly be generalized. Suffice it to say that, for example, the "notice pleading" style may not be what is called for in other jurisdictions, and that a truncated list of mere categories of claims, without more, might arguably fail to constitute a sufficient statement of claim under certain local rules. In any event, it is presumably incumbent upon the defendant to raise the problem, or objection, of incompleteness. Except in egregious cases, it should not necessarily be assumed that the receiving court will do so sua sponte.

The issues identified in the originating complaint or process (as well as in any defense or counterclaim) will largely determine the scope of the discovery, if applicable, available in the subsequent proceedings. Similarly, unless the cause of action is properly pleaded, the plaintiff may find at the conclusion of the hearing that the remedies sought are not supported by the allegations raised in the pleading. The wording of the relief sought, sometimes called the "prayer," should be correct and carefully formulated. For the court, in its judgment, may not go beyond what the plaintiff actually sought, and this is also important for later *res judicata* effect.

In many civil-law jurisdictions, the facts and the allegations may be stated succinctly in the complaint with little argument. This is a reflection of the fact that judgments in such jurisdictions are based primarily on the claims, facts, and allegations as presented orally to the court in the final hearing; the exchange of briefs is meant purely for the purpose of clarifying the delimitation of the subject matter of the case. On the other hand, certain appeals may be decided solely on the pleadings, as discussed in **Chapter 15** below. In such cases, the pleadings of both parties should include the complete argument which otherwise would have been presented orally to the court.

Pleading Facts Versus Law and Evidence

The allegations in the pleading should distinguish between fact and law and between fact and evidence. The evidence by which facts are to be proved is not necessarily to be pleaded in the originating complaint, but rather later in the proceedings. This will also be a function of whether, if at all, pretrial discovery of the common-law variety is available in the relevant jurisdiction. Conclusions of law must not necessarily be pleaded.

In setting out the points of law relied upon, the plaintiff may be expected to refer specifically to the relevant sections of applicable statutes, domestic or foreign. If an action involves foreign law, it will be advisable to provide more detail in the complaint regarding the foreign legal sources. The facts and the allegations are in practice sometimes stated together without a clear distinction. This may cause doubt about the exact allegations. It is often advisable to present facts and allegations in two separate sections of the complaint.

Types of Action and Damages Sought

Depending on the local procedural law, certain different types of actions may be commonly distinguished. First, the plaintiff may seek a judgment ordering the defendant to do something or refrain from doing something, e.g., performing a legal/contractual obligation, paying damages, etc. Second, an action may be aimed at bringing about a change or reversal of an existing legal situation or the establishment of a legal relationship, e.g., dissolution of a legal entity, nullification of corporate resolutions, allocation of real property. Third, an action may be aimed at obtaining declaratory relief upon demonstration of a specific legal interest.

If damages are claimed, the statement of claim should specify the amount claimed with respect to each claim asserted. Under certain circumstances, it may be possible and advisable to file an unspecified claim for the payment of a sum of money. This may be the case (i) if expressly provided for in a statute, (ii) if the amount of damages suffered cannot be specified or is difficult to assess because the final amount will be influenced by uncertain future events, or (iii) if the plaintiff can specify the amount only after the evidence taking. Sometimes, if the plaintiff has a right to obtain information from the defendant, it is admissible first to submit a claim for information from the defendant and to combine this claim with an unspecified damage claim.

Furthermore, according to the principle of the *Dispositionsmaxime* set forth above, local procedural law may allow the plaintiff to submit a partial claim. By so doing, the plaintiff may reduce costs and risks and, depending on the outcome of the case, the plaintiff can subsequently initiate proceedings for the balance of the amount due. However, the defendant who is confronted with a partial claim may file a counterclaim for a negative declaratory judgment, so that in substance the entire claim is pending and must be decided by the court.

Strategic Issues in the Complaint and Answer

The requirements for a complaint involving a foreign party are normally no different from disputes between two local parties. If a party's counsel considers foreign law applicable, he should explain the contents of such law at an early stage. Depending on the jurisdiction and custom, it may be advisable to do so in the statement of claim or answer to the claim. This is normally not required, however, as the content of foreign law may need to be examined on the court's own motion if it considers such law applicable. Where reliance is sought on a point of foreign law, the foreign law may be treated as fact and need to be pleaded. The onus of proof may lie on the party seeking to rely on the foreign law.

Where the local rules and customs require the parties to explicitly name in their pleadings (oral or in writing) evidence for every assertion, this need not initially be complete, and may be amended or supplemented at a later stage. It is often the plaintiff's strategy to assert the minimum required to give a basis to the claim, wait for the opposing party's responses and objections, and then react with an additional pleading and evidence. Moreover, including in the complaint nonessential evidentiary facts, presumptions, inferences or implied facts could open the door to the defendant's raising collateral estoppel and *res judicata* claims in a subsequent case on a different claim. The defendant could argue that the judgment in the prior case conclusively decided all the factual allegations in the complaint and therefore collateral estoppel barred the plaintiff from relitigating those issues.

Under normal circumstances, the "anticipation of objections" in a claim or counterclaim may not be good strategy. It may or may not be necessary or advisable to attach exhaustive corroborating exhibits to the original complaint. At the same time, if a party does not plead material facts, it may not be entitled to rely on them at trial. In this respect, the line between material facts which must be pleaded and evidence which may not be pleaded may sometimes be hard to draw.

Other kinds of evidence, e.g., witnesses, may or may not be stated in the complaint, although this is in fact required in certain jurisdictions. Where permissible, it may be deemed more practical to determine which witness should be heard at the end of the exchange of briefs when the full extent of the case is known.

Local rules will also differ regarding whether the action must include a claim for interest where the plaintiff wants interest on a claimed amount and whether costs can or should be claimed separately. Interest and costs are generally addressed in **Chapter 20.**

Pleading "in the Alternative"

Pleadings in the alternative are normally admissible, but depending on the jurisdiction not necessarily advisable. Theoretically, a party may present as many such alternative pleas as it wants. Indeed, such a tactic may be advisable if the legal and/or factual basis is complicated and it cannot precisely be foreseen which legal conclusion the judge will draw.

The purpose of pleading in the alternative is thus to enable the judge to adjudicate an alternative claim rather than dismiss it, based on his evaluation of the facts or the law. In some cases, alternative pleading may even be necessary under the principle of *Eventualmaxime* set forth above. In case the prayers for relief are unclear, the court may either impose a time-limit on the plaintiff for written clarification or ask for clarification in the course of a hearing.

Dilatory Tactics and Means to Respond

To discourage a party from attempts to protract the proceedings, the judge has various weapons. For example, if the intention to protract is probable and if the evidence could have been presented earlier, then the judge may be entitled to reject the additional pleading and evidence and render his judgment without considering it. Certain judges may prefer to admit the additional evidence in order to avoid making an error which is reviewable on appeal.

The second weapon is the "free evaluation of factual evidence." This can lawfully be extended to an evaluation of why a party did or did not present pleadings and evidence in a certain phase of the proceedings. Depending on the jurisdiction, the jury, and where applicable the judge, may draw adverse inferences based on whether and when evidence was submitted at a given stage of the proceedings.

Moreover, in some jurisdictions local civil procedure law permits the court to dismiss a civil complaint upon first examining it on one or more specific grounds set forth in the law. Among these grounds may be that (i) the complaint is not subject to consideration of the court, (ii) a valid judgment has already been rendered on the dispute involving the same parties, the same subject matter and the same grounds, or (iii) the parties have agreed to submit the case for resolution by arbitration.

Other grounds include that (iv) the case does not fall within the jurisdiction of the particular court, (v) the complaint on behalf of a concerned party has been filed by a person without the necessary power of attorney, (vi) the court is already considering the case involving the same parties, the same subject matter, and the same grounds, and (vii) the application is filed by a person without capacity.

In the United States, upon motion of the defendant Rule 12(b)(6) of the Federal Rules of Civil Procedure permits the court to dismiss the plaintiff's complaint for failure to state a claim upon which relief could be granted. The court will construe the complaint in the light most favorable to the plaintiff and accept as true all material allegations in the complaint, based solely on the content and substance of the pleading. The legal inadequacy of the complaint must appear on the face of the pleading to prevail on a Rule 12(b)(6) motion to dismiss.

Class Actions or Proceedings

Certain jurisdictions, such as the United States and Canada, have specific rules providing for class actions or proceedings. These rules may vary substantially from jurisdiction to jurisdiction, and are generally designed to permit resolution of common issues affecting an identifiable class of persons in a single proceeding. A typical example would be a products liability claim involving a widely-distributed product.

ii. The Answer or Statement of Defense: Form, Substance, Content, Strategic Considerations

Once originating process is filed, the court rules and procedure govern the conduct of the matter. Depending on the jurisdiction and the applicable procedural rules, the court may have the claim served on the defendant either with a summons for a "preliminary hearing" or, as is more customary in common-law jurisdictions, with an order to immediately respond in writing. An order to file the statement of defense includes a deadline which is normally not less than 30 days running from the date of service on the defendant, and perhaps longer in the case of defendants out of jurisdiction. In the United States, an election to waive the service of the summons in federal actions enlarges the time the defendant has to file the answer to 90 days if the defendant is located outside the United States.

If the defendant does not timely file its answer (if required, signed by an attorney), depending on the applicable rules the plaintiff can request the court to issue a default judgment. The defendant may be able to extend the period for delivery of an answer or defense, and in practice such deadlines are frequently extended by agreement between the parties.

Strategic Considerations

Many of the same strategic considerations apply to the defendant as to the plaintiff: pleas and evidence may be withheld if this brings a tactical advantage, but must be carefully balanced against the risk of the court's refusal to admit the evidence and drawing of negative conclusions from late presentation. Depending on the rules, in its statement of defense the defendant should clearly state which facts it accepts and which it denies, and be "consistent."

Certain jurisdictions follow the principle of concentration in which all defenses must be alleged in the defendant's answer, and facts and objections not raised therein may not be brought in a later stage of the proceeding. The defendant must consider each fact alleged in the complaint, stating the reasons of fact and of law with which it rejects the plaintiff's petition. This also relates to the *Verhandlungsmaxime*, discussed earlier, which imposes upon each party the burden to submit the relevant facts upon which it bases its claim or its defense and the means of evidence by which it wishes to furnish proof. In so doing, the defendant need not strictly limit itself to contesting the allegations made by the plaintiff, and may wish to recast the "story" underlining the dispute in a way more advantageous to its position.

Scope of the Answer and Defense

The scope of the answer or defense will depend on the particular circumstances, nature and complexity of the case. It will likewise be a function of the defendant's desire and, in particular, its ability at the time of filing the suit to plead with specificity the factual and legal elements of its case. It will also reflect the customs, style and thinking of the defendant and/or its counsel. The requirements for an answer or defense involving a foreign party are normally no different from disputes between two local parties.

Depending on the jurisdiction, defenses based on statute of limitation, contributory negligence and mitigation of damages must be specifically pleaded. In the United States, under Federal Rule of Civil Procedure 8(c) the defendant must plead all defenses which would avoid liability assuming plaintiff's allegations are true. Courts call these defenses affirmative defenses, and they include accord and satisfaction, assumption of risk, contributory negligence, duress, estoppel, fraud, illegality, laches, *res judicata*, statute of frauds, and waiver.

Other affirmative defenses should be presented as early as possible, whether in the first hearing or in the exchange of briefs. Counsel should confirm whether there is any preclusion or cut-off for defenses such as statute of limitations, mistake, fraud or coercion, release, waiver, contributory negligence, etc. In U.S. litigation, such defenses as lack of personal jurisdiction, improper service of process, or improper venue must be raised the first time that the defendant files a motion by "special appearance" or in its answer, whichever is first; otherwise, the defense is waived.

As stated in **Chapter 3** above, the best known manner in which to exercise party autonomy over the imposition of jurisdiction is to seek dismissal of the entire action as to all or some parties for *forum non conveniens.* However, in certain countries, particularly in Continental Europe, the doctrine of *forum non conveniens* is unknown, and it is not an element in the Brussels and Lugano Conventions. A court having jurisdiction pursuant to the applicable jurisdictional rules of the Conventions must assume jurisdiction as a matter of law and cannot decline it by reference to considerations of convenience.

Pre-Answer Motion Versus Answer

In some jurisdictions, such as the United States, prior to filing a full-fledged answer on the merits the defendant may file a motion and raise any and all of various defenses which may be especially relevant if the named defendant is foreign. These include (i) lack of "subject-matter jurisdiction" (which can be raised at any time until all appeals have been exhausted); (ii) lack of "personal jurisdiction" or improper service of process or improper venue (which must be raised the first time the foreign defendant files a motion, "special appearance," or in its answer, whichever is first); (iii) "failure to state a claim upon which relief can be granted" (which can be raised at any time prior to trial or at trial); and (iv) failure to join an "indispensable party" (which can be raised at any time prior to trial or at trial).

Alternatively, in such jurisdictions including the United States, the foreign defendant may choose not to file such a motion, and instead raise such defenses in its answer. The answer must then contain a specific "denial" or "admission" of each averment of the complaint or a "general denial" with specific admissions. Where the defendant is "without knowledge or information sufficient to form a belief," a statement to that effect constitutes a denial, and a failure to deny constitutes an admission. In some jurisdictions, damage may be deemed to be denied unless specifically admitted.

In short, the tactical advantages for the foreign defendant in appearing only to contest jurisdiction or making a full appearance with a reply in substance are to be assessed in view of the law of the country of prospective enforcement, as to whether a full defense is deemed a tacit submission to jurisdiction. If the law of prospective enforcement does not consider a full defense to be a voluntary submission or if the judgment is to be enforced locally, the defendant may wish to file a full defense in a separate petition, in addition to the jurisdictional defense, if possible.

In relation to defendants from signatory States to the Brussels and Lugano Conventions, Article 18 of the Conventions provides that "a court of a Contracting State before whom a defendant enters an appearance shall have jurisdiction." This rule shall not apply where an appearance "was entered solely to contest the jurisdiction." In contrast to, e.g., the Swiss Private International Law Statute, Article 18 of the Lugano Convention requires that the defendant object to jurisdiction *ab initio*, that is, with its very first communication to or appearance before the court, regardless of the reason for such appearance.

Depending on the local rules, a defendant may also counterclaim in respect of any right or claim that he may have against the plaintiff and by way of counterclaim join a nonparty as a defendant. A defendant may also cross-claim against a co-defendant or initiate a third-party claim against a nonparty to the original action if the co-defendant or nonparty may be liable to the defendant for all or part of the plaintiff's claim.

iii. Further Exchange of Briefs, Further Proceedings, Counterclaims

Parties and their counsel should carefully verify the rules and customs for further pleading after the initial complaint and answer. These may differ vastly from that to which they are accustomed in their home jurisdiction.

In Austria, for example, one of the main characteristics of first-instance civil proceedings is that the first oral hearing is the deadline for written pleadings and that prior to such hearing the parties may exchange pleadings as they like. Thereafter, pleadings may be filed only with explicit leave of the court. Moreover, the deadline for changes in factual allegations is the end of the oral hearing of first instance.

With regard to amendments to pleadings generally, the courts may be reluctant to allow amendments to pleadings after the limitations period has expired, unless the pleading already contains or raises the same substratum of fact which would be relied upon if the amendment were allowed. A party's case may carry more conviction if it does not have to be amended. Amendment can be time-consuming. Further, a party may have to bear the cost not only of its own amendments, but also of the opposing party's consequential amendments.

Counterclaims

Inexperienced defendants have been known to overlook their right to assert a counterclaim at the same time as the answer. In this regard, a problem which occasionally arises is when a defendant characterizes what is in fact a counterclaim as a "defense by way of set-off" or vice versa. Conversely, a defendant may sometimes characterize what is essentially a straightforward defense by way of set-off as a counterclaim.

With regard to counterclaims, certain jurisdictions such as the United States distinguish between "compulsory counterclaims," which arise out of the same transaction or occurrence as one of the plaintiff's claims and must be pleaded or they will be barred, and "permissive counterclaims," which do not arise out of the same transaction or occurrence. Austrian law distinguishes between "connected" and "unconnected" counterclaims, i.e., whether they stem from the same legal relationship as the action or not.

Article 6 no. 3 of the Brussels and Lugano Conventions provides for the making of counterclaims, and applies only to counterclaims for which separate judgment is desired. In jurisdictions in which court fees are assessed as a function of the amount of a claim asserted, counterclaims give rise to payment of court fees in the same way as do plaintiff's claims.

Depending on the jurisdiction, there may be different prerequisites in order for a counterclaim to be admissible. For example, the court dealing with the main claim may need to have jurisdiction over the counterclaim based on general jurisdictional rules, such as the domicile of the defendant. There may also be a requirement that the main claim and the counterclaim have a sufficient factual or legal connection or be based on the same legal relationship. The counterclaim will normally be dismissed if the main action is dismissed due to lack of procedural prerequisites such as absence of jurisdiction. On the other hand, pendency of the counterclaim will not necessarily be affected in case of withdrawal or acknowledgment of the main action.

iv. Joinder of Claims and Parties

Several persons may claim to have a right against one person or one person may claim to have a right against several others based on substantially identical facts or the same legal grounds. Depending on the procedural rules, they may be able to act as joint plaintiffs or be sued as joint defendants, provided the court has jurisdiction over all actions. Where the relationship is so close that conflicting or inconsistent judgments must be avoided, the court may be required to join the various proceedings whether or not the claims were originally brought separately, e.g., in certain kinds of inheritance or status actions. Depending on the applicable law and the legal basis, it may be a legal necessity to act as joint plaintiffs or sue various persons jointly, e.g., in claims by a community of heirs or by a partnership, claims directed at the dissolution of partnerships, or claims in connection with joint real property.

v. Impleader and Intervention

Depending on the applicable law, a party may wish to request support in a pending action from either plaintiff or defendant directed to a third party. Impleaders are often used if either plaintiff or defendant has a reason to assume that it will be sued by such third party, or intends to sue such third party in case the judgment is not in its favor.

Once the request for support has been served, various options exist for the third party to participate in the main proceedings. These include providing internal support to the main party without officially joining, formal representation of the main party by the third party in the proceedings, joinder of the third party to the litigation by way of intervention, or delegation of the conduct of the litigation by the main party to the third party.

Where a third party decides to join a pending litigation prior to the judgment by way of ancillary third-party intervention, the third party aims to support either plaintiff or defendant, since it is interested in a judgment in favor of the supported main party. Ancillary third-party interventions are normally admissible only if the intervening third party can demonstrate that it has a sufficient legal interest in the outcome of the proceedings. Even if an intervention has been validly made, the main party may have the right to withdraw, acknowledge or settle the main action and to withdraw appeals, even if filed by the intervening third party.

vi. Security for Costs

In certain jurisdictions, notably England, the court has discretion to order that a plaintiff resident out of the jurisdiction provide security for costs if the defendant applies for such an order. In the exercise of its discretion, the court must consider all the circumstances of the case; the mere fact that the plaintiff is not resident in the jurisdiction is not enough to warrant such an order. Indeed, an English court will never order security to be obtained from a plaintiff resident in the European Community solely because of nationality. Security for costs is discussed in greater detail in **Chapter 20**.

CHAPTER 8

SUMMARY JUDGMENTS AND EQUIVALENT PROCEEDINGS

Particularly in common-law jurisdictions, a plaintiff or a defendant is able to apply summarily for judgment. The court will normally grant such a judgment only where there is no issue which may go to trial. The defendant must have entered an appearance and the plaintiff must produce affidavit evidence supporting the proposition that the defendant has no defense. Depending on the jurisdiction, actions for fraud, defamation, false imprisonment or seduction will not be capable of a summary-judgment application. A defendant can also apply for summary judgment on a counterclaim after it has served its defense and counterclaim.

Summary judgments as known in some common-law jurisdictions do not exist under most civil-law rules. Under such rules, a party cannot move to obtain a judgment solely on the basis of pleadings and other documents even though the party finds that there is no genuine issue of fact justifying the law suit. Neither can the court render such a judgment on its own motion, or ex officio. However, some proceedings under civil-law rules in fact include elements similar to summary judgments known under common law.

Under the heading of "summary proceeding," a number of different proceedings can be found in civil-law jurisdictions. These may serve different purposes, particularly for the hearing of special requests in civil-law matters and in litigation concerning specific issues as outlined in bankruptcy legislation. Examples are the request for involuntary bankruptcy, the request for recognition of a foreign bankruptcy decree, requests for attachments, and various requests in marital, estate, property, contract and company matters. Furthermore, requests for pretrial interlocutory relief and enforcement requests may be brought in summary proceedings.

Summary proceedings in some civil-law jurisdictions, such as Switzerland, do not encompass default proceedings as is the case in certain other jurisdictions. Special provisions in some codes of civil procedure regulate default proceedings such that if the plaintiff defaults, judgment will be entered against it with the effect of *res judicata.* If the defendant defaults, the defendant will be deemed to have acknowledged the plaintiff's factual narration and the court will base its judgment thereon. If the court seriously doubts the plaintiff's factual narration, it may nevertheless order relevant evidence to be taken. However, the case will not be transferred to summary proceedings.

In some jurisdictions, *jurisdictio voluntaria* or noncontentious procedure is a procedural device for prompt disposition of action without a trial when there is no dispute as to either a material fact or inference to be drawn from undisputed facts, or if only a question of law is involved. A typical feature of these matters is that they are initiated by an application or petition, whereas regular civil disputes are normally initiated by summons.

i. Procedural Requirements

In order to obtain summary judgment, where available, the plaintiff must comply with the procedural requirements of the rules (that is, have properly commenced proceedings and file an application for summary judgment), show that there is no defense to the claim, and apply for the remedy promptly. The defendant must have filed an appearance for the court to have jurisdiction to hear the application. In jurisdictions such as England, unless the defendant has provided acknowledgement and notice of intention to defend in the proper form, any application for summary judgment may be deemed invalid as the appropriate application would be to apply for judgment in default.

The defendant may challenge the application for summary judgment on the basis of the plaintiff's application being irregular, that the claim is of a type that cannot be disposed of by summary proceedings, or that the plaintiff's pleading is inadequate. If the plaintiff's right to bring the suit is seriously in dispute, summary judgment will not normally be granted.

A motion for summary judgment provides a means of allowing the court to deal promptly with issues that do not require a full-fledged trial. It is for the moving party to show that the resolution of some or all of the issues raised does not require the court to make findings on conflicting evidence after hearing from the parties and witnesses through a trial. The court's function is not to resolve an issue of fact but determine whether a genuine issue of fact exists.

Normally, summary judgment applications are in respect of claims for debt, liquidated demand, or unliquidated damages. There are also a number of cases which may be expressly excluded, such as actions that include a claim for libel, slander, malicious prosecution or false imprisonment. In these cases, the defendant may have a right to trial by jury and, therefore, a right to a trial. Also excluded may be admiralty actions *in rem* and claims or counterclaims against the State.

Court Review of Summary Judgment Motion

On a motion for summary judgment, a respondent is presumed to have presented all the available relevant evidence upon which it may rely. It cannot argue that other, better evidence may be available at trial. The court will presume that the respondent has done all that he or she can to accumulate affidavit evidence referencing relevant documentary evidence and opinion evidence if appropriate so as to ensure that the motion for summary judgment is defeated. Certain codes of civil procedure restrict evidence admissible in summary proceedings to interrogation of the parties, written information, judicial inspection, and documents. If the facts can be proven only by other means, such as witnesses, summary proceedings may not be available.

A court may assess the credibility of that evidence in determining whether a genuine issue of fact, law, or mixed fact and law exists for trial. Evidence may be viewed by the court as being so incredible that its credibility is not an issue. In that event, the court may reject the evidence and proceed to grant summary judgment. Apparent factual conflict in evidence does not end the inquiry and the court may, on a common-sense basis, draw inferences from the evidence. Matters of credibility requiring resolution in a case of conflicting evidence ought to go to trial; however, that depends upon the circumstances of the case.

At the hearing of a summary-judgment motion, the court will usually have available before it affidavit evidence filed by both the moving party and the respondent. There will usually also have been cross-examinations on the affidavits, and the court will have transcripts of those cross-examinations. These cross-examinations on the affidavit evidence may be critical to the success of the summary-judgment motion.

Summary Judgment and Foreign Law

The practitioner should check carefully whether the local courts are obliged to research the contents of foreign law applicable to a dispute ex officio or rather transfer the burden of proof for foreign law to the parties involved. Depending on how easily the judge can verify the contents of foreign law, the risk that the judge will come to the conclusion that there is no unanimous interpretation of foreign law certainly is higher than if the judge has to apply his own law. The plaintiff therefore will have to carefully research that issue prior to instituting summary proceedings. Otherwise, the plaintiff risks losing time and money, and must start again in ordinary proceedings if it fails in summary proceedings.

While a motion for summary judgment may lead to a relatively prompt resolution of some issues or the entire action, it should nevertheless be approached with caution. Judgment on such a motion may be subject to appeal, and if the appellate court concludes that a full trial was necessary, a heavy penalty in terms of expense and time lost may be paid depending on the local rules.

It should not be assumed in those jurisdictions where summary judgment is available that the local rules in each and every state or province are identical. The availability of summary judgments may be more circumscribed in one locale than in another. A motion to dismiss an action may not lie to dismiss part of a claim only, but rather for the whole claim or no part of it at all. In those jurisdictions, such as civil-law countries, where summary judgment is not available, there may be other procedures which contain similar elements. These will be in the form of dismissal or default judgment.

Summary Judgment and Dismissal

In the case of dismissal, the court may dismiss the case ex officio if the plaintiff or the appellant does not appear in court for the first preliminary hearing. Generally, the court will also dismiss the case ex officio if the writ of summons is not served properly on the defendant, if the plaintiff does not appear in later preliminary hearings or in the final hearing, or does not file a pleading required by the court.

The court may also dismiss a case for various other reasons, either ex officio or on a motion by the defendant. This applies if the complaint does not include the required information or if the plaintiff is deemed to have no legal interest in the action, e.g., if a judgment will not change the plaintiff's legal position. The court may also dismiss a case if the facts presented to the court are unclear or if the facts have no real connection to the allegations stated by the plaintiff.

If a case is to be decided in accordance with foreign law, and if information about the foreign law cannot be obtained, a possible solution may be a dismissal of the case, although this is rare in practice. Courts and the parties normally solve such problems in practice by finding an approach that fits the needs of each individual case, for instance determining the extent to which foreign law is relevant and how the court may gain knowledge of the foreign law.

In the case of default judgments, if the defendant or the appellee does not appear at a preliminary hearing or at the final hearing, or if the defendant does not submit required pleadings to the court, the plaintiff can move for a default judgment. The court will render the default judgment based on the claims, allegations and facts submitted by the parties to the court. The default judgment will normally be in favor of the plaintiff if the default judgment is rendered after the first preliminary hearing or after the time limit for submitting a statement of defense which the defendant did not submit.

Orders in Response to Motion for Summary Judgment

There are various orders which the judge might make in response to the motion for summary judgment. First, unless the defendant satisfies the court that there is an issue or question which ought to be tried or that there is some other reason why there should be a trial, the court may give such judgment on the claim as it believes is just. Second, if the defendant satisfies the court that there is a triable issue or other reason for a trial to take place, the defendant will be granted unconditional leave to defend the proceedings. Third, even if the defendant raises an arguable defense, leave to defend may be granted unless the court doubts the genuineness or validity of the defense, considers the defense a sham, or one that is bound to fail. Fourth, the court may dismiss the plaintiff's summons if the application was not appropriate for the summary-judgment procedures, or the court believes the plaintiff knew the defendant had a defense to the claim and would be granted unconditional leave to defend.

There may also be rulings of a summary nature made on a creditor's application for collection of monetary sums or reclamation of movable property from the debtor. Collection under such a document is effected according to general rules specified by the law for the enforcement of court judgments. Where applicable, a judge may be able to issue a writ to this effect if the claim is based on a notarized transaction, a written transaction, a protest of a bill of exchange for reasons of nonpayment, nonacceptance or lack of date on the notarized bill of acceptance, collection of alimony for minors not related to paternity identification, collection of tax debt and mandatory state insurance debt from individuals, etc.

A judge can reject the application for the issue of a writ if the subject matter of the claim is not admissible as the object of a writ, no documents have been submitted as confirmation of the claim, the state duty for the claim has not been paid, etc. The judge refuses to issue a writ if the debtor disputes the claim or the dispute involves a right which cannot be settled on the basis of the documents provided. The court's refusal to accept the application for a writ does not preclude the applicant from submitting a similar claim according to usual procedure.

ii. Substantive Requirements

Depending on the jurisdiction, normally summary judgment may be given where there is no real substantial question to be tried or no reasonable doubt that a plaintiff is entitled to judgment. A defendant may show cause against summary judgment by disclosing a triable issue, disclosing an arguable good defense, proving a plausible ground of defense, or showing facts that lead to the inference that at the trial of the action the defendant may be able to establish a defense. This implies that leave to defend should be given where there is a case, either of fact or law, to be investigated.

Both the courts and the rules recognize that there are cases where the defendant may be able to prevent the plaintiff from obtaining summary judgment when the defense is at best dubious or even a sham. To cater for that situation, the court may grant the defendant leave to defend on terms. These terms may relate to security for costs, time, mode of trial (e.g., payment of money into court) or any other matter which the court thinks appropriate. The plaintiff may obtain summary judgment against one defendant without prejudice to any right to proceed against the remaining defendants.

In some jurisdictions, if a defendant makes strong and unambiguous admissions sufficient to support the plaintiff's claim, the plaintiff may apply for judgment based on the admissions. This application may be made at any stage of the proceedings, and it may be based on either formal admissions in the pleadings or on informal admissions. However, judgment is not entered on admissions where a serious question of fact or law requires consideration. It is also possible for a defendant to seek to amend or explain such admissions, even if they are made in court.

Summary Judgment Motions by the Defendant

Some jurisdictions give a defendant the means to apply for summary judgment or dismissal. It is available where the action is frivolous or vexatious, or if there is an obvious defense on the merits. If all the parties consent, the court may dispose of the whole action summarily on the defendant's application for summary judgment. However, if the parties do not consent, the court may only enter judgment for the defendant, if that is justified. The court cannot enter judgment for the plaintiff in the absence of consent to deal with the action summarily.

The outcome of summary proceedings may be one of many. If the plaintiff prevails, the judgment is *res judicata.* It may be enforced against the defendant as if issued in ordinary proceedings. If the court comes to the conclusion that the claim is without merit, the judgment is also *res judicata* and prevents the plaintiff from opening a case in ordinary proceedings for the same claim. Alternatively, the defendant may prevail in summary proceedings but the judgment not be deemed *res judicata.* In that case, the plaintiff may open a case in ordinary proceedings on the same claim, in which proceedings the court must give greater consideration to the applicable law and the full range of evidence is available to the plaintiff.

iii. Practical Problems and Time Factors

Applications for summary judgment should generally be made as early as possible in the proceedings. Delay in making the application may be a reason for the court to refuse to grant it. If the proceedings have been underway for a considerable time, it may be necessary for the plaintiff to explain the delay in the supporting affidavit.

Summary judgment can result in the plaintiff's saving a significant amount of time in the proceedings. Normally, it will see the plaintiff succeed without needing to conduct all the usual interlocutory steps and a final hearing following those steps. A summary judgment motion may also force the opponent to develop the theory of the case and to disclose evidence not yet provided in discovery. A motion for summary judgment may also assist the parties in reaching a settlement by highlighting the strengths and weaknesses of the case and causing the parties to reassess the prospects for ultimate disposition.

Potential Disadvantages to Summary Judgment Motions

There are, however, potential disadvantages which should be considered. First, if the plaintiff is not successful in the application for summary judgment, the court may award the costs of the application against him. Second, an unsuccessful application for summary judgment may have the result that the plaintiff has "shown his hand" quite early in the proceedings. Depending upon the circumstances, this may result in the plaintiff's losing a forensic advantage. On the other hand, it would be expected that a defendant who successfully resists an application for summary judgment will have presented the merits of his case at least equally.

Third, a defense may make partial admissions and, in this event, an application can be made in relation to any amount which is uncontested. Fourth, where the basic nature of the claim is a collection of a debt, and it is suspected that the defendant has acknowledged service merely in an effort to obtain further time to make payment, it may be worth considering waiting for a defense. If a defense is not served, it is possible to obtain a default judgment which is quicker than obtaining a summary judgment. If the defense is a sham, its inadequacy may add support to the plaintiff's application.

iv. Strategic Considerations

An application for summary judgment is made in the court in which the proceedings are being conducted. There can be some strategic advantage to making a summary judgment application for a plaintiff who believes that it is in a relatively strong position and that a defendant is seeking to draw out proceedings. As noted above, it would normally result in the defendant revealing the substance of his defense to the claim at an early point in the proceedings.

From the perspective of the plaintiff, it is important in preparing a claim to carefully analyze all of the material facts so as to assess whether any issues may be determined expeditiously on a summary-judgment motion. In some cases, it may be apparent that a question of liability does not turn on genuine issues of material fact that require a trial. A summary-judgment motion may provide an effective means of determining liability early and leaving a claim for damages to be assessed at trial. Such a positive outcome may facilitate settlement discussions by shifting the balance of bargaining power in favor of the plaintiff. Conversely, the defendant should consider whether the claims advanced may be disposed of in advance of trial. This possibility should be kept in mind in drafting the statement of defense.

As a practical matter, it must be recognized that certain courts are extremely reluctant to dismiss a claim without permitting the party a full opportunity to be heard. Moreover, an unsuccessful motion to dismiss may prejudice the defendant's position at trial. Where there is no appeal from such a judgment and when it is rendered on a point of law, it may become *res judicata.*

If the defendant wishes the action to be dismissed due to lack of jurisdiction of the court, it must normally state this in its first reply or appearance before the court. In such case, the defendant's appearance will not in itself confer jurisdiction on the court pursuant to Article 18 of the Brussels and Lugano Conventions.

Furthermore, despite the summary judgment's nature, the result of the proceedings is not necessarily accelerated. Depending on the rules, the defeated party may appeal to a higher court to have the judgment declared null and void. If the higher court reverses the first-instance judgment, determining the need to produce certain evidence, the proceedings are referred to the trial court so that the evidence may be produced and a new judgment rendered. This whole procedure may take a longer period of time than the common proceedings.

v. Relevance to Later Efforts to Recognize and Enforce

A domestic summary-judgment decision does not face any special difficulty in relation to later efforts to recognize and enforce a judgment.

Recognition and enforcement of a default judgment originating in another Contracting State of the Brussels and Lugano Conventions requires, under Article 46 no. 2, filing of the usual documents as discussed in **Chapter 17** below as well as a document which establishes that the defendant was served with the document instituting proceedings. A default judgment cannot be recognized in another Contracting State if the defendant was not duly served with the documents which instituted the proceedings in sufficient time to enable it to arrange for its defense: Article 27 no. 2 of the Brussels and Lugano Conventions.

CHAPTER 9

INTERIM & CONSERVATORY RELIEF, INJUNCTIONS & SIMILAR EMERGENCY MEASURES

Depending on the jurisdiction, the courts may have available a number of means by which they may preserve the parties' rights on an urgent basis until a trial can be heard and final judgment issued. The principally relevant powers include the power to grant interim and interlocutory injunctions, the power to order the detention or preservation of property that is the subject of proceedings, and the power to appoint a receiver.

Interim and Interlocutory Injunctions

Injunctions are among the most significant tools of interim and conservatory relief in transnational litigation. An interim injunction is one in force for a short period until a hearing involving all parties may be heard. In appropriate cases, interim injunctions will be granted *ex parte*. An interlocutory injunction is one in force until trial.

Such injunctions may be positive or negative in nature. As the injunction is an equitable remedy, it is a matter of the court's discretion whether or not it will be granted. The test usually applied involves, first, determining whether on the plaintiff's case there is a serious question to be tried. The plaintiff need not necessarily show that it has a *prima facie* case, but merely that its claim is not frivolous and that there is a prospect of successfully obtaining a final injunction. The court will normally also weigh the prejudice suffered by the defendant in restoring the original position against any advantage which the plaintiff may derive from the injunction.

The court will consider whether the plaintiff would be adequately compensated at trial by an award of damages for the loss which it would sustain as a result of the defendant's continuing actions. Damages would not be an adequate remedy if the damage suffered cannot be quantified, such as damage to reputation or business. An injunction is more likely to be granted against a defendant if it committed a breach deliberately and in full knowledge of the plaintiff's position. An injunction may not be granted in instances in which a plaintiff delayed too long in taking action or consented to the defendant's behavior. Courts may require as a condition to granting interim or interlocutory injunctions that the plaintiff give the court an undertaking to pay for any damages suffered as a result of the injunction if the plaintiff is unsuccessful at trial.

Certain courts, particularly in the British Commonwealth context, have the power to grant so-called Mareva injunctions. These are injunctions aimed at preventing the dissipation of assets which may frustrate the enforcement of a judgment in favor of the plaintiff. In addition, in appropriate cases a court may grant a Mareva injunction in respect of a defendant present in the jurisdiction who has assets outside the jurisdiction even where the defendant is not a resident of that jurisdiction.

Protective Taking of Evidence

In some jurisdictions, and notably in the civil-law tradition, one important form of interim relief is the protective taking of evidence (known in German, for example, as *Beweissicherung*). This may include judicial inspection (real evidence), witness evidence or expert evidence. It may be requested in any phase of the proceedings if there is a danger of loss of evidence or of impediment in the use of evidence.

As an exception to the principle that evidence must be taken before the deciding court and in the course of proceedings, a party may demand the taking of evidence even prior to commencement of litigation. In this case, the court where the evidence lies has jurisdiction for such purposes. If the party can demonstrate a legal interest in determining the present condition of a piece of evidence, a protective taking of evidence will be made.

The applicant in this case may not be obliged to pay a procedural security deposit. The (future) court of process or, in case of urgency, any court where the evidence is situated is competent for protective judicial inspection such as witness or expert evidence. The costs of the other party or its representation in these proceedings may be required to be reimbursed by the applicant in this first stage, but may be claimed for reimbursement as part of the applicant's litigation costs in subsequent main proceedings.

Protective Execution

Another kind of interim relief, again prevalent in certain civil-law jurisdictions, is protective execution. This measure serves to secure the future enforcement of pecuniary claims (including costs of litigation) stated in a judgment not yet enforceable. This does not include court settlements, authentic instruments and arbitral awards. Pursuant to Article 26 of the Brussels and Lugano Conventions, where applicable, any judgment rendered in a Contracting State must be recognized in another Contracting State. If it is not final, i.e., appeal is pending in the State of origin, and the judgment debtor files appeal against enforcement in the State of enforcement, Article 39 limits enforcement to protective measures.

Therefore, a measure of protective execution in a jurisdiction to which this method applies can be based on foreign decisions as well. For certain kinds of domestic judgments, protective execution, where available, is granted without the need to prove likelihood of success of the claim and without an obligation of the applicant to deposit security. These include default judgments against which a remedy has been taken, confirming decisions of courts of appeal with further appeal, judgments by consent against which appeal has been launched, decisions of second instance against which appeal has been launched, and final orders of payment.

Furthermore, protective execution may be granted by the court of process or by the court of enforcement if the judgment creditor (applicant) alleges and proves that the execution of a pecuniary claim will be more difficult or impossible (danger of bankruptcy, accumulation of executions, etc.). It may also be granted if the enforcement of a judgment would have to be sought in a noncontracting State of the Brussels or Lugano Conventions. In this case, the judgment creditor does not have to deposit security.

Preliminary Injunctions

Preliminary injunctions are a further kind of interim relief in many jurisdictions. Normally, the aim of this injunction is to secure the subsequent performance either of pecuniary claims (even before their maturity) or of claims to refrain from acting. An injunction may be available if performance is endangered by the debtor's dispositions. It may also be available in case of a pecuniary claim if, where applicable, a judgment would have to be enforced in a non-Lugano Convention State. The debtor may be heard prior to the issuance of the court order.

In a Brussels/Lugano Convention State, for securing a nonpecuniary claim the plaintiff may need to prove the likelihood that fulfillment/enforcement of the nonpecuniary claim is endangered. It may also have to prove that enforcement of a final judgment would have to be applied for in a noncontracting State of the Brussels/Lugano Convention without the preliminary order or that the preliminary injunction is indispensable to preventing the claim from being jeopardized.

Only a limited number of means may be available to secure pecuniary claims (e.g., no attachment of real property), although there may be no such limitation with regard to nonpecuniary claims. In practice, preliminary injunctions for securing pecuniary claims are often sought in order to prevent a debtor from dissipating or hiding its assets. Real property, however, cannot be pledged. Only proceeds from the sale of real property (purchase price receivable) may be "frozen" by a stop-payment order on the seller/debtor and the purchaser.

In matters relating to unfair competition, trademarks, patents etc., cease and desist orders are the appropriate means to prohibit (further) infringement until final judgment has been rendered. Furthermore, in disputes between shareholders of a company (possibly involving the company itself), a provisional court order may conserve the present status in the company and prohibit changes.

If the plaintiff loses the case in the main proceedings, or if it has failed to commence action within the prescribed time-limit, depending on the local rules he may be liable to pay actual damages incurred by the opposing party as a result of the injunction, regardless of fault. Also depending on the local rules, disobeying an injunction is a contempt of court punishable by fine and/or imprisonment. It is no defense to contempt proceedings for a defendant to argue either that the order should not have been made or that it has been discharged. A breach may still be contempt even when, at a later stage, the order is discharged. The same principle applies if the original injunction was wrongly granted, in which case the defendant's remedy is to apply for its immediate discharge while adhering to its terms.

Interim Relief And Arbitration

While the subject of arbitration exceeds the scope of this work, it is important to note that judicial supervision, intervention or other assistance parallel to arbitration, including the rendering of interim and conservatory relief either before or after the constitution of the arbitral tribunal, is a tool of potentially great significance in an international dispute. Suffice it to say that this raises, directly or indirectly, two issues. These are the ability of the parties to an arbitration agreement to seek interim or conservatory measures (i) from the municipal courts and (ii) from the arbitral tribunal, which in turn raises the issue of the ability of the courts and that of the tribunal to grant such measures.

With regard to the ability to seek such measures from the courts and their ability to grant such measures, this is governed, and should be governed, not first and foremost by the institutional or other arbitral rules which may have been agreed. Rather, it is governed by the law at the place of the "competent judicial authority," which is not always also the law of the place of arbitration.

In this connection, most countries, with the notable partial exception of the United States, regard attachments in aid of arbitration before the constitution of the tribunal as permissible. They are thus not considered to be in conflict with the courts' obligation under the 1958 New York Convention on the Recognition and Enforcement of Foreign Arbitral Awards to refer parties to arbitration inasmuch as attachments and other provisional measures are subject to an award which the State will later be obligated to execute.

After constitution of the tribunal, the issue of attachments in aid of arbitration is far less problematic than before constitution—except in the United States. Either the tribunal has inherent power or it enjoys specifically granted powers to direct the parties to take provisional measures.

A further problem which often arises is a jurisdictional one: whether a pre-arbitration application to the municipal courts, especially by the plaintiff in the arbitration, in fact "infringed" the agreement to arbitration by constituting an election to have the municipal courts adjudicate not only an issue of interim or conservatory nature, but also the merits of the dispute.

Potential inequities have befallen even the most experienced practitioners who have applied for interim or conservatory measures in the local courts prior to arbitration. No sooner had they done so than the arbitral tribunal subsequently held that notwithstanding the applicant's good-faith belief that its application did not call for adjudication of the merits, the procedure at the place of application dictated otherwise.

With regard to the ability to seek such measures from the arbitral tribunal and its ability to grant such measures, there is a *de facto* disinclination of some arbitrators to grant "orders" for such measures because of the lack of express empowerment to render or enforce such orders. The answer that there is an "indirect" empowerment to do so is inapposite.

In fact, recent internationally accepted jurisprudence and commentary clearly affirms the right and ability of the tribunal to take interim measures of protection, and often couples it with the right to demand security. For example, under French arbitration law, arbitrators may take the same interim measures as judges as long as such measures are within the scope of their "mission" in the sense of Articles 1484(3) and 1504 of the French New Code of Civil Procedure ("NCPC"). Also UNCITRAL Model Law Article 17 provides that unless otherwise agreed by the parties, the arbitral tribunal may, at the request of a party, order any party to take such interim measure of protection as the arbitral tribunal may consider necessary in respect of the subject matter of the dispute. It also provides that the arbitral tribunal may require any party to provide appropriate security in connection with such measure.

It is also commonly viewed that arbitrators have a duty to proceed and determine their own jurisdiction even though a parallel action in a state court may have been commenced, notably by the defendant, to forestall the arbitration. Presumably, the tribunal can in fact proceed unless there is a direct judicial order from a competent court at the seat to stay or dismiss the arbitration.

What is potentially a thornier issue is an attempt, whether legitimate or illegitimate, to interject the courts so as to uphold an absence of arbitral jurisdiction before the tribunal has been constituted. Depending on the jurisdiction in which court intervention is properly sought, the chances of obtaining a stay or dismissal on this basis may vary.

In France, for example, Article 1458 NCPC provides that in "domestic" arbitrations, a competent French court should decline jurisdiction over the issue of arbitral jurisdiction unless the arbitration agreement is manifestly null. The French court may not determine its lack of jurisdiction on its own motion. Moreover, Article 1494 NCPC provides as to "international" arbitrations that specific precedence over French procedural rules shall be given to the rules agreed on by the parties, essentially leaving no room for intervention by the courts except on review or execution of the award.

i. Petitions Abroad in Connection with Domestic Proceedings

In matters concerning measures of execution, when an asset is located abroad the applicable law is the law of that foreign State. Such law determines, *inter alia*, (i) terms of attachment that may be carried out by a claimant; (ii) the persons who may be subject to attachment and those protected from attachment; (iii) the required nature of the claim, i.e., cause of the attachment; (iv) whether the subject matter of the attachment must be confirmed by a writ of execution of by a title; (v) whether the attachment is subject to a claim of urgency evidenced by the claimant; (vi) designation of assets subject to attachment and those that cannot be attached; (vii) instances in which prior authorization is required; (viii) whether this authorization must follow preliminary conciliation attempts; (ix) the procedure for attachment, time-limits, and possible notifications; and (x) issues likely to arise and available remedies.

Normally, a court itself will not make an application for injunctive relief overseas in connection with domestic proceedings. That is the responsibility of the parties. Accordingly, if it is necessary to seek injunctions abroad, the plaintiff will be expected to make the necessary overseas application.

Applying for Injunctive Relief Abroad

The local courts should not generally interfere with parties seeking to obtain injunctions abroad in support of proceedings commenced locally. However, the local courts would not be actively involved in the seeking of such injunctions. A party to local proceedings wishing to obtain an injunction abroad should seek legal advice in the jurisdiction in question as to the likelihood of obtaining an injunction in that jurisdiction, based on the merits of the case as set out by the party's local legal advisors.

The local courts might become involved in the above scenario where, for example, the obtaining of the injunction abroad necessitates the commencement of substantive proceedings in that jurisdiction and the applicant can show that the foreign proceedings interfere with the local process. In those circumstances, the local courts might grant an anti-suit injunction, where applicable (as discussed below).

Recognition and Enforcement of Foreign Interim Relief

Depending on the jurisdiction where the main proceedings are pending, judgments of foreign courts granting interim or conservatory relief in connection with the parties or the issues in the main proceedings are unlikely to be recognized and enforced. This is not necessarily to say that under the law of the place of the main proceedings a litigant is forbidden from seeking interim relief in a foreign court during the course of the local proceedings. At the same time, such a step abroad will likely be useful only if enforcement of the relief sought in the foreign jurisdiction will achieve the desired purpose.

In general, however, only final judgments of foreign courts are recognized in such jurisdictions, a requirement which excludes most forms of interlocutory relief. Final and conclusive judgments are normally those that can no longer be altered by the court that made it. A potential or actual appeal does not prevent recognition unless a stay of execution has been ordered. Orders for specific performance and orders of injunction by a foreign court may not be enforceable locally.

Thus apart from injunctions emanating from Brussels and Lugano Convention countries, the English courts do not generally enforce foreign injunctions because the conditions for enforcing a foreign judgment *in personam* are that it must be for a definite sum of money and that it must be final and conclusive. Accordingly, the English courts will not enforce proceedings of an executive or interim nature, for example interlocutory orders for payments into court. However, foreign petitions *in rem*, e.g., a foreign court order for the sale of moveable goods situated in that country, will be recognized and enforced in England.

Brussels and Lugano Conventions

In the case of the Brussels and Lugano Conventions, the rendering of provisional and protective measures as well as decisions on validity, invalidity, or termination in civil and commercial matters are included in the scope of the Conventions on the enforcement level.

With regard to interim and protective measures, no system of uniform jurisdiction has been established by the Brussels and Lugano Conventions. Article 24 states that legal action for provisional and protective measures may be commenced at the courts of one Contracting State (if the defendant is domiciled in a Contracting State) even if the courts of another Contracting State have jurisdiction as to the substance of the matter (main proceedings). Therefore, preliminary legal protection is granted as available on a national basis. These measures must be based on national jurisdiction rules. According to some opinions, they may also be based on the rules of jurisdiction of the Brussels or Lugano Conventions, but this is unclear.

The enforcement of provisional measures and final decisions in civil and commercial matters are equally within the scope of the Conventions, as the Conventions do not differentiate with regard to enforcement. Under Article 25 of the Brussels and Lugano Conventions, "judgment" includes interim proceedings. Accordingly, the courts of one Contracting State generally recognize and enforce interim measures emanating from another Convention court. At the same time, the enforcement of injunctions and similar protective measures issued by a judge in one State may be denied by the requested State if the opposing party was not summoned beforehand or if the enforcement of a decision is to be executed without foregoing notification (service) of the decision.

Pursuant to Article 26(1) of the Conventions, a judgment rendered in a Contracting State shall be recognized in the other Contracting State without any special procedure being required unless there are grounds for nonrecognition under Articles 27 and 28. For the purposes of Article 26, judgment means any judgment rendered by a court whatever the judgment may be called, including a decree or order. However, provisional measures may be recognized and enforced only if granted or, at least, confirmed in *inter partes* proceedings. Only in these cases can provisional measures have an effect beyond the jurisdiction of the court granting them.

Pursuant to Article 24 of the Brussels and Lugano Conventions, interim measures to secure fulfillment of a claim do not create *lis pendens* for the action on the claim. A plaintiff can submit petitions for interim measures in a country other than the country of the court of proceedings; he may even submit petitions in any country where he expects relief.

Mareva injunctions (see also below) and similar sweeping orders will not be recognized in a Brussels/Lugano Contracting State if they are rendered in a noncontracting State. In the absence of the Convention or a similar bilateral arrangement, if a plaintiff applies for an interim measure in a noncontracting state of the Brussels/Lugano Conventions, it must fulfill the requirements of that country and can make use of the measures available under domestic law.

Conversely, with regard to provisional measures ordered by non-Brussels/Lugano Convention courts, such orders are subject to local procedural rules. Most often, decisions regarding provisional measures rendered by foreign courts are not recognized and enforced locally to the extent that there is a requirement that no further ordinary appeal be available against the foreign decision or that it be final. Depending on the local rules, orders of interim or conservatory relief are invariably not considered to be final.

ii. Petitions Domestically in Support of Foreign Proceedings

In the Brussels/Lugano Convention context, a foreign plaintiff who intends to commence or has commenced action on a claim in civil and commercial matters in a Convention Contracting State may directly apply for the above-described measures and injunctions in a court of a Contracting State.

Brussels/Lugano Convention Bases

In so doing, the foreign plaintiff may not be obliged to deposit security for costs. It can apply for protective execution (for pecuniary claims only) based on a foreign judgment not yet enforceable (because recourse has been taken against the declaration of enforceability in the local court or because of an appeal lodged against the judgment delivered in the country of origin). It may also request a preliminary injunction for pecuniary and other claims. As Article 24 of the Brussels/Lugano Conventions refers to national law, all interim and provisional measures as described above may be obtained in a Contracting State under the rules and prerequisites of its local law.

Among the measures available in this context are a notice of *lis pendens* action concerning real estate to be recorded in the register of rights as a warning to third parties of the fact that some rights in the real estate are disputed. The notice will preserve the rights of the plaintiff against third parties if the plaintiff prevails in the action. If a court of another Contracting State of the Convention, under an action pending in that State, allows notice of *lis pendens* to be recorded in a register of rights in real estate, such a decision must be recognized and enforced under the Convention and must on request be recorded in the local register of rights in real estate.

There are also several types of emergency measures which may be granted by the bailiff in the Convention context, including attachment, injunction, and "revindication." These emergency measures must be recognized and enforced by the other Contracting

States under the Convention. Attachment (or arrest) consists of the seizure of assets of the defendant to secure the execution of the plaintiff's claim after judgment, and may be granted only if the possibility of later enforcement of the claim would otherwise be reduced significantly. An injunction prohibits a person or a legal entity from doing a certain act and may not require the defendant to perform particular acts except as necessary for the compliance with the prohibition ordered by the injunction. A revindication, where applicable, is an emergency measure under which a certain object, for instance chattel, real estate or leased premises in the physical possession of the defendant, is brought into the physical possession of the plaintiff.

Nonconvention Bases

In a nonconvention situation, the plaintiff/applicant (*e.g.*, domiciled in the United States) may obtain interim relief from the courts of a Convention State (provided jurisdiction is established by residence of the opposing party, its assets in the Contracting State, or repetitive infringement, etc.) under the same preconditions as a local plaintiff. The one additional requirement is the making of a security deposit for litigation costs. Care must be taken to verify whether, as is the case in Austria, in contrast to decisions from Convention States the local courts do not enforce decisions on interim measures rendered by such nonconvention States as the United States.

In many countries, and in particular those of the common-law tradition, a wide range of interim and conservatory remedies may be available in the local courts which are potentially of use in connection with disputes abroad. Whether or not such remedies are sought in aid of proceedings pending or proposed outside of the jurisdiction, they obviously must stand or fall on their merits as determined by local law.

Generally, all forms of interlocutory relief are considered to be incidental to a substantive action pending or in some cases imminent in the local jurisdiction. Where an action is pending in a foreign jurisdiction and it becomes necessary to obtain provisional relief locally, it will therefore normally be necessary to institute fresh proceedings locally and to apply for the desired relief as an incident of that action.

Domestic Injunctions in Support of Foreign Proceedings

The most common form of relief is by way of injunction, either a mandatory order requiring a defendant to take certain positive steps or a prohibitive order restraining a defendant from committing specified acts. There is no legal right to an injunction. Rather, it is an equitable remedy that may be granted by a court in the exercise of its discretion. Pretrial injunctions fall into certain subcategories depending on when they are granted: interlocutory, interim, and *ex parte* injunctions.

In the case of interlocutory injunctions, the applicant must generally show that (i) there is a serious question to be tried, (ii) irreparable harm will result if relief is not granted and (iii) the harm to the defendant, if any, which will result from an injunction being granted will be less than the harm to the plaintiff if it is refused, i.e., that the balance of convenience favors the plaintiff. In those jurisdictions where such a test generally applies, there may nevertheless be exceptions.

In Canada, for example, in certain cases it is essential that the strength of the case on the merits be the predominant consideration. The rights of the parties are, in effect, finally determined on the motion for an interlocutory injunction. An example is cases involving covenants in restraint of trade. Also, some cases rest on a pure question of law which can be readily determined. In such situations, the plaintiff is required to establish a strong *prima facie* case on the merits rather than simply a serious issue to be tried. As an equitable remedy, an interlocutory injunction is available only where the ordinary legal remedy of damages would be unavailable in law, inappropriate or inadequate.

With regard to defining irreparable harm, typical examples would include cases where the activities sought to be enjoined would put the plaintiff out of business, prevent the gaining of a livelihood, or cause irrevocable damage to reputation or professional standing. "Irreparable" normally refers to the nature of the harm suffered rather than its magnitude. It is harm which either cannot be quantified in monetary terms or which cannot be cured, usually because one party cannot collect damages from the other. The fact that one party may be impecunious does not automatically determine the application in favor of the other party who will not ultimately be able to collect damages, although it may be a relevant consideration.

In some jurisdictions, such as Australia, an alternative means by which an interlocutory injunction may be made effective is by recognition in equity of a interlocutory order obtained in the forum of the principal litigation. Under this strategy, the plaintiff in the foreign proceedings applies for the granting of a Mareva injunction (see also below) over assets in the jurisdiction (i.e., an injunction prohibiting the removal of property from that jurisdiction). The order takes effect as an order to the foreign court and the plaintiff immediately has the order enforced in the courts of equity in the local court. This possibility is discussed in **Chapter 17** more extensively.

Domestic Interim Injunctions in Support of Foreign Proceedings

In the case of interim injunctions, where available these are orders made on notice to the defendant with a limited duration, generally to permit the defendant to prepare responding material. Apart from this issue of timing, the principles which govern interim injunctions are virtually identical to those governing interlocutory injunctions.

In the case of *ex parte* injunctions, such an injunction may be granted on an emergency basis to prevent a defendant from violating a plaintiff's rights. Such an application may be brought even prior to an action having been commenced. In such case, a plaintiff will be required to undertake to the court to commence an action as soon as is reasonably possible. The normal practice is for the court to expressly limit the effect of *ex parte* injunctions to a stated period of time in the expectation that a contested application for either an interim or interlocutory injunction will soon follow. To justify such an injunction, the delay otherwise necessary to give notice of the application to the defendant must entail serious and irreparable injury to a plaintiff.

Mareva Injunctions

Mareva injunctions (from the decision of the English Court of Appeal in *Mareva Compania Naviera S.A. v. International Bulkcarriers Ltd.* [1980] 1 All E.R. 213 (C.A.)), are orders restraining a defendant from disposing of assets held within the jurisdiction. They are interim orders sought within a proceeding in order to secure a defendant's assets so as to ensure those assets will be available to satisfy any judgment which the plaintiff may receive.

Under the test described by the English Court of Appeal in *Third Chandris Shipping Corp. v. Unimarine S.A.* [1979] Q.B. 645, the plaintiff must make full disclosure of all matters within its knowledge which are material, particularize its claim against the defendant, and show that there is a real risk of the assets being removed before judgment. It is not sufficient to show a possibility that the defendant may become insolvent or that assets may be removed from the jurisdiction in the ordinary course of business.

A Mareva injunction is available to prevent the removal or disposal of almost every kind of asset. This includes a bank account, the goodwill of a company, the proceeds of sale of a flat or even a ship that the plaintiff could not otherwise arrest. The courts, such as in England, may have the power to order a defendant to disclose the whereabouts of its assets in order to make the Mareva injunction more effective and to attend court for cross-examination on this issue. It is possible to obtain a Mareva injunction *ex parte* before the issue of a writ, provided that the applicant gives an undertaking to serve the writ forthwith. An injunction may also be granted postjudgment with the intention of preventing the disposal of assets pending execution of the judgment or taxation of the costs payable by the defendant.

The fact that a Mareva injunction is restricted to freezing assets within the jurisdiction does not prevent an order for disclosure of assets worldwide being made. To assist the plaintiff in determining the location of assets belonging to the defendant, depending on the jurisdiction the court may order discovery of assets in aid of the Mareva injunction. Under such an order, the defendant is required to disclose the location of its assets to the plaintiff. While the purpose of such an order is to allow the plaintiff to properly monitor the Mareva injunction, discovery orders have become an important tactical weapon in their own right.

The injunction does not normally extend to assets outside the jurisdiction. "Worldwide" Mareva injunctions are available only in exceptional circumstances, for example, where the defendant has been extremely unscrupulous, or as a tracing remedy. Some courts, such as those in Canada, have also been willing to grant worldwide Mareva injunctions against a party who is subject to the jurisdiction of that local court.

Where the plaintiff establishes that it has a prima-facie claim against the defendant, the defendant has assets outside the local court's jurisdiction and there is a real risk of removal or dissipation of those assets in order to avoid a judgment, the local court may issue a worldwide Mareva injunction, which will require the defendant to secure assets outside the local court's jurisdiction. Depending on the local rules, such as in Australia, it may be insufficient in disputes involving world-wide Marevas to simply apply for a Mareva injunction in one court without at least at the same time commencing substantive proceedings in that court seeking final relief.

Anton Piller Orders

In some cases, it is vital for a plaintiff to ensure that evidence in the defendant's possession is not destroyed or disposed of before proceedings have commenced. In these circumstances, the plaintiff can apply for an Anton Piller order which is a mandatory injunction to allow the plaintiff's counsel to inspect documents and chattels on the defendant's premises and to take photographs or copies of them: *Anton Piller KG v. Manufacturing Process Ltd* [1976] Ch 55. The plaintiff must show that it has a strong *prima facie* case, that the defendant is in possession of incriminating evidence that the defendant is likely to dispose of before an *inter partes* hearing, and that the plaintiff will suffer serious damage as a result. The plaintiff's draft order must be clear and concise, and he must give full disclosure to the court.

In view of the extraordinary nature of such an order, the ordinary standards for obtaining interlocutory relief do not apply. A plaintiff must make out a strong case and demonstrate a clear risk that the evidence will be destroyed and that the infringing property will not otherwise be recovered. Anton Piller orders commonly provide that seized documents or property are to be held by an independent party, such as an accountant, a secure storage facility or a sheriff.

iii. Property as a Security Device

Certain rules of court contain a variety of procedures designed to preserve property (or its value) until there can be a trial of the proceedings. Examples include orders for the sale of the goods which are perishable or which should be sold immediately for some other reason, or just to preserve property which may be the subject of a contract in dispute so that its quality can be examined in the proceedings. Another example is an order to preserve property which is likely to be destroyed if the court does not intervene.

Other examples include orders of attachment, entries in the public land register, seizure of debt claims, sequestration, judicial custodianship of movable property, prohibition of sale, attachment of movable property, and third-party restraining orders. There are limits on the orders which a court will make of this nature on an interlocutory basis. For example, the order for the sale of goods may not be made if its effect would unduly extend beyond the dispute in the proceedings, e.g., by affecting third parties.

In pecuniary claim matters, the party applying for an injunction may declare its willingness to abstain from enforcement of the injunction if a specific amount is paid in escrow with the court. The court may determine an amount of money for deposit allowing the opponent to avoid the enforcement of the injunction. As a precondition for the enforcement of the injunction, the court may also require the applicant to pay a security deposit equal to the potential damage in the event the claim ultimately proves to be unjustified.

Brussels/Lugano Convention Context

In a Brussels/Lugano Convention situation, the court with which an appeal is lodged against a declaration of enforceability of a foreign judgment may make enforcement conditional on such security as it shall determine pursuant to Article 38 no. 3 of the Conventions. Security measures ordered by a non-Brussels Convention state may not be enforced.

With regard to attachments, the practitioner must study carefully the most recent state of the law in the context of transnational disputes. In the case of Switzerland, for example, an attachment order pursuant to Article 271 of the Bankruptcy Act has traditionally been available in Switzerland to secure the enforcement of a claim for payment of money, regardless of whether an action is pending on the substance of the matter in a non-Lugano Convention court. In transnational litigation, the lack of residence in Switzerland has commonly been the most important ground for attachment. Pursuant to an amendment to the Swiss Bankruptcy Act as of January 1, 1997, however, attachments based on lack of residence in Switzerland will be possible only if the creditor has a title declared enforceable against the foreign debtor or demonstrates a sufficient connection of his claim to Switzerland.

iv. Possible Strategies in the Event of Parallel Suits

To the extent it is possible to have parallel proceedings, it may also be possible to seek an injunction in the local courts where there are also foreign proceedings seeking similar injunctions. If the plaintiff wishes any protective orders to have effect locally, it is necessary to make an application to a local court, and it is not sufficient simply to rely upon the order of a foreign court.

Parallel Suits in Brussels/Lugano Convention States

Article 21 of the Brussels/Lugano Conventions requires any court other than the court first seized to stay on its own motion proceedings involving the same cause of action and the same parties until the jurisdiction of the court first seized is established. The proceedings must be definitely pending, usually in the sense of the writ having been served or, by way of exception, if an Anton Piller order or Mareva injunction has been granted prior to issue of the writ. Where that jurisdiction is established, the court must decline jurisdiction. Where the proceedings brought involve related actions, the court has discretion to stay the proceedings while actions are pending at the first instance.

Under Article 17 of the Brussels/Lugano Conventions, in the event parties (at least one of which is from a Contracting State) have agreed that a court of a Contracting State is to have jurisdiction, then that court has exclusive jurisdiction to hear the case and no court can overrule the jurisdiction agreement. Article 17 takes precedence over Articles 21 and 22 of the Brussels/Lugano Conventions. If, for example, the agreement between the parties contains an exclusive jurisdiction clause conferring jurisdiction on the English courts, all Convention courts should strike out non-English proceedings on the basis that they are vexatious and oppressive.

However, pursuant to Article 24 of the Conventions, a civil action in another Contracting State will not prevent proceedings for attachment or injunction in another Contracting State concerning the same substance of the matter. Thus a civil action may be pending in one Contracting State simultaneously with attachment and injunction proceedings in other Contracting States concerning the same substance of the matter.

In a situation based on Article 24, as well as a nonconvention situation based on the local laws, a party may commence action in one State and apply for interim and protective measures in another. In Convention cases, a party may also seek provisional measures in one State and enforcement in other Contracting States. The European Court of Justice has held that a requested state may refuse to enforce injunctions and similar protective measures if the opposing party was not duly served or was not timely notified of the application for the enforcement of a decision pursuant to Article 27 no. 2 of the Conventions.

A party intending to apply for a interim measure in more than one Convention State must therefore decide beforehand whether it prefers to surprise the opposing party and thus forego international enforceability. Otherwise, the applicant must either apply for the opponent to be heard before the measure is granted or apply for the measures in all countries where enforcement is intended. There is no *lis pendens* of main proceedings in relation to interim measures or between the application for such measures in different States. In nonconvention cases, this option may not exist, and therefore the applicant may have no choice but to move for injunctive relief in all relevant countries.

An emergency measure granted by a court of a Contracting State under the Convention must be enforced by the courts of another Contracting State, even though the particular kind of emergency measure cannot be granted by the courts of the latter State, pursuant to Article 24 of the Conventions. In this regard, the practitioner must take care to verify whether under the local law the courts can grant an emergency measure demanding the defendant to do a certain act as opposed to injunctions prohibiting a certain act.

In international proceedings, *lis pendens* does not apply to precautionary measures under the Brussels and Lugano Conventions. A suit that is already pending on a main issue has no *lis pendens* effect over precautionary measures, and therefore these measures are to proceed according to the law applicable in that State. In the nonconvention context, where there are pending foreign proceedings on a matter a court adjudicating a dispute on the same matter may have discretion to stay its own proceedings. The court may also have the power under its inherent jurisdiction to grant an anti-suit injunction restraining the plaintiff in the foreign proceedings from continuing its foreign action provided it has jurisdiction *in personam* over that person.

Parallel Suits Outside of Brussels/Lugano Conventions

The doctrine of *forum non conveniens*, where applicable, may be relevant in such situations, including in the United States and England. In *Spiliada Maritime Corp. v. Cansulex Ltd.* [1987] AC 460, the House of Lords held that English proceedings will be stayed where the court is satisfied that there is another forum with competent jurisdiction which would be more natural and appropriate, considering the parties' interests and justice. The defendant bears the onus of proof to give the court reasons for exercising its discretion to stay proceedings.

Among the factors which may point in the direction of a stay is prior commencement of legitimate foreign proceedings. It is unlikely that the court would allow a plaintiff to continue two actions in the same dispute in two different jurisdictions. English courts will grant injunctions restraining foreign actions on the basis that to proceed would be vexatious and oppressive, in breach of a contract not to sue, or in breach of a contract to be bound by English proceedings.

Local proceedings will not usually be stayed unless the foreign proceedings were commenced first in time. An application for a stay of proceedings is a request that the court decline to exercise its jurisdiction, and the principles invoked will parallel those relevant to the doctrine of *forum non conveniens* or its equivalent, if any, in the local jurisdiction.

The discretion to dismiss the action in the case of foreign pending proceedings may be seen as existing in order to avoid the confusion and injustice that would follow where both the courts of the forum and foreign countries were prepared to recognize the judgments of each other. The court may take into account whether there are sufficient connecting factors with the forum and whether a stay would deny the plaintiff some legitimate juridical advantage (e.g., where a statute of limitations has expired in the foreign country).

Anti-suit injunctions, where available, will not usually be granted unless the foreign proceedings were instituted second in point of time. To the extent the local court is generally reluctant to interfere with the proceedings of other courts, the principles applicable to an order restraining foreign proceedings are more stringent than those applicable to the staying of the local action. The applicant must show that the foreign proceedings have a tendency to interfere with the due process of the domestic court and that the foreign plaintiff would not lose a substantial juridical advantage if the foreign proceedings were prevented.

With regard to the effect of foreign judgments on local proceedings, the local courts may not take judicial notice of foreign judgments. Consequently, the conclusion of foreign proceedings on a matter will not normally have an effect on local proceedings in the same matter except at the instigation of one of the parties to the proceedings. The party whom the foreign judgment favors should seek either to have the foreign judgment recognized in the local proceedings provided that it satisfies the requirements for common law recognition (see **Chapter 17** below) or to have the judgment "registered," where applicable.

CHAPTER 10

TAKING OF WITNESS EVIDENCE DOMESTICALLY IN SUPPORT OF FOREIGN ACTION

Most countries grant judicial assistance to all States with which they have diplomatic relations in accordance with letters of request of their judicial authorities even in the absence of conventions or treaties. Thus most courts will render judicial assistance as provided by domestic procedural law (*lex fori*) within their area of competence. The requested domestic court will normally not assess the underlying reason for the request, but must nevertheless deny a request if the requested action is either beyond its civil jurisdiction or against local law or public policy.

Unless letters of request explicitly demand the application of a specific foreign rule of procedure, which may or may not be permissible under local law, evidence is taken by (or under the supervision of) the local court in the manner set forth by local law.

Bilateral conventions also allow taking of evidence without intervention of local authorities, namely by diplomatic officers and consular agents of the foreign mission in the country where taking of evidence is sought. This is normally limited to "non-compulsory measures" and therefore requires that the witness be willing to give evidence.

Since the ratification of the 1970 Hague Evidence Convention, discussed below, the term "letter of request" has begun to displace "letter rogatory," but here "letter of request" refers solely to Letters issued in compliance with the Hague Evidence Convention.

i. From Whom Discovery is Possible and When

Depending on the jurisdiction, taking of witness evidence, or "discovery" of witnesses, may or may not be possible to varying degrees. To the extent there is a general opportunity for such taking of evidence, it will normally be possible between and among the parties to an action and, to a limited extent if at all, from nonparties. Certain countries, particularly in the civil-law context, distinguish between "parties" and "witnesses," such that anyone who is not a party to the case and who is present in the country may be obliged to appear as a witness.

Until recently, for example, while parties or witnesses within Canada could be compelled to give evidence in cases pending in a foreign jurisdiction provided that the appropriate letters rogatory were issued to a Canadian court, the Canadian courts followed a strict rule against permitting examination of nonparties for discovery. Now examination of nonparties for discovery is permitted where the party seeking the examination establishes that (i) the evidence sought would not be available from other individuals, (ii) it would be unfair to require the party to proceed to trial without benefit of the examination, and (iii) the examination would not unduly delay the trial, result in unreasonable expense for other parties, or cause any unfairness to the person to be examined.

Availability of "Pretrial Discovery"

Most civil-law countries do not provide for any kind of pretrial discovery procedures apart from the protective taking of (witness) evidence in the context of interim, conservatory and emergency measures. Thus, with some exceptions and gradations, most non-common law jurisdictions do not provide in their local procedure or customs for measures equivalent to pretrial discovery. Accordingly, one party cannot be obligated to provide the other party with information or answers to inquiries, and there is no obligation to disclose the existence and content of documents in possession of the party prior to the trial.

At the same time, even in some civil-law jurisdictions protective taking of evidence may normally be requested at any stage of the proceedings if there is a danger of loss of evidence or of impediment in the use of evidence. In such a situation, it may be possible to have a pretrial hearing of a witness. Whether the taking of witness evidence prior to litigation will be granted when the legal requirements are not fulfilled is doubtful, but could be expected at least as far as the witness gives evidence voluntarily.

Where such a vehicle is available, Austria being a prime example, the court will hear the opposing party before making a final decision on taking evidence, unless the opposing party consents without being heard. In urgent cases, the taking of such evidence may be performed immediately; otherwise, the opposing party is given notice of the summons of the witness and may attend the testimony. The judge must record the testimony and safeguard the protocol until requested by the court in charge of the (subsequent) main proceedings to hand it over.

Pretrial Discovery in Common-Law Jurisdictions

In the case of pretrial discovery in the common-law tradition, expansive taking of evidence of witnesses may be possible from proper filing and service until a court-designated "discovery cut-off" date, where applicable. Such cut-off date is normally a short amount of time before trial. Depending on the jurisdiction and particularly in the case of certain common-law countries, there may in fact be no court involvement unless and until a party or nonparty refuses to comply with a discovery request. Absent such refusal to comply, the degree of involvement of the court in the taking of evidence will invariably be far less than in other countries, particularly of the civil-law tradition.

Depending on the common-law jurisdiction, it may be possible to obtain evidence from any material witness at any stage in foreign proceedings. In certain jurisdictions, e.g., Australia, the State may prohibit the giving of evidence by any person who is a citizen or resident of that State if it is satisfied that the assumption of jurisdiction by the foreign court or the manner of its exercise is contrary to international law or practice.

The courts of a foreign country may assume such exorbitant jurisdiction where, for example, they purport to exercise jurisdiction over a nonresident by sole reason of that person having caused harm to a another person resident in that country. Similarly, depending on the jurisdiction the State may prohibit the production of documents or the giving of evidence if satisfied that the production of the document or the giving of the evidence would be prejudicial to local security.

Generally, where applicable, witnesses are summoned locally by means of a court-issued *subpoena*. The *subpoena* requires the personal attendance of the witness to whom it is addressed. Failure to comply with a *subpoena* normally amounts to contempt of court in relation to which a court will have wide powers to sanction. The law does not necessarily require a party to testify. It will, however, be in the interests of the party to testify if to do so would create no difficulties, since it is possible that a judge or especially a jury, where applicable, might draw adverse inferences from a failure to testify.

The seeking of evidence from corporate entities needs to be approached carefully. Certain courts are generally reluctant to lift the corporate veil and will regard separate companies within corporate groups as distinct legal entities. Accordingly, a *subpoena* served upon a parent of a foreign subsidiary is not necessarily likely to achieve evidence directly from the foreign subsidiary.

With regard to admissibility of evidence in "privileged" documents, where applicable, certain jurisdictions particularly in the common-law area may provide restrictions on the adduction of certain privileged communications. Oral testimony may be treated the same as the adduction of the communication in a document. Adduction of the privileged evidence by whatever means should be prohibited when the corresponding document is protected from production by the privilege. Therefore, although the position is not settled, it appears that where the discovery of documents is not allowed, a witness cannot be compelled to testify on the contents of the documents. Privilege is addressed in **subheading vii.** below.

ii. Conventions

1954 Hague Convention on Civil Procedure

The primary multilateral conventions relevant to the taking of witness evidence domestically in support of foreign actions are the 1954 Hague Convention and the 1970 Hague Evidence Convention respectively, particularly the latter. Certain of the countries addressed in this work are either not a member of either Convention, or for that matter of any other multilateral convention on judicial assistance, or have acceded to only one of the two Hague Conventions in question.

As of July 1, 1997, the 1954 Hague Convention had been acceded to by Argentina, Belgium, Croatia, Czech Republic, Denmark, Egypt, Finland, France (plus some overseas regions), Germany, Hungary, Israel, Italy, Japan, Latvia, Luxembourg, Morocco, Netherlands, Antilles and Aruba, Norway, Poland, Portugal, Rumania, Slovak Republic, Slovenia, Spain, Suriname, Sweden, Switzerland, Turkey and the Vatican.

The 1954 Hague Convention provides that in civil and commercial matters a judicial authority of a Contracting State may, in conformity with the provisions of its legislation, communicate with the competent authority of another Contracting State for the sake of transmitting and effecting letters of request for service of process or letters rogatory for effecting judicial acts within the jurisdiction of the requested State.

The 1954 Convention provides for a minimum of judicial assistance, especially as compared with the 1970 Hague Evidence Convention (discussed below). Under the 1954 Convention, the letter of request must be served in the language of the court from which assistance is requested or must be accompanied by a certified translation into that language. The letter of request must describe the pending proceeding for which judicial assistance is requested, including the names of the parties and a description of the facts and the claim. Furthermore, the letter of request must designate the evidence requested as well as the names and addresses of witnesses to be interrogated. The letter of request may also state that the evidence taking shall be conducted under the law of the foreign proceeding. Finally, it must give the names and addresses of parties who wish to participate in the judicial assistance proceedings.

Under the 1954 Convention, evidence is taken in accordance with the law applicable at the place where the taking of evidence is conducted. Also, the 1954 Convention allows for foreign procedural law to be applied. The restrictions that apply are the same as those under the 1970 Hague Evidence Convention, discussed below. As under the 1970 Hague Evidence Convention, foreign law cannot be applied to compel testimony. Here, only local law is applicable. No force may be used against the parties to the foreign proceeding.

The 1954 Convention does not address the issue of the right to refuse to give testimony. As local law will apply, those rights to refuse testimony granted by local law are available to the person against whom the taking of evidence is directed. As to whether a witness may also refuse testimony based on foreign procedural law, this is not addressed in the 1954 Convention, but it would not appear to be the case. However, the witness, if appearing in the foreign court, could rely on any right to refuse testimony granted by foreign law.

Article 15 of the 1954 Convention allows diplomatic or consular representatives to take evidence if this has been agreed upon in a treaty or if the country in which the representative performs its duties does not object. Certain countries, such as Switzerland, have objected to the taking of evidence by diplomatic or consular representatives, which may extend to the taking of evidence by a foreign diplomatic or consular representative from a citizen of that country. Practically speaking, however, this can hardly be prevented.

1970 Hague Evidence Convention

Many States have acceded to the 1970 Hague Convention on the Taking of Evidence Abroad in Civil and Commercial Matters. Some, such as England, have done so only quite recently. Under the Convention, a letter of request may be sent through the Central Authority or other designated authority of the requesting State to the Central Authority of another Contracting State for the taking of evidence or the performance of some other judicial act for the purpose of judicial proceedings, whether commenced or contemplated.

Among the reservations and declarations to the Convention which may have been made by one or another country, and which must be verified on a case-by-case basis, include those to the effect that (i) taking of evidence by commissioners is prohibited, (ii) taking of evidence by diplomats and consuls requires permission, (iii) requests for "pretrial discovery" of documents as known and practiced primarily in the United States will not be accepted, and (iv) letters of request must be made in the native language of the recipient country.

Requests for pretrial discovery are commonly understood in countries having taken such a reservation to be requests to give information about or produce any relevant documents in a person's possession other than individually specified documents. Interestingly, depending on the country at issue there is either no or very little reported caselaw on this subject.

Taking of Evidence by Consuls Under Hague Convention

Article 15 of the Evidence Convention authorizes consuls to take evidence from nationals of the State that the Consul represents subject to two limitations. First, the Consul cannot use compulsion to require the giving of the evidence and second, the Consul may take evidence only for use in proceedings already commenced in his home State. A Contracting State can also declare at any time that the taking of evidence is allowed only after obtaining permission.

Article 16 authorizes consuls to take evidence from nationals of the country where the consuls are stationed, but no compulsion may be used and evidence can be taken only for use in proceedings already commenced. Article 17 authorizes commissioners to take evidence within the receiving State but only subject to the same limitations imposed by Article 16. Persons taking evidence under Article 15, 16 or 17 are specifically authorized to administer oaths and to take any form of evidence that is not incompatible with local law.

Limitations to the Application of the Hague Evidence Convention

While the Hague Evidence Convention covers a wide range of issues relating to transnational taking of evidence between Contracting States, it is also subject to certain significant limitations. Thus, the Convention is applicable only to the taking of evidence in civil or commercial matters; accordingly, the same principles apply as in the Hague Service Convention, discussed in **Chapters 5** and **6** above. The local and the foreign court may adopt different classifications of law in considering whether proceedings are a civil or commercial matter. In such cases, the court at the place of attempted discovery must normally first determine how the proceedings would be classified under the law and practice of the requesting State.

Second, the Hague Evidence Convention is limited to requests for assistance made by judicial authorities, which it has been argued to exclude administrative agencies and executive bodies, as well as requests by courts in aid of such entities. Furthermore, the Hague Evidence Convention is limited to requests to obtain evidence or perform other judicial acts. While this includes oral depositions, production of documents and inspection of property, it is not entirely clear. In addition, Article 1 of the Hague Evidence Convention makes it clear that it applies to requests relating to proceedings that have not yet commenced.

Contracting States are required to obtain requested evidence by applying the "appropriate measures of compulsion" available under national law. Accordingly, Article 10 of the Hague Evidence Convention enables foreign litigants to obtain evidence even if a local witness is uncooperative. The local courts are then obliged to apply the same degree of compulsion with respect to uncooperative witnesses as is available in purely domestic actions. Depending on the country at issue, this may include threat of fine or suit. Also depending on the country, these local means of compulsion may not be available if the witness is duly served in a foreign country in order to testify before a local court.

Under the Hague Evidence Convention, if a witness is willing to give evidence and produce the requested documents without the issuance of a *subpoena*, depending on the local law such depositions can be taken without an order of a local court and there may be no need for a letter of request. The parties, if they so wish, can appoint an examiner to preside over the taking of any evidence. They can also agree to abide by certain set rules. If a witness will not voluntarily attend, then local jurisdiction must be invoked to compel attendance.

Submission of Letters of Request

The letter of request for the taking of witness testimony by a foreign court is transmitted directly from the requesting judicial authority to the designated Central Authority in the requested State without being transmitted through any other authority of the State of execution (Article 2 para. 2 of the Hague Evidence Convention). The major goal of the Hague Evidence Convention is to simplify the service of letters rogatory (letters of request) and, thereafter, the taking of evidence itself. This is achieved by providing that the same Central Authorities named in the Hague Service Convention will also receive letters rogatory. Unlike requests for service, letters rogatory must mandatorily be written in the official language of the competent Central Authority or must be accompanied by a translation.

The letter of request for the taking of witness testimony by a foreign court is transmitted directly from the requesting judicial authority to the designated Central Authority in the State of execution without being transmitted through any other authority of the State of execution (Article 2 para. 2 of the Hague Evidence Convention). The party seeking the deposition in a foreign country may apply to the court where the proceedings are pending for a letter of request to be issued. The letter will be addressed to the appropriate judicial authority in the relevant foreign country where the witness evidence is sought, and will set out details of the requested deposition.

The letter will ordinarily be sent to an attorney in the foreign jurisdiction where witness evidence is sought, who will deliver the letter to the relevant Central Authority in that foreign jurisdiction at the same time that the application is filed for the commencement of the proceedings. If the opposing party in the principal litigation does not oppose the request, then the appropriate orders (*subpoenas* for attendance, production, etc., as and where applicable) will be made pursuant to the relevant court rules. If the opposing party opposes the request, then the court may hear full argument before orders are given.

Content of Letters of Request

Letters of Request ought to set out all the procedural requirements with which the requesting party, the other party and the foreign court intend the deposition to comply. These requirements may include (i) provision for, e.g., recording of an oath or affirmation; (ii) direct examination or examination-in-chief to be performed by the requesting party; (iii) cross-examination by the requesting party in the case that the witness is hostile; (iv) cross-examination by the nonrequesting party; and (v) redirect examination of witnesses by the requesting party.

They may also include (vi) compulsion of specified persons to attend or produce documents; (vii) an opportunity for the parties to the principal litigation to give objections and for the full recording of these objections; (viii) an opportunity to apply to the court to examine further witnesses; and (ix) sufficient time to be allowed in between direct examination and cross-examination. Finally, they may include (x) application of the procedural rules of the foreign State in place of the procedural rules of the local court; (xi) a specified person to act as the examiner (usually a local attorney); and (xii) a specified person to commence the proceedings (a local attorney).

Taking Evidence Pursuant to Orders from Local Courts

Evidence is taken in accordance with the law applicable at the place where taking of evidence is conducted pursuant to Article 9 para. 1 of the Hague Evidence Convention. Under Article 9 para. 2, the authority issuing a letter of request may request that the local authority apply the law governing the foreign country's domestic procedure of taking evidence. This request must only be followed, however, if the foreign country's domestic law does not irreconcilably conflict with local law. A typical example of such a conflict might be the taking of an oath. Various codes of civil procedure do not allow the taking of an oath, so that such jurisdiction would not follow a request that a witness take an oath when giving testimony.

Where court orders are required, the taking of evidence in most countries for the purpose of foreign proceedings, being a procedural matter, is one over which those local courts have jurisdiction. The jurisdiction is normally determined by the place of residence of the witness to be called to give evidence. However, depending on the rules, a court in one state or province of a jurisdiction may be able to issue a *subpoena* or similar order to a witness in another state or province in the same jurisdiction to attend at a place in the issuing court's jurisdiction and give evidence.

Unless, pursuant to terms in a letter of request as set forth above, the relevant local court orders otherwise, the local procedural rules may apply in relation to specific issues. These may include, where applicable, (i) recording of evidence which can be done either in writing or by video taping or other audio-visual methods; (ii) authentication of the transcript; (iii) imposition of general rules of evidence normally applying in that local court; (iv) privileges which a compelled witness may exercise when giving evidence (e.g., refusal to answer a question on the grounds of self-incrimination); and (v) issuing of *subpoenas* to compel witnesses to attend to give evidence or produce documents (this is not subject to variation in the letters of request).

All the procedural rules relating to the deposition may be varied subject to the discretion of the local court and an application in the letter of request. In the appointment of an examiner, the court has discretion and the parties may or may not be given effective freedom to appoint their own examiner or pose questions themselves. There may or may not be rules prohibiting consuls and other diplomatic agents of foreign states, foreign legal counsel or a foreign court official from taking testimony in the local jurisdiction, even if the witness is from that local jurisdiction or of a third nationality.

Where local rules allow, the evidence may be taken at the premises of the official reporter of the court concerned or by agreement in the offices of the attorneys, by a process of question and answer, with a transcript taken and certified by a court reporter. Also where allowed, in the event that counsel do not agree on the scope of the examination or the propriety of questions asked, the examining party may seek an order of the court as to whether the questions are permissible. Certain countries' courts will generally permit "cross-examination" provided that it is not directed toward credibility issues alone and is relevant to the action as defined by the pleadings. Letters of request should confirm that the witness may be cross-examined and should specify the substantive limits on that cross-examination. Depending on the jurisdiction where the examination is meant to take place, this request may or may not be possible to implement.

Compulsion under Hague Evidence Convention

If compulsion is necessary with respect to the taking of evidence, only local law applies under Article 10 of the Hague Convention. Whether compulsion is available is a matter of the applicable local procedural law. It also depends on whether evidence is taken from a "party" to the foreign domestic procedure or rather from an independent individual such as a "witness." As previously stated, depending on the jurisdiction, a party may have a different status than a third party and often cannot testify as a witness.

While the refusal of a party to cöoperate in the taking of evidence may be taken into account by a judge when rendering the judgment, depending on the applicable law no compulsion is necessarily available against a party. This may yield an unsatisfactory result in the context of international judicial assistance unless the foreign court can take into account the refusal of cooperation when assessing the case and rendering the judgment.

If evidence must be taken from a party unrelated to the foreign proceedings, such a party has the position of a witness. Aside from privileges to refuse testimony, such persons have a legal duty to cooperate in the taking of evidence. If they are in contempt, compulsion may be used against them depending on the applicable law. Also depending on the applicable law, they may be subject to criminal sanction, Article 292 of the Swiss Criminal Code being an example.

In view of the different treatment given parties and witnesses in certain countries, it is important to determine whether foreign law or local law determines whether a person from whom evidence is to be taken is considered a party or witness. On the other hand, under certain procedural laws, both parties and unrelated individuals may refuse cooperation if they would be prejudiced.

In transnational litigation governed by the Hague Evidence Convention, the right to refuse testimony is governed by Article 11 of the Hague Evidence Convention. The witness may refuse testimony based on both local law and foreign law. The foreign law may be important if the attorney-client privilege is involved. For example, a country might recognize a secrecy obligation of attorneys, as many do, but not an attorney-client privilege which also grants the client the right not to produce its attorney's work product. Where a foreign attorney-client privilege is applicable, additional protection is granted to the client who must appear as a witness or is ordered to produce documents. To the extent the attorney-client privilege applies, this person may refuse to cooperate in a context in which he would otherwise have had to testify or to produce documents.

At the same time, Article 11 para. 1(b) of the Hague Evidence Convention provides that only those rights to refuse testimony under foreign law shall apply which are explicitly mentioned in the letter of request. Article 3 of the Hague Service Convention does not require the foreign authority issuing the letter of request to list those rights. However, in the absence of the letter of request listing such right, the local court may insist that the foreign court confirm these rights. Accordingly, persons obliged to cooperate in taking of evidence should therefore insist on being instructed as to which rights to refuse testimony are applicable.

Relevancy and Other Local Evidentiary Rules

If the letter of request does not specify that the evidence is to be taken in accordance with the foreign rules of civil procedure, then it will be taken in accordance with the rules of the relevant local court. This may in fact happen anyway if the local court does not accept such foreign rules in whole or in part.

Thus depending on the jurisdiction it may or may not be possible to take evidence under the foreign rules of civil procedure. However, the request for the evidence to be so taken must be contained in the letter of request. The local courts will more readily grant such a request if the examiner is familiar with the foreign rules of evidence. But this is no guarantee, especially where the local courts as a matter of public policy refuse to allow examination other than by the local court itself.

Objections to Questions

In certain jurisdictions particularly under common law influence, rules and acts respecting evidence provide for objections to questions by a witness. Generally, if a person being examined before an examiner objects to answering any question put to him, the grounds for the objection and the answer to the question shall be set out in the deposition of that person or any statement annexed thereto. The validity of the ground for objecting to answer any such question or for objecting to such question shall normally not be determined by the examiner, but by the corresponding court at whose request the examination is being conducted.

iii. Other Means and Absence of Convention

Certain countries are signatories to bilateral additional agreements to the 1954 Hague Convention on Civil Procedure. Austria, for example, which has not acceded to the 1970 Hague Evidence Convention, has concluded such bilateral agreements with Denmark, France, Germany, Israel, Italy, Luxembourg, Netherlands with Antilles and Aruba, Norway, Sweden, Switzerland, Spain and Turkey. Some countries are also signatories to bilateral treaties on Mutual Assistance in Legal Proceedings (Service of Process) in civil and commercial matters.

Bilateral treaties on judicial assistance contain provisions on the taking of evidence from witnesses, parties, experts, and inspections, etc., and the performing of other judicial acts abroad or in the local jurisdiction. Some bilateral treaties allow the taking of witness and documentary evidence by diplomatic officers and consular agents of the foreign mission in the local jurisdiction without the intervention of the local authorities. This may be limited to taking of evidence from citizens of the requesting country and may not involve the taking of an oath or compulsory measures.

There are also other bilateral and multilateral treaties on this subject which may be relevant. For example, Brazil is not a signatory to the 1970 Hague Convention, but has signed the 1975 Inter-American Convention on the Taking of Evidence Abroad as well as the Additional Protocol to that Convention in 1984 (although neither one has been ratified by the Brazilian Government thus far). The 1975 Inter-American Convention and the 1979 Additional Protocol and Annex have also been signed by such countries as Argentina, Mexico and the United States among others. The 1996 Mercosur (South Common Market) Protocol on Cooperation and Jurisdictional Assistance in Civil, Commercial, Labor and Administrative Matters may also be relevant. Furthermore, the Convention on Nordic Legal Aid in Service of Process and Taking of Evidence between Finland, Iceland, Norway, Sweden, and Denmark is also applicable to the taking of evidence.

Articles 31 and 32 of the Hague Evidence Convention explicitly provide that the Convention does not affect preexisting treaties between Member States to the extent the States have not provided otherwise.

Other Possibilities to Effect Discovery Requests

Quite apart from bilateral conventions and treaties and particularly in the U.S. context, the practitioner should be aware of possibilities to obtain and enforce discovery requests and orders whether or not such means as the Hague Evidence Convention can be availed of or are in fact utilized.

One example which is relevant in transnational litigation is serving a U.S. parent to reach a non-U.S. subsidiary or serving a U.S. subsidiary to reach a non-U.S. parent. U.S. courts may order discovery from a non-U.S. parent or subsidiary on the basis of valid service on the U.S. parent or subsidiary under certain circumstances. This may be possible particularly where the non-U.S. entity has sufficiently interjected itself into the U.S. through the U.S. entity for purposes of personal jurisdiction: e.g., In *re Marc Rich*, 707 F.2d 663, 667 (2d Cir.), *cert. denied*, 463 U.S. 1215 (1983); *Cooper Industries v. British Aerospace*, 102 F.R.D. 918, 919-20 (S.D.N.Y. 1984).

This may result in clashes with the foreign jurisdiction depending on its own law respecting the separateness of identity of parent and subsidiary. For example, Finnish parent companies and their Finnish and non-Finnish subsidiaries are separate legal entities. Therefore, under Finnish law a discovery request on a Finnish parent has no legal effect on its Finnish or non-Finnish subsidiary, which has to be served separately.

A related area in which the caselaw in the U.S. federal courts has taken on interesting new dimensions is how and when a foreign defendant can enforce its right to discovery, or contest a U.S. plaintiff's right to discovery, under the Federal Rules of Civil Procedure. In transnational arbitration, for example, if a party ignores the tribunal's order to produce evidence, the tribunal may not have power to compel attendance of witnesses or production of documents, but it may draw an "adverse inference." Increasingly, the question arises as to whether this is enough for the aggrieved party seeking production and whether there is not some other form of compulsion such as is available in court proceedings in the U.S.

In arbitration taking place in the U.S., discovery under court supervision will normally not be granted except under extraordinary circumstances, and then only on a showing that it is necessary for protection of the rights of a party, especially prior to arbitration. On the other hand, discovery is occasionally ordered where the request is made prior to constitution of the tribunal. After constitution, on the other hand, most U.S. courts have refused to intervene, as exemplified by *Hunt v. Mobil Oil*, 583 F.Supp. 1092 (S.D.N.Y. 1984). Where the tribunal issues a *subpoena* or order to produce evidence which the party ignores, penalties for refusal to obey may be imposed only by a court of competent jurisdiction. Thus a court can be petitioned for an order to compel pursuant to specific statutes, e.g., Chapter 7 of the U.S. Federal Arbitration Act.

Recalcitrant parties in U.S. court proceedings face a different and harsher landscape than in the case of international arbitration. In the face of a complete refusal to respond to a discovery request, the U.S. district court may authorize sanctions. The discovery request may even include an order of inspection of documents located outside the U.S. under Federal Rule 34: e.g., *Graco v. Kremlin, Inc.*, 101 F.R.D. 503, 516 (N.D. Ill. 1984); *Lourance v. Weinig*, 107 F.R.D. 386, 389 (W.D. Tenn. 1985). Such sanctions include (i) designating that certain facts as asserted by the party seeking discovery be considered true, (ii) denying the recalcitrant party an opportunity to support or oppose certain claims or defenses, (iii) striking certain pleadings or dismissing the action entirely, and (iv) holding the recalcitrant party in contempt of court.

Recent decisions on sanctions have also extended to granting partial or complete default judgment for destruction of crucial documents and harassment of witnesses, and assessing fees and expenses: *Shepherd v. American Broadcasting Companies*, 1992 U.S. Dist. LEXIS 4935 (D.C.Dist. April 15, 1992). They have also taken the form of directing a verdict against the non-cooperative party for gross negligence which had led to the loss and destruction of evidence during shipment by a third party: *Jones v. Goodyear Tire and Rubber*, 137 F.R.D. 657 (C.D.Ill. 1991), *aff'd*, *Morocco v. General Motors*, 966 F.2d 220 (7th Cir. 1992).

For some foreign parties, the severity of such sanctions will be perceived as an additional reason to avoid the U.S. courts altogether; for others, it may be regarded as a positive element of protection in the face of discovery abuses which are also becoming more commonplace in transnational arbitration. Indeed Federal Rule 45 sanctions would also apply to a nonparty served with a document *subpoena* as to documents in its possession, custody or control located outside the U.S.: *U.S. v. Chase Manhattan Bank, N.A.*, 590 F. Supp. 1160 (S.D.N.Y. 1984).

iv. Practical Problems and Time Factors

Due to the difficulty in drafting a letter of request and the time delay usually involved, this customary method of discovery is frequently reserved for cases in which the local court cannot assert the requisite personal jurisdiction over the respondent, and in which no convention or bilateral treaty applies. Many letters rogatory take over one year to execute, and the mere transmission to a foreign executing court may take anywhere from several weeks to several months. However, the same delay may in fact apply to letters of request under the Hague Evidence Convention or other multilateral or bilateral treaties.

In jurisdictions where such witness evidence is taken and used, a witness is normally not required to submit unless he would be compellable in the relevant foreign jurisdiction. Thus the court where the action is pending can order attendance only where it is intended to use that evidence at trial, and thus so-called "fishing expeditions" are meant to be ruled out. It may also not be possible, from the standpoint of the right to a fair hearing and equal treatment, for the court to allow only direct examination or examination-in-chief.

Generally, all witnesses who can comply with the testimonial formalities are competent to testify and all competent witnesses are compellable. Therefore, government officials may be compellable witnesses. In certain circumstances, government officials may be able to withhold evidence pursuant to one or another doctrine of sovereign or public interest immunity. Such immunity may arise, depending on the jurisdiction, where non-disclosure is necessary for the proper functioning of the executive government or the public service, in matters that affect national security, and for the protection of the sources of information that can assist government law-enforcement agencies.

With regard to local rules concerning the taking of witness evidence domestically, there may be dramatic differences in the scope depending on the nature of the jurisdiction. Thus in many civil-law countries where taking of evidence is circumscribed in comparison with certain common-law countries, a witness must communicate his observation on facts and occurrences in the past without significant prompting, if any, by examining counsel. In accordance with the principles of immediacy and oral hearing in civil procedure, the witness must give faithful testimony personally and in his own words before the requested judge. It may not be possible for the court to accept any written statements of a witness as evidence.

Furthermore, in many countries the examination of parties to a litigation is not conducted by the standards of witness examination, even if they may be called "party witnesses" in other countries. Their interrogation may not be compelled and they may not be forced to give evidence under oath. In such case, if not under oath, false testimony of a party witness may not be punishable. Analogous to witnesses, the party witness has the duty to appear in court when summoned to give testimony. Nevertheless, direct sanctions against the party's unexcused absence despite summons may not exist under local law.

Agreements of parties to an action by which they are bound to limit the evidence on certain facts and issues to certain types of evidence under exclusion of other types of evidence (e.g., evidence by public instruments but not by witness testimony) are not normally valid or binding.

Apart from a witness's duty to answer questions in a true and complete way, many countries do not contain a general obligation for anybody to "disclose all relevant evidence" to the court or to a party. In countries where a general duty for the parties to reveal evidence does not exist, if a party refuses to present evidence that it obviously must have, the court subject to such procedural rules is free to draw such conclusions therefrom as it finds appropriate.

Particularly in many civil-law countries, the judge questions the witness on the issue of evidence as determined and described in the summons. The attorneys may participate in the examination, but only after the witness has been examined by the judge may the attorneys either ask the judge to put further questions to the witness or, with the judge's consent, question the witness directly. Cross-examination is not allowed. The judge is in command of the process and will reject excessive or irrelevant questions by order and record this in the protocol.

If a lawyer participating in an examination does not comply with these rules or with standards of behavior, the judge may notify this to the local chamber of attorneys who have competence for disciplinary measures over the foreign attorney. At the same time, particularly the common-law lawyer should not prematurely assume that all civil-law jurisdictions look with equal disfavor on direct and cross-examination and have a uniform policy of disallowing attorney involvement in witness questioning using such methods. Each country must be looked at on a case-by-case basis.

For example, although in Finland the common-law notions of examination and cross-examination are not known as such, the witnesses are usually questioned directly by the parties' counsels, first by the party who has called the witness and then by the adverse party. At the same time, Finnish civil procedure law provides that "questions that, due to their content, formulation, or manner of presentation, lead to a certain type of answer shall not be made unless there are specific reasons for doing so," effectively ruling out leading questions of the kind often employed in U.S.-style witness examination.

v. Relevance to Later Efforts to Recognize and Enforce at Place of Service

Taking of witness evidence should normally not have any direct effect on the recognition and enforcement of a judgment or decision. In the European context, Article 29 of the Brussels/Lugano Conventions provides, for example, that a foreign judgment may under no circumstances be reviewed as to its substance, reflecting the principle of "no *revision au fond*." Accordingly, judgments originating from Contracting States of the Brussels/Lugano Conventions undergo recognition *ipso iure*. There are therefore no grounds for refusal with regard to taking of evidence apart from procedures applied which are against public policy.

Bilateral enforcement treaties granting mutual recognition of judgments in which the countries addressed herein are parties do not contain provisions which might be grounds for denying enforcement of a foreign judgment due to unlawful taking of witness abroad. Consequently, a judgment debtor cannot normally object to enforcement because of defective evidence. If a judgment debtor wishes to challenge the authorization of enforcement, it must do so by somehow linking it to an infringement of public policy, if such a link can indeed be made.

In this context, depending on the applicable law there may be restrictions as to who may be a designated witness, and whether the violation of such a restriction constitutes an offense against public policy at the place of ultimate enforcement must be examined on an individual basis. For example, normally anyone may testify except those lacking legal capacity, those legally impeded to testify and, in some cases, those considered suspicious. Legal capacity may relate to insanity, illness, underage, or some physical impairment. Legal impediment may relate to spousal or other relationship. Suspicion, where applicable, may relate to those previously condemned for perjury.

Thus in some cases a violation of public policy can be alleged if the evidence, produced or gathered within the State where enforcement of the foreign judgment is now being sought, was obtained illegally. In Brazil, for example, since the letter of request is the mandatory means of obtaining transnational evidence in that country, one can contest the evidence gathered in some other fashion, and such objection might defeat the "homologation" process as part of the enforcement of the foreign judgment if the contested evidence was fundamental to the foreign judgment. If the foreign judge disregarded Brazilian sovereignty, by ordering or permitting a procedural act to be unduly performed in Brazil, the Brazilian court might deny enforcement of such foreign judgment on that basis.

In other countries, however, the fact that evidence was taken locally in the course of foreign proceedings on consent but without the issuance of otherwise mandatory letters rogatory would not necessarily affect the enforceability of the foreign judgment locally provided the party examined was properly represented.

vi. Special Issues Relating to Expert Evidence

Normally if the letter of request does not specify that the evidence is to be taken in accordance with the foreign rules of civil procedure and evidence, then it will be taken in accordance with the local rules. Accordingly, where applicable and available, the qualification of an expert witness as such is a matter for the trial judge. In such cases, the trial judge must determine, e.g., whether the field of knowledge in which the witness professes expertise is a recognized and organized body of knowledge outside the ordinary experience of people and whether the witness has sufficient expertise in such field as would enable him to assist the tribunal. Local rules on this subject, which exist primarily but not solely in common-law jurisdictions, must be consulted by the practitioner individually.

Whether a particular field of knowledge is shown to be a sufficiently organized branch of science will depend in each case upon the evidence provided in support of such a conclusion, upon the precise question upon which the expert's opinion is to be sought, and also upon the general area of science in question.

Common Law Approaches

As a general rule in common-law jurisdictions, the parties to a trial alone may call evidence. Following from this general rule, in civil cases the court is not empowered to call a witness unless the parties consent, and in criminal trials there must exist exceptional circumstances before the court will call a witness, if it can do so at all. In common-law jurisdictions, the general rule against the court calling witnesses extends to their questioning. That is, principally the parties question witnesses and the judge, on his own motion (or where requested by the jury, if any) asks questions only to remove any ambiguities which arise during party questioning. This situation again exists primarily in common-law jurisdictions.

In such common-law jurisdictions, the court should always show restraint in interfering with party strategy and there is authority to the effect that court intervention in the questioning of witnesses may be grounds for appeal. At the same time, certain local rules may permit the appointment of a court expert to report on a matter before it. In other jurisdictions, such an expert may be appointed only on a party's application.

Civil Law Approaches

In many civil-law jurisdictions, the court of process abroad may demand the taking of expert evidence by means of a letter of request. The parties may propose the experts whom they wish to testify on technical or commercial issues, but the court is not bound by these proposals. Therefore, the choice of the expert is in the discretion of the requested court. A party may have the right to refuse an expert, in particular, if the party suspects that this expert has previously given an expert opinion on the matter at the private request of the other party.

Upon appointment of an expert by the court in most civil-law countries, the requested court transmits a written summary of instructions on the subject of evidence and adds a prepared list of questions explicitly demanded or indicated in the letter of request. The expert opinion is delivered as a written statement. Summons to the hearing is transmitted to the requesting foreign authority and to the parties or their representatives unless they have waived intervention beforehand in the letter of request.

vii. Blocking Statutes and Attorney-Client and Other "Privileges"

Under the Hague Evidence Convention, three separate groups of privileges exist. First, Article 11 permits a witness to refuse to provide evidence that is protected by a privilege provided by the receiving State. Second, witnesses may invoke any privilege of the requesting State, provided that the existence of such privileges is confirmed by the requesting authority; the negotiating history indicates that the receiving State may ignore privileges of the requesting State that are not confirmed. Third, Contracting States may declare that they will recognize privileges recognized in third-party States.

Under the Brussels/Lugano Conventions, the collection of evidence is subject to any claim of privilege under the law of the requesting State and under the laws of the State of collection. Depending on the jurisdiction, there may or may not be privileges under local civil procedure and evidence law which offer protection against disclosure. Particularly in common-law jurisdictions, and notably but by no means exclusively in the United States, "privileged" matter, even if "relevant," may not be discoverable.

Among the kinds of privileged matter which may be withheld from discovery, depending on the jurisdiction, are husband-wife communications and self-incriminating materials to avoid criminal and, in some cases, civil liability. Furthermore, "attorney-client communications" and "attorney work-product" may in some cases be protected from discovery depending on the jurisdiction and the circumstances. In this respect, there are also important differences between and among common-law jurisdictions where such privileges may be particularly important. Such privileges must therefore be examined carefully as practiced or recognized in the particular jurisdiction.

Outside of the Brussels/Lugano Conventions context, care should be taken. Privileges or immunities available under the foreign law but not under the local law of the place where discovery is sought may not necessarily be invoked. Thus in *Appeal Enterprises, Ltd. v. The First National Bank of Chicago* (1984) 46 O.R. 2nd 590 (C.A.), the Ontario Court of Appeal granted an order compelling an accountant to give evidence in Ontario for use in a U.S. proceeding even though Illinois law provided a privilege to the accountant that was not available under Ontario law. Similarly, a person whose evidence was sought by the United States Government for the purpose of criminal proceedings within the United States against others was not permitted to rely upon the Fifth Amendment of the United States Constitution, which would have allowed him to refuse to answer incriminating questions: *United States v. Pressey* 51 D.L.R. 4th 152 (Ont. C.A.) at p. 154.

Attorney-Client Privilege Generally

In the United States, an attorney-client privilege may generally apply if the asserted holder of the privilege is or sought to become a client and additionally the recipient of the communication is a member of the Bar, or is a subordinate of a member. The recipient must be acting as an attorney in connection with that communication and the communication must relate to a fact of which the attorney was informed by the client.

The communication must generally have transpired without the presence of strangers and for the purpose of securing primarily either an opinion on law or legal services or assistance in a legal action, and not for purpose of committing a crime or tort. For the privilege to apply in the United States context, it has been held that membership in a Bar of the U.S. is not required as long as membership in a foreign Bar is established: *Golden Trade S.r.L. v. Lee*, 1992 U.S. Dist. LEXIS 12215 (S.D.N.Y. August 17, 1992) (involving Norwegian counsel).

Common Law Attorney-Client Privilege Outside the U.S.

In other jurisdictions which recognize one or another form of an attorney-client privilege, the requirements and tests may be somewhat different from those of the United States, as can of course be expected. Thus in Australia, for example, for a communication passing between a legal adviser and its client to attract such a privilege, the basic common-law position requires that the communication be made solely for the purpose of enabling the client to obtain legal advice or for the purpose of actual or contemplated litigation and that the communication must be and remain confidential. At the same time, in Australia in some cases the test may be that the communication be made for the dominant, rather than sole, purpose of enabling the client to obtain legal advice or for the purpose of actual or contemplated litigation.

Similarly, in England the "litigation privilege" arises when legal proceedings are anticipated or pending. It covers not only communications between a lawyer and client, but also protects communications between a lawyer or his agent and a third party as well as the client and his agent or a third party. The proviso is that those documents came into existence for the sole or dominant purpose of either giving or getting legal advice in relation to existing or contemplated litigation or collecting evidence for use in litigation.

Attorney-Client Privilege and Business Secrets

In certain countries, there may be less "discovery" before trial, if any, than is the case in the United States and certain other jurisdictions. At the same time, at trial there may be privileges of witnesses and nonparties, including legal counsel, to protect their business and trade secrets which are even broader than, e.g., in the United States. For that reason, among others, issues and disputes regarding privileges of legal counsel in civil litigation are infrequent, and the law establishing attorney-client privileges remains general.

In Germany, for example, if a lawyer is called to give witness evidence before a court, the extent and legal grounds for an attorney-client privilege depend on whether the lawyer is admitted to the German bar, in which case he has the statutory duty and privilege to protect client confidences under the Federal Code for Attorneys. This duty is repeated in the Professional Rules of the Federal Chamber of Lawyers, it is supported as an attorney-client privilege in the German Code of Civil Procedure, and its violation is sanctioned in the German Criminal Code.

In countries like Germany where in-house counsel may be trained lawyers but are not necessarily admitted to the bar, they are then not bound by these duties. The privileges of in-house counsel as employees depend on whether the employer is a party to the litigation. If not, in-house counsel can invoke a privilege to protect the employer's business or trade secrets. If yes, in-house counsel cannot invoke a privilege to protect the employer's business or trade secrets. In recent years, many leading German legal authorities have argued for an attorney-client privilege for in-house counsel with respect to legal advice given to their company. Both the Federal Code for Lawyers (in 1994) and the Professional Rules of the Federal Chamber of Lawyers (in 1997) have undergone extensive amendment recently, and both have maintained the distinction between privileged independent lawyers and nonprivileged in-house counsel.

Attorney-Client Privilege and Classes of Documents

There may also be various classes of documents to which the attorney-client or legal professional privilege may frequently attach. These include communications between a party and his professional legal adviser if they are confidential and made to or by the professional adviser in his professional capacity and with a view to obtaining or giving legal advice or assistance. This may hold notwithstanding that the communication is made through agents of the party and the attorney or agent. These also include documents prepared with a view to their being used as communications of this class, although not in fact used, and communications between and among legal advisers of the client, e.g., between the attorney and his partner or his agent with a view to retaining legal advice or assistance.

Notices, memorandum, minutes or other documents made by the client or its officers or legal adviser are to be handled with care. When such notices record communications which are themselves privileged or containing a record of those communications, or relate to information by the client's legal adviser to enable him to advise the client or to conduct litigation on its behalf, one or another form of the privilege may apply. The same may apply to communications and documents passing between counsel and the third party if made or prepared when litigation is anticipated or commenced, for purposes of litigation, with a view toward obtaining advice as to litigation or evidence to be used, or information which may result in obtaining such evidence.

Depending on the jurisdiction and the applicable rules, communications passing between the party and the third party (who is not the agent of the attorney to receive communication from the party) may be privileged if they were made with reference to litigation either anticipated or commenced, at the request or suggestion of the party's attorney. The privilege may also apply even without any such request or suggestion where the communication was made for the purpose of being put before the attorney with the object of obtaining his advice or enabling him to prosecute the action. Furthermore, the privilege may attach to knowledge, information or a belief of the client derived from a privileged communication made to him by his attorney or his agent.

Attorney "Work-Product" Privilege Generally

The attorney "work-product" privilege exists notably in the United States and may apply even if the attorney-client privilege does not apply pursuant to the Federal Rules of Civil Procedure. In certain common-law jurisdictions including the United States, the privilege has been held to apply to communications from in-house counsel acting in counsel capacity to a client, as well as vice versa. There are generally two such kinds of work-product privilege. These should be borne in mind by a foreign party in any transaction which might result in a civil action involving it in a country such as the United States, Canada, England, or Australia, as a guide regarding the creation and maintenance of documents.

First, "fact work product" may apply to materials prepared in anticipation of litigation or for trial by a party or its representative, whether or not the representative is an attorney. Such materials may enjoy "qualified immunity" from discovery unless the court finds good cause for disclosure. Such good cause might include substantial need and an inability otherwise to obtain the evidence from other sources. Examples of such work product include witness statements, damage calculations by a party, photographs and recordings, and results of tests.

Second, "opinion work product" includes mental impressions, conclusions, opinions, and legal theories of an attorney or other party representative, whether or not the representative is an attorney, concerning the specific litigation. Such opinions may enjoy "absolute immunity" from discovery and may include, e.g., an attorney's notes of interviews, an attorney's research memoranda, and an attorney's assessment of potential claims.

In England and Wales, the "legal advice privilege" extends to communications which come into existence for the purposes of giving or getting legal advice. There is no requirement that such advice be sought or obtained in connection with or in the course of litigation. This privilege embraces all documents generated for the purposes of giving or getting legal advice. It therefore not only includes letters to and from solicitors, but also instructions and opinions of counsel, working papers and drafts.

Outside of the common law, the only institution for the protection of work product of attorneys which may normally be recognized is the trade or business secret privilege. At the same time, while the attorney-client privilege under common law extends only to communications between attorney and client, as opposed to the separate work-product privilege, the law of other countries, such as Austria, comprises both under the attorney-client privilege. Accordingly, an Austrian attorney need never disclose his work-product undertaken for the client in civil litigation. In this regard, the scope of the privilege in certain civil law countries should by no means be underestimated.

Waiver of Attorney-Client and Work-Product Privileges

Whether in the United States or in another jurisdiction which recognizes such forms of privilege, the privilege must normally have been asserted and not waived by the client. In the United States, such waiver may occur by disclosure to a nonparty, thereby waiving the privilege as to all other information on that subject: *McCormick-Morgan v. Teledyne*, 134 F.R.D. 275 (N.D. Cal. 1991), *rev'd in part*, 765 F.Supp. 611 (N.D. Cal. 1991).

Waiver of privilege may be established where it is shown that the possessor of the privilege knows of the existence of the privilege and voluntarily evinces an intention to waive that privilege. Waiver may also occur in the absence of an intention to waive, where fairness and consistency so require. Thus waiver of privilege as to part of a communication may be held to be waiver as to the entire communication. Similarly, where a litigant relies on legal advice as an element of its claim or defense, the privilege which would otherwise attach to that advice may be lost. This may occur, for example, where a party puts into issue its own state of mind with respect to its reliance on representations and legal advice.

In some jurisdictions, the consent of the privilege-holder to waive the privilege may suffice. By contrast, in some civil-law jurisdictions which recognize one or another form of privilege, even when an attorney obtains dispensation from his client, he is still obliged to use his own judgment. Therefore, in Austria, for example, as he considers appropriate the attorney may withhold information known to him in his function if this is or may be in the interest of his client or former client. In Denmark, lawyers may not give evidence on matters of which they have obtained knowledge in their professional capacity unless the client permits it or the court so decides. In the latter case, the decision obliging a lawyer to give evidence may not extend to anything that the lawyer has learned during proceedings in a case which he has conducted for the client or in connection with advice he has given.

Privileges as to Foreign Attorneys in U.S. Litigation

The practitioner should also be particularly aware that in certain jurisdictions including the United States the attorney-client privilege has been held to apply to communications from a lawyer, including in-house counsel (acting in counsel capacity) to a client, as well as vice versa: *American Standard v. Pfizer*, 828 F.2d 734, 745 (Fed. Cir. 1987). In the United Kingdom and Canada, the solicitor-client privilege may also extend to communications between employees of a corporation and the corporate in-house counsel if they concern the employee's function as a lawyer. They are not privileged if the lawyer is performing a business or other function: *Alfred Compton Amusement Machines Ltd. v. Commissioners of Customs & Excise* (No. 2) [1972] 2 All E.R. 246 (C.A.) per Lord Denning M.R. at p. 376.

The U.S. courts may also apply U.S. attorney-client privileges to communications with a foreign lawyer, even though that foreign country might not recognize such a privilege: *Renfield Corp. v. E. Rémy Martin & Co., S.A.*, 98 F.R.D. 442, 444 (D. Del. 1982). In that case, discovery was conducted under the Hague Evidence Convention, and the court held that the witness may invoke privileges available under both the law of the country where discovery is taken or the law of the jurisdiction from which the discovery request originated as provided in Article 11 of the Hague Evidence Convention.

Traditionally, privileges were characterized as "procedural" and governed by the law of the forum. However, the caselaw of some U.S. federal courts reflects a "touch base" rule for determining whether U.S. or foreign law will apply to attorney-client privileges in international litigation. If a communication "touches base" with the United States, a federal court may apply U.S. privilege law: *Chubb Integrated Sys. Ltd. v. National Bank of Washington*, 103 F.R.D. 52, 65 (D.D.C. 1984). If the communication does not "touch base" with the United States, the foreign law will likely apply: *Stryker Corp. v. Intermedics*

Orthopedics, Inc., 145 F.R.D. 298 (E.D.N.Y. 1992). Both of these cases pertained to patent disputes.

Otherwise, U.S. courts seem to be guided by the principle of comity in conflicts of laws between U.S. state and federal jurisdictions, *Cook v. Yellow Freight Sys., Inc.*, 132 F.R.D. 548 (E.D. Cal. 1990) as well as in international disputes, *In re Ampicillin Antitrust Litig.*, 81 F.R.D. 377, 391-94 (D.D.C. 1978). Except where foreign law is contrary to the public policy of the forum, comity requires that the interests of the foreign State be taken into consideration when deciding the scope of discovery. This argument may be more compelling in protecting nonparty rights than when information is in the possession of one of the parties to the litigation.

"Blocking Statutes" and Bank Secrecy Laws

"Blocking statutes" and "secrecy laws" of certain countries are not, strictly speaking, privileges. At the same time, they may prohibit compliance with discovery orders from foreign countries, notably from the United States, requiring production of evidence located within that particular foreign country. For example, in the United Kingdom, Section 4 of the Protection of the Trading Interests Act 1980 provides that the Secretary of State may prohibit compliance with any foreign discovery order that infringes the sovereignty or security of the UK. Also, under Section 3(3) of The Evidence (Proceedings in Other Jurisdictions) Act 1975, a person will not be compelled to give evidence if it is prejudicial to the security of the United Kingdom.

In the Canadian province of Quebec, a blocking statute called the Business Concerns Records Act prevents witnesses from permitting business records of Quebec companies from being taken out of the province or even being referred to during an examination. Danish law contains a blocking statute from 1967 which allows the Minister of Trade to prohibit owners of Danish ships to comply with demands from foreign authorities to give information or deliver documents concerning the shipping company, and which has never been used.

In Switzerland, it is prohibited for foreign individuals or authorities to perform acts which are within the province of Swiss public authorities. This also applies to taking evidence, which under all Swiss procedural laws is left entirely to the courts. Thus taking of evidence within Switzerland must be conducted based on either the Hague Evidence Convention, which entered into force for Switzerland only on January 1, 1995, the 1954 Convention, or the cantonal codes of civil procedure.

With respect to bank secrecy laws, Switzerland is again a particular case. Article 47 of the Swiss Federal Banking Act obligates bankers to keep secret all information entrusted to them while conducting their business. Whether a banker may refuse testimony is governed by applicable cantonal civil procedure codes, which are by no means identical. In Geneva, the banker is fully granted the right to refuse testimony; in Zurich and Ticino, it is left to the court to grant or refuse that right; in Basle, the banker must testify. The secrecy obligation lapses if the third party being protected authorizes the party obligated to secrecy to testify. Switzerland does not accept such waivers, however, if the third party has been forced to grant authorization by an order of foreign court.

Other countries also foresee, although in a different way, a duty of secrecy between a banker and customer. There is a common-law duty in this respect which may have exceptions, including where disclosure is required by law, where the bank has a duty to the public to disclose the information, the interests of the bank require disclosure of information, or either express or implied consent of the customer has been given. In civil law, the bank secrecy privilege is normally a specific form of the trade secret privilege. In those countries which recognize it, it has been developed to protect the secrecy of bank customers vis-à-vis authorities at home and abroad.

Depending on the jurisdiction, the bank's secrecy obligation is general. Exemption is limited to circumstances where no duty of secrecy exists in relation to courts in the event of criminal proceedings against a (legal) person as customer, state authorities investigating illegal money transactions, courts and public notaries in the event of a customer's death, and explicit written consent of the customer. Exception may also be made with regard to general information on the economic situation of a company, information on foreign exchange matters, clarification of legal disputes between banks and customers, and duty of notification pursuant to inheritance and donation tax legislation.

Accordingly, normally only plausible and detailed requests for judicial assistance from foreign criminal authorities against specific persons or legal entities will lead to the lifting of bank secrecy in the specific matter vis-à-vis the requested court. This may occur, for instance, in serious fraud or money laundering cases. In civil proceedings, the bank secret privilege will normally not be lifted unless one of the other grounds is applicable (consent by the customer, clarification of the relationship between bank and customer, etc.).

The practitioner should be aware that a U.S. court may order a party subject to its jurisdiction to produce evidence notwithstanding such blocking statutes and secrecy laws: *Société Nationale Industrielle Aérospatiale v. U.S. District Court*, 482 U.S. 522, 544 n.29 (1987). However, this attitude may be changing to the benefit of the foreign party as a result of Section 442 of the Restatement (Third) of the Foreign Relations Law of the United States (1987).

Trade Secrets and Other Possible Privileges

Depending on the jurisdiction, there may or may not be a privilege or protection with respect to trade secrets and other sensitive information. At common law, trade secrets are protected to a limited degree. While there may be no absolute right to withhold a relevant, unprivileged document, depending on the jurisdiction, courts have on occasion excused production of these documents where they are not necessary. The test of necessity is more strict than the usual test of "relevance," where applicable.

Additionally, there may be means of producing evidence but preventing further disclosure, such as through protective orders. This may be possible if the court is willing to mould an order to reduce the danger of an abuse of discovery procedures, where applicable. The practitioner must verify whether protective orders are available in the particular jurisdiction or, rather, whether once a piece of evidence or information has become known and presented at court, there is no protection against further utilization and disclosure. In the latter case, issues involving disclosure and presentation of evidence must be weighed all the more carefully at an early stage.

In certain civil-law countries, a witness may refuse to answer specific questions in instances in which he might disclose trade secrets or business secrets. This privilege serves as protection against unlawfully taking advantage of the work-product of any private person or corporate entity, whether or not an attorney. The law may not differentiate between secrets of the witness and those of other persons, as the object of protection is the secret itself. The witness may not be obliged to prove his duty of keeping secrecy on behalf of other persons. Only if a party opposes the invocation of the privilege will the court likely examine the witness's right to refuse testimony.

Trade secrets or business secrets are normally technical or commercial facts related to someone's business which are known only to a limited number of persons and are not (easily) accessible to other persons. These secrets are not intended for publication beyond the limited number of persons, and the business owner has a commercial interest in the secrecy of these facts. Such facts may be of technical nature, e.g., techniques of production, models, patents, recipes, constructions, methods of calculation, results of scientific research, computer programs, methods of bank revision, etc.

Facts protected by secrecy may also be derived from the commercial division of the business, such as preference contracts with customers and suppliers, customer lists, sources of commercial information, wage lists, aspects of financing (credit volume, bank connection, financial supporters or investors), turnover, return or profit figures of a company, fiscal status, facts protected by bank secret, and editors' sources of information.

The privilege against self-incrimination has also already been mentioned in other contexts. This privilege, where applicable, may permit a party or nonparty to refuse to answer questions or produce documents. The privilege is personal and does not extend to corporations. The privilege may or may not apply to civil and criminal proceedings alike. The privilege may extend to refusing to answer questions which might cause pecuniary damage to the witness or close relatives. Pecuniary damage may consist in the risk of liability for damages as a consequence of admitting or giving information on certain facts or happenings. The judge must weigh the interest in the testimony against the endangered interest of the witness. It is the duty of the court to instruct a witness of his right to refuse testifying.

Furthermore, in some jurisdictions a privilege extends to doctors with regard to secrets entrusted to them in their profession by or concerning patients, to patent lawyers, public notaries, certified public accountants, newspaper editors and business agents with regard to their professional secrets, and to anyone with regard to questions of election secrecy.

viii. Taking Evidence in U.S. in Support of Foreign Action

The United States is known as the principal exponent of traditional party-and attorney-controlled discovery. At the same time, to a certain degree a shift toward voluntary disclosure at an early stage of litigation may be coming about as a result of the Civil Justice Reform Act of December 1, 1990 and proposals by the Committee on Rules of Practice and Procedure of United States Judicial Conference on September 22, 1992, which became effective December 1, 1993. This new framework includes a duty to disclose, without receiving formal discovery requests, the identity of "each individual likely to have discoverable information relevant to disputed facts alleged with particularity in the pleadings" and a copy or description by category and location of all documents and physical evidence "relevant to" such disputed facts.

The Civil Justice Reform Act required district-by-district plans for all 94 federal districts by December 1993 concerning discovery and case management conferences at which settlement is explored, discovery is limited and issues are narrowed. It also required encouragement of cooperative discovery, including voluntary exchange of information, and prohibition of discovery motions unless they are warranted by unsuccessful good-faith efforts to reach agreement with opposing party.

The practical reality, however, is that individual federal district courts have been allowed to opt out of the new disclosure system and conferencing. Indications are that some two-thirds of the districts have in fact chosen to do so. It has therefore become more important than ever before to consult the particular local rules of court to determine to what extent these discovery reform measures have been implemented locally.

Quite apart from the reform, or attempted reform, of U.S. discovery, the transnational practitioner should also be aware of possibilities to avail itself of discovery mechanisms in the U.S. in support of foreign actions. This requires a familiarity with the specific discovery methods which are available in the U.S. as well as of vehicles to employ such methods even where the main proceeding is pending outside of the U.S.

With regard to specific discovery methods particularly under the U.S. Federal Rules of Civil Procedure, certain summary remarks are appropriate. Generally, certain kinds of discovery are permissible solely against parties. These include so-called interrogatories and requests for admission.

Interrogatories

Interrogatories in the U.S. federal framework are essentially written questions by one party to another party requiring written responses. The responses may constitute admissions by the party which are admissible at trial. Customarily, an interrogatory will call upon the respondent to state each and every fact upon which it bases or supports a contention, identify all persons having or claiming to have knowledge of the facts alleged as supporting such contention, and identify all documents or other tangible things upon which the facts alleged as supporting such contention are based or which the respondent claims contain evidence of such alleged facts.

The "propounding party" of an interrogatory must inform itself of the "local rules," supplementary to the Federal Rules as to, e.g., limitations on a maximum number of interrogatories allowed (often no more than 30). Normally, there are three possible responses to an interrogatory. One is to answer directly and fully; the second is to object based, *inter alia*, on privilege (*see* also below), lack of "relevance" or undue burden; and the third is a partial answer limited by an objection. Responses, signed under oath by the responding party or officer/agent, are normally due within 30 days from service of the interrogatories. The responding party must "furnish such information as is available to the party" and thus must review its own files to assist in giving a full response and may respond by identifying/producing pertinent files.

Request for Admission

Requests for Admission are written requests by one party to another party to admit the truth of a matter, or to admit the genuineness of a document. Such admissions by a party are likewise admissible at trial, and can be in the form of, e.g., "With respect to Plaintiff's contention that Mr. Smith had no authority to enter into the agreement as stated in Count One, Paragraph 25, admit that Mr. Smith was a member in good standing of the Board of Directors of Plaintiff."

Normally there are three possible responses to a request for admission. One is to answer either by admission or by denial without further explanation (a parallel interrogatory will likely ask for such explanation as to each denial). Another is to explain why the responding party is unable to admit or deny, including a statement that it has made a reasonable inquiry to obtain facts to enable it to admit or deny. A third is to object based, *inter alia*, on privilege, lack of "relevance," or undue burden.

The responses, signed by the responding party or officer/agent, are normally due within 30 days from service of the requests; otherwise, they are deemed to be admitted. The responding party must "furnish such information as is available to the party" and thus must review its own files to assist in giving a full response and may respond by identifying/producing pertinent files.

In addition, certain other kinds of discovery are permissible against parties and nonparties. These include "document requests" and "*subpoenas*" as well as "depositions."

Documents Requests and Subpoenas

Document requests and subpoena*s* are requests for production of documents and tangible things (including microfilm, photographs, audio/video recordings, etc.) and for entry of one party upon the land of another to perform inspections and measurements. Requests are to be made with "reasonable particularity" and may be directed against documents located anywhere in world. An example in the U.S. federal scheme would be, e.g., "With respect to Plaintiff's contention that the value of the product has been reduced to 'approximately nothing' as stated in Count One, Paragraph 25, all documents which reflect the valuation method used to determine such alleged value."

Document requests may be addressed solely to parties. Document requests addressed to nonparties within a U.S. court's jurisdiction must be effected through issuance of a subpoena under Federal Rule 45, but may be directed against documents located anywhere in world. If a nonparty cannot be served with a subpoena or is not subject to personal jurisdiction of a U.S. court, documents located outside the U.S. can be obtained from a nonparty solely through foreign judicial assistance via the Hague Evidence Convention or letters rogatory (*see* also below).

There are basically three possible responses to a document request. The respondent agrees to comply; he is unable to comply and sets forth reasons; or the respondent refuses to comply, setting forth reasons, based, *inter alia*, on attorney-client privilege or work-product, lack of "relevance" or undue burden. A partial answer limited by objection may also be given.

The written response by the responding party or officer/agent is normally due within 30 days from service of the requests as to each request. Actual production of the documents may take place later. The responding party must produce all documents in its "possession, custody or control," which may include those in possession of a nonparty over which the requested party exercises control or which it otherwise has the right to obtain.

Depositions

Depositions are attorney examinations of another party or witness under oath before trial, transcribed and sometimes videotaped. They include examination and possible cross-examination of the witness by counsel. A deposition may take place upon "reasonable notice in writing" stating the time and place of deposition. Notice suffices as to a party, including a non-U.S. party.

Deposition notices addressed to nonparties within a U.S. court's jurisdiction must be effected through issuance of one of two types of subpoena under FRCP Rule 45: a subpoena to attend and testify or a subpoena to attend, testify and bring documents in a document request. A deposition notice on a corporation, association or government agency suffices to serve notice on the entity if it sets forth the subject matter of examination, allowing the entity to designate a knowledgeable deponent.

The deposition of a foreign deponent in connection with proceedings based in the U.S. would ordinarily be taken near its place of business, although the court may order the deposition to take place at the U.S. locale: e.g., *Work v. Bier*, 106 F.R.D. 45 (D.D.C. 1985) (German defendants ordered to appear for deposition in U.S.). In the case of the location of the deposition of a foreign nonparty to U.S.-based civil proceedings, the deposition must ordinarily be held within 100 miles of the witness's residence or regular place of business. If the nonparty cannot be served with a subpoena, then its deposition outside the U.S. can be obtained solely through foreign judicial assistance via the Hague Evidence Convention or letters rogatory.

There are essentially two possible objections to deposition questions under oath.

First are objections "to form," that is, how the question was asked, which must be raised by counsel at the deposition or otherwise be waived as to the same question at trial. These objections include that the question is too vague, is compound, (i.e., more than one question at once), is hypothetical, or calls for a speculative answer. Second are objections "to content," that is, as to the subject matter of the question asked. Such objections, which must not be raised by counsel at deposition unless a ground for objection might have been "cured" at the deposition, include that the information is privileged or is not relevant or that the witness is not competent.

Section 1782, US Code Title 28 and Discovery in the U.S.

Section 1782, US Code Title 28 is an important, but until recently little heeded, means to use the U.S. courts to order discovery, from a party or nonparty, in support of a court proceeding or, in certain circumstances, an arbitration outside of the United States. It is essentially a tool which can be used against U.S. parties and nonparties, and by foreign parties, to obtain U.S.-style discovery for non-U.S. proceedings in which such discovery might normally not be possible or permissible. Section 1782 is thus of paramount importance in evaluating the arbitration vs. litigation option, especially from a non-U.S. party's point of view.

Section 1782 provides that "a district court of the district in which a person resides or is found may order him to give his testimony or statement or to produce a document or other thing for use in a proceeding in a foreign or international tribunal." Although this section is over 30 years old, it has come into active use only recently. An increasing number of U.S. court cases have contributed to specifying the requirements and scope of the provision and its permissible application.

The law provides that the U.S. court may order the production of evidence. Accordingly, U.S. courts have taken different approaches as to whether the statutory provision implies that they have broad discretion to decide whether to order production in a particular case. In particular, courts have disagreed on whether it is or should be a requirement for such an order that the evidence sought is "admissible" in the foreign court or arbitration where it would be used.

The Second Circuit Court of Appeals, which also covers the New York region, has more or less consistently held that it will not insist on such a statutory requirement of "discoverability" at the place of foreign proceedings before granting an order of discovery within its jurisdiction in the U.S. Rather, it has generally held that under Section 1782 it is proper to leave the question of discoverability to the foreign court or arbitral tribunal in which the evidence is meant to be used: e.g., *In re Application of Malev Hungarian Airlines*, 964 F.2d 97 (2d Cir. 1992); *In re Application of Silvia Gionoli*, 3 F.3d 54 (2d Cir. 1993); and *Euromepa S. A. v. R. Esmerian, Inc.*, 51 F.3d 1095 (2d Cir. 1995). Other federal appeals courts have not interpreted this statute in the same way as the Second Circuit, holding that the evidence must also be discoverable at the place of intended use before it will be discovered in the U.S.: e.g., *In re Application of Asta Medica*, 981 F.2d 1 (1st Cir. 1992); *In re Letter Rogatory from First Court of First Instance in Civil Matters, Caracas, Venezuela*, 42 F.3d 308 (5th Cir. 1995).

As there is now a substantial body of caselaw sustaining both positions, it is essential to determine the attitude of the particular Circuit where discovery for use abroad is sought. While this split must be resolved by the U.S. Supreme Court, until such time litigants must be aware of the differences, which effectively allow a kind of forum-shopping in the U.S. related to litigation and, in certain circumstances, arbitration taking place outside of the U.S.

There also appears to be confusion and disagreement in the link between Section 1782 and arbitrations taking place outside the United States. In this respect, there have been holdings suggesting that a request for such assistance made to the U.S. court in connection with a pending arbitration outside the U.S. must be made by the arbitral tribunal itself, and not by one of the parties in the arbitration: *e.g., In re Application of Technostroyexport,* 853 F.Supp. 695 (S.D.N.Y. 1994); *Quijada v. Unifrutti of America, Inc.*, 12 Pa. D. & C. 4th 225 (1991). In fact, Section 1782 by its terms allows for the request for discovery in the U.S. to be made by "any interested person," and not solely by the foreign court or tribunal. This issue warrants close study in the near future as it may become the focus of additional rulings in the various Circuits.

Hague Evidence Convention and U.S. Pretrial Discovery

As stated previously, in the context of the Hague Evidence Convention various Contracting States have made declarations or reservations concerning Article 23. The result is that such countries will not execute letters of request for the purpose of obtaining pretrial discovery of documents as known in common-law countries if the letter of request requires a person to state what documents relevant to the proceedings to which the letter of request relates are, or have been, in his possession, custody or control; or to produce any documents other than particular documents specified in the letter of request, which are likely to be in his possession, custody or control.

Generally speaking, a variety of steps may be taken to reduce the risk that the courts of such countries will invoke Article 23 or otherwise refuse to execute letters of request originating from common-law countries, and particularly the United States. The attorney should attempt to persuade the foreign court that the letter of request is seeking evidence which is intended to be used in a trial instead of being an open-ended, no-limits expedition. Furthermore, counsel should describe the requested documents and testimony in as much detail as possible. Moreover, if possible foreign counsel should consider delaying issuing a letter of request until the defendant has answered and factual disputes have been cleared. In addition, letters of request should include findings by the issuing court that the materials sought are actually intended for trial use.

In any event, the foreign counsel should consult with an attorney in the country where such discovery is being sought as to its local law and practice and the kind of requests that the local authorities are likely to approve. Even in England, where common-law discovery rules are closer to those in the United States, Article 23 significantly restricts the scope of the Hague Evidence Convention for U.S. litigants. For instance, a request that is being used as part of a chain of inquiry to discover some material which might lead to obtaining admissible evidence at trial will not be complied within England. This is the case even though the procedure of the foreign court permits such a practice, as do Rule 26 of the U.S. Federal Rules of Civil Procedure and the rules of many state courts in the U.S.

Finally, where there are limitations on or impediments to obtaining pretrial disclosure of documents due to an Article 23 reservation, care should be taken to determine whether the witness with knowledge of such documents can nevertheless still be orally examined on the existence, location, and content of the documents which it is impermissible under local law to physically obtain. In the English context, however, the English court will not make an order requiring a witness to state whether or not documents asked for exist or not.

CHAPTER 11

TAKING OF WITNESS EVIDENCE ABROAD IN SUPPORT OF DOMESTIC ACTION

Many of the observations in **Chapter 10** above apply equally, if also in reverse, to the question of taking of witness evidence abroad in support of domestic action, and reference to **Chapter 10** is hereby made generally. The Conventions mentioned earlier are applicable to taking witness evidence abroad, but their applicability depends in this case on the foreign State and its internal rules and declarations concerning the Conventions.

Courts of most countries generally demand from time to time judicial assistance from all States with which they may have diplomatic relations. In principle, evidence is taken by (or under the supervision of) authorities abroad. This is regularly done in the ways prescribed by local law unless the requesting court has explicitly demanded application of its own rules of procedure and these are not in conflict with national law or irreconcilable with public policy of the requested state.

i. Conventions

The primary multilateral conventions relevant to the taking of witness evidence abroad in support of domestic actions are the 1954 and 1970 Hague Conventions respectively, particularly the latter. Certain of the countries addressed in this work are either not a member of either Convention, or for that matter of any other multilateral convention on judicial assistance, or have acceded to only one of the two Hague Conventions in question. These Conventions are discussed in **Chapter 10** above.

1970 Hague Evidence Convention

Under the 1970 Hague Convention, a letter of request may be sent through the Central Authority or other designated authority of the requesting State to the Central Authority of another Contracting State for the taking of evidence or the performance of some other judicial act for the purpose of judicial proceedings, commenced or contemplated.

The rules of court in each jurisdiction normally provide for the issuance of letters rogatory or letters of request to be issued to foreign courts for orders compelling persons within the jurisdiction of the foreign courts to give evidence as part of the local discovery process or trial. Since discovery is generally confined to an adverse party or his representative, a motion for letters rogatory for such purpose should be supported by affidavit evidence establishing that the person to be examined is the most appropriate representative to be examined. Where an equally appropriate representative is within the jurisdiction, the order will generally be refused.

Where a nonparty is to be examined, the moving party may need to establish that the evidence sought cannot be adduced through a witness within the jurisdiction and that it would be unfair to require the trial to proceed without that evidence. Letters rogatory may nevertheless be refused if the result will be an undue delay, if unreasonable expense will be incurred by other parties, or if the court concludes that their issuance would be otherwise unfair.

Applications to take evidence from a witness abroad are made to the local court, which will issue a commission authorizing a named commissioner to take the evidence and a letter of request directed to the foreign court requesting the issue of the process necessary to compel the witness to attend before the commissioner. The evidence may be taken by questions put to the witness by the commissioner or, more usually, by counsel retained in the foreign jurisdiction or counsel from the jurisdiction where the action is pending, if such is permitted in the foreign jurisdiction. A transcript of the evidence is taken and is filed, together with any accompanying exhibits, in the local court.

The letter of request shall be executed in the requested State by a judicial authority competent to execute it under its own law. That authority shall apply the appropriate measures of compulsion under its domestic law to secure the attendance of witnesses and the production of evidence, subject to any claim of privilege a witness may have either under the law of the State of execution or under the law of the State of origin.

The requesting authority may ask to be notified of the place and time of the proceedings to enable the parties and their representatives to attend. Subject to the consent of the requested State, judicial personnel of the State of origin may be present. The execution of a letter of request may be refused only if execution does not fall within the functions of the judiciary of the requested State or it prejudices that State's sovereignty or security. Execution may not be refused on the grounds that the internal law of the requested State claims exclusive jurisdiction over the subject matter of the action or would not admit a right of action on it.

Under the Hague Evidence Convention, a diplomatic officer or consular agent of a Contracting State may take evidence without compulsion of nationals of the State which that officer or agent represents in aid of proceedings commenced in the courts of the State which that officer or agent represents. Subject to the Contracting State's consent, such officer or agent may also take the evidence without compulsion of nationals of the State in which the evidence is taken. A commissioner appointed under the law of the requesting State may also take such evidence with prior permission of the State concerned.

ii. Other Means and Absence of Convention

As described in **Chapter 10** above, certain countries are signatories to bilateral additional agreements to the 1954 Hague Convention on Civil Procedure. Some countries are also signatories to bilateral treaties on Mutual Assistance in Legal Proceedings (Service of Process) in civil and commercial matters. Such bilateral treaties on judicial assistance hold provisions on the taking of evidence from witnesses, parties, experts and inspections etc., as well as the performance of other judicial acts domestically in connection with actions pending abroad. Where no multilateral or bilateral treaty applies, it may be that service and judicial assistance are granted on the basis of mutual continuous practice and comity.

Local Laws and Legislation

Depending on the jurisdiction, local legislation may provide that in any proceeding, the court may, if it appears in the interest of justice to do so, on the application of a party make an order relating to a person outside the jurisdiction for examination on oath or affirmation at any place outside the jurisdiction before a judge, an officer of the court, or such other person as the court may appoint. Local legislation may also entitle the court to order issuance of a commission for examination of the person on oath or affirmation at any place outside the jurisdiction or for issuance of a letter of request to the judicial authorities of a foreign country to take the evidence of the person.

In deciding whether it is in the interests of justice to make such an order, there are certain matters to which the court is to have regard. These may include (i) whether the person is willing or able to come to the local jurisdiction to give evidence in the proceeding, (ii) whether the person will be able to give evidence material to any issue to be tried in the proceeding, and (iii) whether, having regard to the interests of the parties to the proceeding, justice will be better served by granting or refusing the order.

Local legislation may also provide that any testimony and documents obtained as a result of a request made by or on behalf of the court to a foreign country for testimony, and documents related to such testimony, must have been taken on oath or affirmation or under such admonition as would be accepted, by courts in the foreign country, for purposes of giving testimony before those courts.

The testimony may also need to be signed or certified by a judge, magistrate or officer in or of the foreign country and bear an official or public seal of the country or a minister of State or a department or officer of the Government of the requested country. The testimony may normally be reduced to writing or be recorded on an audio or videotape, but need not necessarily be an affidavit or a transcript of a foreign court proceeding. A court may also direct that the foreign material not be adduced as evidence if it thinks, after considering the parties' interests, that justice would be better served if such evidence were not adduced.

Among the factors which might be taken into account here are (i) the extent to which the foreign material provides evidence that would not otherwise be available, (ii) the probative value of the foreign material with respect to any issue that is likely to be determined in the proceeding, and (iii) the extent to which statements contained in the foreign material could, at the time they were made, be challenged by questioning the persons who made them. Other factors are (iv) whether exclusion of the foreign material would cause undue expense or delay and (v) whether exclusion of the foreign material would unfairly prejudice any party to the proceedings.

iii. Practical Problems and Time Factors

Delays may be anticipated in taking of evidence on the basis of letters of request for local litigation in various parts of the world. Delay may also arise in transmission from one country to the requested country, so that a period of several months should generally be allowed for the execution of a letter of request.

Local courts demand the taking of evidence abroad at the request of each party or on their own motion if the taking of evidence before the court of action is impossible or seriously complicated by specific circumstances. In making such a decision, the local court must consider the cost of immediate taking of evidence, circumstances which prevent the personal attendance of a witness at court, and results to be expected by the taking of evidence abroad. Depending on the applicable law, if the taking of evidence by an authority abroad was deficient under the foreign law, this does not necessarily effect the evidence as long as it was taken in conformance with the law of the court of action.

Because the requested taking of evidence will otherwise be performed under the rules of the internal law of the requested country, the party seeking witness evidence abroad should explicitly request, as required by the domestic court, that the court addressed comply with certain procedural rules on witness evidence of the place where the litigation is pending.

These may include, depending on the jurisdiction, a refusal to accept any written statements of a witness and a right to refuse to answer questions which might bring disgrace, discredit or pecuniary damage upon the witness or his close relatives or entail the danger of criminal prosecution. These may also include various privileges as set forth in **Chapter 10** above, as well as a refusal to give evidence by nonparty witnesses with respect to specific questions and a right not to be forced to give evidence under oath.

The examination abroad of a requested witness (including party witness) may be attended by the parties to the local litigation or their representatives, which may participate in questioning where permitted. Where credibility of witnesses may be an issue, evidence heard out of court is problematical. To the extent the trial judge is in effect the final arbiter on credibility, he has the opportunity to observe the demeanor of the witnesses during their testimony. This opportunity is lost when evidence comes to the court in the form of a transcript. Accuracy of transcripts can also pose a serious problem particularly where the witness is to be examined in jurisdictions where evidence in court proceedings is not usually transcribed. Where the evidence of a witness abroad is required, taking that evidence on commission should be considered a last resort.

Sometimes taking of evidence poses possible conflicts between, for example, common-law and civil-law systems of evidence and discovery. In England under the Civil Evidence Act 1995, which came into force in January 1997 and replaced the provisions of the former 1968 Act, evidence not in person before the English court but rather presented to the court in written form will be "hearsay evidence." Hearsay is an oral or written statement made out of court which is repeated to the court to try and prove the truth of the matter stated. While the 1968 Act prevented a witness from giving hearsay evidence, the 1995 Act abolished the rule of inadmissibility of hearsay evidence.

iv. Relevance to Later Efforts to Recognize and Enforce at Place of Judgment

Taking of witness evidence abroad normally has no direct effect on the issue of recognition and enforcement at home. As the judgment that eventually rendered issues from a local court, the fact that evidence may have been taken abroad by rogatory commission is of no relevance.

At the same time, in common-law jurisdictions which have guidelines on the weight which the court can attach to hearsay evidence, the court where judgment will be rendered will have been prevented from seeing first-hand the witness giving evidence and responding to cross-examination, if any. In such jurisdictions, the taking of first-hand witness evidence is often the most vital stage in a trial and the judge, and jury where applicable, attach importance to the behavior of the witness during his testimony.

Evidence unlawfully gained abroad (e.g., infringing trade secrets protected under the law of the place of judgment) and included in the records does not result in a void judgment as long as the contents of the document are not false or falsified, notwithstanding a possible damage claim by the infringed party against the infringer of the secret obligation. If the evidence taken abroad by means of a letter of request is false, the interested party may file an action aimed at the reversal of the judgment already rendered. In the enforcement proceeding, it is not possible to discuss again the matters of fact already settled by the adjudicating court.

Depending on the local law, false and incomplete testimony of witnesses or expert witnesses may allow resumption of proceedings and a new hearing or a basis for an objection to enforcement (and a motion to stay enforcement). In such actions, the party should submit evidence that the witness has willfully given false testimony and that this was decisive for the loss of the case.

Where the foreign authorities seek to take no active part in the deposition (as for example where the deposition is voluntary), then the applicable procedural rules will be those of the forum (the country of origin). Where the foreign authorities are involved, then a letter of request will be sent by the forum court to the foreign authority stipulating the procedural rules to be applied. Where, in relation to a particular procedural matter (such as discovery), there are no procedural rules specifically included in the letter of request, then the procedural rules of the foreign country will generally apply.

Therefore where it is alleged by one party to the proceedings that the taking of evidence in the foreign country was contrary to the domestic rules, it will be necessary to look to the terms of the foreign court order authorizing the taking of evidence. If, for example, pursuant to an order by an U.S. court there was extensive discovery, the fact that the discovery disclosed material that in another country would have been protected will not matter unless the letter of request (and the orders of the U.S. court) indicated that other country's discovery rules were to apply. Where, however, the extensive discovery was done without a request to, or orders from, a foreign authority, the rules of that other country may apply to rule the discovery of the protected information improper.

v. Special Issues Relating to Expert Evidence

The Hague Evidence Convention makes no distinction between evidence taken abroad from expert witnesses and evidence taken from any other type of witness. An application for a letter of request should specify the name and address of the person to be examined and the questions to be put to that person. However, there will be no need to give notice of the use of an expert's evidence at any hearing, as statements containing expert evidence are recognized as falling outside the parameters of the rule on hearsay evidence.

While witness evidence is given on facts and observations outside the litigation, expert evidence is taken on facts accessible within the proceedings and applies the expert's knowledge and experience to the issue. Certain courts appoint experts to establish facts and/or to offer their expert conclusion (opinion) on the facts established. The letter of request should specify what is needed.

The expert opinion should be delivered as a written statement and may be followed by an oral explanation or specification of the results at a public hearing where the parties may question the expert's opinion. The requested State has the right to require the reimbursement of fees paid to experts as well as costs incurred by the use of special procedures, unless a bilateral treaty states otherwise.

Certain countries' laws also provide for the protective taking of expert evidence even in a pre-litigation stage, but limit it to fact-finding. In such cases, a request for such pre-litigation taking of expert evidence must therefore be limited to the determination of facts and only after litigation has commenced locally can a conclusion or expert opinion be required. The requested State must decide in accordance with its own laws whether to grant this procedure in support of future litigation in the local jurisdiction.

vi. Attorney-Client, Work-Product and Other "Privileges"

The attorney-client privilege and other privileges, as set forth in detail in **Chapter 10** above, must also be respected in taking witness evidence, and letters of request should communicate the rules to the requested court. Article 11 of the 1970 Hague Evidence Convention is relevant here. It provides that the person concerned may refuse to give evidence insofar as he has a privilege or a duty to refuse to give evidence under the law of the State of execution or State of origin, and the privilege or duty has been specified in the letter of request or, at the instance of the requested authority, been otherwise confirmed to that authority by the requesting authority.

If the letter of request, however, contains something incompatible with local law, but the witness gives his testimony, the statement would probably be admissible in the local courts. The same rules apply if the testimony contains something incompatible with foreign rules.

Many courts respect the refusal of production of certain evidence on the grounds that the production would violate a foreign concept of privilege. A blunt refusal with reference to a privilege under local law and without good reason will, however, as with all evidence, be subject to the free evaluation of evidence by the local judge.

Where local law governs the taking of evidence, the privileges of foreign evidence law are not available. A party does not obtain the privileges granted by the evidence law of a foreign country merely because it resides there. Where the law of a foreign country is to govern the taking of evidence (for example, where the deposition is to take place in a foreign country and pursuant to the procedural rules of that country) then the privileges against disclosure that the foreign law grants will apply.

Where evidence is to be taken in a foreign country and a party would benefit from a privilege not given under local law, it would therefore be advisable to apply to include provision for that privilege in the letter of request sent to the courts of that country. However, where taking of evidence and the principal litigation is to be in a jurisdiction in which the party believes that its interests will be significantly prejudiced by disclosure of information permitted under that jurisdiction's law, the only course of action is to contest the jurisdiction of that court.

CHAPTER 12

TAKING OF DOCUMENTARY EVIDENCE DOMESTICALLY IN SUPPORT OF FOREIGN ACTION

Many of the observations in **Chapters 10** and, to a lesser extent, **11** above apply equally or by analogy to the question of taking of documentary evidence domestically in support of a foreign action, and reference to **Chapters 10** and **11** is hereby made generally.

The courts of most countries generally demand from time to time judicial assistance from all States with which they may have diplomatic relations. In principle, evidence is taken by, or under the supervision of, authorities abroad. This is regularly done in the ways prescribed by local law unless the requesting court has explicitly demanded application of its own rules of procedure and these are not in conflict with national law or irreconcilable with public policy of the requested state.

i. From Whom Discovery is Possible and When

As set forth in **Chapter 10** above by analogy, depending on the jurisdiction taking of documentary evidence, or "discovery" of documents, may or may not be possible to varying degrees. To the extent there is a general opportunity for such taking of evidence, it will normally be possible between and among the parties to the action and, to limited extent if at all, from nonparties. Certain countries, particularly in the civil-law context, distinguish between "parties" and "witnesses," such that anyone who is not a party to the case and who is present in the country may be obliged to appear as a witness.

Civil-Law Approaches

Most civil-law countries do not provide for any kind of pretrial discovery procedures apart from the protective taking of (witness) evidence in the context of interim, conservatory and emergency measures. Thus, with some exceptions and gradations, most non-common law jurisdictions do not provide in their local procedure or customs for measures equivalent to pretrial discovery, parties cannot be obligated to provide the other party with information or answers to inquiries, and there is no obligation to disclose the existence and content of documents in possession of the party prior to the trial.

At the same time, it is once again important not to "lump" all civil-law jurisdictions into the same category. One should not assume, erroneously, that all such jurisdictions have a blanket prohibition against pretrial discovery, or court order, of documentary evidence. In some such countries, on a party's request the court may order the other party to submit documents, and regardless of whether the other party or the documents are located in that country or abroad.

In such cases, the request will be granted only under certain circumstances. These include (i) if the court estimates that the document is of importance to the issue, (ii) the proof cannot be provided in another way, (iii) it is reasonable to assist the requesting party in this manner by easing its burden of proof, and (iv) the burden of providing the document for the other party is not excessive. If the other party does not comply with the order, the court may consider it prejudicial to the party's case. The court may not order submission of documents if they relate to circumstances on which the other party would be excluded from giving evidence as a witness. With respect to third parties present in the jurisdiction, the court may order them to produce documents to the same extent that they are obliged to appear as witnesses and subject to the same sanctions.

Common-Law Approaches

In the case of pretrial discovery in the common-law tradition, expansive compulsory production of documentary evidence may be possible after proper filing and service up until a court-designated discovery cut-off date, where applicable. Depending on the jurisdiction and particularly in the case of certain common-law countries, there may in fact be no court involvement unless and until a party or nonparty refuses to comply with a discovery request. The degree of involvement of the court in the taking of evidence will invariably be far greater in other countries, particularly of the civil-law tradition, but depending on the jurisdiction may not involve compulsory production of documents.

With regard to admissibility of evidence in privileged documents, where applicable, certain jurisdictions particularly in the common-law area may provide restrictions on the adduction of certain privileged communications. Adduction of the privileged evidence by whatever means should be prohibited when the document is protected from production by the privilege.

Certain jurisdictions may also have legislation specifically dealing with proceedings before a foreign court, and with the acts of foreign authorities, relating to or affecting trade or commerce with other countries or which constitute or are connected to an external affair. The judicial authorities may then order the prohibition of production of a document in a foreign court, or to or for the purposes of a foreign authority where the document is located in the same jurisdiction at the time the order is made, or at some time when the order is in force. Such orders may be made where the judicial authorities are satisfied that the making of the order is desirable for the protection of the national interest or that the assumption of jurisdiction by the foreign court, or the acts of the foreign authority instituting the action, are inconsistent with international comity or international practice.

As a general matter, parties seeking production of documents domestically in support of foreign actions, where possible, should identify the documents as particularly as possible, the location of the documents, and the person or persons exercising possession, custody or control over the documents. They should also explain the necessity of such documents for ensuring that the foreign action proceeds in a just and fair manner. Even where such requests are normally permitted, the local courts will normally require that the documents subject to an order of production be adequately described. A "fishing expedition," as it has particularly been known in the United States, will not be permitted.

The necessity of adequate description is normally approached flexibly, bearing in mind that the requesting party, not having possession of the documents, may be unable to provide exact descriptions. Thus depending on the local law, the need for specificity may be seen as best served by requiring documents to be identified only with reasonable precision, in view of the circumstances of each case. Thus requiring a witness to search a number of files may in one case be burdensome, and in another quite reasonable. Depending on the situation, documents may be specifically identified, or identified by class, to pass the threshold test for production.

ii. Conventions

The primary multilateral conventions relevant to the taking of documentary evidence domestically in support of foreign actions are the 1954 and 1970 Hague Conventions respectively, as explained in **Chapters 10** and **11** above. Certain countries are either not a member of either Convention, or for that matter of any other multilateral convention on judicial assistance, or have acceded to only one of the two Hague Conventions in question. These Conventions are discussed in **Chapters 10** and **11** above.

1970 Hague Evidence Convention

Under the 1970 Hague Convention, a letter of request may be sent through the Central Authority or other designated authority of the requesting State to the Central Authority of another Contracting State for the taking of evidence or the performance of some other judicial act for the purpose of judicial proceedings, commenced or contemplated.

As stated in **Chapter 10** above but even more relevant here in the context of documentary evidence, among the reservations and declarations to the Convention which may have been made by one or another country, and which must be verified on a case-by-case basis, include those to the effect that requests for "pretrial discovery" of documents as known and practiced primarily in the United States will not be accepted. All but three signatories to the Hague Evidence Convention—former Czechoslovakia, Israel and the United States—had entered Article 23 reservations as of July 1, 1997.

Requests for pretrial discovery are commonly understood in countries having taken such a reservation to include requests to produce any relevant documents in a person's possession other than individually specified documents. Interestingly, depending on the country at issue, there is either no or very little reported caselaw about this subject.

While the Hague Evidence Convention has been held to refer to the taking of documentary evidence separately from oral testimony, depending on the jurisdiction, the local statute which enacts the Convention may not do so. In such cases, local jurisprudence must be examined to verify whether the local courts are deemed to have inherent jurisdiction to issue a letter of request for the production of documentary evidence not arising from statute, as needed to be decided, for example, in Australia in *Elna Australia Pty Ltd v. International Computers (Australia) Pty Ltd*, (1987) 74 ALR 232.

Moreover, as Article 23 of the Hague Evidence Convention allows member countries to exclude pretrial discovery either fully or partially, the extent of exclusion of such methods must be verified on a case-by-case basis. In countries such as Switzerland which have made only a partial exclusion, a letter of request regarding pretrial discovery must be crafted carefully and will not be followed if, for example, the letter does not directly and necessarily relate to the foreign proceeding or requires a person to state which documents relating to the foreign proceeding he possesses or has possessed. Other grounds for refusing to follow the letter might be that it requires documents other than those listed in the letter, which are possibly in the person's possession, or endangers interests of the persons concerned which warrant protection.

Also in this context, the practitioner must bear in mind that the execution of pretrial discovery requests must of course be limited to the parties mentioned in the request, and such parties must normally have their seat or residence within the jurisdiction where the request is meant to be executed. A request that a company produce documents not in its possession may not be executed, depending on the local definition of possession. In Switzerland, for example, it is not relevant whether the third party is under the control of the party receiving the request or whether such third party is within or outside of Switzerland. If the petitioner wishes such third party to be involved in the discovery, he must be named in the request. If the third party is outside of Switzerland, a separate request must be made in the relevant jurisdiction.

Tension between Hague Evidence Convention and U.S. Discovery

In light of the complete and partial exclusions of pretrial document discovery under the Hague Evidence Convention, depending on the jurisdiction, a case-by-case and country-by-country analysis will be called for. Even in civil-law jurisdictions which have not made a complete reservation or exclusion, the requirement of a highly detailed list of documents to be produced, coupled with the discretion granted to the judge to protect interests of persons concerned, normally results in an inability to carry out expansive document discovery of the kind possible in many U.S. litigation proceedings. This is particularly the case under Rule 26(b) of the Federal Rules of Civil Procedure. This rule permits parties to "obtain discovery regarding any matter, not privileged, which is relevant to the subject matter involved in the pending action," even if the information requested is not itself admissible at trial, so long as the request is "reasonably calculated to lead to discovery of admissible evidence."

This tension between the procedures available under the Hague Evidence Convention and under the Federal Rules of Civil Procedure has spurred a debate in the United States over the exclusivity of the Convention. Such exclusivity varies depending on whether the litigant is seeking discovery from a party or nonparty. The U.S. Supreme Court has held that the Hague Evidence Convention does not provide the exclusive means of compelling discovery against a nonresident party: *Société Nationale Industrielle Aérospatiale v. United States District Court*, 482 U.S. 522 (1987).

However, there is no clear rule on whether a litigant desiring a U.S. court to supplant U.S. discovery proceedings with the Hague Evidence Convention procedures bears the burden of demonstrating the propriety of such a request. Nor is a U.S. court's decision to require compliance with the Hague Evidence Convention subject to interlocutory appeal. Often, the U.S. court will strike a compromise, refusing to require compliance with the Hague Evidence Convention, but tailoring the discovery request under the Federal Rules to avoid offending the foreign signatory's sovereign interests. When a U.S. litigant seeks to compel production of documents from a nonresident nonparty witness, the Hague Evidence Convention is the exclusive means unless the U.S. court has *in personam* jurisdiction over the nonresident nonparty.

iii. Other Means and Absence of Convention

As described in **Chapters 10** and **11** above, certain countries are signatories to bilateral additional agreements to the 1954 Hague Convention on Civil Procedure. Some countries are also signatories to bilateral treaties on Mutual Assistance in Legal Proceedings (Service of Process) in civil and commercial matters.

Such bilateral treaties on judicial assistance hold provisions on the taking of documentary evidence from witnesses, parties, experts, and inspections etc., as well as the performance of other judicial acts domestically in connection with actions pending abroad. Where no multilateral or bilateral treaty applies, it may be that service and judicial assistance are granted on the basis of mutual continuous practice and comity.

iv. Practical Problems and Time Factors

To the extent a party is able to be specific in identifying the particular documents to be produced, the location of those documents and the persons having possession, custody, or control over them, the delays experienced in the production of these documents may be minimized. Generally, one of the major reasons for delays in the production of documents relates to the period of time a person requires to search out relevant documents.

Depending on the jurisdiction, "documents" may also be defined somewhat differently. Generally, under most civil procedural laws they include forms of written incorporation of thoughts regarding facts, irrespective of whether the instrument was created coincidentally or with the intent to be used for evidentiary purposes. Documents may also include tape recordings of conversations and cinematograph films.

There may be a separate category of "public documents" or "authentic instruments" encompassing documents executed by a (domestic) authority or person holding the public trust, including notaries within their area of competence. Public documents normally enjoy the presumption of authenticity and have full probative force with regard to what the authority declares or the person of public trust attests. The opposing party is permitted to prove that what is declared or attested is wrong.

All other documents are private documentary evidence whose authenticity may be freely contested in litigation. If, in domestic proceedings, a party presents a document, then the opposing party may be asked by the judge to declare whether it concedes the document's authenticity and correctness. Depending on the local rules, if the opposing party does not explicitly contest the authenticity and the judge has no doubts of his own, the document may be assumed authentic and correct. The court and the opposing party generally have the right to inspect a document in its entirety unless protection of part of the document due to specific reasons (trade secret, etc.) is granted by the court. In this event, only portions of the document are revealed to the other party.

Compelling Production in Support of Foreign Actions

The judge or jury, where applicable, may have full freedom to evaluate acts or omissions of a party including production or nonproduction of evidence that is obviously in its possession. Depending on the local rules, a party in litigation holding documentary evidence may be obliged to produce it to the court if the party itself has based allegations on the respective document, if the party is obliged by specific statute to produce a specific document (e.g., promissory notes, receipts for payment, etc.), or if the documentary evidence is "common evidence" to both parties (such as contracts between the parties, arbitration agreements and arbitral awards, joint protocols, etc.).

A party's duty to produce a document may be exempted if the document refers to matters of family life, would infringe upon a duty of honor, cause disgrace or discredit, or violate a secrecy privilege.

With respect to coercive action and adverse inferences, in some jurisdictions if a party denies possession of a document to be produced as evidence, it may be heard under oath regarding its denial. If the party admits that it has the document, or the court is convinced that this is the case, the court may issue an order to produce the document. While such order may not be enforceable, the court may "freely evaluate" the party's actions and omissions and draw negative conclusions in the event of noncompliance.

Third persons (apart from parties) may be obliged to forward documents to the court or allow inspection if they are obliged by provisions of civil law to submit the documents (e.g., promissory notes, payment receipts, etc.) or the document is "common evidence" among the third party and a party to the action. Depending on the jurisdiction, if the third party admits possession of the documents, and there are no doubts regarding its duty to produce, the court may issue an "order to produce." In contrast to a comparable order to a party to the litigation where such orders may not be enforceable, an order to a third party may be enforceable.

v. Relevance to Later Efforts to Recognize and Enforce at Place of Judgment

Taking of documentary evidence domestically normally has no direct effect on the issue of recognition and enforcement abroad. In the European context, Article 29 of the Brussels/Lugano Conventions provides, for example, that a foreign judgment may under no circumstances be reviewed as to its substance, reflecting the principle of no *revision au fond.* Accordingly, judgments originating from Contracting States of the Brussels/Lugano Conventions undergo recognition *ipso iure.* There are therefore no grounds for refusal with regard to taking of evidence apart from procedures applied which are against public policy.

Bilateral enforcement treaties granting mutual recognition of judgments in which the countries addressed herein are parties do not contain provisions which might be grounds for denying enforcement of a foreign judgment due to unlawful production of documents abroad. Consequently, a judgment debtor cannot normally object to enforcement because of defective evidence.

If a judgment debtor wishes to challenge the authorization of enforcement, it must do so by somehow linking it to an infringement of public policy, if such a link can indeed be made. Thus, as set forth in **Chapter 10** in some cases a violation of public policy can be alleged if the evidence produced or gathered within the state where enforcement of the foreign judgment is now being sought was obtained illegally.

vi. Attorney-Client, Work-Product and Other "Privileges"

As set forth in **Chapter 10**, under the Hague Evidence Convention, three separate groups of privileges exist. Article 11 permits a witness to refuse to provide evidence that is protected by a privilege provided by the receiving State. Witnesses may invoke any privilege of the requesting State, provided that the existence of such privileges is confirmed by the requesting authority; the negotiating history indicates that the receiving State may ignore privileges of the requesting State that are not confirmed. Furthermore, Member States may declare that they will recognize privileges recognized in third-party States.

Under the Brussels/Lugano Conventions, the collection of evidence is subject to any claim of privilege under the law of the requesting State and under the laws of the State of collection. Depending on the jurisdiction, there may or may not be privileges under local civil procedure and evidence law which offer protection against disclosure. Particularly in common-law jurisdictions, and notably but by no means exclusively in the United States, "privileged" matter, even if "relevant," may not be discoverable.

Certain countries have enacted legislation providing for the protection of business records. These statutes may prohibit the taking of business records out of the jurisdiction at the instance of any foreign legislature or court. An example is Section 2 of the Business Concerns Records Act in the Canadian province of Quebec, which the local courts have interpreted broadly to apply not only to the document itself, but also to any record of the document which might result from answers to questions posed in a deposition. If it appears likely that there will be a requirement for a removal of business documents from Quebec, application may be made to the court to oppose the order or apply for an order requiring any person to furnish an undertaking or security to ensure that this person will not violate the Act. Blocking statutes of this kind have not squarely been held to be inapplicable in transnational litigation, as opposed to judicial assistance between and among Canadian provinces.

Recognition of Foreign Privileges in U.S. Courts

Privilege issues in the context of transnational litigation present themselves as conflicts-of-law questions. U.S. federal courts have never developed a comprehensive rule governing the recognition of foreign privileges in U.S. discovery proceedings. Only under the Hague Evidence Convention is the choice-of-law question largely avoided.

While U.S. federal courts may recognize claims of foreign privilege in certain contexts, the available privileges are narrower in the context of a U.S. discovery order than under a Hague Evidence Convention letter of request. In U.S. discovery proceedings, the respondent may assert a claim of privilege under either U.S. law or the law of the State where the requested documents are situated, but not both. The court must resolve the conflict in favor of recognizing the privilege under the law of the State with the "most significant relationship" with the documents at issue: e.g., *Renfield Corp. v. Rémy Martin & Co.*, S.A., 98 F.R.D. 442, 444-45 (D. Del. 1982) (citing Restatement Second Conflict of Laws §139(1) (1971)).

Objections to Discovery on Grounds of Privilege Under U.S. Law

United States courts generally favor broad discovery and so there are in fact few recognized privileges in the United States. Where an element or defense of a claim is governed by state law, claims of privilege are also governed by state law. When all elements and defenses are matters of federal law, then Federal Rules of Evidence Rule 501 dictates that the federal courts may apply the common law of privilege. In addition, a respondent who objects to a discovery request under Federal Rules of Civil Procedure Rules 34 or 45 on the grounds of privilege must make an adequate and timely written statement of the basis of the objection or waive the privilege.

The attorney-client privilege in the United States is uncharacteristically broad compared to its counterparts in many other nations. In *AM & S Europe Ltd. v. Commission*, 1982 E.C.R. 1575, the European Court of Justice held that in the EU the privilege applied only to written communication with an independent attorney in the interest of the client's rights of defense in an ongoing administrative procedure.

In the U.S., on the other hand, the attorney-client privilege encompasses any communication where legal advice of any kind is sought from a professional legal adviser in his capacity as such and the communications relating to that purpose were made in confidence. At the insistence of the client, such communications may be permanently protected from disclosure by himself or the legal adviser unless the protection is waived.

The attorney "work product" privilege complements the attorney-client privilege and protects written statements, private memoranda and personal recollections formed by an adverse party's counsel in the course of his legal duties. This privilege too is broader in the United States than even in many other nations that recognize such a privilege. The English "legal professional privilege" attaches only to documents created primarily for the purpose of preparing for actual or contemplated litigation: *Price Waterhouse v. BCCI Holdings (Luxembourg) S.A.* [1992] BCLC 583; *Waugh v. British Railways Board* [1979] 2 All ER 1169, [1980] AC 521.

vii. Taking of Evidence in U.S. in Support of Foreign Action

As set forth in **Chapter 10** among the kinds of discovery permissible against parties and nonparties in the United States are document requests. Document requests and *subpoenas* are requests for production of documents and tangible things (including microfilm, photographs, audio/video recordings, etc.) and for entry of one party upon the land of another to perform inspections and measurements. Requests are to be made with "reasonable particularity" and may be directed against documents located anywhere in world.

While document requests may be addressed solely to parties, document requests addressed to nonparties within a U.S. court's jurisdiction must be effected through issuance of a *subpoena* under Federal Rules of Civil Procedure Rule 45, but may be directed against documents located anywhere in world. If a nonparty cannot be served with a *subpoena* or is not subject to personal jurisdiction of a U.S. court, documents located outside the U.S. can be obtained from a nonparty solely through foreign judicial assistance via the Hague Evidence Convention or letters rogatory. The three basic responses to a document request are set forth in **Chapter 10** above.

Section 1782, US Code Title 28

As also set forth in **Chapter 10** above, Section 1782, US Code Title 28 is a means to use the U.S. courts to order discovery, from a party or nonparty, in support of a court proceeding or, in certain circumstances, an arbitration outside of the United States. It is essentially a tool which can be used against U.S. parties and nonparties, and by foreign parties, to obtain U.S.-style discovery for non-U.S. proceedings in which such discovery might normally not be possible or permissible.

Hague Evidence Convention and U.S. Pre-Trial Discovery

As stated previously, in the context of the Hague Evidence Convention various Contracting States have made declarations or reservations concerning Article 23. The result is that such countries will not execute letters of request for the purpose of obtaining pretrial discovery of documents as known in common-law countries if the letter of request requires a person to state what documents relevant to the proceedings to which the letter of request relates are, or have been, in his possession, custody or control; or to produce any documents other than particular documents specified in the letter of request, which are likely to be in his possession, custody or control.

CHAPTER 13

TAKING OF DOCUMENTARY EVIDENCE ABROAD IN SUPPORT OF DOMESTIC ACTION

Many of the observations in **Chapters 10, 11,** and **12** apply equally or by analogy to the question of taking of documentary evidence abroad in support of a domestic action, and reference to those Chapters is hereby made generally. The Conventions mentioned earlier are applicable in taking documentary evidence abroad in support of domestic actions, but their applicability depends in this case on the foreign State and its internal rules and declarations concerning the Conventions.

The courts of most countries generally demand from time to time judicial assistance from all states with which they may have diplomatic relations. In principle, evidence is taken by (or under the supervision of) authorities abroad. This is regularly done in the ways prescribed by local law unless the requesting court has explicitly demanded application of its own rules of procedure and these are not in conflict with national law or irreconcilable with public policy of the requested state.

i. From Whom Discovery is Possible and When

As set forth in **Chapter 10** above by analogy, depending on the jurisdiction taking of documentary evidence, or "discovery" of documents, may or may not be possible to varying degrees. To the extent there is a general opportunity for such taking of evidence, it will normally be possible between and among the parties to an action and, to a limited extent if at all, from nonparties. Certain countries, particularly in the civil-law context, distinguish between parties and witnesses, such that anyone who is not a party to the case and who is present in the country may be obliged to appear as a witness.

Civil-Law Approaches

Most civil-law countries do not provide for any kind of pretrial discovery procedures apart from the protective taking of (witness) evidence in the context of interim, conservatory, and emergency measures. Thus, with some exceptions and gradations, most non-common law jurisdictions do not provide in their local procedure or customs for measures equivalent to pretrial discovery. Thus parties cannot be obligated to provide the other party with information or answers to inquiries, and there is no obligation to disclose the existence and content of documents in possession of the party prior to the trial.

In such jurisdictions, if in a local law suit one of the parties wishes evidence to be taken from a person residing or having its registered domicile abroad, such party may so state in its briefs. If, in the subsequent evidence proceeding, the judge comes to the conclusion that the evidence located abroad is indeed necessary to decide essential issues, a letter rogatory or letter of request may be issued. Although the letter will be issued by the court, it is obvious that the party having offered the relevant evidence will need to participate in its preparation.

It is once again important not to lump all civil-law jurisdictions into the same category and to assume erroneously that all such jurisdictions have a blanket prohibition against pretrial discovery, or court order, of documentary evidence. In some such countries, the court may on a party's request order the other party to submit documents, and regardless of whether the other party or the documents are located in that country or abroad. In some of these countries, a party may also ask the court for an order on nonparties to deliver documentary evidence at the cost of the requesting party. Where such an order cannot be compelled and is not complied with, the recourse of the requesting party locally may be limited to suing the holder of the document for its surrender.

A party may object if evidence is taken disregarding legal secrecy protection (e.g., trade secrets). The party must object as early as possible and may request the court to eliminate the infringing piece of evidence from the files; the court's decision whether to remove it from the court file may not be appealed separately, but only together with an appeal against the judgment.

Common-Law Approaches

Depending on the jurisdiction and particularly in the case of certain common-law countries, there may in fact be no court involvement unless and until a party or nonparty refuses to comply with a discovery request. The degree of involvement of the court in the taking of evidence will invariably be far greater in other countries, particularly of the civil-law tradition, but depending on the jurisdiction may not involve compulsory production of documents.

Here again, the common-law jurisdictions should not be lumped together any more than the civil-law jurisdictions. The treatment of document requests abroad in support of proceedings locally is, for example, quite different in the United States and England. The leading case in this area in England is *Panayiotou and Others v. Sony Music Entertainment (UK) Ltd* [1994] 1 All ER 755, the so-called "*George Michael Case.*" Where the plaintiff applied to the English court for a letter of request to seek production of documents held by a New York company associated with the defendant, the defendants contended that the court had no jurisdiction to issue such a letter concerned merely with the production of documents. The court disagreed to the extent the documents were within a party's possession, but held that the letter of request must be confined to particular documents, be admissible in evidence, and be directly material to an issue in the action.

ii. Conventions

As stated in **Chapters 10, 11,** and **12** above and particularly relevant here in the context of documentary evidence, among the reservations and declarations to the Convention which may have been made by one or another country, and which must be verified on a case-by-case basis, include those to the effect that requests for "pretrial discovery" of documents as known and practiced primarily in the United States will not be accepted. Furthermore, implementing legislation in certain countries has had the effect that local courts may have no statutory basis for the issuing of letters of request for the obtaining of purely documentary evidence.

In such cases, including for example Australia, documentary evidence can only be obtained through the Hague Convention as part of a witness examination. This may also mean that documents in the possession of a foreign company cannot be obtained unless the company is willing to attend a witness examination through one of its officers.

iii. Other Means and Absence of Convention

As described in **Chapters 10** and **11** above, certain countries are signatories to bilateral additional agreements to the 1954 Hague Convention on Civil Procedure. Some countries are also signatories to bilateral treaties on Mutual Assistance in Legal Proceedings (Service of Process) in civil and commercial matters.

Such bilateral treaties on judicial assistance hold provisions on the taking of documentary evidence from witnesses, parties, experts and inspections etc. as well as the performance of other judicial acts domestically in connection with actions pending abroad. Where no multilateral or bilateral treaty applies, it may be that service and judicial assistance are granted on the basis of mutual continuous practice and comity.

Also of potential relevance is the Hague Convention Abolishing the Requirement of Legalization for Foreign Public Documents, UNTS 527 p. 198; UKTS 1965 No. 32 (Cmmd. 2617); ATS 1995 No. 11. This convention provides for the acceptability of a certificate issued under the Convention as proof of the authenticity of the foreign public document to which it is attached or annexed.

Many courts, including in jurisdictions which are not signatories to the Hague Evidence Convention, will not issue letters of request for the production of documents from nonparties unless the circumstances are such that the court would grant an order compelling production from a nonparty in a domestic proceeding in similar circumstances. In such cases, the party seeking letters of request should establish that (i) it has been unable to obtain the documents from persons over whom it is entitled to conduct examinations, (ii) it would be unfair to proceed to trial without an opportunity to review the documents sought to be produced, and (iii) an order for production will not result in undue delay or unreasonable expense by adverse parties.

iv. Practical Problems and Time Factors

As stated previously, to the extent a party is able to be specific in identifying the particular documents to be produced, the location of those documents and the persons having possession, custody or control over them, the delays experienced in the production of these documents may be minimized. One of the major reasons for delays in the production of documents relates to the period of time which a person requires to search out relevant documents.

Generally, it is up to the parties to a civil proceeding to present or not present documents that they have from sources located anywhere in the world. Even if in the requested country the means of taking evidence are broader and, in particular, if instruments exist to force a party to produce documents, the judge at the place of the pending action may restrict his own request to a narrower framework that exists in local law. This may mean that he will decline to request inspection of documents or *subpoena* documentary evidence for a local proceeding. Where the party in such jurisdiction directly makes the request of a foreign court, and as long as elementary (constitutional) rights of a party or person involved in the litigation are not infringed, such evidence must be considered by the judge and not be refused as unlawfully presented.

Document Compulsion under U.S. Federal Rules of Civil Procedure

Courts in the United States may compel the production of documents situated abroad without foreign judicial assistance in many instances under the Federal Rules of Civil Procedure. At any time after the requisite "discovery conference" required by Rule 26(b), Rule 34(a) enables a party to request any other party to produce or permit inspection of designated documents which meet the criteria of Rule 26(b) ("any matter, not privileged, which is relevant to the subject matter involved in the pending action"). U.S. courts will, however, refuse to compel discovery if it is unduly burdensome or seeks discovery of information reasonably attainable by other methods, trial preparation materials, or experts not to be called as witnesses at trial.

Federal Rule 34(c) authorizes courts to compel nonparties to produce documents by means of a *subpoena* duces tecum as provided for in Rule 45. Rule 45, in turn authorizes a court to compel production of documents from a nonparty under certain circumstances. Conflict with a foreign law or policy, even one which exposes the respondent to criminal sanctions in the foreign country, does not require a U.S. court to quash a Rule 45 *subpoena* or refuse to impose sanctions under Rule 37 for failure to comply with a request under Rule 34.

Both Rule 34 and Rule 45 require the requesting party to satisfy certain criteria. The court before which the case is pending must have personal jurisdiction over the respondent and only those documents in the respondent's possession or control are discoverable. However, a respondent may have control of documents in the possession of a subsidiary, parent or sister corporation. Discovery is available only if the requesting party effects personal service on the respondent. This precludes discovery under the Federal Rules of foreign nonparty respondents unless an agent is available for service within the U.S. court's jurisdiction.

v. Relevance to Later Efforts to Recognize and Enforce at Place of Judgment

As stated previously, taking of documentary evidence domestically normally has no direct effect on the issue of recognition and enforcement abroad. In the European context, Article 29 of the Brussels/Lugano Conventions provides, for example, that a foreign judgment may under no circumstances be reviewed as to its substance, reflecting the principle of no *revision au fond.* Accordingly, judgments originating from Contracting States of the Brussels/Lugano Conventions undergo recognition *ipso iure.* There are therefore no grounds for refusal with regard to taking of evidence apart from procedures applied which are against public policy.

Bilateral enforcement treaties granting mutual recognition of judgments in which the countries addressed herein are parties do not contain provisions which might be grounds for denying enforcement of a foreign judgment due to unlawful production of documents abroad. Consequently, a judgment debtor cannot normally object to enforcement because of defective evidence. If a judgment debtor wishes to challenge the authorization of enforcement, it must do so by somehow linking it to an infringement of public policy, if such a link can indeed be made. Thus, as set forth in **Chapter 10**, in some cases a violation of public policy can be alleged if the evidence produced or gathered within the State where enforcement of the foreign judgment is now being sought was obtained illegally.

In the United States, the method of discovery of documents located abroad has no profound implications for the enforceability of judgments in the U.S. since the U.S. Supreme Court decision in *Société Nationale Industrielle Aérospatiale v. United States District Court*, 482 U.S. 522, 541 (1987). There, the Court held that it would draw no distinction between evidence that is abroad and evidence that is within the control of a party subject to the jurisdiction of the court with regard to what method of accomplishing discovery is ultimately employed.

An unresolved issue is whether a foreign party waives the right to insist on first use of the Hague Evidence Convention procedures for discovery if the party does not raise objections to unilateral discovery on receipt of a request for evidence or a Rule 45 *subpoena*. No U.S. federal appellate court has decided this issue and there is disagreement among the lower courts on this issue.

In contrast to the United States, certain other countries consider it unacceptable to disregard relevant evidence available to the court. This rule may have its limits where constitutional rights of the parties or persons involved in the litigation are violated. In that case, the use of the unlawfully obtained evidence may provide a basis for nullifying the proceeding.

With regard to nonparties, where those who are a subject of letters of request seeking the production of documents in another State fail to comply with the request, depending on the local law the courts may not be in position to effectively sanction the nonparty. On the other hand, the person who is subject to the request may be a party to the local proceedings and refuse to comply with a request made to produce documents in the possession, custody or control of that party outside the jurisdiction. In such case, the local court may make an adverse inference concerning those documents not produced at trial.

vi. Attorney-Client, Work Product and Other "Privileges"

As set forth in **Chapter 10**, under the Hague Evidence Convention three separate groups of privileges exist. Article 11 permits a witness to refuse to provide evidence that is protected by a privilege provided by the receiving State. Witnesses may invoke any privilege of the requesting State, provided that the existence of such privileges is confirmed by the requesting authority; the negotiating history indicates that the receiving State may ignore privileges of the requesting State that are not confirmed. Furthermore, Member States may declare that they will recognize privileges recognized in third-party States.

Under the Brussels/Lugano Conventions, the collection of evidence is subject to any claim of privilege under the law of the requesting State and under the laws of the State of collection. Depending on the jurisdiction, there may or may not be privileges under local civil procedure and evidence law which offer protection against disclosure.

Particularly in common-law jurisdictions, and notably but by no means exclusively in the United States, "privileged" matter, even if "relevant," may not be discoverable. As stated previously in **Chapters 10**, **11**, and **12** above, certain countries have enacted legislation providing for the protection of business records. These statutes may prohibit the taking of business records out of the jurisdiction at the instance of any foreign legislature or court.

Conflicts Between U.S. Discovery and Foreign Blocking Statutes

U.S. courts' attempts to compel discovery of documents located abroad under the Federal Rules of Civil Procedure have been partially responsible for the proliferation of foreign blocking statutes prohibiting compliance with U.S. discovery proceedings.

A U.S. litigant faced with a respondent's refusal to comply with a discovery request under a blocking statute may petition the court to issue an order compelling production of the requested documents under Federal Rule 37, and may request appropriate sanctions. Alternatively, the litigant can attempt to find a party who has the requisite control over the documents requested, but who is immune from the foreign blocking legislation.

The resolution of conflicts arising between U.S. discovery rules and foreign legislation is an exercise in discretion based on balancing conflicting interests and private hardships. Indeed the U.S. courts have concluded that a U.S. court having jurisdiction to enforce a rule of law is not precluded from exercising its jurisdiction solely because such exercise requires a person to engage in conduct subjecting him to liability under a foreign law having jurisdiction as to that conduct. While the Restatement Third of Foreign Relations Law of the United States incorporates many of the criteria considered by courts in this context, no clear set of rules has emerged to govern these conflicts.

CHAPTER 14

ADMISSIBILITY & PRESENTATION AT TRIAL OF EVIDENCE TAKEN DOMESTICALLY OR ABROAD

i. General Requirements and Practices

Depending on the jurisdiction, it may or may not recognize in varying degrees, if at all, such evidentiary concepts as depositions, interrogatories, requests for admissions, and bills of particulars. Similarly, a particular civil procedure code may or may not contain binding rules regarding admissibility, credibility and weight of individual elements or means of evidence. Accordingly, there may not be any particular or automatic distinction per se between evidence taken domestically and evidence taken abroad.

Applicability of General Principles

The issue of admissibility and presentation at trial of evidence taken domestically or abroad relates back, to a great degree, to the similarities and differences in overarching procedural principles discussed in **Chapter 1** above. Once again, the practitioner should be wise to the differences, sometimes of a subtle nature, in understanding and implementing such principles from one country to the next.

It will be recalled that among the principles of importance here were the principle of "contradiction" (*audiatur et altera pars*) requiring the court to allow all parties to present their claims, evidence, and cause of action. Another was the rule of free disposition, that the party can freely dispose of the matter in dispute, subject to certain limited exceptions, and is free to withdraw its claim or acknowledge a claim brought against it. Still another was the notion of *iura novit curia*, that it is solely for the court and not for the parties to define and apply the law. Furthermore, under exceptional circumstances a party may be ordered by the court to furnish proof of the substance of the applicable foreign law, especially if it is unable to find the law itself.

With regard to the presentation of the facts and the law, another overarching principle is that it is solely for the parties to present and prove those facts and circumstances on which they wish the court to apply the law—as opposed to the competing principle that the judge is under a duty to clarify allegations which are unclear or to consider facts that are in the public domain irrespective of whether they were alleged or not. Another principle is that of immediacy and orality whereby a witness must communicate his observations of facts and past occurrences personally and in his own words before the judge.

The basic provision as to the allocation of the burden of proof is that the party who claims to have rights based on the existence of certain factual circumstances bears the burden of proving these circumstances. It is for the defendant to allege and prove those facts which are apt to rebut or render less likely the rights asserted by claimant. There may also be specific rules as to the allocation of the burden of proof, including various statutory legal and factual presumptions. Finally, it may be possible for the parties to contractually agree on an allocation of the burden of proof deviating from the otherwise applicable rules.

Finally, there is the governing principle of free evaluation of evidence by the judge, which indeed characterizes the judge-dominated system prevalent in most civil-law systems. First, the court is free to consider what weight is to be given to any piece of evidence or testimony received. Second, basically all kinds of evidence are admissible. This principle of free evaluation of evidence is in sharp contrast to the evidence rules in common law countries, such as the United States. There, evidence law is more formalistic, distinguishing, for example, legally obtained evidence from illegally obtained evidence.

In this connection, it makes no difference whether the evidence was obtained domestically or abroad. Of course, if a witness was heard abroad and the local judge must base his assessment on a written transcript of the testimony, such witness statement might be less convincing than that of another witness who appeared in person before the court.

Gaining Information and Taking Evidence Outside the Common Law

As stated previously, it would be a mistake to assume that those jurisdictions which do not allow pretrial discovery conducted by the parties also provide no possibility to gather information and take evidence prior to the main proceeding if certain exceptional circumstances are present. Such a possibility may indeed be open to the parties.

Usually, the party seeking such information must file a request with the competent court sufficiently demonstrating that a particular piece of evidence may be lost or no longer be readily available and that it would suffer irreparable harm if the evidence were not immediately secured. If such motion for early obtaining of information/evidence is granted, then the court (and not the petitioning party) will undertake the necessary steps designed to obtain the information or secure the piece of evidence. The court will, e.g,. order a person to produce a specific document or will hear a specific witness. Such requests/motions for the early production of evidence may not be broad and sweeping, but must be specific and precise.

In such jurisdictions, where evidence is taken only subsequent to the main proceeding, a person considering to file an action must reasonably know or be in a position to assess, prior to commencing proceedings, whether he is likely to succeed in proving his allegations. This includes in particular whether the relevant documents exist and where these documents are located.

Also in such jurisdictions, sometimes a person or entity may have a contractual or statutory right to obtain at any time certain information from another person. Under such circumstances, the person or entity entitled to receive such information may request the other person to provide the information whenever the contractual or statutory prerequisites to do so are fulfilled.

If the person obligated does not comply, the party seeking the information may resort to summary or ordinary proceedings in order to enforce its rights. Sometimes in such jurisdictions the courts will, upon their own initiative or upon motion by one of the parties, initiate the taking of evidence early in the proceedings, in particular if it is thus possible to save time in procuring an expert opinion or when evidence must be gathered abroad or if a quick disposal of the matter may be expected.

Examination of Witnesses and Admissibility

As explained previously, witnesses may enjoy various privileges and, depending on the local law, when examined may refuse to answer questions which might bring disgrace, discredit, the risk of criminal prosecution or pecuniary damage to themselves or close relatives, or might entail the danger of criminal persecution. It is normally the duty of the court to instruct a witness of his right to refuse giving evidence. Depending on the jurisdiction, nonparty witnesses may also refuse to give evidence with respect to specific questions.

For the examination of both party and nonparty witnesses, methods such as examination, cross-examination, etc. may or may not be applicable depending on the jurisdiction, as set forth earlier. A major part of the examination will be conducted by the judge, by counsel or by both depending on the rules. The witness's testimony may be recorded by a stenographer, be preserved by way of a dictated summary by the judge at his discretion, or not be preserved at all.

In jurisdictions such as the United States, there may be complex rules and caselaw relating to permissible kinds of questions and examination of witnesses which must be borne in mind closely. In other jurisdictions notably in the civil-law tradition, the principles of "free evaluation of evidence" and "no binding rules as to admissibility of evidence" may be applied so strictly that even if evidence presented was taken by infringing procedural rules, it may still be used. In short, each jurisdiction is different and must be examined in advance on a case-by-case basis with the aid of local counsel.

In countries such as the United States, Canada and Australia, there may even be significant differences and disparities from one state or province to another. As a general matter, including in the common-law countries, the practitioner should verify the most recent state of the law respecting evidence. Thus in Australia, for example, the Evidence Act 1995 (Cth) now applies in relation to all proceedings in a federal court or a court of the Australian Capital Territory. The states are expected (though not obliged) to shortly pass mirror legislation to the Evidence Act so that a uniform body of law will govern the law of evidence in Australia. Where the Evidence Act is expressed to apply exclusively, the common law and prior statute law are now useful only to assist in understanding changes that have been made in the previous law or terminology employed. Thus, in dealing with evidentiary problems in the relevant courts, it will be necessary to look to the statute for the answer. This is particularly so in relation to the admissibility of evidence, under which common law will be relevant only insofar as it forms a guide to the meaning of the statutory terms.

Discretion and Refusal of Court to Admit Evidence

A characteristic feature of every legal system, whether common-law or civil-law inspired or otherwise, is the ability of the court to refuse to admit evidence on various grounds. As stated earlier, a court will often not be able to be present at the taking of witness evidence obtained outside of the jurisdiction for use in the jurisdiction. In some such cases, there may be an increased likelihood that the court will draw an adverse inference because of its inability to assess the evidence contemporaneously. This is a manifestation of the discretion of the court with regard to admissibility or evaluation of evidence, which takes place in different ways in different legal traditions.

Such discretion of the court may take different forms. Depending on the jurisdiction, the court may have discretion to reject or admit particular pieces of evidence. Furthermore, parties may be relieved from the consequences of noncompliance with particular preconditions for admissibility at the discretion of the court. There may also be discretion rendering evidence admissible or inadmissible depending on whether certain evidentiary standards are met.

For example, in relation to "hearsay" in some jurisdictions which otherwise have restrictions on use of hearsay a previous out-of-court statement made by a person who will testify in court may be admitted into evidence provided that the fact asserted in the statement was fresh in the memory of that person. In addition, a court may refuse to admit evidence if its probative value is substantially outweighed by the danger that the evidence might be unfairly prejudicial to a party, be misleading or confusing, or cause or result in undue waste of time.

Court discretion with regard to the admissibility of evidence also raises the issue of appeal from the exercise of such judicial discretion. Where such appeals are possible, it must normally appear that there has been some error in the exercise of discretion. If it is not apparent from the judgment how a judge reached such a result, an appeal may still be successful if a decision is unreasonable or plainly unjust and the inference can be made that in some way there has been a failure to properly exercise discretion.

Court discretion also raises the issue that normally proof of facts adduced in a foreign State is governed by the law thereof, as to the burden and means of proof, but local courts will not necessarily accept evidence unknown to their local law. At the same time, evidence produced abroad is normally admissible, even if unknown to local law, as long as public policy is not considerably offended.

Burden of Proof and Admissibility

While burdens of proof may differ from jurisdiction to jurisdiction, there are some common threads which are especially relevant to transnational practitioners and serve as guidelines for participation in the evidentiary phase of the dispute. While these guidelines are particularly useful in adversary proceedings where counsel may be expected to criticize the strength of each other's evidence, they are in fact also relevant for inquisitorial proceedings where the judge largely controls the submission of evidence.

First, international jurisprudence demonstrates the emphasis placed on documents prepared in the ordinary course of business, and not for purposes of litigation. Most reliable is evidence in the form of contemporaneous correspondence, minutes, letters and telexes. Indeed on a transnational plane this has been borne out by the experiences of the Iran-United States Claims Tribunal: *see, e.g., Flexi-Van Leasing, Inc. v. Iran*, 1 Iran-U.S. C.T.R. 455 (1982), 12 Iran-U.S. C.T.R. 335 (1986), 13 Iran-U.S. C.T.R. 324 (1986). Second, tribunals have consistently reaffirmed that a mere submission of a list of figures does not constitute evidence of the amounts claimed. Furthermore, the burden of proof may be perceived as being especially high when the evidence is entirely within the hands of the claimant. Courts have typically refused requests to fill evidentiary gaps when they believed that conclusive evidence of a point was readily available and should have been easy to produce.

It is also an accepted principle that presumptive evidence is acceptable only if no other evidence is available. Furthermore, as a matter of evidence selective redacting and "editing" of documents, even for purported reasons of confidentiality, invites the compelling inference that the withheld portions of such documents would not have served the purpose of the party. When a party in possession of evidence that is clearly relevant and would be of assistance to the court opts to make a selective presentation apparently designed not to illuminate the facts but only to support its own arguments, that party assumes the risk that the court will reach its own conclusions as to the content of the material withheld.

Specific Issues of Admissibility

Particularly in the common-law jurisdictions, there tend to be highly complex procedural rules, some of which are codified and others of which emerge from the consensus of caselaw, which may be relevant in transnational litigation. Such rules and customs vary from jurisdiction to jurisdiction, and sometimes between and among states and provinces in the same jurisdiction. For present purposes, it suffices to list some of these characteristics of admissibility which may play a role in the presentation at trial of evidence taken domestically or abroad:

a. In civil cases, the plaintiff bears the burden of proving the facts necessary to support the claim made. The normal standard of proof is known as the balance of probabilities, which means simply that the trier of fact must be satisfied on the evidence that it is more likely than not that the facts are as alleged. Where fraud is alleged in a civil context, the courts may require proof to a high degree of probability but still short of the criminal standard of proof beyond a reasonable doubt.

b. Witnesses testify as to facts which are within their own knowledge. Only expert witnesses, properly qualified as such, may give opinion evidence.

c. The evidence of expert witnesses is permitted to assist the court in dealing with matters which a lay person could not be expected to understand. The qualifications of an expert witness may be tested by cross-examination in court before the expert is permitted to testify.

d. The evidence tendered must be the best available in the circumstances. For example, evidence that the parties entered into a written contract is made by producing the contract unless it is no longer available.

e. Documentary evidence must generally be introduced by a witness who is a party to, or otherwise has personal knowledge of, the document. Certain classes of documents, such as official government reports, may be filed with the court without need of a witness.

f. Business records, including computer records, created in the usual course of business normally constitute acceptable evidence and prove their contents. Prior notice of filing of such records is usually required. As in virtually all cases where documentary evidence is in issue, the opposite party may nevertheless challenge the accuracy of such records and introduce evidence in support of that challenge.

g. Judicial records, foreign judgments, and certain classes of public documents generally prove their contents without more.

h. The legal system being adversarial, the courts are expected to base their judgments on the evidence adduced by the parties. However, judges can and do take judicial knowledge of matters of common knowledge, and the tendency is towards extension rather than restriction of this right.

i. Unsworn evidence may be given by persons incapable of understanding the obligation to give truthful evidence, with the occasional distinction between children and adults.

j. There is an evidentiary burden of raising an issue as to incompetence on the defendant, a persuasive burden of establishing competence beyond reasonable doubt on the plaintiff, and a burden of establishing incompetence on the party alleging it.

k. There may be an exception to compulsion where costs or delay would be caused in rendering the witness capable of hearing, understanding or communicating replies to questions.

l. There may be specific rules on refreshing memory from documents in court.

m. Permission may be given to a party to cross-examine its own witness with leave of the court pursuant to rules on hostile witnesses.

n. Certain questions may be disallowed in cross-examination, such as double questions, questions calling for conclusions, argumentative questions, and questions likely to produce answers which are confusing. Here, a distinction is to be made between the law relating to permissible questions in examination and the law relating to admissibility.

o. Prior inconsistent statements of witnesses may be admitted, whether as relevant to an issue or going to credibility.

p. Leave may be given to a party to recall a witness to give evidence about a matter raised by evidence adduced by another party on which the witness was not cross-examined.

q. Drawing of inferences from what is seen, heard or otherwise noticed during a demonstration, experiment or inspection may be allowed, as opposed to treating such a demonstration only as an aid to understanding the evidence but not as evidence in itself.

r. Statements made outside court by a person other than the witness are generally not admissible, but hearsay evidence may be admitted if it is necessary in the sense that it would be difficult or impossible to prove the point in issue otherwise and if it is inherently reliable.

s. There may be first-hand documentary hearsay exceptions and oral first-hand hearsay exceptions. The result is, where applicable, that the hearsay rule may not apply to oral evidence of a previous representation that is given by a person who saw, heard or otherwise perceived the representation being made, or to a document so far as it contains the representation, or another representation to which it is reasonably necessary to refer in order to understand the representation.

t. There may be an exception to the hearsay rule for business records.

u. There is invariably a privilege against self-incrimination.

In other than common-law jurisdictions, there are often very few specific rules of examination of witnesses. Generally, the examination must be made in such a way that it results in clear and truthful statements, and the witness must be given an opportunity to explain itself coherently. Thus, the witness cannot normally be limited to replying yes or no. It must also be made clear whether the statements are based upon the observations of the witness itself. The court normally determines the extent to which the witness may rely on notes or other material. The court also determines the general reliability of the witness. Where a witness has been heard by another court, including a foreign court, the protocol from that court must normally be read at the trial before the court in which the case is pending.

While the nature of a dispute has no exclusive relevance over admissibility and presentation of evidence, there are certain issues of admissibility and proof which apply more to one area of the law than another. The guidelines below are necessarily of a general international nature and must be viewed against the specific body or bodies of law which apply:

ii. General Commercial

Depending on the jurisdiction, either caselaw or codified law or both may establish specific regulations applicable to merchants (including how merchants are defined) and transactions between or involving merchants. In particular, corporations and limited liability companies are normally understood as "merchants," although the term is not limited to such entities. Commercial law may not be codified only in a commercial code, but also in other statutes relating to, e.g., sales, bankruptcy, checks, promissory notes, commercial registries, intellectual property, agency, etc.

Depending on the local law, certain types of evidence may be admissible concerning commercial obligations. These may include public deeds, private deeds, broker's bills, commercial correspondence, commercial books and witnesses. Some jurisdictions require that contracts submitted to a local judge for evaluation must be written in the local language if agreed and signed in that jurisdiction, unless all parties are foreign. In this case, the contract must be entirely translated. Contracts written in a foreign language but translated into the local language by a sworn translator are also normally admissible evidence.

In some jurisdictions, the "notary" plays a particularly important role and some classes of documents, such as deeds of sale of immoveable property must, and any type of contract may, be executed before a notary rather than a solicitor or attorney. Notarial documents (known as "authentic" documents) prove their contents without more and may be contradicted only by a cumbersome procedure sometimes known as "improbation."

Documents not executed before a notary are then "private writings" and in the ordinary course prove their contents only when identified and produced by one of the parties to the document. Where such distinctions are made, a limited category of private writings, including documents issued by or in the custody of foreign public officers and certified as such and powers of attorney certified by a competent public officer, are deemed to be "semi-authentic." Semi-authentic documents, like authentic documents, prove their contents without more, but if they are contested, the party invoking the document has the burden of proving its accuracy.

Depending on the jurisdiction, a contract or agreement signed by both parties normally proves the agreement it embodies once it has been properly identified and produced by one of those parties, and oral evidence to contradict or vary its otherwise unambiguous terms is then inadmissible. Oral evidence may be introduced to explain the context in which it was signed as an aid to interpretation of ambiguous terms, and oral evidence of a subsequent agreement amending its terms may also be admissible unless the nature of the contract is such that it is required to be made in writing. In certain common law jurisdictions, extensive caselaw and commentary respecting the "parole evidence rule" and "integration agreements" should be consulted on an individual basis.

iii. Sale of Goods

In many disputes over international sale of goods transactions, the 1980 United Nations ("Vienna") Convention on the International Sale of Goods ("CISG") may be applicable where by virtue of the parties the country or countries with a nexus to the transaction are signatories to the CISG and the parties, in a contractual relationship, have not expressly and validly opted out of the CISG. Attempts to include or exclude application of the CISG, whether at the drafting stage or in a subsequent dispute, should be undertaken with care. The practitioner should familiarize himself with Articles 1, 10 and 95 of the CISG in particular, as well as the developing CISG case law which has accumulated notably in such countries as Germany, the Netherlands and Switzerland.

In both international and national sale of goods disputes, the requirement of immediate giving of notice of defects is regularly a major issue. Depending on the applicable law, there may be short periods for implied warranty and somewhat longer periods for damage claims to cover at least part of such implied warranty claims. The most current state of the applicable law with respect to statutes of limitations must be verified in the particular case.

While the rules of evidence do not vary depending on the nature of the civil cause of action, certain rules require that some specific types of contracts must be made in writing. Contracts for the sale of goods may need to be made in writing where the value of the goods exceeds a threshold amount (usually very low) established by legislation. Contracts for the sale of, or imposing charges on, immoveable property may also need to be in writing and be subject to registration requirements.

Goods received may normally be returned if faults or hidden defects make them inappropriate for their use or reduce their value. Depending on the local law, unless otherwise expressly provided for by contract, the seller is liable even if the existence of such faults was unknown. If the seller is aware of a fault or defect at the time of delivery, seller may be obliged to reimburse the purchaser in the amount received plus losses and damage. If the seller was not aware of the defect, the reimbursement may consist of the amount received plus the relevant contractual expenses.

iv. Intellectual Property

Most forms of intellectual property, e.g., trademarks and copyright, may be registered, and ownership may be proved by filing a certificate of registration. Patents that must be registered are similarly proved. In disputes on these issues, the action is frequently accompanied by a motion for preliminary injunction or other interim or conservatory relief. Here, the practitioner must examine the particular law to verify what the standards are for obtaining such relief in the intellectual property realm, and in particular whether a showing of "necessity for immediate action" is required by local statute or caselaw.

Statutes of limitation again play a major role in this area as well. For example, depending on the jurisdiction a claim to refrain from acting in unfair trade matters, including trademark infringement, may be barred soon after the claimant has gained knowledge of the infringement and, regardless of knowledge, a somewhat longer period, but often not longer than three years, after the date of infringement.

Authorship is normally ascribed to the person that registers the intellectual work, unless proven otherwise. If the work is not registered, its authorship is ascribed to the one indicated as or declared to be author, unless otherwise proven. If no indication or declaration is made, the author is presumed to be the one who publicly uses the work.

The European Court of Justice has ruled against all-embracing patents and limitations on prohibitive licensing conditions, especially in the area of telecommunications, which aim at preventing companies from holding a monopoly on future development of telecommunications products. Also the distribution and sale of medicine and medical supplies across borders, where prices for products with identical ingredients differ widely among European Member Countries, has been condoned by the European Court.

On the other hand, regulatory statutes including strict criminal penalties and extensive civil claims for violation of intellectual property rights and, in particular, for product piracy have entered into force. Persons who claim pirating of intellectual property and patented products have been granted broader rights to information in order to find the source and the distribution network of products.

v. Principal-Agent

Particularly in the European Union context, attention should be paid to legislation and directives meant to harmonize law regarding principal-agent relationships, termination of such relationships and termination indemnification to the agent. For example, Austria recently adopted a new Trade Agent Law which harmonizes Austrian law with EU Directive 86/653/EEC. Furthermore, care should be taken to differentiate between principals and agents wholly within the ambit of the Brussels/Lugano Conventions, partially so, or not at all.

In the case of a principal located outside of the Brussels/Lugano Convention scope and an agent located inside the scope, the agent may be able to sue the principal in the home court of the agent as the forum of "assets located" where the principal has a payment claim against customers located in that same Brussels/Lugano jurisdiction. The principal's receivables are the assets, and the location of a receivable may be deemed to be the domicile or usual residence of the third-party debtor.

vi. Tort

Evidence of damage is a basic requirement for reimbursement of the loss. Although it is also necessary to prove the wrongdoer's blame, there are cases in which the burden of proof is reversed, being incumbent on the defendant to prove it is not to blame. Accordingly, if the established situation is the absence of the defendant's fault, it will be incumbent on the plaintiff to prove such fault. If, on the contrary, the situation leads to the belief that the defendant is to blame, it must prove its innocence. There are also legal presumptions of fault according to which the defendant's fault is presumed, being incumbent on it to prove its innocence.

Depending on the jurisdiction, the trend may be to progressively set aside the principle of *actori incumbit probatio* ("proof burdens on the plaintiff") to follow the rule that the evidence shall be produced by the one who makes an allegation against the normality, probability and veracity of the facts.

vii. Product Liability

Particularly in the European Union context, Member States have domestic product-liability legislation which is in line with, and implements, the EU Product Liability Directive.

The United States Context Generally

Product-liability cases play a comparatively minor role in litigation outside of the United States, although obviously there are numerous such suits in various jurisdictions, if also on a somewhat smaller scale. On the other hand, entities who do business in the United States or have a presence there, and who are engaged in manufacturing or other activities which may give rise to product-liability actions, must be aware of the ways in which they may be drawn into product-liability litigation in the U.S. They must also be aware of the ways in which they may shield themselves, at least to a certain extent, from the exercise of jurisdiction over them in the U.S.

As stated earlier under **Chapter 3**, by virtue of the U.S. Federal Rules of Civil Procedure and recent caselaw it is fair to say that "subject matter" and "personal" jurisdiction is exercised expansively; in many cases, therefore, it may be difficult for a non-U.S. defendant to escape the grasp of the U.S. court. State long-arm statutes have for some time authorized service of process on nonresidents arising out of activities related to the forum, as long as the underlying suit does not offend "due process."

In a recent trend, particularly in the state courts, long-arm statutes have been stretched to assert jurisdiction over foreign manufacturers, particularly in the product-liability context. For example, in *Cox v. Hozelock, Ltd.*, 411 S.E.2d 640 (N.C.App. 1992), *cert. denied*, 113 S.Ct. 78 (1992), an English manufacturer purposefully injected a product into the "stream of commerce" without giving any indication that it desired to limit the area of distribution of the product to exclude North Carolina, and jurisdiction was upheld. In *Loral Fairchild v. Victor*, 803 F.Supp. 626 (E.D.N.Y. 1992), a New York federal court applied the Virginia long-arm statute to exercise jurisdiction over a Japanese fax machine manufacturer.

Furthermore, parties with presence or activities in the U.S. should be aware of the December 1993 amendment to Rule 4 of the Federal Rules of Civil Procedure in the U.S, which essentially created a "default" federal long-arm statute for all federal question claims and a "national contacts test." This test may grant jurisdiction if the foreign defendant has substantial U.S. contacts spread thinly over a number of individual U.S. states. The Ninth Circuit Court of Appeals has held that the Fifth Amendment's Due Process clause permits consideration of a defendant's contacts with the entire United States where federal law claims are asserted and a federal jurisdictional statute is relied on: e.g., *Go-Video, Inc. v. Akai Electric Company*, 885 F.2d 1406 (9th Cir. 1989). Other lower courts and commentators have agreed with this analysis.

Moreover, a U.S. court may now assert jurisdiction over a foreign defendant pursuant to new Rule 4(k)(2) in conjunction with U.S. state long-arm statutes under new Federal Rule 4(k)(1)(A). Rule 4(k)(2) is not applicable, however, when the defendant's contacts are focused on some single state so as to support reliance instead on the jurisdiction of that state court.

"Purposeful" Contacts with the United States

"Purposeful" contacts have increasingly been interpreted broadly in U.S. litigation, thereby increasing the likelihood that the net of U.S. court jurisdiction will be successfully cast over the domestic and the foreign defendant. Such contacts have been interpreted recently to include, e.g., (i) presence of an office, warehouse, etc.; (ii) ownership of property or a bank account; (iii) solicitation of business aimed at state residents; (iv) customizing of products for the state market or a particular purchaser; and (v) shipping products from abroad with invoices on the foreign letterhead.

Furthermore, a recent string of decisions from courts in disparate jurisdictions has fixed on other additional contacts to uphold jurisdiction: (vi) employment of personnel in the State; (vii) direct shipping of products to a state subsidiary or distributor which is used as a "marketing conduit;" (viii) presence of a subsidiary, parent, distributor, joint venturer or other entity in the state or with contacts to the state which can be fairly attributed to the defendant on an agent or "alter ego" basis, depending on such criteria as common ownership, financial interdependence, extent of control, observance of formal corporate separateness, etc.; (ix) sending personnel to the state to attend trade shows to demonstrate products or train personnel; and (x) negotiation, signing or performance of part or all of contract within the state or entering into a contract with a company generally in the state.

Finally, agreements to forum selection clauses designating a particular State court as the forum for disputes will generally be upheld even if the foreign defendant has no presence or contacts with that State. Furthermore, even choice of law provisions pointing to that State may also lead to exercise of jurisdiction there: e.g., *Eastern Marketing v. Texas Meridian*, 798 F. Supp. 363, 365 (S.D.W.Va. 1992).

"Reasonableness" and U.S. Jurisdiction Over Foreigners

As for "reasonableness" under the Due Process Clause of the U.S. Constitution, the trend is likewise one of expansiveness. Among the criteria which have emerged from the landmark case of *Asahi Metal v. Superior Court*, 480 U.S. 102, 115 (1987) are (i) the extent of the foreign defendant's purposeful entry into the U.S. State, (ii) the burden on it of defending in that State, (iii) the existence of any conflict with the sovereignty of the defendant's home country, and (iv) the State's interest in adjudicating the dispute. They also include (v) where the most efficient resolution of the suit is deemed to be, (vi) the importance of the State to the U.S. plaintiff's interest in effective and convenient relief, and (vii) the existence of an alternative forum. Here too there has been a recent trend toward expanded application of personal jurisdiction, most particularly in mass tort cases: e.g., *Ashley v. Abbott Laboratories*, 789 F. Supp. 552, 557 (E.D.N.Y. 1992).

With regard to admissibility and presentation at trial of evidence taken domestically or abroad in product-liability suits, it is normally incumbent on the supplier to indemnify the consumer for any damage and defect of products and services. Depending on the jurisdiction, product-liability law is applicable exclusively to manufacturers, producers, builders and importers. It may be incumbent on the supplier, in order to be exempted from indemnification, to prove it has not placed the product on the market, or even though it has placed the product on the market the defect does not exist, or that the consumer or third party is solely to blame. In some jurisdictions, there are statutes and caselaw providing for strict liability for extra-hazardous activity regardless of fault and also for contributory negligence. Case-by-case analysis of the particular jurisdiction is required.

viii. Construction

Statutes of limitation for warranty claims regarding immovable property, and therefore relevant in construction cases, are usually measured from the period of acceptance, unless otherwise agreed by warranty agreement. Particularly in certain civil-law countries, for economic reasons one of the parties to a construction dispute often initiates a "preliminary taking of evidence" procedure (*Beweissicherungsverfahren*), which is carried out by an expert under the direction of the court. This normally results in a written "finding of facts" (*Befund*) which gives the applicant a better basis to decide whether (and which) claim to file.

It is of practical importance that, depending on the jurisdiction, the costs of an expert hired by the court in such preliminary taking of evidence may be reimbursable as "costs of legal proceedings" if the party having applied (and paid) for the taking of evidence then wins the case. Conversely, costs incurred for hiring a "private expert" (even if the same person) are not reimbursable, even with a title for damages.

Certain jurisdictions have statutes and/or caselaw which address in a high degree of detail issues of admissibility of evidence relating to construction relationships. For example, the contractor's fault may be presumed if, prior to delivery of the construction, part of the material supplied by the contractor perishes; it will be incumbent on the plaintiff to provide the evidence of the loss. If the contractor has supplied labor only, but carries out the construction on unsuited land or there are faults or defects in the construction prior to the five-year term, it will be incumbent on the constructor to reverse the presumption of fault.

If the contractor breaches the contract by not carrying out the construction, or carries it out defectively, civil liability for losses and damages resulting therefrom may be demanded. The defaulting builder may be excused from such liability only if it proves that the breach of contract resulted from an act of God, force majeure, etc.

ix. Charterparty

A charterparty is normally defined as a contract for sea transportation of goods which stipulates the provision of an entire ship, part or specified compartments of a ship. Usually, these contracts are accompanied by some supplementary clauses on specific features of a particular mode of transportation.

The charterparty is a special type of contract for the carriage of goods by sea in which a vessel has been rented completely or a certain portion of the vessel or a certain definitive area has been rented for the transport of goods. The charterparty between the charterer (sender) and the carrier can also be concluded for a certain amount of time or a certain number of voyages. The written contract is the actual charterparty and is a document that can be used as evidence of the contractual relationship between the charterer and the carrier.

Charterparty contracts are often governed either by English law and/or by international usage (*lex mercatoria,* or law of merchants). Hence, these sources of law shall apply, in principle, subsidiary to the general requirements and practices adopted in procedural and commercial law, as concerns admissibility and presentation of evidence.

The bill of lading is important for the terms of the charterparty and the contractual liability of the carrier. The bill of lading is issued by the carrier and is a document of title for the goods. Valid terms in the bill of lading are material for the relationship between the carrier and the recipient of the goods. The bill of lading establishes the presumption that the carrier accepted the goods exactly as they are described according to type, measure, number, weight, quality, and value. Once the bona-fide recipient has the bill of lading in its hands, any proof that the carrier did not receive the goods as described in the bill of lading may be inadmissible. Vis-à-vis the recipient, the carrier is normally liable for any discrepancy between the goods and description in the bill of lading.

x. Insurance

Insurance statutes in force normally require insurance contracts to be made in writing. The first requirement to be fulfilled by a policy holder in an indemnity suit is the inclusion of the insurance policy which shall contain the general conditions and the advantages promised by the insurance company, the risks taken, the value of the insured object, the premium payable or paid by the policy holder, the policy validity term, the extent of the risks, and termination of the policy holder's rights, among other requirements.

To the extent the insurance company's liability to indemnify the policy holder is presumed, it will be incumbent on the holder to provide evidence of the facts which exclude or reduce its responsibility to reimburse. Depending on the applicable law, the insurance company may be excused from indemnity if it proves the policy holder's malice, that the policy holder has appraised the object with a higher value than the actual value, that the contract contains some fault capable of rendering it null and void, or that the policy has lapsed because the premium has not been paid according to contractual stipulations. The insurance company may also prove that the policy holder did not make any effort to minimize risks, acting contrary to the stipulated terms.

A major part of insurance disputes relates to refusal of an insurer to pay insurance compensation. The evidence in such cases includes the insurance policy, report of an incident giving rise to insurance compensation, correspondence between the parties, and calculation of incurred damage.

xi. Admiralty and Maritime

In certain countries, there are separate maritime courts which may adjudicate administrative proceedings concerning maritime damages and liability, administrative penalties, naval registries and mortgages, etc. The outcome of such administrative proceedings may be used as factual evidence in judicial courts. They may be contradicted, however, by further evidence produced in subsequent judicial proceedings.

Disputes arising out of delay in loading and unloading a ship and collecting demurrage are most frequent. The parties must provide notices specifying the time of arrival of the ship, timesheets and statements of facts that verify the time of loading/unloading, weather reports as well as official statements of vessel and port administration. The terms and conditions of the charter party as well as international and national trade customs should be taken into account.

Disputes can also occur in relation to a delay of the ship nominated in the charter, its not being sea-worthy, and a ship-owner's lien on cargo. In these instances, the basic evidence is presented by the terms of the respective charter, notices of arrival and technical condition of a ship, and reports and opinions of appropriate officials. Expert investigation can be conducted in order to resolve technical disputes.

The disputes over nonsafety of cargoes have specific features and are settled on the grounds of the terms and information set forth in a respective consignment and the report on acceptance of a cargo at the destination (tallyman's receipts, statements of facts, other paper).

There are also a number of conventions in the area, including the 1924 Brussels Convention on Bills of Lading and the 1978 Hamburg Rules.

CHAPTER 15

APPEAL AND REVIEW OF TRANSNATIONAL JUDGMENTS

To ensure a fair judgment, the law effectively provides a double degree of jurisdiction, i.e., the reexamination of judgments within certain limits and requirements. Procedural law does not stipulate a differentiated treatment toward foreigners, so that judgments rendered by local courts and involving a foreign party are normally appealable in the same manner as in purely domestic litigation. The only requirement may be to provide a guarantee or security to cover cost fees, as discussed in **Chapter 20** below.

Normally, where no appeal is taken or where the appeal is dismissed, the judgment of the lower court becomes final with all of the attributes of such judgments. No form of collateral attack on such a judgment is thereafter permissible. There may be exceptional cases, for example where essential new evidence is uncovered that could not with reasonable diligence have been discovered earlier or where judgment was by default and the defendant, without negligence on his or her part, was not aware of the proceedings. In such cases, steps may be able to be taken to set the judgment aside and obtain a new trial. The procedure to be followed in such cases varies.

In most jurisdictions, the courts may also render various kinds of decisions in a civil action, which in addition to judgments include, e.g., interlocutory and final orders and rulings. The rules on appeal and review may differ depending on the kind of decision at issue.

i. Conclusiveness and Finality of Judgments Generally

Once a judgment has become unappealable (by expiry of the appeal period without filing an appeal or if no appeal to a higher instance is available), then it is "final." If the judgment is for performance (e.g., payment), it forms the basis for enforcement measures if the judgment debtor has not performed within the period set forth in the judgment.

Under most countries' laws, a "final" judgment of a court having jurisdiction is determinative and "conclusive" both as to the overall conclusion reached (*res judicata*) and with regard to all discrete issues which required resolution in order to arrive at the overall conclusion (issue estoppel). A final judgment is "conclusive" only in the sense that it is binding on the parties (material *res judicata*) and enforceable once any ordinary appellate remedy is no longer available, provided no extraordinary appellate remedy is granted suspensive effect (formal *res judicata*). "Finality" thus denotes a judgment that brings the proceedings before a particular court to an end, whereas "conclusiveness" denotes a judgment that is final and no longer challengeable with an ordinary appeal. Conclusiveness is equivalent to enforceability of a judgment.

After a judgment is rendered and cannot be subject to ordinary appeal, the parties cannot bring a new action against each other on the same basis either in the local courts or, where applicable, in a court of other Contracting States under the Brussels and Lugano Conventions (Articles 21, 29 and 34(3)). This corresponds to the principal of conclusiveness (*non bis in idem*) which applies in many jurisdictions irrespective of accession to the Brussels and Lugano Conventions.

Statutory Bases for Appeal

Whether under common law or civil law or otherwise, the right to appeal from, or otherwise have reviewed, a decision of a local court is solely a right recognized pursuant to statutory law, and thus depends upon legislation. The nature of the right of appeal conferred will thus depend upon the relevant legislation. Where a statute provides for a general right of appeal, but another statute deems the order of a lower court "final and conclusive," the general right of appeal is absolved. Rights of appeal in criminal proceedings are not addressed here.

In the strict sense, an appeal involves an assessment of whether the judgment below should or should not have been given on the evidence before the court as it stood at that time. The appellate court is entitled to examine the evidence and the law. Normally, it can consider the conclusions of fact, but only on the basis of the evidence before the court. Importantly, it cannot, on the basis of subsequent events, set aside a judgment correctly made. To do so would be beyond the role of an appeal.

An appeal by way of rehearing, where available, is different. In that instance, the appellate court must determine the rights and liabilities of the parties by applying the circumstances as they exist when the appeal is heard. Accordingly, it is possible to receive and decide the dispute on the basis of fresh evidence. It is also possible to take into account changes in the law.

To enforce a foreign judgment from a court in a Brussels/Lugano Convention Contracting State, the Convention's "specific rules" apply, i.e., the court of enforcement may "suspend" enforcement if appeal was filed in the State of origin against the judgment. For nonconvention matters, enforcement by the local court normally requires a declaration of finality or the equivalent from the court of origin. Depending on the jurisdictions involved, there may or may not be a basis for recognition and enforcement in the absence of a Convention, bilateral treaty or other basis.

Different Kinds of Appeals

While only the most "common" forms of appeal in transnational civil litigation are mentioned below, the practitioner should be aware that it may be possible to contest almost any judicial act which contains a decision and that the type of appeal to be filed to contest a decision will depend on the judgment announced. There may therefore be a wide variety of forms of appeal depending on the jurisdiction, including appellate review, bill of review, request for consideration, appeal requesting clarification of a decision, ordinary appeal, special appeal, extraordinary appeal, and appeal based on diverging judgments, among others. These will obviously be known by different names in different jurisdictions even where the practice may be similar or even substantially the same.

Against decisions held by higher courts, the appellate possibilities may be differentiated. These may include appeals when the judgment rendered in an appellate review or motion for a new trial is not unanimous. These may also include extraordinary appeal when the appealed decision violates a constitutional provision, declares the unconstitutionality of a treaty or federal law, or deems valid a law or act of a local government refuted in view of the Constitution, where applicable.

Within ordinary appeal, certain jurisdictions may also distinguish between ordinary appeal, including *habeas corpus* and writ of *mandamus*, rejection of an *habeas data* or a court injunction, and suits in which among the parties are a foreign State or international organization. Appeals may also based on divergent judgments when a higher court's decision differs from a judgment rendered by another panel or section of the same appellate court.

Depending on the local law, appeals are not only of a voluntary nature, placed at the defeated party's disposal so that the party may resort to them or not. Ex officio appeal cases, such as mandatory re-examination of a judgment granting a writ of *mandamus*, may also be possible.

Furthermore, in some jurisdictions valid judgments and rulings of the courts can be reviewed by court supervision if protested by the Procurator General or other senior judicial officials or judges at the highest level. Such officials, as is the case in the Russian Republic, are entitled to request the appropriate courts to provide them with access to files of civil cases to decide whether sufficient reasons exist for a "protest in the course of supervision." In so doing, they may suspend enforcement of appropriate judgments and rulings until the end of "supervisory litigation."

ii. Procedural Issues

The time period for bringing an appeal and the procedure to be followed vary from jurisdiction to jurisdiction. Depending on the jurisdiction, the kind of appeal and the particular state or province in those countries with such a framework, the time-limit may run from valid formal announcement of the judgment or from the calendar day immediately following the day on which the party concerned or its attorney has formally received the judgment. Also depending on the jurisdiction, the time-limits may or may not be extended, whether upon request of a party concerned or at the discretion of the court. In some cases, the appeal may either be filed with the court of second instance or with the court which has rendered the decision to be challenged.

Normally, an appeal must be lodged in writing. The appellate brief must identify the particular decision to be challenged, specify the precise contents of the request, and substantiate in most instances the particular reasons for the appeal. Some laws provide for a two-step procedure: first, a notice of appeal must be lodged whereupon second, the appealing party is granted a time period for submitting a substantive brief.

Interlocutory Versus Final Agreements

In some courts, there is an important difference between judgments or orders which are "interlocutory" and judgments or orders which are "final" (i.e., finally determine a party's' rights or an issue in dispute under the final judgment rule). In the case of final judgments or orders, a right of appeal normally lies as of right. Most rules of court, however, adopt a distinction between interlocutory and final judgments and orders, and limit appeals from decisions of the former type.

The main limitation is that an appeal cannot be brought from an interlocutory judgment or order given or made by a judge except with the leave of the judge or by the relevant appellate court. The policy purpose behind requirements for leave of this nature is to deny defendants the tactical opportunity to use interlocutory appeals as a way of frustrating the plaintiff and the prosecution of proceedings.

An interlocutory decision is one which involves a direction by the court in relation to the conduct of a proceeding. The grant of an interim or interlocutory injunction is an "interlocutory" decision. A final decision involves the determination of the dispute in respect of which the proceeding was brought.

A strict test is normally applied to determine whether leave to appeal should be given. Normally, the applicant must demonstrate that the order or judgment is attended with sufficient doubt to warrant its being reconsidered on appeal. The application for leave to appeal and the hearing of an appeal pursuant to leave may technically be separate proceedings. Accordingly, in some cases, the appellate court dealing with the issue of leave and the appellate court dealing with the appeal may not be the same. However, where available in urgent cases it will be common to hear the application for leave and any consequential appeal effectively together. To succeed with an appeal from an interlocutory judgment order, the applicant must normally show that the order works a substantial injustice.

Grounds for Appeal

The application for appeal, depending on the applicable rules, must normally include the lower court judgment which is being appealed, the extent to which the lower court judgment is being appealed, and the remedy sought against the lower court judgment. Normally, the reasons for the remedy must be specified and can include, e.g., voidance due to procedural error, reversal of judgment, or remand to the lower court. The application should also include the legal grounds on which the remedy is based, including an exact indication of the part of the lower court's reasoning which is considered erroneous. Therefore, a "general appeal" may not be allowed by merely complaining that the judgment of the lower court is incorrect.

The appellate court normally considers the case only to the extent requested by the appellant. Furthermore, an appellant in a civil case shall normally not refer to circumstances or evidence other than presented in the lower court. Exceptions may be made when it was not able to refer to such circumstances or evidence in the lower court or otherwise had a valid reason for not doing so. This is a reflection of the so-called "principle of concentration" discussed in **Chapter 1** above. This principle aims to have all circumstances and evidence presented at the trial court level and only exceptionally allows the appellant to present new evidence at the appellate level.

Depending on the jurisdiction, the grounds for appeal which must be presented in detail in the appellate brief may include (i) "grounds for nullity," (ii) substantial procedural mistakes, (iii) errors in the determination of facts, and (iv) errors in the legal evaluation. Also depending on local law, the court of appeal may review the first instance court's determination of facts including the evaluation of evidence. While a hearing of witnesses by the appellate court is rare and may require a request from one of the parties, due to the principles of "immediacy and orality" discussed above, the appellate court may not deviate from the evaluation of witness evidence without having heard the witness itself.

If the appellate court finds that the court of first instance failed to take into account substantial and relevant parts of evidence, and the procedure of first instance was therefore incomplete, it may remand the case. In that case, the court of first instance must complete its proceedings in accordance with the second instance court's reasons for the remand. Against such remand, certiorari or the equivalent is admissible, with the general prerequisites.

Further appeal or certiorari to the highest court may be available after service of the appellate court's decision. The main limitation is normally that a relevant question of law must be decided (either because applicable caselaw does not exist or the appellate court's decision deviates from caselaw). Therefore, such certiorari, or *Revision* as it is called in Germany and Austria, can be made only upon "leave to appeal." Depending on the rules, such leave can be granted either by the appellate court in its decision or by the Supreme Court or equivalent itself. To obtain leave from the Supreme Court, the appealing party must file its appeal and in addition state the reasons why leave should be granted. Depending on the jurisdiction, oral hearings may or may not take place before the Supreme Court.

Extraordinary Means of Appeal

The difference between ordinary and extraordinary means of appeal lies in the interaction between the qualification of a judgment as conclusive and nonappealable. If an ordinary remedy is available, the judgment is not conclusive until the ability to raise such an ordinary appeal is exhausted within the time-limit available. A judgment which, by virtue of the nonavailability of ordinary remedies, is conclusive may nevertheless be attacked by extraordinary appeal. Such extraordinary remedy may or may not involve a suspension of effect of the underlying judgment depending on the applicable rules and also whether the appellate court so orders.

In the case of an ordinary appeal, the appellate court generally has the power to set aside the judgment appealed against and replace it with a new judgment on the merits. In some instances, the appellate court may choose, or be restricted, to setting aside the challenged judgment and remanding the matter to the lower court for reconsideration on the basis of the decision rendered by the appellate court. In the case of extraordinary appellate remedies, the appellate court is generally confined to setting aside the challenged judgment and remanding the matter back to the court of lower instance.

Depending on the jurisdiction, extraordinary means of appeal may or may not generally be subsidiary to ordinary means of appeal. Where this is indeed the case, as long as a judgment may still be challenged by ordinary appeal, no extraordinary appeal will be available. However, even in such jurisdictions and in limited cases, the procedural law may allow the challenge of an appellate judgment by extraordinary appeal at the same time as that judgment is also being challenged to the highest instance, e.g., relating to constitutional grounds or other matters of great public interest.

Under certain limited circumstances, specific remedies aim at re-opening or reinstituting the proceedings, or eliminating parts of the proceeding. These include a motion for reinstatement, an action for nullity or to vacate, and an action for reopening the proceedings. Obviously, where these vehicles exist in different jurisdictions, there may be minor or major differences in the way they are employed and one and the same vehicle may be known by different names even in the same language. Extraordinary appeal mechanisms do not normally affect the legal finality of a judgment, i.e., the judgment can be enforced immediately even if a party resorts to an extraordinary appeal.

A party may be able to make a motion for reinstatement if it was unable to make a timely appearance in court or timely file a pleading due to an unforeseeable or unavoidable event, e.g., because through no fault of its own the party was unaware of service of process. The deadlines for filing a reinstatement are likely to be very tight.

This may in practice be the main remedy in instances of defective service (e.g., depositing of the complaint at the post office while the party was on vacation). It can be combined with the appeal for nullity against a default judgment which may also have been rendered in the meantime. If enforcement is underway, provisional suspension can be claimed, which, if the case is reinstated, will become final.

An action for nullity allows a judgment to be challenged after it has become final. Depending on whether this vehicle is available, one or another of several "grounds of nullity" may be raised. These include if a judge was excluded by law from handling the matter (i.e., if the judge is a party or related to a party, etc.) or severe infringement of the right of audience.

The action for nullity is admissible only based on facts which became known to the applicant after finality of the challenged judgment. Lack of jurisdiction cannot be the basis for an action for nullity.

An action for re-opening the proceedings is admissible regardless of whether a proceeding is pending or has already been concluded by final judgment. Where available, it is normally limited to one or more of such grounds as where (i) a document on which the judgment was based proves to be forged; (ii) the judgment is based on false testimony of a witness, expert witness, or party witness; (iii) the judgment is otherwise a result of criminal action (including abuse of his office by the judge), or (iv) if a criminal judgment on which the (civil) judgment was based was replaced by a deviating judgment. Other grounds include (v) if a prior final judgment in the same matter was found and (vi) if a party receives (without fault for the delay) information and/or evidence which would change the judgment. Accordingly, where available such nullity and reopening of claims are not frequent in practice.

After the enforcement procedures have commenced, there may be separate remedies available. Depending on the applicable law, these may include an action to declare enforcement inadmissible, which aims at "invalidating" the judgment as a basis for enforcement. Such an action, where available, may be used most frequently when enforcement is initiated or continued after the judgment debtor has performed (made payment). Counterclaims can also be raised, but only if they could not be raised in the proceeding leading to the judgment. Another such action is one to bar the ongoing method of enforcement, and which aims at suspension and termination of that specific method. It may come into play when the judgment debtor can prove that the creditor has waived this specific enforcement method.

iii. Substantive Issues

Decisions which relate to practice and procedure and those relating to substantive rights are, in the main, clearly distinguishable. Gray areas occur where decisions relating to practice and procedure affect the substantive rights of parties. An example would be a decision to proceed with a matter summarily, which could impact adversely the substantive rights of a party who depends on a comprehensive trial in order to properly assert those rights.

Civil cases in most jurisdictions are normally heard before a judge alone, in other jurisdictions before a panel of judges, and in others occasionally before a judge and jury; the jury normally numbers either six, nine or twelve jurors. In certain common-law jurisdictions, such as Australia, it is well-established practice that only criminal trials are held before a jury.

Errors Warranting Appeal

A party appealing a civil decision will normally identify specific errors on the part of the judge. One is a decision on a question of law, in which case the appellant will challenge the correctness of the legal rule which was applied by the judge. Another is a decision in the exercise of discretion to make or not to make a particular order. In such case, there is a strong presumption in favor of the correctness of the original decision. Such decision should be affirmed unless the appellate court is satisfied that it is clearly wrong.

This may arise where the wrong principle has been adopted, the judge has given weight to extraneous or irrelevant matters, or the judge has failed to give any weight or sufficient weight to relevant considerations. It may also arise because a mistake was made in relation to the facts. An appellate court will normally be more readily disposed to set aside or vary a decision affecting substantive rights than one which relates solely to practice and procedure.

Yet another possible error warranting appeal is a decision on a question of fact. In this instance, the appellate court decides for itself the true effect of the evidence before the court at first instance. A distinction is normally drawn between a finding as to primary facts and a finding of fact which represents an inference.

Appeals and the Lower Court's Findings of Fact

An appellate court will not likely set aside a trial judge's findings as to the primary facts. Such findings often depend upon the credibility of witnesses and the appellate court will not have the opportunity to observe the demeanour of the witness as he testifies. An appellate court may be reluctant to interfere with the amount of an award of damages or whether the awarding of damages was appropriate in a given situation. It may then interfere only if the award was reached erroneously or if the amount of the award was manifestly excessive.

In some jurisdictions, there is an increasing tendency to regard findings of fact by a trial judge as final. In such cases, courts of appeal are not to intervene on factual issues unless the trial judge has made some manifest error in appreciating the evidence that affected the outcome. In view of the ever growing backlogs of trial courts, it may also be difficult to reverse findings of fact by a trial judge that are based on findings of credibility of witnesses who appeared at the trial. Such findings are considered to fall particularly within the province of the judge who actually observed the demeanour of the witnesses at trial. Where the evidence at trial was largely documentary, the same strictures do not apply. In such circumstances, courts of appeal may take the view that they are as well placed as a trial judge to determine issues of fact.

Appeals are normally made in respect of specified parts of a judgment and it is possible for a respondent to the appeal to specify parts of the judgment he wishes to have reviewed. Accordingly, it is possible for both parties to be seeking a review during an appeal and for the outcome of an appeal to be less favorable for an appellant than the original first-instance decision. Other than in such cases of cross-appeals, in view of the prohibition of *reformatio in peius* the appellate court's standard of review is limited to the appellant's complaint. The appellate court is not allowed to set aside or reverse the appealed judgment to appellant's detriment, unless the appellee has also appealed.

Thus in an ordinary appeal the appellant may request the appellate court to consider the case on its full merits within the scope of the original claims and pleadings brought forward in the lower instance. In some cases, the appellant may even bring forward new factual allegations and evidence in support of its original claims or the appeal. It is thus the parties' obligation to present again the whole substance of the dispute to the appellate court, which is bound by the particular motions and requests submitted to it by the parties. Even if it finds other errors in the judgment so reviewed that would influence its judgment, it has no authority to consider them if their effects would not be covered by the parties' motions.

In extraordinary appeals, by contrast, a judgment may normally be challenged primarily for procedural deficiencies or gross errors in applying substantive law. The petition for nullity is generally available only to remedy procedural faults. Accordingly, no new evidence relating to the underlying dispute may be submitted and no pleadings on the merits of the case take place.

iv. Practical Problems and Time Factors

Depending on the local rules, appeals are normally heard before a panel of judges and normally need to be commenced within a relatively short period from the date upon which judgment is delivered, which may be as short as 14 or 21 days. In transnational litigation involving parties and clients in far-flung time zones, this may often pose practical problems. Sometimes, it is necessary to consider making an application for the stay of execution of a court order pending an appeal to a higher court. This may be necessary where, for example, the court order would see payment being made. In addition, there may be circumstances where it is necessary to obtain an extension of an injunction pending the making of an appeal.

In jurisdictions which restrict the basis for appeals to issues already considered in the lower court, the practitioner must take care to frame the arguments in the appeal so as to fit into the allegations raised and the issues considered in the proceedings below. For example, an appeal restricted to either the examination of proper application of substantive law or the reconsideration of issues presented before the lower court may succeed only if the appellant manages to bring its allegations in the appeal within this scope. In the case of federal issues or constitutional appeals, this may be especially problematic inasmuch as the appellant may be permitted to allege solely errors in the application by the court of federal substantive law or an infringement of constitutional principals, and only based on the factual situation as ascertained and described by the lower court in its judgment.

Application for reinstatement, where available, may protract proceedings due to the appeal options granted by law against refusal of reinstatement. As indicated, nullity and reopening actions do not play a major role in practice. If an action for reopening is filed during a proceeding over an appeal against a judgment, then such procedure must be stayed until final decision on the reopening issue. In the two actions against enforcement, it is important that the claimant present all known facts and allegations, because later presentation may not be admissible. In this regard, there may be significant differences between and among countries which appear to have similar procedures in this regard, so that for example Austrian practice is thus more rigid than the practice in Germany in this respect.

Security for Costs and Appeals

Provision is made in some jurisdictions for hearing urgent appeals on an accelerated basis, but ordinary commercial cases are not likely to qualify. Of greater practical utility in such cases is an increasing tendency to require security to be posted when appeals appear to be simply dilatory. The lack of timely payment of such costs, when provided for in law, may terminate the proceeding. In some cases, appeals that are clearly without merit may be dismissed summarily on motion by the respondent.

Where the appellant must pay a court fee when a judgment is appealed, this fee may be a function of the disputed amount. The costs awarded to the winning party in compensation of attorney's fees, where the local rules so provide (*see* **Chapter 20** below), may also be based on the disputed amount. This fee and the risk of such costs should be taken into consideration by the appellant in assessing the size of its claim.

A particular weapon which a respondent to an appeal in England may employ against an appellant who is not resident in the European Union is the application for security for costs. In special circumstances, the Court of Appeal will order that a foreign appellant deposit a sum of money to protect the respondent's costs position in the event the appeal is unsuccessful. One such circumstance identified in the Rules of the Supreme Court is where the successful respondent may suffer unjustifiable difficulty, expense or delay in enforcing a costs order against the appellant.

This may often be the case where the appellant is resident overseas and has no assets within the UK or has conducted itself in such a manner as to suggest that it will attempt to resist enforcement of any costs order. The court always retains discretion to refuse security for costs on the basis that the appeal is likely to succeed or is appropriate in the wider interests of justice. If security for costs is ordered and not provided within the prescribed time limit, the appeal will be automatically dismissed without further order.

v. Strategic Considerations

Strategically, where sufficient doubt as to the correctness of a decision exists, it is often worthwhile preserving one's position by commencing an appeal. There may, of course, be cost consequences of commencing an appeal and failing or not proceeding with the appeal. Generally speaking, however, the costs of conducting an appeal may be significantly less than the costs incurred at trial.

The other side of the coin is the question of whether to accept a particular judgment or to risk on an appeal, and probably a counterappeal, that the appellate court ends up rendering a new judgment which is even less favorable to the appellant than the original decision. This issue may arise in claims for damages where the court of first instance has awarded only part of the claimed amount to the plaintiff, whereupon the appellate court may find higher damages. It is not unusual that although a party may be satisfied with the award received in a particular judgment, an appeal by the losing party provokes it to lodge a cross-appeal, but for the full amount originally claimed.

A foreign party who is a resident of a country that is a party to the Hague Convention on the Service Abroad of Judicial and Extrajudicial Documents in Civil or Commercial Matters may apply under Article 16 of the Convention to set aside a default judgment granted by a court of a Contracting State. The timelimit for doing so following the date of the judgment will be pursuant to declaration by the Contracting State pursuant to the Convention, and is usually one year. The default judgment will be set aside if certain conditions are met. These include if the defendant did not appear, the defendant did not have knowledge of the claim through no fault of its own in sufficient time to defend or knowledge of the judgment with sufficient time to appeal, and the defendant is able to establish a *prima facie* defense to the action on the merits.

Upon filing an appeal, the appellant must also consider the extent of the appeal. The lower court judgment may be contested in whole or in part. In the former case, the court *ad quem* examines the entire disputed issue, in the same manner as it was submitted to the trial court. The faults of the appealed judgment may be reexamined, and the trial-court judgment may be declared null and void. The partial appellate review, contesting a portion of the judgment only, may occur where the judgment included decisions on several joint claims and the appeal refers to only one of them or the opinion of the judgment distinguishes certain issues and the parties appeal from the part in which they were defeated. In this case, where applicable, the appellate court may render judgment only on the appealed portion of the lower court judgment.

vi. Relevance to Later Efforts to Recognize and Enforce

In general, taking an appeal suspends execution of the judgment in appeal at least insofar as that judgment orders the payment of money. In hardship cases, usually involving awards for serious personal injuries, courts may order periodic payments to be made to the successful plaintiff notwithstanding appeal. Stays of execution are normally granted to prevent immediate execution that would render an appeal academic or moot. Appeals from judgments ordering equitable relief, such as injunctions, do not suspend execution, but a stay may be ordered by the appropriate appellate court.

The test for granting a stay of execution is in essence that which applies to injunctions. The party seeking the stay must show that there is a serious issue to be decided, that irreparable harm will be caused if a stay is not granted, and that the balance of convenience favors a stay. In jurisdictions where the appellate remedies provide for suspension or stay of enforcement upon request, the party seeking suspension or stay may be required to file all evidence together with its application so that the court of enforcement is in a position to immediately decide upon the motion for suspension or stay. In this sense, mere cross-reference to evidence attached to the application may be irrelevant. Where the court of enforcement does stay the enforcement proceedings, it may order the applicant to pay a deposit depending on the local rules.

Where a judgment has been rendered despite procedural defects, the practitioner must evaluate whether such allegedly flawed judgment, once conclusive, is likely to be denied enforcement in another jurisdiction by reason of procedural defects. In this context, the benefits of an extraordinary appeal and possibly remanding the proceedings if the appeal is granted must be weighed against the benefits of a determination that such judgment is not recognizable and enforceable in the relevant jurisdiction. The reasons for nonrecognition and nonenforceability are typically restricted to egregious violations of procedure. This evaluation therefore requires careful analysis and coordination with counsel in the enforcing jurisdiction.

Brussels/Lugano Convention Bases

Under Article 30 of the Brussels and Lugano Conventions, a court in which recognition is sought of a judgment rendered in another Contracting State may stay the proceedings if an ordinary appeal against, or request of review of, the judgment has been lodged. Under Article 31, a judgment may be enforced in another Contracting State despite appeal or review of the judgment in the State in which the judgment was rendered if the judgment is enforceable in the latter state. At the same time, under Article 38 of the Convention, the court to which the decision allowing enforcement in another State is appealed may stay the proceedings if an ordinary appeal or request for review has been lodged against the judgment in the State rendering the judgment or if the time for appeal has not yet expired.

With regard to recognition and enforcement of judgments rendered in States other than Contracting States of the Brussels and Lugano Conventions, reference is made in **Chapter 17** below. Generally, if neither the Brussels nor the Lugano Convention is applicable to a judgment rendered in a foreign country whose enforcement is sought in a Brussels/Lugano State, the judgment is not recognizable in that second State until it has gained legal finality.

Arbitral Awards

While arbitration and arbitral awards are intentionally not a focus here, even secondarily, it should be noted that depending on the applicable law, an arbitral award may indeed be final and binding and not subject to any appeal whatsoever. At the same time, in exceptional circumstances corresponding to the applicable law the same arbitral award which is not subject to "appeal" may be subject to vacatur, set aside or annulment proceedings at the place where the award is deemed to have been rendered.

The grounds upon which such action may be granted may or may not correspond closely, or identically, to those set forth for denial of recognition and enforcement of foreign arbitral awards pursuant to, e.g., Article V of the 1958 New York Convention on the Recognition and Enforcement of Foreign Arbitral Awards. The ability, if any, to seek to have an arbitral award set aside at the place of arbitration may also be affected by whether the award is deemed to be a domestic or an "international" award by virtue of the "international" nature of the underlying dispute and/or as a function of the nationalities of the parties to the arbitration.

CHAPTER 16

DAMAGES

The old Roman law principle *casum sentit dominus*, namely that each person normally bears his own accidental damages, finds its reflection, in varying forms, in many countries. Generally, if the damaging incident is caused by someone unlawfully and with fault, that person is liable for compensation to the injured. In a legal sense, an act or omission is only "cause" for an injury if it is a *conditio sine qua non* and the damage was reasonably foreseeable in the normal course of events. Legally, not every causation, but only adequate causation or proximate causation, results in liability, thereby introducing a concept of foreseeability into the law of damages in virtually every jurisdiction.

The requirement that the injury have been caused "in breach of rules of law" relates to statutory or caselaw and derives from the legal protection of "absolute rights" (such as property, personal integrity, personal honor, etc.) or rights as stipulated in contracts. If a party is in breach of contract, it is then liable for reimbursement of the damages ("actual damage") incurred by the other party, provided that the breaching party was at fault. Degrees of fault differ depending on the applicable law, but generally relate to intention, gross negligence and ordinary negligence.

When parties negotiate with the intent of carrying out a contract, incurring expenses and taking commitments towards third parties, the party who abandons the deal with no justification, causing damage to the other party, must account for the blameful behavior. That party is accordingly subject to liability for damages. Doctrinal authority refers to such indemnity as pre-contractual liability, or *culpa in contrahendo*, which is classified as a type of noncontractual civil liability.

Depending on the law, the parties may include liability limitation clauses in a contract. Such clauses often take the form of a penalty clause, which consists of a conventional pre-settlement for losses and damages resulting from the nonfulfillment of the contract. While parties to a contract may provide for liquidated damages in the event of a breach, normally the amount stipulated may not be clearly disproportional to losses which could reasonably arise in the circumstances. Neither negligence nor actual damage is a prerequisite for liquidated damages. If the actual damages exceed the liquidated damages, the breaching party's duty to pay the difference depends on the content of the contract clause.

Contractual provisions limiting or excluding liability may be valid if expressed in clear language, but are always strictly interpreted. They may not exclude liability arising from bodily or moral injury caused to another, nor liability for intentional or gross fault. In considering whether to enforce the clause, the court will take all the relevant factors into account, including bargaining power, other choices available to the contracting parties, the parties' familiarity with the industry, or insurance cover.

i. Acceptable Kinds of Damage Recovery in Contract

In most jurisdictions, whether common law, civil law or other origin, it is possible to recover the following kinds of damages, although the names of the damages theories will obviously differ:

Expectation Damages

The purpose of expectation damages, sometimes called "loss of bargain," is to place the party who has suffered loss in substantially the same situation as had the contract been performed. It is not unusual for an assessment of damages for breach of contract to include the expectation that the plaintiff had of receiving the defendant's performance. For example, where there has been a breach of contract by a party, the nonbreaching party is entitled to damages for the loss of the bargain. This may be the difference between the market value of the contract or its subject matter and the price expressed in the contract.

In essence, expectation damages represent the loss of one's bargain. Expectation damages sometimes are measured by "general damages" or market measures (the difference between the contract price and value that the plaintiff was to receive from the performance), and sometimes by "special damage" measures (see below). In common-law jurisdictions, expectation damage issues will primarily be a question of caselaw and precedent, and to a certain extent of commentary. In civil-law jurisdictions and other countries in which contract relations are codified to a large extent, caselaw and commentary will likewise often be important to give meaning to the inevitable spare wording of codified provisions. Civil-law approaches tend to characterize expectation damages as "positive performance interest."

Particularly in common-law jurisdictions, the law as it relates to damages that may be recovered both in contract and in tort is complex and a full treatment is well beyond the scope of this chapter. The simple general rule that an award of damages for breach of contract is intended to restore the plaintiff to the financial position it would have been in had the breach not occurred is deceptive in its straightforwardness.

Consequential losses, for example, where a breach of contract causes a loss or deprives the plaintiff of an anticipated gain from another transaction, are in principle recoverable if they are not too remote. The classic test of *Hadley v. Baxendale* (1854) 9 Ex. 341, is still a basis for caselaw and commentary: such damages as "... may fairly and reasonably be considered either arising naturally, i.e., according to the usual course of things from such breach of contract itself, or such as may reasonably be supposed to have been in the contemplation of the parties, at the time they made the contract as the probable result of the breach of it."

Reliance Damages

These damages are intended to compensate the plaintiff for monies expended pursuant to the contract, given that a subsequent breach by the defendant means that the money has been wasted. The onus is on the defendant to prove that even if the contract had been performed, the money would nonetheless have been wasted or not recovered. Reliance damages do not feature prominently in cases where the plaintiff is normally adequately compensated by expectation damages.

Generally, a plaintiff is able to choose the method of assessment of damages, whether they be expectation or reliance. Where a plaintiff claims both forms of damage, there may be double-counting, unless it claims in the alternative. It is rare for an injured party to claim reliance loss instead of expectation loss unless the injured party is unable to quantify the value of his expectation or has made a bad bargain.

Reliance damages find their expression in certain civil-law jurisdictions in the form of "negative contract interest." Such remedy may be claimed if at the same time the contract is cancelled, i.e., terminated forthwith by the claimant. Both parties must return any performance received from the other party. In addition, the injured party may then claim damages corresponding to the compensation that will return it to its pre-contractual position. Negative contract interest includes the injured party's costs in connection with the conclusion and cancellation of the contract. Furthermore, negative contract interest may under special circumstances be claimed if negotiations do not result in the conclusion of a contract.

Restitution Damages

There may be situations in which the plaintiff has made a "bad bargain," and by claiming expectation damages, the plaintiff would be worse off than if it could simply be restored to its pre-contract position. If this is the case, the plaintiff is likely to plead a case for damages under the head of restitution. The court will not object to the fact that the plaintiff would be better off in claiming restitution than if the contract had been performed.

These damages are sometimes difficult to distinguish from reliance damages in that the need for restitution invariably arises from reliance on the contract. However, as opposed to lost profits, these damages are more concerned with wasted expenditure. The purpose of restitution damages is to place, as best as possible, the aggrieved party in the situation it was in before it entered into the contract. Generally, the date for assessment of damages is the date of breach of the contract. However, the measure of damages is normally only those that would be in the contemplation of the contracting parties at the time they entered into the contract. In common-law jurisdictions, this notion is often associated with the case of *Hadley v Baxendale* [1854] 9 Ex 314, mentioned above.

Specific Performance

In some jurisdictions and in limited circumstances, the plaintiff might also seek to recover the very performance promised, i.e., specific performance of the contract. This injunctive mechanism is another way of enforcing the plaintiff's expectation. As an "equitable" remedy, specific performance likely will not be available where monetary compensation would be adequate, where the remedy would be impractical or unenforceable, or where the defendant negates the remedy by asserting equitable defenses.

Proportionate Price Reduction

This remedy exists in certain jurisdictions and is not in fact a claim for damages. While it does not require that the breaching party have caused the loss by a negligent or intentional act or omission, it may have a similar effect as a claim for damages. The remedy is available if the injured party does not cancel the contract and provides that the agreed price payable by the injured party will be subject to a reduction. The reduction is proportionate to the reduction of the market value of the breaching party's performance due to the defect. A claim for proportionate price reduction and a claim for damages as positive performance interest may result in the same amount if the injured party cannot prove a consequential loss.

Vienna Sales Convention (CISG)

The 1980 United Nations Convention on the International Sale of Goods (CISG) has come into force in various countries addressed in this work. The CISG is a part of the national law of such countries and may be applicable to international sale of goods contracts between parties residing in different CISG Contracting States unless it is validly excluded in the contract. As stated previously, arguments regarding the intent to include or exclude the CISG should be undertaken with care, both in view of Articles 1, 10 and 95 of the CISG in particular and developing CISG case law in countries like Germany, the Netherlands and Switzerland. Damages, including grounds for damages, scope of damages, and burden of proof, are specifically regulated in the CISG and may supersede other national regulations.

ii. Specific Issues Related to Lost Profit Damages

In general, where liability for damages exists, it relates to "actual damages." Depending on the applicable law, loss of profit need be reimbursed only if the injurer caused the damage intentionally or with gross negligence or, regardless of the degree of fault, if the injurer is a merchant who caused damage during the course of business. The commercial code or equivalent of various jurisdictions will address such issues in addition to the civil code or equivalent and related caselaw.

Where lost profits are recoverable, the issue is basically whether such losses are an immediate and direct result of the breach of contract or tort. Thus profits which are uncertain or too distant in the future are usually denied. Where there are intervening events subsequent to the breach which aggravate the loss, the question will be one of causation. If the intervening event was not a direct result of the original breach, the additional losses caused by that event are not recoverable.

At the same time, entitlement to lost profit is by no means settled in various jurisdictions. The question is whether recovery of economic loss should be allowed only where the plaintiff suffered physical damage or injury or has relied on a negligent misrepresentation. The issue is occasionally resolved in favor of lost profit where there is a high degree of proximity between the plaintiff and the defendant. The trend generally appears to be to broaden rights of recovery under this category of damages.

The calculation of the anticipated profit, limiting the scope of the damaging fact, may be a complex and arduous task. The greatest difficulty in most cases lies in the absence of concrete data to determine with certainty which path would have been taken if the unlawful act had not occurred. Upon the examination of a concrete case, it is important to first investigate if the damaging fact has resulted from an act of God or force majeure and the other cases excluding liability for indemnity set forth in the law, such as the victim's sole guilt and self-defense.

iii. Damages Recovery in Tort, Product Liability and Other Non-Contractual Bases

From an international perspective, the compensation level for personal injuries in most civil-law systems is relatively low compared to most common-law jurisdictions. Indeed most countries generally provide for low damage awards when compared to the United States.

Apart from the concept of fault, caselaw and specific legislation establish liability even for actions or omissions without fault as well as for product liability situations. Furthermore, strict liability in tort may be applicable by statute, caselaw or both depending on the jurisdiction. In such areas, the requirement of "causation" may still apply, but the requirement of unlawful action or omission may be replaced by other, objective criteria.

Generally, the principal purpose of damages awards in tort cases, as in contract, is restitutionary—that is, to put the injured party in (or as close as possible to) the position it would have occupied had the wrongful act not occurred. The damages are restricted to those that are reasonably foreseeable when the tort takes place. Broadly speaking, there are three classifications of damages although the different actions often cut across these distinctions:

First, both pecuniary and nonpecuniary losses may be recoverable. Pecuniary losses are those that can easily be accorded a monetary sum—for example, loss of profit and damage to property. Nonpecuniary losses are those for which it is difficult to accord a monetary value because of their nature. "Pain and suffering" is one such category. Depending on the applicable law and the jurisdiction, nonpecuniary losses may or may not be recoverable at all or, even if so, to any significant extent.

Second, aggravated damages may also be available. These may be awarded, depending on the jurisdiction, where the conduct of the wrongdoer is humiliating or insulting. It is the injury to the plaintiff's feelings that is being compensated. The conduct of the plaintiff is relevant to the amount of aggravated damages that may be awarded. A provocative plaintiff may result in a reduction of the amount of aggravated damages received.

Third, exemplary or punitive damages are to be distinguished from the compensatory damages listed above. That is, exemplary damages are not an attempt to restore the position of the plaintiff, but rather represent the disapproval of the Court with the conduct of the defendant and thus are aimed at deterring similar conduct. Except in certain predetermined areas, exemplary damages are vary rarely awarded in any jurisdiction, including common law countries, other than the United States. The concept of "treble" damages is likewise essentially known only in the United States.

Furthermore, quite many areas of tort law are covered by mandatory insurance, such as traffic insurance and employee insurance systems. Therefore the need for any extra compensation may not exist. Contractual relations are more or less regulated by their own principles, thus limiting the tort law area and its applicability in some countries.

Unlike the common law where contributory negligence by a plaintiff may constitute a complete defense, even statutorily, civil law provides for apportionment of damages where both parties are at fault. The percentage responsibility resting on the plaintiff is determined by the court in giving judgment, and the award of damages is then reduced accordingly.

Particular Losses

Various categories of particular losses can be identified which may occur in transnational litigation as follows:

First, personal injury, covers three basic types: (i) physical pain and suffering and the loss of life expectancy; (ii) destruction or diminution of an existing mental, physical or economic capacity; and (iii) the creation of needs that would not have existed. There are limits to common law damages available in some circumstances by virtue of statute. Some examples of these statutes are workers compensation acts, motor accident acts, victim compensation acts, sporting injuries insurance legislation, etc., depending on the jurisdiction.

Second, reputation losses, are usually compensated via the tort of defamation. Aggravated damages, known as "special damages" in defamation, may be available to compensate for wounded feelings. Exemplary damages may also be available. Again, the law of the particular jurisdiction must be examined closely.

Third, product-liability losses arise from defective products and may be compensated through tortious and contractual remedies, through trade practices legislation, and by way of damages for negligence. Many countries have implemented product-liability legislation, including in the EU in accordance with the European Union Product Liability Directive. Legislation implementing the Directive provides for strict liability and covers compensation for damage caused by a product primarily intended for private use and consumption consisting either of personal injury or of damage to property. The product must have been in private use at the time of the damage. Product-liability cases do not play a predominant role in damage litigation, including measured in terms of damages awards, other than in the courts of the United States.

Fourth, economic loss may be compensated in tort despite the fact that no physical damage or loss has occurred. This is the area known as pure economic loss. Such pure economic loss can be suffered in a number of different ways: where there has been an intentional infliction of economic loss sometimes described as intentional torts, where the economic loss has been suffered as a result of negligence most commonly through the medium of negligent misstatements, and by the loss of services.

With regard to intentional torts, particularly as understood in common law jurisdictions, these may include deceit, conspiracy, injurious falsehood and interference with contractual relations. Deceit involves the making of false statements, whether knowingly or with reckless indifference to the truth of the statement. With conspiracy, the plaintiff must establish economic loss as the result of two or more people plotting to cause this loss. Injurious falsehood is the tort whereby the plaintiff proves that economic loss was suffered as the result of the defendant's publishing written or oral falsehoods with the intention of causing harm to the plaintiff's trade. Interference with contractual relations covers the situation where the plaintiff establishes lost profits or wasted expenditure due to the defendant's either inducing a breach of contract or doing something inconsistent with its due performance.

The most common form of economic loss caused by negligence is that resulting from negligent misstatement. An action may lie in negligence for damage caused by relying upon an honest but carelessly incorrect statement. The reliance on the statement must be reasonable and the relationship between the two parties must be sufficiently close in proximity to warrant special trust and reliance.

Loss of services can be recovered as damages where the plaintiff can prove that an injury has deprived it of the service of an employee or household member. The employer will generally be entitled to money spent on medical bills of the injured employee, as well as any sick leave that is paid over the time of absence.

iv. Standards of Burden of Proof for Recovery

Normally, the loss must be connected to the tortious act by "causation." The burden of proof lies with the plaintiff who must establish, on the balance of probabilities, the cause of the loss suffered by the plaintiff according to the principle of *onus probandi incumbit ei qui decit non qui negat.*

In this regard, the general rule with respect to burden of proof is the same for damage recovery in contract and in tort. The injured party must prove that it has suffered a loss, that the loss is caused by an act or omission including breach of contract, and that the causation of the loss was reasonably foreseeable. The injured party must also prove that a basis of liability exists, and that the conditions for such a basis are fulfilled. Normally, this will require proof of the fact that the loss is caused in a negligent or intentional way.

In some areas, liability in contract or tort is modified by changing the principal rule relating to burden of proof as a result of statute, judicial precedent or the interpretation of a disputed contract. For example, liability may be modified by increasing or diminishing requirements for proof of negligence, or by requiring proof of gross negligence, or by reversing the burden of proof in respect of negligence. Where strict liability applies, the injured party must prove the facts justifying strict liability, loss, causation, and reasonable foreseeability, but not negligence or intent.

In product-liability matters which are not subject to strict liability, the claimant may need to prove the product's defectiveness, damage and causation of the damage by the defectiveness. If in a liability case a specific cause for the damage fits into a general pattern of experience, the burden of proof that the damage in dispute was caused by something or somebody else may shift to the defendant (this burden-of-proof-rule is called "prima-facie proof").

Causation

Depending on the applicable law, there may be different "tests" of causation. A new intervening act (*novus actus interveniens*) may break the chain of causation. International public law cases have also ruled extensively on the absence of supervening events and the subject of "directness" of damages: *see, e.g., German-U.S. Mixed Claims Commission, Administrative Decision No. II* (1923), 2 ILR 199; *see also Samoan Claims Award* (1902), Joint Report No. 2 of 12 August 1904 of the American and the British Commissioners, quoted in 3 M. Whiteman, Damages in International Law 1779-80 (1943). The most commonly used test in damage claims is whether an act was the "proximate cause" of the loss suffered, or whether the act was too remote to create liability.

The principle of adequate causality or proximate cause is also expressed in Article 74 of the CISG. It provides that damages for breach of contract "may not exceed the loss which the party in breach foresaw or ought to have foreseen at the time of the conclusion of the contract, in the light of the facts and matters of which he then knew or ought to have known, as a possible consequence of the breach of contract."

Remoteness

The chain of consequences of an act will be limited by remoteness. The concept of remoteness involves some element of foreseeability and has a policy component. The precise application of the foreseeability element will depend on the tort and the kind of loss as well as of course the particular applicable law. The plaintiff must also establish a loss with sufficient certainty as to its existence and extent. The "likely" future consequences of the wrongful act need to be determined in light of the fact that purely speculative losses will not be recoverable.

Foreseeability

Foreseeability is firmly rooted in the international public law as well as the municipal law experience of common-law, civil-law and other countries alike. International jurisprudence on the subject of reasonable foreseeability includes *Norwegian Shipowners'* claims (1922), RIAA i. 307 at 388; *Lighthouses Arbitration (France v. Greece) (1956), Permanent Court of Arbitration, 23 ILR 299; Sapphire Petroleum Ltd. v. National Iranian Oil Company* (1963), 35 ILR 136, 186; and *Naulilaa* case (1928), RIAA ii. 1013.

Where the wrongdoer intended the consequences of its actions, international jurisprudence recognizes a right of reparation irrespective of whether the consequences are foreseeable. Bin Cheng, General Principles of International Law (1987) at 251; France: Article 1150 French Civil Code ("The debtor can only be liable for the damages which were foreseen or foreseeable at the time the contract was entered into, unless the contractual obligation was not performed due to his own fundamental act"); England: *Hadley v. Baxendale* (1854) 9 Exch. 341; Anson's Law of Contract, 25th (Centenary) Edition, A.G. Guest, Oxford (1982) at 555.

Mitigation

In virtually every jurisdiction, the concept of mitigation plays a role, meaning that the loss recovered may be reduced to the extent that it could have been minimized by actions of the plaintiff. It is normally for the defendant to establish that there has been a failure to mitigate. To minimize its loss, the injured party does not have to enter into a substitute transaction that involves undue risk or burden.

Legal Assumptions and Duties Regarding Third-Party Acts

Depending on the law, the caselaw or statutory law may simplify the linking of cause and effect in certain cases relating to liability for third party's acts. Such categories include parents' responsibility for acts of children in their custody, the guardian's responsibility for its charges (the deaf and mute, the blind who cannot express their will, among others), the employer's (individuals or legal entities) liability for its employees' acts in the exercise of their functions as employees, the hotelier's liability for its guests, etc. Damage recovery caused by animals will be attributed to their owners or possessors. Presumptions, such as the principle *res ipsa loquitur*, may apply depending on the circumstances.

v. Public Policy Constraints on Damage Recovery

For reasons of public policy, certain damages will not be recoverable depending on the applicable law. Thus, for example, where a plaintiff is claiming that part of his loss are monies that were gained illegally, that part of the loss will not be recoverable. However, where loss from illegal activities is argued, the nature and extent of the illegality will be relevant—the more minor offenses are unlikely to raise such public policy objections.

Punitive and Exemplary Damages

Public policy may or may not be a restraint in terms of exemplary damages. The purpose of punitive or exemplary damages is to punish the defendant for conscious wrongdoing in disregard of another's rights. Depending on the jurisdiction, malice on the part of the defendant is not required for the plaintiff to receive exemplary damages. However, all the circumstances of the case will be looked at before exemplary damages will be awarded, including the defendant's financial position. Also, there may be a policy not to impose a greater penalty than would have been imposed under a criminal penalty.

Generally, if there has been reciprocity, or even mitigating circumstances, exemplary damages will not be awarded. Recently, the Supreme Court of Canada held that punitive damages should be awarded only in those circumstances where "the combined award of general and aggravated damages would be insufficient to achieve the goal of punishment and deterrence": *Hill v. Church of Scientology*, [1995] 2 S.C.R. 1130.

In fact, almost all jurisdictions decline to recognize an indemnity intended to punish the defendant for its outrageous conduct, setting an example for similar wrongdoers. Civil liability aims instead to reinstate the condition of the victim prior to suffering the damage, reimbursing it for material and/or moral losses, as well as for what the victim failed to gain as a result of the damaging fact. Most systems of compensation are more concerned with the restoration of the victim's *status quo ante* than with the punishment of the wrongdoer.

Punitive Damages in the United States

The principal jurisdiction in which the municipal courts adjudicate and award punitive or exemplary damages is the United States, which in fact is not a party to any multilateral convention facilitating the mutual recognition and enforcement of foreign civil judgments. The U.S. Supreme Court has recently begun to apply federal constitutional constraints of due process to punitive damage awards. In *BMW of North America, Inc. v. Gore*, 116 S. Ct. 1589 (1996), the U.S. Supreme Court for the first time struck down a state punitive damage award as violating the Due Process Clause of the Fourteenth Amendment of the U.S. Constitution because the award was "grossly excessive." The Court has also suggested that punitive damage awards may be unconstitutional if they are not issued in conjunction with guarantees of fairness (e.g., specified jury instructions and review by trial and appellate courts in light of specified factors): *Pacific Mutual Life Insurance Co. v. Haslip*, 499 U.S. 1 (1991); *Honda v. Oberg*, 512 U.S. 415 (1994).

Depending on the foreign jurisdiction, there may or may not be caselaw holding that a U.S. judgment, or at least that portion of such judgment which orders the payment of punitive or exemplary damages, may not be recognized or enforced in the foreign jurisdiction on the grounds of public policy.

Depending on the country, public policy constraints (ordre public) apply not only as a result of local rules of private international law, but also as stated in Article 16 of the Rome Convention on the Law Applicable to Contractual Obligations and Article 27 no. 1 and Article 34 of the Brussels and Lugano Conventions. Thus most courts will refuse the application of a certain rule of the law of another country if such application is manifestly incompatible with local public policy. Accordingly, they will not recognize or enforce a foreign judgment if such recognition is contrary to local public policy.

The test is normally not whether a foreign rule or judgment is contrary to mandatory local provisions, but whether in a specific case it will lead to a result contrary to fundamental principles of local law. Punitive or exemplary damages, awarded in excess of the economic loss and certain kinds of noneconomic loss, are held to violate most countries' public policy regarding compensatory damages. Thus such a stance will not necessarily prevent a court from agreeing to facilitate Hague Service Convention service, locally against its own citizens, of U.S. civil complaints seeking punitive damages. Yet it will prevent the same court from agreeing to enforce locally the U.S. judgment based on that complaint which later actually awards such damages.

Aggravated and Moral Damages

Punitive or exemplary damages as they are available in the United States should not be confused with "aggravated damages." In theory, aggravated damages link the actual harm suffered by the plaintiff with the characteristics of the defendant's conduct. If that conduct was high-handed or oppressive so as to increase the injury to the plaintiff, aggravated damages may be awarded, for example in Canada.

Nor should punitive or exemplary damages be confused with "moral damages" which may be available in some jurisdictions and which relate to the perceived injury to the individual's intimacy, private life, honor and image as a result of intentional misconduct or omission, negligence or rashness. In the absence of a specific law stipulating the quantum for moral damages, courts will determine such amount taking into account each case's specific circumstances.

Indemnification for moral damages may consider the intensity of the victim's suffering, the seriousness, nature and repercussion of the damaging fact, and the victim's social and political status. It may also consider the intensity of the wrongdoer's malice or degree of fault, his economic status, and existence of previous condemnation in criminal or civil suits grounded on abuse of the exercise of freedom of thought and speech.

vi. Currency Conversion

Under the "breach date conversion" rule often encountered in common law, damages are awarded in local currency and then converted to the foreign currency. The exchange rate to be applied to a loss under this rule is the rate at the time when the loss occurred or the money was owing. This has also been the consistent trend, for example, at the Iran-U.S. Claims Tribunal: *see*, e.g., *American International Group, Inc. v. Iran*, 4 Iran-U.S. C.T.R. 96-104; *Starret Housing Corp. v. Iran*, 16 Iran-U.S. C.T.R. 223. This would mean that in the case of losses which transpired or continued over an extended period of time, the exchange rate for the respective year of loss should be applied, and that the rate for each successive year may change.

In recent years in common-law jurisdictions, this rule has been abandoned in favor of rendering judgments, where applicable, in a foreign currency. Thus, where a loss was sustained in a foreign currency as a result of a tort, the plaintiff would be entitled to an award in the currency which it was reasonably foreseeable he would need to use to remedy the damage. Thus the judgment ought to be in the currency that best expresses the plaintiff's loss, whether in the context of an action for damages for breach of contract or in tort. This more flexible approach is based on the principle that the creditor should be preferred to the debtor (*favor creditoris*), provided that he has exercised due diligence and was not negligent.

Depending on the jurisdiction, this approach may or may not be followed. In some countries, damage claims are always adjudicated by the local courts in the local currency. While contractual obligations for payment in foreign currency may be valid (and actionable) in such countries, the debtor may be ordered to pay in the local currency if the place of payment is in that jurisdiction. In case the creditor is not resident in the local jurisdiction, the conversion of indemnification into foreign currency and its remittance abroad may need to follow the rules of a central bank institution.

CHAPTER 17

RECOGNITION AND ENFORCEMENT OF FOREIGN CIVIL-COMMERCIAL JUDGMENTS

Invariably, enforcement of foreign judgments and acts requires prior declaration of enforceability, also known as leave to issue execution, pursuant to local statute. Such declaration or leave must be sought for foreign judgments in civil and commercial matters, and may include decrees, orders, decisions or writs of execution or the determination of court fees or expenses. The prerequisite, among others, is that under the laws of the originating country they are enforceable and mutual enforcement is guaranteed by multilateral convention, bilateral treaty, a declaration of reciprocity or at common law where applicable.

The subject of inter-state or inter-province enforcement of judgments between and among states or provinces within a single country such as the United States, Canada or Australia, and the extent to which such judgments are entitled to "full faith and credit," exceeds the scope of this general discussion.

i. Conventions

It should be noted that certain countries, such as the United States, are not party to any relevant multilateral convention or treaty meant to facilitate the mutual recognition and enforcement of foreign country money judgments. With regard to such countries, where applicable, the practitioner must pay close attention to bilateral treaties, vehicles at common law and other methods, as also described in **subheading ii.** of this Section below.

Applicability of Brussels and Lugano Conventions

The Brussels and Lugano Conventions and, to a limited extent, the 1954 Hague Convention on Civil Procedure (discussed below) contain provisions on matters of jurisdiction, procedure, and recognition and enforcement which are relevant to Contracting States. Under the Luxembourg Protocol of June 3, 1971, the Member States of the European Union (then: Communities) conferred jurisdiction upon the European Court of Justice to interpret the Brussels Convention.

The Contracting States agreed that when applying and interpreting provisions of the Convention, their courts shall have regard to the principles laid down by any relevant decision delivered by other national courts or the Court of Justice of the European Union. Thereby, the uniform interpretation of both Conventions is secured. The European Court of Justice has rendered some 80 judgments which impact on the interpretation and understanding of both Conventions, including with respect to mutual recognition and enforcement.

For certain recently acceded Member States of the European Union, such as Austria and Finland, the Brussels and Lugano Conventions may not yet apply equally to a variety of issues including mutual recognition and enforcement, and the Lugano Convention may be the sole basis for such matters.

In countries which have ratified only the Lugano Convention, only the Lugano Convention is applicable. If a Member State of the European Union (EU) has ratified both Conventions, the general rule is that between the countries which have ratified the Brussels Convention (original members of the Union) only the Brussels Convention is applicable. As far as those countries' relationship to Lugano Convention Member States is concerned, only the latter Convention is applicable when the latter country has ratified only the Lugano Convention. The Brussels Convention also applies if the defendant's domicile is in a country which has not ratified either Convention.

The Lugano Convention applies where a judgment delivered in a EU Member State is to be enforced in an EFTA State. Furthermore, if a judgment has been delivered in a Member State of the EFTA which is a party to the Lugano Convention and is to be enforced in a Member State of the EU or EFTA, the Lugano Convention applies rather than the Brussels Convention. Once such countries as Austria and Finland have ratified the Brussels Convention, the Lugano Convention will be relevant only for local recognition and enforcement of civil and commercial decisions of courts in such EFTA States as Switzerland, Norway and Iceland and vice versa.

Scope of Brussels and Lugano Conventions

The scope of the Brussels and Lugano Conventions does not differ. Both apply to the enforcement of decisions in civil, commercial and labor (contracts of employment) matters, including authentic instruments, court settlements, decrees, orders, decisions or writs of execution, and the determination of court fees or expenses. Enforcement of criminal or administrative court decisions on civil claims is also covered by the Conventions. The Conventions are to be applied when enforcement of a decision of one State is sought in another State.

Neither Convention applies to the enforcement of judgments on status or legal capacity of natural persons or rights in property arising out of a matrimonial relationship, wills and successions, bankruptcy, proceedings relating to the winding up of insolvent companies or other legal entities, judicial arrangements, compositions and analogous proceedings, social welfare proceedings, or generally arbitration. With regard to arbitration in particular, the interplay with the Brussels and Lugano Conventions is, depending on the circumstances, a complex issue which exceeds the scope of this work. (All signatory States, except Iceland and Portugal, are Contracting States to the 1958 United Nations ("New York") Convention on the Recognition and Enforcement of Foreign Arbitral Awards.)

1954 Hague Convention

Outside the scope of the Brussels and Lugano Conventions, the 1954 Hague Convention provides for the recognition and enforcement of decisions solely on the reimbursement of court fees to the defendant of a litigation which was lost by the plaintiff. This is of interest in relation to countries with which no bilateral enforcement treaties exist. Thus at least court cost decisions against the plaintiff who has lost in the proceedings can be enforced reciprocally on this basis.

A plaintiff domiciled in one of the territories of the Contracting States of the 1954 Hague Convention on Civil Procedure cannot be obliged to deposit security for litigation costs. Therefore, a judgment which orders such a plaintiff to reimburse litigation costs to the defendant is to be deemed enforceable in any of the Contracting States free of charge. For this purpose, court fees do not comprise enforcement costs (e.g., if enforcement was unsuccessful in the country of the decision on costs). These provisions of the 1954 Hague Convention apply only to decisions of countries which have not adopted the Brussels or Lugano Convention.

Other Multilateral Conventions

In special areas related to, e.g., international transportation, multilateral conventions which contain provisions on jurisdiction and enforcement may be relevant. With regard to recognition and enforcement of judgments based on these conventions, enforcement is granted on the basis of reciprocity between the enforcing State and the respective State of origin of the decision.

Among the relevant conventions might be included the Interamerican Convention on Extraterritorial Efficacy of Foreign Judgments and Arbitral Awards, signed in Montevideo on May 8, 1979, which upon enactment will apply, among other countries, to Brazil. Within the scope of the Mercosur (South Common Market) regional agreement, the Protocol of Judicial Cooperation and Assistance in Civil, Commercial, Labor and Administrative Matters was completed in 1992. The 1977 Convention between the Nordic States (Denmark, Finland, Iceland, Norway and Sweden) on the recognition and enforcement of judgments on private law claims has been implemented by practically uniform statutes in each of the countries. Upon the Lugano Convention shortly coming into force in Denmark, it will to a large extent replace the Nordic Convention in relation to Finland, Norway and Sweden, which are so far not parties to the Brussels Convention.

The 1969 International Convention on Civil Liability for Damage Incurred through Oil Pollution provides for recognition and enforcement of judgments concerning claims for compensation of damage incurred through oil pollution. The 1952 Rome Convention on Surface Damage Incurred by Foreign Aircraft to Third Parties allows for enforcement of judgments concerning compensation of such damage. Recognition and enforcement of foreign judgments in respect of disputes involving international carriage is regulated in a number of multilateral and bilateral agreements for goods and passengers. The 1956 Geneva Convention On Contracts for the International Carriage of Goods by Road stipulates that judgments in respect of mutual disputes concerning road carriage addressed in the Convention are subject to mutual enforcement in the Contracting States.

For bankruptcy matters, the Nordic Bankruptcy Convention between Finland, Denmark, Iceland, Norway and Sweden on Bankruptcy Proceedings is meant to ensure that property located in any of the Nordic countries belongs to the bankruptcy estate if proceedings are brought in a court of a Nordic country. It is not superseded by the Brussels and Lugano Conventions, which do not apply to bankruptcy proceedings.

ii. Other Means and Absence of Convention

Foreign civil and commercial judgments not originating from courts or tribunals of Contracting States to the Lugano or Brussels Convention, or any other applicable multilateral convention, are subject to recognition and enforcement abroad either under the terms of bilateral enforcement treaties or, where applicable, at common law or in equity.

Bilateral Enforcement Treaties

Certain of the Brussels/Lugano Contracting States have concluded bilateral treaties on the recognition and enforcement of decisions with other Contracting States which have in turn notified of the extension of such treaties to their overseas territories (e.g., Aruba (NL), until recently Hong Kong (GB), etc.) As the scope of the Brussels and Lugano Conventions does not extend to overseas countries of Contracting States, those bilateral treaties govern and may be useful as to such territories.

Such bilateral treaties normally provide that multilateral conventions prevail in corresponding matters, e.g., in the case of applicability of the Brussels/Lugano Conventions. At the same time, such bilateral arrangements may still be important, if not critical, in the case of noncontracting States or overseas countries of Contracting States to the Conventions. In a given case, the scope of application differs in the bilateral treaty from the relevant Convention. Such bilateral arrangements may also be relevant to the enforcement of judgments, authentic instruments, or court settlements prior to the Convention's entering into force between the State of origin and the enforcing State.

Bilateral treaties, sometimes known as friendship and navigation treaties particularly in the context of the United States, obviously differ somewhat one from another. At the same time, in the context of mutual recognition and enforcement of foreign judgments, they usually provide that decisions rendered in contentious and noncontentious proceedings as well as decisions by criminal courts adjudicating pecuniary claims on the basis of the accused's liability are within the scope of the treaties. With regard to the applicability to interim measures and injunctions, see **Chapter 9** above. As a general rule, enforcement is granted if the deciding court was competent according to the rules of jurisdiction stated in the applicable bilateral treaty, sometimes known as indirect competence or *compétence indirecte*. By contrast, the Brussels and Lugano Conventions set up a uniform system of direct competence which means that the enforcement of a foreign decision regarding the competence of the deciding court may not be reviewed.

Grounds for Opposing Enforcement Under Bilateral Treaties

Such grounds will obviously differ depending on the particular treaty. For present purposes, certain general remarks may be made as an overall orientation.

The public-policy reservation is invariably a principal ground for opposing or denying recognition and enforcement, whether upon motion of the judgment debtor, sua sponte by the enforcing court, or both. Normally, the State requested to enforce a judgment may examine a decision only to the extent of denying recognition or enforcement to judgments, or portions thereof, which are in drastic or egregious contradiction to the established national law and its fundamental values. This examination may not extend to a complete revision of the decision, or *revision au fond*.

It should also be noted that the distinction between domestic public policy and international public policy which is sometimes encountered in the area of recognition and enforcement of foreign arbitral awards, and challenge of such awards at the place of arbitration, does not play quite the same role in transnational litigation. Suffice it to say that in international arbitration a foreign award may be granted enforcement even if it is deemed to violate domestic public policy of the place of enforcement but not deemed to infringe that country's concept of "international public policy," to the extent they are deemed different.

This may also lead, in international arbitration, to the situation where a court at the place of enforcement will reject a petition to set aside an award rendered there on the grounds that it was an "international" arbitration and the award does not offend that country's concept of "international public policy," even if it offends domestic public policy. These distinctions, which in recent years have played an important role in such favored locales of arbitration as France and Switzerland, do not normally figure in the same way in transnational litigation, whether or not a convention basis for enforcement is raised.

With regard to the so-called *exceptio incompetentiae internationalis*, some bilateral treaties give the option to challenge the jurisdiction of a court if jurisdiction is based solely on property abroad. If a defendant objects in time to the jurisdiction of the deciding court (i.e., when making its first appearance) and submits to enforcement only in relation to assets (property) in the State of the deciding court, a decision may not be enforced in the other State, depending on the bilateral agreement.

With regard to indirect jurisdiction (*compétence indirecte*), certain bilateral treaties contain provisions on rules of jurisdiction which have no influence on the national rules of jurisdiction. If a decision is based on a national jurisdictional rule not contained in the enforcement treaty, then the other State may refuse to enforce the decision. As opposed to *exceptio incompetentiae internationalis*, submission or nonobjection during litigation has no influence on indirect jurisdiction, and the competence of the court of decision may be subject to review in the subsequent enforcement procedure in a foreign State.

The provisions on default judgments in bilateral treaties normally do not differ from the Brussels/Lugano Convention. Thus, they provide that judgments on default of appearance will be recognized if the defendant was duly served with the document which instituted the proceedings, leaving sufficient time to arrange for its defense. On a similar basis with regard to judicial payment orders, it must be proven that it is enforceable and has been properly served. The grounds for refusal of recognition are based on the same principles as in the multilateral Conventions.

The practitioner relying on a bilateral treaty for foreign recognition or enforcement must in any event carefully study the treaty bases for any unusual exclusions or other provisions. Such exclusions might include, e.g., that (i) recognition proceedings be commenced within a specific period of time after the rendering of the judgment, (ii) recognition and enforcement is rendered solely on decisions on payment of higher courts, (iii) no interim injunctions or conservatory measures are recognized except as they may relate to litigation costs, (iv) only decisions on pecuniary claims are recognized, and (v) generally that recognition and enforcement is granted with the limitation of indirect competence or of *exceptio incompetentiae internationalis*.

The Dilemma of Absence of Convention, Treaty and Reciprocity

A decision rendered in a third country with which the country of desired enforcement may have no reciprocity, but which was declared enforceable in a Brussels/Lugano Convention State, may normally not be enforced on the basis of such declaration or execution order. The reason is that such an execution order is not considered to be a decision within the meaning of Article 25 of the Brussels/Lugano Conventions, and the same result may ensue from any otherwise applicable bilateral treaty. A decision rendered in a third country without reciprocity can therefore not be made enforceable through the "back door."

This may be of particular relevance to certain countries within the European Union, such as notably Austria and Denmark, in their position on enforceability at home of judgments issued in the United States. Thus the judgment creditor seeking to enforce a U.S. judgment against assets in such a country as Austria might first seek recognition of the U.S. judgment under the Brussels/Lugano Conventions in a third country such as Germany, assuming it could obtain jurisdiction, and then seek enforcement in Austria of that German judgment.

However, recognition and execution in Austria of a German execution order of a U.S. judgment, including one entered into in default, is not provided for by any bilateral or multilateral treaties to which Germany and Austria are both parties. Therefore, the judgment creditor could not enforce any such U.S. judgment against an Austrian judgment debtor in Austria directly or via a German execution order. The German execution order of the U.S. judgment would not be recognized in Austria, as the bilateral treaty between Germany and Austria requires that the foreign judgment be preceded by a formal hearing on disputed claims, whereas the recognition and execution of the U.S. judgment in Germany is a summary proceeding and does not consider substantive law issues. Therefore, the German execution order would not fulfill the definition of "decision" in the bilateral treaty. Furthermore, in this case recognition in Austria may be denied if the debtor had not answered to the German complaint and the jurisdiction of the German court was based merely on the presence of property or assets (*Vermögensgerichtsstand*). Ultimately, the attempt to circumvent Austrian law on recognition and enforcement of foreign judgments would not only be fruitless, but would also constitute an abuse of law.

Another alternative for the creditor so as to produce a judgment in, e.g., Germany that would be recognizable and enforceable in Austria would be to file an independent German action for a declaratory judgment. The declaration would be of recognition of the U.S. judgment (enforceable through the Brussels Convention, but not through the bilateral treaty). To this end, jurisdiction would have to be established on the basis of personal property of the defendant in Germany. Depending on the caselaw and the facts, the assets which the defendant might have in Germany might not be sufficient to establish jurisdiction. The prior U.S. judgment may, of course, be submitted in evidence during the new proceedings, but the case is in principle open for trial on all issues. Caselaw in Contracting States is unclear or contradictory with respect to the importance to be attached to the foreign proceedings, but mostly relates to questions of evidence.

Nonconvention Judgments and Evidence

Even where there is no automatic bar to the recognition and enforcement of a foreign judgment outside of the scope of multilateral and bilateral arrangements, from a practical standpoint such efforts will need to overcome a sobering evidentiary hurdle. That is to say, such nonconvention judgments may not carry significant weight as evidence in proceedings before certain enforcing courts. Thus, depending on the identity of the court of desired enforcement, such previously discussed principles as that of immediacy (and, if the opposing party did not participate in the proceedings which led to such nonconvention foreign judgment, that of right of audience) may play a particular role.

The practical consequence in such cases, depending on the country, may be highly unfavorable to the judgment creditor who assumed that foreign enforcement would be a mere formality. The enforcing court may require that evidence be taken before it or, in instances of judicial assistance, in accordance with its requests and under its direction. Documentary evidence used or even produced by prior proceedings in the foreign country with which there is no reciprocity may be susceptible of full representation in the enforcement proceedings and, where applicable, be subject to the free evaluation of evidence by the judge.

Moreover, the judgment rendered in such foreign proceeding will not be more than of illustrative value. Indeed some countries will go so far as not even to make the foreign judgment a part of the record of the enforcement proceedings, notwithstanding the objection of one or the other party, on the grounds that only "factual" evidence should be entered into the court file. The case may be different if the foreign judgment elaborates on questions of the foreign law which the enforcing court considers to be applicable. However, even in such case, the foreign judgment will not carry the same weight as the enforcing court's own conclusions regarding the application of that foreign law, usually on the basis of opinions obtained from the local judicial authorities.

Enforcement at Common Law

If there is no convention or legislative basis for enforcement, regard may also be had to the common law, where applicable. In such cases, where it is not possible to directly enforce the foreign judgment by levying execution upon it, the foreign judgment may be treated as creating a debt upon which substantive breach of contract proceedings may be commenced for failure to pay the debt. Enforcement at common law may apply, e.g., to enforcement in England and Wales of judgments from, inter alia, the United States, Japan and the countries of the former Soviet Union.

Where applicable, the requirements at common law overlap substantially, but not completely, with those typically encountered in statutes. Thus, the foreign court must have had jurisdiction in the international sense: (i) residence in the foreign country when the proceedings were commenced, (ii) submission to the jurisdiction of the foreign court, or (iii) agreement to submit to the foreign jurisdiction. Such submission will not necessarily be deemed to have arisen by virtue of the entering of an appearance or participation in proceedings only for the purpose of protecting or obtaining the release of property, contesting jurisdiction or inviting the court not to exercise jurisdiction. Additionally, the foreign judgment must be final and conclusive and not subject to abrogation or variation.

If the foreign court lacked jurisdiction over the defendant under its own rules, the judgment may not be conclusive in the foreign country of desired enforcement. In this regard, conflicts of law principles distinguish between complete lack of jurisdiction and a mistake as to the procedure or law in the exercise of jurisdiction. Thus improper service of process by the foreign court relates to the procedure of the court and may not prevent foreign enforcement for lack of finality. Indeed even where the foreign court as a matter of foreign law lacked jurisdiction, unless this is obvious on the face of the judgment the party opposing enforcement on this ground under the law of that court may need to first seek the vacatur of the judgment in the country in which it was made. This follows from the principle that the enforcing forum is not competent to decide whether the foreign court of judgment has properly applied its own law.

Even if the foregoing requirements are met at common law, recognition of the foreign judgment may be attacked on such grounds as the foreign judgment was obtained by fraud, there has been a denial of natural justice in the foreign litigation (overlapping with the public policy exception discussed in **subheading v.** of this Section below), other public policy reasons, and the foreign judgment is penal or involves the enforcement of a revenue debt. Finally, the party seeking recognition may be estopped by reason of a prior contrary judgment in the forum.

Aside from these defenses, the foreign judgment will be regarded as conclusive on its merits and not be open to re-examination locally. Thus to oppose the foreign judgment on the basis that the foreign litigation included practices not allowed under the law of desired enforcement, the judgment debtor must show that the practices amounted to a denial of natural justice or an affront to local public policy. A practice such as extensive pretrial discovery is unlikely to deny natural justice, but the adjudication of the foreign dispute by a person with a pecuniary interest in the outcome would have this result.

Enforcement in Equity

A common-law requirement is that the judgment be for a fixed sum of money. This requirement may not apply to enforcement of the judgment in equity, where available. Equitable remedies originating in foreign courts may therefore be enforced in equity. Certain judgments which require or enjoin the doing of some act have a territorial limitation, and cannot be relied upon to compel the defendant to do, or enjoin him from doing, that act outside of such jurisdictional reach. This may mean that to extraterritorially apply an order to the defendant's conduct or the defendant's assets by means of enforcement in equity, a decree of the foreign court must be obtained.

While orders for common law damages may be enforced by the court making the order only within its own territorial jurisdiction, the obligation to pay is often not restricted to that territory. However, equitable remedies such as restraining orders and orders affecting property may be limited in scope and therefore not be enforceable as to the activity of the judgment debtor in another jurisdiction. Indeed in some cases enforcement of a foreign judgment regulating activities in the enforcing state would be an impermissible impairment of activities conducted in that state or an interference with interests protected by it.

Homologation and Enforcement

Certain countries recognize and enforce foreign judgments pursuant to a procedure known as "homologation." A foreign judgment will be recognized only after homologation is granted by whichever court, e.g., in the case of Brazil the Federal Supreme Court, as provided by the Constitutional provision, has primary and exclusive jurisdiction over such matters. In such system, the foreign judgment's main or accessory effects will be acknowledged by the legal system at the place of enforcement only after such homologation.

This procedure does not transform the foreign judgment into a local one, but does make it enforceable in the local jurisdiction as if it were a local judgment. Such rule may apply to any and all judgments, whether condemnatory, constitutive or declaratory, and to provisional remedies and injunctions as well as to judicial decisions by nonjudicial authorities. The homologation procedure may not apply to decisions declaring the unconstitutionality of rules pertaining to a foreign legal system and judgments by which one intends to prove locally a mere fact, such as the existence of the foreign judgment or the appearance of an individual at trial. Enforcement of the "homologated" judgment is not automatic. If not voluntarily complied with by the judgment debtor, an enforcement proceeding must be commenced.

The homologating court analyzes only conformance to certain extrinsic (formal) requirements and the minimum intrinsic (substantial) requirements, namely the lack of offense of public policy, national sovereignty and social mores. It does not re-adjudicate the foreign claim or confirm the judgment announced in the foreign State. Nor does it carry out a *revision au fond* when the judgment has been rendered in default.

While the homologating court does not require that the foreign judge have applied the law indicated by the conflicts of law rules of the homologating court, homologation will normally be denied if the case falls under the exclusive jurisdiction of the homologating court. If jurisdiction is concurrent, the jurisdiction requirement will be considered as fulfilled if the defendant made an appearance and a full defense in the foreign action. On the other hand, a judgment by default may have been rendered against the defendant domiciled at the place of desired homologation (even if the service of process was valid) or the defendant appeared before the foreign court with the sole purpose of challenging foreign jurisdiction. In such cases, recognition will be granted only if the defendant was obliged by a valid agreement to accept the foreign forum.

iii. Local Procedural Requirements at Place of Action

Brussels/Lugano Convention Bases

Enforceability of judgments rendered in another Contracting State of the Brussels/Lugano Conventions is based on the prerequisites set forth in Article 31 et seq. These include (i) enforceability of the judgment in the country where it was rendered, (ii) proper service of the judgment upon the defendant in accordance with the laws of the country where the judgment was rendered, and (iii) presentation of the necessary documents as provided in Articles 46 and 47. Those necessary documents include an authentic copy of the judgment, proof of proper service of the judgment (in case of default judgments, also of the document initiating the proceeding), and a document demonstrating that the judgment is enforceable in the country where it was rendered.

Nonconvention Bases

In the case of countries which are not parties to any relevant treaties or conventions, recognition (sometimes called registration or confirmation) and enforcement normally take place pursuant to statute. Such legislation normally does not require the commencement of substantive proceedings at the place of desired enforcement. It may permit, in certain cases, direct enforcement of the foreign judgment by its recognition or registration in that jurisdiction.

Normally, such statutes apply to foreign money and nonmoney judgments of certain "types" or given by certain foreign courts as specified in the legislation. This may or may not include foreign interlocutory orders or foreign nonmoney judgments ordering specific performance, Anton Piller injunctions, etc. depending on the jurisdiction. To be susceptible of recognition and enforcement, a foreign judgment must generally be final and conclusive. Default judgments and judgments pending an appeal may nonetheless be final depending on the applicable law and the circumstances.

Reflecting the interests and aspirations of international comity, statutes regulating recognition and enforcement of foreign judgments normally require the enforcing court to recognize and enforce unless the requirements for so doing are not met. Depending on the law and the statute, the grounds for denying enforcement of a foreign judgment must normally be raised either by the judgment debtor or, as to certain grounds such as violation of local public policy even if not raised by the judgment debtor, sua sponte by the local court.

Convention Grounds for Opposing Recognition and Enforcement

The Brussels/Lugano Contracting States generally require a specific declaration of enforceability or leave to issue execution with regard to foreign acts and instruments, including judgments and settlements. Such declaration is granted by the enforcing court and binding for all other courts in that jurisdiction. In Contracting States, this system may extend to enforcement of all foreign judgments, regardless of whether rendered in one of the Contracting States of the Brussels or Lugano Convention or whether recognition and enforcement is granted according to treaties.

The party applying for enforcement must submit documentary evidence establishing that the judgment is enforceable and has been properly served. Normally, this means an original copy of the judgment and documents establishing its authenticity along with a certified translation where needed.

As a rule, a foreign decision must be enforceable (not necessarily final) under the law of the originating State. Reciprocity of enforcement with the State of origin may or may not be a condition of enforceability depending on the jurisdiction. Such prerequisites for domestic enforcement are normally examined only once, in the proceedings leading to the declaration of enforceability, which will be valid as to any subsequent execution in the same jurisdiction. The enforcement itself is then governed by the domestic law at the place of desired enforcement.

If a judgment debtor has no domicile in the country of enforcement, the court where the enforcement measures are to take place is normally competent, e.g., based on the presence of assets against which enforcement is sought. This might also be the court where a third-party debtor is domiciled or has his usual residence or where assets, in particular pledged assets, are situated. Under Article 33 of the Brussels and Lugano Conventions, the applicant not domiciled in the Contracting State where enforcement is sought must appoint a representative for the service of process (merely providing an address for service of process may not be recognized under local law). Authorizing a local attorney should normally satisfy this requirement.

Grounds for appeal against the enforcement of foreign judgments provided in Article 27 of the Brussels/Lugano Convention include (i) contrariness to public policy; (ii) default judgment with improper service of the document instituting the proceedings or not leaving sufficient time to arrange for defense; (iii) the judgment is irreconcilable with a local judgment between the same parties; (iv) specific conflict of laws; and (v) the judgment is irreconcilable with an earlier judgment rendered in a noncontracting state to be recognized in the enforcement state. Under Article 28, grounds may also be raised related to infringement of specific and exclusive jurisdictional rules.

In Brussels/Lugano Convention States, there may be other or different grounds which can be raised in enforcement proceedings outside the Conventions and subordinate to bilateral enforcement treaties which may apply. Such grounds may include (i) lack of jurisdiction of the foreign court of decision by local standards; (ii) improper service (strict personal service not proved) of the document instituting the proceedings unless the defendant made an appearance; (iii) the decision is not final; (iv) irregularity of the proceedings, infringing the defendant's right to defend; and (v) unenforceability of the claim by local standards (reservation on public policy issues).

Nonconvention Grounds for Opposing Recognition and Enforcement

In enforcement situations outside of the scope of any convention or bilateral agreement, the grounds for opposing the recognition and enforcement of foreign country judgments will depend on local statute and caselaw, but certain common threads emerge across borders.

First, it may be possible to oppose on the grounds that the foreign Court had no jurisdiction. Depending on the law, jurisdiction in this context does not normally or necessarily refer to the asserted jurisdiction of the foreign court under its own rules, but rather under the rules of the jurisdiction of desired recognition or enforcement. While such rules may be similar, if not almost identical, depending on the jurisdictions at issue, of course even "related" jurisdictions will differ in some respects as to the one or the other ground for asserting jurisdiction. This is due to divergent statutory or caselaw bases. *See* generally the discussion in **Chapter 3** above.

The fact that even a Contracting State asked to enforce a noncontracting State judgment may review the foreign court's competence is of course a major difference to enforcement proceedings wholly under the Brussels/Lugano Convention, where this is explicitly prohibited under Article 28(3). In cases wholly within the Convention, the Convention itself defines in which cases a court may assume jurisdiction. Provided the foreign court properly applies the Convention, a defendant is sufficiently protected and there is no need for the enforcing court to review the issuing court's competence.

Where the issuing court is not a member of the Convention, however, jurisdiction is solely defined by foreign domestic law. That law may grant jurisdiction to its courts in an overly broad, if not excessive manner, against which the enforcing court may wish to protect the defendant. An example for the practitioner to bear in mind in this context are U.S. "long-arm" statutes used to exercise jurisdiction over foreign defendants and which serve as the basis for judgments which are then sought to be enforced in a Brussels/Lugano Contracting State against that foreign defendant.

Generally, jurisdiction will be proper where the defendant in the foreign proceedings resided in the foreign jurisdiction, submitted or agreed to submit to the jurisdiction (other than by entering a "limited" appearance, or participating in proceedings only to such an extent as was necessary to protect property threatened with seizure or a restraining order) or counterclaimed in the foreign proceedings.

Depending on the jurisdiction, the court of judgment may be deemed to have had no jurisdiction where the subject matter of the proceedings is immovable property situated outside the foreign jurisdiction. Therefore, if the proceedings in the foreign country were contrary to an agreement under which the dispute in question was to be settled, rather than by proceedings in the courts of that foreign country, unless the defendant had submitted or agreed to submit to the jurisdiction or was a plaintiff or counter-claimed, the foreign court may not have properly exercised jurisdiction. This may be the case even where the defendant is resident in the foreign country where the judgment was rendered.

Among other grounds for opposing or denying jurisdiction as exerted by the foreign court are that the judgment was obtained by fraud or that the defendant in the foreign proceedings did not receive notice in sufficient time to enable it to defend, whether or not process had been duly served on the defendant in accordance with the law of the country of the foreign court.

Additionally, the enforcing court may determine that the rights under the foreign judgment are not vested in the person seeking to enforce the judgment, that the judgment has been reversed on appeal or was set aside, that the judgment has been discharged or wholly satisfied, or that prior to the date of the foreign judgment another court having jurisdiction had reached a decision on the matter that was final and conclusive. Finally, it may be found that enforcement of the foreign judgment is contrary to public policy at the place of enforcement. With regard to public policy, see **subheading v.** of this Section below.

Interlocutory Orders and Mareva Injunctions

Chapter I. above described the granting of world-wide Mareva injunctions as an accepted practice in at least some common-law jurisdictions. The practitioner should bear in mind that Mareva injunctions are interlocutory, and the requirement that the judgment be final and conclusive (which applies both to enforcement at common law and in equity) may present an obstacle. It may be contended that interlocutory injunctions should be enforced, at least in other common-law jurisdictions, unless and until altered by the foreign issuing court. However, it may be countered that certain judgments may be enforceable in equity but not at law because they involve collateral and provisional matters. The issue of enforcement of interlocutory judgments in equity, where applicable, must therefore be treated with care and on a case-by-case basis.

iv. *Practical Problems and Time Factors*

Time limits for applying for recognition and enforcement of foreign judgments will vary from jurisdiction to jurisdiction, and will generally be fairly generous, certainly compared to the short time limits in most cases for appealing such judgments at the place where rendered. Normally, recognition and enforcement may be sought simultaneously in any court or courts with appropriate jurisdiction and a link to assets against which enforcement will be sought.

Parallel Proceedings

In some cases, a suit will be pending at the place of desired enforcement whereas a decision has already been reached on the same matter in a foreign court. In such cases, then either party to the dispute (depending on who is favored by the foreign decision) should seek to have that foreign judgment recognized at the place where enforcement is sought or, if it cannot be recognized, enforced at common law, if applicable, or otherwise in the proceedings currently pending in the second jurisdiction. Even if the judgment cannot be enforced but is an "enforceable money judgment," it must normally be recognized in the pending local proceedings as conclusive between the parties on the relevant cause of action.

The only reasons why this might not be the case would be if the reason for nonenforcement was lack of jurisdiction, lack of due service of process, fraud, reversal in the foreign court of appeal, that the rights resulting from the judgment are not vested in the applicant, etc., depending on the specific grounds provided by local statute. If the local decision was in fact reached before the foreign decision, and not the other way around, then the recognition of the foreign judgment may be denied or set aside after the fact.

Under the Brussels/Lugano Conventions, Articles 21-23 apply and Article 27(3) and (5) lead to the denial of recognition of a later judgment when *res judicata* exists. At the same time, an earlier decision in a country with no reciprocity with the Contracting State in which enforcement is sought does not prevent enforcement of a later judgment in the Contracting State. If the later judgment to be enforced in the Contracting State is a judgment of that same Contracting State, and an earlier foreign judgment enforceable in that Contracting State appears, then the earlier foreign judgment can be a basis for an "action for reopening," where available.

Declaration of Enforceability

Normally, the declaration of enforceability is delivered without hearing, or even notifying, the judgment debtor. The judgment debtor will therefore normally be served the declaration of enforceability together with the court decree granting the first enforcement measure when the first enforcement measure is carried out.Upon service of the declaration of enforceability, depending on the applicable law the debtor may either take recourse within a stipulated period of time (e.g., within 14 days) or appeal within a somewhat longer period of time, which may be extended if the debtor has no domicile or residence at the place of desired enforcement.

Such deadlines are mandatory and normally cannot be extended. Recourse is the usual remedy against decrees on enforcement measures while appeal is used specifically to enforce foreign judgments. In the appeal, matters can be raised which include lack of enforceability in the state of origin, lack of reciprocity, improper service of the judgment, etc. Unless the appellant specifies reasons for denial of recognition, depending on the applicable law the court is usually not obliged to consider them on its own motion.

Depending on the applicable law, no enforcement can be made without a declaration of enforceability. If the judgment creditor applies for the declaration of enforceability and simultaneously for specific enforcement measures, the court must decide on both at the same time. If the debtor subsequently lodges an appeal against the declaration of enforceability, the court must stay proceedings on its own motion and may only take protective measures (e.g., pledge, hypothecation) until the declaration of enforceability is final. If damages are expected, the court may also order enforcement to be continued only if the creditor deposits security.

A judgment creditor may avoid delay if it combines the application for declaration of enforceability with the application for execution. Considering the hierarchy of courts and that there are two forms of appeal against the declaration of enforceability, the procedure may be time consuming. In the event of *Widerspruch*, a public hearing is held before judgment is rendered, which may in turn undergo further appeal in two instances.

On the debtor's request, a final declaration of enforceability must be reversed or modified if the judgment has been reversed or modified in the state of origin. For enforcement in Austria, for example, such reversion in the state of origin is grounds for the second court to order a stay of execution. The debtor may also combine the application for modification or reversal of the declaration of enforceability with a request for termination or limitation of enforcement measures.

Depending on the jurisdiction and applicable law, if the foreign judgment is expressed in a foreign currency, the judgment creditor may have the option of obtaining recognition of the judgment in a foreign currency or an equivalent amount in local currency converted on the date of application or according to some other prevailing rule, as discussed in **Chapter 16** above.

v. Public Policy Issues: Default Judgments, Discovery, Punitive Damages and Other Issues Affecting Enforceability

Default Judgments

Normally, whether by virtue of convention, statute or common law, where applicable, a default judgment may be enforced as long as it is a final judgment. This will mean that recognition and enforcement can ensue only once any appeal period as of right has expired. A judgment rendered in default of appearance will not be recognized if the defendant was not duly served with the documents instituting the proceedings or equivalent documents.

Article 27(2) of the Brussels/Lugano Conventions requires the court in which enforcement is sought to examine not only whether service was effected properly, i.e., in accordance with the applicable legal requirements, but also if it was effected in such manner that sufficient time was left to enable the defendant to arrange for a defense. The European Court of Justice and the courts of Convention States have rendered numerous judgments on the issue of proper and timely service.

In assessing such issue, the court must consider exceptional circumstances even after service was duly effected. Thus a judgment rendered without prior service of a summons on the defendant and sought to be enforced without notifying the defendant of judgment cannot be recognized and enforced. Recognition of a default judgment will also be denied if the defendant was not duly served with the documents instituting the proceedings and did not submit to proceedings even if the defendant could have later lodged an appeal after it knew of the decision.

Thus default judgments must meet a twin standards of "due service" and "effected in sufficient time to arrange for the defense." Recognition and enforcement have thus been denied where the defendant had an opportunity to receive (improper) service of process, which would have enabled arranging for defense, but the defendant did not enter an appearance because it correctly considered the service improper.

Under Article 46(2) of the Brussels/Lugano Conventions, a party seeking declaration of enforceability of a default judgment must present, in addition to the judgment itself, an original or certified copy of the document which establishes that the party in default was served with the document instituting the proceedings or an equivalent document. Many bilateral enforcement treaties contain similar provisions on default judgments, but must of course be examined individually for any major divergences from the Brussels/Lugano provisions.

Discovery

As stated previously, in most countries discussed in this work there is no institution by which a party to proceedings may be forced to disclose evidence to the other party. In some of these countries, any judgment originating from countries where pretrial discovery is part of procedural law (e.g., the United States) is *ipso facto* unenforceable. Austria is a case in point. The practitioner must be aware of such impediment at the earliest possible stage when deciding on litigation opportunities, and indeed at the initial contracting stage when assessing workable or unworkable agreements on choice of law and choice of forum.

The reverse situation is a judgment which emanates from a country which does not have any appreciable extent of discovery, any rules as to production of documents, any rights to depose witnesses prior to trial, any right of cross-examination of witnesses by counsel at trial, or any ability to require responses to pretrial interrogatories. When such judgment is then sought to be enforced in a country such as the United States or Canada where such methods are known and accepted, a Canadian or U.S. Court is not likely to construe its enforcement of a judgment "deprived" of such methods at the place of issuance as offending local public policy. While such judgments rest upon forms of procedure far removed from the adversarial process considered indispensable to the common-law tradition, this is not seen as a bar to enforcement.

Defective Service of Process

The manner in which process is served to commence foreign proceedings is normally of little relevance to the enforcing court as long as it does not overlap with a fundamental deprivation of due process or violation of public policy at the place of enforcement. Consequently, depending on the jurisdiction the judgment debtor should not have false hopes about using defective service of originating process to prevent recognition of the judgment abroad.

One of the reasons may be that when the enforcing court must decide whether the defendant was given sufficient notice of the foreign proceedings, it must normally disregard whether service was in accordance with its own law. While the judgment debtor might argue that enforcement would still be contrary to local public policy, if the defective service did not prevent the debtor from obtaining sufficient notice of the proceedings such argument is likely to fail. At common law, where applicable, improper service of process may be used to oppose enforcement of the foreign judgment only if service was so defective as to amount to a denial of natural justice (see also below).

Punitive Damages

Most States, including the Contracting States of the Brussels/Lugano Conventions and many States which have concluded bilateral enforcement treaties with such Contracting States, do not accept the principle of punitive damages. In most such States, the problem of recognition of judgments on punitive damages has not yet arisen. In those in which it has arisen, e.g., attempts to enforce U.S. punitive damages judgments in Germany, the local courts have considered the enforcement of such judgments, or at least that component of the award granting punitive damages, to violate local public policy and therefore be unenforceable. In general, the English courts will not enforce a foreign judgment, including from the U.S., granting punitive damages.

Natural Justice

Denial of natural justice usually involves a denial of the opportunity to fairly present one's case or a lack of impartiality on the part of the Court. Examples of lack of opportunity to fairly present one's case tend to overlap from jurisdiction to jurisdiction. They may include (i) a determination made without a hearing, (ii) intimidation of the defendant by or on behalf of the plaintiff, (iii) bias on the part of a foreign tribunal composed of persons with a pecuniary interest in the action or with a relation to the other party to the proceedings, and (iv) lack of notice of the hearing unless notice was dispensed with *bona fide* and in accordance with the rules of the foreign court, etc. As set forth in **Chapter 5** above, lack of notice does not always amount to a denial of natural justice and must be reviewed on a case-by-case basis.

Public Policy or Ordre Public

"Public policy" is of course not susceptible to a uniform or global definition, even if the practitioner has the sense that certain fundamental rights and notions seem to be embraced by this concept in virtually every foreign jurisdiction with which it has had contact. Again, each jurisdiction must be examined individually, and the general remarks which follow are meant solely as an orientation.

The common-law definition attracting the most significant judicial support is that of the English House of Lords in *Egerton v Brownlow* (1853) 4 HL Cas 1. There, public policy, which is also known in some jurisdictions as *ordre public*, was described as "that principle of law which holds that no subject can lawfully do that which has a tendency to be injurious to the public, or against the public good."

It may arise that a foreign judgment could be denied recognition on public policy grounds if it conflicts with a prior judgment of a court of the enforcing forum. This does not necessarily mean that it would be contrary to public policy to recognize a foreign judgment which conflicts with a prior judgment of another foreign country. Denial of recognition on the latter ground might also be seen as impermissibly examining the merits of the decision. Furthermore, a foreign judgment may also be unenforceable if the manner in which the judgment was obtained is contrary to local public policy, such as by undue influence, duress, or coercion.

If public policy arguments could have been raised in the foreign proceedings and adequately determined there, the court may not permit a public policy defense to be raised at the enforcement stage. This begs the question of whether it would have made sense to raise, in the foreign proceedings, the argument that enforcement in the second jurisdiction would be denied on the grounds of a violation of the public policy of the second jurisdiction and whether the first jurisdiction would even have an interest in hearing, much less ruling, on such an issue.

It is fair to say that the sense and indeed obligation that arbitrators in international arbitration are meant to have, namely to "make every effort to make sure that the award is enforceable at law" (e.g., Article 26 of the current Rules of Arbitration of the International Chamber of Commerce), does not extend to transnational litigation. This is the case even where the judge is made aware of the prospect of seeking enforcement in another jurisdiction.

Another controversial matter concerns foreign judgments that are not accompanied by a statement of grounds. In Brazil, for example, every judicial pronouncement must be justified by a statement of legal and rational grounds for the decision, under penalty of invalidity. This requires that on issues of law, the judge refer expressly to the legal reasoning justifying the decision and its statutory, caselaw and authoritative sources, and on issues of fact, to the evidence gathered in the records.

The Brazilian Federal Supreme Court denies homologation to foreign judgments not accompanied by a statement of grounds, due to the public policy requirement.

Brussels/Lugano Convention Countries

Article 27(1) of the Brussels/Lugano Conventions contains a public policy reservation to enforcement which, where applicable, prevails over other rules of law and bilateral treaties. If the Convention is not applicable, but a bilateral treaty applies, then its provisions prevail. Otherwise, the local domestic enforcement law of the Contracting State is applied. The fact of the matter is, however, that in the case of some Contracting States, but not all, there is little statutory or caselaw guidance as to what exactly contravenes local public policy and what does not.

Recourse to the public policy exception in Article 27(1) of the Brussels/Lugano Conventions is comparatively rare. There must be a drastic and egregious violation of or contradiction with the indispensable and fundamental principles of the country of intended enforcement. Higher court judgments in Convention States on the interpretation of this clause are in fact few and far between. Guidance may be sought from caselaw in Convention States relating to enforcement of non- and pre-Convention foreign judgments, which is more plentiful.

Such examination indicates that depending on the Contracting State, from a practical standpoint it is common court practice to make only limited use of the option to deny enforceability of a foreign judgment on the basis of public policy, and the result of the foreign judgment, including in some cases the nature and magnitude of any damage award, must offend the feeling of justice and equity locally to such an extent as to make recognition and enforcement unbearable.

Article 59 of the Brussels/Lugano Conventions permits Contracting States to undertake an obligation towards a third State not to recognize judgments given in other Contracting States against defendants from the third State in cases where jurisdiction to give judgment is based upon an exorbitant head of jurisdiction.

CHAPTER 18

SETTLEMENT AND COMPROMISE OF PROCEEDINGS

A party, and particularly a defendant, who would prefer to settle may consider various options depending on the jurisdiction. Importantly, the available means of settlement (sometimes called "transaction" or "compromise") differ substantially between and among jurisdictions, even within the same country.

The right of the parties to settle is a manifestation and consequence of the Rule of Free Disposition, also known as the *Dispositionsmaxime*, as discussed in **Chapter 1** above. Namely, the parties can freely dispose of the matter in dispute, subject to certain limited exceptions, and are free to withdraw claims or acknowledge claims brought against them.

The most common form of settlement is the payment into court or, where the rules allow it, the offer to settle. In some jurisdictions, it is possible for either party to serve on the other an offer of compromise. The payment into court provisions may also be augmented in some jurisdictions by the offer to consent to judgment procedure. Depending on the rules, this may extend to plaintiffs as well as defendants.

Court Settlements and Out-of-Court Settlements

It is important to distinguish between court settlements and out-of-court settlements. In-court settlements are settlements which either were entered into in a court hearing with the assistance of the judge or were privately negotiated by the parties but subsequently submitted to the court. Out-of-court settlements are settlements which are privately negotiated and usually for reasons of discretion will subsequently not be submitted to the court. At the same time, normally only a court settlement is an enforceable instrument. An out-of-court settlement is not an enforceable instrument, in certain jurisdictions, unless it has been properly deposited with or certified by the court as applicable. Where such deposit or certification is not available or not employed even if available, the settlement agreement which is then not complied with may require action and judgment to be enforced. An out-of-court settlement can normally be made in any phase of court proceedings without court approval. An in-court settlement may be subject to particular rules and to court approval.

In some jurisdictions, a party intending to sue may ask the district court to issue a summons to the potential defendant to appear before the court to negotiate a settlement ("pretrial settlement"). However, normally no coercive measures may be used to force the other party to appear or settle. While litigation is ongoing, a court settlement can normally be concluded as long as no final (and unappealable) decision exists.

Failure to accept a formal offer of settlement by either the plaintiff or the defendant may lead to a significant award of costs against the refusing party if the final judgment is not more favorable than the offer. A discontinuance of a suit by the plaintiff may also involve an obligation to pay costs generally, depending on the local rules, although these will not usually be significant if the action is at an early stage. Depending on the local rules, where the claimant withdraws its claim and the defendant has made a counterclaim, judgment for that counterclaim may be given on its request.

Certain multilateral and bilateral international agreements, including the Warsaw Convention on Carriage by Air (1929, revised in 1955 in the Hague), also specify the necessity of making settlement offers.

Judicial Involvement in Settlement

Depending on the jurisdiction and the applicable rules, the judge may or may not be entitled, or expected, to broach or attempt a settlement, and the practitioner obviously needs to know at the earliest stage what the possibilities and expectations are in this respect. Where such intervention is possible, it is normally entirely up to the judge whether to attempt a settlement where the parties have not expressly requested him to play such a role. If he does not play such a role, including because he deems the settlement prospects to be nil, there is no recourse open to the parties other than consensual settlement out of court. Depending on the rules and the jurisdiction, the parties may be able to have a settlement on agreed terms recorded in court, with which request the judge must then normally comply.

Certain countries' civil procedure regulations provide that a preliminary "reconciliation" hearing must be held immediately after the closing of the pleading phase of a litigation. Others provide that the judge should attempt to "reconcile" the parties during the merits hearings themselves, at least in claims involving disputes of *in patrimonio* rights of a private nature and family claims. In such cases, "reconciliation" is not tantamount to a settlement, which is an agreement which terminates obligations privately or before the court. Depending on the circumstances, the distinction may not be particularly relevant.

Such a reconciliation procedure is to be distinguished from the conventional way of adjudicating civil disputes in many countries in which the judge as a rule plays the role of conciliator, or *amiable compositeur*, whether or not the parties so request. Thus in some countries it is customary for the court of first instance at the close of the oral hearing to suggest to the parties to wait outside the courtroom while the judge or judges deliberate and decide whether to propose a settlement or even inform the parties of the likely outcome of the dispute.

In such cases, where the parties do not—for reasons of principle or for purposes of an appeal or otherwise—require a judgment, the case may be settled on the basis of the proposal of the judges or on their information about the likely outcome of the case. The judges, instead of writing a full judgment, may give the parties a brief written description of the grounds for their decision and state that the case is settled on that basis. However, if the parties so wish, they will receive a full judgment given in the ordinary manner.

In most jurisdictions, the vast majority of cases are settled or compromised before reaching trial. This is something the courts generally encourage. Hence the courts are usually amenable to adjournments which permit settlement discussions or mediation to proceed and, at times, in some countries courts will order parties to engage in mediation. At least in the common law jurisdictions, however, it is uncommon (and, depending on the circumstances, inappropriate) for a court to give an early indication of its ultimate views in a particular case in an effort to have the parties engage in settlement discussions.

In the United States, the court typically need not be made aware of the terms of a private settlement, and some courts do not want to know the terms out of a concern that their objectivity may be compromised. Moreover, in the U.S. many judges do not want to participate actively in litigants' efforts to settle, aside from simply encouraging a settlement verbally. Other judges are willing to take a more active role or delegate the task to another judge of the same court, or to a magistrate, who may serve as a settlement facilitator.

A prominent example in transnational litigation of settlements in particular types of cases which may require express approval of the court are "class actions" in the United States. Under U.S. Federal Rule of Civil Procedure 23(e) and its state-law equivalents, a class action "shall not be dismissed or compromised without the approval of the court, and notice of the proposed dismissal or compromise shall be given to all members of the class in such manner as the court directs." Settlements in cases involving certain federal statutes, or in which a governmental enforcement agency is involved, may also take the form of a court-approved consent decree that binds one or more parties as an order of the court and may be enforced by the court's contempt power.

Matters Capable of or Amenable to Settlement

Also depending on the jurisdiction and the applicable rules, the settlement, whether in court or out of court, must be of a matter or dispute which is capable of, or amenable to, settlement under the relevant law. Some jurisdictions phrase this in terms of "disposable rights" or *in patrimonio* rights of a private nature. In such cases, (i) rights concerning an individual's personality (e.g., right of name, of image, of honor, of privacy, of freedom, etc.), (ii) rights related to civil status (*status familiae* or "familial status"), (iii) certain property rights (such as the right to alimony), (iv) political rights, (v) public policy matters, and (vi) illegal transactions will not be capable of settlement and any agreement attempting to do so will for that reason be void or voidable.

The same may apply to settlements between counsel, even acting upon due empowerment by the parties, in which agreement is made not to appeal against a future first-instance decision. Such a "settlement" may be deemed void generally or at least if the agreement is made prior to the issuance of the decision. The reason is that appeal is normally considered to be a mandatory procedural right which cannot be validly waived in advance.

In this respect, the practitioner must distinguish such inability to make advance waiver of a right of appeal in litigation from the possibility which does exist, at least in certain jurisdictions, to validly waive in advance any right of appeal or comparable recourse against an arbitral award. Depending on the jurisdiction, such waiver or "exclusion agreement," if available at all, may need to be express and to contain a particular formulation in order to be effective. An example is Article 192(1) of the 1988 Swiss Private International Law Act (PILA), which permits waiver in advance of the right to appeal an arbitral award which is subject to the PILA, but only if all parties are nonresidents of Switzerland and only as long as the waiver is made expressly and in writing. The Swiss Federal Tribunal (e.g., decisions in 116 II 640 and 116 II 722) has held that to be valid, such a waiver must contain an acknowledgement of the availability of setting aside proceedings and the express renunciation of them.

Justiciability Versus Arbitrability

The practitioner should distinguish between the question of matters capable of or amenable to "settlement" and matters capable of or amenable to arbitration. This is especially the case in those jurisdictions, including for example currently Germany, which have defined arbitrable matters as those "capable of being settled." It suffices to say that the question of "arbitrability" differs from country to country and is an entirely different inquiry. In certain countries, claims related to labor, employment and family relationships are viewed as not arbitrable, but this does not necessarily mean that in such jurisdiction all such matters are then also incapable of being settled in litigation.

Indeed to the extent such claims may not be susceptible to adjudication by arbitration, litigation will be precisely the principal forum which is open to litigants as to such claims. Likewise, securities, antitrust and intellectual property claims have been considered nonarbitrable in some countries, but this does not at all necessarily mean that such claims are not subject to litigation and that such litigations are not capable of in-court or out-of-court settlement.

Finally, the practitioner should distinguish between the "compromise," which is sometimes used to refer to a settlement of a dispute, and the "compromise" or *compromis* which is used to refer to a certain kind of agreement to submit disputes to arbitration, withdrawing the dispute from the judiciary's examination. Agreements to submit future disputes to arbitration are usually in the form of an "arbitration clause" within the principal agreement between the parties and are sometimes called a clause compromissoire. Agreements to submit existing disputes are far less common and are often referred to as "submission to arbitration agreements," "submission agreements" or *compromis*.

The historical importance of the distinction between agreements as to future disputes and present ones relates in part to the fact that certain jurisdictions have not recognized the validity of agreements to refer future disputes to arbitration. In such jurisdictions, a clause to submit future disputes to arbitration has not been deemed operative by the local courts when called on to review the validity of such a clause until a submission agreement is executed.

i. Kinds of Settlement and Compromise

Pre-Suit Settlement

Certain jurisdictions provide that legal entities involved in a controversy must apply to the adverse party for a peaceful settlement and compromise before commencing a suit. Depending on the jurisdiction, e.g., the Russian Federation, such requirement may apply only to certain kinds of disputes or parties, for example transport and communication agencies. Even where such a procedure is not required, such "pre-suit settlement" mechanism may frequently be requested by the one or other party in certain jurisdictions.

Pre-suit settlement should be distinguished from consensually agreed provisions for amicable resolution of disputes prior to the right to commence litigation or arbitration. Particularly but by no means exclusively where contractants have agreed to arbitration, they may establish what amounts to a condition precedent to the right to commence proceedings. This in the form of a good-faith effort to amicably resolve the dispute.

Such "cooling off" clauses may require an attempt at settlement, conciliation, mediation or some referee procedure as a condition precedent to the right to commence arbitration or litigation. Provisions of this kind may be a mixed blessing. Cooling off periods often motivate the parties to talk before litigation or arbitration, but just as often instead engender jurisdictional disputes as to whether or when a dispute has "arisen" in the first place.

Payment into Court

Where available, the payment into court mechanism essentially operates so that a defendant may, at any time after an appearance, pay into court a sum of money which is in satisfaction of the claim. The plaintiff must be given notice of a payment into court. The plaintiff may then either accept the money paid in or allow the action to proceed to trial. This choice may be of considerable consequence depending on the applicable rules respecting costs (see **Chapter 20** below).

Offer of Compromise

In some jurisdictions, the parties are allowed to serve an offer of compromise on each other. An offer of compromise, where available, may be served by either party on the other at any stage of proceedings up to judgment. If an offer is not accepted and the trial results in an outcome which is less beneficial than the offer to the party who rejected the offer, then that party may face negative consequences for the period during which the action was unnecessarily continued between the offer and judgment. In some jurisdictions, the rules of procedure provide that formal offers of compromise must be responded to by the opposing side or otherwise risk being penalized with costs.

An offer must be left open for a specified minimum period in accordance with the rules. If an offer is not made in accordance with the rules, it is subject to the principles of contract. The offer of compromise facility is more flexible than payment into court in that any party may avail itself of the procedure. A payment into court can normally be made only by a defendant and only in an action for a debt or damages.

Under Rule 68 of the U.S. Federal Rules of Civil Procedure, which are binding in federal courts and followed by parallel rules in most U.S. states, titled Offer of Judgment, at any time more than 10 days before trial begins a defendant may serve upon the adverse party an offer of judgment for the money or property or to the effect specified in the offer, with costs then accrued. If within 10 days the adverse party accepts the offer, either party may file the offer and notice of acceptance with proof of service and the court clerk shall enter judgment.

An offer not accepted shall be deemed withdrawn and evidence thereof is not admissible except in a proceeding to determine costs. Furthermore, when the liability of one party has been determined by verdict or order or judgment, but the amount or extent of the liability remains to be determined, the party adjudged liable may make an offer of judgment. This shall have the same effect as an offer made before trial if served within a reasonable time not less than 10 days prior to hearings to determine the amount or extent of liability.

Consent to Judgment

If a settlement is reached, a defendant may simply agree to judgment being entered "by consent" or, without formally consenting to it, may submit to judgment without admitting liability. A judgment brings the proceedings to an end finally unless a provision is made for "liberty to apply."

Consent Order

A consent order recording the settlement reached can be entered on the court record without the need for a hearing of any kind. In other instances, a short formal hearing or application may be required. A consent order usually takes the form of proceedings being stayed upon terms agreed. Where the defendant does not contest liability but disagrees with the quantum of money owed, this procedure allows for the action to proceed directly to the assessment of damages. The shortfalls of concluding the settlement without the benefit of a consent order become apparent when one party reneges on a term of the agreement or disputes that a settlement agreement has been reached.

Civil Law In-Court Settlement

In civil-law countries in particular, lawsuits can be settled at any stage from the filing of the claim to the rendering of the final unappealable judgment. They are normally recorded in an agreement between the parties (also known as a contract of transaction) which records the terms of settlement. Such a contract has the effect of a final judgment and must therefore be drawn up with great care. If representation by an attorney is obligatory, the settlement can be recorded validly only in the presence of the attorneys. To validly record the settlement, the judge and the parties or their representatives must normally sign the settlement document.

Reconciliation

As previously stated, certain countries' civil procedure regulations provide that a preliminary "reconciliation" hearing must be held immediately after the closing of the pleading phase of a litigation. Others provide that the judge should attempt to "reconcile" the parties during the merits hearings themselves, at least in claims involving disputes of *in patrimonio* rights of a private nature and family claims.

Out-of-Court Settlement

Any agreement or compromise between the parties which does not involve the intervention of the court must be valid as a matter of statutory requirements, if any, for such agreements and generally as a matter of contract law. Especially in common law countries where such agreements are often entered into extrajudicially, the concern is adhering to general contractual principles (offer, acceptance, consideration, due capacity and authority, and an intention to create legal relations). Like other contracts, a settlement agreement may be invalidated on the same bases as other contracts, e.g., for illegality, fraud, duress or mistake. Parties and their counsel who fail to bear such general requirements in mind run the risk of leaving their terms and conditions of settlement unenforceable.

Deeds of release executed under seal are often utilized in order to make enforceable the terms and conditions of settlement. While this may not be necessary depending on the jurisdiction, it raises the obvious point that in some jurisdictions, and leaving aside special contracts such as those involving land, guarantees and specialties, oral contracts of settlement may be just as binding as written ones. However, the difficulty with oral contracts generally is proving what was agreed when a dispute arises as to the agreement itself. Thus, oral agreements may invite evidentiary problems later on. Accordingly, the practitioner should always take the extra step to reduce the settlement agreement to writing, no matter how "small" the matter may appear to be.

ii. Formalities and Requirements

Pre-Suit Settlement

In those jurisdictions which provide that legal entities involved in a controversy must apply to the adverse party for a peaceful settlement and compromise before commencing a suit, the requirements will be a function of statute and civil procedure code. These need to be consulted on an individual basis.

Payment into Court

Generally, the rules provide for the defendant to make a payment into court only in actions for debt or damages in satisfaction of any or all of the claims in the action. Depending on the rules applicable, the kinds of actions in which a payment into court can be made may be more or less broadly defined. A compromise takes effect as a contract, whereas a payment into court is not contractual.

It is essential for operation of the payment into court mechanism that the relief claimed is monetary. Although this limits the defendants' right to pay into court in actions for debt or damages, numerous areas, such as tort and contract, clearly qualify. Equity suits, however, do not as they seek discretionary orders from the court such as specific performance and injunctions.

Notice of payment into court must be strictly complied with. The defendant must inform the plaintiff in the required manner under the rules in the relevant jurisdiction and, in some jurisdictions, identify the cause(s) of action to which the payment pertains, with proportions clearly identified. If the defendant fails to comply with these requirements, the payment will not be effective in terms of any favorable cost consequences which the defendant may have obtained. In some jurisdictions, the rules allow the court to require the defendant to apportion the payment as the court sees fit. In others, the notice must state the party's position on liability.

Some jurisdictions allow the defendant to pay into court one sum without identifying the separate causes of action. However, the causes of action relevant to the payment must be specified. If the defendant believes that, in a suit for payment of debt, it offered the same sum to the plaintiff prior to the action but that sum was not accepted, the defendant may pay the money into court and rely on this payment in a defense of tender.

Depending on the rules, there is no right for the defendant to alter or withdraw any money paid into court. Leave of the court is required if the defendant wishes, in any way, to change the nature or amount paid in. Leave is obtained by applying to the court with a supporting affidavit. Typically, this is appropriate where circumstances change after the payment in. For example, the discovery of further evidence could affect the amount of the claim. If new evidence is such as to show the payment to be excessive, the defendant would obtain a favorable exercise of discretion.

Generally a payment into court may be accepted at any time before the commencement of the trial, though most jurisdictions specify a short period of time such as 14 days. If the money is accepted within the time limit stipulated in the rules, the plaintiff is entitled to costs up to the date of payment into court. If the plaintiff does not accept the payment and proceeds with the action but recovers less than was originally offered by the defendant in the payment into court, the court may order on costs against the plaintiff in whatever way it sees fit.

Offer of Compromise

The offer of compromise procedure, where available, may be a more flexible and useful procedure for parties who wish to terminate proceedings at an early stage. In some jurisdictions, it acts in replacement of the traditional payment into court facility.

Depending on the jurisdiction, the type of action where an offer of compromise may be utilized is limited to actions for damages. The offer of compromise must be made available to the other party for a specified period. In most jurisdictions this period is at least two to three weeks. An offer of compromise made pursuant to statutory provisions in this way cannot be withdrawn during the period in which it is required to be opened.

The statutory offer of compromise to be distinguished from any informal offer which is made pursuant to general principles of contract. Such offers are usually made as "without prejudice" offers (that is, the fact that the offer is made could be used in evidence). This allows the parties to attempt to put an early end to proceedings without prejudicing their positions if the litigation does proceed. Many jurisdictions recognize the so-called "Calderbank offer," which has its origins in the United Kingdom. This offer allows the compromise to be without prejudice save as to costs. Hence, where the offer contains terms which are ultimately more favorable to the end result or judgment that is obtained by the party which declined the offer, the offer may be made issue when the court is deciding the matter of costs. Practitioners should be wary, as courts have in some cases refused to recognize such offers where the rules in the jurisdiction at hand contained a specific procedure.

A distinct advantage of the offer of compromise procedure is its flexibility and lack of confining or restrictive rules. As a result, there is no specific or prescribed format which an offer of compromise must take. However, it must be specific and precise enough to be directly relevant and comparable to the judgment. The rules in most of the jurisdictions in which the procedure is available require that an offer of compromise be in writing and satisfy numerous standard stipulations which are set out in the rules. An informal offer of compromise does not have these restrictions but must satisfy general principals of contract.

The timing of an offer of compromise can be crucial both with respect to the cost implications and the likelihood of acceptance by the other party. The offer must be served (that is, made to the other party) before any judgment is given. As an official offer of compromise must be left open for a minimum period, this requires considerable foresight. An offer must be made at a stage of proceedings early enough to safeguard against the risk of being void as a result of the timing of judgment.

In the United States, under Rule 68 of the Federal Rules of Civil Procedure if the judgment finally obtained by the offeree is not more favorable than the offer, the offeree must pay the costs incurred after the making of the offer. The fact that an offer is made but not accepted does not preclude a subsequent offer. An offer of judgment under Rule 68 is not filed with the court but served on the adverse party. If it is accepted, the offer and acceptance then will be filed. Because an offer of judgment can be made only by a party "defending against a claim," an offer of compromise by a defendant made before the commencement of the action is not an offer of judgment within Rule 68. The offer must specify a definite sum for which judgment may be entered.

Consent to Judgment

Judgment may be appropriate where a defendant accepts that the plaintiff is entitled to its claimed relief or where the defendant has decided, for whatever reason, not to pursue its defense. The order can be unconditional and simply record the order that judgment be entered, in which case the plaintiff is free to enforce judgment in the normal way.

Alternatively, judgment may be entered for a specified sum but execution of the judgment stayed until defendant fails to abide by the terms of the settlement agreed (normally payments of settlement sums by way of instalment). In this example, the consent order for judgment to be entered should provide that if the defendant defaults, the whole of the balance outstanding should become due and the stay of execution on the judgment automatically lifted as to the unpaid balance of the judgment sum.

Consent Order

As stated earlier, a consent order usually takes the form of proceedings being stayed upon terms agreed. Generally, the terms will involve the defendant's paying specified sums to the plaintiff. It is important to include in this consent order that each party may apply to the court to have the terms of the settlement carried out. If this forms part of the order and the defendant breaches the agreement, the plaintiff will be able to seek the court's assistance in enforcing the agreement.

Civil Law In-Court Settlement

Requirements for a valid court settlement include that domestic jurisdiction and competence of the courts (in general, not of the specific court) are fulfilled, that there is no valid and unappealable court decision on the matter, and that the issue must be "accessible" or "amenable" to settlement. The settlement must be specific so that it can be the basis for enforcement.

The requirements for settlement, where applicable, are determined in the civil code or civil procedure code regulations. Where the judge plays a role, he must normally advise the litigants of the advantages of the agreement and the possible disadvantages of persisting in the dispute. The judge may not coerce the parties since it is a requirement for the validity of the agreement that it be free and voluntary, corresponding to the true will of the parties.

Accordingly, the judge must normally not give any indication of what his ruling would be absent settlement. The judge will normally pay particular attention to whether the form and contents of any in-court settlement agreement are likely to offend public policy or be such as to potentially generate another dispute relating to the terms of the settlement itself.

Reconciliation

Where this vehicle is available, the parties and their attorneys are given legal notice to attend hearings in which they may negotiate with each other through the mediation of the judge. The judge cannot prohibit the party from consulting his attorney during the hearing. The party need not personally appear at the preliminary reconciliation hearing if its attorney is granted special authority to "reconcile." The presence of the attorney is advisable since in both hearings the parties interact with the court as concerns relevant legal issues.

If the party fails to appear in the preliminary reconciliation hearing, this will imply a tacit refusal to settle and compromise. The procedural issues which are settled in such hearing have preclusive effect and are thus not subject to further argument.

Out-of-Court Settlement

In the context of a transnational litigation, the text and content of a privately contracted settlement agreement will obviously vary widely. They will depend on the underlying facts and law and the applicable procedures, as well as the applicable rules and customs respecting contract drafting generally. At the same time, particularly in certain common law jurisdictions certain standard provisions are likely to be encountered. These may include recitals as to the following:

First, a careful description of the underlying contract or contracts, the pending litigations and other proceedings meant to be terminated.

Second, an acknowledgement of the receipt and sufficiency of the "consideration," usually in the form of payment, on the part of each of the parties.

Third, a recital that within a certain finite period of time, e.g., five business days, after the execution of the agreement, one party shall pay the other a sum certain for its damages including, but not limited to, e.g., lost profits, contributions to overhead, unamortized cost of equipment, etc., and any and all other claims "made or which could have been made" by the one party against the other under the relevant agreement or in the legal proceedings as defined.

Fourth, that except as set forth otherwise in the Settlement Agreement, the underlying contract will be cancelled as of the date of the settlement agreement.

Fifth, that in consideration of the payment and the mutual releases contained in the settlement agreement, the one party shall "indemnify, defend and hold harmless" the other from any and all "costs, damages, expenses (including attorneys' fees), losses, suits, claims and liabilities by" third parties.

Sixth, that within, e.g., five business days after the execution of the Settlement Agreement, the plaintiff in the pending litigation or other proceedings will notify the relevant court or institution that the pending case or cases have been "fully settled and compromised" and are to be dismissed "with prejudice," and that each party has agreed to bear a certain percentage, such as 50 percent, of the costs fixed by the court, if any, for the proceedings.

Seventh, that each party shall bear its own costs and attorneys' fees in connection with the proceedings.

Eighth, that as set forth in the settlement agreement and excepting only any claim for nonperformance of one or more obligations arising under the settlement agreement, a certain period of time, e.g., 90 days, after the parties' receipt of payment from each other, each one, "on behalf of itself and all other persons, companies or other entities now or hereafter claiming under, by or through it," will "absolutely, unconditionally and irrevocably release" the other party, "together with any and all corporate parents, subsidiaries and affiliates of such party and the shareholders, officers, directors, employees, agents, servants and attorneys of each of them," "of and from any and all claims of any kind or nature whatsoever, known or unknown, complete or incomplete, now existing or hereafter arising, which arise in whole or in part from any transaction or occurrence taking place on or prior to the date hereof, including without limitation any claims that have been or could have been asserted" in the litigation or other proceedings (as defined). This raises the issue of ensuring that the settlement agreement specifies which claims are being settled where not all claims arising out of the same set of facts or incident may be known at the time of the settlement, and that any sum paid is in full and final satisfaction of future claims arising out of the same facts or circumstances.

Ninth, that during the same (90-day) period, each of the parties shall not take any action whatsoever with respect to any claim subject to the release described in the settlement agreement and shall not take any action inconsistent with the terms of that agreement or effectuating the release of the other party.

Tenth, that if the one party becomes the subject of a bankruptcy case under the relevant federal or other bankruptcy code or statute during the (90-day) period after the other party's receipt of payment from it, the releases will not become effective until the earliest occurrence of one of a number of specified events: (a) the bankrupt party's payment is judicially determined not to constitute a preference or other avoidable transaction under the relevant legislation (collectively called "avoidance actions"); (b) the expiration of applicable statutes of limitations for the commencement of avoidance actions; (c) the "debtor in possession/trustee" or equivalent agrees to ratify the settlement agreement; or (d) counsel for the non-bankrupt party opines in writing that there is no material risk that the bankrupt party's payment could be judicially determined to constitute an avoidance action.

Eleventh, a recital that the parties are entering into the agreement for the purpose of "resolving doubtful and disputed claims and to buy their peace" and that "nothing contained in the agreement constitutes any admission" by the party previously sued of "any liability, culpability or fault" and that "any and all such liability, culpability or fault" by that party "is hereby expressly denied."

Twelfth, that the parties will keep the terms of the agreement and the facts and circumstances of their underlying disputes confidential, except for "disclosure to counsel or to the extent disclosure to regulators, government agencies, insurers, accountants or parties serving legal process is reasonably believed to be required by law."

Thirteenth, that the parties warrant and represent that they have read the agreement, that they understand it, that they have consulted their counsel regarding its legal effect and they have all necessary authority to execute and deliver the agreement.

Fourteenth, that the agreement represents "the complete understanding of the parties with respect to the subject matter" thereof and that the parties "are not entering into the agreement in reliance upon any representation made to it by or on behalf of any other party."

The agreement should contain an express choice of forum or arbitration clause and an express choice of law clause. It may also be appropriate to include a provision concerning the tax implications of the settlement.

Regardless of the jurisdiction and the applicable law, where the parties have entered into a contract of settlement, rescission, revocation or similar remedies with respect to such contract are normally available only according to generally applicable principles of contract law. In some jurisdictions, there are particular provisions further limiting the possibility of rescission of, or withdrawal from, such a settlement agreement.

Such circumstances might include if revocation was expressly reserved by one or both parties (a method widely used in court practice in order to obtain the approval of a client not present or an insurance company, etc.), if the settlement agreement was not validly concluded (e.g., where no attorney was present although required by law), or based on an "error" which affected the settlement basis jointly assumed by both parties. Such bases must be verified and applied on a country-by-country basis.

Role of Attorneys in Settlement

Whether in the case of in-court or out-of-court settlements, the practitioner and his client should take to verify under what circumstances, as is normally the case, settlement discussions and agreements may be entered into by counsel on behalf of their clients. In some countries, neither local attorneys (defined variously as members of the Bar or Bar Association) nor legal aid counsels need to present powers of attorney unless so ordered by the court. In such cases, if a party wants to restrict its lawyer's authority to settle the case, the court must be notified of this restriction, or it must be stated in the power of attorney.

It should be noted in passing that such rules and restrictions may also apply in the case of extrajudicial settlement of arbitral disputes pending before arbitral tribunals locally or at a foreign place of arbitration. Accordingly, the relevant rules respecting the empowerment of attorneys to act in this fashion in the arbitration context must likewise be verified at an early stage.

iii. Effect on Litigation

Prior to Settlement or Upon Failure of Settlement

Quite apart from the issue of a consensual stay or suspension of proceedings pending the outcome of ongoing settlement discussions is the issue of the evidentiary status of such discussions. In the United States, for example, under the Federal Rules of Evidence the parties' attempts to settle a lawsuit generally should not be allowed to affect the ongoing litigation until the settlement is finalized. Rule 408 provides that evidence of offering or accepting "valuable consideration in compromising or attempting to compromise a claim which was disputed as to either validity or amount" is not admissible to prove liability for or invalidity of the claim or its amount. Evidence of conduct or statements made in compromise negotiations is likewise not admissible.

At the same time, this rule of exclusion is not absolute in the United States. Evidence relating to settlement is not excluded by the rule if offered for a purpose other than proving liability for or invalidity of a claim, such as "proving bias or prejudice of a witness, negativing a contention of undue delay, or proving an effort to obstruct a criminal investigation or prosecution."

After the Consummation of Settlement

The in-court or out-of-court settlement, once validly concluded, is considered to be a surrogate for a final and unappealable decision. The proceedings are therefore concluded, and no appeal may be made. A new claim filed on the same dispute would have to be dismissed by the court. In Brussels/Lugano Convention cases, under Article 51 of the Conventions a court settlement equals a final judgment as a basis for enforcement, even in transnational matters, if it is enforceable in the State in which it was concluded.

Thus the judicial or extrajudicial settlement normally produces the effect of *res judicata* between the parties, which can be altered only in the case of bad faith, coercion or essential error as to the controverted object or person. The settlement document, whether or not involving a claim filed at court, will then constitute an enforceable judicial document and legally qualified instrument for the satisfaction of the creditor's right by means of coercive execution in the event the debtor does not fulfill the obligation voluntarily. Depending on the jurisdiction, the *res judicata* effect applies only to settlement and compromise of proceedings when they are properly court-certified, and counsel must therefore take care to obtain such certification if desired.

The *res judicata* effect of the settlement, whereby no new proceedings may be started on the same basis, is obviously to be distinguished from the discontinuance or withdrawal of the suit by the claimant without a settlement, whereby new proceedings may be started on the same basis.

Depending on the applicable law, the parties will normally be able to obtain a stay or suspension of pending proceedings upon a declaration or manifestation that they are currently in settlement discussions and therefore wish to interrupt the litigation pending the outcome. Depending on the rules and customs, the judge may at least expect or insist to be informed by the parties upon an interim cut-off date whether they have indeed achieved settlement by such future date.

Payment into Court

Money paid into court must normally be accepted by a specified time. After this time has expired, the court has exclusive control over the money. If, however, the money is accepted, a stay of the action of indeterminate length commences. There is no formal resolution of proceedings in terms of a judgment. Nor is an estoppel created by the acceptance of such money. Nevertheless, the stay prevents either party from recommencing the action in fresh proceedings.

Offer of Compromise

The offer of compromise is a way of encouraging settlement. Where available, the procedure is laid out in the respective court rules. Generally, the acceptance of an offer of compromise is final and has the effect of concluding proceedings. An offer of compromise that is not accepted is relevant to the ultimate determination of costs, if any.

Most jurisdictions set out the cost ramifications in the rules and distinguish between an offer by the plaintiff and one by the defendant. Where the defendant does not accept an offer of compromise, the defendant may be liable for all attorney/solicitor and client costs where the ultimate judgment against the defendant is less favorable than the offer made initially by the plaintiff. In some jurisdictions, the plaintiff is entitled only to party costs up to the time when the offer was served. After this time, costs are recoverable only on an indemnity basis.

Should the parties settle on a portion of the dispute only, the proceedings will continue so that the remaining part of the claim can be adjudicated. The settlement of part of the claim produces immediate effects for the part of the claim settled. In the event that a party which accepts an offer does not comply with it, the other party is able to apply to the court for judgment.

When there are multiple parties involved in the same suit, nothing precludes a plaintiff from settling with fewer than all of the defendants and proceeding to trial with the remaining defendants. The remaining defendants may be entitled to a setoff or reduction in liability in the amount of the settlement so that the plaintiff does not obtain a double recovery.

Costs

In cases where the defendant makes an offer which the plaintiff rejects and the judgment ultimately delivered is less beneficial to the plaintiff, the defendant may be liable for party costs up to the time at which the offer was served, after which the plaintiff will be liable for the defendant's party costs. In in-court settlement, the court may pay attention to whether the party who served the offer was actually capable of making good on the offer when exercising discretion as to costs.

Even in out-of-court settlement, costs will normally play a role. The normal arrangement in such settlements is that each party shall bear its own costs, including attorney's fees. Where the proceedings have already commenced, and especially in jurisdictions which may assess court fees and provide for legal fees as a function of the asserted amount in dispute and/or the stage of advancement of the proceedings, it is almost inevitable that legal costs or disbursements have been incurred even at an early stage.

In jurisdictions where the basic rule is that the loser pays the winner's costs, unless otherwise agreed a plaintiff who is receiving money in settlement will almost certainly expect to have contribution towards its costs in addition to the settlement sum. If the defendant wishes to pay a fixed sum by way of settlement inclusive of costs, this should be expressly stated, and the agreement should reflect that "each party shall bear its own costs."

Where a defendant agrees, in addition to the settlement sum, to pay the plaintiff's costs, the parties may not be able to agree on what such costs were, or the defendant may consider the costs to be unreasonable and balk at payment on that basis. In a jurisdiction such as England and Wales, in this situation costs can be "taxed" if not agreed. The court assesses a party's detailed bill of costs and makes a decision regarding the reasonableness of the sums claimed. It is invariably worthwhile asking for an estimate of costs and, if none is forthcoming, putting a ceiling upon the amount of costs which will be paid in addition to the settlement sum.

iv. Settlement and Alternative Dispute Resolution ("ADR")

Pre-suit settlement as required by statute or civil procedure code and described above should be distinguished from mandatory pretrial conferences with a judge or more likely a magistrate or mediator. The latter have been introduced in certain jurisdictions, notably in the United States, and normally are triggered only upon formal commencement of the suit. As the backlog of cases in the courts has increased, U.S. courts increasingly encourage settlement by means of voluntary or court-ordered alternative dispute resolution ("ADR") mechanisms such as mediation, arbitration and summary (shortened) trials. In some jurisdictions, cases are assigned to a "calendar" or "track" system that requires some form of alternative dispute resolution before the parties may even commence traditional litigation.

ADR in Name and in Practice

While a thorough discussion of ADR techniques exceeds the scope of this work, certain general comments may be made here. ADR has become well known, and widely used, primarily in the United States and certain other common-law jurisdictions, notably England, Canada and Australia, over roughly the last fifteen years. This is not to say that ADR is not used in other jurisdictions and particularly in countries belonging to other than the common-law tradition. Indeed practitioners in such varied jurisdictions as France, Japan and Saudi Arabia would readily and correctly note that ADR-like methods for settlement, whether in or out of court, have been employed for decades, if not for centuries, in such locales without the need or the desire to attach a special name or a special significance to such methods.

It is in this respect that caution should be exercised in the face of the time-honored observation that well-intentioned efforts to inject aspects of ADR into the legal regimes and cultures of Continental Europe have failed while ADR has increased by quantum leaps in Anglo-American jurisdictions in recent years. At the same time, the increasingly vocal discussion of ADR relates primarily to formalized court-ordered or -recommended or party-initiated techniques. These techniques in some cases take on a highly formalized, if also streamlined, character. They thus distinguish themselves not only from courtroom adjudication and arbitration, but also from traditional forms of negotiation and compromise known in many legal and political traditions.

This development has been particularly marked in the United States. There are systemic causes of ADR and of its popularity in the U.S., and to a certain extent in England, which may not exist in Continental Europe or elsewhere to the same degree. These include disenchantment with and the inability to overcome the high cost, long delay and unpredictability associated with (i) court congestion, (ii) extensive discovery, (iii) the jury system, (iv) motion practice, (v) punitive damages, (vi) the institutionalized plaintiff's bar, (vii) products liability and consumer-driven litigation generally, (viii) non-apportionment of costs or attorney's fees to the victor, and (ix) contingency or success fees.

Certain areas of law usually prove to be especially susceptible to ADR mechanisms. These include complex, long-term international/transnational undertakings, such as take-or-pay contracts, joint ventures, participation agreements, major construction projects, or technology arrangements. They also include relations with administrative agencies, intellectual property disputes and collective bargaining.

Generally, in disputes between companies in different countries, involving competing bodies and rules of law, and complex commercial, construction or other issues, conventional adjudication might not be desired. The reason would be the fear that such disputes might otherwise result in costly, time-consuming adversarial proceedings, final disposition of which may be satisfactory to neither side.

General Characteristics of ADR Procedures

Among the general characteristics of certain ADR procedures are that they are private and confidential and in some cases informal, expeditious, and less expensive or disruptive of business relationships than litigation or arbitration, whether institutional or ad hoc. Depending on the ADR mechanism, it does not result in adjudication, i.e., in a binding decision. This is to be contrasted, of course, with almost any other settlement technique or method described in this Chapter, whether in court or out of court.

There are various situations in which parties may be particularly interested in an ADR resolution, as opposed to settlement. The parties may wish to preserve an amicable and satisfactory relationship or reputation, as opposed to merely saving face, exacting revenge or setting precedent. The parties may wish to maintain the confidentiality of the subject matter, e.g., sensitive hightech or trade secrets. There may be technical or other aspects of the dispute which may lend themselves to a non-adversary method of settlement.

The parties may acknowledge that their legal positions are unclear or that they are a "toss up." Also, the parties may seek a business-oriented solution rather than legal one, but neither one may wish to be accused of weakness by not suing. Finally, and perhaps most important, representatives of the parties need to be available who have not been directly involved in or "tainted" by the dispute and who have sufficient authority to participate in the ADR settlement decisions.

Precautions in ADR Settlements

Where the parties do enter into an agreement resulting from an ADR exercise, they should take certain precautions. The first is to address the issue of suspension of legal proceedings, if any. Subject to any provisions of substantive or procedural law agreed to be applicable to settlement, or otherwise mandatory, the parties may agree to suspend application of all applicable statutes of limitation and contractual prescription periods until the ADR procedure is terminated. Second, the ADR negotiations should be conducted without prejudice to the parties' right and ability to seek interim or conservatory relief in a court of appropriate jurisdiction.

At all times, the parties should take all appropriate measures to verify whether particular provisions of the settlement agreement which ensues from the ADR mechanism are permissible and enforceable. In this respect, they must be guided by the substantive or procedural law agreed applicable to the proceedings and to the settlement agreement or the substantive or procedural law otherwise applicable by virtue of, e.g., the "situs" of proceedings and the place of entry into an initiating agreement or the settlement agreement.

CHAPTER 19

SOVEREIGN IMMUNITY

The principle of "foreign sovereign immunity" has deep historical roots in the practice of most countries and also in international law. Recent developments have restricted traditional notions of sovereign immunity, but the doctrine still remains very important in international litigation.

Depending on the jurisdiction, the issue of extension of sovereign immunity is one of either statute, caselaw or both. The primary concerns here are (i) service of process on foreign sovereigns, (ii) subject-matter and personal jurisdiction, (iii) taking of evidence against foreign sovereign entities, (iv) pre-and post-judgment attachment and other injunctive measures against foreign sovereigns, and (v) recognition and enforcement of judgments against foreign sovereigns.

Absolute Versus Restrictive Sovereign Immunity

The sovereign immunity of foreign States, their governmental entities, and diplomatic and consular officers and employees is a rule of *jus gentium* ("public international law").

The general view is that there is complete immunity in respect of uniquely sovereign acts, or acts *jure imperii*, and in respect of buildings and other real property and other assets owned by a foreign government, which are necessary for the proper functioning of a State. Even in respect of such assets, immunity may, of course, be waived. It is generally assumed that no immunity exists with respect to non-sovereign or commercial acts, or acts *jure gestionis*, and assets not used for governmental purposes. This reflects the restrictive view of sovereign immunity, which has essentially become the international "standard" in this context. It rejects the long-held notion of absolute immunity, under which sovereign States could not be sued in a particular jurisdiction against their will and without their permission.

This position was modified by caselaw over time in many jurisdictions and then codified by statute so that the governing principle became that of restrictive immunity, drawing a distinction between acts by the State that could also be done by a private citizen and acts that flow purely from its sovereign status. An example of such evolution over time and of the interplay between caselaw and statute is the situation in the United States. In 1976, the U.S. Foreign Sovereign Immunities Act (FSIA) was enacted to govern, *inter alia*, obtaining jurisdiction over and perfecting service upon, foreign States and their agencies and instrumentalities in both U.S. federal and state courts. The FSIA codified the "restrictive" theory of sovereign immunity and transferred immunity determinations from the U.S. Department of State to the courts. The restrictive theory had been adopted by the Department of State in policy and practice in 1952.

Defining the Foreign Sovereign and Its "Agents"

Depending on the country and the statute, for purposes of immunity and otherwise the foreign sovereign will normally be defined in a specific way, as expanded upon by caselaw. This definition may include, e.g., an independent sovereign State, the head of a foreign State in his public capacity, a political subdivision of a State when acting in a public capacity, and any government of a foreign State or political subdivision including its departments and agencies. A political subdivision may include a state or province.

Separate entities distinct from the executive organs of the government of the State that are capable of suing or being sued are not necessarily included in the definition. Whether an entity is considered separate will depend on all the circumstances surrounding the case. These may include, for example, (i) the legislative intention of the foreign government in creating and regulating the entity, (ii) the extent to which the entity runs its commercial activities free from governmental interference, and (iii) whether the entity is under government control and exercises government functions. Depending on the statute and caselaw, a separate entity will normally be entitled to State immunity if the proceedings against it relate to something done by it in the exercise of sovereign authority and a State would have been immune in those circumstances.

In this regard, the U.S. FSIA is of particular importance in view of its definition of foreign State and the consequences thereof. The FSIA definition of a "foreign state" includes "a political subdivision of a foreign state or an agency or instrumentality of a foreign state." "Agency" or "instrumentality" in turn means any entity which is a separate legal person, corporate or otherwise, and which is an organ of a foreign State or political subdivision thereof, or a majority of whose shares or other ownership interest is owned by a foreign State or political subdivision thereof, and which is neither a citizen of a state of the United States (as defined in the FSIA), nor created under the laws of any third country.

A political entity typically is considered a State if the other State in question recognizes it as such. In this regard, the Restatement (Third) of the Law, The Foreign Relations Law of the United States (1996), provides that termination of diplomatic relations does not change status as a nation. This approach has been applied to such countries as Iran and the Republic of China (Taiwan). A political entity is also typically considered a State if it meets the international law definition of a State. In this context, regard may be had to whether the entity has ultimate control over its own government or territory and whether it has a defined territory, permanent population, or formal relations with other States.

Unlike a foreign State, a foreign separate entity may bear the burden of proof of showing that it is entitled to State immunity. A recent example is *Kuwait Airways v. Iraqi Airways* [1995] 3 All ER 694, decided in the context of sovereign immunity legislation in the United Kingdom. In that decision, in which Iraqi Airways claimed sovereign immunity as to its seizure and use for itself of the Kuwaiti aircraft fleet, the English House of Lords held that Iraqi Airways was an entity separate from the State, that it had acted in exercise of sovereign authority when it seized the aircraft, and was immune in respect of the seizure. At the same time, it held that subsequent incorporation of the Kuwaiti fleet into the Iraqi commercial fleet was not done in exercise of sovereign authority.

In some jurisdictions, it may be possible to obtain a certificate issued by the Ministry of Foreign Affairs or equivalent to constitute conclusive proof in any local court that any such State or entity is a foreign State or entity to which immunity may extend.

Absence of Statutory Bases and Application of Conventions

In certain jurisdictions, there may be no or virtually no statutory law regulating problems of immunity. However, even in such cases there may be a generally recognized presumption that local law is in accordance with international law, where the opposite cannot be shown. In such cases, the practitioner may be able to rely on internationally accepted notions of sovereign immunity and exceptions thereto. In the reverse situation, where the wording of a statute respecting sovereign immunity is clearly contrary to international law, the local statute may be given preference. This will be the case especially if under the local law international law is not part of the "law of the land" and treaties have to be implemented in order to become part of the local law. Ratification in such cases does not suffice.

A number of conventions may also be relevant to issues of sovereign immunity. These include the 1961 Vienna Convention on Diplomatic Relations, 1963 Vienna Convention on Consular Relations, the 1946 Convention on the Privileges and Immunities of the United Nations and the Special Organizations of the United Nations, the 1926 Convention and 1934 Protocol on Immunity of Ships of Foreign States, and the 1972 Council of Europe Convention on State Immunity. The International Law Commission, a United Nations body specializing in codification and development of public international law principles, has been engaged in drafting a convention on the jurisdictional immunities of States since 1978. As of June 12, 1997, the European Convention on Immunity of States had been acceded to by Belgium, Germany, United Kingdom, Luxembourg, Netherlands, Austria, Switzerland and Cyprus.

Accordingly, in those countries which have no legislation respecting sovereign immunity except via an accession to the 1961 Vienna Convention, the underlying doctrines of sovereign immunity, including an absolute and restrictive theory, have not developed further. In other countries, such as the United States, France, the United Kingdom and Germany, to name just a few, there has been extensive litigation, and therefore voluminous caselaw in the area, which must be heeded by the international practitioner.

i. Service of Process on Foreign Sovereigns

Depending on the applicable legislation and whether absolute or restricted sovereign immunity is followed, there may be several ways of serving process on a foreign State, as distinguished from an agency of the foreign State. First is service in accordance with the agreement to which the State is a party, if any. Second is service through diplomatic channels. Other modes of service on a foreign State may be effective for the purposes of the particular law as long as expressly provided by statute or not expressly forbidden. These would include in accordance with any international convention to which the State is a party. Service of the originating document on an agency of the foreign State may also be made in accordance with an international convention applicable to the agency, in accordance with any applicable rules of court, or where service cannot be made in any of the above manners, a court may direct how service is to be made.

Service on a foreign sovereign to which the U.S. FSIA applies must comply with the statutory list of means of service, also depending on whether the object of service is a sovereign or rather an agency or instrumentality of the foreign State, in "decreasing order of preference." Caselaw explains that the plaintiff must use the more preferred method; a less preferred method of service can be used only if the more preferred means is unavailable. Defective service on an agency will normally preclude default judgment.

If a foreign sovereign is a signatory of the European Convention on Sovereign Immunity, the foreign sovereign must be served through diplomatic channels in accordance with Article 16 of the Convention. The addressee of service is the Foreign Ministry or equivalent of the respective foreign sovereign. Under the Convention, any time-limits start to run at the time of receipt of the documents served by the Ministry and shall not be less than two months. If a foreign sovereign is not a signatory of this Convention, service on foreign sovereigns in civil matters may be subject to bilateral or multilateral treaties on civil procedure. Under the Hague Service and the Hague Evidence Conventions, service usually occurs through diplomatic channels.

If a privileged person appoints a representative or gives proxy to an attorney, the subsequent service of process must normally be effected to the representative or attorney. A certificate issued by the Minister of Foreign Affairs or equivalent constitutes conclusive proof in any court that any such State or entity is a foreign State or entity to which immunity extends.

In countries which have no specific legislation respecting service on foreign sovereigns, they are normally immune to jurisdiction, and thus immune to service. The 1961 Vienna Convention provides no further guidance regarding service of process on foreign sovereigns, and therefore the regular procedural rules of local law are to be followed in attempting to serve a sovereign where this is at all possible.

ii. Subject-Matter and Personal Jurisdiction

Depending on the applicable law, the general position under foreign sovereign immunity legislation based on absolute sovereign immunity is that a foreign State is immune from jurisdiction. For this purpose, the foreign sovereign will normally be defined in a specific way by statute, as expanded upon by caselaw, as including, e.g., an independent sovereign State, the head of a foreign State, and the executive government of a foreign State.

In jurisdictions which subscribe to the concept of restricted sovereign immunity, foreign states may invoke immunity only to the extent that claims brought against them before civil courts are based on *acta iure imperii*, that is, acts particular to their sovereign function, as opposed, e.g., to an act with a commercial nature and/or purpose. In jurisdictions such as the United States which distinguish between subject-matter and personal jurisdiction, the FSIA presumes that a foreign sovereign is immune from both kinds of jurisdiction unless the foreign sovereign falls within one of the exceptions in the FSIA. If an exception applies, the FSIA grants both personal and subject matter jurisdiction over the foreign sovereign.

The applicable law may or may not include a separate entity of the foreign State such as a natural person or a corporation that is an agency or an instrumentality of the foreign State or employees of intergovernmental organizations residing locally. An agency of a foreign State is normally defined to include any legal entity that is an organ of the foreign State. The test applied by the courts is whether the entity is under government control and exercises government functions.

Different jurisdictions have different approaches to the immunity from jurisdiction and when such immunity will not be granted or assumed. Public international law provides exemptions from the general principle that a country's courts have jurisdiction over all persons and all moveable and immoveable goods situated within its borders, i.e., the exemptions of immunity and exterritoriality.

Such limitations are set forth in detail in the 1961 Vienna Convention on Diplomatic Relations, the 1963 Vienna Convention on Consular Relations, the 1972 European Convention on the Immunity of States, and the 1946 Convention on the Privileges and

Immunities of the United Nations and Special Organizations of the United Nations, etc. Since Vienna is the seat of a number of international organizations, the specific "residence conventions" contain additional immunity and exterritoriality rules.

Under public international law, foreign heads of state are exempt from domestic jurisdiction (and domestic law) for the duration of their official function. Foreign States are exempt only in their sovereign activities, not when they act as private subjects. Military actions are invariably *acta iure imperii*, and the state is immune in matters related to these actions. The offices and private residences of diplomats, consular offices, and the residence of international organizations also enjoy exterritoriality. This means that they are not subject to jurisdiction of domestic courts and enforcement proceedings. The heads of diplomatic missions, diplomatic staff, and their relatives are also immune.

Depending on the local law, domestic jurisdiction may be extended to persons who would otherwise enjoy exterritoriality in accordance with public international law if such a person explicitly submits to local jurisdiction or a court dispute involves the person's immoveable property locally or rights *in rem* regarding immovable property of third parties.

Waiver Through "Submission" to Jurisdiction

With regard to "submission" to jurisdiction, some jurisdictions expressly provide by statute that a State is not immune in proceedings as to which it has submitted to jurisdiction. Submission to jurisdiction can take place either by prior written agreement or after the dispute has arisen. A State is normally deemed to have submitted to jurisdiction if it has instituted the proceedings or intervened or taken any step in the proceedings. This does not normally apply to intervention or steps taken for the sole purpose of claiming immunity or asserting an interest in property where the State would have been entitled to immunity if the proceedings had been brought against it.

Depending on the applicable procedure, a notice of intention to defend will not prejudice immunity, but serving a defense will. Accordingly, a defendant State wishing to dispute the jurisdiction of the court is well advised to first enter a notice of intention to defend. This step does not necessarily constitute submission to jurisdiction. The State should then make an application by summons or motion, or limited appearance for the purpose of objecting to jurisdiction, accompanied by an affidavit claiming sovereign immunity. An application for the proceedings to be stayed because the State claims sovereign immunity should not constitute a submission to the jurisdiction, but an application on grounds of *forum non conveniens* risks being a submission if it is made or dealt with before the issue of sovereign immunity.

As to explicit submission, it may be required that a waiver of immunity be obtained through the Ministry of Foreign Affairs or equivalent, and may not be sufficient if obtained from a diplomat personally. Specific consent to a person's subjection under local court jurisdiction must be given by the sending State to be valid. Submission to jurisdiction is normally irrevocable and may not be modified.

If a State takes a step in proceedings in ignorance of facts which entitle it to immunity and if those facts could not reasonably have been ascertained and immunity is claimed as soon as reasonably practicable, the State may not be held to have submitted to jurisdiction.

The mere choice of the law of the country of asserted jurisdiction as the proper law of the contract does not necessarily constitute submission. At the same time, depending on the jurisdiction, where a State agrees that a dispute should be submitted to arbitration, it may lose immunity in relation to proceedings in the courts relating to that arbitration. This provision does not normally apply to arbitration agreements between States and may be subject to, and overridden by, a contrary provision in the parties' arbitration agreement.

Pursuant to Article 32(3) of the Vienna Convention on Diplomatic Relations, once a privileged person raises a claim as a plaintiff he cannot invoke immunity if the defendant files a counter-claim. This applies to contentious as well as non-contentious matters. At the same time, submission to personal jurisdiction is not tantamount to submission to enforcement jurisdiction and the diplomat is not exposed to enforcement proceedings unless he explicitly also submits to enforcement.

In some jurisdictions, there are no special rules or statutes respecting exercise of subject-matter or personal jurisdiction over foreign sovereigns, and there may be no or virtually no caselaw. In such cases, the general rules of procedural law are applicable.

"Commercial Activity" Exception to Immunity

In jurisdictions adhering to the principle of restricted sovereign immunity, waiver of such immunity is normally acceptable only when it is conclusive, specific, unequivocal and duly authorized by government, where applicable. This contrasts with the absolute right of sovereign immunity. A number of specific exceptions are provided for in legislation and caselaw depending on the country at issue. A principal one is that the immunity does not extend to proceedings concerning a "commercial transaction." "Commercial transactions" for the purposes of this limitation include contracts for the supply of goods and services as well as agreements for loans, guarantees or indemnities. They do not normally include contracts of employment or bills of exchange.

Depending on the jurisdiction, the statutory basis for what constitutes a "commercial" transaction for the purposes of immunity may contain an unhelpful, circular definition to the effect that the exception applies to any transaction, act or conduct or any regular course of conduct that by reason of its nature is "of a commercial character." In such cases, clearly the relevant caselaw must be consulted for application of the definition to particular fact patterns.

In particular, certain countries, whether in statute or caselaw or both, distinguish between the commercial "purpose" of an activity and the commercial "nature" of the same activity. In this regard, transactions or proceedings which merely "touch upon" or "incidentally affect" commercial activities may not fall within the exception. For instance, contracts entered into by foreign states and individuals are, in general, considered *acta iure gestionis*, except that employment contracts between foreign states and senior embassy staff are considered *acta iure imperii.*

The FSIA defines "commercial activity" in a manner that focuses on the "nature" of the activity, rather than the stated "purpose" of the foreign state's commercial activity, and recent caselaw has reaffirmed this emphasis. At the same time, the FSIA does not define the term "based upon." Even if a transaction is partly commercial, jurisdiction will not obtain if the cause of action is "based upon" a sovereign activity, for example in the case of promotion of investment.

Absent such a definition, the U.S. Supreme Court has concluded that Congress meant something more than a mere connection with, or relation to, commercial activity. Under the most recent caselaw, the U.S. Supreme Court and lower courts have become more reluctant to find that claims against foreign states are based upon a State's commercial activities than was formerly the case. At the same time, the Court has not expressly stated whether the commercial activity is to be analyzed by norms of private parties engaged in trade, traffic or commerce in the U.S., or whether a foreign State's standards will govern.

Other Exceptions to Sovereign Immunity

Apart from the "commercial activity" exception in some jurisdictions, there are other areas where submission of the sovereign to a foreign State's jurisdiction might come into consideration under the restricted theory of sovereign immunity. In certain jurisdictions, suits for damages and losses resulting from tort or *quasi*-tort, from death, personal injury or damage to or loss of property in the jurisdiction (apart from certain exceptions as to foreign armed forces) may be exempt from immunity.

In this regard, in the United States suits for non-commercial torts in the United States are exempt from immunity under § 1605(a)(5) of the FSIA if the tort "occurred" in the United States "caused by" either the foreign state, or employees of the foreign state acting in the scope of their employment. The potentially broad application of the non-commercial exception is limited to claims "based upon . . . discretionary functions" of the foreign State or State employee. The exception from immunity does not apply to a "claim arising out of malicious prosecution, abuse of process, libel, slander, misrepresentation, deceit, or interference with contract rights."

Among the other exceptions which might be mentioned, depending on the jurisdiction, are (i) *in rem* suits related to property situated within the territory; (ii) suits grounded on the status of heir or legatee, or assignee in a succession within the territory; (iii) suits related to a commercial or industrial establishment, or railway, which the foreign State owns within the territory; and (iv) suits resulting from contracts signed by the foreign State within the territory and enforceable therein.

Other exceptions may include (i) suits filed pursuant to an act not of a public nature and contracts where both parties to the dispute are States; (ii) proceedings relating to a contract of employment made in the jurisdiction or in respect of work wholly or partly performed there (apart from diplomatic staff); (iii) patents, trademarks, and trade or business names; (iv) a State's membership of a local body corporate, unincorporated body or partnership; and (v) value added tax, customs or excise duty, agricultural levies, or business rates in respect of premises. Finally, in the United States immunity is not granted when the action is initiated to enforce certain arbitration agreements or confirm certain arbitration awards or when the foreign State has violated certain international conventions, such as those relating to aircraft sabotage (e.g., 1996 Antiterrorism and Effective Death Penalty Act).

Local Violation of Human Rights by Foreign Sovereigns

The foreign sovereign immunity law of different states shows different approaches to the issue of whether the local courts will investigate or rule upon the validity of acts of a foreign government in its sovereign capacity done in its own territory.

Some States have subscribed to absolute sovereign immunity. Others which subscribe to restrictive sovereign immunity have held that the local statutory basis makes no exception in the case of an act against public international law, such as torture, and therefore a State will be able to rely on immunity in such circumstances: e.g., *Suleiman Al-Adsani v. Government of Kuwait*, English Court of Appeal, 13th March 1996 reported in The Times, 29 March 1996.

Alternatively, in some jurisdictions immunity may be rescinded by principles of public international law. In determining whether the local courts can exercise criminal jurisdiction, an important principle is that limitations of jurisdiction are not to be presumed. Limitations are determined by international customary law. Exercise of criminal jurisdiction against a foreign sovereign would not be excessive if the offense was committed locally, the victims were local nationals, or the acts which violate human rights are crimes against humanity. In the latter case, the courts must have custody of the sovereign.

To come within the definition of "crimes against humanity," the conduct must involve heinous conduct consisting of persecution of a civilian group or crimes of persecution on racial, religious or political grounds or wide acts of terrorization of a civilian population. Crimes against humanity have also been defined in the Statute of the International Tribunal for the former Yugoslavia (1993), Article 5 to include the crimes of murder, enslavement, extermination, deportation, imprisonment, torture, rape, persecution on political, racial and religious grounds, or other inhuman acts. The crimes must be committed in armed conflict, whether internal or international in character, and directed against any civilian population. The Statute of the International Tribunal for Rwanda (1994) gives a wider definition. It includes the same crimes but states that they must be committed as part of a widespread or systematic attack against any civilian population on national, political, ethnic or religious grounds. An "Act of State" defense would normally not be available for this crime and the foreign sovereign would not be immune.

To the extent the underlying issue is related to a specific individual, such individual may be entitled to immunity when the activities complained of were undertaken only on behalf of the foreign sovereign. Courts typically look to the allegations of the complaint to determine whether the individual is being sued in a governmental or private capacity. On a motion to dismiss, the individual claiming foreign State status has the burden of contradicting the allegations of the complaint with affidavits and other evidence.

Under the most recent caselaw in the United States, courts have become more reluctant to find that claims against foreign states are based upon a State's commercial activities than was formerly the case, and this likewise extends to human rights claims under the FSIA. *Saudi Arabia v. Nelson*, 507 U.S. 349 (1993) and its progeny represent a further constriction of the availability of U.S. courts as forums for redressing wrongs committed by foreign States against individuals outside of strictly commercial wrongs. This constriction applies even when such wrongs are committed against U.S. citizens, and even when occurring within the overall context of commercial activity.

There thus appears to be an end of or at least restriction to the ability to bring human rights claims within the rubric of commercial acts, in the sense that an act in the U.S. is required as the basis of the claim against the foreign state. Moreover, the U.S. courts have proven unwilling to imply a waiver of immunity on the basis of a foreign State's ratification of various human rights treaties that make no mention of enforcement proceedings before national courts: e.g., *Denegri v. Chile*, Civ. A. No. 86-3085, 1992 WL 91914 (D.D.C. Apr. 6, 1992).

Suits Against Aliens, Tort Statutes and Head-of-State Immunity

The foregoing should be distinguished from the separate issue of suits against aliens in U.S. courts generally under the Alien Tort Statute, also known as the Alien Tort Claims Act or Alien Tort Act, which provides that the federal courts shall have original jurisdiction of any civil action by an alien for a tort only, committed in violation of the law of nations or a treaty of the United States.

Such jurisdiction is very seldom granted. It can provide a forum to adjudicate transitory tort claims between individuals over whom personal jurisdiction is exercised wherever the tort occurred and to adjudicate tort claims arising outside of territorial jurisdiction as long as the conduct complained of was unlawful where performed. There is an opposing view, namely that the Statute was intended to be limited to torts committed on U.S. soil.

Furthermore, the Alien Tort Statute should be distinguished from the U.S. Torture Victim Protection Act of 1991, providing for federal jurisdiction as a basis for actions based on customary international law, with a private cause of action under international law: e.g., *Kadic v. Karadzic*, 70 F.3d 232 (2d Cir. 1995).

iii. Taking of Evidence Against Foreign Sovereign Entities

Depending on the jurisdiction, evidence may be taken from foreign sovereign entities only with their deliberate consent and without coercive measures. If a foreign sovereign entity may successfully invoke its immunity before a local court, that court has no judicial power over such entity and, as a consequence, may not order the taking of evidence against such entity.

The situation in the United States is instructive, also in view of the comparatively broad scope of "discovery" which may apply in some circumstances to sovereigns. The FSIA does not specifically address discovery against foreign sovereigns. Essentially, ordinary rules of discovery under the Federal Rules of Civil Procedure in federal courts and state law in state courts will apply. At the same time, when foreign sovereign immunity is raised as a defense to jurisdiction, some U.S. courts have postponed discovery until resolution of the threshold issue of whether immunity is to be granted. As the denial of immunity typically is immediately appealable, the court may wait until the resolution of such appeal before allowing or ordering discovery against the sovereign on the underlying claim.

Witness Testimony and Sovereign Immunity

A privileged person may consent or otherwise not be immune from jurisdiction by virtue of one of the exceptions described above. In such cases, he may be summoned as a witness to court proceedings, questioned on his premises, or requested to give written statements on the subject of testimony. Even in cases where a foreign State is subject to local jurisdiction, no penalty or fine may be imposed against it arising from its failure or refusal to produce any document or other information in the course of the proceedings. Even if the foreign sovereign may not or does not invoke its immunity, many courts then abstain from using coercive power to enforce the taking of evidence against foreign sovereigns. However, at its discretion, the court may draw its own conclusions from the foreign sovereign's refusal or omission to submit evidence to the court.

To the extent that unwilling witnesses are subject to the *subpoena* power of the local courts but *subpoenas* cannot be served abroad, there may be difficulties of service on an otherwise compellable witness. This may be the case unless the witness either is resident in or visits the local jurisdiction and can be served while there. If the witness returns abroad, the local court may not be able to compel him to attend, subject to the ability to successfully request foreign judicial authorities to take evidence of a witness in their jurisdiction by deposition for use in the local proceedings. The same opportunities, and constraints, as set forth in **Chapters 10** and **11** above generally apply to compellable witnesses in the sovereign context.

Depending on the applicable law, unless the privileged person consents the parties to the action are not allowed to take part in the questioning of the witness on his premises. In certain countries, the Ministry of Justice or equivalent authority transmits a request for the taking of evidence and must be kept informed of the subject, place and date of the taking of evidence. This privilege may not be extended to agencies of a foreign State. With this exception, evidence is taken under the ordinary rules.

Diplomatic or consular officers are exempted from testifying as witnesses under the applicable conventions unless otherwise provided. Thus under Article 31(2) of the Vienna Convention on Diplomatic Relations, a "diplomatic agent" is not obliged to give evidence as a witness. "Diplomatic agent" in this context relates to "the head of the mission or a member of the diplomatic staff of the mission." Under Article 44 of the Vienna Convention on Consular Relations, members of a consular post may be called upon to give evidence, but are not subject to any penalty or coercive measures if they refuse to do so. Special rules govern the scope of this evidence and the means by which it may be taken. Neither Convention addresses the possibility of *subpoenaing* a head of State. Depending on local legislation, there may or may not be a possible sanction for failure or refusal by or on behalf of a State to disclose or produce documents or other information for the purpose of proceedings to which it is a party.

International law and conventions provide for so-called "immunity of property." Such immunity contains further rules on the exterritoriality of enclosed premises of diplomatic missions and seats of intergovernmental organizations and their assets and property; private accommodation of diplomats; other premises and rooms used for official purposes; and archives, documents, and means of transportation of the diplomatic or consular corps.

In some jurisdictions, there are no special rules or statutes respecting taking of evidence from foreign sovereigns, and there may be no or virtually no caselaw. In such cases, the general rules of procedural law are applicable.

iv. Pre-Judgment Attachment and Other Injunctive Measures Against Foreign Sovereigns

Many jurisdictions provide that no executory or compulsory measures may be applied with regard to premises or assets which are subject to material immunity. Accordingly, as consent of the involved sovereign is not likely to be obtained, neither protective measures nor seizures are available in such cases. Other jurisdictions provide that even in the absence of immunity relief by way of injunctions, specific performance or the recovery of land or other property may not be granted against a foreign State unless the State in question consents in writing to that relief. Where a State so consents, the relief granted may not be greater than the extent of the consent.

In England and Wales, for example, the State Immunity Act 1978 provides that such measures are impermissible unless the State concerned has given its written consent. Submission to the jurisdiction of the English courts would not be sufficient to constitute such consent. At the same time, where a State contractually waives its sovereign immunity from UK proceedings, this waiver would extend to a Mareva injunction freezing assets pending a judgment (see Chapter I. above). The waiver would not extend to such an injunction relating to assets protected by diplomatic immunity such as a diplomat's residence. Express consent to waive sovereign immunity in that case would be required.

Convention Bases

The 1961 Vienna Convention provides in Article 31(3) that no executory measures may be taken against a diplomatic agent, except in the cases referred to in sub-paragraphs (a), (b), and (c) of paragraph 1 of Article 31. Furthermore, the diplomatic agent shall not be subject to any form of arrest or detention.

Nonetheless, the receiving State may at any time notify the sending State that the head of a mission or any other member of the staff is *persona non grata* or not acceptable. No further explanation is needed. Diplomatic agents always remain under the jurisdiction of the sending State. Again, no further provisions dealing with procedural and quasi-procedural issues exist. Therefore, the matter has to be solved case by case considering all the relevant facts and issues, such as foreign public policy, principles of public international law, and comity of nations.

Under the restricted immunity doctrine, enforcement and, therefore, pre-judgment attachments and other injunctive measures against foreign sovereigns are possible under some circumstances. This may be particularly the case with respect to property used in connection with diplomatic representations as well as foreign aircraft owned by a foreign sovereign and used exclusively for State services.

Under Article 23 of the European Convention on State Immunity, enforcement, pre-judgment attachments and injunctive measures against the property of a signatory state are permitted only to the extent that the foreign sovereign has explicitly agreed to such measures in writing. Under Article 26 of the Convention, the rule of Article 23 does not apply to the enforcement of claims based on *acta iure gestionis* of the foreign sovereign defendant and, to the extent enforcement is sought, only against property used for *acta iure gestionis*.

Approaches in the United States

Property in the United States owned by a foreign State cannot be attached, arrested or executed unless it falls within a statutory exception. This includes if the property is "used for a commercial activity in the United States" and the "foreign state" falls within one of six exceptions similar or identical to the exceptions relating to jurisdictional immunity. These are (i) waiver of immunity from attachment; (ii) the claim is based on the commercial activity of the property; (iii) the execution is in violation of international law; (iv) a judgment gives rights in property either acquired by succession or gift or is immovable in the United States; (v) a contractual obligation is the basis for the relationship to the property; or (vi) an arbitration award is the reason for execution of the property.

In the United States, there is a second set of exceptions for agencies or instrumentalities of a foreign state "engaged in commercial activity in the United States" where immunity from attachment is waived or the judgment relates to a claim for which the agency or instrumentality is not immune by virtue of the FSIA "regardless of whether the property is or was used for the activity upon which the claim is based."

Significantly, under the FSIA not only must reasonable notice be given before the court can order such attachment, but also property of a foreign State used for a commercial activity in the United States may be attached prior to entry of judgment in any U.S. action. This is possible if the foreign State explicitly waived its immunity and the purpose of the attachment is to secure satisfaction of a judgment that has been or may ultimately be entered against the foreign State, and not to obtain jurisdiction. Implicit waiver does not apply to this subsection.

In some jurisdictions, there are no special rules or statutes respecting prejudgment attachment and other injunctive measures against foreign sovereigns. In such cases, the general rules of procedural law are applicable.

Central Banks and Monetary Authorities

Unless immunity is explicitly waived, property belonging to the central bank or monetary authority of the foreign State that is held for its own account and is not used or intended for a commercial activity may be immune from attachment and execution. For example, the revised Federal Debt Collection Act which entered into force on January 1, 1997 in Switzerland provides that assets belonging to a foreign sovereign, i.e., a foreign State or central bank, which are used for purposes *de iure imperii* may not be seized or attached in Switzerland. Seizure or attachment will therefore not be possible in the case of accounts maintained with the Swiss National Bank for the purpose of Exchange Control Measures.

Some bilateral enforcement treaties explicitly provide grounds for denial of recognition of a decision if the defendant would have been lawfully privileged by public international law but had not entered an appearance in the proceedings.

As to whether the assets of a foreign central bank can be attached in one jurisdiction prior to a judgment against the central bank in another jurisdiction, in the U.S. context the FSIA proscribes prejudgment attachment of property in the U.S. held for the account of a foreign central bank, with certain exceptions. The FSIA provides that property of a foreign State held in the U.S. shall be immune from attachment, except as outlined elsewhere in the statute. § 1610(a) of the FSIA carves out an exemption for property "used for a commercial activity in the United States." However, § 1611(b)(1) provides that property of a foreign State shall be immune from attachment if it is property "of a foreign central bank or monetary authority held for its own account," unless there has been an explicit waiver of immunity.

For the practitioner, the issue is whether Section 1611(b) is an exception to the "commercial activity" exemption from immunity provided for in § 1610. A showing that property of a central bank is used for a commercial activity does not, of itself, exclude it from the immunity granted by § 1611(b)(1). More important is whether and to what extent the "commercial activity" provisions of the FSIA apply to *prejudgment* attachment. § 1610(d) provides that the property of a foreign State used for commercial activity "shall not be immune from attachment prior to the entry of judgment" where there has been an explicit waiver of immunity. However, it has been argued that § 1611(b)(1) trumps that provision, barring prejudgment attachment of central bank assets altogether. On the other hand, it has been contended that there is no logic to precluding a central bank from voluntarily waiving immunity.

Ultimately, there are certain limited avenues by which prejudgment attachment of central bank assets in the U.S. may be obtained. The primary one is by arguing that the funds of the central bank in the U.S. are not being held "for its own account." It has been held that funds held for a central bank's "own account" are funds used or held in connection with central banking activities, as distinguished from funds used solely to finance the commercial transactions of other entities or of foreign States. Determining which activities are central banking activities is far from a precise science. If a court determined that the debtor's assets in the U.S. were used, even partly, for commercial, non-central bank purposes, the commercial portions of those funds may be attached as long as the court can distinguish between funds used in connection with a central banking activity and funds not so used. Thus a so-called mixed purpose account may not be accorded immunity from attachment merely because some of the assets are used for central bank purposes.

v. Post-Judgment Attachment and Other Measures in Aid of Enforcement of Judgments Against Sovereigns

The rules governing post-judgment attachment and other measures in aid of enforcement against foreign sovereigns after a judgment has been rendered are in many countries not different from those governing pre-judgment attachments and other injunctive relief.

Under Article 32(4) of the 1961 Vienna Convention, waiver of immunity from jurisdiction in respect of civil or administrative proceedings shall not be held to be a waiver of immunity in respect of the execution of the judgment.

The general position under legislation is that the property of a foreign State is immune from execution to satisfy judgment obtained against the foreign State. An important exception may relate to commercial property which is subject to execution. It may also be possible for a foreign State to waive, by agreement, the application of the general rule that there cannot be execution against its property for the purposes of enforcing a judgment. Unless immunity is explicitly waived, property belonging to the central bank or monetary authority of the foreign State that is held for its own account and is not used or intended for a commercial activity is generally immune from attachment and execution.

vi. Recognition and Enforcement of Judgments Against Foreign Sovereigns

The general rules regarding recognition and enforcement of foreign judgments as discussed under **Chapter 17** above are largely applicable to the particular local or convention rules concerning foreign judgments rendered against foreign sovereigns abroad.

The particularity relating to foreign sovereigns is similar in most countries to the treatment of foreign sovereigns for purposes of jurisdiction. Thus, in the case of acts *jure imperii* judgments will not be enforced and no other measures will be taken unless the foreign sovereign waives its immunity. Where acts *jure gestionis* are concerned or the sovereign waives immunity, enforcement may take place and measures in aid of enforcement may be taken. However, only assets which do not serve governmental purposes may be seized.

Under Article 27 no. 1 of the Brussels/Lugano Conventions, where applicable, a foreign sovereign may invoke international *ordre public* or the fact that it has not unconditionally submitted to the foreign court's jurisdiction as a defense before the court of a Contracting State which is requested to recognize or enforce the foreign judgment.

Some jurisdictions, such as Switzerland, have also established an additional requirement for local enforcement of claims against foreign sovereigns, namely that a sufficiently close relationship of the matter concerned to the local jurisdiction of desired enforcement must be shown. The mere fact that a foreign party holds assets in Switzerland, for example, does not constitute such a sufficient relationship. In order to establish such a relationship, it must normally be shown, e.g., that a contract to which the foreign sovereign is a party has been concluded in Switzerland or is to be performed in Switzerland.

Depending on the applicable law, a judgment obtained in default of an appearance against a foreign State is not enforceable unless a copy of the judgment is served on the foreign State through diplomatic channels.

Waiver of Sovereign Immunity Against Enforcement

Article 32(4) of the Vienna Convention on Diplomatic Relations provides that if a state or foreign sovereign subjects itself to local jurisdiction, this does not automatically extend to enforcement proceedings. Therefore, in contracts with foreign sovereigns a "double subjection clause" should be included. The foreign sovereign thereby subjects itself to local jurisdiction as well as enforcement by local courts.

Depending on the local jurisdiction, the property of a foreign State located in that jurisdiction is normally immune from attachment and execution, arrest, detention, seizure and forfeiture in cases of an action *in rem*. The exceptions are where the foreign State in question either explicitly or implicitly waives its immunity with respect to such measures, unless the property of the State is used or is intended for commercial activity, or unless the execution relates to a judgment establishing rights in property acquired by succession or gift, or establishing rights in immoveable property located in the jurisdiction. Such relief may be available against an agency of a foreign State except in respect of military property. Depending on the jurisdiction, the State may give its written consent to measures of enforcement through the head of the State's diplomatic mission at the place of desired enforcement.

Such a restriction on enforcement does not necessarily prevent enforcement efforts against property in use or intended for use for "commercial" purposes. In some jurisdictions such as England and Wales, a certificate issued by the head of the State's diplomatic mission at the place of desired enforcement to the effect that property is not in use or intended for use by or on behalf of the State for commercial purposes may constitute sufficient evidence of that fact unless the contrary is proved.

Property not in use for commercial purposes may include the residence of a diplomat, property of a State's central bank or other monetary authority (see above), and money held by a diplomatic mission in a current account at a commercial bank used to meet day-to-day running of the mission. If the State in question is a party to the European Convention on State Immunity, the certification procedure (except in relation to ships in use for commercial purposes) is available only in proceedings to enforce a final judgment where the State has made a declaration under Article 24 of the European Convention, or to enforce an arbitral award.

In some jurisdictions, there are no special rules or statutes respecting pre-judgment attachment and other injunctive measures against foreign sovereigns. In such cases, the general rules of procedural law are applicable.

Recognition of Foreign Judgment Against the Same State in Which It is Sought

Finally, with respect to recognition and enforcement of foreign judgments against the State in which enforcement is sought (e.g., recognition in the UK of a German judgment against the UK), depending on local legislation a local court may recognize a final judgment of a foreign court against its own State under certain circumstances.

For example, the UK will not recognize a foreign judgment against itself from a European Convention State if it would be manifestly contrary to public policy, or if prior proceedings are pending in the UK or a Convention country between the same parties or a prior judgment has been entered and the current judgment is inconsistent with the previous one. Nor will it do so if the UK was not given proper notice of the proceedings and has not entered an appearance or applied to set the judgment aside. Finally, the UK courts will not extend recognition in relation to proceedings involving the UK's interest in movable or immovable property where the foreign court applied rules different from UK law and, as a result, reached a different decision as to jurisdiction from that which would have been reached in the UK.

Such rules relate to recognition, and not enforcement of judgments. They apply to judgments of European Convention courts only. Depending on the jurisdiction, it may or may not have rules relating to other States' courts generally.

Recognition and Enforcement of Foreign Judgments Against Foreign Sovereigns

The general rules on mutual recognition and enforcement of judgments must first be considered to ascertain whether the judgment in question is directly enforceable in accordance with a multilateral or bilateral treaty between the State where enforcement is sought and the State where the judgment was obtained, irrespective of the identity of the State against which the judgment is sought to be enforced. In this regard, the concerns raised in **Chapter 17** above may be relevant at least in part.

As a second step, if in principle such foreign judgment is directly enforceable, then local rules respecting service of process to recognize and enforce locally must be observed subject to the immunity issues relating to service, jurisdiction and enforcement raised above. Thus, enforcement may be possible only against assets in use for commercial purposes or where the State in question has given its consent.

In this regard, there may be additional rules or statutory provisions respecting such kind of enforcement which need to be heeded. In the UK, for example, a judgment given by a court of an overseas State against a State other than the UK or the State to which that court belongs will be recognized and enforced in the UK only under certain circumstances. For instance, the UK court must be able to affirm that the judgment would be so recognized and enforced if it had not been given against a State and that court would have had jurisdiction if it had applied certain provisions set forth in the State Immunity Act.

CHAPTER 20

COSTS AND FEES

Which party shall bear the costs of the litigation, including costs of legal assistance, or in which proportion those costs should be apportioned between the parties, is naturally an area of paramount concern in litigation. In the transnational litigation context, the issue may be subject to several different jurisdictional influences and therefore must be examined by the practitioner with great care, and ideally at an early stage.

i. Security for Costs

The issue of security for costs is primarily one of interim or conservatory relief, and not so much one of costs and fees attending the end phase of a litigation. For organizational purposes, at the same time, the subject is addressed here in the general category of costs and fees.

On certain occasions in national and international disputes, civil procedural and enforcement law of a particular jurisdiction may provide a basis for a court order requiring a security deposit before a certain action, decree or court activity will be made. Such a deposit will be ordered in most cases upon request of the opponent, sometimes on the court's own motion. It may also be possible to have it ordered as a precondition for granting an interim measure or a stay of enforcement already commenced (i.e., if extraordinary legal remedies such as restitution are sought, or if enforceability of a judgment is challenged).

Accompanying this practice is the risk that a successful defendant, whose costs are ordered to be paid by the plaintiff, may receive no payment if the plaintiff does not have sufficient funds to meet the costs. The same risk arises where the unsuccessful plaintiff is not resident within the jurisdiction, and may not have assets to which a judgment can attach. To protect defendants from this outcome, a defendant can seek a court order requiring the plaintiff to give "security" for the defendant's costs and a stay of the proceedings until the security is provided. Depending on the applicable rules, these applications can be made both at the trial-court level and at the hearing of any appeal. Application may be able to be made for security for costs to date or for future costs.

The court must determine the amount of security. It is normally equal to the potential damage if the applicant does not succeed and the judgment to be enforced is upheld, plus a mark-up. The court will also determine the deadline within which the applicant must pay the security in cash or domestic securities (including savings bank books) to the court.

Procedure

Depending on the jurisdiction, if a foreign national brings a claim before a court, the court may be obliged to order it upon defendant's request to deposit a security to cover the defendant's attorney's costs to be reimbursed if the defendant wins the case. However, depending on the jurisdiction such security is not required if the courts of the country in which the plaintiff is domiciled do not require a similar security of a plaintiff domiciled in the country where the action is being brought.

At the same time, such provision may be of limited importance. Depending on the jurisdiction, it may not apply if the claimant has a permanent domicile in the jurisdiction, if a local decision on reimbursement of litigation costs would be enforced in the state of the claimant's permanent domicile, if the claimant has assets within the jurisdiction, or if state treaties suspend the obligation to deposit a security.

Local rules may require the defendant to move for a security for costs upon its first appearance in the proceedings and specify the amount of security justified by the potential cost to be reimbursed. Depending on the local law, they may provide that the court decree must order the claimant either to deposit a specific amount of money or swear an oath that it is not able to raise the funds (oath of poverty). If neither the security is deposited nor the oath sworn, the plaintiff's action may be considered withdrawn.

Depending on the local rules, security for costs can be provided by agreement between the parties. This request also protects the defendant against an adverse costs award in respect of the application if the plaintiff later agrees to furnish security voluntarily. If the plaintiff refuses to give security by consent, the defendant should then issue an application to the court for security.

Grounds for Obtaining Security

There are certain customary grounds for making an application for security. These include (i) the plaintiff is ordinarily resident out of the jurisdiction; (ii) the plaintiff is conducting litigation for the benefit of a third person and may not be able to meet a costs order; or (iii) the plaintiff, not being an individual, is impecunious. While security may be awarded against an impecunious individual, this is rare. In deciding whether to award security, the court may conduct a balancing exercise between the rights of the plaintiff to maintain proceedings and the possibility that the plaintiff, if unsuccessful, will not be able to meet a costs order. Considerable caselaw has developed concerning the issues to be considered when exercising the discretion to award security in such jurisdictions as England and Australia.

To determine whether there is reason to believe that a plaintiff corporation, if unsuccessful, would be unable to pay the costs of the defendant's defense, the court must examine the corporation's solvency. An affidavit in support of the application should contain this information, including net asset position, ability to service debts, trading figures, the appointment of an external administrator and the liquidity of its assets. The extent of the corporation's solvency must then be compared to the defendant's cost of the action. This is usually estimated in an affidavit sworn by a litigator.

Among the factors considered relevant to the exercise of discretion are the prospects of success or merits of the proceeding. The existence of admissions by the defendant or payments into court beyond nuisance value are indicative of the merits of a matter. Also, if there has been delay in bringing the application for security, this may be considered. Once a defendant becomes aware of the plaintiff's impecuniosity, it should bring an application for security sooner rather than later, so the plaintiff does not incur substantial costs in the belief that an application will not be made.

Furthermore, whether the defendant's conduct is the cause of the plaintiff's impecuniosity will require analysis of the corporation's position prior to the acts complained of. Whether an order for security would stifle the proceedings is not decisive in itself, but also may weigh against the making of an order. Finally, whether the corporation's backers can provide security, especially where those persons will benefit from the successful litigation, may be considered.

Multilateral Conventions and Bilateral Treaties

Multilateral conventions and bilateral treaties may provide for the enforcement of court costs decisions in civil and commercial matters. In this regard, they may therefore suspend the obligation of foreign nationals in convention or treaty countries to deposit security for procedural costs. Many of the countries addressed in this work are parties to such conventions or treaties.

Under the Hague Conventions on Civil Procedure of 1905 and 1954 and the Hague Convention on the Internal Access to the Courts of 1980, security for costs cannot be required of plaintiffs domiciled in Contracting States solely by virtue of being domiciled abroad. Article 45 of the Brussels and Lugano Conventions does not prohibit a requirement of security for costs except as a condition for the enforcement of a judgment given in another Contracting State on the basis that the petitioner is a foreign national or is not domiciled or resident in the Contracting State in which the enforcement is sought.

Security for costs may, however, be prohibited by Articles 6, 59 or 60 of the Maastricht Treaty as a discrimination based on nationality: Judgment of the European Court of Justice of July 1, 1993 in Case C-20/92 (Hubbard); Preliminary Ruling of the European Court of Justice of September 26, 1996 in Case C-43/95, *Data Selecta Aktiebolag and Ronny Sorsberg v. MSL Dynamics*. Thus in recent years and influenced by European law, the principle that a foreign plaintiff is usually required to provide security has been restricted generally, including in England and Wales. Today, the foreign nationality of the plaintiff as a ground for security will be exercised only after proper scrutiny by the court. In general, security will not now be awarded against a plaintiff who is resident in the European Union unless the defendant can prove another ground beyond mere residence abroad. However, if the Plaintiff is resident outside the EU, the court may still usually order security to be provided. Even if a plaintiff is ordinarily resident abroad, if it can show that it has substantial assets situated within the jurisdiction, usually the plaintiff will not be required to give security for costs, provided that those assets are of a fixed and permanent nature and the plaintiff can show that they are available to satisfy the defendant's costs.

Security for Costs and Taking of Evidence

Certain courts may require security for costs caused by the taking of evidence abroad. Such courts may also require security for costs caused by the taking of evidence in another local court under special circumstances, e.g., a party requesting the taking of evidence domestically which is not related to an action pending in the court receiving the request. Furthermore, the court may require payment of or security for costs stated in a default judgment if the defendant petitions for resumption of the action.

ii. Court Costs

Depending on the jurisdiction, court fees may be structured as lump sum charges to be paid in advance, one charge for each court level. The charge may depend on the instance and the subject matter value, regardless of the proceeding's duration, number of hearings, etc.

Many courts operate on a subsidized system which charges a nominal amount to commence proceedings. Others may have more of a "user-pays" system. Generally, a plaintiff must pay a filing fee to commence proceedings in a court, which may be a flat rate to file initiating process. Under the "user-pays" system, additional fees may be payable for the filing of *subpoenas* and other interlocutory documents. Schedules of fees are normally available.

iii. Interest

In many jurisdictions, judgments carry prejudgment simple interest and, in some cases, additionally postjudgment simple interest, at rates set out by statute. If the debtor of a payment obligation is in default, then interest is normally owed. If a plaintiff wishes to recover interest on any damages suffered, this must normally be specifically pleaded in the originating process.

Prejudgment interest normally begins to run from the date the cause of action arose, but this date and the rate of interest may be varied by the court. Interest does not generally run on awards of exemplary or punitive damages or costs, where available. Postjudgment interest runs from the date of judgment.

Depending on the applicable law, a party may succeed in obtaining an order for the payment of interest on the damages owed, in some cases including the party's court fees and costs, so as to make interest run from the date when the interest sum falls due. In the case of court fees and costs, this may be considered to be the date of rendering or of notifying the judgment.

Where an action is based on contract, and interest at a stipulated rate has been provided for in the contract, the judgment will reflect the agreement unless it is usurious. In the absence of an agreement, the local law may determine the interest rate statutorily, in which case there may be differential rates, e.g., where merchants are involved, for amounts owed on promissory notes and checks, etc. If a creditor can prove that it has actually paid higher interest for a loan replacing the payment in dispute, then it may be able to claim such interest as damages if the delay in payment was caused negligently (ordinary negligence being sufficient) or wilfully. In some jurisdictions, unless merchants are involved (commercial matters), interest may only be claimed up to an amount equaling the capital amount (prohibition of the *ultra alterum tantum*).

Under English law, the rate of interest is often fixed at a level somewhat above the inter-bank borrowing rate or rates prevailing during the period of indebtedness. The three-month London Inter-Bank Offering Rate (LIBOR) as of September 6, 1995 was 6.75 percent per annum while the statutory rate of interest applicable to High Court proceedings was 8.0 percent per annum from the time of entering the judgment until the judgment is satisfied. Under New York Civil Practice Law and Rules § 5004, interest shall be at the rate of 9.0 percent per annum "except where otherwise provided by statute."

Where the appropriate damage can be shown to justify such an award, depending on the laws and custom a court may award interest on a compound, rather than simple interest basis. In these cases, strong evidence must normally be shown of an alternate use to which the funds would have been put.

iv. Attorney's Fees, Fee Schedules and Contingencies

In transnational disputes which are subject to arbitration agreements, many parties and practitioners have encountered the principle that the arbitrator's award shall, in addition to dealing with the merits of the case, fix the costs and decide which of the parties shall bear them and in what proportions. Furthermore, certain institutional rules provide at least a modicum of guidance as to what such costs may include. One example is Article 20(2) of the International Chamber of Commerce Rules of Arbitration in its current version, which provides that "[t]he costs of the arbitration shall include the arbitrator's fees and the administrative costs fixed by the International Court of Arbitration in accordance with the scale annexed to the present Rules, the expenses, if any, of the arbitrator, the fees and expenses of any experts, and the normal legal costs incurred by the parties."

In the transnational litigation context, by contrast, there may or may not be fee schedules which are applicable, the expenses of experts may not be a part of the judgment issued, and the "normal legal costs" incurred by the parties may or may not be susceptible of being claimed, or reimbursed, by judgment of the court. In short, the particular rules and customs of the jurisdiction involved must be examined closely, again at the earliest possible stage. Some jurisdictions require a fee agreement to be executed, which may aid in the recovery of costs following successful litigation.

In certain jurisdictions, there are either mandatory or suggested fee schedules for fees to be charged by an attorney for services rendered. Such schedules, which may be statutory, lay down fees for typical services rendered in litigation (court room activities, writs, letters, conferences, telephone conversations, etc.). The rates, where applicable, may be a function of the value of the matter and/or the time expended. For pleadings in normal matters, a fee may be charged regardless of the time expended.

For payment of the attorney by the client, such schedules, where applicable, may be subject to negotiation (mark-up or discount), or other bases such as hourly rates of attorneys may also be applied, instead of or parallel to the fee schedule, depending on local law and custom. In some jurisdictions, in instances in which the schedule does not include a fee for a specific legal service, guidelines for attorneys' fees may apply indicating which attorneys' fees will be considered "reasonable." Hourly rates for attorneys' services are also agreed with increasing frequency for nonlitigation services, even those jurisdictions in which fee schedules for litigation are either mandatory or still heavily used.

Contingency Fee Basis

In most of the countries addressed herein, local attorneys are prohibited from representing a client on the basis of a percentage of the amount recovered (*pactum de quota litis*) or on the basis of whether the intended result is achieved (*pactum de palmario*), generally called contingency fee bases. Such agreements would be null and void and even expose the attorney to disciplinary action, depending on the local rules. Such a prohibition would not necessarily rule out a "success fee" or "bonus" in certain cases. The Code of Conduct for Lawyers in the European Community explicitly prohibits the use of contingent fees. The provision, on the other hand, does not apply to an attorney's fee contract if the contract in question is concluded in accordance with the official fee schedule or otherwise controlled by the attorney's supervising authority.

In some jurisdictions where there is no such formal prohibition, contingency fee bases may nevertheless be frowned upon either by the judicial authorities, the local bar or other group. This effectively results in a low level of reliance on such arrangements. In certain countries, there are also codes of conduct for attorneys and concerning deposits (advance payments) to claim advance payment to cover the actual expenses for services to be performed and fees.

Whatever the rules or customs, particularly foreign attorneys from jurisdictions where such bases may be acceptable must inform themselves about the local parameters. Depending on the country and the circumstances, such foreign attorney could experience difficulties operating on such a contingency basis in connection with a foreign litigation even if his counseling and representation are channelled through a locally admitted co-counsel.

To the extent the attorney must seek payment of outstanding fees from a client by compulsory methods, many of the possible impediments to enforcement across borders generally, including public policy issues as discussed in **Chapter 17** above, could be relevant.

Bearing the Costs of Litigation

In most jurisdictions, each party must initially bear its own litigation costs, consisting of the fees for its attorneys and court charges, if any. Where there is an initial lump sum charge, it is normally paid by the plaintiff in the first instance and by the appealing party in higher instances. Also in most jurisdictions, the allocation and apportionment of the costs of the litigation are directly dependent on the "final" outcome of the proceedings (i.e., regardless of any fault element).

Thus, in most countries the losing party must reimburse the prevailing party for its court fees and attorneys' fees. Also in some systems, where a party prevails only partially, the reimbursement claims may be offset. If, for example, one party succeeds by 80 percent, then its reimbursement claim of 80 percent of its costs is reduced by its reimbursement obligation of 20 percent, so that it would ultimately be entitled to receive a 60-percent compensation of its costs. Under such an arrangement, if the claimant were awarded only 50 percent of the value originally claimed, neither party would have a cost reimbursement claim against the other. This is to a great extent a reflection of the principle, followed in many countries both in arbitration and civil litigation, that "costs follow the event."

Parties and practitioners who have had experience with transnational disputes in the realm of arbitration should be careful to disassociate local rules and customs respecting apportionment of attorneys' fees in arbitration and such apportionment in litigation. In a jurisdiction such as the United States, the principle of "costs follow the event" does not normally follow in civil litigation. At the same time, this does not necessarily mean that such principle, as well as other approaches to apportionment, are not frequently applied in the context of arbitration on U.S. soil or where U.S. law may apply to an arbitration with a foreign situs.

An example is the civil procedure of the State of New York. Under the Civil Practice Law and Rules § 7513 "[u]nless otherwise provided in the agreement to arbitrate, the arbitrator's expenses and fees, together with other expenses, not including attorney's fees, incurred in the conduct of the arbitration, shall be paid as provided in the award." At the same time, the practitioner should be aware that under this provision the court may, on application, "reduce or disallow any fee or expense it finds excessive or allocate it as justice requires." Practitioners who have experienced arbitral awards with a U.S. nexus in which, for example, the victor was awarded substantially all or all of its costs including attorneys' fees should not be lulled into the false assumption that such apportionment can be expected in a U.S. civil judgment.

Direct Costs of Party and Extraordinary Managerial Costs

Depending on the jurisdiction, there may be either a statutory basis or a custom enabling successful claims of extraordinary managerial time, or rather the monetary equivalent thereof, as well as other direct and indirect costs of the party as part of its reimbursable costs. Depending on the complexity, duration and volume of the dispute, and the related testimonial and documentary evidence, such costs could be considerable. Typically, they may include, in addition to out-of-pocket expenses, the fees of experts, expert witnesses, accountants, technicians, consultants and other external advisors. They may also include the value of the managerial time devoted in extraordinary fashion by in-house personnel to the litigation of the case, including in-house counsel.

Such losses may have been a direct result of the cause of action as to which the party is established to be either the successful claimant or the successful defendant. Many practitioners will be familiar with the concept of direct and indirect costs of the party itself, and in particular extraordinary managerial time, in connection with international arbitration disputes. An award of such costs can be regarded as being in conformity with international arbitral jurisprudence and with the laws of leading jurisdictions: e.g., UNCITRAL Rules of Arbitration Article 38.

Of course, whether in the arbitral setting the tribunal actually awards any or all of the direct or indirect costs of the parties, and particularly the value of the time of in-house personnel, will depend on the circumstances. Such an award may by no means be certain even in the case of the "100-percent successful" claimant. Furthermore, the claimant of costs should assert that it took every measure to minimize the amount of time which needed to be invested in the preparation of its claim.

"Reasonableness" of Attorneys' Fees and Other Costs

To the extent the applicable rules allow the judge to exercise discretion as to what constitutes "reasonable" costs and attorneys' fees, "reasonable" will be subject to different interpretations.

One source of difference in interpretation is whether the attorneys' fees which have been incurred were "necessitated" by the complexity of the dispute, by the tactical conduct of the other parties and, occasionally, by the desultory nature of the other party's claims or defenses. Again, in arbitration practice, arbitrators may take into account the conduct of the parties, obstructionist tactics causing delay and costs, and the poorly organized or otherwise inadequate manner in which a party has presented its claims or defenses. Such factors may in turn be seen as having obliged the other party to incur additional time and expense responding to such allegations. Moreover, even a "successful" claimant may be deprived of costs where it grossly exaggerated its claims, so that the "successful" claimant may be ordered to pay the whole of the respondent's costs. In litigation, depending on the rules and customs, such distinctions may also be drawn.

Therefore, the international practitioner must assess, with the assistance of local counsel, what may be "reasonable" in the eyes of the opposing party and particularly of the court. In so doing, it may avoid overreaching—or selling short—a claim for attorneys' fees. This overlaps again with the fact that different systems have different approaches to calculating and assessing attorneys' fees, whether according to mandatory fee schedules or hourly rates or otherwise. Moreover, ever where there is agreement that hourly rates should be the barometer, depending on the jurisdictions involved there may be vastly diverging notions of what hourly rates are "reasonable."

Settlement Proposals and Costs

There may be an interplay between proposals by a party to settle which were rejected, on the one hand, and awards of costs on the other hand. For example, where a party submits a formal offer to settle that is refused, that party may be entitled to full indemnification of its costs from the date of the offer if the eventual judgment is more favorable than the offer. A plaintiff who refuses a formal offer of settlement may be heavily penalized in costs if judgment is eventually given in his favor but for an amount equal to or less than the defendant's offer. This subject is addressed in **Chapter 18** above respecting settlement and cost awards.

Legal Aid

Certain countries have laws which provide legal aid to a party which cannot afford to conduct legal proceedings without endangering its "necessary maintenance." In the European context, such laws are deemed to be in compliance with Article 6 of the European Convention on Human Rights, providing free access to the courts.

In some such countries, a decree granting legal aid may be issued by the court competent for the main proceedings, in which case the party affected is temporarily relieved of any obligation to pay court charges and may be assigned an attorney free of charge. In its application for legal aid, the applicant may need to prove its financial situation. Under certain circumstances, the party granted legal aid may later be required to repay the court charges and attorney fees. Depending on the local law and legislation, legal aid may or may not be limited to local citizens or residents. In some jurisdictions, free legal aid is normally granted only to private parties. Free legal aid covers—in principle—the party's own costs and costs awarded to the other party.

ACCESSIONS TO AND RATIFICATIONS OF THE HAGUE CONVENTIONS as of March 8, 1998

- Service Abroad of Judicial and Extrajudicial Documents in Civil or Commercial Matters, November 15, 1965 (entered into force February 10, 1969)
- Taking of Evidence Abroad in Civil of Commercial Matters, March 18, 1970 (entered into force October 7, 1972)

Member States of Conference	1965: Service	1970: Evidence
Argentina	—	X
Australia	—	X
Austria	—	—
Belgium	X	—
Canada	X	—
Chile	—	—
China	X	X[1]
Croatia	—	—
Cyprus	X	X
Czech Republic	X	X
Denmark	X	X
Egypt	X	—
Finland	X	X
FYROM [2]	—	—
France	X	X
Germany	X	X
Greece	X	—
Hungary	—	—
Ireland	X	—
Israel	X	X
Italy	X	X
Japan	X	—
Latvia	X	X
Luxembourg	X	X
Malta	—	—

1 The Convention applies to the Hong Kong Special Administrative Region only.
2. The Former Yugoslav Republic of Macedonia.

APPENDIX I

THE HAGUE CONVENTIONS

Member States of Conference	**1965: Service**	**1970: Evidence**
Mexico	—	X
Monaco	—	X
Morocco	—	—
Netherlands	X	X
Norway	X	X
Poland	X	X
Portugal	X	X
Romania	—	—
Slovak Republic	X	X
Slovenia	—	—
Spain	X	X
Suriname	—	—
Sweden	X	X
Switzerland	X	X
Turkey	X	—
United Kingdom	X	X
United States	X	X
Uruguay	—	—
Venezuela	X	X

Non-Member States of Conference	1965: Service	1970: Evidence
Andorra	—	—
Antigua and Barbuda	X	—
Armenia	—	—
Bahamas	X	—
Barbados	X	X
Belarus	X	—
Belize	—	—
Bosnia & Herzegovina	—	—
Botswana	X	—
Brazil	—	—
Brunei Darussalam	—	—
Burkina Faso	—	—
Colombia	—	—
Costa Rica	—	—
Ecuador	—	—
El Salvador	—	—
Estonia	X	X
Fiji	—	—
Grenada	—	—
Holy See	—	—
Iceland	—	—
Kyrgyz Republic	—	—
Lebanon	—	—
Lesotho	—	—
Liberia	—	—
Liechtenstein	—	—
Lithuania	—	—
Malawi	X	—
Marshall Islands	—	—
Mauritius	—	—
Moldova	—	—
New Zealand	—	
Niger	—	—
Pakistan	X	—
Panama	—	—

Non-Member States of Conference	1965: Service	1970: Evidence
Andorra	—	—
Peru	—	—
Philippines	—	—
Russian Federation	—	—
St. Kitts and Nevis	—	—
San Marino	—	—
Seychelles	X	—
Singapore	—	X
South Africa	—	X
Sri Lanka	—	—
Swaziland	—	—
Tonga	—	—
Uzbekistan	—	—
Yugoslavia [1]	—	—
Zimbabwe	—	—

CONVENTION ON THE SERVICE ABROAD OF JUDICIAL AND EXTRAJUDICIAL DOCUMENTS IN CIVIL OR COMMERCIAL MATTERS (Concluded November 15, 1965)

The States signatory to the present Convention, Desiring to create appropriate means to ensure that judicial and extrajudicial documents to be served abroad shall be brought to the notice of the addressee in sufficient time, Desiring to improve the organisation of mutual judicial assistance for that purpose by simplifying and expediting the procedure, Have resolved to conclude a Convention to this effect and have agreed upon the following provisions:

Article 1

The present Convention shall apply in all cases, in civil or commercial matters, where there is occasion to transmit a judicial or extrajudicial document for service abroad. This Convention shall not apply where the address of the person to be served with the document is not known.

CHAPTER I - JUDICIAL DOCUMENTS

Article 2

Each contracting State shall designate a Central Authority which will undertake to receive requests for service coming from other contracting States and to proceed in conformity with the provisions of articles 3 to 6. Each State shall organise the Central Authority in conformity with its own law.

Article 3

The authority or judicial officer competent under the law of the State in which the documents originate shall forward to the Central Authority of the State addressed a request conforming to the model annexed to the present Convention, without any requirement of legalisation or other equivalent formality. The document to be served or a copy thereof shall be annexed to the request. The request and the document shall both be furnished in duplicate.

Article 4

If the Central Authority considers that the request does not comply with the provisions of the present Convention it shall promptly inform the applicant and specify its objections to the request.

Article 5

The Central Authority of the State addressed shall itself serve the document or shall arrange to have it served by an appropriate agency, either -

(a) by a method prescribed by its internal law for the service of documents in domestic actions upon persons who are within its territory, or

(b) by a particular method requested by the applicant, unless such a method is incompatible with the law of the State addressed. Subject to sub-paragraph (b) of the first paragraph of this article, the document may always be served by delivery to an addressee who accepts it voluntarily.

If the document is to be served under the first paragraph above, the Central Authority may require the document to be written in, or translated into, the official language or one of the official languages of the State addressed.

That part of the request, in the form attached to the present Convention, which contains a summary of the document to be served, shall be served with the document.

Article 6

The Central Authority of the State addressed or any authority which it may have designated for that purpose, shall complete a certificate in the form of the model annexed to the present Convention. The certificate shall state that the document has been served and shall include the method, the place and the date of service and the person to whom the document was delivered. If the document has not been served, the certificate shall set out the reasons which have prevented service.

The applicant may require that a certificate not completed by a Central Authority or by a judicial authority shall be countersigned by one of these authorities. The certificate shall be forwarded directly to the applicant.

Article 7

The standard terms in the model annexed to the present Convention shall in all cases be written either in French or in English. They may also be written in the official language, or in one of the official languages, of the State in which the documents originate. The corresponding blanks shall be completed either in the language of the State addressed or in French or in English.

Article 8

Each contracting State shall be free to effect service of judicial documents upon persons abroad, without application of any compulsion, directly through its diplomatic or consular agents. Any State may declare that it is opposed to such service within its territory, unless the document is to be served upon a national of the State in which the documents originate.

Article 9

Each contracting State shall be free, in addition, to use consular channels to forward documents, for the purpose of service, to those authorities of another contracting State which are designated by the latter for this purpose.

Each contracting State may, if exceptional circumstances so require, use diplomatic channels for the same purpose.

Article 10

Provided the State of destination does not object, the present Convention shall not interfere with -

(a) the freedom to send judicial documents, by postal channels, directly to persons abroad,

(b) the freedom of judicial officers, officials or other competent persons of the State of origin to effect service of judicial documents directly through the judicial officers, officials or other competent persons of the State of destination,

(c) the freedom of any person interested in a judicial proceeding to effect service of judicial documents directly through the judicial officers, officials or other competent persons of the State of destination.

Article 11

The present Convention shall not prevent two or more contracting States from agreeing to permit, for the purpose of service of judicial documents, channels of transmission other than those provided for in the preceding articles and, in particular, direct communication between their respective authorities.

Article 12

The service of judicial documents coming from a contracting State shall not give rise to any payment or reimbursement of taxes or costs for the services rendered by the State addressed. The applicant shall pay or reimburse the costs occasioned by -

(a) the employment of a judicial officer or of a person competent under the law of the State of destination,

(b) the use of a particular method of service.

Article 13

Where a request for service complies with the terms of the present Convention, the State addressed may refuse to comply therewith only if it deems that compliance would infringe its sovereignty or security.

It may not refuse to comply solely on the ground that, under its internal law, it claims exclusive jurisdiction over the subject-matter of the action or that its internal law would not permit the action upon which the application is based.

The Central Authority shall, in case of refusal, promptly inform the applicant and state the reasons for the refusal.

Article 14

Difficulties which may arise in connection with the transmission of judicial documents for service shall be settled through diplomatic channels.

Article 15

Where a writ of summons or an equivalent document had to be transmitted abroad for the purpose of service, under the provisions of the present Convention, and the defendant has not appeared, judgment shall not be given until it is established that -

(a) the document was served by a method prescribed by the internal law of the State addressed for the service of documents in domestic actions upon persons who are within its territory, or

(b) the document was actually delivered to the defendant or to his residence by another method provided for by this Convention,

and that in either of these cases the service or the delivery was effected in sufficient time to enable the defendant to defend.

Each contracting State shall be free to declare that the judge, notwithstanding the provisions of the first paragraph of this article, may give judgement even if no certificate of service or delivery has been received, if all the following conditions are fulfilled -

(a) the document was transmitted by one of the methods provided for in this Convention,

(b) a period of time of not less than six months, considered adequate by the judge in the particular case, has elapsed since the date of the transmission of the document,

(c) no certificate of any kind has been received, even through every reasonable effort has been made to obtain it through the competent authorities of the State addressed.

Notwithstanding the provisions of the preceding paragraphs the judge may order, in case of urgency, any provisional or protective measures.

Article 16

When a writ of summons or an equivalent document had to be transmitted abroad for the purpose of service, under the provisions of the present Convention, and a judgment has been entered against a defendant who has not appeared, the judge shall have the power to relieve the defendant from the effects of the expiration of the time for appeal from the judgment if the following conditions are fulfilled -

(a) the defendant, without any fault on his part, did not have knowledge of the document in sufficient time to defend, or knowledge of the judgment in sufficient time to appeal, and

(b) the defendant has disclosed a prima facie defence to the action on the merits. An application for relief may be filed only within a reasonable time after the defendant has knowledge of the judgment.

Each contracting State may declare that the application will not be entertained if it is filed after the expiration of a time to be stated in the declaration, but which shall in no case be less than one year following the date of the judgment.

This article shall not apply to judgments concerning status or capacity of persons.

CHAPTER II - EXTRAJUDICIAL DOCUMENTS

Article 17

Extrajudicial documents emanating from authorities and judicial officers of a contracting State may be transmitted for the purpose of service in another contracting State by the methods and under the provisions of the present Convention.

CHAPTER III - GENERAL CLAUSES

Article 18

Each contracting State may designate other authorities in addition to the Central Authority and shall determine the extent of their competence.

The applicant shall, however, in all cases, have the right to address a request directly to the Central Authority. Federal States shall be free to designate more than one Central Authority.

Article 19

To the extent that the internal law of a contracting State permits methods of transmission, other than those provided for in the preceding articles, of documents coming from abroad, for service within its territory, the present Convention shall not affect such provisions.

Article 20

The present Convention shall not prevent an agreement between any two or more contracting States to dispense with -

(a) the necessity for duplicate copies of transmitted documents as required by the second paragraph of article 3,

(b) the language requirements of the third paragraph of article 5 and article 7,

(c) the provisions of the fourth paragraph of article 5,

(d) the provisions of the second paragraph of article 12.

Article 21

Each contracting State shall, at the time of the deposit of its instrument of ratification or accession, or at a later date, inform the Ministry of Foreign Affairs of the Netherlands of the following -

(a) the designation of authorities, pursuant to articles 2 and 18,

(b) the designation of the authority competent to complete the certificate pursuant to article 6,

(c) the designation of the authority competent to receive documents transmitted by consular channels, pursuant to article 9.

Each contracting State shall similarly inform the Ministry, where appropriate, of -

(a) opposition to the use of methods of transmission pursuant to articles 8 and 10,

(b) declarations pursuant to the second paragraph of article 15 and the third paragraph of article 16,

(c) all modifications of the above designations, oppositions and declarations.

Article 22

Where Parties to the present Convention are also Parties to one or both of the Conventions on civil procedure signed at the Hague on 17th July 1905, and on 1st March 1954, this Convention shall replace as between them articles 1 to 7 of the earlier Conventions.

Article 23

The present Convention shall not affect the application of article 23 of the Convention on civil procedure signed at The Hague on 17th July 1905, or of article 24 of the Convention on civil procedure signed at The Hague on 1st March 1954.

These articles shall, however, apply only if methods of communication, identical to those provided for in these Conventions, are used.

Article 24

Supplementary agreements between parties to the Conventions of 1905 and 1954 shall be considered as equally applicable to the present Convention, unless the parties have otherwise agreed.

Article 25

Without prejudice to the provisions of articles 22 and 24, the present Convention shall not derogate from Conventions containing provisions on the matters governed by this Convention to which the contracting States are, or shall become, Parties.

Article 26

The present Convention shall be open for signature by the States represented at the Tenth Session of the Hague Conference on Private International Law.

It shall be ratified, and the instruments of ratification shall be deposited with the Ministry of Foreign Affairs of the Netherlands.

Article 27

The present Convention shall enter into force on the sixtieth day after the deposit of the third instrument of ratification referred to in the second paragraph of article 26. The Convention shall enter into force for each signatory State which ratifies subsequently on the sixtieth day after the deposit of its instrument of ratification.

Article 28

Any State not represented at the Tenth Session of the Hague Conference on Private International Law may accede to the present Convention after it has entered into force in accordance with the first paragraph of article 27. The instrument of accession shall be deposited with the Ministry of Foreign Affairs of the Netherlands. The Convention shall enter into force for such a State in the absence of any objection from a State, which has ratified the Convention before such deposits, notified to the Ministry of Foreign Affairs of the Netherlands within a period of six months after the date on which the said Ministry has notified it of such accession.

In the absence of any such objection, the Convention shall enter into force for the acceding State on the first day of the month following the expiration of the last of the periods referred to in the preceding paragraph.

Article 29

Any State may, at the time of signature, ratification or accession, declare that the present Convention shall extend to all the territories for the international relations of which it is responsible, or to one or more of them. Such a declaration shall take effect on the date of entry into force of the Convention for the State concerned.

At any time thereafter, such extensions shall be notified to the Ministry of Foreign Affairs of the Netherlands.

The Convention shall enter into force for the territories mentioned in such an extention on the sixtieth day after the notification referred to in the preceding paragraph.

Article 30

The present Convention shall remain in force for five years from the date of its entry into force in accordance with the first paragraph of article 27, even for States which have ratified it or acceded to it subsequently.

If there has been no denunciation, it shall be renewed tacitly every five years.

Any denunciation shall be notified to the Ministry of Foreign Affairs of the Netherlands at least six months before the end of the five year period.

It may be limited to certain of the territories to which the Convention applies.

The denunciation shall have effect only as regards the State which has notified it. The Convention shall remain in force for the other contracting States.

Article 31

The Ministry of Foreign Affairs of the Netherlands shall give notice to the States referred to in article 26, and to the States which have acceded in accordance with article 28, of the following -

(a) the signatures and ratifications referred to in article 26;

(b) the date on which the present Convention enters into force in accordance with the first paragraph of article 27;

(c) the accessions referred to in article 28 and the dates on which they take effect;

(d) the extensions referred to in article 29 and the dates on which they take effect;

(e) the designations, oppositions and declarations referred to in article 21;

(f) the denunciations referred to in the third paragraph of article 30.

IN WITNESS WHEREOF the undersigned, being duly authorised thereto, have signed the present Convention.

DONE at The Hague, on the 15th day of November, 1965, in the English and French languages, both texts being equally authentic, in a single copy which shall be deposited in the archives of the Government of the Netherlands, and of which a certified copy shall be sent, through the diplomatic channel, to each of the States represented at the Tenth Session of the Hague Conference on Private International Law.

ANNEX TO THE CONVENTION

FORMS

REQUEST

FOR SERVICE ABROAD OF JUDICIAL OR EXTRAJUDICIAL DOCUMENTS

Convention on the Service Abroad of Judicial and Extrajudicial Documents In Civil or Commercial Matters, signed at The Hague, November 15, 1965.

Identity and address of the applicant	Address of receiving authority

The undersigned applicant has the honour to transmit–in duplicate–the documents listed below and, in conformity with article 5 of the above-mentioned Convention, requests prompt service of one copy thereof on the addressee, i.e.,

(identity and address) ______________________________

____

(a) in accordance with the provisions of sub-paragraph (a) of the first paragraph of article 5 of the Convention.*

(b) in accordance with the following particular method (sub-paragraph (b) of the first paragraph of article 5):* ______________________________

____

____

____

(c) by delivery to the addressee, if he accepts it voluntarily (second paragraph of article 5).

The authority is requested to return or to have returned to the applicant a copy of the documents–and of the annexes*–with a certificate as provided on the reverse side.

List of documents

____

____

____

____

____

____

____

______________________________ Done at __________, the __________

Signature and/or stamp.

Reverse of the request

CERTIFICATE

The undersigned authority has the honour to certify, in conformity with article 6 of the Convention,

1) that the document has been served*

- the (date) ____________________
- at (place, street, number) ____________________
____

- in one of the following methods authorized by article 5–

  (a) in accordance with the provisions of sub-paragraph (a) of the first paragraph of article 5 of the Convention.*

  (b) in accordance with the following particular method:* ____________________
  ____

  (c) by delivery to the addressee, who accepted it voluntarily*.

The documents referred to in the request have been delivered to:

- (identity and description of person) ____________________
____

- relationship to the addressee (family, business or other): ____________________
____

2) that the document has not been served, by reason of the following facts:* ____
____
____
____

In conformity with the second paragraph of article 12 of the Convention, the applicant is requested to pay or reimburse the expenses detailed in the attached statement.*

Annexes

Documents returned: ____________________
____
– ____________________

In appropriate cases, documents establishing the service: ____________________
____________________ Done at ________, the ________
____
____________________ Signature and/or stamp.

* Delete if inappropriate

SUMMARY OF THE DOCUMENT TO BE SERVED

Convention on the service abroad of judicial and extrajudicial documents in civil or commercial matters, signed at The Hague, the 15th of November 1965

(article 5, fourth paragraph)

Name and address of the requesting authority: ______________________________

____

Particulars of the parties:** ______________________________

____

JUDICIAL DOCUMENT**

Nature and purpose of the document: ______________________________

____

Nature and purpose of the proceedings and, where appropriate the amount in dispute:

____

____

Date and place for entering appearance:* ______________________________

____

Court which has given judgment:* ______________________________

____

Date of judgment:* ______________________________

Time limits stated in the document:* ______________________________

____

EXTRAJUDICIAL DOCUMENT**

Nature and purpose of the document: ______________________________

____

Time limits stated in the document:** ______________________________

____

* Delete if inappropriate

DECLARATIONS BY CONTRACTING STATES

ANTIGUA AND BARBUDA

Notification in conformity with Article 31 of the Convention

By note of 1 May 1985, received at the Ministry of Foreign Affairs of the Kingdom of Netherlands on 17 May 1985, the Government of Antigua and Barbuda informed the Ministry of Foreign Affairs it does consider itself bound by the abovementioned Convention, declared applicable to Antigua by the Government of the United Kingdom of Great Britain and Northern Ireland on 20 May 1970.

Notification in conformity with Article 31, letter e, of the Convention

The Government of Antigua and Barbuda informed the Ministry of Foreign Affairs of the Kingdom of the Netherlands by Note of 2 May 1986 that as the authority referred to in Article 21 has been designated:

The Registrar-Eastern Caribbean Supreme Court.

Notification in conformity with Article 31, letter e, of the Convention

Rectification of the Notifications Judicial and Extrajudicial Documents Nos. 2 and 3/ 1987 of 14 July 1987 and 28 August 1987.

The competent authorities under Article 21 of the above-mentioned Convention, designated by the Government of Antigua and Barbuda, are:

a) The Governor-General, Antigua and Barbuda;

b) The Registrar of the High Court of Antigua and Barbuda, St. John's, Antigua.

The Hague, 18 November 1987

Notification in conformity with Article 31, paragraph e, of the Convention

Referring to the extension of the Convention in 1970 to Hong Kong and the designation of the Central Authority for Hong Kong the Government of the United Kingdom of Great Britain and Northern Ireland informed the Ministry of Foreign Affairs of the Kingdom of the Netherlands by letter of 3 May 1984 that "the Colonial Secretary of Hong Kong" has been re-designated as "the Chief Secretary of Hong Kong". Requests for documents to be served in Hong Kong should be addressed accordingly.

BARBADOS

With the following declaration:

"The Government of Barbados has designated the Registrar of the Supreme Court of Barbados as the Central Authority for the purposes of Articles 2 and 18, in accordance with the provisions of Article 21 of the Convention."

BELGIUM

With the following declaration:

"1. In conformity with the first paragraph of Article 2 of the Convention, the Ministry of Justice. Administration de la Législation. Place Poelaert, 4, 1.000 Brussels is designated as the Central Authority;

"2. The Ministry of Justice is also designated as the competent authority to receive documents forwarded by the channels provided for in the first paragraph of Article 9 of the Convention;

"3. The Belgian Government is opposed to use being made within its territory of the freedom to effect service provided for in the first paragraph of Article 8;

"4. The Belgian Government declares that it will avail itself of the provision contained in the second paragraph of Article 15;

"5. In conformity with the third paragraph of Article 16, the Belgian Government declares that the applications mentioned in the second paragraph of Article 16 will not be entertained if they are filed after the expiration of a period of one year following the date of the judgment;

* Delete if inappropriate

** If appropriate, identify and address of the person interested in the transmission of the document.

"6. The Belgian Government believes it should draw attention to the fact that any request for the service of documents made under sections a) or b) of the first paragraph of Article 5 requires the agency of a process-server (huissier de justice) and that the resulting costs should be reimbursed in conformity with Article 12 of the Convention."

BOTSWANA

With the following declaration:

"1. Pursuant to the first paragraph of Article 2 of the Convention the Minister of State in the Office of the President of the Republic of Botswana has been designated the Central Authority to receive requests for service from other contracting states.

"2. The Registrar of the High Court of Botswana is designated as the authority competent to complete the certificate in the form of the Model annexed to the Convention pursuant to the first paragraph of Article 6.

"3. In accordance with the provisions of Article 9 of the Convention the Minister of State in the Office of the President is designated as the receiver of process sent through Consular channels.

"4. It is declared that the Government of Botswana objects to the method of service referred to in sub-paragraphs (b) and (c) of Article 10.

"5. It is declared that a judge of the High Court of Botswana may give judgment if all the conditions specified in paragraph 2 of Article 15 are fulfilled."

All documents forwarded for service must be in duplicate and written in or translated into the English language.

CANADA

Notification in conformity with Article 31, paragraph c, of the Convention.

Canada deposited its instrument of accession to the above-mentioned Convention with the Ministry of Foreign Affairs of the Kingdom of the Netherlands on 26 September 1988 in accordance with Article 28, paragraph 1.

The States which have ratified the Convention were notified by the Dutch Government of the accession on 29 September 1988. Since none of these States raised an objection to the accession within the period of six months specified in Article 28, paragraph 2, the said accession became perfect on 10 April 1989.

In accordance with Article 28, paragraph 3, the provisions of the Convention will enter into force for Canada on 1 May 1989.

A copy of a document transmitted by Canada and containing the designations and declarations referred to in Article 21 of the Convention is attached to this Notification.

CANADA

A. *Transmission and execution of requests for service*

1. Central Authority

(Article 2 and Article 18, paragraph 3)

comment: To save time, requests should be forwarded directly to the Central Authority of the province or territory concerned. They may, however, also be forwarded to the Federal Central Authority which will transmit them to the relevant Central Authority.

Alberta

name:	Attorney–General for Alberta Att: Executive Director–Court Services
address:	9833–109th Street Edmonton, Alberta Canada T5K 2E
telephone:	(403) 427–4992

British Columbia

name:	Ministry of the Attorney–General for British Columbia Office of the Deputy Minister
address:	Fifth Floor, 910 Government Street Victoria, British Columbia Canada V8V 1X4
telephone:	(604) 387–5211

Manitoba

name:	Attorney–General for Manitoba c/o Director–Civil Legal Services
address:	Woodsworth Building, 6th Floor 405 Broadway Winnipeg, Manitoba Canada, R3C 0V8
telephone:	(204) 945–2847

New Brunswick

name:	Attorney–General for New Brunswick
address:	P.O. Box 6000 Fredericton, New Brunswick Canada, E3B 5H1
telephone:	(506) 453–2208

Newfoundland

name:	Department of Justice
address:	Confederation Building St. John's, Newfoundland Canada A1C 517
telephone:	(709) 576–2869

Nova Scotia

name:	Attorney General of Nova Scotia Legal Services Division
address:	P.O. Box 7 Halifax, Nova Scotia B3J 2L6
telephone:	(902) 424–4024

Ontario

name:	Ministry of the Attorney General for Ontario Reciprocity Office: Civil Law Division
address:	18 King Street East Toronto, Ontario Canada M5C 1C5
telephone:	(416) 965–2570

Prince Edward Island

name:	Attorney General of Prince Edward Island Office of the Deputy Minister
address:	P.O. Box 2000 Charlottetown, Prince Edward Island Canada C1A 7N8
telephone:	(902) 368–4570

Québec

name:	Minister de la Justice du Québec a/s Le service juridique
address:	1200 route de l'Église 5 ième étage Ste-Foy, Québec Canada G1V 4M1
telephone:	(418) 643–1436

Saskatchewan

name:	Minister of Justice for Saskatchewan Att. of Director of Sheriff Services
address:	1874 Scarth St., 10th Floor Regina, Saskatchewan Canada S4P 3V7
telephone:	(306) 787–5488

Yukon

name:	Director of Court Services
address:	Department of Justice, Box 2703 Whitehorse, Yukon Y1A 2C6
telephone:	(403) 667–5942

Northwest Territories

name:	Deputy Minister of Justice Government of the Northwest Territories
address:	Box 1320 Yellowknife, Northwest Territories Canada X1A 2L9
telephone:	(613) 995–0119

CANADA

name:	Director, Legal Advisory Division Department of External Affairs
address:	125 Sussex Drive Ottawa, Ontario Canada K1A 0G2
telephone:	(613) 995-0119

Payment of Service Costs:

The payment of Service costs should be made to:

Alberta:	Provincial Treasurer of Alberta
British Columbia:	Minister of Finance of British Columbia
Prince Edward Island:	Minister of Finance of Prince Edward Island
Manitoba:	Minister of Finance of Manitoba
New Brunswick:	Minister of Finance of New Brunswick
Nova Scotia:	Minister of Finance of Nova Scotia
Ontario:	Treasurer of Ontario
Quebec:	"Ministre des Finances du Québec"
Saskatchewan:	Department of Justice of Saskatchewan–Sheriff Services
Newfoundland:	Newfoundland Exchequer Account
Yukon:	Territorial Treasurer of the Government of Yukon
Northwest Territories:	Government of the Northwest Territories.

2. Methods of service employed by the Central Authority (Article 5)

2.1 Formal service (Article 5, paragraph 1, sub-paragraph a)

In Canada, service will be effected according to the methods of service prescribed by the laws in force in each province and territory.

The normal procedure that will be used by central authorities in Canada is personal service made by a sheriff or deputy sheriff or a huissier in Quebec, on an individual or on a corporation by handing a copy of the document to the defendant in person, wherever he may be, or to the President, Chairman or other Chief Officer of a corporation at the place of business.

Service may also be effected by leaving a copy of the document with a person of a reasonable age at the defendant's domicile or residence.

Where service is made on a corporation, provincial laws usually provide for service on a director or senior officer of the corporation or, in some cases, on a registered agent or on a responsible person at the registered office of the corporation.

2.2 Informal delivery (Article 5, paragraph 2)

The practice of informal delivery ("par simple remise") of judicial or extra-judicial documents is not known in Canada.

2.3 Service by a particular method (Article 5, paragraph 1, sub-paragraph b)

In Alberta, New Brunswick and Ontario, service will be made by certified mail at the option of the requesting party. In Ontario, the Central Authority will serve by any form of mail, at the option of the requesting party.

2.4 Translation requirements (Article 5, paragraph 3)

For both Formal service and Service by a particular method, translation requirements will depend on the province or territory concerned.

For Alberta, British Columbia, Newfoundland, Nova Scotia, Prince Edward Island, Saskatchewan, all documents must be written in or translated into English.

For Ontario, Manitoba, and the Northwest Territories, all documents must be written in or translated into English or French.

For New Brunswick and the Yukon, all documents must be written in or translated into English or French. The Central Authority of New Brunswick or the Yukon may reserve the right to require documents to be translated into English or French depending on the language understood by the addressee.

For Quebec, translation will be required in all cases where the recipient does not understand the language in which the document is written. All documents which commence actions must be translated. Summary translation of all other documents is acceptable if the recipient agrees. Translation is to be done into the French language, however, the Quebec central authority may, upon request, allow a translation in English at the condition that the recipient understands this language.

Costs (Article 12, paragraph 2, sub-paragraph a)

Costs for execution of service will be of $50.-Can.

3. Authority competent to complete the certificate of service (Article 6)

In addition to the Central Authorities, the sheriffs, deputy-sheriffs, sub-sheriffs, clerk of the court or his/her deputy for the judicial district (except in Manitoba where there are no judicial districts) in which the person is to be served or the huissiers (only in Quebec) are competent to complete the certificate of service.

B. *Forwarding of requests for service to the Central Authority of another Contracting State*

Forwarding Authorities (Article 3)

Requests for service to Central Authorities of other States may be transmitted by:

The Attorney General for Canada

The Attorneys General or the Ministry of Attorney General or Minister of Justice of a province or a territory–as the case may be

Clerks of the courts and their deputies for a judicial or a court district

The members of the law societies of all provinces and territories

The member of the Board of Notaries of the Province of Quebec (for non-litigious matters only)

Local registrars

The huissiers and sheriffs

The prothonotaries and deputy prothonotaries

The "Percepteur des pensions alimentaires" in Quebec

CANADA

I *Transmission through consular or diplomatic channels (Articles 8 and 9)*

A Acceptance

On accession, Canada has not declared that it objects to service by consular or diplomatic channels on its territory.

Receiving authority (Article 9, paragraph 1)

The Central Authorities in Canada designated in accordance with Articles 2 and 18 of the *Convention* are competent to receive requests for service transmitted by a foreign consul within Canada.

B Forwarding to the Contracting States

Canada does not object to service by consular channels of Canadian documents abroad providing that the recipient accepts this method of service.

II *Transmission through postal channels (Article 10, sub-paragraph a)*

A Acceptance

Canada does not object to service by postal channels.

B Forwarding to other contracting States

Canadian law allows the use of postal channels to serve Canadian documents to persons abroad.

III *Service through judicial officers, notably "huissiers", etc. of the requested State (Article 10, sub-paragraphs b) and c))*

On accession, Canada has not declared to object to methods of service of Article 10, sub-paragraphs b) and c).

IV *Other direct channels (Article 11); special agreements (Articles 24 and 25)*

Canada is party to bilateral conventions on civil procedure with the following States:

Austria	Canada Treaty Series	1935	n° 16
Belgium	Canada Treaty Series	1928	n° 16
Czechoslovakia	Canada Treaty Series	1928	n° 17
Denmark	Canada Treaty Series	1936	n° 4
Finland	Canada Treaty Series	1936	n° 5
France	Canada Treaty Series	1928	n° 15
Germany	Canada Treaty Series	1935	n° 11
Greece	Canada Treaty Series	1938	n°11
Hungary	Canada Treaty Series	1939	n° 6
Iraq	Canada Treaty Series	1938	n° 12
Italy	Canada Treaty Series	1938	n° 14
Netherlands	Canada Treaty Series	1936	n° 2
Norway	Canada Treaty Series	1935	n° 15
Poland	Canada Treaty Series	1935	n° 18
Portugal	Canada Treaty Series	1935	n° 17
Spain	Canada Treaty Series	1935	n° 12
Sweden	Canada Treaty Series	1935	n° 13
Turkey	Canada Treaty Series	1935	n° 19
Yugoslavia	Canada Treaty Series	1939	n° 4

CANADA
GUARANTEES UNDER THE CONVENTION

Declarations made pursuant to Articles 15, paragraph 1 or 16, paragraph 3.

1. *Stays of entry* (Article 15, paragraph 2)

   Canada declares that the judges may give judgment under the conditions stated in Article 15 of the Convention.

2. *Relief from expiration of the period of time for appeal* (Article 16, paragraph 3)

   Canada declares that an application filed under Article 16 of the Convention will not be entertained if it is filed after the expiration of one year following the date of the judgment, except in exceptional cases determined by the rules of the Court seized of the matter.

CHINA, PEOPLE'S REPUBLIC OF

The People's Republic of China deposited its instrument of accession with the Ministry of Foreign Affairs of the Kingdom of the Netherlands on May 6, 1991, in accordance with Article 28, paragraph 1, of the Convention.

The instrument of accession contains the following declarations:

"1. to designate according to Article 2 and Article 9 of the Convention the Ministry of Justice of the People's Republic of China as the Central Authority and the authority competent to receive documents transmitted by foreign States through consular channels.

"The communication address is:

"Bureau of International Judicial Assistance

Ministry of Justice of the People's Republic of China

No 11, Xiaguangli

Niuwangmiao, Chaoyang district

BEIJING, 100016

The People's Republic of China

"2. to declare according to the second paragraph of Article 8 that the means of service stipulated in the first paragraph of that Article may be used within the territory of the People's Republic of China only when the document is to be served upon a national of the State in which the documents originate.

"3. to oppose the service of documents in the territory of the People's Republic of China by the methods provided by Article 10 of the Convention.

"4. to declare in accordance with the second paragraph of Article 15 of the Convention that if all the conditions provided in that paragraph are fulfilled, the judge, notwithstanding the provisions of the first paragraph of that Article, may give judgment even if no certificate of service or delivery has been received.

"5. to declare in accordance with the third paragraph of Article 16 of the Convention that the application for relief from the effects of the expiration of the time for appeal shall not be entertained except that it is filed within one year following the date of the judgment."

(courtesy translation)

In accordance with the terms of Article 28, paragraph 1, of the Convention any State not represented at the Tenth Session of the Hague Conference on private international law may accede to the present Convention after it has entered into force in accordance with the first paragraph of article 27, (viz: 10 February 1969).

In accordance with Article 28, paragraph 2, the Convention shall enter into force for the People's Republic of China in the absence of any objection from a state which has ratified the Convention (at present: Belgium, Denmark, Egypt, Finland, France, the Federal Republic of Germany, Greece, Israel, Italy, Japan, Luxembourg, the Kingdom of the Netherlands, Norway, Portugal, Spain, Sweden, Turkey, the United Kingdom of Great Britain and Northern Ireland and the United States of America) before such deposit, notified to the Ministry of Foreign Affairs of the Kingdom of the Netherlands within a period of six months after the date on which the said Ministry has notified it of such accession. For practical reasons this six months' period in this case is running from 1 June 1991 till 1 December 1991.

The States which ratified the Convention were notified of the accession by the Dutch Government on 17 May 1991. Since none of these States raised an objection to the accession within the period of six months specified in Article 28, paragraph 2, the said accession became perfect on 1 December 1991.

The provisions of the Convention will enter into force for the People's Republic of China on 1 January 1992 in accordance with Article 28, paragraph 3.

CYPRUS

Notification in conformity with Article 31, paragraph c, of the Convention.

The Republic of Cyprus deposited its instrument of accession with the Ministry of Foreign Affairs of the Kingdom of the Netherlands on 26 October 1982 in accordance with Article 28, paragraph 1, of the Convention.

In accordance with Article 28, paragraph 3, the provisions of the Convention will enter into force for the Republic of Cyprus on 1 June 1983.

The States which have ratified the Convention were notified by the Netherlands Government of the accession on 3 November 1982. Since none of these States raised an objection to the accession within the period of six months specified in Article 28, paragraph 2, the said accession became perfect on 15 May 1983.

Referring to the accession of Cyprus to the above-mentioned Convention the Embassy of Turkey at the Hague addressed a Note dated 6 April 1983 to the Ministry of Foreign Affairs of the Kingdom of the Netherlands. [See note 13.]

Notification in conformity with Article 31, paragraph e of the Convention

In conformity with Article 21 of the Convention the Government of Cyprus informed the Ministry of Foreign Affairs of the Kingdom of the Netherlands by Note dated 5 January 1984 of the designation of the following authorities and made the following declarations:

"(a) *Article 2:*

Designation of Central Authority which will undertake to receive requests for service:—Ministry of Justice.

(b) *Article 6:*

Designation of the authority competent to complete the certificate of Service-Ministry of Justice.

(c) *Article 9:*

Designation of the authority competent to receive documents transmitted by Consular Channels:–Ministry of Justice.

(d) *Articles 8 and 10:*

No opposition to the methods of transmission of documents provided by these articles.

(e) *Article 15:*

Declaration that judgement may be given if all conditions laid down in paragraph 2 are fulfilled.

(f) *Article 16:*

Declaration pursuant to paragraph 3 that the application will not be entertained if it is filed after the expiration of one year from the date of the judgement.

(g) *Article 18:*

Designation of other authorities in addition to the Central Authorities. The Courts of the Republic. Competence:

Service of documents through their Registries."

CZECH REPUBLIC

Notification in conformity with Article 31, paragraphs c and e, of the Convention

By notification dated January 28, 1993 the Czech Republic communicated the following: "In accordance with the valid principles of international law and to the extent defined by it, the Czech Republic, as a successor state created as a result of the division of the Czech and Slovak Federal Republic, considers itself bound, as of January 1, 1993, i.e. the date of the division of the Czechoslovak federation, by multilateral international treaties to which the Czech and Slovak Federal Republic was a party on that date, including reservations and declarations to their provisions made earlier by Czechoslovakia", which are as follow:

Translation

"In accordance with Article 8 of the Convention, within the territory of the Socialist Republic of Czechoslovakia judicial documents may not be served directly through the diplomatic or consular agents of another contracting State unless the document is to be served upon a national of the State in which the documents originate;

"In accordance with Article 10 of the Convention, within the territory of the Socialist Republic of Czechoslovakia judicial documents may not be served by another contracting State through postal channels nor through the judicial officers, officials or other competent persons;

"In accordance with Article 15, paragraph 2 of the Convention, Czechoslovakian judges may give judgement even if the conditions pursuant to Article 15, paragraph 1, have not been fulfilled;

"The provisions of Article 29 of the Convention concerning the extension of the Convention to territories for the international relations of which the contracting States are responsible are at variance with the Declaration of the United Nations General Assembly on the Granting of Independence to Colonial Countries and Peoples of 14 December 1960, and for this reason the Socialist Republic of Czechoslovakia does not consider itself to be bound by these provisions."

"A copy of the original text of the declaration is attached."

By Note dated 31 March 1982 and received at the Ministry of Foreign Affairs on 1 April 1982, the Embassy of the Czechoslovak Socialist Republic communicated the following with regard to the above-cited declaration concerning Article 29 of the Convention:

"This declaration cannot be considered a reserve in view of the fact that it does not follow other purposes than a similar declaration made at the ratification of the Convention on the Taking of Evidence Abroad in Civil or Commercial Matters, though a different formulation was used.

"By this declaration the Czechoslovak Socialist Republic expresses its disagreement of principle with the status of colonies and other dependent territories which is in contradiction with the Declaration of the United Nations General Assembly on the Granting of Independence to Colonial Countries and Peoples of December 14, 1960.

"The Czechoslovak Socialist Republic, however, has no intention to exclude the application of the Convention on the relations with the territories on which the use of the Convention has been extended in accordance with its Art. 29."

"The States which have ratified the Convention were notified by the Netherlands Government of the accession on 26 October 1981. Since none of these States raised an objection to the accession within the period of six months specified in Article 28, paragraph 2, the said accession became perfect on 9 May 1982.

"The provisions of the Convention will enter into force for the Czechoslovak Socialist Republic on 1 June 1982.

"The Czechoslovak Government has designated the following authorities as the authorities referred to in Articles 2, 6 and 9 of the Convention;

"competent for the Czech Socialist Republic: Ministerstvo spravodlnosti Ceské socialistické republiky/Ministry of Justice of the Czech Socialist Republic, 128 10 Praha 2, Vysehradskà 16;

"competent for the Slovak Socialist Republic: Ministerstvo spravodlivosti Slovenskej socialistickej republiky/Ministry of Justice of the Slovak Socialist Republic 883 11 Bratislava, Suvorovova 12.

DENMARK

With the following declarations:

re Art. 2 and 18

The Ministry of Justice is designated as the Central Authority.

re Art. 6

The Danish court of law that has asked for the service to be made is designated as competent to complete the certificate in accordance with Article 6.

re Art. 9

The local judge of first instance–though, as regards the court of first instance at Copenhagen and the court of first instance of the city and of the canton of Arhus, the president of the court–is designated as competent to receive documents forwarded through consular channels in accordance with Art. 9.

re Art. 10

Denmark is unable to recognize the method of effecting service set out in Art. 10, para. c.

re Art. 15

Denmark avails itself of the power, provided for in Art. 15, second paragraph, to declare that the judge may give judgment in a matter even if the provisions of Art. 15, first paragraph, are not fulfilled.

re Art. 16

Denmark avails itself of the power, provided for in Art. 16, third paragraph, to declare that an application will not be entertained if it is made after the expiration of a period of one year following the date of judgment. The question of the re-hearing of a matter in which a person has been judged by default shall be decided in accordance with the rules of the code of procedure, Art. 373 and Art. 374, cf. Art. 434. According to these rules, any person against whom judgment is given by default in an action, in first instance may apply for a re-hearing of the matter if he can prove that the default cannot be imputed to him. The application for a re-hearing should be filed as soon as possible and may not be submitted after the expiration of a period of one year following the date of judgment.

EGYPT

With a declaration that the signing of the Agreement "does not mean in any way a recognition of Israel" by the Arab Republic of Egypt and that "no treaty relation" will arise "between" the two countries.

The Arab Republic of Egypt also declared that it "opposes the use of the methods of transmitting abroad the judicial and extrajudicial documents according to Articles 8 and 10 of the Convention."

In conformity with article 21 of the Convention the Arab Republic of Egypt has designated the Ministry of Justice as the central authority as provided for in Articles 2 and 18.

First paragraph of declaration withdrawn effective Jan. 25, 1980.

FINLAND

With the following declarations:

"1. The Ministry of Justice has been designated Central Authority, pursuant to the first paragraph of article 2 of the Convention.

"2. The Central Authority (The Ministry of Justice) is acting as the authority presupposed in art. 9 of the Convention.

"3. Finnish authorities are not obliged to assist in serving documents transmitted by using any of the methods referred to in sub-paragraphs (b) and (c) of art. 10 of the Convention."

"(Ministry of Justice was substituted for Ministry of Foreign Affairs as Central Authority by Note dated 31 March 1982, effective 1 June 1982.)

FRANCE

With the following declarations:

"1. In conformity with Articles 2 and 18 of the Convention, the Ministry of Justice, Civil Division of International Judicial Assistance (Ministere de la Justice, Service Civil de l'Entraide judiciaire internationale), 13 Place Vendôme, Paris (1 er), is designated as the Central Authority to the exclusion of all other authorities.

"2. The authority competent to complete the certificate referred to in Article 6 is the Public Prosecutor of the Republic (Procureur de la Republique) in whose district the addressee of the document to be served resides.

"3. The Public Prosecutor of the Republic (Procureur de la Republique) is likewise authorized to receive documents forwarded through consular channels in accordance with Article 9.

"4. The Government of the French Republic declares that it is opposed, as has been provided for in Article 8, to the direct service, through diplomatic and consular agents of the contracting States, of documents upon persons who are not nationals of those States.

"5. The Government of the French Republic declares that the provisions of the second paragraph of Article 15 have its approval. It furthermore declares, with reference to Article 16, paragraph 3, that an application for relief from the effects of the expiration of the time for appeal from a judgment will not be entertained if it is filed more than twelve months following the date of the judgment."

GERMANY

On October 3, 1990 the German Democratic Republic acceded to the Federal Republic of Germany.

With the following declarations:

"(1) Requests for service shall be addressed to the Central Authority of the Land where the request is to be complied with. The Central Authority pursuant to Article 2 and paragraph 3 of Article 18 of the Convention shall be for

Baden-Württemberg	das Justizministerium Baden-Württemberg *(The Ministry of Justice of Baden-Württemberg)* D 7000 Stuttgart
Bavaria	das Bayerische Staats-ministerium der Justiz (The Bavarian State Ministry of Justice) D 8000 München
Berlin	der Senator fur Justiz (The Senator of Justice) D 1000 Berlin
Bremen	der Prasident des Landgerichts Bremen (The President of the Regional Court of Bremen) D 2800 Bremen
Hamburg	der Präsident des Amts-gerichts Hamburg (The President of the Local Court of Hamburg) D 2000 Hamburg
Hesse	der Hessische Minister der Justiz (The Hessian Minister of Justice) D 6200 Wiesbaden
Lower Saxony	der Niedersächsische Minister der Justiz (The Minister of Justice of Lower Saxony) D 3000 Hannover
Northrhine-Westphalia	der Justizminister des Landes Nordrhein-Westfalen (The Minister of Justice of the Land Northrhine-Westphalia) D 4000 Dusseldorf

Rhineland-Palatinate	das Ministerium der Justiz (The Minister of Justice) D 6500 Mainz
Saarland	der Minister für Rechtspflege (The Minister of Justice) D 6500 Saarbrucken
Schleswig-Holstein	der Justizminister des Landes Schleswig-Holstein (The Minister of Justice of the Land Schleswig-Holstein) D 2300 Kiel

"The Central Authorities are empowered to have requests for service complied with directly by postal channels if the conditions for service in accordance with paragraph 1(a) of Article 5 of the Convention have been fulfilled. In that case the competent Central Authority will hand over the document to the postal authorities for service. In all other cases the local court (Amtsgericht) in whose district the documents are to be served shall be competent to comply with requests for service. Service shall be effected by the registry of the local court.

"Formal service (paragraph 1 of Article 5 of the Convention) shall be permissible only if the document to be served is written in or translated into, the German language.

"(2) The Central Authority shall complete the certificate (paragraphs 1 and 2 of Article 6 of the Convention) if it has itself arranged for the request for service to be complied with directly by postal channels; in all other cases this shall be done by the registry of the local court.

"(3) The Central Authority of the Land where the documents are to be served and the authorities competent under Section 1 of the Act of 18th December 1958 implementing the Convention on Civil Procedure, signed at The Hague on 1st March 1954, to receive requests from consuls of foreign States, shall be competent to receive requests for service transmitted by a foreign consul within the Federal Republic of Germany (paragraph 1 of Article 9 of the Convention). Under that Act the president of the regional court (Landgericht) in whose district the documents are to be served shall be competent; in his place the president of the local court shall be competent if the request for service is to be complied with in the district of the local court which is subject to his administrative supervision.

"(4) In accordance with paragraph 2(a) of Article 21 of the Convention, the Government of the Federal Republic of Germany objects to the use of methods of transmission pursuant to Articles 8 and 10. Service through diplomatic or consular agents (Article 8 of the Convention) is therefore only permissible if the document is to be served upon a national of the State sending the document. Service pursuant to Article 10 of the Convention shall not be effected. At the time of the deposit of its instrument of ratification the Federal Republic of Germany declared that the said Convention shall also apply to Land Berlin with effect from the date on which it enters into force for the Federal Republic of Germany."

By a Note dated November 19, 1992 addressed to the Ministry of Foreign Affairs of the Kingdom of the Netherlands, the Government of the Federal Republic of Germany made in conformity with Article 21, second paragraph, letter *b*, of the above mentioned Convention the following declaration:

"1. Notwithstanding the provisions of the first paragraph of Article 15, a German judge may give judgement even if no certificate of service or delivery has been received, if all the following conditions are fulfilled:

- the document was transmitted by one of the methods provided for in this Convention,
- a period of time of not less than six months, considered adequate by the judge in the particular case, has elapsed since the date of the transmission of the document,
- no certificate of any kind has been received, even though every reasonable effort has been made to obtain it through the competent authorities of the State addressed.

2. An application for relief in accordance with Article 16 will not be entertained if it is filed after the expiration of one year following the termination of the time-limit which has not been observed."

GREECE

Notification in conformity with Article 31 of the Convention

In accordance with Article 26 of the Convention the Ambassador of Greece at The Hague signed on 20 July 1983 for the Hellenic Republic the above-mentioned Convention as follows:

P.ECONOMOU 20 juillet 1983

and deposited on the same date the instrument of ratification by the Hellenic Republic of the Convention.

In conformity with its Article 27, paragraph 2, the Convention will enter into force for the Hellenic Republic on 18 September 1983.

The Greek Government designated the Department of Administrative and Judicial Affairs of the Ministry of Foreign Affairs of the Hellenic Republic as the Central Authority pursuant to Article 2 of the Convention.

The Permanent Bureau of the Hague Conference on private international law presents its compliments to the Diplomatic Missions of the Member States and to the National Organs and has the honour to inform them that, by a Note dated 23 November 1989 addressed to the Ministry of Foreign Affairs of the Kingdom of the Netherlands, the Government of the Hellenic Republic made in conformity with Article 15, second paragraph, and Article 21, second paragraph, of the above-mentioned Convention the following declaration:

The judges of the Hellenic Republic may give judgment if all the conditions in Article 15, paragraph 2, letters (a), (b), and (c) of the Convention are fulfilled even if no certificate of service or delivery has been received.

[Translation]

With the following declarations and reservations:

"a) The Central Authority in Israel within the meaning of Articles 2, 6 and 18 of the Convention is: The Director of Courts, Directorate of Courts, Russian Compound, Jerusalem;

"b) The State of Israel, in its quality as State of destination, will, in what concerns Article 10, paragraphs b) and c), of the Convention, effect the service of judicial documents only through the Directorate of Courts, and only where an application for such service emanates from a judicial authority or from the diplomatic or consular representation of a Contracting State;

"c) An application to relieve a defendant from the effects of the expiration of the time of appeal from a judgment within the meaning of Article 16 of the Convention will be entertained only if filed within one year from the date of the judgment in question."

ITALY

Notification in conformity with Article 31, paragraph a and e of the Convention

"In accordance with Article 26, paragraph 2, the Italian Republic deposited its instrument of ratification of the Convention with the Ministry of Foreign Affairs of the Kingdom of the Netherlands on 25 November 1981.

"On the occasion of the deposit of the instrument of ratification the Italian Government notified of the following:

Translation

> "a) pursuant to Articles 2 and 18, 'l'Ufficio unico degli ufficiali giudiziari presso la corte d'appello di Roma' (the registry of the court of appeal in Rome) is designated as the Central Authority for the purpose of Article 5;
>
> "b) 'gli uffici unici degli ufficiali giudiziari costituiti presso le corti di appello e i tribunali e gli ufficiali giudiziari addetti alle preture' (the registries of the courts of appeal and other courts, and the bailiffs appointed to the courts of first instance) are competent to issue the certificate pursuant to Article 6;

"c) 'gli uffici unici degli ufficiali giudiziari presso le corti di appello e i tribunali e gli ufficiali giudiziari addetti alle preture' (the registries of the courts of appeal and other courts and the bailiffs appointed to the courts of first instance) are competent to receive for the purpose of service, documents forwarded by consular or diplomatic authorities pursuant to Article 9;

"d) the costs proceeding from each request for service in accordance with Article 5, first paragraph, under a and b, which requires the employment of a bailiff, have to be paid in advance in the size of 6.000 lire, except adjustment at the time of restitution of the notified document.

"However, the costs in relation to the notified document pursuant to Article 12, paragraph 2, of the Convention, can be paid after the restitution in a way specifically fixed by the bailiff. The Italian State shall not require any advance or repayment of costs for service of documents requested by the Contracting States in so far as those States for their parts shall not require the payment or repayment of costs for documents originated from Italy."

"In accordance with Article 27, paragraph 2, the Convention shall enter into force for the Italian Republic on 24 January 1982.

JAPAN

With the following declarations and reservations:

"(1) The Minister for Foreign Affairs is designated as the Central Authority which receives requests for service from other contracting States, pursuant to the first paragraph of Article 2.

"(2) The District Court which has rendered judicial aid with respect to the service is designated as the authority competent to complete the certificate in the form of the model annexed to the Convention, pursuant to the first paragraph of Article 6.

"(3) The Minister for Foreign Affairs is designated as the authority competent to receive documents transmitted through consular channels, pursuant to the first paragraph of Article 9.

"(4) It is declared that the Government of Japan objects to the use of the methods of service referred to in subparagraphs (b) and (c) of Article 10.

"(5) It is declared that Japanese courts may give judgment if all the conditions specified in the second paragraph of Article 15 are fulfilled."

LUXEMBOURG

With the following declarations:

"1. The Public Prosecutor at the Superior Court of Justice has been designated as the Central Authority within the meaning of Article 2 of the Convention. He is also competent to receive the documents forwarded through the channels referred to in Article 9, para. 1, of the Convention.

"2. In accordance with Article 8, the Luxembourg Government is opposed to diplomatic and consular agents directly serving within its territory judicial documents on persons other than nationals of their own country.

"3. [Withdrawn by Note dated June 2, 1978.]

"4. When foreign judicial documents are served, in connection with Articles 5(a) and 10(b) and (c), through the intermediary of a Luxembourg official, they must be drawn up in French or German or accompanied by a translation into one of those languages.

"5. The Luxembourg Government declares that notwithstanding the provisions of Article 15, para. 1, of the Convention, its judges can enter judgment if the conditions set out in para. 2 of the said Article are fulfilled.

"6. In accordance with Article 16, para. 3, of the Convention, the Luxembourg Government declares that the applications referred to in para. 2 of the said Article will not be entertained if they are filed after the expiration of a period of one year following the date of the judgment."

MALAWI

With a declaration designating the Registrar of the High Court of Malawi, P.O. Box 30244, Chichiri, Blantyre, 3, Malawi, as the Central Authority referred to in Article 2.

NETHERLANDS

With the following declarations:

"1. The Public Prosecutor at the District Court of The Hague is designated for the Netherlands as the Central Authority referred to in Article 2 of the Convention.

"The office of the Public Prosecutor is situated at Juliana van Stolberglaan 2-4, The Hague.

"2. Pursuant to Article 18, paragraph 1, of the Convention, the Public Prosecutor at a District Court other than that of The Hague is likewise competent to receive requests and serve documents in accordance with Articles 3 to 6 of the Convention within the area of jurisdiction of such other Court.

"3. The Public Prosecutor at the District Court in the area of jurisdiction where service of the document has been requested is competent to complete a certificate as referred to under Article 6 of the Convention.

"4. The Public Prosecutor at the District Court in the area of jurisdiction where service of the document is requested has been designated for the Netherlands as the authority referred to in Article 9, paragraph 1, of the Convention which is competent to serve documents forwarded through consular channels.

"5. Notwithstanding the provisions of Article 15, paragraph 1, of the Convention, the Netherlands Court may give judgment, even if no certificate of service or delivery has been received, if all the following conditions are fulfilled:

"a) the document was transmitted by one of the methods provided for in this Convention;

"b) a period of time of not less than six months, considered adequate by the judge in the particular case, has elapsed since the date of the transmission of the document;

"c) no certificate, either of service or of delivery, has been received even though every reasonable effort has been made to obtain it through the competent authorities.

"6. An application for relief from the effects of the expiration of the time for appeal as provided for in Article 16 is only admissible if it is submitted within a year, to be calculated from the date on which the judgment is given."

In accordance with Article 27, paragraph 2, the Convention shall enter into force for the Kingdom of the Netherlands (for the Kingdom in Europe) on January 2, 1976.

In accordance with Article 29, paragraph 2, the Kingdom of the Netherlands declared on 28 May 1986 that the above-mentioned Convention shall extend to Aruba.

In conformity with Article 29, paragraph 3, the Convention will enter into force for Aruba on 27 July 1986.

Notification in conformity with Article 31, letter e, of the Convention.

The Ministry of Foreign Affairs of the Kingdom of the Netherlands notifies hereby the designation of the

Head, Central Office for General
Legal Affairs
L.G. Smith Boulevard 76
Oranjestad
Aruba

as the authority for Aruba referred to in Article 21 of the Convention.

NORWAY

With the following declarations:

"1. In accordance with Article 2, the Ministry of Justice, Oslo/Dep, is designated as the Central Authority.

"2. In accordance with Article 6, the County or Town Court in whose district the document has been served is designated for the purpose of completing the certificate in the form annexed to the Convention.

"3. In accordance with Article 9 first paragraph, the County or Town Court in whose district the person to be served is a resident or is staying, is designated as receiver of documents forwarded through consular channels.

"4. The Government of Norway is opposed to the use of such methods of service or transmission of documents on its territory as mentioned in Articles 8 and 10 of the Convention.

"5. Norwegian courts may give judgment when all the conditions specified in the second paragraph of Article 15 are fulfilled.

"6. In accordance with the third paragraph of Article 16, applications for relief according to Article 16 will not be entertained if they are delivered to the competent Norwegian authorities after the expiration of three years following the date of the judgment."

PAKISTAN

Notification in conformity with Article 31, paragraph c, of the Convention

Pakistan deposited its instrument of accession to the above-mentioned Convention with the Ministry of Foreign Affairs of the Kingdom of the Netherlands on 7 December 1988 in accordance with Article 28, paragraph 1.

The States which have ratified the Convention were notified by the Dutch Government of the accession on 19 December 1988. Since none of these States raised an objection to the accession within the period of six months specified in Article 28, paragraph 2, the said accession became perfect on 6 July 1989.

The provisions of the Convention will enter into force for Pakistan on 1 August 1989 in accordance with Article 28, paragraph 3.

The Permanent Bureau of the Hague Conference on private international law presents its compliments to the Diplomatic Missions of the Member States and to the National Organs and has the honour to inform them that, by a Note dated 1 February 1990, the Government of Pakistan informed the Ministry of Foreign Affairs of the Kingdom of the Netherlands of the designation of authorities, in conformity with Article 21 of the above-mentioned convention, and made declarations. The text of the communication is as follows:

> "the Government of Pakistan has designated the Solicitor, Ministry of Law and Justice to the Government of Pakistan in Islamabad, as the central authority, for receiving requests for service coming from other Contracting States and Registrars of Lahore High Court Lahore, Peshawar High Court Peshwar, Baluchistan High Court Quetta, and the High Court of Sind, Karochi, 'other authorities' in addition to the Central Authority, within their respective territorial jurisdictions.
>
> The certificate prescribed by Article 6 of the Convention if not completed by a judicial authority shall be completed or counter-signed by the Registrars of the High Courts.
>
> For the purposes of Article 8 of the Convention it is hereby declared that the Government of Pakistan is opposed to service of Judicial Documents upon persons other than nationals of the requesting States, residing in Pakistan, directly through the Diplomatic and Consular agents of the requesting States. However, it has no objection to such service by postal channels directly to the persons concerned [Article 10(a)] or directly through the judicial officers of Pakistan in terms of Article 10(b) of the Convention if such service is recognized by the law of the requesting State.
>
> In terms of the second paragraph of Article 15 of the Convention, it is hereby declared that notwithstanding the provision of the first paragraph there-of the judge may give judgement even if no certificate of service or delivery has been received, if the following conditions are fulfilled:-

a) the document was transmitted by one of the methods provided for in the Convention;
b) the period of time of not less than 6 months, considered adequate by the Judge in the particular case, has elapsed since the date of transmission of the document; and
c) no certificate of any kind has been received even though every reasonable effort has been made to obtain it through the competent authorities of the State addressed.
As regards Article 16, paragraph 3, of the Convention it is hereby declared that in case of ex-parte decisions, an application for setting it aside will not be entertained if it is filed after the expiration of the period of limitation prescribed by law of Pakistan."

PORTUGAL

Declaration of Portugal.

1. Legal Affairs Department of Ministry of Justice has been designated as Central Authority, in accordance with Art. 2, paragraph 1, of Convention.

2. Justice Department officials: court clerks (escrivaes) and process-servers (officiais de diligencias) have been designated as persons competent to prepare certificate referred to in Article 6 of Convention.

3. In accordance with Art. 8, paragraph 2, of Convention, the Portuguese government grants diplomatic and consular agents power to serve documents on their own nationals only.

4. Portuguese government declares that, notwithstanding provisions of first paragraph of Art. 15 of Convention its judges may give judgment if conditions listed in paragraph 2 of said Art. are fulfilled.

5. In accordance with Art. 16, paragraph 3 of Convention, Portuguese government states that applications referred to in Art. 16, paragraph 2, will not be considered if they are made after expiration of a period of one year from date of judgment.

SEYCHELLES

Notification in conformity with Article 31, paragraph e of the Convention

By Note dated 4 June 1981 and received at the Ministry of Foreign Affairs of the Kingdom of the Netherlands on 14 July 1981 the Republic of Seychelles informed the Ministry in accordance with Article 21 of the Convention of the following:

"Article 2

"The Central Authority designated is:

The Registrar,
Supreme Court,
Victoria,
Mahé,
Republic of Seychelles.

"Article 8

"The Government of the Republic of Seychelles declares that it is opposed to service by a contracting state of judicial documents upon persons abroad, without application of any compulsion, directly through the diplomatic or consular agents of that contracting state unless the document is to be served upon a national of the state in which the documents originate.

"Article 10

"The Government of the Republic of Seychelles declares that it objects to paragraph (b) and (c) of this Article, in so far as they permit service of judicial documents through officials or persons *other than* judicial officers.

"Article 15

"The Government of the Republic of Seychelles declares that notwithstanding the provisions of the first paragraph of this Article, the judge may give judgment even if no certificate of service or delivery has been received, if all the following conditions are fulfilled.

"a) the document was transmitted by one of the methods provided for in this Convention, "b) a period of time of not less than six months, considered adequate by the judge in the particular case, has elapsed since the date of the transmission of the document,

"c) no certificate of any kind has been received, even though every reasonable effort has been made to obtain it through the competent authorities of the State addressed.

"Article 16

"The Government of the Republic of Seychelles declares that it will not entertain an application for relief if filed later than one year following the date of the judgment."

SLOVAK REPUBLIC

By notification dated March 15, 1993 the Slovak Republic communicated the following:

"In accordance with relevant principles and norms of international law and to extent defined by it, the Slovak Republic, as a successor State, born from the division of the Czech and Slovak Federal Republic, considers itself bound, as of January 1, 1993, i.e. the date of the division of the Czechoslovak Federation, by multilateral international treaties to which the Czech and Slovak Federal Republic was a party at that date, including reservations and declarations in respect of provisions made earlier by Czechoslovakia, as well as objections by Czechoslovakia in respect of reservations made by other treaty parties", which are as follows: [Same declarations and reservations, *mutatis mutandis,* under Czech Republic, see footnote 8].

SPAIN

The Permanent Bureau of the Hague Conference on private international law presents its compliments to the Diplomatic Missions of the Member States and to the National Organs and has the honour to inform them that, by instrument deposited on 4 June 1987 with the Ministry of Foreign Affairs of the Kingdom of the Netherlands,

Spain

ratified the above-mentioned Convention.

In accordance with Article 27, paragraph 2, the Convention will enter into force for Spain on 3 August 1987.

The instrument of ratification contains the following declarations:

"1) The Spanish State declares that its judges, notwithstanding the provisions of Article 15, may give judgment even if no certificate of service or delivery of documents has been received, if all the conditions enumerated in the said Article 15, paragraph 2, are fulfilled.

"2) The Spanish State declares that the time of expiration, referred to in Article 16, is sixteen months from the date of the judgment.

"3) The Spanish State designates as the Central Authority to issue the certificates in the form of the model annexed to the Convention:

Secretaría General Técnica,
Subdirección de Cooperación Jurídica Internacional,
Ministerio de Justicia.
San Bernardo, 45.
28015 MADRID."

[Translation]

SWEDEN

With the following declarations:

"a) The Ministry for Foreign Affairs (address: Utrikesdepartementet, Juridiska byran, Box 16121, S-103 23 Stockholm 16, Sweden) has been designated Central Authority.

"b) The Central Authority (the Ministry for Foreign Affairs) has been designated to receive documents transmitted through consular channels, pursuant to art. 9.

"c) Swedish authorities are not obliged to assist in serving documents transmitted by using any of the methods referred to in sub-paragraphs (b) and (c) of art. 10.

"By virtue of the third paragraph of art. 5 of the Convention the Central Authority requires that any document to be served under the first paragraph of the same article must be written in or translated into Swedish."

SWITZERLAND

With the following reservations and declarations:

Re Article 1

1.With regard to Article 1, Switzerland takes the view that the Convention applies exclusively to the Contracting States. In particular, it believes that documents which are effectively addressed to a person resident abroad cannot be served on a legal entity who is not authorized to receive them in the country in which they were drawn up without derogating from Articles 1 and 15, first paragraph, of the Convention.

Re Articles 2 and 18

2.In accordance with Article 21, first paragraph (a), Switzerland designates the cantonal authorities listed in the annex as Central Authorities as referred to in Articles 2 and 18 of the Convention. Requests for the service of documents may also be addressed to the Federal Justice and Police Department in Bern, which will forward them to the appropriate Central Authority.

Re Article 5, third paragraph

3.Switzerland declares that in cases where the addressee does not voluntarily accept a document, it cannot officially be served on him or her in accordance with Article 5, first paragraph, unless it is in the language of the authority addressed, *i. e.* in German, French or Italian, or accompanied by a translation into one of these languages, depending on the part of Switzerland in which the document is to be served.

Re Article 6

4.In accordance with Article 21, first paragraph (b), Switzerland designates the competent cantonal court or the cantonal Central Authority as the body responsible for completing the certificate referred to in Article 6.

Re Articles 8 and 10

5.In accordance with Article 21, second paragraph (a), Switzerland declares that it is opposed to the use in its territory of the methods of transmission provided for in Articles 8 and 10.

Re Article 9

6.In accordance with Article 21, first paragraph (c), Switzerland designates the cantonal Central Authorities as the authorities competent to receive documents transmitted by consular channels pursuant to Article 9 of the Convention.

Cantonal Central Authorities:

Canton	Official Language(s)	Addresses	Telephone Numbers
Appenzell Ausserrhoden	German	Kantonsgericht Appenzell A.Rh. 9403 Trogen	[41] (71) 94 24 61
Appenzell Innerrhoden	German	Kantonsgericht Appenzell I.Rh. 9050 Appenzell	[41] (71) 87 95 51
Aargau	German	Obergericht des Kantons Aargau 5000 Aarau	[41] (64) 21 19 40
Basel-Landschaft	German	Obergericht des Kantons Basel-Landschaft 4410 Liestal	[41] (61) 925 51 11
Basel-Stadt	German	Appellationsgericht Basel-Stadt 4054 Basel	[41] (61) 267 81 81

Canton	Official Language(s)	Addresses	Telephone Numbers
Bern	German/French	Justizdirektion des Kantons Bern 3011 Bern	[41] (31) 633 76 76
Fribourg	French/German	Tribunal cantonal 1700 Fribourg	[41] (37) 25 39 10
Genève	French	Parquet du Procureur géneral 1211 Genève 3	[41] (22) 319 21 11
Glarus	German	Obergericht des Kantons Glarus	[41] (58) 61 15 32
Graubünden	German	Justiz-, Polizei- und Sanitätsdepartment Graubünden 7001 Chur	[41] (81) 21 21 21
Jura	French	Département de la Justice 2800 Delémont	[41] (66) 21 51 11
Luzern	German	Obergericht des Kantons Luzern 6002 Luzern	[41] (41) 24 51 11
Neuchâtel	French	Département de Justice 2001 Neuchâtel	[41] (38) 22 31 11
Nidwalden	German	Kantonsgericht Nidwalden 6370 Stans	[41] (41) 63 79 50
Obwalden	German	Kantonsgericht des Kantons Obwalden 6060 Sarnen	[41] (41) 66 92 22
St. Gallen	German	Kantonsgericht St. Gallen 9001 St. Gallen	[41] (71) 21 31 11
Schaffhausen	German	Kantonsgericht des Kantons Schaffhausen 8201 Schaffhausen	[41] (53) 82 74 22
Schwyz	German	Kantonsgericht Schwyz 6430 Schwyz	[41] (43) 24 11 24
Solothurn	German	Obergericht des Kantons Solothurn 4500 Solothurn	[41] (65) 21 73 11
Tessin	Italian	Tribunale di appello 6901 Lugano	[41] (91) 21 51 11
Thurgau	German	Obergericht des Kantons Thurgau 8500 Frauenfeld	[41] (54) 22 31 21
Uri	German	Gerichtskanzlei Uri 6460 Altdorf	[41] (44) 4 22 44
Valais	French/ German	Tribunal cantonal 1950 Sion	[41] (27) 22 93 93
Vaud	French	Tribunal cantonal 1014 Lausanne	[41] (21) 313 15 11
Zug	German	Obergericht des Kantons Zug Rechtshilfe 6300 Zug	[41] (42) 25 33 11
Zürich	German	Obergericht des Kantons Zürich Rechtshilfe 8023 Zürich	[41] (1) 257 91 91

TURKEY

With the following declaration:

"1. Pursuant to Article 2, paragraph 1 of the Convention, the Directorate General of Civil Affairs of the Ministry of Justice (Adalet Bakanligi Hukuk Isleri Genel Mudurlugu, Ankara) is designated as the Central Authority.

"2. The Directorate General of Civil Affairs of the Ministry of Justice is also competent to complete certificates as referred to in Article 6 of the Convention.

"3. The Directorate General of Civil Affairs is also designated as the authority competent to receive documents forwarded through the channels specified in Article 9, paragraph 1 of the Convention.

"4. Pursuant to Article 8 of the Convention, the Government of the Republic of Turkey acknowledges the freedom of diplomatic and consular agents to serve judicial documents upon their own nationals only.

"5. The Government of the Republic of Turkey declares that it is opposed to the use of the methods of serving judicial documents listed in Article 10 of the Convention.

"6. The Government of the Republic of Turkey declares that its judges, notwithstanding the provisions of the first paragraph of Article 15, may give judgment if all the conditions set out in the second paragraph of the said Article are fulfilled.

"7. Pursuant to Article 16, paragraph 3, the Government of the Republic of Turkey declares that applications for relief as referred to in Article 16, paragraph 2, will not be entertained if they are filed after the expiration of a period of one year following the date of the judgment."

Embassy of the Republic of Turkey [at the Hague]

No. $18^{313}/_{328}$-78

The Embassy of Turkey presents its compliments to the Ministry of Foreign Affairs, the depositary of the Convention on the service abroad of judicial and extrajudicial documents in civil or commercial matters, and has the honour to inform it of the text of the declaration of the Turkish Government regarding the accession to the aforementioned Convention by the Greek Cypriot Government:

Quote:

The Republic of Turkey, although not exercising its right of opposition as set forth in Article 28(2) of the Convention, declares that it does not consider itself bound to apply the provisions of the Convention with respect to the Greek Cypriot Government which, in constitutional terms, is not authorized to represent the 'Republic of Cyprus' as a whole.

The Embassy of Turkey avails itself of this opportunity to renew to the Ministry of Foreign Affairs the assurances of its highest considerations.

The Hague, April 6, 1983

[Initialed]

[Official stamp]

UNITED KINGDOM

With the following declarations:

"(1)(a) In accordance with the provisions of Articles 2 and 18 of the Convention, Her Majesty's Principal Secretary of State for Foreign Affairs is designated as the Central Authority; and the Senior Master of the Supreme Court, Royal Courts of Justice, Strand, London, W.C. 2, the Crown Agent for Scotland, Lord Advocate's Department, Crown Office, 9 Parliament Square, Edinburg 1, and the [as per letter dated 10 June 1980] the Master (Queen's Bench and Appeals), Royal Courts of Justice, Belfast 1, are designated as additional authorities for England and Wales, Scotland, and Northern Ireland respectively.

"(b) The authorities competent under Article 6 of the Convention to complete the Certificate of Service are the authorities designated under Articles 2 and 18.

"(c) In accordance with the provisions of Article 9 of the Convention, the United Kingdom designates as receivers of process through consular channels the same authorities as those designated under Articles 2 and 18.

"(d) With reference to the provisions of paragraphs (b) and (c) of Article 10 of the Convention, documents for service through official channels will be accepted in the United Kingdom only by the central or additional authorities and only from judicial consular or diplomatic officers of other Contracting States.

"(e) The United Kingdom declares its acceptance of the provisions of the second paragraph of Article 15 of the Convention.

"(f) In accordance with the provisions of the third paragraph of Article 16 of the Convention, the United Kingdom declares, in relation to Scotland only, that applications for setting aside judgments on the grounds that the defendant did not have knowledge of the proceedings in sufficient time to defend the action will not be entertained if filed more than one year after the date of judgment.

"The authorities designated by the United Kingdom will require all documents forwarded to them for service under the provisions of the Convention to be in duplicate and, pursuant to the third paragraph of Article 5 of the Convention, will require the documents to be written in, or translated into, the English language.

"A notification under the second and third paragraphs of Article 29 regarding the extension of the Convention to the territories for the international relations of which the United Kingdom is responsible will be addressed to the Royal Netherlands Government in due course."

"(2)(a) In accordance with Article 18 of the Convention the Colonial Secretary of Hong Kong is designated as the Authority competent to receive requests for service in accordance with Article 2 of the Convention.

"(b) The authority competent under Article 6 of the Convention to complete the Certificate of Service is the Registrar of the Supreme Court of Hong Kong.

"(c) In accordance with the provisions of Article 9 of the Convention the Registrar of the Supreme Court of Hong Kong is designated as the receiver of process sent through consular channels.

"(d) With reference to the provisions of paragraph (b) and (c) of Article 10 of the Convention, documents sent for service through official channels will be accepted in Hong Kong only by the central or additional authority and only from judicial, consular or diplomatic officers of other Contracting States.

"(e) The acceptance by the United Kingdom of the provisions of the second paragraph of Article 15 of the Convention shall equally apply to Hong Kong.

"The authorities designated above will require all documents forwarded to them for service under the provisions of the Convention to be in duplicate and, pursuant to the third paragraph of Article 5 of the Convention, will require the documents to be written in, or translated into, the English language."

"(3)(a) In accordance with Article 18 of the Convention the authority shown against the name of each territory in the Annex (hereinafter severally called "the designated authority") is designated as the authority in that territory competent to receive requests for service in accordance with Article 2 of the Convention.

"(b) The authority in each territory competent under Article 6 of the Convention to complete the Certificate of Service is the designated authority.

"(c) In accordance with the provisions of Article 9 of the Convention, the designated Authority shall receive process sent through consular channels.

"(d) With reference to the provisions of paragraphs and (b) and (c) of Article 10 of the Convention, documents sent for service through official channels will be accepted in a territory listed in the Annex by the designated authority and only from judicial, consular or diplomatic officers of other Contracting States.

"(e) The acceptance by the United Kingdom of the provisions of the second paragraph of Article 15 of the Convention shall equally apply to the territories named in the Annex.

"The authorities designated in the Annex will require all documents forwarded to them for service under the provisions of the Convention to be in duplicate and, pursuant to the third paragraph of Article 5 of the Convention, will require the documents to be written in, or translated into, the English language."

ANNEX

Antigua and Barbuda,[1] The Governor General, Antigua and Barbuda.

The Registrar of the High Court of Antigua and Barbuda, St. John's, Antigua.

Bermuda, The Registrar of the Supreme Court, Bermuda.

British Honduras, The Supreme Court Registry, British Honduras.

British Solomon Islands Protectorate, The Registrar of the High Court, Honiara, British Solomon Islands Protectorate.

British Virgin Islands, The Registrar of the Supreme Court, British Virgin Islands.

Cayman Islands, The Clerk of the Courts, Grand Cayman, Cayman Islands

Central and Southern Line Islands, The Registrar of the High Court, Honiara, British Solomon Island Protectorate.

Falkland Islands and Dependencies, The Registrar of the Supreme Court, Stanley, Falkland Islands.

Fiji, The Registrar of the Supreme Court, Fiji.

Gibraltar, The Registrar of the Supreme Court, Gibraltar.

Gilbert and Ellice Islands Colony, The Registrar of the High Court, Tarawa, Gilbert and Ellice Islands Colony.

Guernsey, The Bailiff, Bailiff's Office, Royal Court House, Guernsey, Channel Islands.

Isle of Man, The First Deemster and Clerk of the Rolls, Rolls Office, Douglas, Isle of Man.

Jersey, The Attorney General, Jersey, Channel Islands.

Montserrat, The Registrar of the High Court, Montserrat.

Pitcairn, The Governor and Commander-in-Chief, Pitcairn.

St. Helena and Dependencies, The Supreme Court, St. Helena.

St. Lucia, The Registrar of the High Court of Justice, St. Lucia.

St. Vincent, The Registrar of the Supreme Court, St. Vincent.

Seychelles, The Supreme Court, Seychelles.

Turks and Caicos Islands., The Registrar of the Supreme Court, Turks and Caicos Islands.

Extension to Anguilla–

Notification in conformity with Article 31, paragraphs d and e, of the Convention

"In accordance with Article 29, paragraph 2, of the Convention the Ambassador of the United Kingdom of Great Britain and Northern Ireland at The Hague notified the Minister of Foreign Affairs of the Kingdom of the Netherlands, by a Letter dated 30 July 1982 and received on 3 August 1982, the extension of the Convention to Anguilla.

"In accordance with Article 29, paragraph 3, the Convention will enter into force for Anguilla on 28 September 1982.

"The extension was accompanied by the following declarations:

"(a) in accordance with Article 18 of the Convention the Registrar of the Supreme Court of Anguilla (hereinafter called the designated authority) is designated as the authority competent to receive requests for service in accordance with Article 2 of the Convention.

"(b) the authority competent under Article 6 of the Convention to complete the Certificate of Service is the designated authority.

"(c) in accordance with the provisions of Article 9 of the Convention the designated authority shall receive process sent through consular channels.

1 Ed. note—Now independent parties to the Convention. See also country footnote.

"(d) with reference to the provisions of paragraphs (b) and (c) of Article 10 of the Convention, documents sent for service through official channels will be accepted by the designated authority and only from judicial, consular or diplomatic officers of other contracting states.

"(e) the acceptance by the United Kingdom of the provisions of the second paragraph of Article 15 of the Convention shall apply to Anguilla.

"The designated authority will require all documents forwarded to it for service under the provisions of the Convention to be in duplicate and, pursuant to the third paragraph of Article 5 of the Convention, will require the documents to be written in, or translated into, the English language.

"Extension to the Associated State of Saint Christopher and Nevis–

Notification in conformity with Article 31, paragraphs d and e, of the Convention.

"In accordance with Article 29, paragraph 2, of the Convention the Ambassador of the United Kingdom of Great Britain and Northern Ireland at The Hague notified the Minister of Foreign Affairs of the Kingdom of the Netherlands by Letter dated 1 March 1983 and received on 2 March 1983 of the extension of the Convention to the Associated State of Saint Christopher and Nevis.

"In accordance with Article 29, paragraph 3, the Convention will enter into force for Saint Christopher and Nevis on 1 May 1983.

"The Letter contains the following declarations:

"a) in accordance with Article 18 of the Convention the Registrar of the West Indies Associated State Supreme Court, Saint Christopher and Nevis circuit (hereinafter called the designated authority) is designated as the authority competent to receive requests for service in accordance with Article 2 of the Convention;

"b) the authority competent under Article 6 of the Convention to complete the Certificate of Service is the designated authority;

"c) in accordance with the provisions of Article 9 of the Convention the designated authority shall receive process sent through consular channels;

"d) with reference to the provisions of paragraphs (b) and (c) of Article 10 of the Convention, documents sent for service through official channels will be accepted by the designated authority and only from judicial, consular or diplomatic officers of other contracting states;

"e) the acceptance by the United Kingdom of the provisions of the second paragraph of Article 15 of the Convention shall apply to Saint Christopher and Nevis.

"The designated authority will require all documents forwarded to it for service under the provisions of the Convention to be in duplicate and, pursuant to the third paragraph of Article 5 of the Convention, will require the documents to be written in, or translated into, the English language."

UNITED STATES

With the following declarations:

"1. In accordance with Article 2, the United States Department of Justice is designated as the Central Authority to receive requests for service from other Contracting States and to proceed in conformity with Articles 3 to 6.

"2. In accordance with Article 6, in addition to the United States Department of Justice, the United States Marshal or Deputy Marshal for the judicial district in which service is made are designated for the purpose of completing the certificate in the form annexed to the Convention.

"3. In accordance with the second paragraph of Article 15, it is declared that the judge may, notwithstanding the provisions of the first paragraph of Article 15, give judgment even if no certificate of service or delivery has been received, if all the conditions specified in subdivisions (a), (b) and (c) of the second paragraph of Article 15 are fulfilled.

"4. In accordance with the third paragraph of Article 16, it is declared that an application under Article 16 will not be entertained if it is filed (a) after the expiration of the period within which the same may be filed under the procedural regulations of the court in which the judgment has been entered, or (b) after the expiration of one year following the date of the judgment, whichever is later.

"5. In accordance with Article 29, it is declared that the Convention shall extend to all the States of the United States, the District of Columbia, Guam, Puerto Rico, and the Virgin Islands."

Each request for service should be accompanied by an international money order (not 'postal' money order) made payable to the 'Treasurer of the United States' in the sum of $15.00. No fee will be charged for a request for service from any State party to the Convention which does not impose a charge for the service of documents sent from the United states for service under the Convention.

(The address of the U.S. Central Authority for purposes of service under the Convention is: Office of International Judicial Assistance, Department of Justice, Washington D.C. 20530.)

VENEZUELA

1. With regard to Article 5(b)(3):

"The Republic of Venezuela declares that notices and documents and other items annexed to the notices will be accepted only when they are properly translated into the Spanish language."

2. With regard to Article 8

"The Republic of Venezuela does not agree to the exercise of the faculty provided for in the first paragraph of this Article within its territory, in respect of other persons who are not nationals of the country of origin."

3. With regard to Article 10(a)

"The Republic of Venezuela does not agree to the transmission of documents through postal channels."

4. With regard to Article 10(a)

"The Republic of Venezuela declares that Venezuelan judges shall be empowered to decide when the conditions contained in sections (a), (b) and (c) of this Article are fulfilled, even though they have not received any communication evidencing either the notice or transfer, or delivery of the document."

5. With regard to Article 16

"The Republic of Venezuela declares that the request allowed by the third paragraph of this Article shall not be admissible if it is made after the expiration of the period specified in Venezuelan law."

CONVENTION ON THE TAKING OF EVIDENCE ABROAD IN CIVIL OR COMMERCIAL MATTERS (Concluded March 18, 1970)

The States signatory to the present Convention,

Desiring to facilitate the transmission and execution of Letters of Request and to further the accommodation of the different methods which they use for this purpose.

Desiring to improve mutual judicial co-operation in civil or commercial matters.

Have resolved to conclude a Convention to this effect and have agreed upon the following provisions–

CHAPTER I
LETTERS OF REQUEST

Article 1

In civil or commercial matters a judicial authority of a Contracting State may, in accordance with the provisions of the law of that State, request the competent authority of another Contracting State, by means of a Letter of Request, to obtain evidence, or to perform some other judicial act.

A Letter shall not be used to obtain evidence which is not intended for use in judicial proceedings, commenced or contemplated.

The expression "other judicial act" does not cover the service of judicial documents or the issuance of any process by which judgments or orders are executed or enforced, or orders for provisional or protective measures.

Article 2

A Contracting State shall designate a Central Authority which will undertake to receive Letters of Request coming from a judicial authority of another Contracting State and to transmit them to the authority competent to execute them. Each State shall organize the Central Authority in accordance with its own law.

Letters shall be sent to the Central Authority of the State of execution without being transmitted through any other authority of that State.

Article 3

A Letter of Request shall specify–

(a) the authority requesting its execution and the authority requested to execute it, if known to the requesting authority;

(b) the names and addresses of the parties to the proceedings and their representatives, if any;

(c) the nature of the proceedings for which the evidence is required, giving all necessary information in regard thereto;

(d) the evidence to be obtained or other judicial act to be performed.

Where appropriate, the Letter shall specify, inter alia–

(e) the names and addresses of the persons to be examined;

(f) the questions to be put to the persons to be examined or a statement of the subject-matter about which they are to be examined;

(g) the documents or other property, real or personal, to be inspected;

(h) any requirement that the evidence is to be given on oath or affirmation, and any special form to be used;

(i) any special method or procedure to be followed under Article 9.

A Letter may also mention any information necessary for the application of Article 11.

No legalization or other like formality may be required.

Article 4

A Letter of Request shall be in the language of the authority requested to execute it or be accompanied by a translation into that language.

Nevertheless, a Contracting State shall accept a Letter in either English or French, or a translation into one of these languages, unless it has made the reservation authorized by Article 33.

A Contracting State which has more than one official language and cannot, for reasons of internal law, accept Letters in one of these languages for the whole of its territory, shall, by declaration, specify the language in which the Letter or translation thereof shall be expressed for execution in the specified parts of its territory. In case of failure to comply with this declaration, without justifiable excuse, the costs of translation into the required language shall be borne by the State of origin.

A Contracting State may, by declaration, specify the language or languages other than those referred to in the preceding paragraphs, in which a Letter may be sent to its Central Authority.

Any translation accompanying a Letter shall be certified as correct, either by a diplomatic officer or consular agent or by a sworn translator or by any other person so authorized in either State.

Article 5

If the Central Authority considers that the request does not comply with the provisions of the present Convention, it shall promptly inform the authority of the State of origin which transmitted the Letter of Request, specifying the objections to the Letter.

Article 6

If the authority to whom a Letter of Request has been transmitted is not competent to execute it, the Letter shall be sent forthwith to the authority in the same State which is competent to execute it in accordance with the provisions of its own law.

Article 7

The requesting authority shall, if it so desires, be informed of the time when, and the place where, the proceedings will take place, in order that the parties concerned, and their representatives, if any, may be present. This information shall be sent directly to the parties or their representatives when the authority of the State of origin so requests.

Article 8

A Contracting State may declare that members of the judicial personnel of the requesting authority of another Contracting State may be present at the execution of a Letter of Request. Prior authorization by the competent authority designated by the declaring State may be required.

Article 9

The judicial authority which executes a Letter of Request shall apply its own law as to the methods and procedures to be followed.

However, it will follow a request of the requesting authority that a special method or procedure be followed, unless this is incompatible with the internal law of the State of execution or is impossible of performance by reason of its internal practice and procedure or by reason of practical difficulties.

A Letter of Request shall be executed expeditiously.

Article 10

In executing a Letter of Request the requested authority shall apply the appropriate measures of compulsion in the instances and to the same extent as are provided by its internal law for the execution of orders issued by the authorities of its own country or of requests made by parties in internal proceedings.

Article 11

In the execution of a Letter of Request the person concerned may refuse to give evidence in so far as he has a privilege or duty to refuse to give the evidence–

(a) under the law of the State of execution; or

(b) under the law of the State of origin, and the privilege or duty has been specified in the Letter, or, at the instance of the requested authority, has been otherwise confirmed to that authority by the requesting authority.

A Contracting State may declare that, in addition, it will respect privileges and duties existing under the law of States other than the State of origin and the State of execution, to the extent specified in that declaration.

Article 12

The execution of a Letter of Request may be refused only to the extent that–

(a) in the State of execution the execution of the Letter does not fall within the functions of the judiciary; or

(b) the State addressed considers that its sovereignty or security would be prejudiced thereby.

Execution may not be refused solely on the ground that under its internal law the State of execution claims exclusive jurisdiction over the subject-matter of the action or that its internal law would not admit a right of action on it.

Article 13

The documents establishing the execution of the Letter of Request shall be sent by the requested authority to the requesting authority by the same channel which was used by the latter.

In every instance where the Letter is not executed in whole or in part, the requesting authority shall be informed immediately through the same channel and advised of the reasons.

Article 14

The execution of the Letter of Request shall not give rise to any reimbursement of taxes or costs of any nature.

Nevertheless, the State of execution has the right to require the State of origin to reimburse the fees paid to experts and interpreters and the costs occasioned by the use of a special procedure requested by the State of origin under Article 9, paragraph 2.

The requested authority whose law obliges the parties themselves to secure evidence, and which is not able itself to execute the Letter, may, after having obtained the consent of the requesting authority, appoint a suitable person to do so. When seeking this consent the requested authority shall indicate the approximate costs which would result from this procedure. If the requesting authority gives its consent it shall reimburse any costs incurred; without such consent the requesting authority shall not be liable for the costs.

CHAPTER II
TAKING OF EVIDENCE BY DIPLOMATIC OFFICERS, CONSULAR AGENTS AND COMMISSIONERS

Article 15

In a civil or commercial matter, a diplomatic officer or consular agent of a Contracting State may, in the territory of another Contracting State and within the area where he exercises his functions, take the evidence without compulsion of nationals of a State which he represents in aid of proceedings commenced in the courts of a State which he represents.

A Contracting State may declare that evidence may be taken by a diplomatic officer or consular agent only if permission to that effect is given upon application made by him or on his behalf to the appropriate authority designated by the declaring State.

Article 16

A diplomatic officer or consular agent of a Contracting State may, in the territory of another Contracting State and within the area where he exercises his functions, also take the evidence, without compulsion, of nationals of the State in which he exercises his functions or of a third State, in aid of proceedings commenced in the courts of a State which he represents, if–

(a) a competent authority designated by the State in which he exercises his functions has given its permission either generally or in the particular case, and

(b) he complies with the conditions which the competent authority has specified in the permission.

A Contracting State may declare that evidence may be taken under this Article without its prior permission.

Article 17

In a civil or commercial matter, a person duly appointed as a commissioner for the purpose may, without compulsion, take evidence in the territory of a Contracting State in aid of proceedings commenced in the courts of another Contracting State if–

(a) a competent authority designated by the State where the evidence is to be taken has given its permission either generally or in the particular case; and

(b) he complies with the conditions which the competent authority has specified in the permission.

A Contracting State may declare that evidence may be taken under this Article without its prior permission.

Article 18

A Contracting State may declare that a diplomatic officer, consular agent or commissioner authorized to take evidence under Articles 15, 16 or 17, may apply to the competent authority designated by the declaring State for appropriate assistance to obtain the evidence by compulsion. The declaration may contain such conditions as the declaring State may see fit to impose.

If the authority grants the application it shall apply any measures of compulsion which are appropriate and are prescribed by its law for use in internal proceedings.

Article 19

The competent authority, in giving the permission referred to in Articles 15, 16 or 17, or in granting the application referred to in Article 18, may lay down such conditions as it deems fit, *inter alia*, as to the time and place of the taking of the evidence. Similarly it may require that it be given reasonable advance notice of the time, date and place of the taking of the evidence; in such a case a representative of the authority shall be entitled to be present at the taking of the evidence.

Article 20

In the taking of evidence under any Article of this Chapter persons concerned may be legally represented.

Article 21

Where a diplomatic officer, consular agent or commissioner is authorized under Articles 15, 16 or 17 to take evidence–

(a) he may take all kinds of evidence which are not incompatible with the law of the State where the evidence is taken or contrary to any permission granted pursuant to the above Articles, and shall have power within such limits to administer an oath or take an affirmation;

(b) a request to a person to appear or to give evidence shall, unless the recipient is a national of the State where the action is pending, be drawn up in the language of the place where the evidence is taken or be accompanied by a translation into such language;

(c) the request shall inform the person that he may be legally represented and, in any State that has not filed a declaration under Article 18, shall also inform him that he is not compelled to appear or to give evidence;

(d) the evidence may be taken in the manner provided by the law applicable to the court in which the action is pending provided that such manner is not forbidden by the law of the State where the evidence is taken;

(e) a person requested to give evidence may invoke the privileges and duties to refuse to give the evidence contained in Article 11.

Article 22

The fact that an attempt to take evidence under the procedure laid down in this Chapter has failed, owing to the refusal of a person to give evidence, shall not prevent an application being subsequently made to take the evidence in accordance with Chapter I.

CHAPTER III–GENERAL CLAUSES

Article 23

A Contracting State may at the time of signature, ratification or accession, declare that it will not execute Letters of Request issued for the purpose of obtaining pretrial discovery of documents as known in Common Law countries.

Article 24

A Contracting State may designate other authorities in addition to the Central Authority and shall determine the extent of their competence. However, Letters of Request may in all cases be sent to the Central Authority.

Federal States shall be free to designate more than one Central Authority.

Article 25

A Contracting State which has more than one legal system may designate the authorities of one of such systems, which shall have exclusive competence to execute Letters of Request pursuant to this Convention.

Article 26

A Contracting State, if required to do so because of constitutional limitations, may request the reimbursement by the State of origin of fees and costs, in connection with the execution of Letters of Request, for the service of process necessary to compel the appearance of a person to give evidence, the costs of attendance of such persons, and the cost of any transcript of the evidence.

Where a State has made a request pursuant to the above paragraph, any other Contracting State may request from that State the reimbursement of similar fees and costs.

Article 27

The provisions of the present Convention shall not prevent a Contracting State from-

(a) declaring that Letters of Request may be transmitted to its judicial authorities through channels other than those provided for in Article 2;

(b) permitting, by internal law or practice, any act provided for in this Convention to be performed upon less restrictive conditions;

(c) permitting, by internal law or practice, methods of taking evidence other than those provided for in this Convention.

Article 28

The present Convention shall not prevent an agreement between any two or more Contracting States to derogate from–

(a) the provisions of Article 2 with respect to methods of transmitting Letters of Request;

(b) the provisions of Article 4 with respect to the languages which may be used;

(c) the provisions of Article 8 with respect to the presence of judicial personnel at the execution of Letters;

(d) the provisions of Article 11 with respect to the privileges and duties of witnesses to refuse to give evidence;

(e) the provisions of Article 13 with respect to the methods of returning executed Letters to the requesting authority;

(f) the provisions of Article 14 with respect to fees and costs;

(g) the provisions of Chapter II.

Article 29

Between Parties to the present Convention who are also Parties to one or both of the Conventions on Civil Procedure signed at the Hague on the 17th of July 1905 [99 British Foreign and State Papers 990] and the 1st of March 1954 [286 UNTS 265], this Convention shall replace Articles 8-16 of the earlier Conventions.

Article 30

The present Convention shall not affect the application of Article 23 of the Convention of 1905, or of Article 24 of the Convention of 1954.

Article 31

Supplementary Agreements between Parties to the Conventions of 1905 and 1954 shall be considered as equally applicable to the present Convention unless the Parties have otherwise agreed.

Article 32

Without prejudice to the provisions of Articles 29 and 31, the present Convention shall not derogate from conventions containing provisions on the matters covered by this Convention to which the Contracting States are, or shall become Parties.

Article 33

A State may, at the time of signature, ratification or accession exclude, in whole or in part, the application of the provisions of paragraph 2 of Article 4 and of Chapter II. No other reservation shall be permitted.

Each Contracting State may at any time withdraw a reservation it has made; the reservation shall cease to have effect on the sixtieth day after notification of the withdrawal.

When a State has made a reservation, any other State affected thereby may apply the same rule against the reserving State.

Article 34

A State may at any time withdraw or modify a declaration.

Article 35

A Contracting State shall, at the time of the deposit of its instrument of ratification or accession, or at a later date, inform the Ministry of Foreign Affairs of the Netherlands of the designation of authorities, pursuant to Articles 2, 8, 24 and 25.

A Contracting State shall likewise inform the Ministry, where appropriate, of the following–

(a) The designation of the authorities to whom notice must be given, whose permission may be required, and whose assistance may be invoked in the taking of evidence by diplomatic officers and consular agents, pursuant to Articles 15, 16 and 18 respectively;

(b) the designation of the authorities whose permission may be required in the taking of evidence by commissioners pursuant to Article 17 and of those who may grant the assistance provided for in Article 18;

(c) declarations pursuant to Articles 4, 8, 11, 15, 16, 17, 18, 23 and 27;

(d) any withdrawal or modification of the above designations and declarations;

(e) the withdrawal of any reservation.

Article 36

Any difficulties which may arise between Contracting States in connection with the operation of this Convention shall be settled through diplomatic channels.

Article 37

The present Convention shall be open for signature by the States represented at the Eleventh Session of the Hague Conference on Private International Law.

It shall be ratified, and the instruments of ratification shall be deposited with the Ministry of Foreign Affairs of the Netherlands.

Article 38

The present Convention shall enter into force on the sixtieth day after the deposit of the third instrument of ratification referred to in the second paragraph of Article 37.

The Convention shall enter into force for each signatory State which ratifies subsequently on the sixtieth day after the deposit of its instrument of ratification.

Article 39

Any State not represented at the Eleventh Session of the Hague Conference on Private International Law which is a Member of this Conference or of the United Nations or of a specialized agency of that Organization, or a Party to the Statute of the International

Court of Justice[1] may accede to the present Convention after it has entered into force in accordance with the first paragraph of Article 38.

The instrument of accession shall be deposited with the Ministry of Foreign Affairs of the Netherlands.

The Convention shall enter into force for a State acceding to it on the sixtieth day after the deposit of its instrument of accession.

The accession will have effect only as regards the relations between the acceding State and such Contracting States as will have declared their acceptance of the accession. Such declaration shall be deposited at the Ministry of Foreign Affairs of the Netherlands; this Ministry shall forward, through diplomatic channels, a certified copy to each of the Contracting States.

The Convention will enter into force as between the acceding State and the State that has declared its acceptance of the accession on the sixtieth day after the deposit of the declaration of acceptance.

Article 40

Any State may, at the time of signature, ratification or accession, declare that the present Convention shall extend to all the territories for the international relations of which it is responsible, or to one or more of them. Such a declaration shall take effect on the date of entry into force of the Convention for the State concerned. At any time thereafter, such extensions shall be notified to the Ministry of Foreign Affairs of the Netherlands.

The Convention shall enter into force for the territories mentioned in such an extension on the sixtieth day after the notification indicated in the preceding paragraph.

Article 41

The present Convention shall remain in force for five years from the date of its entry into force in accordance with the first paragraph of Article 38, even for States which have ratified it or acceded to it subsequently.

If there has been no denunciation, it shall be renewed tacitly every five years.

Any denunciation shall be notified to the Ministry of Foreign Affairs of the Netherlands at least six months before the end of the five year period.

It may be limited to certain of the territories to which the Convention applies.

The denunciation shall have effect only as regards the State which has notified it. The Convention shall remain in force for the other Contracting States.

Article 42

The Ministry of Foreign Affairs of the Netherlands shall give notice to the States referred to in Article 37, and to the States which have acceded in accordance with Article 39, of the following–

(a) the signatures and ratifications referred to in Article 37;

(b) the date on which the present Convention enters into force in accordance with the first paragraph of Article 38;

(c) the accessions referred to in Article 39 and the dates on which they take effect;

(d) the extensions referred to in Article 40 and the dates on which they take effect;

(e) the designations, reservations and declarations referred to in Articles 33 and 35;

(f) the denunciations referred to in the third paragraph of Article 41.

IN WITNESS WHEREOF the undersigned, being duly authorised [sic] thereto, have signed the present Convention.

DONE at The Hague, on the 18th day of March 1970, in the English and French languages, both texts being equally authentic, in a single copy which shall be deposited in the archives of the Government of the Netherlands, and of which a certified copy shall be sent, through the diplomatic channel to each of the States represented at the Eleventh Session of the Hague Conference on Private International Law.

Done at The Hague March 18, 1970; entered into force for the United States October 7, 1972. TIAS 7444; 23 UST 2555 States which are parties:

DECLARATIONS BY CONTRACTING STATES

ARGENTINA

Notification pursuant to Article 42 of the Convention

In conformity with Article 39, paragraph 2, the instrument of accession by the Argentine Republic to the above-mentioned Convention was deposited with the Ministry of Foreign Affairs of the Kingdom of the Netherlands on 8 May 1987.

The instrument of accession of the Argentine Republic contains the following reservation, referred to in Article 33, first paragraph, of the Convention:

"The Argentine Republic totally excludes the application of the provisions of paragraph 2 of Article 4, as well as those of Chapter II.";

and the following declaration regarding Article 23 of the Convention:

"The Argentine Republic will not execute Letters of Request issued for the purpose of obtaining pre-trial discovery of documents as known in the Common Law Countries."

Furthermore, the instrument contains the declaration annexed to this notification.

In accordance with paragraph 3 of Article 39, the Convention will enter into force for the Argentine Republic on 7 July 1987.

According to Article 39, paragraph 4 of the Convention, the accession will have effect only as regards the relations between the Argentine Republic and such Contracting States as will have declared their acceptance of the accession. Such declarations shall be deposited at the Ministry of Foreign Affairs of the Kingdom of the Netherlands.

The Hague 20, May 1987

"The Argentine Republic excludes the extension of the application of the Convention on the taking of evidence abroad in civil or commercial matters, adopted at The Hague on March 18, 1970, to the Malvinas, South Georgia, and South Sandwich Islands, which was notified by the United Kingdom of Great Britain and Northern Ireland to the Ministry of Foreign Affairs of the Kingdom of the Netherlands on November 23, 1979, and reaffirms its rights of sovereignty over the Malvinas, South Georgia and South Sandwich Islands, which form an integral part of its national territory."

The General Assembly of the United Nations has adopted resolutions 2065 (XX), 3160 (XXVIII), 31/49, 37/9, 38/12, 39/6, 40/21 and 41/40 in which the existence of a dispute of sovereignty is recognized in reference to the Malvinas Islands, and it urges the Argentine Republic and the United Kingdom of Great Britain and Northern Ireland to maintain negotiations with the purpose of finding a peaceful and definitive solution to the dispute as soon as possible, with the good offices of the Secretary General of the United Nations, who will inform the General Assembly of the progress that has been accomplished.

In like manner, "the Argentine Republic excludes the June 19, 1986 approval formulated by the United Kingdom of Great Britain and Northern Ireland for the Malvinas, South Georgia and South Sandwich Islands with respect to the accession of the Principality of Monaco to the aforementioned Convention." (Translation provided by the Division of Language Services, Department of State)

In accordance with Article 35 of the Convention the Government of the Argentine Republic designated the following competent authority:

Ministerio de Relaciones Exteriores y Culto

Reconquista 1088
Buenos Aires

Notification pursuant to Article 42 of the Convention

The following States declared their acceptance of the accession of the Argentine Republic to the Convention:

the United States of America	December 1, 1987
Finland	5 February 1990

In accordance with Article 39 the Convention will enter into force between

Argentina and the United States of America	January 30, 1988
Finland	6 April 1990

AUSTRALIA

Notification pursuant to Article 42 of the Convention.

In conformity with Article 39, paragraph 2, the instrument of accession by Australia to the above-mentioned Convention was deposited with the Ministry of Foreign Affairs of the Kingdom of the Netherlands on 23 October 1992.

The instrument of accession of Australia contains the following reservation and declarations:

Pursuant to Article 33, it excludes the operation of paragraph 2 of Article 4.

The Government of Australia hereby declares, for and on behalf of Australia, that:

- pursuant to Article 2, the Secretary to the Attorney-General's Department of the Commonwealth of Australia will be its Central Authority;
- pursuant to Article 8, members of the judicial personnel of the requesting authority of another Contracting State may be present at the execution of a Letter of Request, subject to prior authorisation by the judicial authority executing the Letter of Request;
- pursuant to Article 15, evidence may be taken by a diplomatic officer or consular agent only if permission to that effect is given upon application to the Secretary of the Attorney-General's Department of the Commonwealth of Australia;
- pursuant to Article 16, the Secretary to the Attorney-General's Department of the Commonwealth of Australia will be its competent authority for the purposes of that Article and is empowered to specify conditions with respect to any permission given under that Article; and
- pursuant to Article 23, it will not execute Letters of Request issued for the purpose of obtaining pre-trial discovery of documents as known in Common Law Countries.
- pursuant to Article 24, it designates the Registrars of the State and Territory Supreme Courts as additional authorities.
- pursuant to Article 40, the Convention extends to all the territories for the international relations of which it is responsible.

In accordance with paragraph 3 of Article 39, the Convention will enter into force for Australia on 22 December 1992.

According to Article 39, paragraph 4, of the Convention the accession will have effect only as regards the relations between Australia and such Contracting States as will have declared their acceptance of the accession. Such declarations shall be deposited at the Ministry of Foreign Affairs of the Kingdom of the Netherlands.

The following States have declared their acceptance of Australia's accession to the Convention: Aruba, Cyprus, Finland, the Federal Republic of Germany, Luxembourg, the Kingdom of the Netherlands (for the Kingdom in Europe), the United States of America.

In accordance with Article 39 the Convention will enter into force between Australia and

the United States of America	22 August 1993
France	27 March 1993
Denmark	12 April 1993
the United Kingdom of Great Britain and Northern Ireland	20 April 1993
Cyprus	19 June 1993
the Federal Republic of Germany	3 July 1993
Luxembourg	9 February 1993
the Kingdom of the Netherlands (for the Kingdom in Europe)	14 February 1993
Aruba	19 July 1993
Finland	23 July 1993

BARBADOS

Notification in conformity with Article 42, sub. e, of the Convention

By a Letter of 2 September 1982, received at The Ministry of Foreign Affairs of the Kingdom of the Netherlands on 29 September 1982, Barbados informed the Depositary in accordance with Article 35 of the above-mentioned Convention of the following: ". . . for the purpose of the said Convention, the Central Authority is the Registrar of the Supreme Court of Barbados."

CYPRUS

Notification in conformity with Article 42, sub. e, of the Convention.–

After having designated the Central Authority on 3 May 1984 (see Notification No. 2/1984) the Government of Cyprus informed the Ministry of Foreign Affairs of the Kingdom of the Netherlands of the following on 15 May 1984:

"The Republic of Cyprus makes the following declarations:

"1. Under Article 2 the Ministry of Justice is designated as the Competent Authority.

"2. Under Article 16 the Ministry of Justice is designated as the Competent Authority.

"3. Under Article 17 the Ministry of Justice is designated as the Competent Authority.

"4. In accordance with Article 18 the Republic of Cyprus declares that a diplomatic officer, consular agent or commissioner authorized to take evidence under Articles 15, 16 or 17 may apply to the Competent Authority for appropriate assistance to obtain such evidence by compulsion as prescribes by the law for internal proceedings, provided that the requesting Contracting State has made a declaration affording reciprocal facilities under Article 18.

"5. In accordance with Article 23, the Government of the Republic of Cyprus declares that the Republic of Cyprus will not execute Letters of Request issued for the purpose of obtaining pre-trial discovery of documents. The Government of the Republic of Cyprus further declares that the Republic of Cyprus understands 'Letters of Request issued for the purpose of obtaining pre-trial discovery of documents' for the purposes of the foregoing declaration as including any Letter of Request which requires a person:

"a. to state what documents relevant to the proceedings to which the Letter of Request relates are, or have been, in his possession, custody or power; or

"b. to produce any documents other than particular documents specified in the Letter of Request as being documents appearing to the requested court to be, in his possession, custody or power.

"The Republic of Cyprus makes the following reservations:

"1. In accordance with Article 8 the Republic of Cyprus declares that members of the judicial personnel of the requesting authority may be present at the execution of a Letter of Request.

"2. In accordance with the provisions of article 33 the Republic of Cyprus will not accept a Letter of Request in French."

According to the depositary the declaration under 5 and the reservation under 2 should have been made at the time of accession. The States which have declared to accept Cyprus' accession to the Convention, namely: the Federal Republic of Germany, Finland, France, Israel, Italy, the Kingdom of the Netherlands, Luxembourg, Portugal, the United Kingdom of Great Britain and Northern Ireland, Sweden and Czechoslovakia, are requested to inform the Ministry of Foreign Affairs of the Kingdom of the Netherlands whether they accept the declaration and the reservation concerned.

Notification pursuant to Article 42 of the Convention

The following State declared its acceptance of the accession of Cyprus to the above-mentioned Convention:

the United States of America 1 December 1987

In accordance with Article 39 the Convention will enter into force between Cyprus and the United States of America 30 January 1988

CZECH REPUBLIC

By notification dated January 28, 1993 the Czech Republic communicated the following:

"In accordance with the valid principles of international law and to the extent defined by it, the Czech Republic, as a successor state created as a result of the division of the Czech and Slovak Federal Republic, considers itself bound, as of January 1, 1993, i.e. the date of the division of the Czechoslovak federation, by multilateral international treaties to which the Czech and Slovak Federal Republic was a party on that date, including reservations and declarations to their provisions made earlier by Czechoslovakia", which are as follow:

(Translation)

"The Socialist Republic of Czechoslovakia declares, with reference to Article 16 of the Convention on the taking of evidence abroad in civil or commercial matters, concluded at The Hague on 18 March 1970, that evidence may be taken in accordance with Chapter II without its prior permission provided the principle of reciprocity is applied.

"The Socialist Republic of Czechoslovakia also decisions, in connection with Article 18 of the said Convention, that a diplomatic officer, consular agent or commissioner authorized to take evidence under Articles 15, 16 and 17, may request the competent Czechoslovak court or the Czechoslovak state notary to carry out procedural action and that such a diplomatic officer, consular agent or commissioner will transmit the dossier to that court or notary through the intermediary of the Minister of Justice of the Czech Socialist Republic in Prague or the Minister of Justice of the Slovak Socialist Republic in Bratislava, provided the principle of reciprocity is applied.

"The Socialist Republic of Czechoslovakia wishes to state, in connection with Article 40 of the Convention according to all states the right to declare that the convention shall be applicable to all territories for the international relations of which it is responsible, that keeping certain countries in a state of dependence is in its opinion contrary to the spirit and objectives of the United Nations Declaration of 14 December 1960 on the granting of independence to colonial countries and peoples, which declares the necessity for a speedy and unconditional end to colonialism in all its forms.".

By notification contained in Note dated May 28, 1978, the Minister of Justice of the Czech Socialist Republic and the Minister of Justice of the Slovak Socialist Republic have been designated as central authorities in accordance with Articles 2 and 24 of the Convention.

DENMARK

With the following reservations:

"1) Availing itself of the provisions laid down in Article 33, the Danish Government hereby declares, in accordance with Article 4, that Denmark will not accept Letters of Request which are sent in French.

"2) Availing itself of the provisions laid down in Article 33, the Danish Government hereby declares, in accordance with Article 17, that Denmark will not accept the taking of evidence by commissioners." And with the following declarations in accordance with Article 35:

"Article 2

"The Ministry of Justice is hereby designated as Central Authority.

"Article 4

"Letters of Request may be sent in Norwegian and Swedish, and Denmark accepts no obligation to return evidence taken in other languages than Danish.

"Article 8

"Members of the judicial personnel of the requesting authority of another contracting State may be present at the execution of a Letter of Request if they have obtained prior authorization from the competent Danish authority.

"Article 15

"A diplomatic officer or consular agent may take evidence if he has been authorized to do so by the Ministry of Justice.

"Article 16

"The Ministry of Justice will issue authorizations to take evidence.

"Article 23

"Letters of Request issued for the purpose of obtaining pre-trial discovery of documents may not be executed in Denmark.

"Article 27a

"As has been the case hitherto, Letters of Request may be transmitted directly to the competent Danish court by the consular agents of foreign States."

Additional declaration of July 23, 1980:

"The declaration made by the Kingdom of Denmark in accordance with article 23 concerning 'Letters of Request issued for the purpose of obtaining pre-trial discovery of documents' shall apply to any Letter of Request which requires a person:

"a) to state what documents relevant to the proceedings to which the Letter of Request relates are, or have been, in his possession, other than particular documents specified in the Letter of Request; or

"b) to produce any documents other than particular documents which are specified in the Letter of Request, and which are likely to be in his possession."

FINLAND

With the following reservation and declaration:

Reservation:

"In conformity with Article 33, Finland enters a reservation to paragraph 2 of Article 4 to the effect that Letters of Request in the English or French languages will not be accepted."

Declaration:

"1. In Finland the Ministry for Foreign Affairs shall be the Central Authority referred to in Article 2.

"2. Swedish is the second official language of Finland. Finland will therefore in accordance with paragraph 1 of Article 4 accept Letters of Request in the Swedish language. The answer shall be given in the Swedish language if in connection with the Letter of Request this has been specifically requested.

"3. A member of the judicial personnel of the requesting authority may in accordance with Article 8 be present at the execution of a Letter of Request, provided that the Finnish Ministry of Justice has given its consent.

"4. The evidence referred to in Articles 16 and 17 of the Convention may be taken without the prior permission of the Finnish authorities.

"5. Finland is not going to execute Letters of Request referred to in Article 23 issued for the purpose of obtaining pre-trial discovery of documents as known in Common Law countries."

Notification in conformity with Article 42, paragraph e, of the Convention

By note dated 11 December 1980 and received at the Ministry of Foreign Affairs of the Kingdom of the Netherlands on 12 December 1980 the Government of Finland informed the Ministry of the withdrawal in part of the reservation to Article 4, paragraph 2, of the above-mentioned Convention made at the time of ratification and declared that it hereafter accepts the Letters of Request done in or translated into the English language. In accordance with Article 35, sub. c, the Government of Finland made the following declaration:

> "By accepting Letters of Request in English, the Republic of Finland does not undertake to execute the request, or transmit the evidence thus obtained in the English language; nor to have translated the documents which establish the execution of the Letter of Request."

Furthermore the Government of Finland modified the declaration concerning Article 23 of the above-mentioned Convention made at the time of ratification. The modified declaration is worded as follows:

"The declaration made by the Republic of Finland in accordance with Article 23 concerning 'Letters of Request issued for the purpose of obtaining pre-trial discovery of documents' shall apply only to Letters of Request which require a person:

"a) to state what documents relevant to the proceedings to which the Letter of Request relates are, or have been, in his possession, custody or power;

"b) to produce any documents other than particular documents specified in the Letter of Request, which are likely to be in his possession, custody or power.".

FRANCE

With the following declarations:

With respect to the first paragraph of Article 40 of the Convention, France declares that the Convention shall apply to all the Territory of the French Republic.

In conformity with the provisions of Article 33, the French Government declares:

That, in application of the second paragraph of Article 4, it will execute only Letters in French or accompanied by a translation in French.

That, in application of Article 23, it will not execute Letters of Request issued for the purpose of obtaining pre-trial discovery of documents as known in Common Law countries;

In conformity with the provisions of Article 2, the Ministry of Justice, Civil Division of International Judicial Assistance, 13 Place Vendome, Paris (1er), is designated as the Central Authority to the exclusion of any other authority.

In conformity with the provisions of Article 16, the Ministry of Justice, Civil Division of International Judicial Assistance, 13 Place Vendome, Paris (1er), is designated as the competent authority to give permission to diplomatic officers or consular agents of a Contracting State to take the evidence, without compulsion, of persons other than nationals of that State in aid of proceedings commenced in the courts of a State which they represent.

That permission, which shall be given for each specific case and shall be accompanied by special conditions when appropriate, shall be granted under the following general conditions:

1. Evidence shall be taken only within the confines of the Embassies or Consulates;
2. The date and time of taking the evidence shall be notified in due time to the Civil Division of International Judicial Assistance so that it may have the opportunity to be represented at the proceedings;
3. Evidence shall be taken in premises accessible to the public;
4. Persons requested to give evidence shall be served with an official instrument in French or accompanied by a translation into French, and that instrument shall mention:
    a. That evidence is being taken in conformity with the provisions of The Hague Convention of March 18, 1970 on the Taking of Evidence Abroad in Civil or Commercial Matters and relates to legal proceedings pending before a jurisdiction specifically designated by a Contracting State;
    b. That appearance is voluntary and failure to appear will not give rise to criminal proceedings in the State of origin;
    c. That the parties to the trial are consenting or, if not, the grounds of their objections;

d. That in the taking of evidence the person concerned may be legally represented;

e. That a person requested to give evidence may invoke a privilege or duty to refuse to give evidence.

A copy of these requests shall be transmitted to the Ministry of Justice.

5. The Civil Division of International Judicial Assistance shall be kept informed of any difficulty.

In conformity with the provisions of Article 17, the Ministry of Justice, Civil Division of International Judicial Assistance, 13 Place Vendôme, Paris (1er), is appointed as the competent authority to give permission to persons duly appointed as commissioners to proceed, without compulsion, to take any evidence in aid of proceedings commenced in the courts of a Contracting State.

This permission, which shall be given for each specific case and shall be accompanied by special conditions when appropriate, shall be granted under the following general conditions:

1. Evidence shall be taken only within the Embassy confines;

2. The date and time of taking the evidence shall be notified in due time to the Civil Division of International Judicial Assistance so that it may have the opportunity to be represented at the proceedings;

3. Evidence shall be taken in premises accessible to the public;

4. Persons requested to give evidence shall be served with an official instrument in French or accompanied by a translation in French, and that instrument shall mention:

a. That evidence is being taken in conformity with the provisions of The Hague Convention of March 18, 1970 on the Taking of Evidence Abroad in Civil or Commercial Matters and relates to legal proceedings pending before a jurisdiction specifically designated by a Contracting State;

b. That appearance is voluntary and failure to appear will not give rise to criminal proceedings in the State of origin;

c. That the parties to the trial are consenting and, if not, the grounds of their objections;

d. That in the taking of evidence the person concerned may be legally represented;

e. That a person requested to give evidence may invoke the privilege and duty to refuse to give evidence.

A copy of these requests shall be transmitted to the Ministry of Justice.

5. The Civil Division of International Judicial Assistance shall be kept informed of any difficulty.

The request for permission transmitted by the requesting authority to the Ministry of Justice shall specify:

1. The motives that led to choosing this method of taking evidence in preference to that of a Letter of Request, considering the judiciary costs incurred;

2. The criteria for appointing commissioners when the person appointed does not reside in France.

The French Government declares that, in application of the provisions of Article 8, members of the judicial personnel of the requesting authority of a Contracting State may be present at the execution of a Letter of Request.

The Permanent Bureau of the Hague Conference on private international law presents its compliments to the Diplomatic Missions of the Member States and to the National Organs and has the honour to inform them that, by a letter received at the Ministry of Foreign Affairs of the Kingdom of the Netherlands on 19 January 1987, in accordance with Article 34 of the Convention, France has modified its declaration regarding Article 23 as follows:

The declaration made by the French Republic in accordance with Article 23 relating to Letters of Request issued for the purpose of obtaining pre-trial discovery of documents does not apply when the requested documents are enumerated limitatively in the Letter of Request and have a direct and precise link with the object of the procedure. (Translation)

The Permanent Bureau avails itself of this opportunity to renew to the Diplomatic Missions of the Member States and to the National Organs an assurance of its highest consideration and esteem.

GERMANY

"A. The Government of the Federal Republic of Germany makes the following declarations in accordance with paragraph 1 of Article 33 of the Convention of 18th March 1970:

"The Federal Republic of Germany makes the reservation provided for in the first sentence of paragraph 1 of Article 33 of the Convention excluding the application of the provisions of paragraph 2 of Article 4 of the Convention. Letters of Request to be executed under Chapter 1 of the Convention must, in accordance with paragraphs 1 and 5 of Article 4 of the Convention, be in the German language or be accompanied by a translation into that language.

"The Federal Republic of Germany declares in accordance with the option provided for in the first sentence of paragraph 1 of Article 33 of the Convention to make a reservation excluding the application of the provisions of Chapter II of the Convention that the taking of evidence by diplomatic officers or consular agents is not permissible in its territory if German nationals are involved.

"B. The Government of the Federal Republic of Germany makes the following declarations pursuant to Article 35 of the Convention of 18th March 1970:

"(1) The authority competent to execute a Letter of Request shall be the local court (Amtsgericht) in whose district the official act is to be performed.

Letters of Request shall be addressed to the Central Authority of the Land in which the respective request is to be executed. The Central Authority pursuant to Article 2 and paragraph 2 of Article 24 of the Convention shall be for

Baden-Württemberg	das Justizministerium Baden-Württemberg (The Ministry of Justice of Baden-Württemberg), D 7000 Stuttgart
Bavaria	das Bayerische Staatsministerium der Justiz (The Bavarian State Ministry of Justice), D 8000 München
Berlin	der Senator fur Justiz (The Senator of Justice), D 1000 Berlin

By Note of 29 September 1992 the following central authority was designated

Brandenburg	Das Ministerium der Justiz des Landes Brandenburg, D-0-1561 Potsdam
Bremen	der Präsident des Landgerichts Bremen (The President of the Regional Court of Bremen), D 2800 Bremen
Hamburg	der Prasident des Amtsgerichts Hamburg (The President of the Local Court of Hamburg), D 2000 Hamburg
Hesse	der Hessische Minister der Justiz (The Minister of Justice), D 6200 Wiesbaden
Lower Saxony	der Niedersachsische Minister der Justiz (The Minister of Justice of Lower Saxony), D 3000 Hannover

By Note of 29 September 1992 the following central authority was designated

Mecklenburg–Western Pomerania	Der Minister fur Justiz, Bundes-und Europaangelegen heiten, D-0-2754 Schwerin
Northrhine-Westphalia	der Prasident des Oberlandesgerichts Düsseldorf, D 4000 Düsseldorf
Rhineland-Palatinate	das Ministerium der Justiz (The Ministry of Justice), D 6500 Mainz
Saarland	der Minister fur Rechtspflege (The Minister of Justice), D 6600 Saarbrücken

By note of 29 September 1992 the following central authority was designated

Saxony	Das Sächsische Staatsministerium der Justiz D-0 8060 Dresden

By note of 29 September 1992 the following central authority was designated

Saxony-Anhalt	Das Ministerium der Justiz des Landes Sachsen-Anhalt, D-0 3037 Magdeburg
Schleswig-Holstein	der Justizminister des Landes Schleswig-Holstein (The Minister of Justice of the Land Schleswig-Holstein), D 2300 Kiel

By Note of 29 September 1992 the following central authority was designated

Thuringia	Das Justizministerium Thuringen, D-0-5082 Erfurt

"(2) Pursuant to Article 8 of the Convention, the Government of the Federal Republic of Germany declares that members of the requesting court of another Contracting State may be present at the execution of a Letter of Request by the local court if prior authorization has been given by the Central Authority of the Land where the request is to be executed.

"(3) The taking of evidence by diplomatic officers or consular agents pursuant to paragraph 1 of Article 16 of the Convention which involves nationals of a third State or stateless persons shall be subject to permission from the Central Authority of the Land where the evidence is to be taken. Pursuant to paragraph 2 of Article 16 of the Convention, permission shall not be required if the national of the third State is also a national of the State of the requesting court.

"(4) A commissioner of the requesting court may not take evidence pursuant to Article 17 of the Convention unless the Central Authority of the Land where the evidence is to be taken has given its permission. Such permission may be made subject to conditions. The local court in whose district official acts would have to be performed by virtue of a Letter of Request in the same matter shall be entitled to control the preparation and the actual taking of the evidence. Under the second sentence of Article 19 of the Convention, a member of the court may be present at the taking of the evidence.

"(5) The Federal Republic of Germany declares in pursuance of Article 23 of the Convention that it will not, in its territory, execute Letters of Request issued for the purpose of obtaining pre-trial discovery of documents as known in Common Law countries."

ISRAEL

Notification in conformity with Article 42, paragraph e, of the convention

In accordance with Article 35 of the Convention Israel notified by a Note dated April 17, 1980 and received at the Ministry of Foreign Affairs of the Kingdom of the Netherlands on April 25, 1980, that the Central Authority designated by the State of Israel in accordance with Article 2 of the above-mentioned Convention, is the Director of Courts, 19 Jaffa Road, Jerusalem.

ITALY

Notification in conformity with Article 42, subs. a and e, of the Convention

The Italian Republic deposited its instrument of ratification of the above-mentioned Convention with the Ministry of Foreign Affairs of the Kingdom of the Netherlands on 22 June 1982, in accordance with Article 37, paragraph 2, of the Convention.

In accordance with Article 38, paragraph 2, the Convention will enter into force for Italy on 21 August 1982.

At the time of the deposit of the instrument of ratification the Italian Government notified the Ministry of Foreign Affairs of the following:

Translation

"(1) The Italian Government declares, in accordance with Article 8, that members of the judicial personnel of the requesting authority of another Contracting State may be present at the execution of a Letter of Request, subject to prior authorization by the competent authority designated by the Italian State under (4) paragraph 2 below.

"(2) The Italian Government declares, in accordance with Article 18, that a diplomatic officer, consular agent or commissioner who is taking evidence under Article 15, 16 or 17, may apply to the Authority designated by the Italian State under (4) paragraph 2 below, for appropriate assistance to obtain the evidence by compulsion.

"(3) The Italian Government declares, in accordance with Article 23, that it will not execute Letters of Request issued for the purpose of obtaining pre-trial discovery of documents as known in Common Law countries.

"(4) In accordance with Article 35 the Italian Government designates the Ministry of Foreign Affairs pursuant to Article 2 as the Central Authority which will undertake to receive Letters of Request coming from a judicial authority of another Contracting State and to transmit them to the authority competent to execute them.

"In accordance with the abovementioned Article the Italian Government designates the Court of Appeal within whose jurisdiction proceedings are to take place as the authority competent to:

"–authorize foreign judicial personnel to be present at the execution of a Letter of Request, pursuant to Article 8;

"–authorize foreign diplomatic officers, consular agents or commissioners to take evidence under Article 16 or 17;

"–grant the judicial assistance provided for in Article 18."

LUXEMBOURG

Notification in accordance with Article 42, subs. a and e, of the Convention

In accordance with Article 37, paragraph 2, Luxemburg deposited on 26 July 1977 its instrument of ratification of the Convention with the Ministry of Foreign Affairs of the Kingdom of the Netherlands.

In conformity with Article 38, paragraph 2, the Convention shall enter into force for Luxemburg on 24 September 1977.

On the occasion of the deposit of the said instrument of ratification the Government of Luxemburg made the following declarations and reservations:

"–In accordance with Article 2 the Parquet Général is designated as the Central Authority.

"–In pursuance of Article 4, paragraph 4, Letters of Request in German shall also be accepted.

"–In pursuance of Article 23, Letters of Request issued for the purpose of obtaining pre-trial discovery of documents as known in Common Law countries shall not be executed.

"–In accordance with the provisions of Article 16, the Parquet Général is designated as the authority competent to authorise the diplomatic officers or consular agents of a Contracting State to take, without compulsion, the evidence of persons other than the nationals of that State in aid of proceedings commenced in the courts of the State which they represent.

"This authorization, which is given in each specific case and to which specific conditions, where appropriate, are attached, is granted under the following general conditions:

"1–The evidence shall be taken only within the precincts of an Embassy or Consulate.

"2–The Parquet Général shall be given reasonable advance notice of the time, date and place of the taking of evidence so that it can, if it wishes, be represented.

"3–A request to a person to appear shall, in accordance with the regulations, be in the form of an official document in French or German or accompanied by and [sic] translation into one of these languages stating:

"a) that the evidence is to be taken in accordance with the provisions of the Convention on the taking of evidence abroad in civil or commercial matters concluded at The Hague on 18 March 1970, and in the framework of a judicial procedure followed in a jurisdiction designated by a Contracting State;

"b) that the appearance is voluntary and that no prosecution in the requesting State will result from failure to appear;

"c) that the parties to the action, where appropriate, consent to the taking of the evidence or are opposed to it for reasons to be given;

"d) that the person requested to appear may be legally represented;

"e) that the person requested to appear may invoke a privilege or a duty to refuse to give evidence.

"–In accordance with the provisions of Article 17, the Parquet Général is designated as the authority competent to authorize persons designated in accordance with the regulations as commissioners to take evidence, without compulsion, in aid of proceedings commenced in the courts of another Contracting State.

"This authorization, which is given in the particular case and to which specific conditions, where appropriate, are attached, is granted under the following general conditions:

"1–The Parquet Général shall be given reasonable advance notice of the time, date and place of the taking of evidence so that it can, if it wishes, be represented.

"2–A request to a person to appear shall, in accordance with the regulations, be in the form of an official document in French or German or accompanied by a translation into one of these languages stating:

"a) that the evidence is to be taken in accordance with the provisions of the Convention on the taking of evidence abroad in civil or commercial matters concluded at The Hague on 18 March 1970, and in the framework of a judicial procedure followed in a jurisdiction designated by a Contracting State;

"b) that the appearance is voluntary and that no prosecution in the requesting State will result from failure to appear;

"c) that the parties to the action, where appropriate, consent to the taking of the evidence or are opposed to it for reasons to be given;

"d) that the person requested to appear may be legally represented;

"e) that the person requested to appear may invoke a privilege or a duty to refuse to give evidence.

"–In pursuance of Article 8, members of the judicial personnel of the requesting authority of a Contracting State may be present at the execution of a Letter of Request."

MEXICO

Notification pursuant to Article 42 of the Convention

In conformity with Article 39, paragraph 2, the instrument of accession by the United Mexican States to the above-mentioned Convention was deposited with the Ministry of Foreign Affairs of the Kingdom of the Netherlands on 27 July 1989.

The instrument of accession of the United Mexican States contains the declarations and reservations the text of which together with a translation in English is annexed to this notification.

In accordance with paragraph 3 of Article 39, the Convention will enter into force for the United Mexican States on 25 September 1989.

According to Article 39, paragraph 4, of the Convention the accession will have effect only as regards the relations between the United Mexican States and such Contracting States as will have declared their acceptance of the accession. Such declarations shall be deposited at the Ministry of Foreign Affairs of the Kingdom of the Netherlands.

A) TRANSMISSION AND EXECUTION OF LETTERS OF REQUEST

1. Central Authority (Article 2)

Name: Secretaria de Relaciones Exteriores,
Direccion General de Asuntos Juridicos.
Address: Ricardo Flores Magon No. 1
Telephone: 782-3440
Telex: 01762090

2. Language requirements (Article 4)

2.1 The United Mexican States does hereby make a special reservation related to the provisions of paragraph 2 of Article 4, and declares in accordance with paragraph 4 of the same Article, that letters of request sent to its Central Authority or judicial authorities shall be written in the spanish language or shall otherwise be accompanied by a translation into said language.

B) TAKING OF EVIDENCE ABROAD BY DIPLOMATIC OFFICERS, CONSULAR AGENTS AND COMMISSIONS (CHAPTER II)

3. The United Mexican States makes a special and complete reservation concerning the provisions contained in Articles 17 and 18 of this Chapter in relation to the "commissioners" and the use of measures to compulsion by diplomatic officers and consular agents.

C) FORMULATION OF PRE-TRIAL DISCOVERY OF DOCUMENTS

4. With reference to Article 23 of the Convention, the United Mexican States declares that according to Mexican law, it shall only be able to comply with letters of request issued for the purpose of obtaining the production and transcription of documents when the following requirements are met:

a) that the judicial proceeding has been commenced;

b) that the documents are reasonably identifiable as to date, subject and other relevant information and that the request specifies those facts and circumstances that lead the requesting party to reasonable belief that the requested documents are known to the person from whom they are requested or that they are in his possession or under his control or custody;

c) that the direct relationship between the evidence or information sought and the pending proceeding be identified.

D) OTHER TRANSMISSION CHANNEL TO THE JUDICIAL AUTHORITIES DIFFERENT FROM THOSE PROVIDED FOR IN ARTICLE 2

5. In regard to Article 27, paragraph a) of the Convention, the United Mexican States does hereby declare that the letters of request may be transmitted to its judicial authorities not only through the Central Authority but also through diplomatic or consular channels or through judicial channels (directly sent from the foreign court to the Mexican Court), providing that in the latter case all requirements relating to legalization of signatures are fulfilled.

6. In regard to Article 32 of the Convention, the United Mexican States informs that it is a State Party to the Interamerican Convention on the Taking of Evidence Abroad, signed in Panama on January the thirtieth, nineteen hundred and seventy-five, as well as to its Additional Protocol signed in La Paz, Bolivia, on May the twenty-fourth, nineteen hundred and eighty-four.

In accordance with Article 39 the Convention will enter into force between the United Mexican States and

Norway	20 November 1989
Israel	17 December 1989
the United States of America	24 December 1989

Argentina	25 December 1989
Finland	16 January 1990
Denmark	22 January 1990
the United Kingdom of Great Britain and Northern Ireland	16 March 1990
(also for Anguilla, the Cayman Islands, the Falkland Islands, Gibraltar, Guernsey, Hong Kong, the Isle of Man, Jersey, South Georgia and the South Sandwich Islands and Sovereign Base Areas of Akrotiri and Dheklia in the Island of Cyprus)	
the Federal Republic of Germany	3 March 1990
Czechoslovakia	2 April 1990
the Kingdom of the Netherlands (for the Kingdom in Europe)	16 April 1990
Aruba	18 May 1991
Sweden	17 April 1990
Portugal	14 October 1991

Notification in conformity with Article 42, sub c and e, of the Convention

In accordance with Article 39, paragraph 2, the Principality of Monaco deposited its instrument of accession to the above-mentioned Convention with the Ministry of Foreign Affairs of the Kingdom of the Netherlands on 17 January 1986, with the following declarations and reservations:

Translation

1. In accordance with article 2, the Directorate of Judicial Services, MC 98025 MONACO CEDEX, is designated as the Central Authority.

2. Under article 4, paragraph 2, only Letters of Request drawn up in French or accompanied by a translation in that language shall be accepted.

3. Under article 23, Letters of Request issued for the purpose of obtaining pre-trial discovery of documents shall not be executed.

4. In accordance with articles 16 and 17, the Directorate of Judicial Services is designated as a competent authority for the purpose of authorising, as appropriate:

- the consular authorities of a Contracting State to take the evidence without compulsion of persons other than nationals of that State and in aid of proceedings commenced in a court of the State which they represent, or
- persons duly designated as commissioners to take evidence without compulsion in aid of proceedings commenced in a court of the Contracting State.

Such authorisation, which shall be granted for each particular case and may contain specific conditions, shall be subject to the following general conditions:

a) evidence shall be taken solely on the premises of consulates when the latter are situated within the Principality, and in other cases in the Palais de Justice of Monaco;

b) the Directorate of Judicial Services shall be informed of the date and time of the taking of the evidence in time to permit the Directorate to be represented, and, if necessary, to provide courtroom accommodation at the Palais de Justice of Monaco;

c) the persons concerned in the taking of evidence shall be duly summoned by an official document drawn up in French or accompanied by a translation in that language; this document shall indicate:

- that the taking of the evidence in question is being conducted in accordance with the provisions of the Hague Convention of 18 March 1970 on the Taking of Evidence Abroad in Civil or Commercial Matters, and that the procedure constitutes part of legal proceedings pursued under the specially designated jurisdiction of a Contracting State;
- that appearance is voluntary and non-appearance would not entail legal proceedings in the requesting State;

- that the person concerned in the taking of evidence may be represented by a lawyer or defence counsel;
- that the parties in the proceedings, should they be instituted, give their consent, and if not the document shall state the reasons for their opposition;
- that the person concerned in the taking of evidence may apply to be exempted or barred from testifying.

A copy of the summonses shall be sent to the Directorate of Judicial Services, which is also to be kept informed of any difficulties.

Pursuant to Article 39, paragraph 3, the Convention will enter into force for the Principality of Monaco on 18 March 1986.

The accession will have effect only as regards the relations between Monaco and such Contracting States as will have declared their acceptance of the accession.

Notification pursuant to Article 42 of the Convention

In accordance with Article 39 the Convention will enter into force between Monaco and

the United States of America	January 30, 1988
the Kingdom of the Netherlands (Kingdom in Europe)	14 July 1986
Portugal	14 October 1991

NETHERLANDS

Notification in conformity with Article 42, subs. a and e of the Convention.

"The Kingdom of the Netherlands deposited on 8 April 1981, in accordance with Article 37, paragraph 2, of the Convention its instrument of ratification for the Kingdom in Europe of the above-mentioned Convention.

"Upon the deposit of the instrument of ratification the Government of the Kingdom of the Netherlands has made the following declarations:

"In the Netherlands the Convention shall be applied as follows:

"Article 2

"The Public Prosecutor at The Hague District Court is designated as the Central Authority.

"Article 4

"Letters of Request will be accepted in Dutch, German, English or French, or if they are accompanied by a translation into one of these languages.

"The Netherlands does not undertake to translate documents for the execution of a Letter of Request.

"Article 8

"Members of the judicial personnel of another Contracting State may be present at the execution of a Letter of Request provided that the court which is responsible for execution authorizes this and provided that any conditions which the court may impose are respected.

"Article 11

"Only the court which is responsible for executing the Letter of Request shall be competent to decide whether any person concerned by the execution has a privilege or duty to refuse to give evidence under the law of a State other than the State of origin; no such privilege or duty exists under Dutch law.

"Article 14

"Fees paid to experts and interpreters and costs occasioned by the use of a special procedure requested by the State of origin under Article 9, paragraph 2 of the Convention shall be borne by the State of origin.

"Article 16

"In the Netherlands, no prior permission is required for the taking of evidence as provided for in Article 16.

"Article 17

"The permission referred to in Article 17 must be requested from the President of the District Court in the area in which evidence is to be taken. If evidence is to be taken from witnesses or experts, the area in question will be that in which the witnesses or experts, or the majority of them, reside. If the President gives permission, he may impose any conditions which he considers necessary to ensure that the evidence is taken in a proper manner. He may decide that the evidence should be taken at the court, under the supervision of a judge designated by him. Permission will only be granted if the following conditions are met:

"a) the witness or expert concerned must have been duly summoned; the summons must be in Dutch, or must be accompanied by a Dutch translation and must contain:

"–the facts of the case and a summary of the proceedings in connection with which the evidence is to be taken, and details of the court which has requested the evidence;

"–a statement to the effect that there is no obligation for the witness or expert to appear, and that if he refuses to appear, to take an oath, to give his word of honour or to give evidence, he will not incur any penalty or measure of any kind, either in the Netherlands or in the State where the proceedings have been instituted;

"–a statement to the effect that the person concerned may be legally represented;

"–a statement to the effect that in so far as the person concerned has a privilege or duty to refuse to give evidence, he may do so;

"–a statement to the effect that the commissioner will reimburse expenses incurred by the witness or expert in connection with his appearance to give evidence.

"b) A copy of the summons must be forwarded to the President.

"c) The request for permission must state the reasons why the taking of evidence has been entrusted to a commissioner and it must state the commissioner's official status unless he is a lawyer competent to practise in the Netherlands.

"d) The costs of taking the evidence, i.e., the expenses of the witnesses, experts or interpreters, must be reimbursed in full.

"Article 23

"The Netherlands will not execute Letters of Request issued for the purpose of obtaining pre-trial discovery of documents as known in Common Law countries.

"For the purposes of Article 23 of the Convention, "Letters of Request issued for the purpose of obtaining pre-trial discovery of documents as known in Common Law countries", which the Netherlands will not execute, are defined by the Government of the Kingdom of the Netherlands as being any Letters of Request which require a person:

"a. to state which of the documents which are of relevance to the proceedings to which the Letter of Request relates have been in his possession, custody or power, or

"b. to produce any document other than particular documents specified in the Letter of Request as being documents which the court which is conducting the proceedings believes to be in his possession, custody or power.

"Article 26

"The Netherlands will request that any State of origin which has made a request pursuant to paragraph 1 of Article 26 should reimburse the fees and costs to which this paragraph refers.

"In accordance with Article 38, paragraph 2, the Convention will enter into force for the Kingdom of the Netherlands (the Kingdom in Europe) on 7 June 1981."

In accordance with Article 40, paragraph 2, the Kingdom of the Netherlands declared on 28 May 1986 that the Convention shall extend to Aruba.

In conformity with Article 40, paragraph 3, the Convention will enter into force for Aruba on 27 July 1986.

The Permanent Bureau of the Hague Conference on private international law presents its compliments to the Diplomatic Missions of the Member States and to the National Organs and has the honour to inform them that, in accordance with Article 2 of the above-mentioned Convention, the

Kingdom of the Netherlands

has designated the *"Procureur-Generaal in Aruba van het Gemeenschappelijk Hof van Justitie van de Nederlandse Antillen en Aruba" (the Attorney-General in Aruba of the joint Court of Justice of the Netherlands Antilles and of Aruba) as Central Authority for Aruba.*

The Convention is being applied in Aruba subject to the same declarations as made upon ratification of the Convention on 8 April 1981 by the Kingdom of the Netherlands for the Kingdom in Europe. In addition, in conformity with Article 4, paragraphs 3 and 4, Aruba will not accept Letters of Request in French, unless accompanied by a translation into Dutch, English, or Spanish.

The Permanent Bureau avails itself of this opportunity to renew to the Diplomatic Missions of the Members States and to the National Organs an assurance of its highest consideration and esteem.

NORWAY

With the following reservation:

"In conformity with article 33, Norway enters a reservation to paragraph 2 of article 4 to the effect that Letters of Request in the French language will not be accepted."

And with the following declarations:

"I. The Royal Ministry of Justice and Police is designated as the Central Authority with reference to article 2 and as the Competent Authority with reference to articles 15, 16 and 17.

"II. With reference to article 4, paragraph 3, the Kingdom of Norway declares that letters in the Danish or Swedish languages can be sent to the Central Authority.

"III. By accepting Letters of Request in another language than the Norwegian, the Kingdom of Norway does not undertake to execute the request, or transmit the evidence thus obtained in this other language; nor to have translated the documents which establish the execution of the letter of request.

"IV. By virtue of article 15, evidence can be taken by diplomatic officers or consular agents only if, upon application, prior permission to that effect has been granted.

"V. By virtue of article 23, the Kingdom of Norway declares that it will not execute Letters of Request issued for the purpose of obtaining pre-trial discovery of documents as known in Common Law countries."

The declaration made by the Kingdom of Norway in accordance with article 23 concerning "Letters of Request issued for the purpose of obtaining pre-trial discovery of documents" shall apply only to Letters of Request which require a person

a) to state what documents relevant to the proceedings, to which the Letter of Request relates, are, or have been, in his possession, other than particular documents specified in the Letter of Request; or

b) to produce any documents other than particular documents, which are specified in the Letter of Request, and which are likely to be in his possession.

PORTUGAL

With the following reservations and declarations:

"a) In accordance with Article 33 of the Convention, the Portuguese State makes the following reservations:

"1. exclusion of the application of paragraph 2 Article 4;

"2. exclusion of the application of Chapter II, with the exception of Article 15.

"b) In accordance with Articles 15 and 23 of the Convention, the Portuguese State makes the following declarations:

"1. The Portuguese State declares that the evidence as referred to in Article 15, can only be taken if permission to that effect is given by the appropriate authority designated by it upon application made by the diplomatic or consular agent;

"2. The Portuguese State declares that it will not execute Letters of Request issued for the purpose of obtaining pre-trial discovery of documents as known in Common Law Countries.

"c) With regard to Articles 2 and 15 of the Convention, the competent Portuguese authority will be the Director-General of the Judiciary Department ("Direccao-Geral dos Servicas Judiciarios") of the Ministry of Justice.".

SINGAPORE

In accordance with Article 39, paragraph 3, the Convention shall enter into force for the Republic of Singapore on December 26, 1978.

Notification in accordance with Convention Article 42(c) and (e):

On October 27, 1978, the Ministry of Foreign Affairs of the Kingdom of the Netherlands received the instrument of accession of the Republic of Singapore to the Convention on the Taking of Evidence Abroad in Civil and Commercial Matters in accordance with Article 39, Paragraph 2, of the aforesaid Convention.

At the time of its accession the Government of the Republic of Singapore made the following reservations:

"(i) The entire Chapter II of the Convention is not applicable to the Republic of Singapore; and

"(ii) With regard to Article 4, paragraph 2, the Republic of Singapore will not accept a Letter of Request in a language other than English, since this language is the one used by the judicial personnel in Singapore."

In accordance with Article 23 the Government of the Republic of Singapore has declared that the Republic of Singapore will not execute Letters of Request issued for the purpose of obtaining pretrial discovery of documents as known in Common Law countries.

The Government of the Republic of Singapore has further declared that it understands "Letters of Request issued for the purpose of obtaining pretrial discovery of documents" for the purposes of the foregoing declaration as including any Letter of Request which requires a person:

(a) to state what documents relevant to the proceedings to which the Letter of Request relates are, or have been, in his possession, custody or power, or

(b) to produce any documents other than particular documents specified in the Letter of Request as being documents appearing to the requested court to be, or likely to be, in his possession, custody or power. It is also understood that the reference to civil or commercial actions in the Convention does not include tax matters for the Republic of Singapore.

In accordance with Article 39, paragraph 3, the Convention shall enter into force for the Republic of Singapore on December 26, 1978.

The accession shall be effective only for relations between the Republic of Singapore and contracting States that declare that they accept this accession.

Notification in conformity with Article 42, paragraph e, of the Convention:

In accordance with Article 35 of the Convention Singapore notified the Ministry of Foreign Affairs of the Kingdom of the Netherlands by a Note dated August 4, 1979, that the Central Authority which will undertake to receive Letters of Request referred to in Article 2 of the Convention, is the Registrar of the Supreme Court.

SLOVAK REPUBLIC

By notification dated March 15, 1993 the Slovak Republic communicated the following:

"In accordance with relevant principles and norms of international law and to extent defined by it, the Slovak Republic, as a successor State, born from the division of the Czech and Slovak Federal Republic, considers itself bound, as of January 1, 1993, i.e. the date of the division of the Czechoslovak Federation, by multilateral international treaties to which the Czech and Slovak Federal Republic was a party at that date, including reservations and declarations in respect of provisions made earlier by Czechoslovakia, as well as objections by Czechoslovakia in respect of reservations made by other treaty parties", which are as follows: [Same declarations and reservations, *mutatis mutandis*, under Czech Republic, see footnote 5].

SPAIN

Notification pursuant to Article 42 of the Convention

In accordance with Article 37, paragraph 2, of the above-mentioned Convention Spain deposited its instrument of ratification with the Ministry of Foreign Affairs of the Kingdom of the Netherlands on 22 May 1987.

The instrument of ratification contains the following reservation:

"In accordance with Article 33 in relation with Article 4, paragraph 2, Spain will not accept Letters of Request which are not drawn up in Spanish or accompanied by a translation."

and the following declarations:

"a) The Spanish Central Authority referred to in Article 2 will be: The Ministry of Justice-Technical Secretariat General-(San Bernardo, 45-28015 MADRID), with exclusion of any other Authority.

"b) With prior authorization of the Spanish Ministry of Justice, a Judge of the requesting State may intervene in the execution of a Letter of Request, in accordance with Article 8.

"c) In accordance with Articles 16 and 17, the evidence may be taken, without prior permission of the Spanish Authority, in the premises of the diplomatic or consular representation of the requesting State.

"d) Pursuant to Article 23 Spain does not accept Letters of Request derived from the "pre-trial discovery of documents" procedure known in Common Law countries."

The Convention will enter into force for Spain on 21 July 1987.

SWEDEN

With the following declarations:

(Translation)

- That, in pursuance of Article 4, para. 4, Letters of Request in the Danish and Norwegian languages will be accepted;
- That, in pursuance of Article 8, members of the judicial personnel of the requesting authority of another Contracting State may be present at the execution of a Letter of Request without prior authorisation;
- That, in pursuance of Article 15, para. 2, a diplomatic officer or consular agent may only take evidence if permission to do so has been granted by the competent Swedish authority;
- That, in pursuance of Article 23, Letters of Request issued for the purpose of obtaining pre-trial discovery of documents as known in Common Law countries will not be executed;
- That documents provided by Sweden which establish that a Letter of Request has been executed will be in the Swedish language only.

Ministry of Foreign Affairs, Stockholm, has been designated as the Central Authority referred to in Article 2 and also as the Competent Authority referred to in Article 15-17.

Additional declaration on July 11, 1980: "The Swedish Government understands 'Letters of Request issued for the purpose of pre-trial discovery of documents' for the purposes of the foregoing Declaration as including any Letter of Request which requires a person:

"a) to state what documents relevant to the proceedings to which the Letter of Request relates are, or have been, in his possession, custody or power, or

"b) to produce any documents other than particular documents specified in the Letter of Request, which are likely to be in his possession, custody or power."

SWITZERLAND

With the following reservations and declarations:

Re Article 1

·1. With regard to Article 1, Switzerland takes the view that the Convention applies exclusively to the Contracting States. Moreover, regarding the conclusions of the Special Commission which met in The Hague in April 1989, Switzerland believes that, whatever the opinion of the contracting states on the exclusive application of the Convention, priority should in any event be given to the procedures provided for in the Convention regarding requests for the taking of evidence abroad.

Re Articles 2 and 24

2. In accordance with Article 35, first paragraph, Switzerland designates the cantonal authorities listed in the annex as Central Authorities as referred to in Articles 2 and 24 of the Convention. Requests for the taking of evidence or the execution of any other judicial act may also be addressed to the Federal Justice and Police Department in Bern, which will forward them to the appropriate Central Authority.

Re Article 4, second and third paragraphs

3. In accordance with Articles 33 and 35, Switzerland declares, with regard to Article 4, second and third paragraphs, that Letters of Request and any accompanying documents must be in the language of the authority requested to execute them, *i. e.* in German, French or Italian, or accompanied by a translation into one of these languages, depending on the part of Switzerland in which the document is to be executed. The documents confirming execution will be drawn up in the official language of the requested authority.

Re Article 8

4. In accordance with Article 35, second paragraph, Switzerland declares, with regard to Article 8, that members of the judicial personnel of the requesting authority of another Contracting State may be present at the execution of a Letter of Request provided they have obtained prior authorization from the executing authority.

Re Articles 15, 16 and 17

5. In accordance with Article 35, Switzerland declares that evidence may be taken according to Articles 15, 16 and 17 subject to prior authorization by the Federal Justice and Police Department. A request for authorization must be addressed to the Central Authority in the canton where the evidence is to be taken.

Re Article 23

6. In accordance with Article 23, Switzerland declares that Letters of Request issued for the purpose of obtaining pre-trial discovery of documents will not be executed if:

a)the request has no direct and necessary link with the proceedings in quesion; or

b) a person is required to indicate what documents relating to the case are or were in his/her possession or keeping or at his/her disposal; or

c) a person is required to produce documents other that those mentioned in the request for legal assistance, which are probably in his/her possession or keeping or at his/her disposal; or

d) interests worthy of protection of the concerned persons are endangered.

Cantonal Central Authorities:

Canton	Official Language(s)	Addresses	Telephone Numbers
Appenzell Ausserrhoden	German	Kantonsgericht Appenzell A.Rh. 9403 Trogen	[41] (71) 94 24 61
Appenzell Innerrhoden	German	Kantonsgericht Appenzell I.Rh. 9050 Appenzell	[41] (71) 87 95 51
Aargau	German	Obergericht des Kantons Aargau 5000 Aarau	[41] (64) 21 19 40
Basel-Landschaft	German	Obergericht des Kantons Basel-Landschaft 4410 Liestal	[41] (61) 925 51 11
Basel-Stadt	German	Appellationsgericht Basel-Stadt 4054 Basel	[41] (61) 267 81 81
Bern	German/ French	Justizdirektion des Kantons Bern 3011 Bern	[41] (31) 633 76 76
Fribourg	French/ German	Tribunal cantonal 1700 Fribourg	[41] (37) 25 39 10
Genève	French	Parquet du Procureur géneral 1211 Genève 3	[41] (22) 319 21 11
Glarus	German	Obergericht des Kantons Glarus	[41] (58) 61 15 32
Graubünden	German	Justiz-, Polizei-und Sanitätsdepartment Graubünden 7001 Chur	[41] (81) 21 21 21
Jura	French	Département de la Justice 2800 Delémont	[41] (66) 21 51 11
Luzern	German	Obergericht des Kantons Luzern 6002 Luzern	[41] (41) 24 51 11
Neuchâtel	French	Département de Justice 2001 Neuchâtel	[41] (38) 22 31 11
Nidwalden	German	Kantonsgericht Nidwalden 6370 Stans	[41] (41) 63 79 50
Obwalden	German	Kantonsgericht des Kantons Obwalden 6060 Sarnen	[41] (41) 66 92 22
St. Gallen	German	Kantonsgericht St. Gallen 9001 St. Gallen	[41] (71) 21 31 11
Schaffhausen	German	Kantonsgericht des Kantons Schaffhausen 8201 Schaffhausen	[41] (53) 82 74 22
Schwyz	German	Kantonsgericht Schwyz 6430 Schwyz	[41] (43) 24 11 24
Solothurn	German	Obergericht des Kantons Solothurn 4500 Solothurn	[41] (65) 21 73 11
Tessin	Italian	Tribunale di appello 6901 Lugano	[41] (91) 21 51 11
Thurgau	German	Obergericht des Kantons Thurgau 8500 Frauenfeld	[41] (54) 22 31 21
Uri	German	Gerichtskanzlei Uri 6460 Altdorf	[41] (44) 4 22 44

Canton	Official Language(s)	Addresses	Telephone Numbers
Valais	French/ German	Tribunal cantonal 1950 Sion	[41] (27) 22 93 93
Vaud	French	Tribunal cantonal 1014 Lausanne	[41] (21) 313 15 11
Zug	German	Obergericht des Kantons Zug Rechtshilfe 6300 Zug	[41] (42) 25 33 11
Zürich	German	Obergericht des Kantons Zürich Rechtshilfe 8023 Zürich	[41] (1) 257 91 91

UNITED KINGDOM

Notification in conformity with Article 42, under a and e, of the Convention:

In accordance with Article 37, paragraph 2, the United Kingdom of Great Britain and Northern Ireland deposited on July 16, 1976 its instrument of ratification with the Ministry of Foreign Affairs of the Netherlands.

In conformity with Article 38, paragraph 2, the Convention shall enter into force for the United Kingdom on September 14, 1976.

The instrument of ratification mentioned above, contains the following reservation:

"... in accordance with the provisions of Article 33 the United Kingdom will not accept a Letter of Request in French.".

On the occasion of the deposit of the said instrument of ratification the Government of the United Kingdom of Great Britain and Northern Ireland made the following declarations:

"1. In accordance with Article 8 Her Majesty's Government declare that members of the judicial personnel of the requesting authority may be present at the execution of a Letter of Request.

"2. In accordance with Article 18 Her Majesty's Government declare that a diplomatic officer, consular agent or commissioner authorised to take evidence under Articles 15, 16 and 17 may apply to the competent authority designated hereinbefore for appropriate assistance to obtain such evidence by compulsion provided that the Contracting State whose diplomatic officer, consular agent or commissioner makes the application has made a declaration affording reciprocal facilities under Article 18.

"3. In accordance with Article 23 Her Majesty's Government declare that the United Kingdom will not execute Letters of Request issued for the purpose of obtaining pre-trial discovery of documents. Her Majesty's Government further declare that Her Majesty's Government understand "Letters of Request issued for the purpose of obtaining pre-trial discovery of documents" for the purposes of the foregoing Declaration as including any Letter of Request which requires a person:–

"a. to state what documents relevant to the proceedings to which the Letter of Request relates are, or have been, in his possession, custody, or power, or

"b. to produce any documents other than particular documents specified in the Letter of Request as being documents appearing to the requesting court to be, or to be likely to be, in his possession, custody or power.

"4. In accordance with Article 27 Her Majesty's Government declare that by the law and practice of the United Kingdom the prior permission referred to in Articles 16 and 17 is not required in respect of diplomatic officers, consular agents or commissioners of a Contracting State which does not require permission to be obtained for the purposes of taking evidence under Articles 16 and 17."

In accordance with Article 35 of the Convention, the Government of the United Kingdom made the following designations:

1. Under Article 2: the Foreign and Commonwealth Office.

2. Under Article 16: the Foreign and Commonwealth Office.

3. Under Article 17: the Foreign and Commonwealth Office.

4. Under Article 18: the Senior Master of the Supreme Court (Queen's Bench Division) for England and Wales; the Crown Agent for Scotland, for Scotland; the Master (Queen's Bench and Appeals). The address of the Master (Queen's Bench and Appeals) is Royal Courts of Justice Belfast 1.

5. Under Article 24: the Senior Master of the Supreme Court (Queen's Bench Division) in England and Wales; the Crown Agent for Scotland, for Scotland; the Master (Queen's Bench and Appeals). The address of the Master (Queen's Bench and Appeals) is Royal Courts of Justice, Belfast 1.

By notification received on June 23, 1978 by the Ministry of Foreign Affairs of the Netherlands, the Convention was extended to Hong Kong effective Aug. 22, 1978, with the following declaration:

"(a) In accordance with the provisions of article 4 and article 33 of the Convention, Hong Kong will not accept a Letter of Request in French.

"(b) In accordance with article 35 and article 24 of the Convention, the Registrar of the Supreme Court of Hong Kong is designated as an additional authority competent to receive Letters of Request for execution in Hong Kong.

"(c) In accordance with article 35 and articles 16 and 17 of the Convention, the Chief Secretary is designated as the competent authority of Hong Kong."

Extension to Gibraltar.–

In accordance with Article 40, Paragraph 3, the Convention shall enter into force for Gibraltar on January 20, 1979.

The extension declaration contains the following reservation: "In accordance with the provisions of Article 4 and Article 33 of the Convention, Gibraltar will not accept a Letter of Request in French."

In accordance with Article 35 of the Convention the following designations have been made:

"(a) Under Articles 16 and 17 of the Convention, the Deputy Governor is designated as the competent authority for Gibraltar;

"(b) Under Article 18 of the Convention, the Registrar of the Supreme Court of Gibraltar is designated as the competent authority;

"(c) Under Article 24 of the Convention, the Deputy Governor is designated as an additional authority competent to receive Letters of Request for execution in Gibraltar."

[For declarations see the original note.]

Notification in conformity with Article 42, subs. d and e, of the Convention

By a letter dated November 20, 1978, and received at the Ministry of Foreign Affairs of the Kingdom of the Netherlands on November 21, 1978, the Ambassador of the United Kingdom of Great Britain and Northern Ireland at The Hague, referring to the deposit on July 16, 1976 of the instrument of ratification of the above-mentioned Convention by the United Kingdom of Great Britain and Northern Ireland, declared in accordance with article 40 that the Convention shall extend to Gibraltar. The Convention shall enter into force for Gibraltar on January 20, 1979.

With the following designations and declarations:

The declaration of extension contains the following reservation:

"...in accordance with the provisions of Article 4 and Article 33 of the Convention, Gibraltar will not accept a Letter of Request in French." In accordance with Article 35 of the Convention the following designations have been made:

a) under Articles 16 and 17 of the Convention the Deputy Governor is designated as the competent authority for Gibraltar;

b) under Article 18 of the Convention, the Registrar of the Supreme Court of Gibraltar is designated as the competent authority;

c) under Article 24 of the Convention, the Deputy Governor is designated as an additional authority competent to receive Letters of Request for execution in Gibraltar.

and the following declarations:

1. In accordance with Article 8, members of the judicial personnel of the requesting authority may be present at the execution of a Letter of Request in Gibraltar.

2. In accordance with Article 18, a diplomatic officer, consular agent or commissioner authorised to take evidence under Articles 15, 16 and 17 of the Convention may apply to the competent authority in Gibraltar designated hereinbefore for appropriate assistance to obtain such evidence by compulsion provided that the Contracting State whose diplomatic officer, consular agent or commissioner makes the application has made a declaration affording reciprocal facilities under Article 18.

3. In accordance with Article 23, Gibraltar will not execute Letters of Request issued for the purpose of obtaining pre-trial discovery of documents. The Government of Gibraltar understands "Letters of Request issued for the purpose of obtaining pre-trial discovery of documents" for the purposes of the foregoing Declaration as including any Letter of Request which requires a person:

a) to state what documents relevant to the proceedings to which the Letter of Request relates are, or have been, in his possession, custody or power; or

b) to produce any documents other than particular documents specified in the Letter of Request as being documents appearing to the requested court to be, or likely to be, in his possession, custody or power.

4. In accordance with Article 27, by the law and practice of Gibraltar the prior permission referred to in Articles 16 and 17 of the Convention is not required in respect of diplomatic officers, consular agents or commissioners of a Contracting State which does not require permission to be obtained for the purposes of taking evidence under Articles 16 or 17.

Extension to Sovereign Base Areas of Akrotiri and Dhekelia in the Island of Cyprus.–

"The Convention shall enter into force for the Sovereign Base Areas of Akrotiri and Dhekelia in the Island of Cyprus on August 24, 1979."

The declaration of extension contains the following reservation:

"...in accordance with the provisions of Article 4 and Article 33 of the Convention, the Sovereign Base Areas will not accept a Letter of Request in French.".

In accordance with Article 35 of the Convention the following designations have been made:

a) under Articles 16 and 17 of the Convention the Chief Officer, Sovereign Base Areas, is designated as the competent authority for the Sovereign Base Areas;

b) under Article 18 of the Convention, the Senior Registrar of the Judge's Court of the Sovereign Base Areas of Akrotiri and Dhekelia is designated as the competent authority;

c) under Article 24 of the Convention, the Senior Registrar of the Judge's Court of the Sovereign Base Areas of Akrotiri and Dhekelia is designated as an additional authority competent to receive Letters of Request for execution in the Sovereign Base Areas.

and the following declarations:

1. In accordance with Article 8, members of the judicial personnel of the requesting authority may be present at the execution of a Letter of Request in the Sovereign Base Areas.

2. In accordance with Article 18, a diplomatic officer, consular agent or commissioner authorised to take evidence under Articles 15, 16 and 17 of the Convention may apply to the competent authority in the Sovereign Base Areas designated hereinbefore for appropriate assistance to obtain such evidence by compulsion provided that the Contracting State whose diplomatic officer, consular agent or commissioner makes the application has made a declaration affording reciprocal facilities under Article 18.

3. In accordance with Article 23, the Sovereign Base Areas will not execute Letters of Request issued for the purpose of obtaining pre-trial discovery of documents. The Administration of the Sovereign Base Areas understands "Letters of Request issued for the purpose of obtaining pre-trial discovery of documents" for the purposes of the foregoing Declaration as including any Letter of Request which requires a person:

a) to state what documents relevant to the proceedings to which the Letter of Request relates are, or have been, in his possession, custody or power; or

b) to produce any documents other than particular documents specified in the Letter of Request as being documents appearing to the requested court to be, or likely to be, in his possession, custody or power.

4. In accordance with Article 27, by the law and practice of the Sovereign Base Areas the prior permission referred to in Articles 16 and 17 of the Convention is not required in respect of diplomatic officers, consular agents or commissioners of a Contracting State which does not require permission to be obtained for the purposes of taking evidence under Articles 16 or 17.

Extension to Falkland Islands and Dependencies.–

Notification in conformity with Article 42, subs. d and e, of the Convention

By a letter dated November 23, 1979, and received at the Ministry of Foreign Affairs of the Kingdom of the Netherlands on November 26, 1979, the Ambassador of the United Kingdom of Great Britain and Northern Ireland at The Hague, referring to the deposit on July 16, 1976 of the instrument of ratification of the above-mentioned Convention by the United Kingdom of Great Britain and Northern Ireland, declared in accordance with Article 40 that the Convention shall extend to the Falkland Islands and Dependencies.

The Convention shall enter into force for the Falkland Islands and Dependencies of January 25, 1980.

The declaration of extension contains the following reservation:

"...in accordance with the provisions of Article 4 and Article 33 of the Convention, the Falkland Islands and Dependencies will not accept a Letter of Request in French.". In accordance with Article 35 of the Convention the following designations have been made:

a) under Articles 16, 17 and 18 of the Convention the Judge of the Supreme Court of the Falkland Islands, is designated as the competent authority for the Falkland Islands and Dependencies;

b) under Article 24 of the Convention, the Governor of the Falkland Islands and its dependencies is designated as an additional authority competent to receive Letters of Request for execution in the Falkland Islands and Dependencies.

and the following declarations:

1. In accordance with Article 8, members of the judicial personnel of the requesting authority may be present at the execution of a Letter of Request in the Falkland Islands and Dependencies.

2. In accordance with Article 18, a diplomatic officer, consular agent or commissioner authorised to take evidence under Articles 15, 16 and 17 of the Convention may apply to the competent authority in the Falkland Islands and Dependencies designated hereinbefore for appropriate assistance to obtain such evidence by compulsion provided that the Contracting State whose diplomatic officer, consular agent or commissioner makes the application has made a declaration affording reciprocal facilities under Article 18.

3. In accordance with Article 23, the Falkland Islands and Dependencies will not execute Letters of Request issued for the purpose of obtaining pre-trial discovery of documents.

The Governor of the Falkland Islands and its Dependencies understands "Letters of Request issued for the purpose of obtaining pre-trial discovery of documents" for the purposes of the foregoing declaration as including any Letter of Request which requires a person:

a) to state what documents relevant to the proceedings to which the Letter of Request relates are, or have been, in his possession, custody or power; or

b) to produce any documents other than particular documents specified in the Letter of Request as being documents appearing to the requested court to be, or likely to be, in his possession, custody or power.

4. In accordance with Article 27, by the law and practice of the Falkland Islands and Dependencies the prior permission referred to in Article 16 and 17 of the Convention is not required in respect of diplomatic officers, consular agents or commissioners of a Contracting State which does not require permission to be obtained for the purposes of taking evidence under Article 16 or 17.

Extension to Isle of Man.–

Notification in conformity with article 42, subs. d and e, of the Convention

By a letter dated April 16, 1980, and received at the Ministry of Foreign Affairs of the Kingdom of the Netherlands on April 16, 1980, the Ambassador of the United Kingdom of Great Britain and Northern Ireland at The Hague, referring to the deposit on July 16, 1976 of the instrument of ratification of the above-mentioned Convention by the United Kingdom of Great Britain and Northern Ireland, declared in accordance with article 40 that the Convention shall extend to the Isle of Man.

The Convention shall enter into force for the Isle of Man of June 15, 1980.

The declaration of extension contains the following reservation:

". . . in accordance with the provisions of Article 4 and Article 33 of the Convention, the Isle of Man will not accept a Letter of Request in French.".

In accordance with Article 35 of the Convention the following designations have been made:

a) under Articles 16, 17 and 18 of the Convention Her Majesty's First Deemster and Clerk of the Rolls is designated as the competent authority for the Isle of Man;

b) under Article 24 of the Convention, Her Majesty's First Deemster and Clerk of the Rolls is designated as an additional authority competent to receive Letters of Request for execution in the Isle of Man.

and the following declarations:

1. In accordance with Article 8, members of the judicial personnel of the requesting authority may be present at the execution of a Letter of Request in the Isle of Man.

2. In accordance with Article 18, a diplomatic officer, consular agent or commissioner authorised to take evidence under Article 15, 16 and 17 of the Convention may apply to the competent authority in the Isle of Man designated hereinbefore for appropriate assistance to obtain such evidence by compulsion provided that the Contracting State whose diplomatic officer, consular agent or commissioner makes the application has made a declaration affording reciprocal facilities under Article 18.

3. In accordance with Article 23, the Isle of Man will not execute Letters of Request issued for the purpose of obtaining pre-trial discovery of documents.

The Government of the Isle of Man understands "Letters of Request issued for the purpose of obtaining pre-trial discovery of documents" for the purposes of the foregoing declaration as including any Letter of Request which requires a person:

a) to state what documents relevant to the proceedings to which the Letter of Request relates are, or have been, in his possession, custody or power; or

b) to produce any documents other than particular documents specified in the Letter of Request as being documents appearing to the requested court to be, or likely to be in his possession, custody or power.

4. In accordance with Article 27, by the law and practice of the Isle of Man the prior permission referred to in Articles 16 and 17 of the Convention is not required in respect of diplomatic officers, consular agents or commissioners of a Contracting State which does not require permission to be obtained for the purposes of taking evidence under Article 16 or 17.

Extension to Cayman Islands.–

Notification in conformity with Article 42, subs. d and e of the Convention

By letter dated 16 September 1980 and received at the Ministry of Foreign Affairs of the Kingdom of the Netherlands on that same date, the Ambassador of the United Kingdom of Great Britain and Northern Ireland at The Hague referring to the deposit on 16 July 1976 of the instrument of ratification of the above-mentioned Convention by the United Kingdom of Great Britain and Northern Ireland declared in accordance with Article 40 that the Convention shall extend to the Cayman Islands.

The Convention will enter into force for the Cayman Islands on 15 November 1980.

The declaration of extension contains the following reservation:

". . . in accordance with the provisions of Article 4 and Article 33 of the Convention, . . .the Cayman Islands will not accept a Letter of Request in French."

In accordance with Article 35 of the Convention the following designations have been made:

a) Under Articles 16 and 17 of the Convention, the Attorney General is designation as the competent authority for the Cayman Islands;

b) Under Article 18 of the Convention, the Clerk of the Grand Court is designated as the competent authority;

c) Under Article 24 of the Convention, His Excellency the Governor is designated as an additional authority competent to receive Letters of Request for execution in the Cayman Islands.

and the following declarations:

1. In accordance with Article 8, members of the judicial personnel of the requesting authority may be present at the execution of a Letter of Request in the Cayman Islands.

2. In accordance with Article 18, a diplomatic officer, consular agent or commissioner authorised to take evidence under Articles 15, 16 and 17 of the Convention may apply to the competent authority in the Cayman Islands designated hereinbefore for appropriate assistance to obtain such evidence by compulsion provided that the Contracting State whose diplomatic officer, consular agent or commissioner makes the application has made a declaration affording reciprocal facilities under Article 18.

3. In accordance with Article 23, the Cayman Islands will not execute Letters of Request issued for the purpose of obtaining pre-trial discovery of documents. The Government of the Cayman Islands understand "Letters of Request issued for the purpose of obtaining pre-trial discovery of documents" for the purposes of the foregoing declaration as including any Letter of Request which requires a person:

a) to state what documents relevant to the proceedings to which the Letter of Request relates are, or have been, in his possession, custody or power; or

b) to produce any documents other than particular documents specified in the Letter of Request as being documents appearing to the requested court to be, or likely to be, in his possession, custody or power.

4. In accordance with Article 27, by the law and practice of the Cayman Islands the prior permission referred to in Articles 16 and 17 of the Convention is not required in respect of diplomatic officers, consular agents or commissioners of a Contracting State which does not require permission to be obtained for the purposes of taking evidence under Article 16 or 17.

Extension to Guernsey.–

Notification in accordance with Article 42, sub. d and e, of the Convention

With reference to the deposit of its instrument of ratification of the above-mentioned Convention on 16 July 1985 the Government of the United Kingdom of Great Britain and Northern Ireland declared by letter of 13 November 1985 which was received by the Ministry of Foreign Affairs of the Kingdom of the Netherlands on 19 November 1985, in accordance with Article 40, second paragraph, that the Convention shall extend to Guernsey.

In accordance with Article 35 the Government of the United Kingdom furthermore declared that:

"(a) under Articles 8 and 25 of the Convention, the Bailiff, Deputy Bailiff, and Jurat of the Royal Court of Guernsey, the Chairman or a Jurat of the Court of Alderney and the Seneschal (or Deputy) of the Seneschal of Sark are designated as the competent authorities for Guernsey;

"(b) under Article 23 of the Convention, Guernsey will not execute Letters of Request issued for the purpose of obtaining pre-trial discovery of documents.".

In accordance with Article 40, third paragraph, the Convention will enter into force for Guernsey on 18 January 1986.

Extension to Anguilla.–

Notification pursuant to Article 42, paragraph c, d and e, of the Convention

In accordance with Article 40, paragraph 2, the Kingdom of Great Britain and Northern Ireland declared, by a Letter dated 1 July 1986, received at the Ministry of Foreign Affairs on 3 July 1986, that the present Convention shall extend to Anguilla. In accordance with Article 35 of the Convention, the following designations have been made:

"a. Under Articles 16, 17 and 18 of the Convention the Registrar of the East Caribbean Supreme Court is designated as the competent authority for Anguilla.

"b. Under Article 24 of the Convention, the Governor of Anguilla is designated as an additional authority competent to receive Letters of Request for execution in Anguilla."

and the following declarations

". . . . in accordance with the provisions of Articles 4 and 33 of the Convention, Anguilla will not accept a Letter of Request in French.

"In accordance with Article 8, members of the judicial personnel of the requesting authority may be present at the execution of a Letter of Request in Anguilla. In accordance with Article 18, a diplomatic officer, consular agent or commissioner authorized to take evidence under Articles 15, 16 and 17 of the Convention may apply to the competent authority in Anguilla designated above for appropriate assistance to obtain such evidence by compulsion provided that the contracting State, whose diplomatic officer, consular agent or commissioner makes (sic) the application has made a declaration affording reciprocal facilities under Article 18.

In accordance with Article 23, Anguilla will not execute Letters of Request issued for the purpose of obtaining pre-trial discovery of documents. Anguilla understands 'Letters of Request issued for the purpose of obtaining pre-trial discovery of documents' for the purposes of the foregoing declaration as including any Letter of Request which requires a person:

"i. to state what documents relevant to the proceedings to which the Letter of Request relates are, or have been, in his possession, custody or power; or

"ii. to produce any documents other than particular documents specified in the Letter of Request as being documents appearing to the requested court to be, or likely to be, in his possession, custody or power.

In accordance with Article 27, by the law and practice of Anguilla the prior permission referred to in Articles 16 and 17 of the Convention is not required in respect of diplomatic officers, consular agents or commissioners of a Contracting State which does not require permission to be obtained for the purposes of taking evidence under Articles 16 or 17."

In accordance with Article 40, the Convention entered into force for Anquilla on 1 September 1986.

UNITED STATES

The United States Department of Justice, Washington, D.C., 20530, is designated as the Central Authority referred to in Article 2 of the Convention.

Under paragraph 2 of Article 4 of the United States has agreed to accept a Letter of Request in or translated into French. The United States wishes to point out that owing to the necessity of translating such documents into English it will take the Central Authority longer to comply with a Letter of Request in or translated into French than with a similar request received in English.

In accordance with paragraph 3 of Article 4 the United States declares that it will also accept Letters of Request in Spanish for execution in the Commonwealth of Puerto Rico.

In accordance with Article 8 the United States declares that subject to prior authorization members of the judicial personnel of the requesting authority of another Contracting State may be present at the execution of a Letter of Request. The Department of Justice is the competent authority for the purposes of this Article.

The United States declares that evidence may be taken in the United States under Articles 16 and 17 without its prior permission.

In accordance with Article 18 the United States declares that a diplomatic or consular officer or a commissioner authorized to take evidence under Articles 15, 16 or 17 may apply for appropriate assistance to obtain the evidence by compulsion. The competent authority for the purposes of Article 18 is the United States district court of the district in which a person resides or is found. Such court may order him to give his testimony or statement or to produce a document or thing for use in a proceeding in a foreign tribunal. The order may direct that the testimony or statement be given, or the document or other thing be produced, before a person appointed by the court.

In accordance with Article 40 the United States declares that the Convention shall extend to Guam, Puerto Rico and the Virgin Islands.

In accordance with the provisions of Article 39 of the Convention, the United States declared its acceptance of the accessions by Argentina, Barbados, Cyprus, Monaco, and Singapore.

I. *(Items to be included in all Letters of Request.)*

1. Sender	_____*(identity and address)*_____
2. Central Authority of the Requested State	_____*(identity and address)*_____
3. Person to whom the executed request is to be returned	_____*(identity and address)*_____

II. *(Items to be included in all Letters of Request.)*

4. In conformity with article 3 of the Convention, the undersigned applicant has the honour to submit the following request:

5. a. Requesting judicial authority (article 3,a)	*(identity and address)*
b. To the competent authority of (article 3,a)	*(the requested State)*
6. Names and addresses of the parties and their representatives (article 3,b)	
a. Plaintiff	
b. Defendant	
c. Other parties	
7. Nature and purpose of the proceedings and summary of the facts (article 3,c)	
8. Evidence to be obtained or other judicial act to be performed (article 3,d)	

III. *(Items to be completed where applicable.)*

9. Identity and address of any person to be examined (article 3,e)	
10. Questions to be put to the persons to be examined or statement of the subject-matter about which they are to be examined (article 3,f)	_____*(see attached list)*_____

11. Documents or other property to be inspected (article 3,g)	_____*(specify whether it is to be produced, copied, valued, etc.)* ________________
12. Any requirement that the evidence be given on oath or affirmation and any special form to be used (article 3,h)	_________*(In the event that the evicende cannot be taken in the manner requested, specify whether it is to be taken in such manner s provided by local law for the formal taking of evidence.*____________
13. Special methods or procedure to be followed (articles 3,i and 9)	________________
14. Request for notification of the time and place for the execution of the Request and identity and address of any person to be notified (article 7)	________________
15. Request for attendance or participation of judicial personnel of the requesting authority at the execution of the letter of Request	________________
16. Specification of privilege or duty to refuse to give evidence under the law of the State of origin (article 11,b)	________________
17. The fees and costs incurred which are reimbursable under the second paragraph of article 14 or under article 26 of the Convention will be borne by	__________*(identity and address)*__________

IV. ***(Items to be included in all Letters of Request.)***

18. Date of request	________________
19. Signature and seal of the requesting authority	________________

APPENDIX II

UNITED NATIONS CONVENTIONS

CONTRACTING STATES TO THE UN CONVENTIONS

(as of April 8, 1998)

- Contracts for the International Sale of Goods, Vienna, April 11, 1980 (entered into force January 1, 1988)
- Recognition and Enforcement of Foreign Arbitral Awards, New York, June 10, 1958 (entered into force June 7, 1959)

Contracting States	**1958: Arbitral Awards (New York)**	**1980: CISG (Vienna Sales)**
Afghanistan		
Albania		
Algeria	X	
Andorra		
Angola		
Antigua and Barbuda	X	
Argentina	X	X
Armenia[1]	X	
Australia	X	X
Austria	X	X
Azerbaijan [1]		
Bahamas		
Bahrain	X	
Bangladesh	X	
Barbados	X	
Belarus[1]	X	X
Belgium	X	X
Benin`	X	
Bhutan		
Bolivia	X	
Bosnia and Herzegovina[2]	X	X
Botswana	X	
Brazil		
Brunei Darussalam	X	
Bulgaria	X	X
Burkina Faso	X	
Burundi		
Cambodia	X	
Cameroon	X	
Canada [3]	X	X

Contracting States	**1958: Arbitral Awards (New York)**	**1980: CISG (Vienna Sales)**
Cape Verde		
Central African Republic	X	
Chad		
Chile	X	X
China (People's Republic)	X	X
Colombia	X	
Congo		
Congo (Democratic Republic of)		
Costa Rica	X	
Cote d'Ivoire	X	
Croatia[2]	X	
Cuba	X	X
Cyprus	X	
Czech Republic[4]	X	X
Denmark[5]	X	X
Djibouti	X	
Dominica	X	
Dominican Republic		
Ecuador	X	X
Egypt	X	X
El Salvador	X	
Equatorial Guinea		
Eritrea		
Estonia	X	X
Ethiopia		
Fiji		
Finland	X	X
France[6]	X	X
Gabon		
Gambia		
Georgia[1]	X	X
Germany[7]	X	X
Ghana	X	X
Greece	X	X
Grenada		
Guatemala	X	
Guinea	X	X

Contracting States	**1958: Arbitral Awards (New York)**	**1980: CISG (Vienna Sales)**
Guinea-Bissau		
Guyana		
Haiti	X	
Holy See[8]	X	
Honduras		
Hungary	X	X
Iceland		
India	X	
Indonesia	X	
Iran (Islamic Republic of)		
Iraq		X
Ireland	X	
Israel	X	
Italy	X	X
Jamaica		
Japan	X	
Jordan	X	
Kazakstan [1]	X	
Kenya	X	
Kiribati[8]		
Korea (Democratic People's Republic)		
Korea (Republic)	X	
Kuwait	X	
Kyrgyzstan [1]	X	
Lao People's Democratic Republic		
Latvia	X	X
Lebanon		
Lesotho	X	X
Liberia		
Libyan Arab Jamahiriya		
Liechtenstein		
Lithuania	X	X
Luxembourg	X	X as of 01-02-48
Macedonia Former Yugoslaw Republic of [2]	X	
Madagascar	X	

Contracting States	**1958: Arbitral Awards (New York)**	**1980: CISG (Vienna Sales)**
Malawi		
Malaysia	X	
Maldives		
Mali	X	
Malta		
Marshall Islands		
Mauritania	X	
Mauritius	X	
Mexico	X	X
Micronesia (Federal States)		
Moldova (Republic)[1]		X
Monaco	X	
Mongolia	X	X
Morocco	X	
Mozambique		
Myanmar (Burma)		
Namibia		
Nauru[8]		
Nepal	X	
Netherlands[9]	X	X
New Zealand[10]	X	X
Nicaragua		
Niger	X	
Nigeria	X	
Norway	X	X
Oman		
Pakistan		
Palau		
Panama	X	
Papua New Guinea		
Paraguay	X	
Peru	X	
Phillippines	X	
Poland	X	X
Portugal	X	
Qatar		
Romania	X	X

Contracting States	1958: Arbitral Awards (New York)	1980: CISG (Vienna Sales)
Russian Federation[1]	X	X
Rwanda		
Saint Kitts & Nevis		
Saint Lucia		
Saint Vincent & the Grenadines		
Samoa		
San Marino	X	
Sao Tome and Principe		
Saudi Arabia	X	
Senegal	X	
Seychelles		
Sierra Leone		
Singapore	X	X
Slovakia[4]	X	X
Slovenia[2]	X	X
Solomon Islands		
Somalia		
South Africa	X	
Spain	X	X
Sri Lanka	X	
Sudan		
Suriname[11]	X	
Swaziland		
Sweden	X	X
Switzerland[8]	X	X
Syrian Arab Republic	X	X
Taiwan[8]		
Tajikistan[1]		
Tanzania (United Republic)	X	
Thailand	X	
Togo		
Tonga[8]		
Trinidad & Tobago	X	
Tunisia	X	
Turkey	X	
Turkmenistan[1]		
Tuvalu[8]		

Contracting States	1958: Arbitral Awards (New York)	1980: CISG (Vienna Sales)
Uganda	X	X
Ukraine[1]	X	X
United Arab Emirates		
United Kingdom[12]	X	
United States of America[13]	X	X
Uruguay	X	
Uzbekistan[1]	X	X
Vanuatu		
Venezuela	X	X
Viet Nam	X	
West Bank/Gaza[8]		
Western Samoa		
Yemen		
Yugoslavia[2]	X	X
Zambia		X
Zimbabwe	X	

1 Separated successor state of the former USSR. Belarus, the Russian Federation, and Ukraine are treated here as automatically bound by prior ratifications of N.Y. Convention

2 Bosnia & Herzegovina, Croatia, the former Yugoslaw Republic of Macedonia, and Slovenia are treated here as seprated successor states to parts of Yugoslavia. Serbia and Montenegro have jointly claimed successor status to former Yugoslavia, but to date the UN has not accepted the claim. The former Yugoslavia ratified the N.Y. Convention and an entry has been retained for "Yugoslavia". Bosnia & Herzegovina, Croatia, the former Yugoslav Republic of Macedonia, and Slovenia have expressly declared succession to the N.Y. Convention.

3 Includes federal, all 10 provincial and both territorial jurisdictions

4 Former Czechoslovakia seprated into two states, the Czech Republic and Slovakia, on January 1, 1993. Both Republics have succeeded to the N.Y. Convention.

5 Includes Farce Islands and Greenland

6 Includes, *inter alia*, French Guinea, French Polynesia, Guadeloupe, Martinique, Mayotte, New Caledonia, Réunion, and Miquelon.

7 The Federal Republic of Germany (FRG) absorbed the German Democratic Republic (GDR) on October 3, 1990, and became simply "Germany."

8 Not member of the UN on January 1, 1997.

9 Includes Aruba and Netherlands Antilles.

10 Excludes Cook Islands and Tokelau.

11 Some secondary sources list Suriname as successor party to the N.Y. Convention on basis of the declaration of November 29, 1975, following independence from the Netherlands.

12 Includes, *inter alia*, Bermuda, Gibraltar, Guernsey, Isle of Man and Cayman Islands.

13 Includes, *inter alia*, American Samoa, Guam, Northern Mariana Islands, Puerto Rico, and U.S. Virgin Islands.

UNITED NATIONS CONVENTION ON CONTRACTS FOR THE INTERNATIONAL SALE OF GOODS

Done at Vienna April 11, 1980, Entered into force January 1, 1988

THE STATES PARTIES TO THIS CONVENTION,

BEARING IN MIND the broad objectives in the resolutions adopted by the sixth special session of the General Assembly of the United Nations on the establishment of a New International Economic Order,

CONSIDERING that the development of international trade on the basis of equality and mutual benefit is an important element in promoting friendly relations among States,

BEING OF THE OPINION that the adoption of uniform rules which govern contracts for the international sale of goods and take into account the different social, economic and legal systems would contribute to the removal of legal barriers in international trade and promote the development of international trade,

HAVE AGREED as follows:

PART I
SPHERE OF APPLICATION AND GENERAL PROVISIONS

CHAPTER I - SPHERE OF APPLICATION

Article 1

(1) This Convention applies to contracts of sale of goods between parties whose places of business are in different States:

(a) when the States are Contracting States; or

(b) when the rules of private international law lead to the application of the law of a Contracting State.

(2) The fact that the parties have their places of business in different States is to be disregarded whenever this fact does not appear either from the contract or from any dealings between, or from information disclosed by, the parties at any time before or at the conclusion of the contract.

(3) Neither the nationality of the parties nor the civil or commercial character of the parties or of the contract is to be taken into consideration in determining the application of this Convention.

Article 2

This Convention does not apply to sales:

(a) of goods bought for personal, family or household use, unless the seller, at any time before or at the conclusion of the contract, neither knew nor ought to have known that the goods were bought for any such use:

(b) by auction;

(c) on execution or otherwise by authority of law;

(d) of stocks, shares, investment securities, negotiable instruments or money;

(e) of ships, vessels, hovercraft or aircraft;

(f) of electricity.

Article 3

(1) Contracts for the supply of goods to be manufactured or produced are to be considered sales unless the party who orders the goods undertakes to supply a substantial part of the materials necessary for such manufacture or production.

(2) This Convention does not apply to contracts in which the preponderant part of the obligations of the party who furnishes the goods consists in the supply of labor or other services.

Article 4

This Convention governs only the formation of the contract of sale and the rights and obligations of the seller and the buyer arising from such a contract. In particular, except as otherwise expressly provided in this Convention, it is not concerned with:

(a) the validity of the contract or of any of its provisions or of any usage:

(b) the effect which the contract may have on the property in the goods sold.

Article 5

This Convention does not apply to the liability of the seller for death or personal injury caused by the goods to any person.

Article 6

The parties may exclude the application of this Convention or, subject to article 12, derogate from or vary the effect of any of its provisions.

CHAPTER II - GENERAL PROVISIONS

Article 7

(1) In the interpretation of this Convention, regard is to be had to its international character and to the need to promote uniformity in its application and the observance of good faith in international trade.

(2) Questions concerning matters governed by this Convention which are not expressly settled in it are to be settled in conformity with the general principles on which it is based or, in the absence of such principles, in conformity with the law applicable by virtue of the rules of private international law.

Article 8

(1) For the purposes of this Convention statements made by and other conduct of a party are to be interpreted according to his intent where the other party knew or could not have been unaware what that intent was.

(2) If the preceding paragraph is not applicable, statements made by and other conduct of a party are to be interpreted according to the understanding that a reasonable person of the same kind as the other party would have had in the same circumstances.

(3) In determining the intent of a party or the understanding a reasonable person would have had, due consideration is to be given to all relevant circumstances of the case including the negotiations, any practices which the parties have established between themselves, usages and any subsequent conduct of the parties.

Article 9

(1) The parties are bound by any usage to which they have agreed and by any practices which they have established between themselves.

(2) The parties are considered, unless otherwise agreed, to have impliedly made applicable to their contract or its formation a usage of which the parties knew or ought to have known and which in international trade is widely known to, and regularly observed by, parties to contracts of the type involved in the particular trade concerned.

Article 10

For the purposes of this Convention:

(a) if a party has more than one place of business, the place of business is that which has the closest relationship to the contract and its performance, having regard to the circumstances known to or contemplated by the parties at any time before or at the conclusion of the contract;

(b) if a party does not have a place of business, reference is to be made to his habitual residence.

Article 11

A contract of sale need not be concluded in or evidenced by writing and is not subject to any other requirement as to form. It may be proved by any means, including witnesses.

Article 12

Any provision of article 11, article 29 or Part II of this Convention that allows a contract of sale or its modification or termination by agreement or any offer, acceptance or other indication of intention to be made in any form other than in writing does not apply where any party has his place of business in a Contracting State which has made a declaration under article 96 of this Convention. The parties may not derogate from or vary the effect of this article.

Article 13

For the purposes of this Convention "writing" includes telegram and telex.

PART II
FORMATION OF THE CONTRACT

Article 14

(1) A proposal for concluding a contract addressed to one or more specific persons constitutes an offer if it is sufficiently definite and indicates the intention of the offeror to be bound in case of acceptance. A proposal is sufficiently definite if it indicates the goods and expressly or implicitly fixes or makes provision for determining the quantity and the price.

(2) A proposal other than one addressed to one or more specific persons is to be considered merely as an invitation to make offers, unless the contrary is clearly indicated by the person making the proposal.

Article 15

(1) An offer becomes effective when it reaches the offeree.

(2) An offer, even if it is irrevocable, may be withdrawn if the withdrawal reaches the offeree before or at the same time as the offer.

Article 16

(1) Until a contract is concluded an offer may be revoked if the revocation reaches the offeree before he has dispatched an acceptance.

(2) However, an offer cannot be revoked:

(a) if it indicates, whether by stating a fixed time for acceptance or otherwise, that it is irrevocable; or

(b) if it was reasonable for the offeree to rely on the offer as being irrevocable and the offeree has acted in reliance on the offer.

Article 17

An offer, even if it is irrevocable, is terminated when a rejection reaches the offeror.

Article 18

(1) A statement made by or other conduct of the offeree indicating assent to an offer is an acceptance. Silence or inactivity does not in itself amount to acceptance.

(2) An acceptance of an offer becomes effective at the moment the indication of assent reaches the offeror. An acceptance is not effective if the indication of assent does not reach the offeror within the time he has fixed or, if no time is fixed, within a reasonable time, due account being taken of the circumstances of the transaction, including the rapidity of the means of communication employed by the offeror. An oral offer must be accepted immediately unless the circumstances indicate otherwise.

(3) However, if, by virtue of the offer or as a result of practices which the parties have established between themselves or of usage, the offeree may indicate assent by performing an act, such as one relating to the dispatch of the goods or payment of the price, without notice to the offeror, the acceptance is effective at the moment the act is performed, provided that the act is performed within the period of time laid down in the preceding paragraph.

Article 19

(1) A reply to an offer which purports to be an acceptance but contains additions, limitations or other modifications is a rejection of the offer and constitutes a counter-offer.

(2) However, a reply to an offer which purports to be an acceptance but contains additional or different terms which do not materially alter the terms of the offer constitutes an acceptance, unless the offeror, without undue delay, objects orally to the discrepancy or dispatches a notice to that effect. If he does not so object, the terms of the contract are the terms of the offer with the modifications contained in the acceptance.

(3) Additional or different terms relating, among other things, to the price, payment, quality and quantity of the goods, place and time of delivery, extent of one party's liability to the other or the settlement of disputes are considered to alter the terms of the offer materially.

Article 20

(1) A period of time for acceptance fixed by the offeror in a telegram or a letter begins to run from the moment the telegram is handed in for dispatch or from the date shown on the letter or, if no such date is shown, from the date shown on the envelope. A period of time for acceptance fixed by the offeror by telephone, telex or other means of instantaneous communication, begins to run from the moment that the offer reaches the offeree.

(2) Official holidays or non-business days occurring during the period for acceptance are included in calculating the period. However, if a notice of acceptance cannot be delivered at the address of the offeror on the last day of the period because that day falls on an official holiday or a non-business day at the place of business of the offeror, the period is extended until the first business day which follows.

Article 21

(1) A late acceptance is nevertheless effective as an acceptance if without delay the offeror orally so informs the offeree or dispatches a notice to that effect.

(2) If a letter or other writing containing a late acceptance shows that it has been sent in such circumstances that if its transmission had been normal it would have reached the offeror in due time, the late acceptance is effective as an acceptance unless, without delay, the offeror orally informs the offeree that he considers his offer as having lapsed or dispatches a notice to that effect.

Article 22

An acceptance may be withdrawn if the withdrawal reaches the offeror before or at the same time as the acceptance would have become effective.

Article 23

A contract is concluded at the moment when an acceptance of an offer becomes effective in accordance with the provisions of this Convention.

Article 24

For the purposes of this Part of the Convention, an offer, declaration of acceptance or any other indication of intention "reaches" the addressee when it is made orally to him or delivered by any other means to his personally, to his place of business or mailing address or, if he does not have a place of business or mailing address, to his habitual residence.

PART III
SALE OF GOODS

CHAPTER I - GENERAL PROVISIONS

Article 25

A breach of contract committed by one of the parties is fundamental if it results in such detriment to the other party as substantially to deprive him of what he is entitled to expect under the contract, unless the party in breach did not foresee and a reasonable person of the same kind in the same circumstances would not have foreseen such a result.

Article 26

A declaration of avoidance of the contract is effective only if made by notice to the other party.

Article 27

Unless otherwise expressly provided in this Part of the Convention, if any notice, request or other communication is given or made by a party in accordance with this Part and by means appropriate in the circumstances, a delay or error in the transmission of the communication or its failure to arrive does not deprive that party of the right to rely on the communication.

Article 28

If, in accordance with the provisions of this Convention, one party is entitled to require performance of any obligation by the other party, a court is not bound to enter a judgement for specific performance unless the court would do so under its own law in respect of similar contracts of sale not governed by this Convention.

Article 29

(1) A contract may be modified or terminated by the mere agreement of the parties.

(2) A contract in writing which contains a provision requiring any modification or termination by agreement to be in writing may not be otherwise modified or terminated by agreement. However, a party may be precluded by his conduct from asserting such a provision to the extent that the other party has relied on that conduct.

CHAPTER II - OBLIGATIONS OF THE SELLER

Article 30

The seller must deliver the goods, hand over any documents relating to them and transfer the property in the goods, as required by the contract and this Convention.

SECTION I
DELIVERY OF THE GOODS AND HANDING OVER OF DOCUMENTS

Article 31

If the seller is not bound to deliver the goods at any other particular place, his obligation to deliver consists:

(a) if the contract of sale involves carriage of the goods - in handing the goods over to the first carrier for transmission to the buyer;

(b) if, in cases not within the preceding subparagraph, the contract relates to specific goods, or unidentified goods to be drawn from a specific stock or to be manufactured or produced, and at the time of the conclusion of the contract the parties knew that the goods were at, or were to be manufactured or produced at, a particular place - in placing the goods at the buyer's disposal at that place;

(c) in other cases - in placing the goods at the buyer's disposal at the place where the seller had his place of business at the time of the conclusion of the contract.

Article 32

(1) If the seller, in accordance with the contract or this Convention, hands the goods over to a carrier and if the goods are not clearly identified to the contract by markings on the

goods, by shipping documents or otherwise, the seller must give the buyer notice of the consignment specifying the goods.

(2) If the seller is bound to arrange for carriage of the goods, he must make such contracts as are necessary for carriage to the place fixed by means of transportation appropriate in the circumstances and according to the usual terms for such transportation.

(3) If the seller is not bound to effect insurance in respect of the carriage of the goods, he must, at the buyer's request, provide him with all available information necessary to enable him to effect such insurance.

Article 33

The seller must deliver the goods:

(a) if a date is fixed by or determinable from the contract, on that date;

(b) if a period of time is fixed by or determinable from the contract, at any time within that period unless circumstances indicate that the buyer is to choose a date; or

(c) in any other case, within a reasonable time after the conclusion of the contract.

Article 34

If the seller is bound to hand over documents relating to the goods, he must hand them over at the time and place and in the form required by the contract. If the seller has handed over documents before that time, he may, up to that time, cure any lack of conformity in the documents, if the exercise of this right does not cause the buyer unreasonable inconvenience or unreasonable expense. However, the buyer retains any right to claim damages as provided for in this Convention.

SECTION II
CONFORMITY OF THE GOODS AND THIRD PARTY CLAIMS

Article 35

(1) The seller must deliver goods which are of the quantity, quality and description required by the contract and which are contained or packaged in the manner required by the contract.

(2) Except where the parties have agreed otherwise, the goods do not conform with the contract unless they:

(a) are fit for the purposes for which goods of the same description would ordinarily be used;

(b) are fit for any particular purpose expressly or impliedly made known to the seller at the time of the conclusion of the contract, except where the circumstances show that the buyer did not rely, or that it was unreasonable for him to rely, on the seller's skill and judgement;

(c) possess the qualities of goods which the seller has held out to the buyer as a sample or model;

(d) are contained or packaged in the manner usual for such goods or, where there is no such manner, in a manner adequate to preserve and protect the goods.

(3) The seller is not liable under subparagraphs (a) to (d) of the preceding paragraph for any lack of conformity of the goods if at the time of the conclusion of the contract the buyer knew or could not have been unaware of such lack of conformity.

Article 36

(1) The seller is liable in accordance with the contract and this Convention for any lack of conformity which exists at the time when the risk passes to the buyer, even though the lack of conformity becomes apparent only after that time.

(2) The seller is also liable for any lack of conformity which occurs after the time indicated in the preceding paragraph and which is due to a breach of any of his obligations, including a breach of any guarantee that for a period of time the goods will remain fit for their ordinary purpose or for some particular purpose or will retain specified qualities or characteristics.

Article 37

If the seller has delivered goods before the date for delivery, he may, up to that date, deliver any missing part or make up any deficiency in the quantity of the goods delivered, or deliver goods in replacement of any non-conforming goods delivered or remedy any lack of conformity in the goods delivered, provided that the exercise of this right does not cause the buyer unreasonable inconvenience or unreasonable expense. However, the buyer retains any right to claim damages as provided for in this Convention.

Article 38

(1) The buyer must examine the goods, or cause them to be examined, within as short a period as is practicable in the circumstances.

(2) If the contract involves carriage of the goods, examination may be deferred until after the goods have arrived at their destination.

(3) If the goods are redirected in transit or redispatched by the buyer without a reasonable opportunity for examination by him and at the time of the conclusion of the contract the seller knew or ought to have known of the possibility of such redirection or redispatch, examination may be deferred until after the goods have arrived at the new destination.

Article 39

(1) The buyer loses the right to rely on a lack of conformity of the goods if he does not give notice to the seller specifying the nature of the lack of conformity within a reasonable time after he has discovered it or ought to have discovered it.

(2) In any event, the buyer loses the right to rely on a lack of conformity of the goods if he does not give the seller notice thereof at the latest within a period of two years from the date on which the goods were actually handed over to the buyer, unless this time-limit is inconsistent with a contractual period of guarantee.

Article 40

The seller is not entitled to rely on the provisions of articles 38 and 39 if the lack of conformity relates to facts of which he knew or could not have been unaware and which he did not disclose to the buyer.

Article 41

The seller must deliver goods which are free from any right or claim of a third party, unless the buyer agreed to take the goods subject to that right or claim. However, if such right or claim is based on industrial property or other intellectual property, the seller's obligation is governed by article 42.

Article 42

(1) The seller must deliver goods which are free from any right or claim of a third party based on industrial property or other intellectual property, of which at the time of the conclusion of the contract the seller knew or could not have been unaware, provided that the right or claim is based on industrial property or other intellectual property:

(a) under the law of the State where the goods will be resold or otherwise used, if it was contemplated by the parties at the time of the conclusion of the contract that the goods would be resold or otherwise used in that State; or

(b) in any other case, under the law of the State where the buyer has his place of business.

(2) The obligation of the seller under the preceding paragraph does not extend to cases where:

(a) at the time of the conclusion of the contract the buyer knew or could not have been unaware of the right or claim; or

(b) the right or claim results from the seller's compliance with technical drawings, designs, formulae or other such specifications furnished by the buyer.

Article 43

(1) The buyer loses the right to rely on the provisions of article 41 or article 42 if he does not give notice to the seller specifying the nature of the right or claim of the third party within a reasonable time after he has become aware or ought to have become aware of the right or claim.

(2) The seller is not entitled to rely on the provisions of the preceding paragraph if he knew of the right or claim of the third party and the nature of it.

Article 44

Notwithstanding the provisions of paragraph (1) of article 39 and paragraph (1) of article 43, the buyer say reduce the price in accordance with article 50 or claim damages, except for loss of profit, if he has a reasonable excuse for his failure to give the required notice.

SECTION III
REMEDIES FOR BREACH OF CONTRACT BY THE SELLER

Article 45

(1) If the seller fails to perform any of his obligations under the contract or this Convention, the buyer say:

(a) exercise the rights provided in articles 46 to 52;

(b) claim damages as provided in articles 74 to 77.

(2) The buyer is not deprived of any right he may have to claim damages by exercising his right to other remedies.

(3) No period of grace may be granted to the seller by a court or arbitral tribunal when the buyer resorts to a remedy for breach of contract.

Article 46

(1) The buyer may require performance by the seller of his obligations unless the buyer has resorted to a remedy which is inconsistent with this requirement.

(2) If the goods do not conform with the contract, the buyer may require delivery of substitute goods only if the lack of conformity constitutes a fundamental breach of contract and a request for substitute goods is made either in conjunction with notice given under article 39 or within a reasonable time thereafter.

(3) If the goods do not conform with the contract, the buyer may require the seller to remedy the lack of conformity by repair, unless this is unreasonable having regard to all the circumstances. A request for repair must be made either in conjunction with notice given under article 39 or within a reasonable time thereafter.

Article 47

(1) The buyer may fix an additional period of time of reasonable length for performance by the seller of his obligations.

(2) Unless the buyer has received notice from the seller that he will not perform within the period so fixed, the buyer may not, during that period, resort to any remedy for breach of contract. However, the buyer is not deprived thereby of any right he may have to claim damages for delay in performance.

Article 48

(1) Subject to article 49, the seller may, even after the date for delivery, remedy at his own expense any failure to perform his obligations, if he can do so without unreasonable delay and without causing the buyer unreasonable inconvenience or uncertainty of reimbursement by the seller of expenses advanced by the buyer. However, the buyer retains any right to claim damages as provided for in this Convention.

(2) If the seller requests the buyer to make known whether he will accept performance and the buyer does not comply with the request within a reasonable time, the seller may perform within the time indicated in his request. The buyer may not, during that period of time, resort to any remedy which is inconsistent with performance by the seller.

(3) A notice by the seller that he will perform within a specified period of time is assumed to include a request, under the preceding paragraph, that the buyer make known his decision.

(4) A request of notice by the seller under paragraph (2) or (3) of this article is not effective unless received by the buyer.

Article 49

(1) The buyer may declare the contract avoided:

(a) if the failure by the seller to perform any of his obligations under the contract or this Convention amounts to a fundamental breach of contract; or

(b) in case of non-delivery, if the seller does not deliver the goods within the additional period of time fixed by the buyer in accordance with paragraph (1) of article 47 or declares that he will not deliver within the period so fixed.

(2) However, in cases where the seller has delivered the goods, the buyer loses the right to declare the contract avoided unless he does so:

(a) in respect of late delivery, within a reasonable time after he has become aware that delivery has been made;

(b) in respect of any breach other than late delivery, within a reasonable time:

(i) after he knew or ought to have known of the breach;

(ii) after the expiration of any additional period of time fixed by the buyer in accordance with paragraph (1) of article 47, or after the seller has declared that he will not perform his obligations within such an additional period; or

(iii) after the expiration of any additional period of time indicated by the seller in accordance with paragraph (2) of article 48, or after the buyer has declared that he will not accept performance.

Article 50

If the goods do not conform with the contract and whether or not the price has already been paid, the buyer may reduce the price in the same proportion as the value that the goods actually delivered had at the time of the delivery bears to the value that conforming goods would have had at that time. However, if the seller remedies any failure to perform his obligations in accordance with article 37 or article 48 or if the buyer refuses to accept performance by the seller in accordance with those articles, the buyer may not reduce the price.

Article 51

(1) If the seller delivers only a part of the goods or if only a part of the goods delivered is in conformity with the contract, articles 46 to 50 apply in respect of the part which is missing or which does not conform.

(2) The buyer may declare the contract avoided in its entirety only if the failure to make delivery completely or in conformity with the contract amounts to a fundamental breach of the contract.

Article 52

(1) If the seller delivers the goods before the date fixed, the buyer may take delivery or refuse to take delivery.

(2) If the seller delivers a quantity of goods greater than that provided for in the contract, the buyer may take delivery or refuse to take delivery of the excess quantity. If the buyer takes delivery of all or part of the excess quantity, he must pay for it at the contract rate.

CHAPTER III
OBLIGATIONS OF THE BUYER

Article 53

The buyer must pay the price for the goods and take delivery of them as required by the contract and this Convention.

SECTION I
PAYMENT OF THE PRICE ARTICLE 54

The buyer's obligation to pay the price includes taking such steps and complying with such formalities as may be required under the contract or any laws and regulations to enable payment to be made.

Article 55

Where a contract has been validly concluded but does not expressly or implicitly fix or make provision for determining the price, the parties are considered, in the absence of any indication to the contrary, to have impliedly made reference to the price generally charged at the time of the conclusion of the contract for such goods sold under comparable circumstances in the trade concerned.

Article 56

If the price is fixed according to the weight of the goods, in case of doubt it is to be determined by the net weight.

Article 57

(1) If the buyer is not bound to pay the price at any other particular place, he must pay it to the seller:

(a) at the seller's place of business; or

(b) if the payment is to be made against the handing over of the goods or of documents, at the place where the handing over takes place.

(2) The seller must bear any increase in the expenses incidental to payment which is caused by a change in his place of business subsequent to the conclusion of the contract.

Article 58

(1) If the buyer is not bound to pay the price at any other specific time, he must pay it when the seller places either the goods or documents controlling their disposition at the buyer's disposal in accordance with the contract and this Convention. The seller may make such payment a condition for handing over the goods or documents.

(2) If the contract involves carriage of the goods, the seller may dispatch the goods on terms whereby the goods, or documents controlling their disposition, will not be handed over to the buyer except against payment of the price.

(3) The buyer is not bound to pay the price until he has had an opportunity to examine the goods, unless the procedures for delivery or payment agreed upon by the parties are inconsistent with his having such an opportunity.

Article 59

The buyer must pay the price on the date fixed by or determinable from the contract and this Convention without the need for any request or compliance with any formality on the part of the seller.

SECTION II
TAKING DELIVERY

Article 60

The buyer's obligation to take delivery consists:

(a) in doing all the acts which could reasonably be expected of him in order to enable the seller to make delivery; and

(b) in taking over this goods.

SECTION III
REMEDIES FOR BREACH OF CONTRACT BY THE BUYER

Article 61

(1) If the buyer fails to perform any of his obligations under the contract or this Convention, the seller may:

(a) exercise the rights provided in articles 62 to 65;

(b) claim damages as provided in articles 74 to 77.

(2) The seller is not deprived of any right he may have to claim damages by exercising his right to other remedies.

(3) No period of grace may be granted to the buyer by a court or arbitral tribunal when the seller resorts to a remedy for breach of contract.

Article 62

The seller may require the buyer to pay the price, take delivery or perform his other obligations, unless the seller has resorted to a remedy which is inconsistent with this requirement.

Article 63

(1) The seller may fix an additional period of time of reasonable length for performance by the buyer of his obligations.

(2) Unless the seller has received notice from the buyer that he will not perform within the period so fixed, the seller may not, during that period, resort to any remedy for breach of contract. However, the seller is not deprived thereby of any right he may have to claim damages for delay in performance.

Article 64

(1) The seller may declare the contract avoided:

(a) If the failure by the buyer to perform any of his obligations under the contract or this Convention amounts to a fundamental breach of contract; or

(b) if the buyer does not, within the additional period of time fixed by the seller in accordance with paragraph (1) of article 63, perform his obligation to pay the price or take delivery of the goods, or if he declares that he will not do so within the period so fixed.

(2) However, in cases where the buyer has paid the price, the seller loses the right to declare the contract avoided unless he does so:

(a) in respect of late performance by the buyer, before the seller has become aware that performance has been rendered; or

(b) in respect of any breach other than late performance by the buyer, within a reasonable time:

(i) after the seller knew or ought to have known of the breach; or

(ii) after the expiration of any additional period of time fixed by the seller in accordance with paragraph (1) of article 63, or after the buyer has declared that he will not perform his obligations within such an additional period.

Article 65

(1) If under the contract the buyer is to specify the form, measurement or other features of the goods and he fails to make such specification either on the date agreed upon or within a reasonable time after receipt of a request from the seller, the seller may, without prejudice to any other rights he may have, make the specification himself in accordance with the requirements of the buyer that may be known to him.

(2) If the seller makes the specification himself, he must inform the buyer of the details thereof and must fix a reasonable time within which the buyer may make a different specification. If, after receipt of such a communication, the buyer fails to do so within the time so fixed, the specification made by the seller is binding.

CHAPTER IV - PASSING OF RISK

Article 66

Loss of or damage to the goods after the risk has passed to the buyer does not discharge him from his obligation to pay the price, unless the loss or damage is due to an act or omission of the seller.

Article 67

(1) If the contract of sale involves carriage of the goods and the seller is not bound to hand them over at a particular place, the risk passes to the buyer when the goods are handed over to the first carrier for transmission to the buyer in accordance with the contract of sale. If the seller is bound to hand the goods over to a carrier at a particular place, the risk does not pass to the buyer until the goods are handed over to the carrier at that place. The fact that the seller is authorized to retain documents controlling the disposition of the goods does not affect the passage of the risk.

(2) Nevertheless, the risk does not pass to the buyer until the goods are clearly identified to the contract, whether by markings on the goods, by shipping documents, by notice given to the buyer or otherwise.

Article 68

The risk in respect of goods sold in transit passes to the buyer from the time of the conclusion of the contract. However, if the circumstances so indicate, the risk is assumed by the buyer from the time the goods were handed over to the carrier who issued the documents embodying the contract of carriage. Nevertheless, if at the time of the conclusion of the contract of sale the seller knew or ought to have known that the goods had been lost or damaged and did not disclose this to the buyer, the loss or damage is at the risk of the seller.

Article 69

(1) In cases not within articles 67 and 68, the risk passes to the buyer when he takes over the goods or, if he does not do so in due time, from the time when the goods are placed at his disposal and he commits a breach of contract by failing to take delivery.

(2) However, if the buyer is bound to take over the goods at a place other than a place of business of the seller, the risk passes when delivery is due and the buyer is aware of the fact that the goods are placed at his disposal at that place.

(3) If the contract relates to goods not then identified, the goods are considered not to be placed at the disposal of the buyer until they are clearly identified to the contract.

Article 70

If the seller has committed a fundamental breach of contract, articles 67, 68 and 69 do not impair the remedies available to the buyer on account of the breach.

CHAPTER V - PROVISIONS COMMON TO THE OBLIGATIONS OF THE SELLER AND OF THE BUYER

SECTION I ANTICIPATORY BREACH AND INSTALMENT CONTRACTS

Article 71

(1) A party may suspend the performance of his obligations if, after the conclusion of the contract, it becomes apparent that the other party will not perform a substantial part of his obligations as a result of:

(a) a serious deficiency in his ability to perform or in his creditworthiness; or

(b) his conduct in preparing to perform or in performing the contract.

(2) If the seller has already dispatched the goods before the grounds described in the preceding paragraph become evident, he may prevent the handing over of the goods to the buyer even though the buyer holds a document which entitles him to obtain them. The present paragraph relates only to the rights in the goods as between the buyer and the seller.

(3) A party suspending performance, whether before or after dispatch of the goods, must immediately give notice of the suspension to the other party and must continue with performance if the other party provides adequate assurance of his performance.

Article 72

(1) If prior to the date for performance of the contract it is clear that one of the parties will commit a fundamental breach of contract, the other party may declare the contract avoided.

(2) If time allows, the party intending to declare the contract avoided must give reasonable notice to the other party in order to permit him to provide adequate assurance of his performance.

(3` The requirements of the preceding paragraph do not apply if the other party has declared that he will not perform his obligations.

Article 73

(1) In the case of a contract for delivery of goods by installments, if the failure of one party to perform any of his obligations in respect of any instalment constitutes a fundamental breach of contract with respect to that instalment, the other party may declare the contract avoided with respect to that instalment.

(2) If one party's failure to perform any of his obligations in respect of any instalment gives the other party good grounds to conclude that a fundamental breach of contract will occur with respect to future installments, he may declare the contract avoided for the future, provided that he does so within a reasonable time.

(3) A buyer who declares the contract avoided in respect of any delivery may, at the same time, declare it avoided in respect of deliveries already made or of future deliveries if, by reason of their interdependence, those deliveries could not be used for the purpose contemplated by the parties at the time of the conclusion of the contract.

SECTION II
DAMAGES

Article 74

Damages for breach of contract by one party consist of a sum equal to the loss, including loss of profit, suffered by the other party as a consequence of the breach. Such damages may not exceed the loss which the party in breach foresaw or ought to have foreseen at the time of the conclusion of the contract, in the light of the facts and matters of which he then knew or ought to have known, as a possible consequence of the breach of contract.

Article 75

If the contract is avoided and if, in a reasonable manner and within a reasonable time after avoidance, the buyer has bought goods in replacement or the seller has resold the goods, the party claiming damages may recover the difference between the contract price and the price in the substitute transaction as well as any further damages recoverable under article 74.

Article 76

(1) If the contract is avoided and there is a current price for the goods, the party claiming damages may, if he has not made a purchase or resale under article 75, recover the difference between the price fixed by the contract and the current price at the time of avoidance as well as any further damages recoverable under article 74. If, however, the party claiming damages has avoided the contract after taking over the goods, the current price at the time of such taking over shall be applied instead of the current price at the time of avoidance.

(2) For the purposes of the preceding paragraph, the current price is the price prevailing at the place where delivery of the goods should have been made or, if there is no current price at that place, the price at such other place as serves as a reasonable substitute, making due allowance for differences in the cost of transporting the goods.

Article 77

A party who relies on a breach of contract must take such measures as are reasonable in the circumstances to mitigate the loss, including loss of profit, resulting from the breach. If he fails to take such measures, the party in breach may claim a reduction in the damages in the amount by which the loss should have been mitigated.

SECTION III
INTEREST

Article 78

If a party fails to pay the price or any other sum that is in arrears, the other party is entitled to interest on it, without prejudice to any claim for damages recoverable under article 74.

SECTION IV
EXEMPTIONS

Article 79

(1) A party is not liable for a failure to perform any of his obligations if he proves that the failure was due to an impediment beyond his control and that he could not reasonably be expected to have taken the impediment into account at the time of the conclusion of the contract or to have avoided or overcome it, or its consequences.

(2) If the party's failure is due to the failure by a third person whom he has engaged to perform the whole or a part of the contract, that party is exempt from liability only if:

(a) he is exempt under the preceding paragraph; and

(b) the person whom he has so engaged would be so exempt if the provisions of that paragraph were applied to him.

(3) The exemption provided by this article has effect for the period during which the impediment exists.

(4) The party who fails to perform must give notice to the other party of the impediment and its effect on his ability to perform. If the notice is not received by the other party within a reasonable time after the party who fails to perform know or ought to have known of the impediment, he is liable for damages resulting from such non-receipt.

(5) Nothing in this article prevents either party from exercising any right other than to claim damages under this Convention.

Article 80

A party may not rely on a failure of the other party to perform, to the extent that such failure was caused by the first party's act or omission.

SECTION V
EFFECTS OF AVOIDANCE

Article 81

(1) Avoidance of the contract releases both parties from their obligations under it, subject to any damages which may be due. Avoidance does not affect any provision of the contract for the settlement of disputes or any other provision of the contract governing the rights and obligations of the parties consequent upon the avoidance of the contract.

(2) A party who has performed the contract either wholly or in part may claim restitution from the other party of whatever the first party has supplied or paid under the contract. If both parties are bound to make restitution, they must do so concurrently.

Article 82

(1) The buyer loses the right to declare the contract avoided or to require the seller to deliver substitute goods if it is impossible for him to make restitution of the goods substantially in the condition in which he received them.

(2) The preceding paragraph does not apply:

(a) if the impossibility of making restitution of the goods or of making restitution of the goods substantially in the condition in which the buyer received them is not due to his act or omission;

(b) if the goods or part of the goods have perished or deteriorated as a result of the examination provided for in article 38; or

(c) if the goods or part of the goods have been sold in the normal course business or have been consumed or transformed by the buyer in the course of normal use before he discovered or ought to have discovered the lack of conformity.

Article 83

A buyer who has lost the right to declare the contract avoided or to require the seller to deliver substitute goods in accordance with article 82 retains all other remedies under the contract and this Convention.

Article 84

(1) If the seller is bound to refund the price, he must also pay interest on it, from the date on which the price was paid.

(2) The buyer must account to the seller for all benefits which he has derived from the goods or part of them:

(a) if he must make restitution of the goods or part of them; or

(b) if it is impossible for him to make restitution of all or part of the goods or to make restitution of all or part of the goods substantially in the condition in which he received them, but he has nevertheless declared the contract avoided or required the seller to deliver substitute goods.

SECTION VI
PRESERVATION OF THE GOODS

Article 85

If the buyer is in delay in taking delivery of the goods or, where payment of the price and delivery of the goods are to be made concurrently, if he fails to pay the price, and the seller is either in possession of the goods or otherwise able to control their disposition, the seller must take such steps as are reasonable in the circumstances to preserve them. He is entitled to retain them until he has been reimbursed his reasonable expenses by the buyer.

Article 86

(1) If the buyer has received the goods and intends to exercise any right under the contract or this Convention to reject them, he must take such steps to preserve them as are reasonable in the circumstances. He is entitled to retain them until he has been reimbursed his reasonable expenses by the seller.

(2) If goods dispatched to the buyer have been placed at his disposal at their destination and he exercises the right to reject them, he must take possession of them on behalf of

the seller, provided that this can be done without payment of the price and without unreasonable inconvenience or unreasonable expense. This provision does not apply if the seller or a person authorized to take charge of the goods on his behalf is present at the destination. If the buyer takes possession of the goods under this paragraph, his rights and obligations are governed by the preceding paragraph.

Article 87

A party who is bound to take steps to preserve the goods may deposit them in a warehouse of a third person at the expense of the other party provided that the expense incurred is not unreasonable.

Article 88

(1) A party who is bound to preserve the goods in accordance with article 85 or 86 may sell them by any appropriate means if there has been an unreasonable delay by the other party in taking possession of the goods or in taking them back or in paying the price or the cost of preservation, provided that reasonable notice of the intention to sell has been given to the other party.

(2) If the goods are subject to rapid deterioration or their preservation would involve unreasonable expense, a party who is bound to preserve the goods in accordance with article 85 or 86 must take reasonable measures to sell them. To the extent possible he must give notice to the other party of his intention to sell.

(3) A party selling the goods has the right to retain out of the proceeds of sale an amount equal to the reasonable expenses of preserving the goods and of selling them. He must account to the other party for the balance.

PART IV
FINAL PROVISIONS

Article 89

The Secretary-General of the United Nations is hereby designated as the depositary for this Convention.

Article 90

This Convention does not prevail over any international agreement which has already been or may be entered into and which contains provisions concerning the matters governed by this Convention, provided that the parties have their places of business in States parties to such agreement.

Article 91

(1) This Convention is open for signature at the concluding meeting of the United Nations Conference on Contracts for the International Sale of Goods and will remain open for signature by all States at the Headquarters of the United Nations, New York until 30 September 1981.

(2) This Convention is subject to ratification, acceptance or approval by the signatory States.

(3) This Convention is open for accession by all States which are not signatory States as from the date it is open for signature.

(4) Instruments of ratification, acceptance, approval and accession are to be deposited with the Secretary-General of the United Nations.

Article 92

(1) A Contracting State may declare at the time of signature, ratification, acceptance, approval or accession that it will not be bound by Part II of this Convention or that it will not be bound by Part III of this convention.

(2) A Contracting State which makes a declaration in accordance with the preceding paragraph in respect of Part II or Part III of this Convention is not to be considered a Contracting State within paragraph (1) of article 1 of this Convention in respect of matters governed by the Part to which the declaration applies.

Article 93

(1) If a Contracting State has two or more territorial units in which, according to its constitution, different systems of law are applicable in relation to the matters dealt with in this Convention, it may, at the time of signature, ratification, acceptance, approval or accession, declare that this Convention is to extend to all its territorial units or only to one or more of them, and may amend its declaration by submitting another declaration at any time.

(2) These declarations are to be notified to the depositary and are to state expressly the territorial units to which the Convention extends.

(3) If, by virtue of a declaration under this article, this Convention extends to one or more but not all of the territorial units of a Contracting State, and if the place of business of a party is located in that State, this place of business, for the purposes of this Convention, is considered not to be in a Contracting State, unless it is in a territorial unit to which the Convention extends.

(4) If a Contracting State makes no declaration under paragraph (1) of this article, the Convention is to extend to all territorial units of that State.

Article 94

(1) Two or more Contracting States which have the same or closely related legal rules on matters governed by this Convention may at any time declare that the Convention is not to apply to contracts of sale or to their formation where the parties have their places of business in those States. Such declarations may be made jointly or by reciprocal unilateral declarations.

(2) A Contracting State which has the same or closely related legal rules on matters governed by this Convention as one or more non-Contracting States may at any time declare that the Convention is not to apply to contracts of sale or to their formation where the parties have their places of business in those States.

(3) If a State which is the object of a declaration under the preceding paragraph subsequently becomes a Contracting State, the declaration made will, as from the date on which the Convention enters into force in respect of the new Contracting State, have the effect of a declaration made under paragraph (1), provided that the new Contracting State joins in such declaration or makes a reciprocal unilateral declaration.

Article 95

Any State may declare at the time of the deposit of its instrument of ratification, acceptance, approval or accession that it will not be bound by subparagraph (1)(b) of article 1 of this Convention.

Article 96

A Contracting State whose legislation requires contracts of sale to be concluded in or evidenced by writing may at any time make a declaration in accordance with article 12 that any provision of article 11, article 29, or Part II of this Convention, that allows a contract of sale or its modification or termination by agreement or any offer, acceptance, or other indication of intention to be made in any form other than in writing, does not apply where any party has his place of business in that State.

Article 97

(1) Declarations made under this Convention at the time of signature are subject to confirmation upon ratification, acceptance or approval.

(2) Declarations and confirmations of declarations are to be in writing and be formally notified to the depositary.

(3) A declaration takes effect simultaneously with the entry into force of this Convention in respect of the State concerned. However, a declaration of which the depositary receives formal notification after such entry into force takes effect on the first day of the month following the expiration of six months after the date of its receipt by the depositary. Reciprocal unilateral declarations under article 94 take effect on the first day of the month following the expiration of six months after the receipt of the latest declaration by the depositary.

(4) Any State which makes a declaration under this Convention may withdraw it at any time by a formal notification in writing addressed to the depositary. Such withdrawal is to take effect on the first day of the month following the expiration of six months after the date of the receipt of the notification by the depositary.

(5) A withdrawal of a declaration made under article 94 renders inoperative, as from the date on which the withdrawal takes effect, any reciprocal declaration made by another State under that article.

Article 98

No reservations are permitted except those expressly authorized in this Convention.

Article 99

(1) This Convention enters into force, subject to the provisions of paragraph (6) of this article, on the first day of the month following the expiration of twelve months after the date of deposit of the tenth instrument of ratification, acceptance, approval or accession, including an instrument which contains a declaration made under article 92.

(2) When a State ratifies, accepts, approves or accedes to this Convention after the deposit of the tenth instrument of ratification, acceptance, approval or accession, this Convention, with the exception of the Part excluded, enters into force in respect of that State, subject to the provisions of paragraph (6) of this article, on the first day of the month following the expiration of twelve months after the date of the deposit of its instrument of ratification, acceptance, approval or accession.

(3) A State which ratifies, accepts, approves or accedes to this Convention and is a party to either or both the Convention relating to a Uniform Law on the Formation of Contracts for the International Sale of Goods done at The Hague on 1 July 1964 (1964 Hague Formation Convention) and the Convention relating to a Uniform Law on the International Sale of Goods done at The Hague on 1 July 1964 (1964 Hague Sales Con-

vention) shall at the same time denounce, as the case may be, either or both the 1964 Hague Sales Convention and the 1964 Hague Formation Convention by notifying the Government of the Netherlands to that effect.

(4) A State party to the 1964 Hague Sales Convention which ratifies, accepts, approves or accedes to the present Convention and declares or has declared under article 92 that it will not be bound by Part II of this Convention shall at the time of ratification, acceptance, approval or accession denounce the 1964 Hague Sales Convention by notifying the Government of the Netherlands to that effect.

(5) A State party to the 1964 Hague Formation Convention which ratifies, accepts, approves or accedes to the present Convention and declares or has declared under article 92 that it will not be bound by Part III of this Convention shall at the time of ratification, acceptance, approval or accession denounce the 1964 Hague Formation Convention by notifying the Government of the Netherlands to that effect.

(6) For the purpose of this article, ratifications, acceptances, approvals and accessions in respect of this Convention by States parties to the 1964 Hague Formation Convention or to the 1964 Hague Sales Convention shall not be effective until such denunciations as may be required on the part of those States in respect of the latter two Conventions have themselves become effective. The depositary of this Convention shall consult with the Government of the Netherlands, as the depositary of the 1964 Conventions, so as to ensure necessary co-ordination in this respect.

Article 100

(1) This Convention applies to the formation of a contract only when the proposal for concluding the contract is made on or after the date when the Convention enters into force in respect of the Contracting States referred to in subparagraph (1)(a) or the Contracting State referred to in subparagraph (1)(b) of article 1.

(2) This Convention applies only to contracts concluded on or after the date when the Convention enters into force in respect of the Contracting States referred to in subparagraph (1)(a) or the Contracting State referred to in subparagraph (1)(b) of article 1.

Article 101

(1) A Contracting State may denounce this Convention, or Part II or Part III of the Convention, by a formal notification in writing addressed to the depositary.

(2) The denunciation takes effect on the first day of the month following the expiration of twelve months after the notification is received by the depositary. Where a longer period for the denunciation to take effect is specified in the notification, the denunciation takes effect upon the expiration of such longer period after the notification is received by the depositary.

DONE at Vienna, this day of eleventh day of April, one thousand nine hundred and eighty, in a single original, of which the Arabic, Chinese, English, French, Russian and Spanish texts are equally authentic.

IN WITNESS WHEREOF the undersigned plenipotentiaries, being duly authorized by their respective Governments, have signed this Convention.

CONVENTION ON THE RECOGNITION AND ENFORCEMENT OF FOREIGN ARBITRAL AWARDS
New York, June 10, 1958

Article I

1. This Convention shall apply to the recognition and enforcement of arbitral awards made in the territory of a State other than the State where the recognition and enforcement of such awards are sought, and arising out of differences between persons, whether physical or legal. It shall also apply to arbitral awards not considered as domestic awards in the State where their recognition and enforcement are sought.

2. The term "arbitral awards" shall include not only awards made by arbitrators appointed for each case but also those made by permanent arbitral bodies to which the parties have submitted.

3. When signing, ratifying or acceding to this Convention, or notifying extension under article X hereof, any State may on the basis of reciprocity declare that it will apply the Convention to the recognition and enforcement of awards made only in the territory of another Contracting State. It may also declare that it will apply the Convention only to differences arising out of legal relationships, whether contractual or not, which are considered as commercial under the national law of the State making such declaration.

Article II

1. Each Contracting State shall recognize an agreement in writing under which the parties undertake to submit to arbitration all or any differences which have arisen or which may arise between them in respect of a defined legal relationship, whether contractual or not, concerning a subject matter capable of settlement by arbitration.

2. The term "agreement in writing" shall include an arbitral clause in a contract or an arbitration agreement, signed by the parties or contained in an exchange of letters or telegrams.

3. The court of a Contracting State, when seized of an action in matter in respect of which the parties have made an agreement within the meaning of this article, shall, at the request of one of the parties, refer the parties to arbitration, unless it finds that the said agreement is null and void, inoperative or incapable of being performed.

Article III

Each Contracting State shall recognize arbitral awards as binding and enforce them in accordance with the rules of procedure of the territory where the award is relied upon, under the conditions laid down in the following articles. There shall not be imposed substantially more onerous conditions or higher fees or charges on the recognition or enforcement of arbitral awards to which this Convention applies than are imposed on the recognition or enforcement of domestic arbitral awards.

Article IV

1. To obtain the recognition and enforcement mentioned in the preceding article, the party applying for recognition and enforcement shall, at the time of application, supply:

(a) The duly authenticated original award or a duly certified copy thereof;

(b) The original agreement referred to in article II or a duly certified copy thereof.

2. If the said award or agreement is not made in an official language of the country in which the award is relied upon, the party applying for recognition and enforcement of the award shall produce a translation of these documents into such language. The translation shall be certified by an official or sworn translator or by a diplomatic or consular agent.

Article V

1. Recognition and enforcement of the award may be refused, at the request of the party against whom it is invoked, only if that party furnishes to the competent authority where the recognition and enforcement is sought, proof that:

(a) The parties to the agreement referred to in Article II were, under the law applicable to them, under some incapacity, or the said agreement is not valid under the law to which the parties have subjected it or, failing any indication thereon, under the law of the country where the award was made; or

(b) The party against whom the award is invoked was not given proper notice of the appointment of the arbitrator or of the arbitration proceedings or was otherwise unable to present his case; or

(c) The award deals with a difference not contemplated by or not falling within the terms of the submission to arbitration, or it contains decisions on matters beyond the scope of the submission to arbitration, provided that, if the decisions on matters submitted to arbitration can be separated from those not so submitted, that part of the award which contains decisions on matters submitted to arbitration may be recognized and enforced; or

(d) The composition of the arbitral authority or the arbitral procedure was not in accordance with the agreement of the parties, or, failing such agreement, was not in accordance with the law of the country where the arbitration took place; or

(e) The award has not yet become binding on the parties, or has been set aside or suspended by a competent authority of the country in which, or under the law of which, that award was made.

2. Recognition and enforcement of an arbitral award may also be refused if the competent authority in the country where recognition and enforcement is sought finds that:

(a) The subject matter of the difference is not capable of settlement by arbitration under the law of that country; or

(b) The recognition or enforcement of the award would be contrary to the public policy of that country.

Article VI

If an application for the setting aside or suspension of the award has been made to a competent authority referred to in article V (1) (e), the authority before which the award is sought to be relied upon may, if it considers it proper, adjourn the decision on the enforcement of the award and may also, on the application of the party claiming enforcement of the award, order the other party to give suitable security.

Article VII

1. The provisions of the present Convention shall not affect the validity of multilateral or bilateral agreements concerning the recognition and enforcement of arbitral awards entered into by the Contracting States nor deprive any interested party of any right he may have to avail himself of an arbitral award in the manner and to the extent allowed by the law or the treaties of the country where such award is sought to be relied upon.

2. The Geneva Protocol on Arbitration Clauses of 1923 and the Geneva Convention on the Execution of Foreign Arbitral Awards of 1927 shall cease to have effect between Contracting States on their becoming bound and to the extent that they become bound, by this Convention.

Article VIII

1. This Convention shall be open until 31 December 1958 for signature on behalf of any Member of the United Nations and also on behalf of any other State which is or hereafter becomes a member of any specialized agency of the United Nations, or which is or hereafter becomes a party to the Statute of the International Court of Justice, or any other State to which an invitation has been addressed by the General Assembly of the United Nations.

2. This Convention shall be ratified and the instrument of ratification shall be deposited with the Secretary-General of the United Nations.

Article IX

1. This Convention shall be open for accession to all States referred to in Article VIII.

2. Accession shall be effected by the deposit of an instrument of accession with the Secretary-General of the United Nations.

Article X

1. Any State may, at the time of signature, ratification or accession, declare that this Convention shall extend to all or any of the territories for the international relations of which it is responsible. Such a declaration shall take effect when the Convention enters into force for the State concerned.

2. At any time thereafter any such extension shall be made by notification addressed to the Secretary-General of the United Nations and shall take effect as from the ninetieth day after the day of receipt by the Secretary-General of the United Nations of this notification, or as from the date of entry into force of the Convention for the State concerned, whichever is the later.

3. With respect to those territories to which this Convention is not extended at the time of signature, ratification or accession, each State concerned shall consider the possibility of taking the necessary steps in order to extend the application of this Convention to such territories, subject, where necessary for constitutional reasons, to the consent of the Governments of such territories.

Article XI

In the case of a federal or non-unitary State, the following provisions shall apply:

(a) With respect to those articles of this Convention that come within the legislative jurisdiction of the federal authority, the obligations of the federal Government shall to this extent be the same as those of Contracting States which are not federal States;

(b) With respect to those articles of this Convention that come within the legislative jurisdiction of constituent states or provinces which are not, under the constitutional system of the federation, bound to take legislative action, the federal Government shall bring such articles with a favourable recommendation to the notice of the appropriate authorities of constituent states or provinces at the earliest possible moment;

(c) A federal State Party to this Convention shall, at the request of any other Contracting State transmitted through the Secretary-General of the United Nations, supply a statement of the law and practice of the federation and its constituent units in regard to any particular provision of this Convention, showing the extent to which effect has been given to that provision by legislative or other action.

Article XII

1. This Convention shall come into force on the ninetieth day following the date of deposit of the third instrument of ratification or accession.

2. For each State ratifying or acceding to this Convention after the deposit of the third instrument of ratification or accession, this Convention shall enter into force on the ninetieth day after deposit by such State of its instrument of ratification or accession.

Article XIII

1. Any Contracting State may denounce this Convention by a written notification to the Secretary-General of the United Nations. Denunciation shall take effect one year after the date of receipt of the notification by the Secretary-General.

2. Any State which has made a declaration or notification under article X may, at any time thereafter, by notification to the Secretary-General of the United Nations, declare that this Convention shall cease to extend to the territory concerned one year after the date of the receipt of the notification by the Secretary-General.

3. This Convention shall continue to be applicable to arbitral awards in respect of which recognition or enforcement proceedings have been instituted before the denunciation takes effect.

Article XIV

A Contracting State shall not be entitled to avail itself of the present Convention against other Contracting States except to the extent that it is itself bound to apply the Convention.

Article XV

The Secretary-General of the United Nations shall notify the States contemplated in article VIII of the following:

(a) Signatures and ratifications in accordance with Article VIII;

(b) Accessions in accordance with Article IX;

(c) Declarations and notifications under Articles I,X and XI;

(d) The date upon which this Convention enters into force in accordance with Article XII;

(e) Denunciations and notifications in accordance with article XIII.

Article XVI

1. This Convention, of which the Chinese, English, French, Russian and Spanish texts shall be equally authentic, shall be deposited in the archives of the United Nations.

2. The Secretary-General of the United Nations shall transmit a certified copy of this Convention to the States contemplated in article VIII.

APPENDIX III

CONVENTIONS OF THE EUROPEAN COMMUNITES AND THE EUROPEAN UNION

EUROPEAN COMMUNITY/EUROPEAN UNION CONVENTIONS
(as of January 1997)

- EC Convention on Jurisdiction and Enforcement of Judgments in Civil and Commercial Matters, Brussels, September 27, 1968 (Brussels Convention), as amended on October 25, 1982
- Brussels Convention as amended, San Sebastian, May 26, 1989
- Jurisdiction and the Enforcement of Judgments in Civil and Commercial Matters, Lugano, September 16, 1988
- Service in the Member States of the European Union of Judicial and Extra-judicial Documents in Civil or Commercial Matters, drawn up on the basis of Article K.3 of the Treaty of the European Union, May 26, 1997

EU-Countries	Brussels Conv. as amended 1982	Brussels Conv. as amended 1989	Lugano Conv. 1988	Service Conv. 1997
Austria	—	—	X	—
Belgium	X	X	—	—
Denmark	X	X	X	—
Finland	—	—	X	—
France	X	X	X	—
Germany	X	X	X	—
Greece	X	X	—	—
Ireland	X	X	X	—
Italy	X	X	X	—
Luxembourg	X	X	X	—
Netherlands	X	X	X	—
Portugal	—	X	X	—
Spain	—	X	X	—
Sweden	—	—	X	—
United Kingdom	X	X	X	—
EFTA Countries				
Iceland	—	—	X	—
Norway	—	—	X	—
Switzerland	—	—	X	—

EUROPEAN COMMUNITIES CONVENTION ON THE LAW APPLICABLE TO CONTRACTUAL OBLIGATIONS (Rome 1980)

Preamble

The High Contracting Parties to the Treaty establishing the European Economic Community,

Anxious to continue in the field of private international law the work of unification of law which has already been done within the Community, in particular in the field of jurisdiction and enforcement of judgments,

Wishing to establish uniform rules concerning the law applicable to contractual obligations.

Have agreed as follows:

TITLE I - SCOPE OF THE CONVENTION

Article 1 - Scope of the Convention

1 . The rules of this Convention shall apply to contractual obligations in any situation involving a choice between the laws of different countries.

2 . They shall not apply to:

(a) questions involving the status or legal capacity of natural persons, without prejudice to Article 11;

(b) contractual obligations relating to:

- wills and succession,
- rights in property arising out of a matrimonial relationship,
- rights and duties arising out of a family relationship, parentage, marriage or affinity, including maintenance obligations in respect of children who are not legitimate;

(c) obligations arising under bills of exchange, cheques and promissory notes and other negotiable instruments to the extent that the obligations under such other negotiable instruments arise out of their negotiable character;

(d) arbitration agreements and agreements on the choice of court;

(e) questions governed by the law of companies and other bodies corporate or unincorporate such as the creation, by registration or otherwise, legal capacity, internal organisation or winding up of companies and other bodies corporate or unincorporate and the personal liability of officers and members as such for the obligations of the company or body;

(f) the question whether an agent is able to bind a principal, or an organ to bind a company or body corporate or unincorporate, to a third party;

(g) the constitution of trusts and the relationship between settlors, trustees and beneficiaries;

(h) evidence and procedure, without prejudice to Article 14.

3 . The rules of this Convention do not apply to contracts of insurance which cover risks situated in the territories of the Member States of the European Economic Community. In order to determine whether a risk is situated in these territories the court shall apply its internal law.

4 . The preceding paragraph does not apply to contracts of re-insurance.

Article 2 - Application of law of non - contracting States

Any law specified by this Convention shall be applied whether or not it is the law of a Contracting State.

TITLE II - UNIFORM RULES

Article 3 - Freedom of choice

1 . A contract shall be governed by the law chosen by the parties. The choice must be expressed or demonstrated with reasonable certainty by the terms of the contract or the circumstances of the case. By their choice the parties can select the law applicable to the whole or a part only of the contract.

2 . The parties may at any time agree to subject the contract to a law other than that which previously governed it, whether as a result of an earlier choice under this Article or of other provisions of this Convention. Any variation by the parties of the law to be applied made after the conclusion of the contract shall not prejudice its formal validity under Article 9 or adversely affect the rights of third parties.

3 . The fact that the parties have chosen a foreign law, whether or not accompanied by the choice of a foreign tribunal, shall not, where all the other elements relevant to the situation at the time of the choice are connected with one country only, prejudice the application of rules of the law of that country which cannot be derogated from by contract, hereinafter called "mandatory rules".

4 . The existence and validity of the consent of the parties as to the choice of the applicable law shall be determined in accordance with the provisions of Articles 8, 9 and 11.

Article 4 - Applicable law in the absence of choice

1 . To the extent that the law applicable to the contract has not been chosen in accordance with article 3, the contract shall be governed by the law of the country with which it is most closely connected. Nevertheless, a severable part of the contract which has a closer connection with another country may by way of exception be governed by the law of that other country.

2 . Subject to the provisions of paragraph 5 of this Article, it shall be presumed that the contract is most closely connected with the country where the party who is to effect the performance which is characteristic of the contract has, at the time of conclusion of the contract, his habitual residence, or, in the case of a body corporate or unincorporate, its central administration. However, if the contract is entered into in the course of that

party's trade or profession, that country shall be the country in which the principal place of business is situated or, where under the terms of the contract the performance is to be effected through a place of business other than the principal place of business, the country in which that other place of business is situated.

3 . Notwithstanding the provisions of paragraph 2 of this Article, to the extent that the subject matter of the contract is a right in immovable property or a right to use immovable property it shall be presumed that the contract is most closely connected with the country where the immovable property is situated.

4 . A contract for the carriage of goods shall not be subject to the presumption in paragraph 2. In such a contract if the country in which, at the time the contract is concluded, the carrier has his principal place of business is also the country in which the place of loading or the place of discharge or the principal place of business of the consignor is situated, it shall be presumed that the contract is most closely connected with that country. In applying this paragraph single voyage charter-parties and other contracts the main purpose of which is the carriage of goods shall be treated as contracts for the carriage of goods.

5 . Paragraph 2 shall not apply if the characteristic performance cannot be determined, and the presumptions in paragraphs 2, 3 and 4 shall be disregarded if it appears from the circumstances as a whole that the contract is more closely connected with another country.

Article 5 - Certain consumer contracts

1 . This Article applies to a contract the object of which is the supply of goods or services to a person ("the consumer") for a purpose which can be regarded as being outside his trade or profession, or a contract for the provision of credit for that object.

2 . Notwithstanding the provisions of Article 3, a choice of law made by the parties shall not have the result of depriving the consumer of the protection afforded to him by the mandatory rules of the law of the country in which he has his habitual residence:

- if in that country the conclusion of the contract was preceded by a specific invitation addressed to him or by advertising, and he had taken in that country all the steps necessary on his part for the conclusion of the contract, or
- if the other party or his agent received the consumer's order in that country, or
- if the contract is for the sale of goods and the consumer travelled from that country to another country and there gave his order, provided that the consumer's journey was arranged by the seller for the purpose of inducing the consumer to buy.

3 . Notwithstanding the provisions of Article 4, a contract to which this Article applies shall, in the absence of choice in accordance with Article 3, be governed by the law of the country in which the consumer has his habitual residence if it is entered into in the circumstances described in paragraph 2 of this Article.

4 . This Article shall not apply to:

(a) a contract of carriage;

(b) a contract for the supply of services where the services are to be supplied to the consumer exclusively in a country other than that in which he has his habitual residence.

5 . Notwithstanding the provisions of paragraph 4, this Article shall apply to a contract which, for an inclusive price, provides for a combination of travel and accommodation.

Article 6 - Individual employment contracts

1 . Notwithstanding the provisions of Article 3, in a contract of employment a choice of law made by the parties shall not have the result of depriving the employee of the protection afforded to him by the mandatory rules of the law which would be applicable under paragraph 2 in the absence of choice.

2 . Notwithstanding the provisions of Article 4, a contract of employment shall, in the absence of choice in accordance with Article 3, be governed:

(a) by the law of the country in which the employee habitually carries out his work in performance of the contract, even if he is temporarily employed in another country; or

(b) if the employee does not habitually carry out his work in any one country, by the law of the country in which the place of business through which he was engaged is situated;

unless it appears from the circumstances as a whole that the contract is more closely connected with another country, in which case the contract shall be governed by the law of that country.

Article 7 - Mandatory rules

1 . When applying under this Convention the law of a country, effect may be given to the mandatory rules of the law of another country with which the situation has a close connection, if and in so far as, under the law of the latter country, those rules must be applied whatever the law applicable to the contract. In considering whether to give effect to these mandatory rules, regard shall be had to their nature and purpose and to the consequences of their application or non-application.

2 . Nothing in this Convention shall restrict the application of the rules of the law of the forum in a situation where they are mandatory irrespective of the law otherwise applicable to the contract.

Article 8 - Material validity

1 . The existence and validity of a contract, or of any term of a contract, shall be determined by the law which would govern it under this Convention if the contract or term were valid.

2 . Nevertheless a party may rely upon the law of the country in which he has his habitual residence to establish that he did not consent if it appears from the circumstances that it would not be reasonable to determine the effect of his conduct in accordance with the law specified in the preceding paragraph.

Article 9 - Formal validity

1 . A contract concluded between persons who are in the same country is formally valid if it satisfies the formal requirements of the law which governs it under this Convention or of the law of the country where it is concluded.

2 . A contract concluded between persons who are in different countries is formally valid if it satisfies the formal requirements of the law which governs it under this Convention or of the law of one of those countries.

3 . Where a contract is concluded by an agent, the country in which the agent acts is the relevant country for the purposes of paragraphs 1 and 2.

4 . An act intended to have legal effect relating to an existing or contemplated contract is formally valid if it satisfies the formal requirements of the law which under this Convention governs or would govern the contract or of the law of the country where the act was done.

5 . The provisions of the preceding paragraphs shall not apply to a contract to which Article 5 applies, concluded in the circumstances described in paragraph 2 of Article 5. The formal validity of such a contract is governed by the law of the country in which the consumer has his habitual residence.

6 . Notwithstanding paragraphs 1 to 4 of this Article, a contract the subject matter of which is a right in immovable property or a right to use immovable property shall be subject to the mandatory requirements of form of the law of the country where the property is situated if by that law those requirements are imposed irrespective of the country where the contract is concluded and irrespective of the law governing the contract.

Article 10 - Scope of the applicable law

1 . The law applicable to a contract by virtue of Articles 3 to 6 and 12 of this Convention shall govern in particular:

(a) interpretation;

(b) performance;

(c) within the limits of the powers conferred on the court by its procedural law, the consequences of breach, including the assessment of damages in so far as it is governed by rules of law;

(d) the various ways of extinguishing obligations, and prescription and limitation of actions;

(e) the consequences of nullity of the contract.

2 . In relation to the manner of performance and the steps to be taken in the event of defective performance regard shall be had to the law of the country in which performance takes place.

Article 11 - Incapacity

In a contract concluded between persons who are in the same country, a natural person who would have capacity under the law of that country may invoke his incapacity resulting from another law only if the other party to the contract was aware of this incapacity at the time of the conclusion of the contract or was not aware thereof as a result of negligence.

Article 12 - Voluntary assignment

1 . The mutual obligations of assignor and assignee under a voluntary assignment of a right against another person ("the debtor") shall be governed by the law which under this Convention applies to the contract between the assignor and assignee.

2 . The law governing the right to which the assignment relates shall determine its assignabiity, the relationship between the assignee and the debtor, the conditions under which the assignment can be invoked against the debtor and any question whether the debtor's obligations have been discharged.

Article 13 - Subrogation

1 . Where a person ("the creditor") has a contractual claim upon another ("the debtor"), and a third person has a duty to satisfy the creditor, or has in fact satisfied the creditor in discharge of that duty, the law which governs the third person's duty to satisfy the creditor shall determine whether the third person is entitled to exercise against the debtor the rights which the creditor had against the debtor under the law governing their relationship and, if so, whether he may do so in full or only to a limited extent.

2 . The same rule applies where several persons are subject to the same contractual claim and one of them has satisfied the creditor.

Article 14 - Burden of proof, etc.

1 . The law governing the contract under this Convention applies to the extent that it contains, in the law of contract, rules which raise presumptions of law or determine the burden of proof.

2 . A contract or an act intended to have legal effect may be proved by any mode of proof recognised by the law of the forum or by any of the laws referred to in Article 9 under which that contract or act is formally valid, provided that such mode of proof can be administered by the forum.

Article 15 - Exclusion of renvoi

The application of the law of any country specified by this Convention means the application of the rules of law in force in that country other than its rules of private international law.

Article 16 - "Ordre public"

The application of a rule of the law of any country specified by this Convention may be refused only if such application is manifestly incompatible with the public policy ("ordre public") of the forum.

Article 17 - No retrospective effect

This Convention shall apply in a Contracting State to contracts made after the date on which this Convention has entered into force with respect to that State.

Article 18 - Uniform interpretation

In the interpretation and application of the preceding uniform rules, regard shall be had to their international character and to the desirability of achieving uniformity in their interpretation and application.

Article 19 - States with more than one legal system

1 . Where a State comprises several territorial units each of which has its own rules of law in respect of contractual obligations, each territorial unit shall be considered as a country for the purposes of identifying the law applicable under this Convention.

2 . A State within which different territorial units have their own rules of law in respect of contractual obligations shall not be bound to apply this Convention to conflicts solely between the laws of such units.

Article 20 - Precedence of Community law

This Convention shall not affect the application of provisions which, in relation to particular matters, lay down choice of law rules relating to contractual obligations and which are or will be contained in acts of the institutions of the European Communities or in national laws harmonised in implementation of such acts.

Article 21 - Relationship with other conventions

This Convention shall not prejudice the application of international conventions to which a Contracting State is, or becomes, a party.

Article 22 - Reservations

1 . Any Contracting State may, at the time of signature, ratification, acceptance or approval, reserve the right not to apply:

(a) the provisions of Article 7 (1);

(b) the provisions of Article 10 (1) (e).

2 . Any Contracting State may also, when notifying an extension of the Convention in accordance with Article 27 (2), make one or more of these reservations, with its effect limited to all or some of the territories mentioned in the extension.

3 . Any Contracting State may at any time withdraw a reservation which it has made; the reservation shall cease to have effect on the first day of the third calendar month after notification of the withdrawal.

TITLE III - FINAL PROVISIONS

Article 23

1 . If, after the date on which this Convention has entered into force for a Contracting State, that State wishes to adopt any new choice of law rule in regard to any particular category of contract within the scope of this Convention, it shall communicate its intention to the other signatory States through the Secretary-General of the Council of the European Communities.

2 . Any signatory State may, within six months from the date of the communication made to the Secretary-General, request him to arrange consultations between signatory States in order to reach agreement.

3 . If no signatory State has requested consultations within this period or if within two years following the communication made to the Secretary-General no agreement is reached in the course of consultations, the Contracting State concerned may amend its law in the manner indicated. The measures taken by that State shall be brought to the knowledge of the other signatory States through the Secretary-General of the Council of the European Communities.

Article 24

1 . If, after the date on which this Convention has entered into force with respect to a Contracting State, that State wishes to become a party to a multilateral convention whose principal aim or one of whose principal aims is to lay down rules of private international law concerning any of the matters governed by this Convention, the procedure set out in Article 23 shall apply. However, the period of two years, referred to in paragraph 3 of that Article, shall be reduced to one year.

2 . The procedure referred to in the preceding paragraph need not be followed if a Contracting State or one of the European Communities is already a party to the multilateral convention, or if its object is to revise a convention to which the State concerned is already a party, or if it is a convention concluded within the framework of the Treaties establishing the European Communities.

Article 25

If a Contracting State considers that the unification achieved by this Convention is prejudiced by the conclusion of agreements not covered by Article 24 (1), that State may request the Secretary-General of the Council of the European Communities to arrange consultations between the signatory States of this Convention.

Article 26

Any Contracting State may request the revision of this Convention. In this event a revision conference shall be convened by the President of the Council of the European Communities.

Article 27

1 . This Convention shall apply to the European territories of the Contracting States, including Greenland, and to the entire territory of the French Republic.

2 . Notwithstanding paragraph 1:

(a) this Convention shall not apply to the Faroe Islands, unless the Kingdom of Denmark makes a declaration to the contrary;

(b) this Convention shall not apply to any European territory situated outside the United Kingdom for the international relations of which the United Kingdom is responsible, unless the United Kingdom makes a declaration to the contrary in respect of any such territory;

(c) this Convention shall apply to the Netherlands Antilles, if the Kingdom of the Netherlands makes a declaration to that effect.

3 . Such declarations may be made at any time by notifying the SecretaryGeneral of the Council of the European Communities.

4 . Proceedings brought in the United Kingdom on appeal from courts in one of the territories referred to in paragraph 2 (b) shall be deemed to be proceedings taking place in those courts.

Article 28

1 . This Convention shall be open from 19 June 1980 for signature by the States party to the Treaty establishing the European Economic Community.

2 . This Convention shall be subject to ratification, acceptance or approval by the signatory States. The instruments of ratification, acceptance or approval shall be deposited with the Secretary-General of the Council of the European Communities.

Article 29

1 . This Convention shall enter into force on the first day of the third month following the deposit of the seventh instrument of ratification, acceptance or approval.

2 . This Convention shall enter into force for each signatory State ratifying, accepting or approving at a later date on the first day of the third month following the deposit of its instrument of ratification, acceptance or approval.

Article 30

1 . This Convention shall remain in force for 10 years from the date of its entry into force in accordance with Article 29 (1), even for States for which it enters into force at a later date.

2 . If there has been no denunciation it shall be renewed tacitly every five years.

3 . A Contracting State which wishes to denounce shall, not less than six months before the expiration of the period of 10 or five years, as the case may be, give notice to the Secretary-General of the Council of the European Communities. Denunciation may be limited to any territory to which the Convention has been extended by a declaration under Article 27 (2).

4 . The denunciation shall have effect only in relation to the State which has notified it. The Convention will remain in force as between all other Contracting States.

Article 31

The Secretary-General of the Council of the European Communities shall notify the States party to the Treaty establishing the European Economic Community

(a) the signatures;

(b) the deposit of each instrument of ratification, acceptance or approval;

(c) the date of entry into force of this Convention;

(d) communications made in pursuance of Articles 23, 24, 25, 26, 27 and 30;

(e) the reservations and withdrawals of reservations referred to in Article 22.

Article 32

The Protocol annexed to this Convention shall form an integral part thereof.

Article 33

This Convention, drawn up in a single original in the Danish, Dutch, English, French, German, Irish and Italian languages, these texts being equally authentic, shall be deposited in the archives of the Secretariat of the Council of the European Communities. The Secretary-General shall transmit a certified copy thereof to the Government of each signatory State.

EUROPEAN COMMUNITIES CONVENTION ON JURISDICTION AND ENFORCEMENT OF JUDGMENTS IN CIVIL AND COMMERCIAL MATTERS[1]

Brussels, September 27, 1968,
(As amended by the 1978, 1982, and 1989 Accession Conventions)

PREAMBLE

THE HIGH CONTRACTING PARTIES TO THE TREATY ESTABLISHING THE EUROPEAN ECONOMIC COMMUNITY,

DESIRING to implement the provisions of Article 220 of that Treaty by virtue of which they undertook to secure the simplification of formalities governing the reciprocal recognition and enforcement of judgments of courts or tribunals;

ANXIOUS to strengthen in the Community the legal protection of persons therein established;

CONSIDERING that it is necessary for this purpose to determine the international jurisdiction of their courts, to facilitate recognition and to introduce an expeditious procedure for securing the enforcement of judgments, authentic instruments and court settlements;[2]

HAVE DECIDED to conclude this Convention and to this end have designated as their Plenipotentiaries:

HIS MAJESTY THE KING OF THE BELGIANS:

Mr Pierre HARMEL, Minister for Foreign Affairs;

THE PRESIDENT OF THE FEDERAL REPUBLIC OF GERMANY:

Mr Willy BRANDT, Vice-Chancellor, Minister for Foreign Affairs;

THE PRESIDENT OF THE FRENCH REPUBLIC:

Mr Michel DEBRÉ, Minister for Foreign Affairs;

THE PRESIDENT OF THE ITALIAN REPUBLIC:

---

1 Text as amended by the Convention of 9 October 1978 on the accession of the Kingdom of Denmark, Ireland and the United Kingdom of Great Britain and Northern Ireland - hereafter referred to as the '1978 Accession Convention' - by the Convention of 25 October 1982 on the accession of the Hellenic Republic -hereafter referred to as the '1982 Accession Convention' - and by the Convention of 26 May 1989 on the accession of the Kingdom of Spain and the Portuguese Republic - hereafter referred to as the '1989 Accession Convention'.

2 The Preamble of the 1989 Accession Convention contained the following text: 'MINDFUL that on 16 September 1988 the Member States of the Community and the Member States of the European Free Trade Association concluded in Lugano the Convention on jurisdiction and the enforcement of judgments in civil and commercial matters, which extends the principles of the Brussels Convention to the States becoming parties to that Convention'.

Mr Giuseppe MEDICI, Minister for Foreign Affairs;

HIS ROYAL HIGHNESS THE GRAND DUKE OF LUXEMBOURG:

Mr Pierre GRÉGOIRE, Minister for Foreign Affairs;

HER MAJESTY THE QUEEN OF THE NETHERLANDS:

Mr J.M.A.H. LUNS, Minister for Foreign Affairs;

WHO, meeting within the Council, having exchanged their Full Powers, found in good and due form,

HAVE AGREED AS FOLLOWS:

TITLE I
Scope

Article 1

This Convention shall apply in civil and commercial matters whatever the nature of the court or tribunal. It shall not extend, in particular, to revenue, customs or administrative matters.[3]

The Convention shall not apply to:

1. the status or legal capacity of natural persons, rights in property arising out of a matrimonial relationship, wills and succession;
2. bankruptcy, proceedings relating to the winding-up of insolvent companies or other legal persons, judicial arrangements, compositions and analogous proceedings;
3. social security;
4. arbitration.

TITLE II
JURISDICTION
Section 1

General provisions

Article 2

Subject to the provisions of this Convention, persons domiciled in a Contracting State shall, whatever their nationality, be sued in the courts of that State.

Persons who are not nationals of the State in which they are domiciled shall be governed by the rules of jurisdiction applicable to nationals of that State.

Article 3

Persons domiciled in a Contracting State may be sued in the courts of another Contracting State only by virtue of the rules set out in Sections 2 to 6 of this Title.

3 Second sentence added by Article 3 of the 1978 Accession Convention.

In particular the following provisions shall not be applicable as against them:

- in Belgium: Article 15 of the civil code (Code civil — Burgerlijk Wetboek) and Article 638 of the judicial code (Code judiciaire —Gerechtelijk Wetboek),
- in Denmark: Article 246(2) and (3) of the law on civil procedure (Lov om rettens pleje),[4]
- in the Federal Republic of Germany: Article 23 of the code of civil procedure (Zivilprozeßordnung),
- in Greece: Article 40 of the code of civil procedure (Code of Political Economy, [Translation]).
- in France: Articles 14 and 15 of the civil code (Code civil),
- in Ireland: the rules which enable jurisdiction to be founded on the document instituting the proceedings having been served on the defendant during his temporary presence in Ireland,
- in Italy: Articles 2 and 4, Nos 1 and 2 of the code of civil procedure (Codice di procedura civile),
- in Luxembourg: Articles 14 and 15 of the civil code (Code civil),
- in the Netherlands: Articles 126(3) and 127 of the code of civil procedure (Wetboek van Burgerlijke Rechtsvordering),
- in Portugal: Article 65 (1) (c), Article 65 (2) and Article 65A (c) of the code of civil procedure (Código de Processo Civil) and Article 11 of the code of labour procedure (Código de Processo de Trabalho),
- in the United Kingdom: the rules which enable jurisdiction to be founded on:

  (a) the document instituting the proceedings having been served on the defendant during his temporary presence in the United Kingdom; or

  (b) the presence within the United Kingdom of property belonging to the defendant; or

  (c) the seizure by the plaintiff of property situated in the United Kingdom.[5]

Article 4

If the defendant is not domiciled in a Contracting State, the jurisdiction of the courts of each Contracting State shall, subject to the provisions of Article 16, be determined by the law of that State.

As against such a defendant, any person domiciled in a Contracting State may, whatever his nationality, avail himself in that State of the rules of jurisdiction there in force, and in particular those specified in the second paragraph of Article 3, in the same way as the nationals of that State.

4 As amended by a Communication of 8 February 1988 made in accordance with Article VI of the annexed Protocol, and confirmed by Annex I (d) (1) to the 1989 Accession Convention.

5 Second subparagraph as amended by Article 4 of the 1978 Accession Convention, by Article 3 of the 1982 Accession Convention and by Article 3 of the 1989 Accession Convention.

Section 2
Special jurisdiction

Article 5

A person domiciled in a Contracting State may, in another Contracting State, be sued:

1. in matters relating to a contract, in the courts for the place of performance of the obligation in question; in matters relating to individual contracts of employment, this place is that where the employee habitually carries out his work, or if the employee does not habitually carry out his work in any one country, the employer may also be sued in the courts for the place where the business which engaged the employee was or is now situated;[6]

2. in matters relating to maintenance, in the courts for the place where the maintenance creditor is domiciled or habitually resident or, if the matter is ancillary to proceedings concerning the status of a person, in the court which, according to its own law, has jurisdiction to entertain those proceedings, unless that jurisdiction is based solely on the nationality of one of the parties;[7]

3. in matters relating to tort, delict or quasi-delict, in the courts for the place where the harmful event occurred;

4. as regards a civil claim for damages or restitution which is based on an act giving rise to criminal proceedings, in the court seised of those proceedings, to the extent that that court has jurisdiction under its own law to entertain civil proceedings;

5. as regards a dispute arising out of the operations of a branch, agency or other establishment, in the courts for the place in which the branch, agency or other establishment is situated;

6. as settlor, trustee or beneficiary of a trust created by the operation of a statute, or by a written instrument, or created orally and evidenced in writing, in the courts of the Contracting State in which the trust is domiciled;[8]

7. as regards a dispute concerning the payment of remuneration claimed in respect of the salvage of a cargo or freight, in the court under the authority of which the cargo or freight in question:

   (a) has been arrested to secure such payment, or

   (b) could have been so arrested, but bail or other security has been given;

   provided that this provision shall apply only if it is claimed that the defendant has an interest in the cargo or freight or had such an interest at the time of salvage.[9]

Article 6

A person domiciled in a Contracting State may also be sued:

6 Point 1 as amended by Article 4 of the 1989 Accession Convention.

7 Point 2 as amended by Article 5(3) of the 1978 Accession Convention.

8 Point 6 added by Article 5(4) of the 1978 Accession Convention.

9 Point 7 added by Article 5(4) of the 1978 Accession Convention.

1. where he is one of a number of defendants, in the courts for the place where any one of them is domiciled;
2. as a third party in an action on a warranty or guarantee or in any other third party proceedings, in the court seised of the original proceedings, unless these were instituted solely with the object of removing him from the jurisdiction of the court which would be competent in his case;
3. on a counter-claim arising from the same contract or facts on which the original claim was based, in the court in which the original claim is pending;
4. in matters relating to a contract, if the action may be combined with an action against the same defendant in matters relating to rights *in rem* in immovable property, in the court of the Contracting State in which the property is situated.[10]

Article 6a[11]

Where by virtue of this Convention a court of a Contracting State has jurisdiction in actions relating to liability from the use or operation of a ship, that court, or any other court substituted for this purpose by the internal law of that State, shall also have jurisdiction over claims for limitation of such liability.

Section 3
Jurisdiction in matters relating to insurance

Article 7

In matters relating to insurance, jurisdiction shall be determined by this Section, without prejudice to the provisions of Articles 4 and 5 point 5.

Article 8[12]

An insurer domiciled in a Contracting State may be issued:

1. in the courts of the State where he is domiciled, or
2. in another Contracting State, in the courts for the place where the policy-holder is domiciled, or
3. if he is a co-insurer, in the courts of a Contracting State in which proceedings are brought against the leading insurer.

An insurer who is not domiciled in a Contracting State but has a branch, agency or other establishment in one of the Contracting States shall, in disputes arising out of the operations of the branch, agency or establishment, be deemed to be domiciled in that State.

Article 9

In respect of liability insurance or insurance of immovable property, the insurer may in addition be sued in the courts for the place where the harmful event occurred. The same

10 Point 4 added by Article 5 of the 1989 Accession Convention.

11 Article added by Article 6 of the 1978 Accession Convention.

12 Text as amended by Article 7 of the 1978 Accession Convention.

applies if movable and immovable property are covered by the same insurance policy and both are adversely affected by the same contingency.

Article 10

In respect of liability insurance, the insurer may also, if the law of the court permits it, be joined in proceedings which the injured party had brought against the insured.

The provisions of Articles 7, 8 and 9 shall apply to actions brought by the injured party directly against the insurer, where such direct actions are permitted.

If the law governing such direct actions provides that the policy-holder or the insured may be joined as a party to the action, the same court shall have jurisdiction over them.

Article 11

Without prejudice to the provisions of the third paragraph of Article 10, an insurer may bring proceedings only in the courts of the Contracting State in which the defendant is domiciled, irrespective of whether he is the policy-holder, the insured or a beneficiary.

The provisions of this Section shall not affect the right to bring a counterclaim in the court in which, in accordance with this Section, the original claim is pending.

Article 12[13]

The provisions of this Section may be departed from only by an agreement on jurisdiction:

1. which is entered into after the dispute has arisen, or
2. which allows the policy-holder, the insured or a beneficiary to bring proceedings in courts other than those indicated in this Section, or
3. which is concluded between a policy-holder and an insurer, both of whom are domiciled in the same Contracting State, and which has the effect of conferring jurisdiction on the courts of that State even if the harmful event were to occur abroad, provided that such an agreement is not contrary to the law of that State, or
4. which is concluded with a policy-holder who is not domiciled in a Contracting State, except in so far as the insurance is compulsory or relates to immovable property in a Contracting State, or
5. which relates to a contract of insurance in so far as it covers one or more of the risks set out in Article 12a.

Article 12a[14]

The following are the risks referred to in point 5 of Article 12:

1. Any loss of or damage to

    (a) sea-going ships, installations situated offshore or on the high seas, or aircraft, arising from perils which relate to their use for commercial purposes;

---

13 Text as amended by Article 8 of the 1978 Accession Convention.

14 Article added by Article 9 of the 1978 Accession Convention.

(b) goods in transit other than passengers' baggage where the transit consists of or includes carriage by such ships or aircraft;

2. Any liability, other than for bodily injury to passengers or loss of or damage to their baggage:

   (a) arising out of the use or operation of ships, installations or aircraft as referred to in point 1(a) above in so far as the law of the Contracting State in which such aircraft are registered does not prohibit agreements on jurisdiction regarding insurance of such risks;

   (b) for loss or damage caused by goods in transit as described in point 1(b) above;

3. Any financial loss connected with the use or operation of ships, installations or aircraft as referred to in point 1(a) above, in particular loss of freight or charter-hire;

4. Any risk or interest connected with any of those referred to in points 1 to 3 above.

Section 4[15]
Jurisdiction over consumer contracts

Article 13

In proceedings concerning a contract concluded by a person for a purpose which can be regarded as being outside his trade or profession, hereinafter called 'the consumer,' jurisdiction shall be determined by this Section, without prejudice to the provisions of point 5 of Articles 4 and 5, if it is:

1. a contract for the sale of goods on instalment credit terms; or

2. a contract for a loan repayable by instalments, or for any other form of credit, made to finance the sale of goods; or

3. any other contract for the supply of goods or a contract for the supply of services, and

   (a) in the State of the consumer's domicile the conclusion of the contract was preceded by a specific invitation addressed to him or by advertising; and

   (b) the consumer took in that State the steps necessary for the conclusion of the contract.

Where a consumer enters into a contract with a party who is not domiciled in a Contracting State but has a branch, agency or other establishment in one of the Contracting States, that party shall, in disputes arising out of the operations of the branch, agency or establishment, be deemed to be domiciled in that State.

This Section shall not apply to contracts of transport.

15 Text as amended by Article 10 of the 1978 Accession Convention.

Article 14

A consumer may bring proceedings against the other party to a contract either in the courts of the Contracting State in which that party is domiciled or in the courts of the Contracting State in which he is himself domiciled.

Proceedings may be brought against a consumer by the other party to the contract only in the courts of the Contracting State in which the consumer is domiciled.

These provisions shall not affect the right to bring a counter-claim in the court in which, in accordance with this Section, the original claim is pending.

Article 15

The provisions of this Section may be departed from only by an agreement:

1. which is entered into after the dispute has arisen; or
2. which allows the consumer to bring proceedings in courts other than those indicated in this Section; or
3. which is entered into by the consumer and the other party to the contract, both of whom are at the time of conclusion of the contract domiciled or habitually resident in the same Contracting State, and which confers jurisdiction on the courts of that State, provided that such an agreement is not contrary to the law of that State.

Section 5
Exclusive jurisdiction

Article 16

The following courts shall have exclusive jurisdiction, regardless of domicile:

1. (a) in proceedings which have as their object rights *in rem* in immovable property or tenancies of immovable property, the courts of the Contracting State in which the property is situated;

   (b) however, in proceedings which have as their object tenancies of immovable property concluded for temporary private use for a maximum period of six consecutive months, the courts of the Contracting State in which the defendant is domiciled shall also have jurisdiction, provided that the landlord and the tenant are natural persons and are domiciled in the same Contracting State;[16]
2. in proceedings which have as their object the validity of the constitution, the nullity or the dissolution of companies or other legal persons or associations of natural or legal persons, or the decisions of their organs, the courts of the Contracting State in which the company, legal person or association has its seat;
3. in proceedings which have as their object the validity of entries in public registers, the courts of the Contracting State in which the register is kept;
4. in proceedings concerned with the registration or validity of patents, trade marks, designs, or other similar rights required to be deposited or registered, the courts

16 Point 1 as amended by Article 6 of the 1989 Accession Convention.

of the Contracting State in which the deposit or registration has been applied for, has taken place or is under the terms of an international convention deemed to have taken place;

5. in proceedings concerned with the enforcement of judgments, the courts of the Contracting State in which the judgment has been or is to be enforced.

Section 6
Prorogation of jurisdiction

Article 17[17]

If the parties, one or more of whom is domiciled in a Contracting State, have agreed that a court or the courts of a Contracting State are to have jurisdiction to settle any disputes which have arisen or which may arise in connection with a particular legal relationship, that court or those courts shall have exclusive jurisdiction. Such an agreement conferring jurisdiction shall be either:

(a) in writing or evidenced in writing; or

(b) in a form which accords with practices which the parties have established between themselves; or

(c) in international trade or commerce, in a form which accords with a usage of which the parties are or ought to have been aware and which in such trade or commerce is widely known to, and regularly observed by, parties to contracts of the type involved in the particular trade or commerce concerned.

Where such an agreement is concluded by parties, none of whom is domiciled in a Contracting State, the courts of other Contracting States shall have no jurisdiction over their disputes unless the court or courts chosen have declined jurisdiction.

The court or courts of a Contracting State on which a trust instrument has conferred jurisdiction shall have exclusive jurisdiction in any proceedings brought against a settlor, trustee or beneficiary, if relations between these persons or their rights or obligations under the trust are involved.

Agreements or provisions of a trust instrument conferring jurisdiction shall have no legal force if they are contrary to the provisions of Articles 12 or 15, or if the courts whose jurisdiction they purport to exclude have exclusive jurisdiction by virtue of Article 16.

If an agreement conferring jurisdiction was concluded for the benefit of only one of the parties, that party shall retain the right to bring proceedings in any other court which has jurisdiction by virtue of this Convention.

In matters relating to individual contracts of employment an agreement conferring jurisdiction shall have legal force only if it is entered into after the dispute has arisen or if the employee invokes it to seise courts other than those for the defendant's domicile or those specified in Article 5(1).

---

17 Text as amended by Article 11 of the 1978 Accession Convention and by Article 7 of the 1989 Accession Convention.

Article 18

Apart from jurisdiction derived from other provisions of this Convention, a court of a Contracting State before whom a defendant enters an appearance shall have jurisdiction. This rule shall not apply where appearance was entered solely to contest the jurisdiction, or where another court has exclusive jurisdiction by virtue of Article 16.

Section 7
Examination as to jurisdiction and admissibility

Article 19

Where a court of a Contracting State is seised of a claim which is principally concerned with a matter over which the courts of another Contracting State have exclusive jurisdiction by virtue of Article 16, it shall declare of its own motion that it has no jurisdiction.

Article 20

Where a defendant domiciled in one Contracting State is sued in a court of another Contracting State and does not enter an appearance, the court shall declare of its own motion that it has no jurisdiction unless its jurisdiction is derived from the provisions of this Convention.

The court shall stay the proceedings so long as it is not shown that the defendant has been able to receive the document instituting the proceedings or an equivalent document in sufficient time to enable him to arrange for his defense, or that all necessary steps have been taken to this end.[18]

The provisions of the foregoing paragraph shall be replaced by those of Article 15 of the Hague Convention of 15 November 1965 on the service abroad of judicial and extrajudicial documents in civil or commercial matters, if the document instituting the proceedings or notice thereof had to be transmitted abroad in accordance with that Convention.

Section 8
Lis pendens — related actions

Article 21[19]

Where proceedings involving the same cause of action and between the same parties are brought in the courts of different Contracting States, any court other than the court first seised shall of its own motion stay its proceedings until such time as the jurisdiction of the court first seised is established.

Where the jurisdiction of the court first seised is established, any court other than the court first seised shall decline jurisdiction in favour of that court.

Article 22

Where related actions are brought in the courts of different Contracting States, any court other than the court first seised may, while the actions are pending at first instance, stay its proceedings.

---

18 Second subparagraph as amended by Article 12 of the 1978 Accession Convention.

19 Text as amended by Article 8 of the 1989 Accession Convention.

A court other than the court first seised may also, on the application of one of the parties, decline jurisdiction if the law of that court permits the consolidation of related actions and the court first seised has jurisdiction over both actions.

For the purposes of this Article, actions are deemed to be related where they are so closely connected that it is expedient to hear and determine them together to avoid the risk of irreconcilable judgments resulting from separate proceedings.

Article 23

Where actions come within the exclusive jurisdiction of several courts, any court other than the court first seised shall decline jurisdiction in favour of that court.

Section 9
Provisional, including protective, measures

Article 24

Application may be made to the courts of a Contracting State for such provisional, including protective, measures as may be available under the law of that State, even if, under this Convention, the courts of another Contracting State have jurisdiction as to the substance of the matter.

Title III
RECOGNITION AND ENFORCEMENT

Article 25

For the purposes of this Convention, 'judgment' means any judgment given by a court or tribunal of a Contracting State, whatever the judgment may be called, including a decree, order, decision or writ of execution, as well as the determination of costs or expenses by an officer of the court.

Section 1
Recognition

Article 26

A judgment given in a Contracting State shall be recognized in the other Contracting States without any special procedure being required.

Any interested party who raises the recognition of a judgment as the principal issue in a dispute may, in accordance with the procedures provided for in Sections 2 and 3 of this Title, apply for a decision that the judgment be recognized.

If the outcome of proceedings in a court of a Contracting State depends on the determination of an incidental question of recognition that court shall have jurisdiction over that question.

Article 27

A judgment shall not be recognized:

1. if such recognition is contrary to public policy in the State in which recognition is sought;

2. where it was given in default of appearance, if the defendant was not duly served with the document which instituted the proceedings or with an equivalent document in sufficient time to enable him to arrange for his defense;[20]

3. if the judgment is irreconcilable with a judgment given in a dispute between the same parties in the State in which recognition is sought;

4. if the court of the State of origin, in order to arrive at its judgment, has decided a preliminary question concerning the status or legal capacity of natural persons, rights in property arising out of a matrimonial relationship, wills or succession in a way that conflicts with a rule of the private international law of the State in which the recognition is sought, unless the same result would have been reached by the application of the rules of private international law of that State;[21]

5. if the judgment is irreconcilable with an earlier judgment given in a non-contracting State involving the same cause of action and between the same parties, provided that this latter judgment fulfils the conditions necessary for its recognition in the State addressed.[22]

Article 28

Moreover, a judgment shall not be recognized if it conflicts with the provisions of Sections 3, 4 or 5 of Title II, or in a case provided for in Article 59.

In its examination of the grounds of jurisdiction referred to in the foregoing paragraph, the court or authority applied to shall be bound by the findings of fact on which the court of the State of origin based its jurisdiction.[23]

Subject to the provisions of the first paragraph, the jurisdiction of the court of the State of origin may not be reviewed; the test of public policy referred to in point 1 of Article 27, may not be applied to the rules relating to jurisdiction.[24]

Article 29

Under no circumstances may a foreign judgment be reviewed as to its substance.

Article 30

A court of a Contracting State in which recognition is sought of a judgment given in another Contracting State may stay the proceedings if an ordinary appeal against the judgment has been lodged.

A court of a Contracting State in which recognition is sought of a judgment given in Ireland or the United Kingdom may stay the proceedings if enforcement is suspended in the State of origin by reason of an appeal.[25]

---

20 Point 2 as amended by Article 13(1) of the 1978 Accession Convention.

21 Point 4 as amended by Annex I (a) (2) first subparagraph to the 1989 Accession Convention.

22 Point 5 added by Article 13(2) of the 1978 Accession Convention and amended by Annex I(d)(2) second subparagraph to the 1989 Accession Convention.

23 As amended by Annex I(d)(3) first subparagraph to the 1989 Accession Convention.

24 As amended by Annex I(d)(3) second subparagraph to the 1989 Accession Convention.

25 Second subparagraph added by Article 14 of the 1978 Accession Convention and amended by Annex I(d)(4) to the 1989 Accession Convention.

Section 2
Enforcement

Article 31

A judgment given in a Contracting State and enforceable in that State shall be enforced in another Contracting State when, on the application of any interested party, it has been declared enforceable there.[26]

However, in the United Kingdom, such a judgment shall be enforced in England and Wales, in Scotland, or in Northern Ireland when, on the application of any interested party, it has been registered for enforcement in that part of the United Kingdom.[27]

Article 32

The application shall be submitted:

- in Belgium, to the tribunal de premiére instance or rechtbank van eerste aanleg,
- in Denmark, to the byret;[28]
- in the Federal Republic of Germany, to the presiding judge of a chamber of the Landgericht,
- in Greece, to the Monomeles Protodikeio.
- in Spain, to the Juzgado de Primera Instancia,
- in France, to the presiding judge of the tribunal de grande instance,
- in Ireland, to the High Court,
- in Italy, to the corte d'appello,
- in Luxembourg, to the presiding judge of the tribunal d'arrondissement,
- in the Netherlands, to the presiding judge of the arrondissementsrechtbank,
- in Portugal, to the Tribunal Judicial de Círculo
- in the United Kingdom:

  1. in England and Wales, to the High Court of Justice, or in the case of maintenance judgment to the Magistrates' Court on transmission by the Secretary of State;
  2. in Scotland, to the Court of Session, or in the case of a maintenance judgment to the Sheriff Court on transmission by the Secretary of State;
  3. in Northern Ireland, to the High Court of Justice, or in the case of maintenance judgment to the Magistrates' Court on transmission by the Secretary of State.[29]

The jurisdiction of local courts shall be determined by reference to the place of domicile of the party against whom enforcement is sought. If he is not domiciled in the State in which enforcement is sought, it shall be determined by reference to the place of enforcement.

---

26 Text as amended by Article 9 of the 1989 Accession Convention.

27 Second subparagraph added by Article 15 of the 1978 Accession Convention.

28 As amended by a Communication of 8 February 1988 made in accordance with Article VI of the annexed Protocol, and confirmed by Annex I(d)(5) to the 1989 Accession Convention.

29 First subparagraph as amended by Article 16 of the 1978 Accession Convention and by Article 4 of the 1982 Accession Convention and by Article 10 of the 1989 Accession Convention.

Article 33

The procedure for making the application shall be governed by the law of the State in which enforcement is sought.

The applicant must give an address for service of process within the area of jurisdiction of the court applied to. However, if the law of the State in which enforcement is sought does not provide for the furnishing of such an address, the applicant shall appoint a representative *ad litem*.

The documents referred to in Articles 46 and 47 shall be attached to the application.

Article 34

The court applied to shall give its decision without delay; the party against whom enforcement is sought shall not at this stage of the proceedings be entitled to make any submissions on the application.

The application may be refused only for one of the reasons specified in Articles 27 and 28.

Under no circumstances may the foreign judgment be reviewed as to its substance.

Article 35

The appropriate officer of the court shall without delay bring the decision given on the application to the notice of the applicant in accordance with the procedure laid down by the law of the State in which enforcement is sought.

Article 36

If enforcement is authorized, the party against whom enforcement is sought may appeal against the decision within one month of service thereof.

If that party is domiciled in a Contracting State other than that in which the decision authorizing enforcement was given, the time for appealing shall be two months and shall run from the date of service, either on him in person or at his residence. No extension of time may be granted on account of distance.

Article 37[30]

1. An appeal against the decision authorizing enforcement shall be lodged in accordance with the rules governing procedure in contentious matters:

- in Belgium, with the tribunal de premiére instance or rechtbank van eerste aanleg,
- in Denmark, with the landsret,
- in the Federal Republic of Germany, with the Oberlandesgericht,
- in Greece, with the Epheteio,
- in Spain, with the Audiencia Provincial,
- in France, with the cour d'appel,
- in Ireland, with the High Court,

30 Text as amended by Article 17 of the 1978 Accession Convention, by Article 5 of the 1982 Accession Convention and by Article 11 of the 1989 Accession Convention.

- in Italy, with the corte d'appello,
- in Luxembourg, with the Cour supérieure de justice sitting as a court of civil appeal,
- in the Netherlands, with the arrondissementsrechtbank,
- in Portugal, with the Tribunal de Relação,
- in the United Kingdom:

  (a) in England and Wales, with the High Court of Justice, or in the case of a maintenance judgment with the Magistrates' Court;

  (b) in Scotland, with the Court of Session, or in the case of a maintenance judgment with the Sheriff Court;

  (c) in Northern Ireland, with the High Court of Justice, or in the case of a maintenance judgment with the Magistrates' Court.

2. The judgment given on the appeal may be contested only:

- in Belgium, Greece, Spain, France, Italy, Luxembourg and in the Netherlands, by an appeal in cassation,
- in Denmark, by an appeal to the højesteret, with the leave of the Minister of Justice,
- in the Federal Republic of Germany, by a Rechtsbeschwerde,
- in Ireland, by an appeal on a point of law to the Supreme Court,
- in Portugal, by an appeal on a point of law,
- in the United Kingdom, by a single further appeal on a point of law.

Article 38

The court with which the appeal under Article 37(1) is lodged may, on the application of the appellant, stay the proceedings if an ordinary appeal has been lodged against the judgment in the State of origin or if the time for such an appeal has not yet expired; in the latter case, the court may specify the time within which such an appeal is to be lodged.[31]

Where the judgment was given in Ireland or the United Kingdom, any form of appeal available in the State of origin shall be treated as an ordinary appeal for the purposes of the first paragraph.[32]

The court may also make enforcement conditional on the provision of such security as it shall determine.

Article 39

During the time specified for an appeal pursuant to Article 36 and until any such appeal has been determined, no measures of enforcement may be taken other than protective measures taken against the property of the party against whom enforcement is sought.

31 As amended by Annex I(d)(6) first subparagraph to the 1989 Accession Convention.

32 Second subparagraph added by Article 18 of the 1978 Accession Convention and amended by Annex I(d)(6) second subparagraph to the 1989 Accession Convention.

The decision authorizing enforcement shall carry with it the power to proceed to any such protective measures.

Article 40

If the application for enforcement is refused, the applicant may appeal:

- in Belgium, to the cour d'appel or hof van beroep,
- in Denmark, to the landsret,
- in the Federal Republic of Germany, to the Oberlandesgericht,
- in Greece, to the Epheteio,
- in Spain, to the Audiencia Provincial,
- in France, to the cour d'appel,
- in Ireland, to the High Court,
- in Italy, to the corte d'appello,
- in Luxembourg, to the Cour superieure de justice sitting as a court of civil appeal,
- in the Netherlands, to the gerechtshof,
- in Portugal, to the Tribunal da Relação,
- in the United Kingdom:

  (a) in England and Wales, to the High Court of Justice, or in the case of a maintenance judgment to the Magistrates' Court;

  (b) in Scotland, to the Court of Session, or in the case of a maintenance judgment to the Sheriff Court;

  (c) in Northern Ireland, to the High Court of Justice, or in the case of a maintenance judgment to the Magistrates' Court.[33]

2. The party against whom enforcement is sought shall be summoned to appear before the appellate court. If he fails to appear, the provisions of the second and third paragraphs of Article 20 shall apply even where he is not domiciled in any of the Contracting States.

Article 41[34]

A judgment given on an appeal provided for in Article 40 may be contested only:

- in Belgium, Greece, France, Italy, Luxembourg and in the Netherlands, by an appeal in cassation,
- in Denmark, by an appeal to the højesteret, with the leave of the Minister of Justice,
- in the Federal Republic of Germany, by a Rechtsbeschwerde,
- in Ireland, by an appeal on a point of law to the Supreme Court,
- in Portugal, by an appeal on a point of law,

33 First subparagraph as amended by Article 19 of the 1978 Accession Convention and by Article 6 of the 1982 Accession Convention and by Article 12 of the 1989 Accession Convention.

34 Text as amended by Article 20 of the 1978 Accession Convention, by Article 7 of the 1982 Accession Convention and by Article 13 of the 1989 Accession Convention.

- in the United Kingdom, by a single further appeal on a point of law.

Article 42

Where a foreign judgment has been given in respect of several matters and enforcement cannot be authorized for all of them, the court shall authorize enforcement for one or more of them.

An applicant may request partial enforcement of a judgment.

Article 43

A foreign judgment which orders a periodic payment by way of a penalty shall be enforceable in the State in which enforcement is sought only if the amount of the payment has been finally determined by the courts of the State of origin.[35]

Article 44 [36]

An applicant who, in the State of origin, has benefited from complete or partial legal aid or exemption from costs or expenses, shall be entitled, in the procedures provided for in Articles 32 to 35, to benefit from the most favourable legal aid or the most extensive exemption from costs or expenses provided for by the law of the State addressed.

However, an applicant who requests the enforcement of a decision given by an administrative authority in Denmark in respect of a maintenance order may, in the State addressed, claim the benefits referred to in the first paragraph if he presents a statement from the Danish Ministry of Justice to the effect that he fulfils the economic requirements to qualify for the grant of complete or partial legal aid or exemption from costs or expenses.

Article 45

No security, bond or deposit, however described, shall be required of a party who in one Contracting State applies for enforcement of a judgment given in another Contracting State on the ground that he is a foreign national or that he is not domiciled or resident in the State in which enforcement is sought.

Section 3
Common provisions

Article 46

A party seeking recognition or applying for enforcement of a judgment shall produce:

1. a copy of the judgment which satisfies the conditions necessary to establish its authenticity;
2. in the case of a judgment given in default, the original or a certified true copy of the document which establishes that the party in default was served with the document instituting the proceedings or with an equivalent document.[37]

---

35 As amended by Annex I(d)(7) to the 1989 Accession Convention.

36 Text as amended by Article 21 of the 1978 Accession Convention and by Annex I(d)(8) to the 1989 Accession Convention.

37 Point 2 as amended by Article 22 of the 1978 Accession Convention.

Article 47[38]

A party applying for enforcement shall also produce:

1. documents which establish that, according to the law of the State of origin the judgment is enforceable and has been served;
2. where appropriate, a document showing that the applicant is in receipt of legal aid in the State of origin.

Article 48

If the documents specified in point 2 of Articles 46 and 47 are not produced, the court may specify a time for their production, accept equivalent documents or, if it considers that it has sufficient information before it, dispense with their production.

If the court so requires, a translation of the documents shall be produced; the translation shall be certified by a person qualified to do so in one of the Contracting States.

Article 49

No legalization or other similar formality shall be required in respect of the documents referred to in Articles 46 or 47 or the second paragraph of Article 48, or in respect of a document appointing a representative *ad litem*.

Title IV
AUTHENTIC INSTRUMENTS AND COURT SETTLEMENTS

Article 50

A document which has been formally drawn up or registered as an authentic instrument and is enforceable in one Contracting State shall, in another Contracting State, be declared enforceable there, on application made in accordance with the procedures provided for in Article 31 *et seq.* The application may be refused only if enforcement of the instrument is contrary to public policy in the State addressed.[39]

The instrument produced must satisfy the conditions necessary to establish its authenticity in the State of origin.

The provisions of Section 3 of Title III shall apply as appropriate.

Article 51

A settlement which has been approved by a court in the course of proceedings and is enforceable in the State in which it was concluded shall be enforceable in the State addressed under the same conditions as authentic instruments.[40]

---

38 As amended by Annex I(d)(9) to the 1989 Accession Convention.

39 First paragraph as amended by Article 14 of the 1989 Accession Convention.

40 As amended by Annex I(d)(10) to the 1989 Accession Convention.

Title V
GENERAL PROVISIONS

Article 52

In order to determine whether a party is domiciled in the Contracting State whose courts are seised of a matter, the Court shall apply its internal law.

If a party is not domiciled in the State whose courts are seised of the matter, then, in order to determine whether the party is domiciled in another Contracting State, the court shall apply the law of that State.

. . .[41]

Article 53

For the purposes of this Convention, the seat of a company or other legal person or association of natural or legal persons shall be treated as its domicile. However, in order to determine that seat, the court shall apply its rules of private international law.

In order to determine whether a trust is domiciled in the Contracting State whose courts are seised of the matter, the court shall apply its rules of private international law.[42]

Title VI
TRANSITIONAL PROVISIONS

Article 54[43]

The provisions of this Convention shall apply only to legal proceedings instituted and to documents formally drawn up or registered as authentic instruments after its entry into force in the State of origin and, where recognition or enforcement of a judgment or authentic instruments is sought, in the State addressed.

However, judgments given after the date of entry into force of this Convention between the State of origin and the State addressed in proceedings instituted before that date shall be recognized and enforced in accordance with the provisions of Title III if jurisdiction was founded upon rules which accorded with those provided for either in Title II of this Convention or in a convention concluded between the State of origin and the State addressed which was in force when the proceedings were instituted.[44]

---

41 Third paragraph deleted by Article 15 of the 1989 Accession Convention.

42 Second subparagraph added by Article 23 of the 1978 Accession Convention.

43 Text as replaced by Article 16 of the 1989 Accession Convention.

44 Title V of the 1978 Accession Convention contains the following transitional provisions:
'Article 34

1. The 1968 Convention and the 1971 Protocol, with the amendments made by this Convention, shall apply only to legal proceedings instituted and to authentic instruments formally drawn up or registered after the entry into force of this Convention in the State of origin and, where recognition or enforcement of a judgment or authentic instrument is sought, in the State addressed.

2. However, as between the six Contracting States to the 1968 Convention, judgments given after the date of entry into force of this Convention in proceedings instituted before that date shall be recognized and enforced in accordance with the provisions of Title III of the 1968 Convention as amended.

3. Moreover, as between the six Contracting States to the 1968 Convention and the three States mentioned in Article 1 of this Convention, and as between those three States, judgments given after the date of entry into force of this Convention between the State of origin and the State addressed in proceedings instituted before that date shall also be recognized and enforced in accordance with the provisions of Title III of the

If the parties to a dispute concerning a contract had agreed in writing before 1 June 1988 for Ireland or before 1 January 1987 for the United Kingdom that the contract was to be governed by the law of Ireland or of a part of the United Kingdom, the courts of Ireland or of that part of the United Kingdom shall retain the right to exercise jurisdiction in the dispute.[45]

Article 54a[46]

For a period of three years from 1 November 1986 for Denmark and from 1 June 1988 for Ireland, jurisdiction in maritime matters shall be determined in these States not only in accordance with the provisions of Title II, but also in accordance with the provisions of paragraphs 1 to 6 following. However, upon the entry into force of the International Convention relating to the arrest of sea-going ships, signed at Brussels on 10 May 1952, for one of these States, these provisions shall cease to have effect for that State.

1. A person who is domiciled in a Contracting State may be sued in the courts of one of the States mentioned above in respect of a maritime claim if the ship to which the claim relates or any other ship owned by him has been arrested by judicial process within the territory of the latter State to secure the claim, or could have been so arrested there but bail or other security has been given, and either:

   (a) the claimant is domiciled in the latter State; or

1968 Convention as amended if jurisdiction was founded upon rules which accorded with the provisions of Title II, as amended, or with provisions of a convention concluded between the State of origin and the State addressed which was in force when the proceedings were instituted.'

Title V of the 1982 Accession Convention contains the following transitional provisions:

'*Article 12*

1. The 1968 Convention and the 1971 Protocol, as amended by the 1978 Convention, shall apply only to legal proceedings instituted and to authentic instruments formally drawn up or registered after the entry into force of this Convention in the State of origin and, where recognition or enforcement of a judgment or authentic instrument is sought, in the State addressed.

2. However, as between the State of origin and the State addressed, judgments given after the date of entry into force of this Convention in proceedings instituted before that date shall be recognized and enforced in accordance with the provisions of Title III of the 1968 Convention, as amended by the 1978 Convention, and by this Convention if jurisdiction was founded upon rules which accorded with the provisions of Title II, as amended by the 1968 Convention or with provisions of a convention concluded between the State of origin and the State addressed which was in force when the proceedings were instituted.'

Title VI of the 1989 Accession Convention contains the following transitional provisions:

'*Article 29*

1. The 1968 Convention and the 1971 Protocol, as amended by the 1978 Convention, the 1982 Convention and this Convention, shall apply only to legal proceedings instituted and to authentic instruments formally drawn up or registered after the entry into force of this Convention in the State of origin and, where recognition or enforcement of a judgment or authentic instrument is sought, in the State addressed.

2. However, judgments given after the date of entry into force of this Convention between the State of origin and the State addressed in proceedings instituted before that date shall be recognized and enforced in accordance with the provisions of Title III of the 1968 Convention, as amended by the 1978 Convention, the 1982 Convention and this Convention, if jurisdiction was founded upon rules which accorded with the provisions of Title II of the 1968 Convention, as amended, or with the provisions of a convention which was in force between the State of origin and the State addressed when the proceedings were instituted.'

45 This paragraph replaces Article 35 of Title V of the 1978 Accession Convention which was extended to the Hellenic Republic by Article 1(2) of the 1982 Accession Convention. Article 28 of the 1989 Accession Convention provided for the deletion of both these provisions.

46 Article added by Article 17 of the 1989 Accession Convention. It corresponds to Article 36 of Title V of the 1978 Accession Convention which was extended to the Hellenic Republic by Article I(2) of the 1982 Accession Convention. Article 28 of the 1989 Accession Convention provided for the deletion of both these provisions.

(b) the claim arose in the latter State; or

(c) the claim concerns the voyage during which the arrest was made or could have been made; or

(d) the claim arises out of a collision or out of damage caused by a ship to another ship or to goods or persons on board either ship, either by the execution or non-execution of a manoeuvre or by the non-observance of regulations; or

(e) the claim is for salvage; or

(f) the claim is in respect of a mortgage or hypothecation of the ship arrested.

2. A claimant may arrest either the particular ship to which the maritime claim relates, or any other ship which is owned by the person who was, at the time when the maritime claim arose, the owner of the particular ship. However, only the particular ship to which the maritime claim relates may be arrested in respect of the maritime claims set out in (5)(o), (p) or (q) of this Article.

3. Ships shall be deemed to be in the same ownership when all the shares therein are owned by the same person or persons.

4. When in the case of a charter by demise of a ship the charterer alone is liable in respect of a maritime claim relating to that ship, the claimant may arrest that ship or any other ship owned by the charterer, but no other ship owned by the owner may be arrested in respect of such claim. The same shall apply to any case in which a person other than the owner of a ship is liable in respect of a maritime claim relating to that ship.

5. The expression 'maritime claim' means a claim arising out of one or more of the following:

(a) damage caused by any ship either in collision or otherwise;

(b) loss of life or personal injury caused by any ship or occurring in connection with the operation on any ship;

(c) salvage;

(d) agreement relating to the use or hire of any ship whether by charterparty or otherwise;

(e) agreement relating to the carriage of goods in any ship whether by charterparty or otherwise;

(f) loss of or damage to goods including baggage carried in any ship;

(g) general average;

(h) bottomry;

(i) towage;

(j) pilotage;

(k) goods or materials wherever supplied to a ship for her operation or maintenance;

(l) construction, repair or equipment of any ship or dock charges and dues;

(m) wages of masters, officers or crew;

(n) mater's disbursements, including disbursements made by shippers, charterers or agents on behalf of a ship or her owner;

(o) dispute as to the title to or ownership of any ship;

(p) disputes between co-owners of any ship as to the ownership, possession, employment or earnings of that ship;

(q) the mortgage or hypothecation of any ship

6. In Denmark, the expression 'arrest' shall be deemed as regards the maritime claims referred to in 5(o) and (p) of this Article, to include a 'forbud', where that is the only procedure allowed in respect of such a claim under Articles 646 to 653 of the law on civil procedure (lov om rettens pleje).

Title VII
RELATIONSHIP TO OTHER CONVENTIONS

Article 55

Subject to the provisions of the second subparagraph of Article 54, and of Article 56, this Convention shall, for the States which are parties to it, supersede the following conventions concluded between two or more of them:

- the Convention between Belgium and France on jurisdiction and the validity and enforcement of judgments, arbitration awards and authentic instruments, signed at Paris on 8 July 1899,
- the Convention between Belgium and the Netherlands on jurisdiction, bankruptcy, and the validity and enforcement of judgments, arbitration awards and authentic instruments, signed at Brussels on 28 March 1925,
- the Convention between France and Italy on the enforcement of judgments in civil and commercial matters, signed at Rome on 3 June 1930,
- the Convention between the United Kingdom and the French Republic providing for the reciprocal enforcement of judgments in civil and commercial matters, with Protocol, signed at Paris on 18 January 1934,[47]
- the Convention between the United Kingdom and the Kingdom of Belgium providing for the reciprocal enforcement of judgments in civil and commercial matters, with Protocol, signed at Brussels on 2 May 1934,[48]
- the Convention between Germany and Italy on the recognition and enforcement of judgments in civil and commercial matters, signed at Rome on 9 March 1936,
- the Convention between the Federal Republic of Germany and the Kingdom of Belgium on the mutual recognition and enforcement of judgments, arbitration awards and authentic instruments in civil and commercial matters, signed at Bonn on 30 June 1958,

47 Fourth and fifth indents added by Article 24 of the 1978 Accession Convention.

48 Fourth and fifth indents added by Article 24 of the 1978 Accession Convention.

- the Convention between the Kingdom of the Netherlands and the Italian Republic on the recognition and enforcement of judgments in civil and commercial matters, signed at Rome on 17 April 1959,
- the Convention between the United Kingdom and the Federal Republic of Germany for the reciprocal recognition and enforcement of judgments in civil and commercial matters, signed at Bonn on 14 July 1960,[49]
- the Convention between the Kingdom of Greece and the Federal Republic of Germany for the reciprocal recognition and enforcement of judgments, settlements and authentic instruments in civil and commercial matters, signed in Athens on 4 November 1961,[50]
- the Convention between the Kingdom of Belgium and the Italian Republic on the recognition and enforcement of judgments and other enforceable instruments in civil and commercial matters, signed at Rome on 6 April 1962,
- the Convention between the Kingdom of the Netherlands and the Federal Republic of Germany on the mutual recognition and enforcement of judgments and other enforceable instruments in civil and commercial matters, signed at The Hague on 30 August 1962,
- the Convention between the United Kingdom and the Republic of Italy for the reciprocal recognition and enforcement of judgments in civil and commercial matters, signed at Rome on 7 February 1964, with amending Protocol signed at Rome on 14 July 1970,[51]
- the Convention between the United Kingdom and the Kingdom of the Netherlands providing for the reciprocal recognition and enforcement of judgments in civil matters, signed at The Hague on 17 November 1967[52]
- the Convention between Spain and France on the recognition and enforcement of judgments and arbitration awards in civil and commercial matters, signed at Paris on 28 May 1969,[53]
- the Convention between Spain and Italy regarding legal aid and the recognition and enforcement of judgments in civil and commercial matters, signed at Madrid on 22 May 1973,[54]
- the Convention between Spain and the Federal Republic of Germany on the recognition and enforcement of judgments, settlements and enforceable authentic instruments in civil and commercial matters, signed at Bonn on 14 November 1983,[55]

and, in so far as it is in force:

---

49 Ninth indent added by Article 24 of the 1978 Accession Convention.

50 10th indent added by Article 8 of the 1982 Accession Convention.

51 13th and 14th indents added by Article 24 of the 1978 Accession Convention.

52 13th and 14th indents added by Article 24 of the 1978 Accession Convention.

53 15th, 16th and 17th indents added by Article 18 of the 1989 Accession Convention.

54 15th, 16th and 17th indents added by Article 18 of the 1989 Accession Convention.

55 15th, 16th and 17th indents added by Article 18 of the 1989 Accession Convention.

- the Treaty between Belgium, the Netherlands and Luxembourg on jurisdiction, bankruptcy, and the validity and enforcement of judgments, arbitration awards and authentic instruments, signed at Brussels on 24 November 1961.

Article 56

The Treaty and the conventions referred to in Article 55 shall continue to have effect in relation to matters to which this Convention does not apply.

They shall continue to have effect in respect of judgments given and documents formally drawn up or registered as authentic instruments before the entry into force of this Convention.

Article 57

1. This Convention shall not affect any conventions to which the Contracting States are or will be parties and which, in relation to particular matters, govern jurisdiction or the recognition or enforcement of judgments.[56]

2. With a view to its uniform interpretation, paragraph 1 shall be applied in the following manner:

(a) this Convention shall not prevent a court of a Contracting State which is a party to a convention on a particular matter from assuming jurisdiction in accordance with that Convention, even where the defendant is domiciled in another Contracting State which is not a party to that Convention. The court hearing the action shall, in any event, apply Article 20 of this Convention;

(b) judgments given in a Contracting State by a court in the exercise of jurisdiction provided for in a convention on a particular matter shall be recognized and enforced in the other Contracting State in accordance with this Convention.

Where a convention on a particular matter to which both the State of origin and the State addressed are parties lays down conditions for the recognition or enforcement of judgments, those conditions shall apply. In any event, the provisions of this Convention which concern the procedure for recognition and enforcement of judgments may be applied.[57]

3. This Convention shall not affect the application of provisions which, in relation to particular matters, govern jurisdiction or the recognition or enforcement of judgments and which are or will be contained in acts of the institutions of the European Communities or in national laws harmonized in implementation of such acts.[58]

---

56 First paragraph as amended by Article 25(1) of the 1978 Accession Convention and by Article 19 of the 1989 Accession Convention.

57 Paragraph 2 added by Article 19 of the 1989 Accession Convention. This paragraph corresponds to Article 25(2) of the 1978 Accession Convention which was extended to the Hellenic Republic by Article 1(2) of the 1982 Accession Convention. Article 28 of the 1989 Accession Convention provided for the deletion of both these provisions.

58 Paragraph added by Article 25(1) of the 1978 Accession Convention.

Article 58[59]

Until such time as the Convention on jurisdiction and the enforcement of judgments in civil and commercial matters, signed at Lugano on 16 September 1988, takes effect with regard to France and the Swiss Confederation, this Convention shall not affect the rights granted to Swiss nationals by the Convention between France and the Swiss Confederation on jurisdiction and enforcement of judgments in civil matters, signed at Paris on 15 June 1869.

Article 59

This Convention shall not prevent a Contracting State from assuming, in a convention on the recognition and enforcement of judgments, an obligation towards a third State not to recognize judgments given in other Contracting States against defendants domiciled or habitually resident in the third State where, in cases provided for in Article 4, the judgment could only be founded on a ground of jurisdiction specified in the second paragraph of Article 3.

However, a Contracting State may not assume an obligation towards a third State not to recognize a judgment given in another Contracting State by a court basing its jurisdiction on the presence within that State of property belonging to the defendant, or the seizure by the plaintiff of property situated there:

1. if the action is brought to assert or declare proprietary or possessory rights in that property, seeks to obtain authority to dispose of it, or arises from another issue relating to such property; or

2. if the property constitutes the security for a debt which is the subject-matter of the action.[60]

Title VIII
FINAL PROVISIONS

Article 60

. . .[61]

Article 61[62]

This Convention shall be ratified by the signatory States. The instruments of ratification shall be deposited with the Secretary-General of the Council of the European Communities.

---

59 Text as amended by Article 20 of the 1989 Accession Convention.

60 Second subparagraph added by Article 26 of the 1978 Accession Convention.

61 Article 21 of the 1989 Accession Convention provides for the deletion of Article 60 as amended by Article 27 of the 1978 Convention.

62 Ratification of the 1978 and 1982 Accession Conventions was governed by Articles 38 and 14 of those Conventions. The ratification of the 1989 Accession Convention is governed by Article 31 of that Convention, which reads as follows:
'*Article 31*
This Convention shall be ratified by the signatory States. The instruments of ratification shall be deposited with the Secretary-General of the Council of the European Communities.'

Article 62[63]

This Convention shall enter into force on the first day of the third month following the deposit of the instrument of ratification by the last signatory State to take this step.

Article 63

The Contracting States recognize that any State which becomes a member of the European Economic Community shall be required to accept this Convention as a basis for the negotiations between the Contracting States and that State necessary to ensure the implementation of the last paragraph of Article 220 of the Treaty establishing the European Economic Community.

The necessary adjustments may be the subject of a special convention between the Contracting States of one part and the new Member States of the other part.

Article 64[64]

The Secretary-General of the Council of the European Communities shall notify the signatory States of:

(a) the deposit of each instrument of ratification;

(b) the date of entry into force of this Convention;

(c) . . .[65]

(d) any declaration received pursuant to Article IV of the Protocol;

(e) any communication made pursuant to Article VI of the Protocol.

Article 65

The Protocol annexed to this Convention by common accord of the Contracting States shall form an integral part thereof.

---

63 The entry into force of the 1978 and 1982 Accession Conventions was governed by Articles 39 and 15 of those Conventions.
The entry into force of the 1989 Accession Convention is governed by Article 32 of that Convention, which reads as follows:
'*Article 32*
1. This Convention shall enter into force on the first day of the third month following the date on which two signatory States, of which one is the Kingdom of Spain or the Portuguese Republic, deposit their instruments of ratification.
2. This Convention shall take effect in relation to any other signatory State on the first day of the third month following the deposit of its instrument of ratification.'

64 Notification concerning the 1978 and 1982 Accession Conventions is governed by Articles 40 and 16 of those Conventions.
Notification concerning the 1989 Accession Convention is governed by Article 33 of that Convention, which reads as follows:
'*Article 33*
The Secretary-General of the Council of the European Communities shall notify the signatory States of:
(a) the deposit of each instrument of ratification;
(b) the dates of entry into force of this Convention for the Contracting States.'

65 Article 22 of the 1989 Accession Convention provides for the deletion of letter (c) as amended by Article 28 of the 1978 Accession Convention.

Article 66

This Convention is concluded for an unlimited period.

Article 67

Any Contracting State may request the revision of this Convention. In this event, a revision conference shall be convened by the President of the Council of the European Communities.

Article 68[66]

This Convention, drawn up in a single original in the Dutch, French, German and Italian languages, all four texts being equally authentic, shall be deposited in the archives of the Secretariat of the Council of the European Communities. The Secretary-General shall transmit a certified copy to the Government of each signatory State.[67]

---

66 An indication of the authentic texts of the Accession Conventions is to be found in the following provisions:
— with regard to the 1978 Accession Convention, in Article 41 of that Convention, which reads as follows:
'*Article 41*
This Convention, drawn up in a single original in the Danish, Dutch, English, French, German, Irish and Italian languages, all seven texts being equally authentic, shall be deposited in the archives of the Secretariat of the Council of the European Communities. The Secretary-General shall transmit a certified copy to the Government of each signatory State.'
— with regard to the 1982 Accession Convention, in Article 17 of that Convention, which reads as follows:
'*Article 17*
This Convention, drawn up in a single original in the Danish, Dutch, English, French, German, Greek, Irish and Italian languages, all eight texts being equally authentic, shall be deposited in the archives of the General Secretariat of the Council of the European Communities. The Secretary-General shall transmit a certified copy to the Government of each signatory State.'
— with regard to the 1989 Accession Convention, in Article 34 of that Convention, which reads as follows:
'*Article 34*
This Convention, drawn up in a single original in the Danish, Dutch, English, French, German, Greek, Irish, Italian, Portuguese and Spanish languages, all 10 texts being equally authentic, shall be deposited in the archives of the General Secretariat of the Council of the European Communities. The Secretary-General shall transmit a certified copy to the Government of each signatory State.'

67 Legal backing for the drawing-up of the authentic texts of the 1968 Convention in the official languages of the acceding Member States is to be found:
— with regard to the 1978 Accession Convention, in Article 37 of that Convention, which reads as follows:
'*Article 37*
The Secretary-General of the Council of the European Communities shall transmit a certified copy of the 1968 Convention and of the 1971 Protocol in the Dutch, French, German and Italian languages to the Governments of the Kingdom of Denmark, Ireland and the United Kingdom of Great Britain and Northern Ireland.
The texts of the 1968 Convention and the 1971 Protocol, drawn up in the Danish, English and Irish languages, shall be annexed to this Convention. The texts drawn up in the Danish, English and Irish languages shall be authentic under the same conditions as the original texts of the 1968 Convention and the 1971 Protocol.'
— with regard to the 1982 Accession Convention, in Article 13 of that Convention, which reads as follows:
'*Article 13*
The Secretary-General of the Council of the European Communities shall transmit a certified copy of the 1968 Convention, of the 1971 Protocol and of the 1978 Convention in the Danish, Dutch, English, French, German, Irish and Italian languages to the Government of the Hellenic Republic.
The texts of the 1968 Convention, of the 1971 Protocol and of the 1978 Convention, drawn up in the Greek language, shall be annexed to this Convention. The texts drawn up in the Greek language shall be authentic under the same conditions as the other texts of the 1968 Convention, the 1971 Protocol and the 1978 Convention.'
— with regard to the 1989 Accession Convention, in Article 30 of that Convention, which reads as follows:
'*Article 30*
1. The Secretary-General of the Council of the European Communities shall transmit a certified copy of

the 1968 Convention, of the 1971 Protocol, of the 1978 Convention and of the 1982 Convention in the Danish, Dutch, English, French, German, Greek, Irish and Italian languages to the Governments of the Kingdom of Spain and of the Portuguese Republic.

2. The texts of the 1968 Convention, of the 1971 Protocol, of the 1978 Convention and of the 1982 Convention, drawn up in the Portuguese and Spanish languages, are set out in Annexes II, III, IV and V to this Convention. The texts drawn up in the Portuguese and Spanish languages shall be authentic under the same conditions as the other texts of the 1968 Convention, the 1971 Protocol, the 1978 Convention and the 1982 Convention.

CONVENTION ON JURISDICTION AND THE ENFORCEMENT OF JUDGMENTS IN CIVIL AND COMMERCIAL MATTERS

Done at Lugano on 16 September 1988

PREAMBLE

THE HIGH CONTRACTING PARTIES TO THIS CONVENTION,

ANXIOUS to strengthen in their territories the legal protection of persons therein established,

CONSIDERING that it is necessary for this purpose to determine the international jurisdiction of their courts, to facilitate recognition and to introduce an expeditious procedure for securing the enforcement of judgments, authentic instruments and court settlements,

AWARE of the links between them, which have been sanctioned in the economic field by the free trade agreements concluded between the European Economic Community and the States members of the European Free Trade Association,

TAKING INTO ACCOUNT the Brussels Convention of 27 September 1968 on jurisdiction and the enforcement of judgments in civil and commercial matters, as amended by the Accession Conventions under the successive enlargements of the European Communities,

PERSUADED that the extension of the principles of that Convention to the States parties to this instrument will strengthen legal and economic cooperation in Europe,

DESIRING to ensure as uniform an interpretation as possible of this instrument,

HAVE in this spirit DECIDED to conclude this Convention and

HAVE AGREED AS FOLLOWS:

TITLE I
SCOPE

Article 1

This Convention shall apply in civil and commercial matters whatever the nature of the court or tribunal. It shall not extend, in particular, to revenue, customs or administrative matters.

The Convention shall not apply to:

1. the status or legal capacity of natural persons, rights in property arising out of a matrimonial relationship, wills and succession;
2. bankruptcy, proceedings relating to the winding-up of insolvent companies or other legal persons, judicial arrangements, compositions and analogous proceedings;
3. social security;
4. arbitration.

TITLE II
JURISDICTION

Section 1
General provisions

Article 2

Subject to the provisions of this Convention, persons domiciled in a Contracting State shall, whatever their nationality, be sued in the courts of that State.

Persons who are not nationals of the State in which they are domiciled shall be governed by the rules of jurisdiction applicable to Article 3 nationals of that State.

Persons domiciled in a Contracting State may be sued in the courts of another Contracting State only by virtue of the rules set out in Sections 2 to 6 of this Title.

In particular the following provisions shall not be applicable as against them:

- in Belgium: Article 15 of the civil code (Code civil-Burgerlijk Wetboek) and Article 638 of the judicial code (Code judiciaire-Gerechtelijk Wetboek),
- in Denmark: Article 246 (2) and (3) of the law on civil procedure (Lov om rettens pleje),
- in the Federal Republic of Germany: Article 23 of the code of civil procedure (Zivilpozeßordnung),
- in Greece: Article 40 of the code of civil procedure
- in France: Articles 14 and 15 of the civil code (Code civil),
- in Ireland: the rules which enable jurisdiction to be founded on the document instituting the proceedings having been served on the defendant during his temporary presence in Ireland,
- in Iceland: Article 77 of the Civil Proceedings Act (lög um me_fer_ einkamála í héra_i),
- in Italy: Articles 2 and 4, Nos 1 and 2 of the code of civil procedure (Codice di procedura civile),
- in Luxembourg: Articles 14 and 15 of the civil code (Code civil),
- in the Netherlands: Articles 126 (3) and 127 of the code of civil procedure (Wetboek van Burgerlijke Rechtsvordering),
- in Norway: Section 32 of the Civil Proceedings Act (tvistemålsloven),
- in Austria: Article 99 of the Law on Court Jurisdiction (Jurisdiktionsnorm)
- in Portugal: Articles 65 (1) (c), 65 (2) and 65A (c) of the code of civil procedure (Código de Processo Civil) and Article 11 of the code of labour procedure (Código de Processo de Trabalho),
- in Switzerland: le for du lieu du séquestre/Gerichtsstand des Arrestortes/foro del luogo del sequestro within the meaning of Article 4 of the loi fédérale sur le droit international privé/Bundesgesetz über das internationale Privatrecht/legge federale sul diritto internazionale privato,
- in Finland: the second, third and fourth sentences of Section 1 of Chapter 10 of the Code of Judicial Procedure (oikeudenkäymiskaari/rättegångsbalken),

- in Sweden: the first sentence of Section 3 of Chapter 10 of the Code of Judicial Procedure (Rättegångsbalken),
- in the United Kingdom: the rules which enable jurisdiction to be founded on:
  - (a) the document instituting the proceedings having been served on the defendant during his temporary presence in the United Kingdom; or
  - (b) the presence within the United Kingdom of property belonging to the defendant; or
  - (c) the seizure by the plaintiff of property situated in the United Kingdom.

Article 4

If the defendant is not domiciled in a Contracting State, the jurisdiction of the courts of each Contracting State shall, subject to the provisions of Article 16, be determined by the law of that State.

As against such a defendant, any person domiciled in a Contracting State may, whatever his nationality, avail himself in that State of the rules of jurisdiction there in force, and in particular those specified in the second paragraph of Article 3, in the same way as the nationals of that State.

Section 2
Special jurisdiction

Article 5

A person domiciled in a Contracting State may, in another Contracting State, be sued:

1. in matters relating to a contract, in the courts for the place of performance of the obligation in question; in matters relating to individual contracts of employment, this place is that where the employee habitually carries out his work, or if the employee does not habitually carry out his work in any one country, this place shall be the place of business through which he was engaged;
2. in matters relating to maintenance, in the courts for the place where the maintenance creditor is domiciled or habitually resident or, if the matter is ancillary to proceedings concerning the status of a person, in the court which, according to its own law, has jurisdiction to entertain those proceedings, unless that jurisdiction is based solely on the nationality of one of the parties;
3. in matters relating to tort, delict or quasi-delict, in the courts for the place where the harmful event occurred;
4. as regards a civil claim for damages or restitution which is based on an act giving rise to criminal proceedings, in the court seised of those proceedings, to the extent that that court has jurisdiction under its own law to entertain civil proceedings;
5. as regards a dispute arising out of the operations of a branch, agency or other establishment, in the courts for the place in which the branch, agency or other establishment is situated;
6. in his capacity as settlor, trustee or beneficiary of a trust created by the operation of a statute, or by a written instrument, or created orally and evidenced in writing, in the courts of the Contracting State in which the trust is domiciled;

7. as regards a dispute concerning the payment of remuneration claimed in respect of the salvage of a cargo or freight, in the court under the authority of which the cargo or freight in question:

   (a) has been arrested to secure such payment,

   or

   (b) could have been so arrested, but bail or other security has been given;

   provided that this provision shall apply only if it is claimed that the defendant has an interest in the cargo or freight or had such an interest at the time of salvage.

Article 6

A person domiciled in a Contracting State may also be sued:

1. where he is one of a number of defendants, in the courts for the place where any one of them is domiciled;
2. as a third party in an action on a warranty or guarantee or in any other third party proceedings, in the court seised of the original proceedings, unless these were instituted solely with the object of removing him from the jurisdiction of the court which would be competent in his case;
3. on a counterclaim arising from the same contract or facts on which the original claim was based, in the court in which the original claim is pending;
4. in matters relating to a contract, if the action may be combined with an action against the same defendant in matters relating to rights *in rem* in immovable property, in the court of the Contracting State in which the property is situated.

Article 6A

Where by virtue of this Convention a court of a Contracting State has jurisdiction in actions relating to liability arising from the use or operation of a ship, that court, or any other court substituted for this purpose by the internal law of that State, shall also have jurisdiction over claims for limitation of such liability.

Section 3
Jurisdiction in matters relating to insurance

Article 7

In matters relating to insurance, jurisdiction shall be determined by this Section, without prejudice to the provisions of Articles 4 and 5 (5).

Article 8

An insurer domiciled in a Contracting State may be sued:

1. in the courts of the State where he is domiciled; or
2. in another Contracting State, in the courts for the place where the policy-holder is domiciled; or
3. if he is a co-insurer, in the courts of a Contracting State in which proceedings are brought against the leading insurer.

An insurer who is not domiciled in a Contracting State but has a branch, agency or other establishment in one of the Contracting States shall, in disputes arising out of the operations of the branch, agency or establishment, be deemed to be domiciled in that State.

Article 9

In respect of liability insurance or insurance of immovable property, the insurer may in addition be sued in the courts for the place where the harmful event occurred. The same applies if movable and immovable property are covered by the same insurance policy and both are adversely affected by the same contingency.

Article 10

In respect of liability insurance, the insurer may also, if the law of the court permits it, be joined in proceedings which the injured party has brought against the insured.

The provisions of Articles 7, 8 and 9 shall apply to actions brought by the injured party directly against the insurer, where such direct actions are permitted.

If the law governing such direct actions provides that the policy-holder or the insured may be joined as a party to the action, the same court shall have jurisdiction over them.

Article 11

Without prejudice to the provisions of the third paragraph of Article 10, an insurer may bring proceedings only in the courts of the Contracting State in which the defendant is domiciled, irrespective of whether he is the policy-holder, the insured or a beneficiary.

The provisions of this Section shall not affect the right to bring a counterclaim in the court in which, in accordance with this Section, the original claim is pending.

Article 12

The provisions of this Section may be departed from only by an agreement on jurisdiction:

1. which is entered into after the dispute has arisen; or
2. which allows the policy-holder, the insured or a beneficiary to bring proceedings in courts other than those indicated in this Section; or
3. which is concluded between a policy-holder and an insurer, both of whom are at the time of conclusion of the contract domiciled or habitually resident in the same Contracting State, and which has the effect of conferring jurisdiction on the courts of that State even if the harmful event were to occur abroad, provided that such an agreement is not contrary to the law of the State; or
4. which is concluded with a policy-holder who is not domiciled in a Contracting State, except in so far as the insurance is compulsory or relates to immovable property in a Contracting State; or
5. which relates to a contract of insurance in so far as it covers one or more of the risks set out in Article 12A.

Article 12A

The following are the risks referred to in Article 12 (5):

1. any loss of or damage to:

(a) sea-going ships, installations situated off shore or on the high seas, or aircraft, arising from perils which relate to their use for commercial purposes;

(b) goods in transit other than passengers' baggage where the transit consists of or includes carriage by such ships or aircraft;

2. any liability, other than for bodily injury to passengers or loss of or damage to their baggage;

(a) arising out of the use or operation of ships, installations or aircraft as referred to in (1) (a) above in so far as the law of the Contracting State in which such aircraft are registered does not prohibit agreements on jurisdiction regarding insurance of such risks;

(b) for loss or damage caused by goods in transit as described in (1) (b) above;

3. any financial loss connected with the use or operation of ships, installations or aircraft as referred to in (1) (a) above, in particular loss of freight or charter-hire;

4. any risk or interest connected with any of those referred to in (1) to (3) above.

Section 4
Jurisdiction over consumer contracts

Article 13

In proceedings concerning a contract concluded by a person for a purpose which can be regarded as being outside his trade or profession, hereinafter called 'the consumer', jurisdiction shall be determined by this Section, without prejudice to the provisions of Articles 4 and 5 (5), if it is:

1. a contract for the sale of goods on instalment credit terms; or

2. a contract for a loan repayable by instalments, or for any other form of credit, made to finance the sale of goods; or

3. any other contract for the supply of goods or a contract for the supply of services, and

(a) in the State of the consumer's domicile the conclusion of the contract was preceded by a specific invitation addressed to him or by advertising, and

(b) the consumer took in that State the steps necessary for the conclusion of the contract.

Where a consumer enters into a contract with a party who is not domiciled in a Contracting State but has a branch, agency or other establishment in one of the Contracting States, that party shall, in disputes arising out of the operations of the branch, agency or establishment, be deemed to be domiciled in that State.

This Section shall not apply to contracts of transport.

Article 14

A consumer may bring proceedings against the other party to a contract either in the courts of the Contracting State in which that party is domiciled or in the courts of the Contracting State in which he is himself domiciled.

Proceedings may be brought against a consumer by the other party to the contract only in the courts of the Contracting State in which the consumer is domiciled.

These provisions shall not affect the right to bring a counterclaim in the court in which, in accordance with this Section, the original claim is pending.

Article 15

The provisions of this Section may be departed from only by an agreement:

1. which is entered into after the dispute has arisen; or
2. which allows the consumer to bring proceedings in courts other than those indicated in this Section; or
3. which is entered into by the consumer and the other party to the contract, both of whom are at the time of conclusion of the contract domiciled or habitually resident in the same Contracting State, and which confers jurisdiction on the courts of that State, provided that such an agreement is not contrary to the law of that State.

Section 5
Exclusive jurisdiction

Article 16

The following courts shall have exclusive jurisdiction, regardless of domicile:

1. 27

(a) in proceedings which have as their object rights *in rem* in immovable property or tenancies of immovable property, the courts of the Contracting State in which the property is situated;

(b) however, in proceedings which have as their object tenancies of immovable property concluded for temporary private use for a maximum period of six consecutive months, the courts of the Contracting State in which the defendant is domiciled shall also have jurisdiction, provided that the tenant is a natural person and neither party is domiciled in the Contracting State in which the property is situated;

2. in proceedings which have as their object the validity of the constitution, the nullity or the dissolution of companies or other legal persons or associations of natural or legal persons, or the decisions of their organs, the courts of the Contracting State in which the company, legal person or association has its seat;
3. in proceedings which have as their object the validity of entries in public registers, the courts of the Contracting State in which the register is kept;
4. in proceedings concerned with the registration or validity of patents, trade marks, designs, or other similar rights required to be deposited or registered, the courts of the Contracting State in which the deposit or registration has been applied for, has taken place or is under the terms of an international convention deemed to have taken place;
5. in proceedings concerned with the enforcement of judgments, the courts of the Contracting State in which the judgment has been or is to be enforced.

Section 6
Prorogation of jurisdiction

Article 17

1. If the parties, one or more of whom is domiciled in a Contracting State, have agreed that a court or the courts of a Contracting State are to have jurisdiction to settle any disputes which have arisen or which may arise in connection with a particular legal relationship, that court or those courts shall have exclusive jurisdiction. Such an agreement conferring jurisdiction shall be either:

(a) in writing or evidenced in writing, or

(b) in a form which accords with practices which the parties have established between themselves, or

(c) in international trade or commerce, in a form which accords with a usage of which the parties are or ought to have been aware and which in such trade or commerce is widely known to, and regularly observed by, parties to contracts of the type involved in the particular trade or commerce concerned.

Where such an agreement is concluded by parties, none of whom is domiciled in a Contracting State, the courts of other Contracting States shall have no jurisdiction over their disputes unless the court or courts chosen have declined jurisdiction.

2. The court or courts of a Contracting State on which a trust instrument has conferred jurisdiction shall have exclusive jurisdiction in any proceedings brought against a settlor, trustee or beneficiary, if relations between these persons or their rights or obligations under the trust are involved.

3. Agreements or provisions of a trust instrument conferring jurisdiction shall have no legal force if they are contrary to the provisions of Article 12 or 15, or if the courts whose jurisdiction they purport to exclude have exclusive jurisdiction by virtue of Article 16.

4. If an agreement conferring jurisdiction was concluded for the benefit of only one of the parties, that party shall retain the right to bring proceedings in any other court which has jurisdiction by virtue of this Convention.

5. In matters relating to individual contracts of employment an agreement conferring jurisdiction shall have legal force only if it is entered into after the dispute has arisen.

Article 18

Apart from jurisdiction derived from other provisions of this Convention, a court of a Contracting State before whom a defendant enters an appearance shall have jurisdiction. This rule shall not apply where appearance was entered solely to contest the jurisdiction, or where another court has exclusive jurisdiction by virtue of Article 16.

Section 7
Examination as to jurisdiction and admissibility

Article 19

Where a court of a Contracting State is seised of a claim which is principally concerned with a matter over which the courts of another Contracting State have exclusive jurisdiction by virtue of Article 16, it shall declare of its own motion that it has no jurisdiction.

Article 20

Where a defendant domiciled in one Contracting State is sued in a court of another Contracting State and does not enter an appearance, the court shall declare of its own motion that it has no jurisdiction unless its jurisdiction is derived from the provisions of this Convention.

The court shall stay the proceedings so long as it is not shown that the defendant has been able to receive the document instituting the proceedings or an equivalent document in sufficient time to enable him to arrange for his defence, or that all necessary steps have been taken to this end.

The provisions of the foregoing paragraph shall be replaced by those of Article 15 of the Hague Convention of 15 November 1965 on the service abroad of judicial and extrajudicial documents in civil or commercial matters, if the document instituting the proceedings or notice thereof had to be transmitted abroad in accordance with that Convention.

Section 8
Lis Pendens - related actions

Article 21

Where proceedings involving the same cause of action and between the same parties are brought in the courts of different Contracting States, any court other than the court first seised shall of its own motion stay its proceedings until such time as the jurisdiction of the court first seised is established.

Where the jurisdiction of the court first seised is established, any court other than the court first seised shall decline jurisdiction in favour of that court.

Article 22

Where related actions are brought in the courts of different Contracting States, any court other than the court first seised may, while the actions are pending at first instance, stay its proceedings.

A court other than the court first seised may also, on the application of one of the parties, decline jurisdiction if the law of that court permits the consolidation of related actions and the court first seised has jurisdiction over both actions.

For the purposes of this Article, actions are deemed to be related where they are so closely connected that it is expedient to hear and determine them together to avoid the risk of irreconcilable judgments resulting from separate proceedings.

Article 23

Where actions come within the exclusive jurisdiction of several courts, any court other than the court first seised shall decline jurisdiction in favour of that court.

Section 9
Provisional, including protective, measures

Article 24

Application may be made to the courts of a Contracting State for such provisional, including protective, measures as may be available under the law of that State, even if, under this Convention, the courts of another Contracting State have jurisdiction as to the substance of the matter.

TITLE III
RECOGNITION AND ENFORCEMENT

Article 25

For the purposes of this Convention, 'judgment' means any judgment given by a court or tribunal of a Contracting State, whatever the judgment may be called, including a decree, order, decision or writ of execution, as well as the determination of costs or expenses by an officer of the court.

Section 1
Recognition

Article 26

A judgment given in a Contracting State shall be recognized in the other Contracting States without any special procedure being required.

Any interested party who raises the recognition of a judgment as the principal issue in a dispute may, in accordance with the procedures provided for in Section 2 and 3 of this Title, apply for a decision that the judgment be recognized.

If the outcome of proceedings in a court of a Contracting State depends on the determination of an incidental question of recognition that court shall have jurisdiction over that question.

Article 27

A judgment shall not be recognized:

1. if such recognition is contrary to public policy in the State in which recognition is sought;
2. where it was given in default of appearance, if the defendant was not duly served with the document which instituted the proceedings or with an equivalent document in sufficient time to enable him to arrange for his defence;
3. if the judgment is irreconcilable with a judgment given in a dispute between the same parties in the State in which recognition is sought;
4. if the court of the State of origin, in order to arrive at its judgment, has decided a preliminary question concerning the status or legal capacity of natural persons, rights in property arising out of a matrimonial relationship, wills or succession in a way that conflicts with a rule of the private international law of the State in which the recognition is sought, unless the same result would have been reached by the application of the rules of private international law of that State;
5. if the judgment is irreconcilable with an earlier judgment given in a non-contracting State involving the same cause of action and between the same parties, provided that this latter judgment fulfils the conditions necessary for its recognition in the State addressed.

Article 28

Moreover, a judgment shall not be recognized if it conflicts with the provisions of Sections 3, 4 or 5 of Title II or in a case provided for in Article 59.

A judgment may furthermore be refused recognition in any case provided for in Article 54B (3) or 57 (4).

In its examination of the grounds of jurisdiction referred to in the foregoing paragraphs, the court or authority applied to shall be bound by the findings of fact on which the court of the State of origin based its jurisdiction.

Subject to the provisions of the first and second paragraphs, the jurisdiction of the court of the State of origin may not be reviewed; the test of public policy referred to in Article 27 (1) may not be applied to the rules relating to jurisdiction.

Article 29

Under no circumstances may a foreign judgment be reviewed as to its substance.

Article 30

A court of a Contracting State in which recognition is sought of a judgment given in another Contracting State may stay the proceedings if an ordinary appeal against the judgment has been lodged.

A court of a Contracting State in which recognition is sought of a judgment given in Ireland or the United Kingdom may stay the proceedings if enforcement is suspended in the State of origin by reason of an appeal.

Section 2
Enforcement

Article 31

A judgment given in a Contracting State and enforceable in that State shall be enforced in another Contracting State when, on the application of any interested party, it has been declared enforceable there.

However, in the United Kingdom, such a judgment shall be enforced in England and Wales, in Scotland, or in Northern Ireland when, on the application of any interested party, it has been registered for enforcement in that part of the United Kingdom.

Article 32

1. The application shall be submitted:

- in Belgium, to the tribunal de première instance or rechtbank van eerste aanleg,
- in Denmark, to the byret,
- in the Federal Republic of Germany, to the presiding judge of a chamber of the Landgericht,
- in Greece, to the Monomeles protodikeio,
- in Spain, to the Juzgado de Primera Instancia,
- in France, to the presiding judge of the tribunal de grande instance,
- in Ireland, to the High Court,

- in Iceland, to the héra_sdómari,
- in Italy, to the corte d'appello,
- in Luxembourg, to the presiding judge of the tribunal d'arrondissement,
- in the Netherlands, to the presiding judge of the arrondissementsrechtbank,
- in Norway, to the herredsrett or byrett as namsrett,
- in Austria, to the Landesgericht or the Kreisgericht,
- in Portugal, to the Tribunal Judicial de Círculo,
- in Switzerland:

  (a) in respect of judgments ordering the payment of a sum of money, to the juge de la mainlevée / Rechtsöffnungsrichter / giudice competente a pronunciare sul rigetto dell'opposizione, within the framework of the procedure governed by Articles 80 and 81 of the loi fédérale sur la poursuite pour dettes et la faillite / Bundesgesetz über Schuldbetreibung und Konkurs / legge federale sulla esecuzione e sul fallimento;

  (b) in respect of judgments ordering a performance other than the payment of a sum of money, to the juge cantonal d'exequatur compétent / zuständiger kantonaler Vollstreckungsrichter / giudice cantonale competente a pronunciare l'exequatur,

- in Finland, to the ulosotonhaltija / överexekutor,
- in Sweden, to the Svea hovrätt,
- in the United Kingdom:

  (a) in England and Wales, to the High Court of Justice, or in the case of a maintenance judgment to the Magistrates' Court on transmission by the Secretary of State;

  (b) in Scotland, to the Court of Session, or in the case of a maintenance judgment to the Sheriff Court on transmission by the Secretary of State;

  (c) in Northern Ireland, to the High Court of Justice, or in the case of a maintenance judgment to the Magistrates' Court on transmission by the Secretary of State.

2. The jurisdiction of local courts shall be determined by reference to the place of domicile of the party against whom enforcement is sought. If he is not domiciled in the State in which enforcement is sought, it shall be determined by reference to the place of enforcement.

Article 33

The procedure for making the application shall be governed by the law of the State in which enforcement is sought.

The applicant must give an address for service of process within the area of jurisdiction of the court applied to. However, if the law of the State in which enforcement is sought does not provide for the furnishing of such an address, the applicant shall appoint a representative *ad litem*.

The documents referred to in Articles 46 and 47 shall be attached to the application.

Article 34

The court applied to shall give its decision without delay; the party against whom enforcement is sought shall not at this stage of the proceedings be entitled to make any submissions on the application.

The application may be refused only for one of the reasons specified in Articles 27 and 28.

Under no circumstances may the foreign judgment be reviewed as to its substance.

Article 35

The appropriate officer of the court shall without delay bring the decision given on the application to the notice of the applicant in accordance with the procedure laid down by the law of the State in which enforcement is sought.

Article 36

If enforcement is authorized, the party against whom enforcement is sought may appeal against the decision within one month of service thereof.

If that party is domiciled in a Contracting State other than that in which the decision authorizing enforcement was given, the time for appealing shall be two months and shall run from the date of service, either on him in person or at his residence. No extension of time may be granted on account of distance.

Article 37

1. An appeal against the decision authorizing enforcement shall be lodged in accordance with the rules governing procedure in contentious matters:

- in Belgium, with the tribunal de première instance or rechtsbank van eerste aanleg,
- in Denmark, with the landsret,
- in the Federal Republic of Germany, with the Oberlandesgericht,
- in Greece, with the epheteio,
- in Spain, with the Audiencia Provincial,
- in France, with the cour d'appel,
- in Ireland, with the High Court,
- in Iceland, with the héra_sdómari,
- in Italy, with the corte d'appello,
- in Luxembourg, with the Cour supérieure de justice sitting as a court of civil appeal,
- in the Netherlands, with the arrondissementsrechtsbank,
- in Norway, with the lagmannsrett,
- in Austria, with the Landesgericht or the Kreisgericht,
- in Portugal, with the Tribunal da Relação,
- in Switzerland, with the tribunal cantonal / Kantonsgericht / tribunale cantonale,
- in Finland, with the hovioikeus / hovrätt,
- in Sweden, with the Svea hovrätt,
- in the United Kingdom:

(a) in England and Wales, with the High Court of Justice, or in the case of a maintenance judgment with the Magistrates' Court;

(b) in Scotland, with the Court of Session, or in the case of a maintenance judgment with the Sheriff Court;

(c) in Northern Ireland, with the High Court of Justice, or in the case of a maintenance judgment with the Magistrates' Court.

2. The judgment given on the appeal may be contested only:

- in Belgium, Greece, Spain, France, Italy, Luxembourg and in the Netherlands, by an appeal in cassation,
- in Denmark, by an appeal to the højesteret, with the leave of the Minister of Justice,
- in the Federal Republic of Germany, by a Rechtsbeschwerde,
- in Ireland, by an appeal on a point of law to the Supreme Court,
- in Iceland, by an appeal to the Hæstiréttur,
- in Norway, by an appeal (kjæremål or anke) to the Hoyesteretts Kjæremålsutvalg or Hoyesterett,
- in Austria, in the case of an appeal, by a Revisionsrekurs and, in the case of opposition proceedings, by a Berufung with the possibility of a Revision,
- in Portugal, by an appeal on a point of law,
- in Switzerland, by a recours de droit public devant le tribunal fédéral / staatsrechtliche Beschwerde beim Bundesgericht / ricorso di diritto pubblico davanti al tribunale federale,
- in Finland, by an appeal to the korkein oikeus / högsta domstolen,
- in Sweden, by an appeal to the högsta domstolen,
- in the United Kingdom, by a single further appeal on a point of law.

Article 38

The court with which the appeal under Article 37 (1) is lodged may, on the application of the appellant, stay the proceedings if an ordinary appeal has been lodged against the judgment in the State of origin or if the time for such an appeal has not yet expired; in the latter case, the court may specify the time within which such an appeal is to be lodged.

Where the judgment was given in Ireland or the United Kingdom, any form of appeal available in the State of origin shall be treated as an ordinary appeal for the purposes of the first paragraph.

The court may also make enforcement conditional on the provision of such security as it shall determine.

Article 39

During the time specified for an appeal pursuant to Article 36 and until any such appeal has been determined, no measures of enforcement may be taken other than protective measures taken against the property of the party against whom enforcement is sought.

The decision authorizing enforcement shall carry with it the power to proceed to any such protective measures.

Article 40

1. If the application for enforcement is refused, the applicant may appeal:

- in Belgium, to the cour d'appel or hof van beroep,
- in Denmark, to the landsret,
- in the Federal Republic of Germany, to the Oberlandesgericht,
- in Greece, to the epheteio,
- in Spain, to the Audiencia Provincial,
- in France, to the cour d'appel,
- in Ireland, to the High Court,
- in Iceland, to the héra_sdómari,
- in Italy, to the corte d'appello,
- in Luxembourg, to the Cour supérieure de justice sitting as a court of civil appeal,
- in the Netherlands, to the gerechtshof,
- in Norway, to the lagmannsrett,
- in Austria, to the Landesgericht or the Kreisgericht,
- in Portugal, to the Tribunal da Relação,
- in Switzerland, to the tribunal cantonal / Kantonsgericht / tribunale cantonale,
- in Finland, to the hovioikeus / hovrätt,
- in Sweden, to the Svea hovrätt,
- in the United Kingdom:
  - (a) in England and Wales, to the High Court of Justice, or in the case of a maintenance judgment to the Magistrates' Court;
  - (b) in Scotland, to the Court of Session, or in the case of a maintenance judgment to the Sheriff Court;
  - (c) in Northern Ireland, to the High Court of Justice, or in the case of a maintenance judgment to the Magistrates' Court.

2. The party against whom enforcement is sought shall be summoned to appear before the appellate court. If he fails to appear, the provisions of the second and third paragraphs of Article 20 shall apply even where he is not domiciled in any of the Contracting States.

Article 41

A judgment given on an appeal provided for in Article 40 may be contested only:

- in Belgium, Greece, Spain, France, Italy, Luxembourg and in the Netherlands, by an appeal in cassation,
- in Denmark, by an appeal to the højesteret, with the leave of the Minister of Justice,

- in the Federal Republic of Germany, by a Rechtsbeschwerde,
- in Ireland, by an appeal on a point of law to the Supreme Court,
- in Iceland, by an appeal to the Hæstiréttur,
- in Norway, by an appeal (kjæremål or anke) to the Hoyesteretts kjæremålsutvalg or Hoyesterett,
- in Austria, by a Revisionsrekurs,
- in Portugal, by an appeal on a point of law,
- in Switzerland, by a recours de droit public devant le tribunal fédéral / staatsrechtliche Beschwerde beim Bundesgericht / ricorso di diritto pubblico davanti al tribunale federale,
- in Finland, by an appeal to the korkein oikeus / högsta domstolen,
- in Sweden, by an appeal to the högsta domstolen,
- in the United Kingdom, by a single further appeal on a point of law.

Article 42

Where a foreign judgment has been given in respect of several matters and enforcement cannot be authorized for all of them, the court shall authorize enforcement for one or more of them.

An applicant may request partial enforcement of a judgment.

Article 43

A foreign judgment which orders a periodic payment by way of a penalty shall be enforceable in the State in which enforcement is sought only if the amount of the payment has been finally determined by the courts of the State of origin.

Article 44

An applicant who, in the State of origin, has benefited from complete or partial legal aid or exemption from costs or expenses, shall be entitled, in the procedures provided for in Articles 32 to 35, to benefit from the most favourable legal aids or the most extensive exemption from costs or expenses provided for by the law of the State addressed.

However, an applicant who requests the enforcement of a decision given by an administrative authority in Denmark or in Iceland in respect of a maintenance order may, in the State addressed, claim the benefits referred to in the first paragraph if he presents a statement from, respectively, the Danish Ministry of Justice or the Icelandic Ministry of Justice to the effect that he fulfils the economic requirements to qualify for the grant of complete or partial legal aid or exemption from costs or expenses.

Article 45

No security, bond or deposit, however described, shall be required of a party who in one Contracting State applies for enforcement of a judgment given in another Contracting State on the ground that he is a foreign national or that he is not domiciled or resident in the State in which enforcement is sought.

Section 3
Common provisions

Article 46

A party seeking recognition or applying for enforcement of a judgment shall produce:

1. a copy of the judgment which satisfies the conditions necessary to establish its authenticity;
2. in the case of a judgment given in default, the original or a certified true copy of the document which establishes that the party in default was served with the document instituting the proceedings or with an equivalent document.

Article 47

A party applying for enforcement shall also produce:

1. documents which establish that, according to the law of the State of origin, the judgment is enforceable and has been served;
2. where appropriate, a document showing that the applicant is in receipt of legal aid in the State of origin.

Article 48

If the documents specified in Articles 46 (2) and 47 (2) are not produced, the court may specify a time for their production, accept equivalent documents or, if it considers that it has sufficient information before it, dispense with their production.

If the court so requires, a translation of the document shall be produced; the translation shall be certified by a person qualified to do so in one of the Contracting States.

Article 49

No legalization or other similar formality shall be required in respect of the documents referred to in Articles 46 or 47 or the second paragraph of Article 48, or in respect of a document appointing a representative *ad litem.*

TITLE IV
AUTHENTIC INSTRUMENTS AND COURT SETTLEMENTS

Article 50

A document which has been formally drawn up or registered as an authentic instrument and is enforceable in one Contracting State shall, in another Contracting State, be declared enforceable there, on application made in accordance with the procedures provided for in Article 31 *et seq.* The application may be refused only if enforcement of the instrument is contrary to public policy in the State addressed.

The instrument produced must satisfy the conditions necessary to establish its authenticity in the State of origin.

The provisions of Section 3 of Title III shall apply as appropriate.

Article 51

A settlement which has been approved by a court in the course of proceedings and is enforceable in the State in which it was concluded shall be enforceable in the State addressed under the same conditions as authentic instruments.

TITLE V
GENERAL PROVISIONS

Article 52

In order to determine whether a party is domiciled in the Contracting State whose courts are seised of a matter, the Court shall apply its internal law.

If a party is not domiciled in the State whose courts are seised of the matter, then, in order to determine whether the party is domiciled in another Contracting State, the court shall apply the law of that State.

Article 53

For the purposes of this Convention, the seat of a company or other legal person or association of natural or legal persons shall be treated as its domicile. However, in order to determine that seat, the court shall apply its rules of private international law.

In order to determine whether a trust is domiciled in the Contracting State whose courts are seised of the matter, the court shall apply its rules of private international law.

TITLE VI
TRANSITIONAL PROVISIONS

Article 54

The provisions of this Convention shall apply only to legal proceedings instituted and to documents formally drawn up or registered as authentic instruments after its entry into force in the State of origin and, where recognition or enforcement of a judgment or authentic instrument is sought, in the State addressed.

However, judgments given after the date of entry into force of this Convention between the State of origin and the State addressed in proceedings instituted before that date shall be recognized and enforced in accordance with the provisions of Title III if jurisdiction was founded upon rules which accorded with those provided for either in Title II of this Convention or in a convention concluded between the State of origin and the State addressed which was in force when the proceedings were instituted.

If the parties to a dispute concerning a contract had agreed in writing before the entry into force of this Convention that the contract was to be governed by the law of Ireland or of a part of the United Kingdom, the courts of Ireland or of that part of the United Kingdom shall retain the right to exercise jurisdiction in the dispute.

Article 54A

For a period of three years from the entry into force of this Convention for Denmark, Greece, Ireland, Iceland, Norway, Finland and Sweden, respectively, jurisdiction in maritime matters shall be determined in these States not only in accordance with the provisions of Title II, but also in accordance with the provisions of paragraphs 1 to 7 following. However, upon the entry into force of the International Convention relating to the arrest of sea-going ships, signed at Brussels on 10 May 1952, for one of these States, these provisions shall cease to have effect for that State.

1. A person who is domiciled in a Contracting State may be sued in the courts of one of the States mentioned above in respect of a maritime claim if the ship to which the claim relates or any other ship owned by him has been arrested by judicial process within the territory of the latter State to secure the claim, or could have been so arrested there but bail or other security has been given, and either:

   (a) the claimant is domiciled in the latter State; or

   (b) the claim arose in the latter State; or

   (c) the claim concerns the voyage during which the arrest was made or could have been made; or

   (d) the claim arises out of a collision or out of damage caused by a ship to another ship or to goods or persons on board either ship, either by the execution or non-execution of a manoeuvre or by the non-observance of regulations; or

   (e) the claim is for salvage; or

   (f) the claim is in respect of a mortgage or hypothecation of the ship arrested.

2. A claimant may arrest either the particular ship to which the maritime claim relates, or any other ship which is owned by the person who was, at the time when the maritime claim arose, the owner of the particular ship. However, only the particular ship to which the maritime claim relates may be arrested in respect of the maritime claims set out under 5. (o), (p) or (q) of this Article.

3. Ships shall be deemed to be in the same ownership when all the shares therein are owned by the same person or persons.

4. When in the case of a charter by demise of a ship the charterer alone is liable in respect of a maritime claim relating to that ship, the claimant may arrest that ship or any other ship owned by the charterer, but no other ship owned by the owner may be arrested in respect of such claim. The same shall apply to any case in which a person other than the owner of a ship is liable in respect of a maritime claim relating to that ship.

5. The expression 'maritime claim' means a claim arising out of one or more of the following:

   (a) damage caused by any ship either in collision or otherwise;

   (b) loss of life or personal injury caused by any ship or occurring in connection with the operation on any ship;

   (c) salvage;

   (d) agreement relating to the use or hire of any ship whether by charterparty or otherwise;

   (e) agreement relating to the carriage of goods in any ship whether by charterparty or otherwise;

   (f) loss of or damage to goods including baggage carried in any ship;

   (g) general average;

(h) bottomry;

(i) towage;

(j) pilotage;

(k) goods or materials wherever supplied to a ship for her operation or maintenance;

(l) construction, repair or equipment of any ship or dock charges and dues;

(m) wages of masters, officers or crew;

(n) master's disbursements, including disbursements made by shippers, charterers or agents on behalf of a ship or her owner;

(o) dispute as to the title to or ownership of any ship;

(p) disputes between co-owners of any ship as to the ownership, possession, employment or earnings of that ship;

(q) the mortgage or hypothecation of any ship.

6. In Denmark, the expression 'arrest' shall be deemed as regards the maritime claims referred to under 5. (o) and (p) of this Article, to include a 'forbud', where that is the only procedure allowed in respect of such a claim under Articles 646 to 653 of the law on civil procedure (lov om rettens pleje).

7. In Iceland, the expression 'arrest' shall be deemed, as regards the maritime claims referred to under 5. (o) and (p) of this Article, to include a 'lögbann', where that is the only procedure allowed in respect of such a claim under Chapter III of the law on arrest and injunction (lög um kyrrsetningu og lögbann).

TITLE VII
RELATIONSHIP TO THE BRUSSELS CONVENTION AND TO OTHER CONVENTIONS

Article 54B

1. This Convention shall not prejudice the application by the Member States of the European Communities of the Convention on Jurisdiction and the Enforcement of Judgments in Civil and Commercial Matters, signed at Brussels on 27 September 1968 and of the Protocol on interpretation of that Convention by the Court of Justice, signed at Luxembourg on 3 June 1971, as amended by the Conventions of Accession to the said Convention and the said Protocol by the States acceding to the European Communities, all of these Conventions and the Protocol being hereinafter referred to as the 'Brussels Convention'.

2. However, this Convention shall in any event be applied:

(a) in matters of jurisdiction, where the defendant is domiciled in the territory of a Contracting State which is not a member of the European Communities, or where Article 16 or 17 of this Convention confer a jurisdiction on the courts of such a Contracting State;

(b) in relation to a *lis pendens* or to related actions as provided for in Articles 21 and 22, when proceedings are instituted in a Contracting State which is not a member of the European Communities and in a Contracting State which is a member of the European Communities;

(c) in matters of recognition and enforcement, where either the State of origin or the State addressed is not a member of the European Communities.

3. In addition to the grounds provided for in Title III recognition or enforcement may be refused if the ground of jurisdiction on which the judgment has been based differs from that resulting from this Convention and recognition or enforcement is sought against a party who is domiciled in a Contracting State which is not a member of the European Communities, unless the judgment may otherwise be recognized or enforced under any rule of law in the State addressed.

Article 55

Subject to the provisions of Articles 54 (2) and 56, this Convention shall, for the States which are parties to it, supersede the following conventions concluded between two or more of them:

- the Convention between the Swiss Confederation and France on jurisdiction and enforcement of judgments in civil matters, signed at Paris on 15 June 1869,
- the Treaty between the Swiss Confederation and Spain on the mutual enforcement of judgments in civil or commercial matters, signed at Madrid on 19 November 1896,
- the Convention between the Swiss Confederation and the German Reich on the recognition and enforcement of judgments and arbitration awards, signed at Berne on 2 November 1929,
- the Convention between Denmark, Finland, Iceland, Norway and Sweden on the recognition and enforcement of judgments, signed at Copenhagen on 16 March 1932,
- the Convention between the Swiss Confederation and Italy on the recognition and enforcement of judgments, signed at Rome on 3 January 1933,
- the Convention between Sweden and the Swiss Confederation on the recognition and enforcement of judgments and arbitral awards signed at Stockholm on 15 January 1936,
- the Convention between the Kingdom of Belgium and Austria on the reciprocal recognition and enforcement of judgments and authentic instruments relating to maintenance obligations, signed at Vienna on 25 October 1957,
- the Convention between the Swiss Confederation and Belgium on the recognition and enforcement of judgments and arbitration awards, signed at Berne on 29 April 1959,
- the Convention between the Federal Republic of Germany and Austria on the reciprocal recognition and enforcement of judgments, settlements and authentic instruments in civil and commercial matters, signed at Vienna on 6 June 1959,
- the Convention between the Kingdom of Belgium and Austria on the reciprocal recognition and enforcement of judgments, arbitral awards and authentic instruments in civil and commercial matters, signed at Vienna on 16 June 1959,
- the Convention between Austria and the Swiss Confederation on the recognition and enforcement of judgments, signed at Berne on 16 December 1960,

- the Convention between Norway and the United Kingdom providing for the reciprocal recognition and enforcement of judgments in civil matters, signed at London on 12 June 1961,
- the Convention between the United Kingdom and Austria providing for the reciprocal recognition and enforcement of judgments in civil and commercial matters, signed at Vienna on 14 July 1961, with amending Protocol signed at London on 6 March 1970,
- the Convention between the Kingdom of the Netherlands and Austria on the reciprocal recognition and enforcement of judgments and authentic instruments in civil and commercial matters, signed at The Hague on 6 February 1963,
- the Convention between France and Austria on the recognition and enforcement of judgments and authentic instruments in civil and commercial matters, signed at Vienna on 15 July 1966,
- the Convention between Luxembourg and Austria on the recognition and enforcement of judgments and authentic instruments in civil and commercial matters, signed at Luxembourg on 29 July 1971,
- the Convention between Italy and Austria on the recognition and enforcement of judgments in civil and commercial matters, of judicial settlements and of authentic instruments, signed at Rome on 16 November 1971,
- the Convention between Norway and the Federal Republic of Germany on the recognition and enforcement of judgments and enforceable documents, in civil and commercial matters, signed at Oslo on 17 June 1977,
- the Convention between Denmark, Finland, Iceland, Norway and Sweden on the recognition and enforcement of judgments in civil matters, signed at Copenhagen on 11 October 1977,
- the Convention between Austria and Sweden on the recognition and enforcement of judgments in civil matters, signed at Stockholm on 16 September 1982,
- the Convention between Austria and Spain on the recognition and enforcement of judgments, settlements and enforceable authentic instruments in civil and commercial matters, signed at Vienna on 17 February 1984,
- the Convention between Norway and Austria on the recognition and enforcement of judgments in civil matters, signed at Vienna on 21 May 1984, and
- the Convention between Finland and Austria on the recognition and enforcement of judgments in civil matters, signed at Vienna on 17 November 1986.

Article 56

The Treaty and the conventions referred to in Article 55 shall continue to have effect in relation to matters to which this Convention does not apply.

They shall continue to have effect in respect of judgments given and documents formally drawn up or registered as authentic instruments before the entry into force of this Convention.

Article 57

1. This Convention shall not affect any conventions to which the Contracting States are or will be parties and which in relation to particular matters, govern jurisdiction or the recognition or enforcement of judgments.

2. This Convention shall not prevent a court of a Contracting State which is party to a convention referred to in the first paragraph from assuming jurisdiction in accordance with that convention, even where the defendant is domiciled in a Contracting State which is not a party to that convention. The court hearing the action shall, in any event, apply Article 20 of this Convention.

3. Judgments given in a Contracting State by a court in the exercise of jurisdiction provided for in a convention referred to in the first paragraph shall be recognized and enforced in the other Contracting States in accordance with Title III of this Convention.

4. In addition to the grounds provided for in Title III, recognition or enforcement may be refused if the State addressed is not a contracting party to a convention referred to in the first paragraph and the person against whom recognition or enforcement is sought is domiciled in that State, unless the judgment may otherwise be recognized or enforced under any rule of law in the State addressed.

5. Where a convention referred to in the first paragraph to which both the State of origin and the State addressed are parties lays down conditions for the recognition or enforcement of judgments, those conditions shall apply. In any event, the provisions of this Convention which concern the procedures for recognition and enforcement of judgments may be applied.

Article 58
(None)

Article 59

This Convention shall not prevent a Contracting State from assuming, in a convention on the recognition and enforcement of judgments, an obligation towards a third State not to recognize judgments given in other Contracting States against defendants domiciled or habitually resident in the third State where, in cases provided for in Article 4, the judgment could only be founded on a ground of jurisdiction specified in the second paragraph of Article 3.

However, a Contracting State may not assume an obligation towards a third State not to recognize a judgment given in another Contracting State by a court basing its jurisdiction on the presence within that State of property belonging to the defendant, or the seizure by the plaintiff of property situated there:

1. if the action is brought to assert or declare proprietary or possessory rights in that property, seeks to obtain authority to dispose of it, or arises from another issue relating to such property, or
2. if the property constitutes the security for a debt which is the subject-matter of the action.

TITLE VIII
FINAL PROVISIONS

Article 60

The following may be parties to this Convention:

(a) States which, at the time of the opening of this Convention for signature, are members of the European Communities or of the European Free Trade Association;

(b) States which, after the opening of this Convention for signature, become members of the European Communities or of the European Free Trade Association;

(c) States invited to accede in accordance with Article 62 (1) (b).

Article 61

1. This Convention shall be opened for signature by the States member of the European Communities or of the European Free Trade Association.

2. The Convention shall be submitted for ratification by the signatory States. The instruments of ratification shall be deposited with the Swiss Federal Council.

3. The Convention shall enter into force on the first day of the third month following the date on which two States, of which one is a member of the European Communities and the other a member of the European Free Trade Association, deposit their instruments of ratification.

4. The Convention shall take effect in relation to any other signatory State on the first day of the third month following the deposit of its instrument of ratification.

Article 62

1. After entering into force this Convention shall be open to accession by:

(a) the States referred to in Article 60 (b);

(b) other States which have been invited to accede upon a request made by one of the Contracting States to the depositary State. The depositary State shall invite the State concerned to accede only if, after having communicated the contents of the communications that this State intends to make in accordance with Article 63, it has obtained the unanimous agreement of the signatory States and the Contracting States referred to in Article 60 (a) and (b).

2. If an acceding State wishes to furnish details for the purposes of Protocol 1, negotiations shall be entered into to that end. A negotiating conference shall be convened by the Swiss Federal Council.

3. In respect of an acceding State, the Convention shall take effect on the first day of the third month following the deposit of its instrument of accession.

4. However, in respect of an acceding State referred to in paragraph 1 (a) or (b), the Convention shall take effect only in relations between the acceding State and the Contracting States which have not made any objections to the accession before the first day of the third month following the deposit of the instrument of accession.

Article 63

Each acceding State shall, when depositing its instrument of accession, communicate the information required for the application of Articles 3, 32, 37, 40, 41 and 55 of this Convention and furnish, if need be, the details prescribed during the negotiations for the purposes of Protocol 1.

Article 64

1. This Convention is concluded for an initial period of five years from the date of its entry into force in accordance with Article 61 (3), even in the case of States which ratify it or accede to it after that date.

2. At the end of the initial five-year period, the Convention shall be automatically renewed from year to year.

3. Upon the expiry of the initial five-year period, any contracting State may, at any time, denounce the Convention by sending a notification to the Swiss Federal Council.

4. The denunciation shall take effect at the end of the calendar year following the expiry of a period of six months from the date of receipt by the Swiss Federal Council of the notification of denunciation.

Article 65

The following are annexed to this Convention:

- a Protocol 1, on certain questions of jurisdiction, procedure and enforcement,
- a Protocol 2, on the uniform interpretation of the Convention,
- a Protocol 3, on the application of Article 57.

These Protocols shall form an integral part of the Convention.

Article 66

Any Contracting State may request the revision of this Convention. To that end, the Swiss Federal Council shall issue invitations to a revision conference within a period of six months from the date of the request for revision.

Article 67

The Swiss Federal Council shall notify the States represented at the Diplomatic Conference of Lugano and the States who have later acceded to the Convention of:

(a) the deposit of each instrument of ratification or accession;

(b) the dates of entry into force of this Convention in respect of the Contracting States;

(c) any denunciation received pursuant to Article 64;

(d) any declaration received pursuant to Article Ia of Protocol 1;

(e) any declaration received pursuant to Article Ib of Protocol 1;

(f) any declaration received pursuant to Article IV of Protocol 1;

(g) any communication made pursuant to Article VI of Protocol 1.

Article 68

This Convention, drawn up in a single original in the Danish, Dutch, English, Finnish, French, German, Greek, Icelandic, Irish, Italian, Norwegian, Portuguese, Spanish and Swedish languages, all fourteen texts being equally authentic, shall be deposited in the archives of the Swiss Federal Council. The Swiss Federal Council shall transmit a certified copy to the Government of each State represented at the Diplomatic Conference of Lugano and to the Government of each acceding State.

PROTOCOL 1

on certain questions of jurisdiction, procedure and enforcement

THE HIGH CONTRACTING PARTIES HAVE AGREED UPON THE FOLLOWING PROVISIONS, WHICH SHALL BE ANNEXED TO THE CONVENTION:

Article I

Any person domiciled in Luxembourg who is sued in a court of another Contracting State pursuant to Article 5 (1) may refuse to submit to the jurisdiction of that court. If the defendant does not enter an appearance the court shall declare of its own motion that it has no jurisdiction.

An agreement conferring jurisdiction, within the meaning of Article 17, shall be valid with respect to a person domiciled in Luxembourg only if that person has expressly and specifically so agreed.

Article Ia

1. Switzerland reserves the right to declare, at the time of depositing its instrument of ratification, that a judgment given in another Contracting State shall be neither recognized nor enforced in Switzerland if the following conditions are met:

(a) the jurisdiction of the court which has given the judgment is based only on Article 5 (1) of this Convention; and

(b) the defendant was domiciled in Switzerland at the time of the introduction of the proceedings; for the purposes of this Article, a company or other legal person is considered to be domiciled in Switzerland if it has its registered seat and the effective centre of activities in Switzerland; and

(c) the defendant raises an objection to the recognition or enforcement of the judgment in Switzerland, provided that he has not waived the benefit of the declaration foreseen under this paragraph.

2. This reservation shall not apply to the extent that at the time recognition or enforcement is sought a derogation has been granted from Article 59 of the Swiss Federal Constitution. The Swiss Government shall communicate such derogations to the signatory States and the acceding States.

3. This reservation shall cease to have effect on 31 December 1999. It may be withdrawn at any time.

Article Ib

Any Contracting State may, by declaration made at the time of signing or of deposit of its instrument of ratification or of accession, reserve the right, notwithstanding the provisions of Article 28, not to recognize and enforce judgments given in the other Contracting States if the jurisdiction of the court of the State of origin is based, pursuant to Article 16 (1) (b), exclusively on the domicile of the defendant in the State of origin, and the property is situated in the territory of the State which entered the reservation.

Article II

Without prejudice to any more favourable provisions of national laws, persons domiciled in a Contracting State who are being prosecuted in the criminal courts of another

Contracting State of which they are not nationals for an offence which was not intentionally committed may be defended by persons qualified to do so, even if they do not appear in person.

However, the court seised of the matter may order appearance in person; in the case of failure to appear, a judgment given in the civil action without the person concerned having had the opportunity to arrange for his defence need not be recognized or enforced in the other Contracting States.

Article III

In proceedings for the issue of an order for enforcement, no charge, duty or fee calculated by reference to the value of the matter in issue may be levied in the State in which enforcement is sought.

Article IV

Judicial and extrajudicial documents drawn up in one Contracting State which have to be served on persons in another Contracting State shall be transmitted in accordance with the procedures laid down in the conventions and agreements concluded between the Contracting States.

Unless the State in which service is to take place objects by declaration to the Swiss Federal Council, such documents may also be sent by the appropriate public officers of the State in which the document has been drawn up directly to the appropriate public officers of the State in which the addressee is to be found. In this case the officer of the State of origin shall send a copy of the document to the officer of the State applied to who is competent to forward it to the addressee. The document shall be forwarded in the manner specified by the law of the State applied to. The forwarding shall be recorded by a certificate sent directly to the officer of the State of origin.

Article V

The jurisdiction specified in Articles 6 (2) and 10 in actions on a warranty or guarantee or in any other third party proceedings may not be resorted to in the Federal Republic of Germany, in Spain, in Austria and in Switzerland. Any person domiciled in another Contracting State may be sued in the courts:

- of the Federal Republic of Germany, pursuant to Articles 68, 72, 73 and 74 of the code of civil procedure (Zivilprozeßordnung) concerning third-party notices,
- of Spain, pursuant to Article 1482 of the civil code,
- of Austria, pursuant to Article 21 of the code of civil procedure (Zivilprozeßordnung) concerning third-party notices,
- of Switzerland, pursuant to the appropriate provisions concerning third-party notices of the cantonal codes of civil procedure.

Judgments given in the other Contracting States by virtue of Article 6 (2) or 10 shall be recognized and enforced in the Federal Republic of Germany, in Spain, in Austria and in Switzerland in accordance with Title III. Any effects which judgments given in these States may have on third parties by application of the provisions in the preceding paragraph shall also be recognized in the other Contracting States.

Article Va

In matters relating to maintenance, the expression 'court' includes the Danish, Icelandic and Norwegian administrative authorities.

In civil and commercial matters, the expression 'court' includes the Finnish ulosotonhaltija /överexekutor.

Article Vb

In proceedings involving a dispute between the master and a member of the crew of a sea-going ship registered in Denmark, in Greece, in Ireland, in Iceland, in Norway, in Portugal or in Sweden concerning remuneration or other conditions of service, a court in a Contracting State shall establish whether the diplomatic or consular officer responsible for the ship has been notified of the dispute. It shall stay the proceedings so long as he has not been notified. It shall of its own motion decline jurisdiction if the officer, having been duly notified, has exercised the powers accorded to him in the matter by a consular convention, or in the absence of such a convention has, within the time allowed, raised any objection to the exercise of such jurisdiction.

Article Vc
(None)

Article Vd

Without prejudice to the jurisdiction of the European Patent Office under the Convention on the grant of European patents, signed at Munich on 5 October 1973, the courts of each Contracting State shall have exclusive jurisdiction, regardless of domicile, in proceedings concerned with the registration or validity of any European patent granted for that State which is not a Community patent by virtue of the provision of Article 86 of the Convention for the European patent for the common market, signed at Luxembourg on 15 December 1975.

Article VI

The Contracting States shall communicate to the Swiss Federal Council the text of any provisions of their laws which amend either those provisions of their laws mentioned in the Convention or the lists of courts specified in Section 2 of Title III.

PROTOCOL 2
on the uniform interpretation of the Convention

PREAMBLE

THE HIGH CONTRACTING PARTIES,

HAVING REGARD to Article 65 of this Convention,

CONSIDERING the substantial link between this Convention and the Brussels Convention,

CONSIDERING that the Court of Justice of the European Communities by virtue of the Protocol of 3 June 1971 has jurisdiction to give rulings on the interpretation of the provisions of the Brussels Convention,

BEING AWARE of the rulings delivered by the Court of Justice of the European Communities on the interpretation of the Brussels Convention up to the time of signature of this Convention,

CONSIDERING that the negotiations which led to the conclusion of the Convention were based on the Brussels Convention in the light of these rulings,

DESIRING to prevent, in full deference to the independence of the courts, divergent interpretations and to arrive at as uniform an interpretation as possible of the provisions of the Convention, and of these provisions and those of the Brussels Convention which are substantially reproduced in this Convention,

HAVE AGREED AS FOLLOWS:

Article 1

The courts of each Contracting State shall, when applying and interpreting the provisions of the Convention, pay due account to the principles laid down by any relevant decision delivered by courts of the other Contracting States concerning provisions of this Convention.

Article 2

1. The Contracting Parties agree to set up a system of exchange of information concerning judgments delivered pursuant to this Convention as well as relevant judgments under the Brussels Convention. This system shall comprise:

- transmission to a central body by the competent authorities of judgments delivered by courts of last instance and the Court of Justice of the European Communities as well as judgments of particular importance which have become final and have been delivered pursuant to this Convention or the Brussels Convention,
- classification of these judgments by the central body including, as far as necessary, the drawing-up and publication of translations and abstracts,
- communication by the central body of the relevant documents to the competent national authorities of all signatories and acceding States to the Convention and to the Commission of the European Communities.

2. The central body is the Registrar of the Court of Justice of the European Communities.

Article 3

1. A Standing Committee shall be set up for the purposes of this Protocol.

2. The Committee shall be composed of representatives appointed by each signatory and acceding State.

3. The European Communities (Commission, Court of Justice and General Secretariat of the Council) and the European Free Trade Association may attend the meetings as observers.

Article 4

1. At the request of a Contracting Party, the depositary of the Convention shall convene meetings of the Committee for the purpose of exchanging views on the functioning of the Convention and in particular on:

- the development of the case-law as communicated under the first indent of Article 2 (1),
- the application of Article 57 of the Convention.

2. The Committee, in the light of these exchanges, may also examine the appropriateness of starting on particular topics a revision of the Convention and make recommendations.

PROTOCOL 3
on the application of Article 57

THE HIGH CONTRACTING PARTIES HAVE AGREED AS FOLLOWS:

1. For the purposes of the Convention, provisions which, in relation to particular matters, govern jurisdiction or the recognition or enforcement of judgments and which are, or will be contained in acts of the institutions of the European Communities shall be treated in the same way as the conventions referred to in Article 57 (1).
2. If one Contracting State is of the opinion that a provision contained in an act of the institutions of the European Communities is incompatible with the Convention, the Contracting States shall promptly consider amending the Convention pursuant to Article 66, without prejudice to the procedure established by Protocol 2.

DECLARATION
by the representatives of the Governments of the States signatories to the Lugano Convention which are members of the European Communities on Protocol 3 on the application of Article 57 of the Convention

Upon signature of the Convention on jurisdiction and the enforcement of judgments in civil and commercial matters done at Lugano on 16 September 1988,

THE REPRESENTATIVES OF THE GOVERNMENTS OF THE MEMBER STATES OF THE EUROPEAN COMMUNITIES,

taking into account the undertakings entered into *vis-á-vis* the member states of the European Free Trade Association,

anxious not to prejudice the unity of the legal system set up by the Convention,

declare that they will take all measures in their power to ensure, when Community acts referred to in paragraph 1 of Protocol 3 on the application of Article 57 are being drawn up, respect for the rules of jurisdiction and recognition and enforcement of judgments established by the Convention.

DECLARATION
by the Representatives of the Governments of the States signatories to the Lugano Convention which are members of the European Communities

Upon signature of the Convention on jurisdiction and the enforcement of judgments in civil and commercial matters done at Lugano on 16 September 1988,

THE REPRESENTATIVES OF THE GOVERNMENTS OF THE MEMBER STATES OF THE EUROPEAN COMMUNITIES

declare that they consider as appropriate that the Court of Justice of the European Communities, when interpreting the Brussels Convention, pay due account to the rulings contained in the case-law of the Lugano Convention.

Done at Lugano on the sixteen day of September in the year one thousand nine hundred and eighty-eight.

DECLARATION
by the Representatives of the Governments of the States signatories to the Lugano Convention which are members of the European Free Trade Association

Upon signature of the Convention on jurisdiction and the enforcement of judgments in civil and commercial matters done at Lugano on 16 September 1988,

THE REPRESENTATIVES OF THE GOVERNMENTS OF THE MEMBER STATES OF THE EUROPEAN FREE TRADE ASSOCIATION *declare* that they consider as appropriate that their courts, when interpreting the Lugano Convention, pay due account to the rulings contained in the case law of the Court of Justice of the European Communities and of courts of the Member States of the European Communities in respect of provisions of the Brussels Convention which are substantially reproduced in the Lugano Convention.

CONVENTION ON THE SERVICE IN THE MEMBER STATES OF THE EUROPEAN UNION OF JUDICIAL AND EXTRAJUDICIAL DOCUMENTS IN CIVIL OR COMMERCIAL MATTERS

(Brussels, 26 May 1997)

THE COUNCIL OF THE EUROPEAN UNION.

Having regard to the Treaty on European Union, and in particular Article K.3 (2) (c) thereof,

Having examined the views of the European Parliament following the consultation conducted by the Presidency in accordance with Article K.6 of the Treaty,

Considering that, for the purposes of achieving the objectives of the European Union, the Member States view the rules on cooperation in the service of judicial and extrajudicial documents in civil or commercial matters as a matter of common interest falling within the scope of judicial cooperation in civil matters as laid down in Title VI of the Treaty,

HAVING DECIDED that the Convention, the text of which is attached, which has been signed today by the Representatives of the Governments of the Member States, is hereby drawn up,

RECOMMENDS that it be adopted by the Member States in accordance with their respective constitutional requirements.

Done at Brussels, 26 May 1997.

For the Council
The President
W. SORGDRAGER

CONVENTION

drawn up on the basis of Article K.3 of the Treaty on European Union, on the service in the Member States of the European Union of judicial and extrajudicial documents in civil or commercial matters

THE HIGH CONTRACTING PARTIES to this Convention, Member States of the European Union:

REFERRING to the Act of the Council of the European Union of 26 May 1997,

DESIRING to improve and expedite the transmission of judicial and extrajudicial documents in civil or commercial matters for service between the Member States,

WHEREAS, to that end, the transmission of these documents shall be effected directly and by rapid means, between the agencies designated by the Member States;

WHEREAS Article K.3 (2) (c) of the Treaty on European Union provides that conventions drawn up on the basis of Article K.3 thereof may stipulate that the Court of Justice of the European Communities shall have jurisdiction to interpret their provisions, in accordance with such arrangements as they may lay down;

BEARING IN MIND the Hague Convention of 15 November 1965 on the service abroad of judicial and extrajudicial documents in civil or commercial matters and, in particular, the provisions in Article 25 thereof that that Convention does not derogate from conventions which contain provisions on the matters governed by it and to which Contracting States are, or shall become, Parties.

HAVE AGREED AS FOLLOWS:

TITLE I

Article 1
Scope

1. This Convention shall apply in civil and commercial matters where a judicial or extrajudicial document has to be transmitted from one Member State to another for service there.

2. This Convention shall not apply where the address of the person to be served with the document is not known.

Article 2
Transmitting and receiving agencies

1. Each Member State shall designate the public officers, authorities or other persons, hereinafter referred to as 'transmitting agencies', competent for the transmission of judicial or extrajudicial documents to be served in another Member State.

2. Each Member State shall designate the public officers, authorities or other persons, hereinafter referred to as 'receiving agencies', competent for the receipt of judicial or extrajudicial documents from another Member State.

3. A Member State may declare, when giving the notification referred to in Article 24 (2), that it will designate one transmitting agency or/and one receiving agency. A federal State, a State in which several legal systems apply or a State with autonomous territorial units shall be free to designate more than one such agency. The designation shall have effect for a period of five years and may be renewed at five-year intervals.

4. Each Member State, when giving the notification referred to in Article 24 (2), shall provide the following information:

(a) the names and addresses of the receiving agencies referred to in paragraphs 2 and 3;

(b) the geographical areas in which they have jurisdiction;

(c) the means of receipt of documents available to them; and

(d) the languages that may be used for the completion of the standard form in the Annex.

The Member States shall notify the depositary of any subsequent modification of such information.

Article 3
Central body

Each Member State shall, when giving the notification referred to in Article 24 (2), designate a central body responsible for:

(a) supplying information to the transmitting agencies;

(b) seeking solutions to any difficulties which may arise during transmission of documents for service;

(c) forwarding, in exceptional cases, at the request of a transmitting agency, a request for service to the competent receiving agency.

A federal State, a State in which several legal systems apply or a State with autonomous territorial units shall be free to designate more than one central body.

TITLE II
JUDICIAL DOCUMENTS

Section 1
Transmission and service of judicial documents

Article 4
Transmission of documents

1. Judicial documents shall be transmitted directly and as soon as possible between the agencies designated on the basis of Article 2.

2. The transmission of documents, requests, confirmations, receipts, certificates and any other papers between transmitting agencies and receiving agencies may be carried out by any appropriate means, provided that the content of the document received is true and faithful to that of the document forwarded and that all information in it is easily legible.

3. The document to be transmitted shall be accompanied by a request drawn up using the standard form in the Annex. The form shall be completed in the official language of the Member State addressed or, if there are several official languages in that Member State, the official language or one of the official languages of the place where service is to be effected, or in another language, which that Member State has indicated it can accept. When giving the notification referred to in Article 24 (2), each Member State shall indicate the official language or languages of the European Union other than its own which is or are acceptable to it for completion of the form.

4. The documents and all papers that are transmitted shall be exempted from legalization or any equivalent formality.

5. When the transmitting agency wishes a copy of the document to be returned together with the certificate referred to in Article 10, it shall send the document in duplicate.

Article 5
Translation of documents

1. The applicant shall be advised by the transmitting agency to which he or she forwards the document for transmission that the addressee may refuse to accept it if it is not in one of the languages provided for in Article 8.

2. The applicant shall bear any costs of translation prior to the transmission of the document, without prejudice to any possible subsequent decision by the court or competent authority on liability for such costs.

Article 6
Receipt of documents by receiving agency

1. A receiving agency, on receipt of a document, shall, as soon as possible and in any event within seven days of receipt thereof, send a receipt to the transmitting agency by the swiftest possible means of transmission using the standard form in the Annex.

2. Where the request for service cannot be fulfilled on the basis of the information or documents transmitted, the receiving agency shall contact the transmitting agency by the swiftest possible means in order to secure the missing information or documents.

3. If the request for service is manifestly outside the scope of this Convention or if non-compliance with the formal conditions required makes service impossible, the request and the documents transmitted shall be returned, on receipt, to the transmitting agency, together with the notice of return in the standard form in the Annex.

4. A receiving agency receiving a document for service but not having territorial jurisdiction to serve it shall forward it, as well as the request, to the competent receiving agency in the same Member State if the request complies with the conditions laid down in Article 4 (3) and shall inform the transmitting agency accordingly, using the standard form in the Annex. That receiving agency shall inform the transmitting agency when it receives the document, in the manner provided for in paragraph 1.

Article 7
Service of documents

1. The receiving agency shall itself serve the document or have it served, either in accordance with the law of the Member State addressed or by a particular form requested by the transmitting agency, unless such a method is incompatible with the law of that Member State.

2. All steps required for service of the document shall be effected as soon as possible. In any event, if it has not been possible to effect service within one month of receipt, the receiving agency shall inform the transmitting agency by means of the certificate in the standard form in the Annex, which shall be drawn up under the conditions referred to in Article 10 (2). The period shall be calculated in accordance with the law of the Member State addressed.

Article 8
Refusal to accept a document

1. The receiving agency shall inform the addressee that he or she may refuse to accept the document to be served if it is in a language other than either of the following languages:

(a) the official language of the Member State addressed or, if there are several official languages in that Member State, the official language or one of the official languages of the place where service is to be effected;

or

(b) a language of the Member State of transmission which the addressee understands.

2. Where the receiving agency is informed that the addressee refuses to accept the document in accordance with paragraph 1, it shall immediately inform the transmitting

agency by means of the certificate provided for in Article 10 and return the request and the documents of which a translation is requested.

Article 9
Date of service

1. The date of service of a document pursuant to Article 7 shall be the date on which it is served in accordance with the law of the Member State addressed, without prejudice to Article 8.

2. However, where a document must be served within a particular period in the context of proceedings to be brought or pending in the Member State of origin, the date to be taken into account with respect to the applicant shall be that fixed by the law of that Member State.

3. When giving the notification referred to in Article 24 (2), each Member State may declare that it will not apply paragraphs 1 and 2 of this Article.

Article 10
Certificate of service and copy of the document served

1. When the formalities concerning the service of the document have been completed, a certificate of completion of those formalities shall be drawn up in the standard form in the Annex and addressed to the transmitting agency, together with, where Article 4 (5) applies, a copy of the document served.

2. The certificate shall be completed in the official language or one of the official languages of the Member State of origin or in another language which the Member State of origin has indicated that it can accept. Each Member State shall, when giving the notification referred to in Article 24 (2), indicate the official language or languages of the European Union other than its own which is or are acceptable to it for completion of the form.

Article 11
Costs of service

1. The service of judicial documents coming from a Member State shall not give rise to any payment or reimbursement of taxes or costs for services rendered by the Member State addressed.

2. The applicant shall pay or reimburse the costs occasioned by:

(a) the employment of a judicial officer or of a person competent under the law of the Member State addressed;

(b) the use of a particular method of service.

Section 2
Other means of transmission and service of judicial documents

Article 12
Transmission by consular or diplomatic channels

Each Member State shall be free, in exceptional circumstances, to use consular or diplomatic channels to forward judicial documents, for the purpose of service, to those agencies of another Member State which are designated pursuant to Article 2 or 3.

Article 13
Service by diplomatic or consular agents

1. Each Member State shall be free to effect service of judicial documents on persons residing in another Member State, without application of any compulsion, directly through its diplomatic or consular agents.

2. Any Member State may, when giving the notification referred to in Article 24 (2), declare that it is opposed to such service within its territory, unless the documents are to be served on nationals of the Member State in which the documents originate.

Article 14
Service by post

1. Each Member State shall be free to effect service of judicial documents directly by post to persons residing in another Member State.

2. Any Member State may, when giving the notification referred to in Article 24 (2), or at any other time, specify the conditions under which it will accept service of judicial documents by post.

Article 15
Direct service

1. This Convention shall not interfere with the freedom of any person interested in a judicial proceeding to effect service of judicial documents directly through the judicial officers, officials or other competent persons of the Member State addressed.

2. Any Member State may, when giving the notification referred to in Article 24 (2), declare that it is opposed to the service of judicial documents in its territory pursuant to paragraph 1.

TITLE III
EXTRAJUDICIAL DOCUMENTS

Article 16

Extrajudicial documents may be transmitted for service in another Member State in accordance with the provisions of this Convention.

TITLE IV
INTERPRETATION BY THE COURT OF JUSTICE

Article 17

The Court of Justice of the European Communities shall have jurisdiction to give rulings on the interpretation of this Convention in accordance with the provisions of the Protocol drawn up by the act of the Council of the European Union of 26 May 1997.

TITLE V
FINAL PROVISIONS

Article 18
Executive Committee

1. A Committee shall be established with responsibility for examining all general questions relating to the application of this Convention.

2. The Committee shall meet at least once a year. It shall meet for the first time as soon as this Convention is applied, as provided for in Article 24 (4), between three Member States. It shall monitor the functioning of this Convention and, in particular, the effectiveness of the agencies designated pursuant to Article 2 and the practical application of Articles 3 (c) and 9. It shall report to the Council thereon within three years of its first meeting and every five years thereafter.

3. The Committee's tasks shall also include:

(a) drawing up and annually updating a manual containing the information provided by Member States in accordance with Article 2 (4);

(b) drawing up a glossary in the official language of the European Union of documents which can be served under this Convention.

4. The Committee may also make proposals designed to:

(a) expedite the transmission and service of documents;

(b) make adjustments to the form in the Annex;

(c) initiate negotiations for the revision of this Convention.

Article 19
Application of Articles 15 and 16 of the Hague Convention of 1965

Articles 15 and 16 of the Hague Convention of 15 November 1965 on the service abroad of judicial and extrajudicial documents in civil or commercial matters shall apply in relation to writs of summons or equivalent documents under this Convention as they apply to such documents transmitted under the Hague Convention, and accordingly:

1. (a) Where a writ of summons or an equivalent document had to be transmitted to another Member State for the purpose of service, under the provisions of this Convention, and the defendant has not appeared, judgement shall not be given until it is established that;

(i) the document was served by a method prescribed by the internal law of the Member State addressed for the service of documents in domestic actions upon persons who are within its territory;

or

(ii) the document was actually delivered to the defendant or to his residency by another method provided for by this Convention;

and that in either of these cases the service or the delivery was affected in sufficient time to enable the defendant to defend.

(b) Each Member State shall be free, when giving the notification referred to in Article 24 (2), to declare that the judge, notwithstanding the provisions of subparagraph (a), may give judgement even if no certificate of service or delivery has been received, if all the following conditions are fulfilled:

(i) the document was transmitted by one of the methods provided for in this Convention;

(ii) a period of time of not less than six months, considered adequate by the judge in the particular case, has elapsed since the date of the transmission of the document;

(iii) no certificate of any kind has been received, even though every reasonable effort has been made to obtain it through the competent authorities of the State addressed.

(c) Notwithstanding the provisions of subparagraphs (a) and (b), the judge may order, in case of urgency, any provisional or protective measures.

2. (a) When a writ of summons or an equivalent document had to be transmitted to another Member State for the purpose of service, under the provisions of this Convention, and a judgement has been entered against a defendant who has not appeared, the judge shall have the power to relieve the defendant from the effects of the expiration of the time for appeal from the judgement if the following conditions are fulfilled:

(i) the defendant, without any fault on his part, did not have knowledge of the document in sufficient time to defend, or knowledge of the judgement in sufficient time to appeal; and

(ii) the defendant has disclosed a *prima facie* defence to the action on the merits.

(b) An application for relief may be filed only within a reasonable time after the defendant has knowledge of the judgement.

(c) Each Member State may declare, when giving the notification referred to in Article 24 (2), that the application will not be entertained if it is filed after the expiration of a time to be stated in the declaration, but which shall in no case be less than one year following the date of the judgement.

(d) This paragraph shall not apply to judgments concerning status or capacity of persons.

Article 20
Relationship with other agreements or arrangements

1. This Convention shall not affect existing or future agreements which fulfil the conditions laid down in Article K.7 of the Treaty on European Union between two or more Member States and which contain provisions on matters governed by this Convention.

2. Member States shall send to the depositary of this Convention:

(a) a copy of the agreements or arrangements referred to in paragraph 1;

(b) any denunciations of those agreements or arrangements.

Article 21
Legal aid

This Convention shall not affect the application of Article 23 of the Convention on civil procedure of 17 July 1905, Article 24 of the Convention on civil procedure of 1 March

1954 or Article 13 of the Convention on international access to justice of 25 October 1980 between the Member States parties to these Conventions.

Article 22
Protection of information transmitted

1. Information, including in particular personal data, transmitted under this Convention shall be used by the receiving agency only for the purpose for which it was transmitted.

2. Receiving agencies shall ensure the confidentiality of such information, in accordance with their national law.

3. Paragraphs 1 and 2 shall not affect national laws enabling data subjects to be informed of the use made of information transmitted under this Convention.

Article 23
Reservations

1. Each Member State, when giving the notification referred to in Article 24 (2), shall declare that it avails itself of one or more of the reservations provided for in:

(a) Article 2 (3);

(b) Article 9 (3);

(c) Article 13 (2);

(d) Article 15 (2).

2. No reservations other than those expressly provided for shall be permitted.

3. Any Member State may, at any time, withdraw a reservation which it has made. The reservation shall cease to have effect 90 days after the notification of the withdrawal.

Article 24
Adoption and entry into force

1. This Convention shall be subject to adoption by the Member States in accordance with their respective constitutional requirements.

2. Member States shall notify the depositary of the completion of the constitutional procedures for the adoption of this Convention.

3. This Convention shall enter into force 90 days after the notification referred to in paragraph 2 by the last Member State to complete that formality.

4. Until this Convention enters into force, any Member State, may, when giving the notification referred to in paragraph 2, or at any later date, declare that as far as it is concerned the Convention, with the exception of Article 17, shall apply to its relations with Member States that have made the same declaration. Such declarations shall apply 90 days after the date of deposit.

Article 25
Accession

1. This Convention shall be open to accession by any State that becomes a member of the European Union.

2. The text of this Convention in the language of the acceding State, drawn up by the Council of the European Union, shall be authentic.

3. Instruments of accession shall be deposited with the depositary.

4. This Convention shall enter into force with respect to any State that accedes to it 90 days after the deposit of its instrument of accession or on the date of entry into force of the Convention if it has not already entered into force at the time of expiry of the said period of 90 days.

5. Where this Convention is not yet in force at the time of the deposit of their instruments of accession, Article 24 (4) shall apply to acceding Member States.

Article 26
Amendments

1. Amendments to this Convention may be proposed by any Member State, being a Party to this Convention, or by the Commission. Any proposal for an amendment shall be sent to the depositary, who shall forward it to the Council.

2. Amendments shall be adopted by the Council, which shall recommend that they be adopted by the Member States in accordance with their respective constitutional requirements.

3. Amendments thus adopted shall enter into force in accordance with the provisions of Article 24 (3).

4. Notwithstanding paragraphs 1, 2 and 3, the forms in the Annex may be amended by decisions of the Council, acting on a proposal from the Executive Committee in accordance with Article 18 (4) (b), any Member State, being a party to this Convention, or the Commission.

Article 27
Depositary and publications

1. The Secretary-General of the Council of the European Union shall act as depositary of this Convention.

2. The depositary shall publish in the *Official Journal of the European Communities:*

   (a) adoptions and accessions;

   (b) the date on which this Convention enters into force;

   (c) the date on which this Convention is applied as between three Member States;

   (d) declarations referred to in Articles 2 (1) and (2), 3, 4 (3), 10 (2), 14 (2), 19 (1) (b) and (2) (c), and 24 (4);

   (e) reservations and withdrawals of reservations referred to in Article 23 (1).

In witness whereof, the undersigned Plenipotentiaries have signed this Protocol.

Done at Brussels, on the twenty-sixth day of May in the year one thousand nine hundred and ninety-seven, in a single original, in the Danish, Dutch, English, Finnish, French, German, Greek, Irish, Italian, Portuguese, Spanish and Swedish languages, each text being equally authentic, such original remaining deposited in the archives of the General Secretariat of the Council of the European Union.

ANNEX

Convention on the service in the Member States of the European Union of judicial and extrajudicial documents in civil or commercial matters

(English, in languages)

REQUEST FOR SERVICE OF DOCUMENTS

(Article 4 (3) of the Convention)

Reference No. (*) This item is optional

1. TRANSMITTING AGENCY

1.1. Identity:

1.2. Address:

1.2.1. Street and Number/PO Box:

1.2.2. Place and Code:

1.2.3. Country:

1.3. Tel. No.:

1.4. Fax No.:(*)

1.5. E-mail (*):

2. RECEIVING AGENCY

2.1. Identity:

2.2. Address:

2.2.1. Street and Number/PO Box:

2.2.2. Place and Code:

2.2.3. Country:

2.3. Tel. No. :

2.4. Fax No.:(*)

2.5. E-mail (*):

3. APPLICANT

3.1. Identity:

3.2. Address:

3.2.1. Street and Number/PO Box:

3.2.2. Place and Code:

3.2.3. Country:

3.3. Tel. No.:(*)

3.4. Fax No.: (*)

3.5. E-mail (*):

4. ADDRESSEE

4.1. Identity:

4.2. Address:

4.2.1. Street and Number/PO Box:

4.2.2. Place and Code:

4.2.3. Country:

4.3. Tel. No.: (*)

4.4. Fax No.: (*)

4.5 E-mail (*):

4.6. Identification number/social security number/organization number/or equivalent (*):

5. METHOD OF SERVICE

5.1. In accordance with the law of the Member State addressed

5.2. By the following particular method:

5.2.1. If this method is incompatible with the law of the Member State addressed, the document(s) should be served in accordance with the law:

5.2.1.1. yes

5.2.1.2. no

6. DOCUMENT TO BE SERVED

(a) 6.1. Nature of the document

6.1.1. Judicial

6.1.1.1. writ of summons

6.1.1.2. judgment

6.1.1.3. appeal

6.1.1.4. other:

6.1.2. Extrajudicial

(b) 6.2. Date or timelimit stated in the document (*):

(c) 6.3. Language of document:

–6.3.1. original D

EN

DK

ES

FIN

FR

GR

IT

NL

P

S

others:

–6.3.2. translation(*) D

EN

DK

ES

FIN

FR

GR

IT

NL

P

S

others:

(d) 6.4. Number of enclosures:

7. A COPY OF DOCUMENT TO BE RETURNED WITH THE CERTIFICATE OF SERVICE (Article 4 (5) of the Convention)

7.1. Yes (in this case send two copies of the document to be served)

7.2. No

1.

2.

Done at:

Date:

Signature and/or stamp:

Reference No. of the receiving agency:

ACKNOWLEDGMENT OF RECEIPT

(Article 6 (1) of the Convention)

This acknowledgment must be sent by the swiftest possible means of transmission as soon as possible after receipt of the document and in any event within seven days of receipt.

8. DATE OF RECEIPT:

Done at:

date:

Signature and/or stamp:

NOTICE OF RETURN OF REQUEST AND DOCUMENT

(Article 6 (3) of the Convention)

The request and document must be returned on receipt.

9. REASON FOR RETURN:

9.1. The request is manifestly outside the scope of the Convention:

9.1.1. the document is not civil or commercial.

9.1.2. the service is not from one Member State to another Member State

9.2. Non-compliance with formal conditions required makes service impossible:

9.2.1. the document is not easily

9.2.2. the language used to complete the form is incorrect

9.2.3. the document received is not a true and faithful copy

9.2.4. other (please give details):

9.3. The method of service is incompatible with the law of that Member State (Article 7 (1) of the Convention)

Done at:

date:

Signature and/or stamp:

NOTICE OF RETRANSMISSION OF REQUEST AND DOCUMENT TO THE APPROPRIATE RECEIVING AGENCY

(Article 6 (4) of the Convention)

The request and document were forwarded on to the following receiving agency, which has territorial jurisdiction to serve it:

10.1. IDENTITY:

10.2. Address:

10.2.1. Street and Number/PO Box:

10.2.2. Place and Code:

10.2.3. Country

10.3. Tel No.:

10.4. Fax No. (*):

10.5. E-mail (*):

Done at:

date:

Signature and/or stamp:

Reference No of the appropriate receiving agency:

NOTICE OF RECEIPT BY THE APPROPRIATE RECEIVING AGENCY TO THE TRANSMITTING AGENCY

(Article 6 (4) of the Convention)

This notice must be sent by the swiftest possible means of transmission as soon as possible after receipt of the document and in any event within seven days of receipt.

11. DATE OF RECEIPT:

Done at:

date:

Signature and/or stamp:

CERTIFICATE OF SERVICE OR NON-SERVICE OF DOCUMENTS

(Article 10 of the Convention)

The service shall be effected as soon as possible, in any event, if it has not been possible to effect the service within one month of receipt, the receiving agency shall inform the transmitting agency (according to Article 7 (2) of the Convention).

12. COMPLETION OF SERVICE

(a) 12.1. Date and address of service:

(b) 12.2. The document was

(A) 12.2.1. served in accordance with the law of the Member State addressed, namely

12.2.1.1. handed to

12.2.1.1.1. the addressee in person

12.2.1.1.2. another person

12.2.1.1.2.1. Name:

12.2.1.1.2.2. Address:

12.2.1.1.2.2.1. Street and Number/PO Box:

12.2.1.1.2.2.2. Place and Code:

12.2.1.1.2.2.3. Country:

12.2.1.1.2.3. Relation to the addressee:

Family

Employee

others

12.2.1.1.3. the addressee's address

12.2.1.2. served by post

12.2.1.2.1. without acknowledgment of receipt

12.2.1.2.2. with the enclosed acknowledgment of receipt

12.2.1.2.2.1. from the addressee

12.2.1.2.2.2. another person

12.2.1.2.2.2.1. Name:

12.2.1.2.2.2.2. Address:

12.2.1.2.2.2.2.1. Street and Number/PO Box:

12.2.1.2.2.2.2.2. Place and Code:

12.2.1.2.2.2.2.3. Country:

12.2.1.2.2.2.3. Relation to the addressee:

Family

Employee

others

12.2.1.3. other method (please say how)

(B) 12.2.2. served by the following particular method (please say how):

(c) 1.2.3. The addressee of the document was informed (orally) (in writing) that he or she may refuse to accept it if it was not in an official language of the place of service or in an official language of the state of transmission which he or she understands.

13. INFORMATION IN ACCORDANCE WITH ARTICLE 7(2)

It was not possible to effect service within one month of receipt.

14. REFUSAL OF DOCUMENT

The addressee refused to accept the document on account of the language used. The documents are annexed to this certificate.

15. REASON FOR NON-SERVICE OF DOCUMENT

15.1. Address unknown

15.2. Addressee cannot be located

15.3. Document could not be served before the date or time-limit stated in point 6.2.

15.4 Others (please specify):

The documents are annexed to this certificate.

Done at:

date:

Signature and/or stamp:

APPENDIX IV

COUNCIL OF EUROPE CONVENTIONS

CONVENTIONS OF THE COUNCIL OF EUROPE
(as of April 8, 1998)

- Information on Foreign Law, London, June 7, 1968, ETS No. 62 (London) and Additional Protocol, Strasbourg, March 15, 1978, ETS No. 97
- Abolition of Legalization of Documents Executed by Diplomatic Agents or Consular Officers, London, June 7, 1968, ETS No. 63
- State Immunity and Additional Protocol, Basle, May 16, 1972, ETS Nos. 74, 74 A

Contracting States	Foreign Law 1968		Legalization 1968	State Immunity 1972	
	ETS No. 62	ETS No. 97	ETS No. 63	ETS No. 74	ETS No. 74A
Albania		—	—	—	—
Andorra		—	—	—	—
Austria	X	X	X	X	X
Belgium	X	X	—	X	X
Bulgaria	X	X	—	—	—
Croatia		—	—	—	—
Cyprus	X	X	X	X	X
Czech Republic		—	—	—	
Denmark	X	X	—	—	—
Estonia	X	X	—	—	—
Finland	X	X	—	—	—
France	X	X	X	—	—
Germany	X	X	X	X	—
Greece	X	X	X	—	—
Hungary	X	X	—	—	—
Iceland	X	X	—	—	—
Ireland		—	—	—	—
Italy	X	X	X	—	X
Latvia		—	—	—	—
Liechtenstein	X	—	X	—	—
Lithuania	X	—	—	—	—
Luxembourg	X	X	X	X	X
Malta	X	X	—	—	—
Moldova		—	—	—	—
Netherlands	X	X	X	X	X
Norway	X	X	X	—	—
Poland	X	X	X	—	—

Contracting States	**Foreign Law 1968**		**Legalization 1968**	**State Immunity 1972**	
	ETS No. 62	**ETS No. 97**	**ETS No. 63**	**ETS No. 74**	**ETS No. 74A**
Portugal	X	X	X	—	—
Romania	X	X	—	—	—
Russia	X	—	—	—	—
San Marino		—	—	—	—
Slovakia	X	X	—	—	—
Slovenia	X	—	—	—	—
Spain	X	X	X	—	—
Sweden	X	X	X	—	—
Switzerland	X	X	X	X	X
The former Yugoslav Republic of Macedonia		—	—	—	—
Turkey	X	—	X	—	—
Ukraine	X	X	—	—	—
United Kingdom	X	X	X	X	—
Non Member States					
Belarus	X	X	—	—	—
Costa Rica	X				
Morocco		—	—	—	—

EUROPEAN CONVENTION ON INFORMATION ON FOREIGN LAW London, June 7, 1968

Preamble

The member States of the Council of Europe, signatories hereto,

Considering that the aim of the Council of Europe is the achievement of greater unity between its members;

Convinced that the creation of a system of international mutual assistance in order to facilitate the task of judicial authorities in obtaining information on foreign law, will contribute to the attainment of this aim,

Have agreed as follows:

Article 1 - Scope of the Convention

1. The Contracting Parties undertake to supply one another, in accordance with the provisions of the present Convention, with information on their law and procedure in civil and commercial fields as well as on their judicial organisation.

2. However, two or more Contracting Parties may decide to extend as between themselves the scope of the present Convention to fields other than those mentioned in the preceding paragraph. The text of such agreements shall be communicated to the Secretary General of the Council of Europe.

Article 2 - National liaison bodies

1. In order to carry out the provisions of the present Convention each Contracting Party shall set up or appoint a single body (hereinafter referred to as the "receiving agency"):

(a) to receive requests for the information referred to in Article 1, paragraph 1, of the present Convention from another Contracting Party;

(b) to take action on these requests in accordance with Article 6.

The receiving agency may be either a ministerial department or other State body.

2. Each Contracting Party may set up or appoint one or more bodies (hereinafter referred to as "transmitting agency") to receive requests for information from its judicial authorities and to transmit them to the competent foreign receiving agency. The receiving agency may be appointed as a transmitting agency.

3. Each Contracting Party shall communicate to the Secretary General of the Council of Europe the name and address of its receiving agency and, where appropriate, of its transmitting agency or agencies.

Article 3 - Authorities entitled to make a request for information

1. A request for information shall always emanate from a judicial authority, even when it has not been drawn up by that authority. The request may be made only where proceedings have actually been instituted.

2. Any Contracting Party may, if it has not set up or appointed a transmitting agency, indicate, by a declaration addressed to the Secretary General of the Council of Europe, which of its authorities it will deem a judicial authority within the meaning of the preceding paragraph.

3. Two or more Contracting Parties may decide to extend as between themselves the present Convention to requests from authorities other than judicial authorities. The text of such agreements shall be communicated to the Secretary General of the Council of Europe.

Article 4 - Contents of a request for information

1. A request for information shall state the judicial authority from which it emanates as well as the nature of the case. It shall specify as exactly as possible the questions on which information concerning the law of the requested State is desired, and where there is more than one legal system in the requested State, the system of the law on which information is requested.

2. The request shall also state the facts necessary both for its proper understanding and for the formulation of an exact and precise reply. Copies of documents may be attached where necessary to clarify the scope of the request.

3. The request may include questions in fields other than those referred to in Article 1, paragraph (1), where they relate to the principal questions specified in the request.

4. Where a request is not drawn up by a judicial authority it shall be accompanied by the decision of that authority authorising it.

Article 5 - Transmission of a request for information

A request for information shall be transmitted directly to the receiving agency of the requested State by a transmitting agency or, in the absence of such an agency, by the judicial authority from which it emanates.

Article 6 - Authorities empowered to reply

1. The receiving agency which has received a request for information may either draw up the reply itself or transmit the request to another State or official body to draw up the reply.

2. The receiving agency may, in appropriate cases or for reasons of administrative organisation, transmit the request to a private body or to a qualified lawyer to draw up the reply.

3. Where the application of the preceding paragraph is likely to involve costs, the receiving agency shall, before making the transmission referred to in the said paragraph, indicate to the authority from which the request emanated the private body or lawyer to whom the request will be transmitted, inform the said authority as accurately as possible of the probable cost, and request its consent.

Article 7 - Content of the reply

The object of the reply shall be to give information in an objective and impartial manner on the law of the requested State to the judicial authority from which the request emanated. The reply shall contain, as appropriate, relevant legal texts and relevant judicial decisions. It shall be accompanied, to the extent deemed necessary for the proper information of the requesting authority, by any additional documents, such as extracts from doctrinal works and "travaux preparatoires". It may also be accompanied by explanatory commentaries.

Article 8 - Effects of the reply

The information given in the reply shall not bind the judicial authority from which the request emanated.

Article 9 - Communication of the reply

The reply shall be addressed by the receiving agency to the transmitting agency, if the request had been transmitted by this agency, or to the judicial authority, if the request was sent directly by the latter.

Article 10 - Duty to reply

1. The receiving agency to whom a request for information has been sent shall, subject to the provisions of Article 11, take action on the request in accordance with Article 6. 2. Where the reply is not drawn up by the receiving agency, the latter shall be bound to ensure that a reply is sent subject to the conditions specified in Article 12.

Article 11 - Exceptions to the obligation to reply

The requested State may refuse to take action on the request for information if its interests are affected by the case giving rise to the request or if it considers that the reply might prejudice its sovereignty or security.

Article 12 - Time-limit for the reply

The reply to a request for information shall be furnished as rapidly as possible. However, if the preparation of the reply requires a long time, the receiving agency shall so inform the requesting foreign authority and shall, if possible, indicate at the same time the probable date on which the reply will be communicated.

Article 13 - Additional information

1. The receiving agency, as well as the body or the person whom it has instructed to reply, in accordance with Article 6, may request the authority from which the request emanates to provide any additional information it deems necessary to draw up the reply.

2. The request for additional information shall be transmitted by the receiving agency in the same way as is provided by Article 9 for the communication of the reply.

Article 14 - Languages

1. The request for information and annexes shall be in the language or in one of the official languages of the requested State or be accompanied by a translation into that language. The reply shall be in the language of the requested State.

2. However, two or more Contracting Parties may decide to derogate, as between themselves, from the provisions of the preceding paragraph.

Article 15 - Costs

1. The reply shall not entail payment of any charges or expenses except those referred to in Article 6, paragraph 3, which shall be borne by the State from which the request emanates.

2. However, two or more Contracting Parties may decide to derogate, as between themselves, from the provisions of the preceding paragraph.

Article 16 - Federal States

In Federal States, the functions of the receiving agency other than those exercised under Article 2, paragraph 1(a) may, for constitutional reasons, be conferred on other State bodies.

Article 17 - Entry into force of the Convention

1. This Convention shall be open to signature by the member States of the Council of Europe. It shall be subject to ratification or acceptance. Instruments of ratification or acceptance shall be deposited with the Secretary General of the Council of Europe.

2. This Convention shall enter into force three months after the date of the deposit of the third instrument of ratification or acceptance.

3. In respect of a signatory State ratifying or accepting subsequently, the Convention shall come into force three months after the date of the deposit of its instrument of ratification or acceptance.

Article 18 - Accession of a State not a member of the Council of Europe

1. After the entry into force of this Convention, the Committee of Ministers of the Council of Europe may invite any non-member State to accede thereto.

2. Such accession shall be effected by depositing with the Secretary General of the Council of Europe an instrument of accession which shall take effect three months after the date of its deposit.

Article 19 - Territorial scope of the Convention

1. Any Contracting Party may, at the time of signature or when depositing its instrument of ratification, acceptance or accession, specify the territory or territories to which this Convention shall apply.

2. Any Contracting Party may, when depositing its instrument of ratification, acceptance or accession or at any later date, by declaration addressed to the Secretary General of the Council of Europe, extend this Convention to any other territory or territories specified in the declaration and for whose international relations it is responsible or on whose behalf it is authorised to give undertakings.

3. Any declaration made in pursuance of the preceding paragraph may, in respect of any territory mentioned in such declaration, be withdrawn according to the procedure laid down in Article 20 of this Convention.

Article 20 - Duration of the Convention and denunciation

1. This Convention shall remain in force indefinitely.

2. Any Contracting Party may, in so far as it is concerned, denounce this Convention by means of a notification addressed to the Secretary General of the Council of Europe.

3. Such denunciation shall take effect six months after the date of receipt by the Secretary General of such notification.

Article 21 - Functions of the Secretary General of the Council of Europe

The Secretary General of the Council of Europe shall notify the member States of the Council and any State which has acceded to this Convention of:

(a) any signature;

(b) any deposit of an instrument of ratification, acceptance or accession;

(c) any date of entry into force of this Convention in accordance with Article 17 thereof;

(d) any declaration received in pursuance of the provisions of paragraph 2 of Article 1, paragraph 3 of Article 2, paragraph 2 of Article 3 and paragraphs 2 and 3 of Article 19;

(e) any notification received in pursuance of the provisions of Article 20 and the date on which denunciation takes effect.

In witness whereof the undersigned, being duly authorised thereto, have signed this Convention.

Done at London, this 7th June 1968, in French and English, both texts being equally authoritative, in a single copy which shall remain deposited in the archives of the Council of Europe. The Secretary General of the Council of Europe shall transmit certified copies to each of the signatory and acceding States.

ADDITIONAL PROTOCOL TO THE EUROPEAN CONVENTION ON INFORMATION ON FOREIGN LAW
Strasbourg, March 15, 1978

The member States of the Council of Europe, signatory hereto,

Having regard to the provisions of the European Convention on Information on Foreign Law, opened for signature in London on 7 June 1968 (hereinafter referred to as "the Convention");

Considering that it is desirable to extend the system of international mutual assistance established by that Convention in the field of criminal law and procedure, in a multilateral framework open to all the Contracting Parties to the Convention;

Considering that, with a view to eliminating economic obstacles to legal proceedings and permitting persons in an economically weak position more easily to exercise their rights in member States, it is also desirable to extend the system established by the Convention to the field of legal aid and advice in civil and commercial matters;

Noting that Article 1, paragraph 2, of the Convention provides that two or more Contracting Parties may decide to extend as between themselves the scope of the Convention to fields other than those referred to in the Convention;

Noting that Article 3, paragraph 3, of the Convention provides that two or more Contracting Parties may decide to extend as between themselves the Convention to requests from authorities other than judicial authorities,

Have agreed as follows:

CHAPTER I

Article 1

The Contracting Parties undertake to supply one another, in accordance with the provisions of the Convention, with information on their substantive and procedural law and judicial organisation in the criminal field, including prosecuting authorities, as well as on the law concerning the enforcement of penal measures. This undertaking applies to all proceedings in respect of offences the prosecution of which, at the time of the request for information, falls within the jurisdiction of the judicial authorities of the requesting Party.

Article 2

A request for information on questions in the field referred to in Article 1 may:

(a) emanate not only from a court, but from any judicial authority having jurisdiction to prosecute offences or execute sentences that have been imposed with final and binding effect; and

(b.) be made not only where proceedings have actually been instituted, but also when the institution of proceedings is envisaged.

CHAPTER II

ARTICLE 3

Within the framework of the undertaking contained in Article 1, paragraph 1 of the Convention, the Contracting Parties agree that requests for information may:

(a.) emanate not only from a judicial authority but also from any authority or person acting within official systems of legal aid or legal advice on behalf of persons in an economically weak position;

(b) be made not only where proceedings have actually been instituted but also when the institution of proceedings is envisaged.

Article 4

1. Each Contracting Party which has not set up or appointed one or more bodies to act as a transmitting agency as provided for in Article 2, paragraph 2 of the Convention, shall set up or appoint such an agency or agencies for the purpose of transmitting any request for information in accordance with Article 3 of this Protocol to the competent foreign receiving agency.

2. Each Contracting Party shall communicate to the Secretary General of the Council of Europe the name and address of the transmitting agency or agencies set up or appointed in accordance with the preceding paragraph.

CHAPTER III

Article 5

1. Any State may, at the time of signature or when depositing its instrument of ratification, acceptance, approval or accession, declare that it will only be bound by one or the other of Chapters I and II of this Protocol.

2. Any State having made such a declaration may, at any subsequent time, declare by means of a notification addressed to the Secretary General of the Council of Europe that it will be bound by the provisions of both Chapters I and II. Such notification shall take effect from the date of its reception.

3. Any Contracting Party which is bound by the provisions of both Chapters I and II may at any time declare by means of a notification addressed to the Secretary General of the Council of Europe that it will only be bound by one or the other of Chapters I and II. Such notification shall take effect six months after the date of the receipt of such notification.

4. The provisions of Chapter I or II, as the case may be, shall be applicable only between Contracting Parties which are bound by the Chapter in question.

Article 6

1. This Protocol shall be open to signature by the member States of the Council of Europe, signatory to the Convention, who may become Parties to it either by:

(a) signature without reservation in respect of ratification, acceptance or approval;

(b) signature with reservation in respect of ratification, acceptance or approval, followed by ratification, acceptance or approval.

2. Instruments of ratification, acceptance or approval shall be deposited with the Secretary General of the Council of Europe.

3. A member State of the Council of Europe may not sign this Protocol without reservation in respect of ratification, acceptance or approval, nor ratify, accept or approve it, unless it has, simultaneously or previously, ratified or accepted the Convention.

Article 7

1. This Protocol shall enter into force three months after the date on which three member States of the Council of Europe shall have become Parties to the Protocol in accordance with the provisions of Article 6.

2. In the case of any member State which shall subsequently sign the Protocol without reservation in respect of ratification, acceptance or approval or which shall ratify, accept or approve it, the Protocol shall enter into force three months after the date of such signature or after the date of deposit of the instrument of ratification, acceptance or approval.

Article 8

1. After the entry into force of this Protocol, any State which has acceded, or has been invited to accede, to the Convention, may be invited by the Committee of Ministers to accede also to this Protocol.

2. Such accession shall be effected by depositing with the Secretary General of the Council of Europe an instrument of accession which shall take effect three months after the date of its deposit.

Article 9

1. Any State may, at the time of signature or when depositing its instrument of ratification, acceptance, approval or accession, specify the territory or territories to which this Protocol shall apply.

2. Any State may, when depositing its instrument of ratification, acceptance, approval or accession or at any later date, by declaration addressed to the Secretary General of the Council of Europe, extend this Protocol to any other territory or territories specified in the declaration and for those international relations it is responsible or on whose behalf it is authorised to give undertakings.

3. Any declaration made in pursuance of the preceding paragraph may, in respect of any territory mentioned in such declaration, be withdrawn by means of a notification addressed to the Secretary General of the Council of Europe. Such withdrawal shall take effect six months after the date of receipt by the Secretary General of the Council of Europe of the notification.

Article 10

1. Any Contracting Party may, in so far as it is concerned, denounce this Protocol by means of a notification addressed to the Secretary General of the Council of Europe.

2. Such denunciation shall take effect six months after the date of receipt by the Secretary General of the Council of Europe of such notification.

3. Denunciation of the Convention shall automatically entail denunciation of this Protocol.

Article 11

The Secretary General of the Council of Europe shall notify the member States of the Council and any State which has acceded to the Convention of:

(a) any signature without reservation in respect of ratification, acceptance or approval;

(b) any signature with reservation in respect of ratification, acceptance or approval;

(c) any deposit of an instrument of ratification, acceptance, approval or accession;

(d) any date of entry into force of this Protocol in accordance with Article 7 thereof;

(e) any notification received in pursuance of the provisions of Article 4;

(f) any declaration or notification received in pursuance of the provisions of Article 5;

(g) any declaration received in pursuance of the provisions of Article 9 and any withdrawal of any such declaration;

(h) any notification received in pursuance of the provisions of Article 10 and the date on which denunciation takes effect.

In witness whereof the undersigned, being duly authorised thereto, have signed this Protocol.

Done at Strasbourg, this 15th day of March 1978, in English and in French, both texts being equally authoritative, in a single copy which shall remain deposited in the archives of the Council of Europe. The Secretary General of the Council of Europe shall transmit certified copies to each of the signatory and acceding States.

EUROPEAN CONVENTION ON THE ABOLITION OF LEGALISATION OF DOCUMENTS EXECUTED BY DIPLOMATIC AGENTS OR CONSULAR OFFICERS

London, June 7, 1968

The member States of the Council of Europe, signatory hereto,

Considering that the aim of the Council of Europe is to achieve a greater unity between its members;

Considering that relations between the member States, as well as relations between their diplomatic agents or consular officers, are increasingly based on mutual trust;

Considering that the abolition of legalisation is likely to strengthen the ties between the member States by making it possible to use foreign documents in the same manner as documents emanating from national authorities;

Convinced of the need to abolish the requirement of legalisation of documents executed by their diplomatic agents or consular officers,

Have agreed as follows:

Article 1

For the purposes of this Convention, legalisation means only the formality used to certify the authenticity of the signature on a document, the capacity in which the person signing such document has acted and, where appropriate, the identity of the seal or stamp which such document bears.

Article 2

1. This Convention shall apply to documents which have been executed by diplomatic agents or consular officers of a Contracting Party, acting in their official capacity and exercising their functions in the territory of any state, and which have to be produced:

(a) either in the territory of another Contracting Party, or

(b) to the diplomatic agents or consular officers of another Contracting Party exercising their functions in the territory of a State which is not a party to this Convention.

2. This Convention shall also apply to official certificates, such as those recording the registration of a document or the fact that it was in existence on a certain date, and authentications of signatures, appended by diplomatic agents or consular officers to documents other than those referred to in paragraph 1.

Article 3

Each Contracting Party shall exempt from legalisation documents to which this Convention applies.

Article 4

1. Each Contracting Party shall take the measures necessary to avoid the carrying out by its authorities of legalisations in cases where this Convention abolishes legalisation.

2. Each Contracting Party shall provide for the verification, where necessary, of the authenticity of the documents to which this Convention applies. Such verification shall not give rise to payment of any taxes or expenses and shall be carried out as quickly as possible.

Article 5

This Convention shall, as between the Contracting Parties, prevail over the provisions of any treaties, conventions or agreements which provide, or shall provide, for legalisation of the authenticity of the signature of a diplomatic agent or consular officer, the capacity in which such person signing the document has acted, and, where appropriate, the identity of the seal or stamp which the document bears.

Article 6

1. This Convention shall be open to signature by the member States of the Council of Europe. It shall be subject to ratification or acceptance. Instruments of ratification or acceptance shall be deposited with the Secretary General of the Council of Europe.

2. This Convention shall enter into force three months after the date of the deposit of the third instrument of ratification or acceptance.

3. In respect of a signatory State ratifying or accepting subsequently, the Convention shall come into force three months after the date of the deposit of its instrument of ratification or acceptance.

Article 7

1. After the entry into force of this Convention, the Committee of Ministers of the Council of Europe may invite any State not a member of the Council of Europe to accede to this Convention.

2. Such accession shall be effected by depositing with the Secretary General of the Council of Europe an instrument of accession which shall take effect three months after the date of its deposit.

Article 8

1. Any Contracting Party may, at the time of signature or when depositing its instrument of ratification, acceptance or accession, specify the territory or territories to which this Convention shall apply.

2. Any Contracting Party may, when depositing its instrument of ratification, acceptance or accession or at any later date, by declaration addressed to the Secretary General of the Council of Europe, extend this Convention to any other territory or territories specified in the declaration and for whose international relations it is responsible or on whose behalf it is authorised to give undertakings.

3. Any declaration made in pursuance of the preceding paragraph may, in respect of any territory mentioned in such declaration, be withdrawn according to the procedure laid down in Article 9 of this Convention.

Article 9

1. This Convention shall remain in force indefinitely.

2. Any Contracting Party may, in so far as it is concerned, denounce this Convention by means of a notification addressed to the Secretary General of the Council of Europe.

3. Such denunciation shall take effect six months after the date of receipt by the Secretary General of such notification.

Article 10

The Secretary General of the Council of Europe shall notify the member States of the Council and any State which has acceded to this Convention of:

(a) any signature;

(b) any deposit of an instrument of ratification, acceptance or accession;

(c) any date of entry into force of this Convention;

(d) any declaration received in pursuance of the provisions of Article 8;

(e) any notification received in pursuance of the provisions of Article 9 and the date on which denunciation takes effect.

In witness whereof the undersigned, being duly authorised thereto, have signed this Convention.

Done at London, this 7th June 1968, in English and French, both texts being equally authoritative, in a single copy which shall remain deposited in the archives of the Council of Europe. The Secretary General of the Council of Europe shall transmit certified copies to each of the signatory and acceding States.

EUROPEAN CONVENTION ON STATE IMMUNITY AND ADDITIONAL PROTOCOL

Basle, May 16, 1972

Preamble

The member States of the Council of Europe, signatory hereto,

Considering that the aim of the Council of Europe is to achieve a greater unity between its members;

Taking into account the fact that there is in international law a tendency to restrict the cases in which a State may claim immunity before foreign courts;

Desiring to establish in their mutual relations common rules relating to the scope of the immunity of one State from the jurisdiction of the courts of another State, and designed to ensure compliance with judgments given against another State;

Considering that the adoption of such rules will tend to advance the work of harmonisation undertaken by the member States of the Council of Europe in the legal field,

Have agreed as follows:

CHAPTER I - IMMUNITY FROM JURISDICTION

Article 1

1. A Contracting State which institutes or intervenes in proceedings before a court of another Contracting State submits, for the purpose of those proceedings, to the jurisdiction of the courts of that State.

2. Such a Contracting State cannot claim immunity from the jurisdiction of the courts of the other Contracting State in respect of any counterclaim:

(a) arising out of the legal relationship or the facts on which the principal claim is based;

(b) if, according to the provisions of this Convention, it would not have been entitled to invoke immunity in respect of that counterclaim had separate proceedings been brought against it in those courts.

3. A Contracting State which makes a counterclaim in proceedings before a court of another Contracting State submits to the jurisdiction of the courts of that State with respect not only to the counterclaim but also to the principal claim.

Article 2

A Contracting State cannot claim immunity from the jurisdiction of a court of another Contracting State if it has undertaken to submit to the jurisdiction of that court either:

(a) by international agreement;

(b) by an express term contained in a contract in writing; or

(c) by an express consent given after a dispute between the parties has arisen.

Article 3

1. A Contracting State cannot claim immunity from the jurisdiction of a court of another Contracting State if, before claiming immunity, it takes any step in the proceedings relating to the merits. However, if the State satisfies the Court that it could not have acquired knowledge of facts on which a claim to immunity can be based until after it has taken such a step, it can claim immunity based on these facts if it does so at the earliest possible moment.

2. A Contracting State is not deemed to have waived immunity if it appears before a court of another Contracting State in order to assert immunity.

Article 4

1. Subject to the provisions of Article 5, a Contracting State cannot claim immunity from the jurisdiction of the courts of another Contracting State if the proceedings relate to an obligation of the State, which, by virtue of a contract, falls to be discharged in the territory of the State of the forum.

2. Paragraph 1 shall not apply:

(a) in the case of a contract concluded between States;

(b) if the parties to the contract have otherwise agreed in writing;

(c) if the State is party to a contract concluded on its territory and the obligation of the State is governed by its administrative law.

Article 5

1. A Contracting State cannot claim immunity from the jurisdiction of a court of another Contracting State if the proceedings relate to a contract of employment between the State and an individual where the work has to be performed on the territory of the State of the forum.

2. Paragraph 1 shall not apply where:

(a) the individual is a national of the employing State at the time when the proceedings are brought;

(b) at the time when the contract was entered into the individual was neither a national of the State of the forum nor habitually resident in that State; or

(c) the parties to the contract have otherwise agreed in writing, unless, in accordance with the law of the State of the forum, the courts of that State have exclusive jurisdiction by reason of the subject-matter.

3. Where the work is done for an office, agency or other establishment referred to in Article 7, paragraphs 2(a) and (b) of the present article apply only if, at the time the contract was entered into, the individual had his habitual residence in the Contracting State which employs him.

Article 6

1. A Contracting State cannot claim immunity from the jurisdiction of a court of another Contracting State if it participates with one or more private persons in a company, association or other legal entity having its seat, registered office or principal place of business on the territory of the State of the forum, and the proceedings concern the relationship, in matters arising out of that participation, between the State on the one hand and the entity or any other participant on the other hand.

2. Paragraph 1 shall not apply if it is otherwise agreed in writing.

Article 7

1. A Contracting State cannot claim immunity from the jurisdiction of a court of another Contracting State if it has on the territory of the State of the forum an office, agency or other establishment through which it engages, in the same manner as a private person, in an industrial, commercial or financial activity, and the proceedings relate to that activity of the office, agency or establishment.

2. Paragraph 1 shall not apply if all the parties to the dispute are States, or if the parties have otherwise agreed in writing.

Article 8

A Contracting State cannot claim immunity from the jurisdiction of a court of another Contracting State if the proceedings relate:

(a) to a patent, industrial design, trade-mark, service mark or other similar right which, in the State of the forum, has been applied for, registered or deposited or is otherwise protected, and in respect of which the State is the applicant or owner;

(b) to an alleged infringement by it, in the territory of the State of the forum, of such a right belonging to a third person and protected in that State;

(c) to an alleged infringement by it, in the territory of the State of the forum, of copyright belonging to a third person and protected in that State;

(d) to the right to use a trade name in the State of the forum.

Article 9

A Contracting State cannot claim immunity from the jurisdiction of a court of another Contracting State if the proceedings relate to:

(a) its rights or interests in, or its use or possession of, immovable property; or

(b) its obligations arising out of its rights or interests in, or use or possession of, immovable property and the property is situated in the territory of the State of the forum.

Article 10

A Contracting State cannot claim immunity from the jurisdiction of a court of another Contracting State if the proceedings relate to a right in movable or immovable property arising by way of succession, gift or bona vacantia.

Article 11

A Contracting State cannot claim immunity from the jurisdiction of a court of another Contracting State in proceedings which relate to redress for injury to the person or damage to tangible property, if the facts which occasioned the injury or damage occurred in the territory of the State of the forum, and if the author of the injury or damage was present in that territory at the time when those facts occurred.

Article 12

1. Where a Contracting State has agreed in writing to submit to arbitration a dispute which has arisen or may arise out of a civil or commercial matter, that State may not claim immunity from the jurisdiction of a court of another Contracting State on the ter-

ritory or according to the law of which the arbitration has taken or will take place in respect of any proceedings relating to:

(a) the validity or interpretation of the arbitration agreement;

(b) the arbitration procedure;

(c) the setting aside of the award,

unless the arbitration agreement otherwises provides.

2. Paragraph 1 shall not apply to an arbitration agreement between States.

Article 13

Paragraph 1 of Article 1 shall not apply where a Contracting State asserts, in proceedings pending before a court of another Contracting State to which it is not a party, that it has a right or interest in property which is the subject-matter of the proceedings, and the circumstances are such that it would have been entitled to immunity if the proceedings had been brought against it.

Article 14

Nothing in this Convention shall be interpreted as preventing a court of a Contracting State from administering or supervising or arranging for the administration of property, such as trust property or the estate of a bankrupt, solely on account of the fact that another Contracting State has a right or interest in the property.

Article 15

A Contracting State shall be entitled to immunity from the jurisdiction of the courts of another Contracting State if the proceedings do not fall within Articles 1 to 14; the court shall decline to entertain such proceedings even if the State does not appear.

Chapter II - Procedural rules

Article 16

1. In proceedings against a Contracting State in a court of another Contracting State, the following rules shall apply.

2. The competent authorities of the State of the forum shall transmit

- the original or a copy of the document by which the proceedings are instituted;
- a copy of any judgment given by default against a State which was defendant in the proceedings,

through the diplomatic channel to the Ministry of Foreign Affairs of the defendant State, for onward transmission, where appropriate, to the competent authority. These documents shall be accompanied, if necessary, by a translation into the official language, or one of the official languages, of the defendant State.

3. Service of the documents referred to in paragraph 2 is deemed to have been effected by their receipt by the Ministry of Foreign Affairs.

4. The time-limits within which the State must enter an appearance or appeal against any judgment given by default shall begin to run two months after the date on which the document by which the proceedings were instituted or the copy of the judgment is received by the Ministry of Foreign Affairs.

5. If it rests with the court to prescribe the time-limits for entering an appearance or for appealing against a judgment given by default, the court shall allow the State not less than two months after the date on which the document by which the proceedings are instituted or the copy of the judgment is received by the Ministry of Foreign Affairs.

6. A Contracting State which appears in the proceedings is deemed to have waived any objection to the method of service.

7. If the Contracting State has not appeared, judgment by default may be given against it only if it is established that the document by which the proceedings were instituted has been transmitted in conformity with paragraph 2, and that the time-limits for entering an appearance provided for in paragraphs 4 and 5 have been observed.

Article 17

No security, bond or deposit, however described, which could not have been required in the State of the forum of a national of that State or a person domiciled or resident there, shall be required of a Contracting State to guarantee the payment of judicial costs or expenses. A State which is a claimant in the courts of another Contracting State shall pay any judicial costs or expenses for which it may become liable.

Article 18

A Contracting State party to proceedings before a court of another Contracting State may not be subjected to any measure of coercion, or any penalty, by reason of its failure or refusal to disclose any documents or other evidence. However the court may draw any conclusion it thinks fit from such failure or refusal.

Article 19

1. A court before which proceedings to which a Contracting State is a party are instituted shall, at the request of one of the parties or, if its national law so permits, of its own motion, decline to proceed with the case or shall stay the proceedings if other proceedings between the same parties, based on the same facts and having the same purpose:

(a) are pending before a court of that Contracting State, and were the first to be instituted; or

(b) are pending before a court of any other Contracting State, were the first to be instituted and may result in a judgment to which the State party to the proceedings must give effect by virtue of Article 20 or Article 25.

2. Any Contracting State whose law gives the courts a discretion to decline to proceed with a case or to stay the the proceedings in cases where proceedings between the same parties, based on the same facts and having the same purpose, are pending before a court of another Contracting State, may, by notification addressed to the Secretary General of the Council of Europe, declare that its courts shall not be bound by the provisions of paragraph 1.

Chapter III - Effect of Judgment

Article 20

1. A Contracting State shall give effect to a judgment given against it by a court of another Contracting State:

(a) if, in accordance with the provisions of Articles 1 to 13, the State could not claim immunity from jurisdiction; and

(b) if the judgment cannot or can no longer be set aside if obtained by default, or if it is not or is no longer subject to appeal or any other form of ordinary review or to annulment.

2. Nevertheless, a Contracting State is not obliged to give effect to such a judgment in any case:

(a) where it would be manifestly contrary to public policy in that State to do so, or where, in the circumstances, either party had no adequate opportunity fairly to present his case;

(b) where proceedings between the same parties, based on the same facts and having the same purpose:

(i) are pending before a court of that State and were the first to be instituted;

(ii) are pending before a court of another Contracting State, were the first to be instituted and may result in a judgment to which the State party to the proceedings must give effect under the terms of this Convention;

(c) where the result of the judgment is inconsistent with the result of another judgment given between the same parties:

(i) by a court of the Contracting State, if the proceedings before that court were the first to be instituted or if the other judgment has been given before the judgment satisfied the conditions specified in paragraph 1. b; or

(ii) by a court of another Contracting State where the other judgment is the first to satisfy the requirements laid down in the present Convention;

(d) where the provisions of Article 16 have not been observed and the State has not entered an appearance or has not appealed against a judgment by default.

3. In addition, in the cases provided for in Article 10, a Contracting State is not obliged to give effect to the judgment:

(a) if the courts of the State of the forum would not have been entitled to assume jurisdiction had they applied, mutatis mutandis, the rules of jurisdiction (other than those mentioned in the annex to the present Convention) which operate in the State against which judgment is given; or

(b) if the court, by applying a law other than that which would have been applied in accordance with the rules of private international law of that State, has reached a result different from that which would have been reached by applying the law determined by those rules.

However, a Contracting State may not rely upon the grounds of refusal specified in sub-paragraphs (a) and (b) above if it is bound by an agreement with the State of the forum on the recognition and enforcement of judgments and the judgment fulfils the requirement of that agreement as regards jurisdiction and, where appropriate, the law applied.

Article 21

1. Where a judgment has been given against a Contracting State and that State does not give effect thereto, the party which seeks to invoke the judgment shall be entitled to have determined by the competent court of that State the question whether effect should be given to the judgment in accordance with Article 20. Proceedings may also be brought before this court by the State against which judgment has been given, if its law so permits.

2. Save in so far as may be necessary for the application of Article 20, the competent court of the State in question may not review the merits of the judgment.

3. Where proceedings are instituted before a court of a State in accordance with paragraph 1:

(a) the parties shall be given an opportunity to be heard in the proceedings;

(b) documents produced by the party seeking to invoke the judgment shall not be subject to legalisation or any other like formality;

(c) no security, bond or deposit, however described, shall be required of the party invoking the judgment by reason of his nationality, domicile or residence;

(d) the party invoking the judgment shall be entitled to legal aid under conditions no less favourable than those applicable to nationals of the State who are domiciled and resident therein.

4. Each Contracting State shall, when depositing its instrument of ratification, acceptance or accession, designate the court or courts referred to in paragraph 1, and inform the Secretary General of the Council of Europe thereof.

Article 22

1. A Contracting State shall give effect to a settlement to which it is a party and which has been made before a court of another Contracting State in the course of the proceedings; the provisions of Article 20 do not apply to such a settlement.

2. If the State does not give effect to the settlement, the procedure provided for in Article 21 may be used.

Article 23

No measures of execution or preventive measures against the property of a Contracting State may be taken in the territory of another Contracting State except where and to the extent that the State has expressly consented thereto in writing in any particular case.

CHAPTER IV - OPTIONAL PROVISIONS

Article 24

1. Notwithstanding the provisions of Article 15, any State may, when signing this Convention or depositing its instrument of ratification, acceptance or accession, or at any later date, by notification addressed to the Secretary General of the Council of Europe, declare that, in cases not falling within Articles 1 to 13, its courts shall be entitled to entertain proceedings against another Contracting State to the extent that its courts are entitled to entertain proceedings against States not party to the present Convention. Such a declaration shall be without prejudice to the immunity from jurisdiction which foreign States enjoy in respect of acts performed in the exercise of sovereign authority (*acta jure imperii*).

2. The courts of a State which has made the declaration provided for in paragraph 1 shall not however be entitled to entertain such proceedings against another Contracting State if their jurisdiction could have been based solely on one or more of the grounds mentioned in the annex to the present Convention, unless that other Contracting State has taken a step in the proceedings relating to the merits without first challenging the jurisdiction of the court.

3. The provisions of Chapter II apply to proceedings instituted against a Contracting State in accordance with the present article.

4. The declaration made under paragraph 1 may be withdrawn by notification addressed to the Secretary General of the Council of Europe. The withdrawal shall take effect three months after the date of its receipt, but this shall not affect proceedings instituted before the date on which the withdrawal becomes effective.

Article 25

1. Any Contracting State which has made a declaration under Article 24 shall, in cases not falling within Articles 1 to 13, give effect to a judgment given by a court of another Contracting State which has made a like declaration:

(a) if the conditions prescribed in paragraph 1. b of Article 20 have been fulfilled; and

(b) if the court is considered to have jurisdiction in accordance with the following paragraphs.

2. However, the Contracting State is not obliged to give effect to such a judgment:

(a) if there is a ground for refusal as provided for in paragraph 2 of Article 20; or

(b) if the provisions of paragraph 2 of Article 24 have not been observed.

3. Subject to the provisions of paragraph 4, a court of a Contracting State shall be considered to have jurisdiction for the purpose of paragraph 1. b:

(a) if its jurisdiction is recognised in accordance with the provisions of an agreement to which the State of the forum and the other Contracting State are Parties;

(b) where there is no agreement between the two States concerning the recognition and enforcement of judgments in civil matters, if the courts of the State of the forum would have been entitled to assume jurisdiction had they applied, mutatis mutandis, the rules of jurisdiction (other than those mentioned in the annex to the present Convention) which operate in the State against which the judgment was given. This provision does not apply to questions arising out of contracts.

4. The Contracting States having made the declaration provided for in Article 24 may, by means of a supplementary agreement to this Convention, determine the circumstances in which their courts shall be considered to have jurisdiction for the purposes of paragraph 1. b of this article.

5. If the Contracting State does not give effect to the judgment, the procedure provided for in Article 21 may be used.

Article 26

Notwithstanding the provisions of Article 23, a judgment rendered against a Contracting State in proceedings relating to an industrial or commercial activity, in which the State is engaged in the same manner as a private person, may be enforced in the State of the forum against property of the State against which judgment has been given, used exclusively in connection with such an activity, if:

(a) both the State of the forum and the State against which the judgment has been given have made declarations under Article 24;

(b) the proceedings which resulted in the judgment fell within Articles 1 to 13 or were instituted in accordance with paragraphs 1 and 2 of Article 24; and

(c) the judgment satisfies the requirements laid down in paragraph 1(b) of Article 20.

CHAPTER V - GENERAL PROVISIONS

Article 27

1. For the purposes of the present Convention, the expression "Contracting State" shall not include any legal entity of a Contracting State which is distinct therefrom and is capable of suing or being sued, even if that entity has been entrusted with public functions.

2. Proceedings may be instituted against any entity referred to in paragraph 1 before the courts of another Contracting State in the same manner as against a private person; however, the courts may not entertain proceedings in respect of acts performed by the entity in the exercise of sovereign authority (acta jure imperii).

3. Proceedings may in any event be instituted against any such entity before those courts if, in corresponding circumstances, the courts would have had jurisdiction if the proceedings had been instituted against a Contracting State.

Article 28

1. Without prejudice to the provisions of Article 27, the constituent States of a Federal State do not enjoy immunity.

2. However, a Federal State Party to the present Convention, may, by notification addressed to the Secretary General of the Council of Europe, declare that its constituent States may invoke the provisions of the Convention applicable to Contracting States, and have the same obligations.

3. Where a Federal State has made a declaration in accordance with paragraph 2, service of documents on a constituent State of a Federation shall be made on the Ministry of Foreign Affairs of the Federal State, in conformity with Article 16.

4. The Federal State alone is competent to make the declarations, notifications and communications provided for in the present Convention, and the Federal State alone may be party to proceedings pursuant to Article 34.

Article 29

The present Convention shall not apply to proceedings concerning:

(a) social security;

(b) damage or injury in nuclear matters;

(c) customs duties, taxes or penalties.

Article 30

The present Convention shall not apply to proceedings in respect of claims relating to the operation of seagoing vessels owned or operated by a Contracting State or to the carriage of cargoes and of passengers by such vessels or to the carriage of cargoes owned by a Contracting State and carried on board merchant vessels.

Article 31

Nothing in this Convention shall affect any immunities or privileges enjoyed by a Contracting State in respect of anything done or omitted to be done by, or in relation to, its armed forces when on the territory of another Contracting State.

Article 32

Nothing in the present Convention shall affect privileges and immunities relating to the exercise of the functions of diplomatic missions and consular posts and of persons connected with them.

Article 33

Nothing in the present Convention shall affect existing or future international agreements in special fields which relate to matters dealt with in the present Convention.

Article 34

1. Any dispute which might arise between two or more Contracting States concerning the interpretation or application of the present Convention shall be submitted to the International Court of Justice on the application of one of the parties to the dispute or by special agreement unless the parties agree on a different method of peaceful settlement of the dispute.

2. However, proceedings may not be instituted before the International Court of Justice which relate to:

(a) a dispute concerning a question arising in proceedings instituted against a Contracting State before a court of another Contracting State, before the court has given a judgment which fulfils the condition provided for in paragraph 1. b of Article 20;

(b) a dispute concerning a question arising in proceedings instituted before a court of a Contracting State in accordance with paragraph 1 of Article 21, before the court has rendered a final decision in such proceedings.

Article 35

1. The present Convention shall apply only to proceedings introduced after its entry into force.

2. When a State has become Party to this Convention after it has entered into force, the Convention shall apply only to proceedings introduced after it has entered into force with respect to that State.

3. Nothing in this Convention shall apply to proceedings arising out of, or judgments based on, acts, omissions or facts prior to the date on which the present Convention is opened for signature.

CHAPTER VI - FINAL PROVISIONS

Article 36

1. The present Convention shall be open to signature by the member States of the Council of Europe. It shall be subject to ratification or acceptance. Instruments of ratification or acceptance shall be deposited with the Secretary General of the Council of Europe.

2. The Convention shall enter into force three months after the date of the deposit of the third instrument of ratification or acceptance.

3. In respect of a signatory State ratifying or accepting subsequently, the Convention shall enter into force three months after the date of the deposit of its instrument of ratification or acceptance.

Article 37

1. After the entry into force of the present Convention, the Committee of Ministers of the Council of Europe may, by a decision taken by a unanimous vote of the members casting a vote, invite any non-member State to accede thereto.

2. Such accession shall be effected by depositing with the Secretary General of the Council of Europe an instrument of accession which shall take effect three months after the date of its deposit.

3. However, if a State having already acceded to the Convention notifies the Secretary General of the Council of Europe of its objection to the accession of another non-member State, before the entry into force of this accession, the Convention shall not apply to the relations between these two States.

Article 38

1. Any State may, at the time of signature or when depositing its instrument of ratification, acceptance or accession, specify the territory or territories to which the present Convention shall apply.

2. Any State may, when depositing its instrument of ratification, acceptance or accession or at any later date, by declaration addressed to the Secretary General of the Council of Europe, extend this Convention to any other territory or territories specified in the declaration and for whose international relations it is responsible or on whose behalf it is authorised to give undertakings.

3. Any declaration made in pursuance of the preceding paragraph may, in respect of any territory mentioned in such declaration, be withdrawn according to the procedure laid down in Article 40 of this Convention.

Article 39

No reservation is permitted to the present Convention.

Article 40

1. Any Contracting State may, in so far as it is concerned, denounce this Convention by means of notification addressed to the Secretary General of the Council of Europe.

2. Such denunciation shall take effect six months after the date of receipt by the Secretary General of such notification. This Convention shall, however, continue to apply to proceedings introduced before the date on which the denunciation takes effect, and to judgments given in such proceedings.

Article 41

The Secretary General of the Council of Europe shall notify the member States of the Council of Europe and any State which has acceded to this Convention of:

(a) any signature;

(b) any deposit of an instrument of ratification, acceptance or accession;

(c) any date of entry into force of this Convention in accordance with Articles 36 and 37 thereof;

(d) any notification received in pursuance of the provisions of paragraph 2 of Article 19;

(e) any communication received in pursuance of the provisions of paragraph 4 of Article 21;

(f) any notification received in pursuance of the provisions of paragraph 1 of Article 24;

(g) the withdrawal of any notification made in pursuance of the provisions of paragraph 4 of Article 24;

(h) any notification received in pursuance of the provisions of paragraph 2 of Article 28;

(i) any notification received in pursuance of the provisions of paragraph 3 or Article 37;

(j) any declaration received in pursuance of the provisions of Article 38;

(k) any notification received in pursuance of the provisions of Article 40 and the date on which denunciation takes effect.

In witness whereof the undersigned, being duly authorised thereto, have signed this Convention.

Done at Basle, this 16th day of May 1972, in English and French, both texts being equally authoritative, in a single copy which shall remain deposited in the archives of the Council of Europe. The Secretary General of the Council of Europe shall transmit certified copies to each of the signatory and acceding States.

ANNEX

The grounds of jurisdiction referred to in paragraph 3, sub-paragraph (a), of Article 20, paragraph 2 of Article 24 and paragraph 3, sub-paragraph (b), of Article 25 are the following:

(a) the presence in the territory of the State of the forum of property belonging to the defendant, or the seizure by the plaintiff of property situated there, unless:

- the action is brought to assert proprietary or possessory rights in that property, or arises from another issue relating to such property; or
- the property constitutes the security for a debt which is the subject-matter of the action;

(b) the nationality of the plaintiff;

(c) the domicile, habitual residence or ordinary residence of the plaintiff within the territory of the State of the forum unless the assumption of jurisdiction on such a ground is permitted by way of an exception made on account of the particular subject-matter of a class of contracts;

(d) the fact that the defendant carried on business within the territory of the State of the forum, unless the action arises from that business;

(e) a unilateral specification of the forum by the plaintiff, particularly in an invoice.

a legal person shall be considered to have its domicile or habitual residence where it has its seat, registered office or principal place of business.

ADDITIONAL PROTOCOL TO THE EUROPEAN CONVENTION ON STATE IMMUNITY
Basle, May 16, 1972

The member States of the Council of Europe, signatory to the present Protocol,

Having taken note of the European Convention on State Immunity -hereinafter referred to as "the Convention" - and in particular Articles 21 and 34 thereof;

Desiring to develop the work of harmonisation in the field covered by the Convention by the addition of provisions concerning a European procedure for the settlement of disputes,

Have agreed as follows:

PART I

Article 1

1. Where a judgment has been given against a State Party to the Convention and that State does not give effect thereto, the party which seeks to invoke the judgment shall be entitled to have determined the question whether effect should be given to the judgment in conformity with Article 20 or Article 25 of the Convention, by instituting proceedings before either:

(a) the competent court of that State in application of Article 21 of the Convention; or

(b) the European Tribunal constituted in conformity with the provisions of Part III of the present Protocol, provided that that State is a Party to the present Protocol and has not made the declaration referred to in Part IV thereof.

The choice between these two possibilites shall be final.

2. If the State intends to institute proceedings before its court in accordance with the provisions of paragraph 1 or Article 21 of the Convention, it must give notice of its intention to do so to the party in whose favour the judgment has been given; the State may thereafter institute such proceedings only if the party has not, within three months of receiving notice, instituted proceedings before the European Tribunal. Once this period has elapsed, the party in whose favour the judgment has been given may no longer institute proceedings before the European Tribunal.

3. Save in so far as may be necessary for the application of Articles 20 and 25 of the Convention, the European Tribunal may not review the merits of the judgment.

PART II

Article 2

1. Any dispute which might arise between two or more States parties to the present Protocol concerning the interpretation or application of the Convention shall be submitted, on the application of one of the parties to the dispute or by special agreement, to the

European Tribunal constituted in conformity with the provisions of Part III of the present Protocol. The States parties to the present Protocol undertake not to submit such a dispute to a different mode of settlement.

2. If the dispute concerns a question arising in proceedings instituted before a court of one State Party to the Convention against another State Party to the Convention, or a question arising in proceedings instituted before a court of a State Party to the Convention in accordance with Article 21 of the Convention, it may not be referred to the European Tribunal until the court has given a final decision in such proceedings.

3. Proceedings may not be instituted before the European Tribunal which relate to a dispute concerning a judgment which it has already determined or is required to determine by virtue of Part I of this Protocol.

Article 3

Nothing in the present Protocol shall be interpreted as preventing the European Tribunal from determining any dispute which might arise between two or more States parties to the Convention concerning the interpretation or application thereof and which might be submitted to it by special agreement, even if these States, or any of them, are not parties to the present Protocol.

PART III

Article 4

1. There shall be established a European Tribunal in matters of State Immunity to determine cases brought before it in conformity with the provisions of Parts I and II of the present Protocol.

2. The European Tribunal shall consist of the members of the European Court of Human Rights and, in respect of each non-member State of the Council of Europe which has acceded to the present Protocol, a person possessing the qualifications required of members of that Court designated, with the agreement of the Committee of Ministers of the Council of Europe, by the government of that State for a period of nine years.

3. The President of the European Tribunal shall be the President of the European Court of Human Rights.

Article 5

1. Where proceedings are instituted before the European Tribunal in accordance with the provisions of Part I of the present Protocol, the European Tribunal shall consist of a Chamber composed of seven members. There shall sit as ex officio members of the Chamber the member of the European Tribunal who is a national of the State against which the judgment has been given and the member of the European Tribunal who is a national of the State of the forum, or, should there be no such member in one or the other case, a person designated by the government of the State concerned to sit in the capacity of a member of the Chamber. The names of the other five members shall be chosen by lot by the President of the European Tribunal in the presence of the Registrar.

2. Where proceedings are instituted before the European Tribunal in accordance with the provisions of Part II of the present Protocol, the Chamber shall be constituted in the manner provided for in the preceding paragraph. However, there shall sit as ex officio members of the Chamber the members of the European Tribunal who are nationals of the States parties to the dispute or, should there be no such member, a person designated

by the government of the State concerned to sit in the capacity of a member of the Chamber.

3. Where a case pending before a Chamber raises a serious question affecting the interpretation of the Convention or of the present Protocol, the Chamber may, at any time, relinquish jurisdiction in favour of the European Tribunal meeting in plenary session. The relinquishment of jurisdiction shall be obligatory where the resolution of such question might have a result inconsistent with a judgment previously delivered by a Chamber or by the European Tribunal meeting in plenary session. The relinquishment of jurisdiction shall be final. Reasons need not be given for the decision to relinquish jurisdiction.

Article 6

1. The European Tribunal shall decide any disputes as to whether the Tribunal has jurisdiction.

2. The hearings of the European Tribunal shall be public unless the Tribunal in exceptional circumstances decides otherwise.

3. The judgments of the European Tribunal, taken by a majority of the members present, are to be delivered in public session. Reasons shall be given for the judgment of the European Tribunal. If the judgment does not represent in whole or in part the unanimous opinion of the European Tribunal, any member shall be entitled to deliver a separate opinion.

4. The judgments of the European Tribunal shall be final and binding upon the parties.

Article 7

1. The European Tribunal shall draw up its own rules and fix its own procedure.

2. The Registry of the European Tribunal shall be provided by the Registrar of the European Court of Human Rights.

Article 8

1. The operating costs of the European Tribunal shall be borne by the Council of Europe. States non-members of the Council of Europe having acceded to the present Protocol shall contribute thereto in a manner to be decided by the Committee of Ministers after agreement with these States.

2. The members of the European Tribunal shall receive for each day of duty a compensation to be determined by the Committee of Ministers.

PART IV

Article 9

1. Any State may, by notification addressed to the Secretary General of the Council of Europe at the moment of its signature of the present Protocol, or of the deposit of its instrument of ratification, acceptance or accession thereto, declare that it will only be bound by Parts II to V of the present Protocol.

2. Such a notification may be withdrawn at any time.

PART V

Article 10

1. The present Protocol shall be open to signature by the member States of the Council of Europe which have signed the Convention. It shall be subject to ratification or acceptance. Instruments of ratification or acceptance shall be deposited with the Secretary General of the Council of Europe.

2. The present Protocol shall enter into force three months after the date of the deposit of the fifth instrument of ratification or acceptance.

3. In respect of a signatory State ratifying or accepting subsequently, the Protocol shall enter into force three months after the date of the deposit of its instrument of ratification or acceptance.

4. A member State of the Council of Europe may not ratify or accept the present Protocol without having ratified or accepted the Convention.

Article 11

1. A State which has acceded to the Convention may accede to the present Protocol after the Protocol has entered into force.

2. Such accession shall be effected by depositing with the Secretary General of the Council of Europe an instrument of accession which shall take effect three months after the date of its deposit.

Article 12

No reservation is permitted to the present Protocol.

Article 13

1. Any Contracting State may, in so far as it is concerned, denounce the present Protocol by means of a notification addressed to the Secretary General of the Council of Europe.

2. Such denunciation shall take effect six months after the date of receipt by the Secretary General of such notification. The Protocol shall, however, continue to apply to proceedings introduced in conformity with the provisions of the protocol before the date on which such denunciation takes effect.

3. Denunciation of the Convention shall automatically entail denunciation of the present Protocol.

Article 14

The Secretary General of the Council of Europe shall notify the member States of the Council and any State which has acceded to the Convention of:

(a) any signature of the present Protocol;

(b) any deposit of an instrument of ratification, acceptance or accession;

(c) any date of entry into force of the present Protocol in accordance with Articles 10 and 11 thereof;

(d) any notification received in pursuance of the provisions of Part IV and any withdrawal of any such notification;

(e) any notification received in pursuance of the provisions of Article 13 and the date on which such denunciation takes effect.

In witness whereof the undersigned, being duly authorised thereto, have signed the present Protocol.

Done at Basle, this 16th day of May 1972, in English and French, both texts being equally authoritative, in a single copy which shall remain deposited in the archives of the Council of Europe. The Secretary General of the Council of Europe shall transmit certified copies to each of the signatory and acceding States.

RESOLUTION (72) 2 OF THE COMMITTEE OF MINISTERS OF THE COUNCIL OF EUROPE CONCERNING THE EUROPEAN CONVENTION ON STATE IMMUNITY

adopted at the 206th meeting of the Ministers' Deputies on 18 January 1972

The Committee of Ministers of the Council of Europe,

Having taken note of the text of the European Convention on State Immunity;

Considering that one of the aims of this Convention is to ensure compliance with judgments given against a State,

Recommends the governments of those member States which shall become parties to this Convention to establish, for the purpose of Article 21 of the Convention, a procedure which shall be as expeditious and simple as possible.

APPENDIX V

INTER-AMERICAN CONVENTIONS

INTER-AMERICAN CONVENTIONS
(as of October 15, 1997)

- Letters Rogatory and Additional Protocol, Panama City, January 30, 1975
- Additional Protocol, Montevideo, May 8, 1979
- Taking of Evidence, Panama City, January 30, 1975
- Additional Protocol, La Paz, May 24, 1984

Countries	Letter Rogatory 1975	Additional Protocol 1979	Evidence 1975	Additional Protocol 1984
Argentina	X	X	X	X
Bolivia	—	—	—	—
Brazil	X	X	—	—
Chile	X	X	X	—
Columbia	X	X	X	—
Costa Rica	X	—	X	—
Dominican Republic	—	—	X	—
Ecuador	X	X	X	X
El Salvador	X	—	X	—
Guatemala	X	X	X	—
Haiti	—	—	—	—
Honduras	X	—	X	—
Mexico	X	X	X	X
Nicaragua	—	—	—	—
Panama	X	X	X	—
Paraguay	X	X	X	—
Peru	X	X	X	—
Spain	X	—	—	—
United States of America	X	X	—	—
Uruguay	X	X	X	—
Venezuela	X	X	X	X

INTER-AMERICAN CONVENTION ON LETTERS ROGATORY
Done at Panama, January 30, 1975
Entered into force January 16, 1976

The Governments of the Member States of the Organization of American States, desirous of concluding a convention on letters rogatory, have agreed as follows:

I. USE OF TERMS
Article 1

For the purposes of this Convention the terms "exhortos" and "cartas rogatorias" are synonymous in the Spanish text. The terms "letters rogatory", "commissions rogatories," and "cartae rogatorias" used in the English, French and Portuguese texts, respectively, cover both "exhortos" and "cartas rogatorias."

II. SCOPE OF THE CONVENTION
Article 2

This Convention shall apply to letters rogatory, issued in conjunction with proceedings in civil and commercial matters held before the appropriate judicial or other adjudicatory authority of one of the States Parties to this Convention, that have as their purpose;

a. The performance of procedural acts of a merely formal nature, such as service of process, summonses or subpoenas abroad;

b. The taking of evidence and the obtaining of information abroad, unless a reservation is made in this respect.

Article 3

This Convention shall not apply to letters rogatory relating to procedural acts other than those specified in the preceding article; and in particular it shall not apply to acts involving measures of compulsion.

III. TRANSMISSION OF LETTERS ROGATORY
Article 4

Letters rogatory may be transmitted to the authority to which they are addressed by the interested parties, through judicial channels, diplomatic or consular agents, or the Central Authority of the State of origin or of the State of destination, as the case may be.

Each State Party shall inform the General Secretarist of the Organization of American States of the Central Authority competent to receive and distribute letters rogatory.

IV. REQUIREMENTS FOR EXECUTION
Article 5

Letters rogatory shall be executed in the States Parties provided they meet the following requirements:

a. The letter regatory is legalized, except as provided for in Article 6 and 7 of this Convention. The letter rogatory shall be presumed to be duly legalized in the State of origin when legalized by the competent consular or diplomatic agent;

b. The letter rogatory and the appended documentation are duly translated into the official language of the State of destination.

Article 6

Whenever letters rogatory are transmitted through consular or diplomatic channels or through the Central Authority, legalization shall not be required.

Article 7

Courts in border areas of the States Parties may directly execute the letters rogatory contemplated in this Convention and such letters shall not require legalization.

Article 8

Letters rogatory shall be accompanied by the following documents to be delivered to the person on whom process, summons or subpoena is being served:

a. An authenticated copy of the complaint with its supporting documents, and of other exhibits or rulings that serve as the basis for the measure requested;

b. Written information identifying the judicial or other adjudicatory authority issuing the letter, indicating the time-limits allowed the person affected to act upon the request, and warning of the consequences of failure to do so;

c. Where appropriate, information on the existence and address of the court-appointed defense counsel or of competent legal-aid societies in the State of origin.

Article 9

Execution of letters rogatory shall not imply ultimate recognition of the jurisdiction of the judicial or other adjudicatory authority issuing the letter rogatory or a commitment to recognize the validity of the judgment it may render or to execute it.

V. EXECUTION
Article 10

Letters rogatory shall be executed in accordance with the laws and procedural rules of the State of destination.

At the request of the judicial or other adjudicatory authority, issuing the letter rogatory, the authority of the State of destination may execute the letter through a special procedure, or accept the observance of additional formalities in performing the act requested, provided this procedure or the observance of those formalities is not contrary to the law of the State of destination.

Article 11

The authority of the State of destination shall have jurisdiction to determine any issue arising as a result of the execution of the measure requested in the letter rogatory.

Should such authority find that it lacks jurisdiction to execute the letter rogatory, it shall ex officio forward the documents and antecedents of the case to the authority of the State which has jurisdiction.

Article 12

The costs and other expenses involved in the processing and execution of letters rogatory shall be borne by the interested parties.

The State of destination may, in its discretion, execute a letter rogatory that does not indicate the person to be held responsible for costs and other expenses when incurred. The identity of the person empowered to represent the applicant for legal purposes may be indicated in the letter rogatory or in the documents relating to its execution.

The effects of a declaration in forma pauperis shall be regulated by the law of the State of destination.

Article 13

Consular or diplomatic agents of the States Parties to this Convention may perform the acts referred to in Article 2 in the State in which they are accredited, provided the performance of such acts is not contrary to the laws of that State. In so doing, they shall not perform any acts involving measures of compulsion.

VI. GENERAL PROVISIONS

Article 14

States Parties belonging to economic integration systems may agree directly between themselves upon special methods and procedures more expeditious than those provided for in this Convention. These agreements may be extended to include other States in the manner in which the parties may agree.

Article 15

This Convention shall not limit any provisions regarding letters rogatory in bilateral or multilateral agreements that may have been signed or may be signed in the future by the States Parties or preclude the continuation of more favorable practices in this regard that may be followed by these States.

Article 16

The States Parties to this Convention may declare that its provisions cover the execution of letters rogatory in criminal, labor, and "contentious-administrative" cases, as well as in arbitrations and other matters within the jurisdiction of special courts. Such declarations shall be transmitted to the General Secretariat of the Organization of American States.

Article 17

The State of destination may refuse to execute a letter rogatory that is manifestly contrary to its public policy ("ordre public").

Article 18

The States Parties shall inform the General Secretariat of the Organization of American States of the requirements stipulated in their laws for the legalization and the translation of letters rogatory.

VII. FINAL PROVISIONS

Article 19

This Convention shall be open for signature by the Member States of the Organization of American States.

Article 20

This Convention is subject to ratification. The instruments of ratification shall be deposited with the General Secretariat of the Organization of American States.

Article 21

This Convention shall remain open for accession by any other State. The instrument of accession shall be deposited with the General Secretariat of the Organization of American States.

Article 22

This Convention shall enter into force on the thirtieth day following the date of deposit of the second instrument of ratification.

For each State ratifying or acceding to the Convention after the deposit of the second instrument of ratification, the Convention shall enter into force on the thirtieth day after deposit by such State of its instrument of ratification or accession.

Article 23

If a State Party has two or more territorial units in which different systems of law apply in relation to the matters dealt with in this Convention, it may, at the time of signature, ratification or accession, declare that this Convention shall extend to all its territorial units or only to one or more of them.

Such declaration may be modified by subsequent declarations, which shall expressly indicate the territorial unit or units to which the Convention applies. Such subsequent declarations shall be transmitted to the General Secretariat of the Organization of American States, and shall become effective thirty days after the date of their receipt.

Article 24

This Convention shall remain in force indefinitely, but any of the States Parties may denounce it. The instrument of denunciation shall be deposited with the General Secretariat of the Organization of American States. After one year from the date of deposit of the instrument of denunciation, the Convention shall no longer be in effect for the denouncing State, but shall remain in effect for the other States Parties.

Article 25

The original instrument of this Convention, the English, French, Portuguese and Spanish texts of which are equally authentic, shall be deposited with the General Secretariat of the Organization of American States. The Secretariat shall notify the Member State of the Organization of American States and the States that have accoded to the Convention of the signatures, deposits of instruments of ratification, accession, and denunciation as well as of reservations, if any. It shall also transmit the information mentioned in the second paragraph of Article 4 and in Article 18 and the declarations referred to in Article 16 and 23 of this Convention.

IN WITNESS WHEREOF the undersigned Plenipotentiaries, being duly authorized thereto by their respective Governments, have signed this Convention.

DONE AT PANAMA CITY, Republic of Panama, this thirtieth day of January one thousand nine hundred and seventy-five.

ADDITIONAL PROTOCOL TO THE INTER-AMERICAN CONVENTION ON LETTERS ROGATORY WITH ANNEX

Done at Montevideo, May 8, 1979

Entered into force June 14, 1980

The Government of the Member States of the Organization of American States, desirous of strengthening and facilitating international cooperation in judicial procedures as provided for in the Inter-American Convention on Letters Rogatory, done in Panama on January 30, 1975, have agreed as follows;

1. SCOPE OF PROTOCOL
Article 1

This Protocol shall apply only to those procedural acts set forth in Article 2 (a) of the Inter-American Convention on Letters Rogatory, hereinafter referred to as "the Convention". For the purposes of this Protocol, such acts shall be understood to mean procedural acts (pleadings, motions, orders, and subpoenas) that are served and requests for information that are made by a judicial or other adjudicatory authority of a State Party to a judicial or administrative authority of another State Party and are transmitted by a letter rogatory from the Central Authority of the State of origin to the Central Authority of the State of destination.

II. CENTRAL AUTHORITY
Article 2

Each State Party shall designate a central authority that shall perform the functions assigned to it in the Convention and in this Protocol. At the time of deposit of their instruments of ratification or accession to this Protocol, the States Parties shall communicate the designations to the General Secretariat of the Organization of American States, which shall distribute to the States Parties to the Convention a list containing the designations received. The Central Authority designated by a State Party in accordance with Article 4 of the Convention may be changed at any time. The State Party shall inform the above-mentioned Secretariat of such change as promptly as possible.

III. PREPARATION OF LETTERS ROGATORY
Article 3

Letters rogatory shall be prepared on forms that are printed in the four official languages of the Organization of American States or in the languages of the State of origin and of the State of destination and conform to form A contained in the Annex to this Protocol.

Letter rogatory shall be accompanied by the following:

a. Copy of the complaint or pleading that initiated the action in which the letter rogatory was issued, as well as a translation thereof into the language of the State of destination;

b. Untranslated copy of the documents attached to the complaint or pleading;

c. Untranslated copy of any rulings ordering issuance of the letter rogatory;

d. Form conforming to Form U annexed to this Protocol and containing essential information for the person to be served or the authority to receive the documents, and

e. Certificate conforming to Form C annexed to this Protocol on which the Central Authority of the State of destination shall attest to execution or non-execution of the letter rogatory.

The copies shall be regarded as authenticated for the purposes of Article 8 (a) of the Convention if they bear the seal of the judicial or other adjudicatory authority that issued the letter rogatory.

A copy of the letter rogatory together with Form G and the copies referred to in items a, b, and c of this Article shall be delivered to the person notified or to the authority to which the request is addressed. One of the copies of the letter rogatory and the documents attached to it shall remain in the possession of the State of destination; the untranslated original, the certificate of execution and the documents attached to them shall be returned to the Central Authority of the State of origin through appropriate channels.

If a State Party has more than one official language, it shall, at the time of signature, ratification or accession to this Protocol, declare which language or languages shall be considered official for the purposes of the Convention and of this Protocol. If a State Party comprises territorial units that have different official languages, it shall, at the time of signature, ratification or accession to this Protocol, declare which language or languages in each territorial unit shall be considered official for the purposes of the Convention and of this Protocol. The General Secretariat of the Organization of American States shall distribute to the States Parties to this Protocol the information contained in such declarations.

IV. TRANSMISSION AND PROCESSING OF LETTERS ROGATORY

Article 4

Upon receipt of a letter rogatory from the Central Authority in another State Party, the Central Authority in the State of destination shall transmit the letter rogatory to the appropriate judicial or administrative authority for processing in accordance with the applicable local law.

Upon execution of the letter rogatory, the judicial or administrative authority or authorities that processed it shall attest to the execution thereof in the manner prescribed in their local law, and shall transmit it with the relevant documents to the Central Authority. The Central Authority of the State Party of destination shall certify execution of the letter rogatory to the Central Authority of the State Party of origin on a form conforming to Form C of the Annex, which shall not require legalization. In addition, the Central Authority of the State of destination shall return the letter rogatory and attached documents to the Central Authority of the State of origin for delivery to the judicial or other adjudicatory authority that issued it.

V. COSTS AND EXPENSES

Article 5

The processing of letters rogatory by the Central Authority of the State Party of destination and its judicial or administrative authorities shall be free of charge. However, this State Party may seek payment by parties requesting execution of letters rogatory for those services which, in accordance with its local law, are required to be paid for directly by those parties.

The party requesting the execution of a letter rogatory shall, at its election, either select and indicate in the letter rogatory the person who is responsible in the State of destination for the cost of such services or, alternatively, shall attach to the letter rogatory a check for the fixed amount that is specified in Article 6 of this Protocol for its processing by the State of destination and will cover the cost of such services or a document proving that such amount has been transferred by some other means to the Central Authority of the State of destination.

The fact that the cost of such services ultimately exceeds the fixed amount shall not delay or prevent the processing or execution of the letter rogatory by the Central Authority or the judicial or administrative authorities of the State of destination. Should the cost exceed that amount, the Central Authority of the State of destination may, when returning the executed letter rogatory, seek payment of the outstanding amount due from the party requesting execution of the letter rogatory.

Article 6

At the time of deposit of its instrument of ratification or accession to this Protocol with the General Secretariat of the Organization of American States, each State Party shall attach a schedule of the services and the costs and other expenses that, in accordance with its local law, shall be paid directly by the party requesting execution of the letter rogatory. In addition, each State Party shall specify in the above-mentioned schedule the single amount which it considers will reasonably cover the cost of such services, regardless of the number or nature thereof. This amount shall be paid when the person requesting execution of the letter rogatory has not designated a person responsible for the payment of such services in the State of destination but has decided to pay for them directly in the manner provided for in Article 5 of this Protocol.

The General Secretariat of the Organization of American States shall distribute the information received to the States Parties to this Protocol. A State Party may at any time notify the General Secretariat of the Organization of American States of changes in the above-mentioned schedules, which shall be communicated by the General Secretariat to the other States Parties to this Protocol.

Article 7

States Parties may declare in the schedules mentioned in the foregoing articles that, provided there is reciprocity, they will not charge parties requesting execution of letters rogatory for the services necessary for executing them, or will accept in complete satisfaction of the cost of such services either the single fixed amount specified in Article 6 or another specified amount.

Article 8

This Protocol shall be open for signature and subject to ratification or accession by those Member States of the Organization of American States that have signed, ratified, or acceded to the Inter-American Convention on Letters Rogatory signed in Panama on January 30, 1975.

This Protocol shall remain open for accession by any other State that accedes or has acceded to the Inter-American Convention on Letters Rogatory, under the conditions set forth in this article.

The instruments of ratification and accession shall be deposited with the General Secretariat of the Organization of American States.

Article 9

This Protocol shall enter into force on the thirtieth day following the date on which two States Parties to the Convention have deposited their instruments of ratification or accession to this Protocol.

For each State ratifying or acceding to the Protocol after its entry into force, the Protocol shall enter into force on the thirtieth day following deposit by such State of its instrument of ratification or accession, provided that such State is a Party to the Convention.

Article 10

If a State Party has two or more territorial units in which different systems of law apply in relation to matters dealt with in this Protocol, it may, at the time of signature, ratification or accession, declare that this Protocol shall extend to all its territorial units or only to one or more of them.

Such declaration may be modified by subsequent declarations that shall expressly indicate the territorial unit or units to which this Protocol applies. Such subsequent declaration shall be transmitted to the General Secretariat of the Organization of American States, and shall become effective thirty days after the date of their receipt.

Article 11

This Protocol shall remain in force indefinitely, but any of the States Parties may denounce it. The instrument of denunciation shall be deposited with the General Secretariat of the Organization of American States. After one year from the date of deposit of the instrument of denunciation, the Protocol shall no longer be in effect for the denouncing State, but shall remain in effect for the other States Parties.

Article 12

The original instrument of this Protocol and its Annex (Forms A, B and C), the English, French, Portuguese and Spanish texts of which are equally authentic, shall be deposited with the General Secretariat of the Organization of American States, which will forward an authenticated copy of the text to the Secretariat of the United Nations for registration and publication in accordance with Article 102 of its Charter. The General Secretariat of the Organization of American States shall notify the Member States of that Organization and the States that have acceded to the Protocol of the signatures, deposits of instruments of ratification, accession and denunciation, as well as of reservations, if any. It shall also transmit to them the information mentioned in Article 2, the last paragraph of Article 3, and Article 6 and the declarations referred to in Article 10 of this Protocol.

IN WITNESS WHEREOF the undersigned Plenipotentiaries, being duly authorized thereto by their respective Governments, have signed this Protocol.

DONE AT MONTEVIDEO, Republic of Uruguay, this eighth day of May, one thousand nine hundred and seventy-nine.

ANNEX TO THE ADDITIONAL PROTOCOL TO THE INTER-AMERICAN CONVENTION ON LETTERS ROGATORY

FORM A
LETTER ROGATORY[1]

1. REQUESTING JUDICIAL OR OTHER ADJUDICATORY AUTHORITY
Name
Address
2. CASE:
DO CKET No.:
3. CENTRAL AUTHORITY OF THE STATE OF ORIGIN
Name
Address
4. CENTRAL AUTHORITY OF THE STATE OF DESTINATION
Name
Address
5. REQUESTING PARTY
Name
Address
6. COUNSEL TO THE REQUESTING PARTY
Name
Address
7. PERSON DESIGNATED TO ACT IN CONNECTION WITH THE LETTER ROGATORY
Name
Address
Is this person responsible for costs and expenses?
Yes
No
If not, check in the amount of _____ is attached
Or proof of payment is attached [2]

The Central Authority signing this letter rogatory has the honor to transmit to you in triplicate the documents listed below and, in conformity with the Protocol to the Inter-American Convention on Letters Rogatory:

A. Requests their prompt service on:[3]

The undersigned authority requests that service be carried out in the following manner:

(1) In accordance with the special procedure or additional formalities that are described below, as provided for in the second paragraph of Article 10 of the abovementioned Convention; or

1 Complete the original and two copies of this form, if A(1) is applicable, attach the original and two copies of the translation of this item in the language of the State of destination.

2 Delete if inapplicable.

3 Delete if inapplicable.

(2) By service personally on the identified addressee or, in the case of a legal entity, on its authorized agent; or

(3) If the person or the authorized agent of the entity to be served is not found, service shall be made in accordance with the law of the State of destination.

B. Requests the delivery of the documents listed below to the following judicial or administrative authority:

Authority:

C. Requests the Central Authority of the State of destination to return to the Central Authority of the State of origin one copy of the documents listed below and attached to this letter rogatory, and an executed Certificate on the attached Form C.[4]

Done at this date of , 19 .

Signature and stamp of the judicial or other adjudicatory authority of the State of origin

Signature and stamp of the Central Authority of the State of origin

Title or other identification of each document to be delivered:

(Attach additional pages, if necessary.)

4 Delete if inapplicable.

ANNEX TO THE ADDITIONAL PROTOCOL TO THE INTER-AMERICAN CONVENTION ON LETTERS ROGATORY

FORM B
ESSENTIAL INFORMATION FOR THE ADDRESSEE[5]

To (Name and address of the person being served)

You are hereby informed that (Brief statement of nature of service)

A copy of the letter rogatory that gives rise to the service or delivery of these documents is attached to this document. This copy also contains essential information for you. Also attached are copies of the complaint or pleading initiating the action in which the letter rogatory was issued, of the documents attached to the complaint or pleading, and of any rulings that ordered the issuance of the letter rogatory.

I. ADDITIONAL INFORMATION FOR SERVICE[6]

A. The document being served on you (original or copy) concerns the following:

B. The remedies sought or the amount in dispute is as follows:

C. By this service, you are requested:

D. In case of service on you as a defendant you can answer the complaint before the judicial or other adjudicatory authority specified in Form A, Box 1 (State place, date and hour):[7]

You are being summoned to appear as:[8]

If some other action is being requested of the person served, please describe:[9]

E. If you fail to comply, the consequences might be:

F. You are hereby informed that a defense counsel appointed by the Court or the following legal aid societies are available to you at the place where the proceeding is pending.

Name:

Address:

The documents listed in Part III are being furnished to you so that you may better understand and defend your interests.

---

5 Complete the original and two copies of this form in the language of the State of origin and two copies in the language of the State of destination.

6 Delete if inapplicable.

7 Delete if inapplicable.

8 Delete if inapplicable.

9 Delete if inapplicable.

II. FOR INFORMATION FROM JUDICIAL OR ADMINISTRATIVE AUTHORITY [10]

To:

(Name and address of the judicial or administrative authority)

You are respectfully requested to furnish the undersigned authority with the following information:

The documents listed in Part III are being furnished to you to facilitate your reply.

III. LIST OF ATTACHED DOCUMENTS

(Attach additional) pages if necessary.)

Done at this day of ,19 .

Signature and stamp of thc judicial or other adjudicatory authority of the State of origin

Signature and stamp of the Central Authority of the State of Origin

10 Delete if inapplicable.

ANNEX TO THE ADDITIONAL PROTOCOL TO THE INTER-AMERICAN CONVENTION ON LETTERS ROGATORY

FORM C
CERTIFICATE OF EXECUTION[11]

To:

(Name and address of judicial or other adjudicatory authority that issued the letter rogatory)

In conformity with the Additional Protocol to the Inter-American Convention on Letters Rogatory, signed at Montevideo on May 8, 1979, and in accordance with the attached original letter rogatory, the undersigned Central Authority has the honor to certify the following:

A. That one copy of the documents attached to this Certificate has been served or delivered as follows:

Date:

At (Address)

By one of the following methods authorized by the Convention.

(1) In accordance with the special procedure or additional formalities that are described below, as provided for in the second paragraph of Article 10 of the above-mentioned Convention, or

(2) By service personally on the identified addressee or, in the case of a legal entity, on its authorized agent, or

(3) If the person or the authorized agent of the entity to be served was not found, in accordance with the law of the State of destination: (Specify method used)[12]

B. That the documents referred to in the letter rogatory have been delivered to

identity of person

Relationship to the addressee

(family, business or other)

C. That the documents attacted to the Certificater have not been served or delivered for the following reason(s):

D. In conformity with the Protcol, the party requesting execution of the letter rogatory is resquested to pay the outstanding balance of costs in the amount indicated in the attached statement.[13]

Done at the day of 19

---

11 Complete the original and one copy in the language of the State of destination.

12 Delete if inapplicable.

13 Delete if inappliacable.

Signature and stamp of Central Authority of the State of destination

Where appropriate, attach originals or copies of any additional documents proving service or delivery, and identify them.

INTER-AMERICAN CONVENTION ON THE TAKING OF EVIDENCE ABROAD

Signed at Panama City, January 30, 1975

The Governments of the Member States of the Organization of American States, desirous of concluding a convention on the taking of evidence abroad, have agreed as follows:

Article 1

For the purposes of this Convention the terms "exhortos" and "cartas rogatorias" are synonymous in the Spanish text. The terms "letters rogatory", "commissions rogatoires", and "cartas rogatórias" used in the English, French and Portuguese texts, respectively, cover both "exhortos" and "cartas rogatorias".

Article 2

Letters rogatory issued in conjunction with proceedings in civil or commercial matters for the purpose of taking evidence or obtaining information abroad and addressed by a judicial authority of one of the States Parties to this Convention to the competent authority of another, shall be executed in accordance with the terms specified therein, provided:

1. The procedure requested is not contrary to legal provisions in the State of destination that expressly prohibit it;

2. The interested party places at the disposal of the authority of the State of destination the financial and other means necessary to secure compliance with the request.

Article 3

The authority of the State of destination shall have jurisdiction over disputes arising in connection with the execution of the measure requested.

Should the authority of the State of destination find that it lacks jurisdiction to execute the letter rogatory but consider that another authority of the same State has jurisdiction, it shall ex officio forward to it, through the appropriate channels, the documents and antecedents of the case.

In the execution of letters rogatory, the authority of the State of destination may apply the measures of compulsion provided for in its law.

Article 4

Letters rogatory requesting the taking of evidence or the obtaining of information abroad shall specify the following information needed for fulfilling the request:

1. A clear and precise statement of the purpose of the evidence requested;

2. Copies of the documents and decisions that serve as the basis and justification of the letter rogatory, as well as such interrogatories and documents as may be needed for its execution;

3. Names and addresses of the parties to the proceeding, as well as of witnesses, expert witnesses, and other persons involved and all information needed for the taking of the evidence;

4. A summary report on the proceeding and the facts giving rise to it, if needed for the taking of the evidence;

5. A clear and precise statement of such special requirements or procedures as may be requested by the authority of the State of origin for the taking of the evidence, except as provided in Article 2.1 and Article 6.

Article 5

Letters rogatory concerning the taking of evidence shall be executed in accordance with the laws and procedural rules of the State of destination.

Article 6

At the request of the authority issuing the letter rogatory, the authority of the State of destination may accept the observance of additional formalities or special procedures in performing the act requested, unless the observance of those procedures or of those formalities is contrary to the laws of the State of destination or impossible of performance.

Article 7

The costs and other expenses involved in the processing and execution of letters rogatory shall be borne by the interested parties.

The State of destination may, in its discretion, execute a letter rogatory that does not indicate the person to be held responsible for costs and other expenses when incurred. The identity of the person empowered to represent the applicant for legal purposes may be indicated in the letter rogatory or in the documents relating to its execution.

The effects of a declaration *in forma pauperis* shall be regulated by the law of the State of destination.

Article 8

Execution of letters rogatory shall not imply ultimate recognition of the jurisdiction of the authority issuing the letter rogatory or a commitment to recognize the validity of the judgment it may render or to execute it.

Article 9

Pursuant to Article 2.1, the authority of the State of destination may refuse execution of a letter rogatory whose purpose is the taking of evidence prior to judicial proceedings or "pretrial discovery of documents" as the procedure is known in Common Law countries.

Article 10

Letters rogatory shall be executed in the States Parties provided they meet the following requirements:

1. The letter rogatory is legalized, except as provided for in Article 13 of this Convention. The letter rogatory shall be presumed to be duly legalized in the State of origin when legalized by the competent consular or diplomatic agent;

2. The letter rogatory and the appended documentation are duly translated into the official language of the State of destination.

The States Parties shall inform the General Secretariat of the Organization of American States of the requirements stipulated in their laws for the legalization and the translation of letters rogatory.

Article 11

Letters rogatory may be transmitted to the authority to which they are addressed through judicial channels, diplomatic or consular agents, or the Central Authority of the State of origin or of the State of destination, as the case may be.

Each State Party shall inform the General Secretariat of the Organization of American States of the Central Authority competent to receive and distribute letters rogatory.

Article 12

A person called to give evidence in the State of destination pursuant to a letter rogatory may refuse to do so when he invokes impediment, exception or duty to refuse to testify:

1. Under the law of the State of destination; or
2. Under the law of the State of origin, if the invoked impediment, exception or duty to refuse has been specified in the letter rogatory or has been confirmed by the requesting authority at the instance of the court of destination.

Article 13

Whenever letters rogatory are transmitted or returned through consular or diplomatic channels or through the Central Authority, legalization shall not be required.

Article 14

This Convention shall not limit any provisions regarding letters rogatory for the taking of evidence abroad in bilateral or multilateral agreements that may have been signed or may be signed in the future by the States Parties or preclude the continuation of more favorable practices in this regard that may be followed by these States Parties.

This Convention shall not limit the application of any provisions on the taking of evidence by consuls that may be in force in other conventions or preclude the continuation of accepted practices in this regard.

Article 15

The States Parties to this Convention may declare that its provisions cover the execution of letters rogatory for the taking of evidence abroad in criminal, labor, and "contentious-administrative" cases, as well as in arbitrations and other matters within the jurisdiction of special courts. Such declarations shall be transmitted to the General Secretariat of the Organization of American States.

Article 16

The State of destination may refuse to execute a letter rogatory that is manifestly contrary to its public policy ("ordre public").

Article 17

This Convention shall be open for signature by the Member States of the Organization of American States.

Article 18

This Convention is subject to ratification. The instruments of ratification shall be deposited with the General Secretariat of the Organization of American States.

Article 19

This Convention shall remain open for accession by any other State. The instruments of accession shall be deposited with the General Secretariat of the Organization of American States.

Article 20

This Convention shall enter into force on the thirtieth day following the date of deposit of the second instrument of ratification.

For each State ratifying or acceding to the Convention after the deposit of the second instrument of ratification, the Convention shall enter into force on the thirtieth day after deposit by such State of its instrument of ratification or accession.

Article 21

If a State Party has two or more territorial units in which different systems of law apply in relation to the matters dealt with in this Convention, it may, at the time of signature, ratification or accession, declare that this Convention shall extend to all its territorial units or only to one or more of them.

Such declaration may be modified by subsequent declarations, which shall expressly indicate the territorial unit or units to which the Convention applies. Such subsequent declarations shall be transmitted to the General Secretariat of the Organization of American States, and shall become effective thirty days after the date of their receipt.

Article 22

This Convention shall remain in force indefinitely, but any of the States Parties may denounce it. The instrument of denunciation shall be deposited with the General Secretariat of the Organization of American States. After one year from the date of deposit of the instrument of denunciation, the Convention shall no longer be in effect for the denouncing State, but shall remain in effect for the other States Parties.

Article 23

The original instrument of this Convention, the English, French, Portuguese and Spanish texts of which are equally authentic, shall be deposited with the General Secretariat of the Organization of American States. The Secretariat shall notify the Member States of the Organization of American States and the States that have acceded to the Convention of the signatures, deposits of instruments of ratification, accession, and denunciation as well as reservations, if any. It shall also transmit the information mentioned in Article 10 and in the second paragraph of Article 11, and the declarations referred to in Articles 15 and 21 of this Convention.

IN WITNESS WHEREOF the undersigned Plenipotentiaries, being duly authorized thereto by their respective Governments, have signed this Convention.

DONE AT PANAMA CITY, Republic of Panama, this thirtieth day of January, one thousand nine hundred and seventy-five.

ADDITIONAL PROTOCOL TO THE INTER-AMERICAN CONVENTION ON THE TAKING OF EVIDENCE ABROAD

Signed at La Paz, May 24, 1984.

The Government of the Member States of the Organization of American States, desirous of strengthening and facilitating international cooperation in judicial procedures as provided for in the Inter-American Convention on the Taking of Evidence Abroad, have agreed as follows:

I. CENTRAL AUTHORITY

Article 1

Each State Party shall designate a central authority that shall perform the functions assigned to it in the Inter-American Convention on the Taking of Evidence Abroad (hereinafter referred to as "the Convention") and in this Protocol. At the time of deposit of its instrument of ratification of or accession to this Protocol, each State Party shall communicate its designation to the General Secretariat of the Organization of American States, which shall distribute to the State Parties to the Convention a list containing the designations receives. The Central Authority designated by a State Party in accordance with Article 11 of the Convention may be changed at any time. The State Party shall inform the above-mentioned Secretariat of such change as promptly as possible.

A State Party that is also a Party to the Additional Protocol to the Inter-American Convention on Letters Rogatory shall designate the same Central Authority for the purposes indicated in the two Protocols.

II. PREPARATION OF LETTERS ROGATORY REQUESTING THE TAKING OF EVIDENCE

Article 2

Letters rogatory requesting the taking of evidence shall be prepared on a form conforming to Form A of the Annex to this Protocol, and shall be accompanied by the documentation to which Article 4 of the Convention refers and a form conforming to Form B of the Annex to this Protocol.

If a State Party has more than one official language, it shall, at the time of signature or ratification of this Protocol, or of accession to it, declare which language or languages shall be considered official for the purpose of the Convention and of this Protocol. If a State Party comprises territorial units that have different languages, it shall, at the time of signature or ratification of this Protocol, or of accession to it, declare which language or languages in each territorial unit shall be considered official for the purpose of the Convention and of this Protocol. The General Secretariat of the Organization of American States shall distribute to the States Parties to this Protocol the information contained in such declarations.

III. TRANSMISSION AND PROCESSING OF LETTERS ROGATORY REQUESTING THE TAKING OF EVIDENCE

Article 3

Upon receipt of a letter rogatory from the Central Authority of another State Party, the Central Authority of a State Party shall transmit the letter rogatory to the appropriate judicial or other adjudicatory authority for processing in accordance with applicable local law.

The judicial or other adjudicatory authority or authorities that processed the letter rogatory shall certify the execution thereof in accordance with their local law, or the reasons for its non-execution, and shall transmit it with the relevant documents to their Central Authority. The Central Authority of the State Party of destination shall certify execution of the letter rogatory, or the reasons that prevented it from executing the letter rogatory, to the Central Authority of the State Party of origin on a form conforming to Form B of the Annex, which shall not require legalization. In addition, the Central Authority of the State of destination shall return the letter rogatory and attached documentation to the Central Authority of the State of origin for delivery to the judicial or other adjudicatory authority that issued it.

Article 4

In processing letters rogatory pursuant to the Convention and this Protocol, the judicial or other adjudicatory authority of the State of destination shall apply the appropriate measures of compulsion provided for in its legislation when it finds that the requirements set forth in that legislation for the application of such measures in domestic proceedings have been met.

Article 5

The judicial or other adjudicatory authority of the State of origin may request notice of the date, time, and place of the execution of a letter rogatory transmitted to the competent authority of a State Party. The judicial or other adjudicatory authority of the State of destination that will execute the letter shall provide notice of the date, time, and place to the judicial or other adjudicatory authority of the State of origin, as requested. The legal representatives of the parties or their lawyers may attend the execution of the letter; their intervention shall be subject to the law of the State of destination.

IV. COSTS AND EXPENSES

Article 6

The processing of letters rogatory by the Central Authority of the State of destination and by its judicial or other adjudicatory authorities shall be free of charge. However, this State Party may seek payment by the party requesting the evidence or information for those services which, in accordance with its local law, are required to be paid for directly by that party.

The party requesting the evidence or information shall, at its election, either select and indicate in the letter rogatory the person who is responsible in the State of destination for the cost of the above-mentioned services or attach to the letter rogatory a check for the fixed amount that is specified in Article 7 of this Protocol and will cover the cost of such services or a document proving that such amount has been transferred by some other means to the Central Authority of the State of destination.

The fact that the cost of such services ultimately exceeds the fixed amount shall not delay or prevent the processing or execution of the letter rogatory by the Central Authority or the judicial or other adjudicatory authorities of the State of destination. Should the cost exceed that amount, the Central Authority of the State of destination may, when returning the executed letter rogatory, seek payment of the outstanding amount due from the party requesting execution of the letter rogatory.

Article 7

At the time of deposit of its instrument of ratification of or accession to this Protocol with the General Secretariat of the Organization of American States, each State Party shall attach a schedule of services, itemizing the pertinent costs and expenses that, in accordance with its local law, shall be paid for directly by the party requesting the evidence or information. In addition, each State Party shall specify in the above-mentioned schedule the single amount that it considers will reasonably cover the cost of such services, regardless of the number or nature thereof. This amount shall be paid when the person requesting the evidence or information has not designated a person responsible for the payment of such services in the State of destination, but has decided to pay for them directly in the manner provided for in Article 6 of this Protocol.

The General Secretariat of the Organization of American States shall distribute the information received to the States Parties to this Protocol. A State Party may at any time notify the General Secretariat of the Organization of American States of changes in the above-mentioned schedules, which shall be communicated by the General Secretariat to the other States Parties to this Protocol.

Article 8

States Parties may declare in the schedules mentioned in Article 7 that, provided there is reciprocity, they will not, in certain matters, charge the party requesting the evidence or information for the services necessary for executing the letter rogatory, or that they will accept in complete satisfaction of the cost of such services the single amount that is specified in Article 7 or another fixed amount.

V. THE TAKING OF EVIDENCE BY DIPLOMATIC OR CONSULAR AGENTS

Article 9

The Convention shall not preclude a diplomatic or consular agent of a State Party, acting within his territorial jurisdiction, from taking evidence or obtaining information in the State Party in which he performs his functions, but in so doing he may not use measures of compulsion.

However, whenever evidence is taken or information obtained from persons whose nationality is not that of the State accrediting the diplomatic or consular agent, the provisions of Article 10 shall apply.

Article 10

In the case provided for in the second paragraph of Article 9 and without prejudice to the provisions of Article 12, the States Parties may limit the powers of the diplomatic or consular agents of the other States Parties to specified matters and stipulate such conditions for the taking of evidence or obtaining of information, including those relating to the time and place at which it shall be taken or obtained, as they deem necessary or advisable:

A declaration to this effect shall be made at the time of signature or ratification of, or accession to this Protocol.

Article 11

In the cases provided for in Article 9 of this Protocol, a diplomatic or consular agent may, through the appropriate channels, request the competent judicial or other adjudicatory authority to apply the appropriate measures of compulsion provided for under the laws of the State Party in which he performs his functions. The judicial or other adjudicatory authority shall apply those measures of compulsion when it finds that the requirements set forth in its legislation for the application of such measures in local proceedings have been met.

Article 12

When evidence is taken or information obtained pursuant to Article 9 of this Protocol, the rules and procedures in force in the State of origin may be observed, provided they do not conflict with the provisions of Article 2 (1) of the Convention; however, the grounds for refusal to testify specified in Article 12 of the Convention shall also apply to the taking of evidence or obtaining of information.

In the cases provided for in Article 9 of this Protocol, the persons from whom evidence is being taken or information obtained may be assisted by legal counsel and, where appropriate, by interpreters and by persons they trust.

Article 13

The failure of an attempt to take evidence or obtain information pursuant to Article 9 of this Protocol because of the refusal of the person called upon to provide it shall not preclude a request that evidence be taken or information obtained in accordance with Chapters I to IV of this Protocol.

VI. GENERAL PROVISIONS

Article 14

At the time of signing, ratifying or acceding to this Protocol, the States Parties may declare that the rules relating to the preparation and processing of letters rogatory for the taking of evidence or obtaining of information also apply to criminal and other matters provided for in Article 15 of the Convention.

Article 15

The judicial or other adjudicatory authority of the State of destination shall honor a request to follow special procedures pursuant to Article 6 of the Convention, unless they cannot be followed by it or they are incompatible with the fundamental principles of the legislation or the mandatory rules of the State of destination.

Article 16

The States Parties to this Protocol shall process a letter rogatory that requests the exhibition and copying of documents if it meets the following requirements:

a. The proceeding has been initiated;

b. The documents are reasonably identified by date, contents, or other appropriate information, and

c. The letter rogatory specifies those facts and circumstances causing the requesting party reasonably to believe that the requested documents are or were in the possession, control, or custody of, or are known to the person from whom the documents are requested.

The person from whom documents are requested may, where appropriate, deny that he has possession, control, or custody of the requested documents, or may object to the exhibition and copying of the documents, in accordance with the rules of the Convention.

At the time of signing, ratifying or acceding to this Protocol a State may declare that it will process the letters rogatory to which this article applies only if they identify the relationship between the evidence or information requested and the pending proceeding.

Article 17

The provisions of this Protocol shall be interpreted in such a way as to complement those of the Inter-American Convention on the Taking of Evidence Abroad.

VII. FINAL PROVISIONS

Article 18

This Protocol shall be open for signature and ratification or accession by those Member States of the Organization of American States that have signed, ratified, or acceded to the Inter-American Convention on the Taking of Evidence Abroad signed in Panama on January 30, 1975.

This Protocol shall remain open for accession by any other State that accedes or has acceded to the Inter-American Convention on the Taking of Evidence Abroad under the conditions set forth in this article.

The instruments of ratification and accession shall be deposited with the General Secretariat of the Organization of American States.

Article 19

Each State may, at the time of signature, ratification or accession, make reservations to this Protocol, provided that each reservation concerns one or more specific provisions.

Article 20

This Protocol shall enter into force on the thirtieth day following the date on which two States Parties to the Convention have deposited their instruments of ratification of or accession to this Protocol.

For each State ratifying or acceding to the Protocol after its entry into force, the Protocol shall enter into force on the thirtieth day following deposit by such State of its instrument of ratification or accession, provided that such State is a party to the Convention.

Article 21

If a State Party has two or more territorial units in which different systems of law apply in relation to the matters dealt with in this Protocol, it may, at the time of signature, ratification or accession, declare that this Protocol shall extend to all its territorial units or to only one or more of them.

Such declaration may be modified by subsequent declarations that shall expressly indicate the territorial unit or units to which this Protocol applies. Such subsequent declarations shall be transmitted to the General Secretariat of the Organization of American States, and shall become effective thirty days after the date of their receipt.

Article 22

This Protocol shall remain in force indefinitely, but any of the States Parties may denounce it. The instrument of denunciation shall be deposited with the General Secretariat of the Organization of American States. After one year from the date of deposit of the instrument of denunciation, the Protocol shall no longer be in effect for the denouncing State, but shall remain in effect for the other States Parties.

Article 23

The original instrument of this Protocol and its Annex (Forms A and B), the English, French, Portuguese and Spanish texts of which are equally authentic, shall be deposited with the General Secretariat of the Organization of American States, which shall forward an authenticated copy of its text to the Secretariat of the United Nations for registration and publication in accordance with Article 102 of its Charter. The General Secretariat of the Organization of American States shall notify the Member States of that Organization and the States that have acceded to the Protocol of the signatures, deposits of instruments of ratification, accession and denunciation, as well as of reservations, if any. It shall also transmit to them the information mentioned in Article 1, the last paragraph of Article 2, Article 7, and declarations pursuant to Articles 8, 10, 14, 16, and 21 of this Protocol.

IN WITNESS WHEREOF, the undersigned Plenipotentiaries, being duly authorized thereto by their respective Governments, have signed this Protocol.

DONE AT LA PAZ, Republic of Bolivia, this twenty-fourth day of May, one thousand nine hundred and eighty-four.

ANNEX TO THE ADDITIONAL PROTOCOL TO THE INTER-AMERICAN CONVENTION ON THE TAKING OF EVIDENCE ABROAD

FORM A

LETTER ROGATORY REQUESTING THE TAKING OF EVIDENCE OR OBTAINING OF INFORMATION ABROAD[1]

1 REQUESTING JUDICIAL OR OTHER ADJUDICATORY AUTHORITY Name Address	2 CASE DOCKET No.
3 CENTRAL AUTHORITY OF THE STATE OF ORIGIN Name Address	4 CENTRAL AUTHORITY OF THE STATE OF DESTINATION[2] Name Address Country
5 REQUESTING PARTY Name Address	6 COUNSEL TO THE REQUESTING PARTY IN THE STATE OF ORIGIN Name Address

7

PERSON DESIGNATED TO ACT IN CONNECTION WITH THE LETTER ROGATORY

1. Local counsel designated to represent the requesting party before the judicial or other adjudicatory authority of the State of destination.

Name
Address

2. Person designated to carry out formalities on behalf of the requesting party.

Name
Address

3. Person designated to meet the costs and expenses.

Name

Address

If no person is designated, attach the following payment document:
*Check in the amount of________________
*Receipt________________________________
*Other proof of payment________________

1. Complete the original and one copy of this form with known data.

2. Fill in country only; name and address of the Central Authority of the State of Destination to be completed by the Central Authority of the State of Origin.

* Delete if not applicable.

To the Central Authority of____

The undersigned Central Authority has the honor to transmit to you the letter rogatory presented below and respectfully requests its processing in accordance with the provisions of the Inter-American Convention on the Taking of Evidence Abroad and the Additional Protocol thereto.

____
Signature and stamp of the Central Authority
of the State of origin

The judicial or other adjudicatory authority signing this letter rogatory has the honor to request the cooperation of the judicial or other adjudicatory authority with jurisdiction to take evidence in ____________________
(City, Country)

and, in conformity with the Inter-American Convention on the Taking of Evidence Abroad and its Additional Protocol, respectfully requests the evidence or information set forth below, which is necessary for the preparation of or a decision in the civil, commercial or______________* proceedings noted in Box 2 of the first page of this form. Two copies of the documentation required by Article 4 of the Convention and by the Additional Protocol are attached to this letter rogatory.

1. Parties to the proceeding (Convention, Article 4 (3))

a. Plaintiff

Name______________________________

Address______________________________

Counsel______________________________

Counsel's Address______________________________

b. Defendant

Name______________________________

Address______________________________

Counsel______________________________

Counsel's Address______________________________

c. Other parties

Name______________________________

Address______________________________

Counsel______________________________

Counsel's Address______________________________

2. Clear and precise statement of purpose of evidence to be taken (Convention, Article 4 (1))

a. Type of evidence or information requested (testimony, examination of documents, etc.)

____

b. Type of proceeding (contract, tort, succession, etc.)

____

* If Article 14 of the Additional Protocol is applicable, indicate in the space provided whether the proceeding concerns a criminal or other matter provided for in Article 15 of the Convention.

c. Relation between the evidence or information requested and the pending proceeding (Be specific)

3. If needed, summary report on the status of the proceedings and the facts giving rise to the proceedings (Convention, Article 4 (4))
(State "None" if not needed)

4. Clear and precise statement of any basic or additional formalities and procedures, special requirements or procedures to be followed (Articles 4 (5) and 6 of the Convention and Article 15 of the Additional Protocol). (Explain the form in which evidence is to be taken (oral or in writing, transcript or summary, etc.))

5. Person (or persons) whose evidence is to be taken and capacity in which person will give evidence.

Name

Address

Capacity
(Party, Witness, Expert, etc.)

6. Attach as an appendix a list of the questions that will be asked and indicate the person (or persons) who should reply, or state that questions will be asked at the time evidence is taken.

Attach documents or objects that should be presented to the person whose evidence will be taken.

Attach copies of provisions (laws or regulations) relating to any impediments that might be invoked by the person giving evidence pursuant to Article 12 (2) of the Convention.

7. Documents or other objects to be inspected or information to be obtained. (Specify whether documents or objects are to be exhibited, copied, valued, etc.)

8. Specify whether the evidence should be taken under oath or affirmation.

In the event that the evidence cannot be taken in the manner requested, specify whether it should be taken as provided by the local law.

9. Specify whether the evidence should be taken at a particular location and, if so, identify that location.

Address

10. Specify whether the requesting judicial or other adjudicatory authority wishes to be informed of the date, time, and place at which evidence will be taken and, if so, indicate address to which notice should be sent (Article 5 of the Additional Protocol).

Address

11. Specify whether the notice of date, time, and place should be sent to any other person and, if so, provide the information requested.

Name

Address

12. Specify the date by which the requesting judicial or other adjudicatory authority requires receipt of the response to the letter rogatory.

Date____

Reason for time limit____

Done at ________________ , this_________________

day of ________ , 19__________

____
Signat ure and stamp of Judicial or other Adjudicatory Authority
of the State of origin

[States Parties may include additional lines in Form A]

ANNEX TO THE ADDITIONAL PROTOCOL TO THE INTER-AMERICAN CONVENTION ON THE TAKING OF EVIDENCE ABROAD

FORM B

CERTIFICATE OF EXECUTION OF LETTER ROGATORY REQUESTING THE TAKING OF EVIDENCE [1]

TO: CENTRAL AUTHORITY OF____

____

____

(Name and address of Central Authority of the State of origin)

In conformity with the Additional Protocol to the Inter-American Convention on the Taking of Evidence Abroad, signed at La Paz, Bolivia, on the twenty-fourth day of May, one thousand nine hundred and eighty-four, and in accordance with the attached original letter rogatory, the undersigned Central Authority has the honor to certify the following:

* A. That the evidence requested in the Request (verso) has been taken:

Date____

Name of person who provided the evidence____

Place where evidence was taken____

By one of the following methods authorized by the Convention:

* (1) In accordance with the laws and procedural rules of the State of destination.

* (2) In accordance with the following requirements, additional formalities or special procedures:

____

____

____

* B. That the information requested has been obtained:

Date____

Place where information was obtained____

C. Annexed is:

* (a) A certified copy of the testimony (transcript or summary) or the information obtained.

* (b) The document (or documents) that were secured as a result of such request, if the person to whom the request was made voluntarily surrendered them or, if not, copies thereof.

* (c) Other (Specify)____

*D. In Conformity with the Additional Protocol, the party requesting the evidence or information is requested to pay. The outstanding balance of costs or expenses in the amount indicated in the attached statement.

*E. That the evidence or information requested has not been obtained for the following reason(s):

____

____

1. Fill out this form in original and one copy.

* Delete if not applicable.

Done at____________________, this__________ day ________
of____________________, 19__________

Signature and stamp of the Central Authority
of the State of destination

APPENDIX VI

UNITED STATES STATUTES

United States Statutes

TABLE OF CONTENTS

I.
Uniform Foreign Money-Judgments Recognition Act
13 U.L.A. 263 (1962)

§ 1. Definitions.

As used in this Act:

(1) "foreign state" means any governmental unit other than the United States, or any state, district, commonwealth, territory, insular possession thereof, or the Panama Canal Zone, the Trust Territory of the Pacific Islands, or the Ryukyu Islands;

(2) "foreign judgment" means any judgment of a foreign state granting or denying recovery of a sum of money, other than a judgment for taxes, a fine or other penalty, or a judgment for support in matrimonial or family matters.

§ 2. Applicability.

This Act applies to any foreign judgment that is final and conclusive and enforceable where rendered even though an appeal therefrom is pending or it is subject to appeal.

§ 3. Recognition and Enforcement.

Except as provided in section 4, a foreign judgment meeting the requirements of section 2 is conclusive between the parties to the extent that it grants or denies recovery of a sum of money. The foreign judgment is enforceable in the same manner as the judgment of a sister state which is entitled to full faith and credit.

§ 4. Grounds for Non-recognition.

(a) A foreign judgment is not conclusive if

(1) the judgment was rendered under a system which does not provide impartial tribunals or procedures compatible with the requirements of due process of law;

(2) the foreign court did not have personal jurisdiction over the defendant; or

(3) the foreign court did not have jurisdiction over the subject matter.

(3) the foreign court did not have jurisdiction over the subject matter.

(b) A foreign judgment need not be recognized if

(1) the defendant in the proceedings in the foreign court did not receive notice of the proceedings in sufficient time to enable him to defend;

(2) the judgment was obtained by fraud;

(3) the [cause of action][claim for relief] on which the judgment is based is repugnant to the public policy of this state;

(4) the judgment conflicts with another final and conclusive judgment;

(5) the proceeding in the foreign court was contrary to an agreement between the parties under which the dispute in question was to be settled otherwise than by proceedings in that court; or

(6) in the case of jurisdiction based only on personal service, the foreign court was a seriously inconvenient forum for the trial of the action.

§ 5. Personal Jurisdiction.

(a) The foreign judgment shall not be refused recognition for lack of personal jurisdiction if

(1) the defendant was served personally in the foreign state;

(2) the defendant voluntarily appeared in the proceedings, other than for the purpose of protecting property seized or threatened with seizure in the proceedings or of contesting the jurisdiction of the court over him;

(3) the defendant prior to the commencement of the proceeding had agreed to submit to the jurisdiction of the foreign court with respect to the subject matter involved;

(4) the defendant was domiciled in the foreign state when the proceedings were instituted, or, being a body corporate had its principal place of business, was incorporated, or had otherwise acquired corporate status, in the foreign state;

(5) the defendant had a business office in the foreign state and the proceedings in the foreign court involved a [cause of action][claim for relief] arising out of business done by the defendant through that office in the foreign state; or

(6) the defendant operated a motor vehicle or airplane in the foreign state and the proceedings involved a [cause of action][claim for relief] arising out of such operation.

(b) The courts of this state may recognize other bases of jurisdiction.

§ 6. Stay in Case of Appeal.

If the defendant satisfies the court either than an appeal is pending or that he is entitled and intends to appeal from the foreign judgment, the court may stay the proceedings until the appeal has been determined or until the expiration of a period of time sufficient to enable the defendant to prosecute the appeal.

§ 7. Savings Clause.

This Act does not prevent the recognition of a foreign judgment in situations not covered by this Act.

§ 8. Uniformity of Interpretation.

This Act shall be so construed as to effectuate its general purpose to make uniform the law of those states which enact it.

§ 9. Short Title.

This Act may be cited as the Uniform Money-Judgments Recognition Act.

§ 10. Repeal.

The following Acts are repealed:

(1)

(2)

(3)

§ 11. Time of Taking Effect.

This Act shall take effect ___________.

JURISDICTIONS THAT HAVE ADOPTED THE UNIFORM FOREIGN MONEY-JUDGMENT RECOGNITION ACT

JURISDICTION	DATE	JURISDICTION	DATE
Alaska	8-16-1972	Missouri.	6-21-1984
California	11-8-1967	Montana	10-1-1993
Colorado	7-1-1977	New Mexico	7-1-1991
Connecticut	4-13-1988	New York	9-1-1970
Connecticut	10-1-1994	North Carolina	19-1-1993
Georgia	1975	Ohio	1985
Idaho	1990	Oklahoma	6-30-1965
Illinois	7-15-1963	Oregon	10-4-1977
Iowa	5-18-1989	Pennsylvania	11-21-1990
Maryland	6-1-1963	Texas	6-17-1981
Massachusetts	9-3-1966	Virgin Islands	2-18-1992
Michigan	11-2-1967	Virginia	1990
Minnesota	5-23-1985	Washington	6-26-1975

II.
Jurisdictional Immunities of Foreign States (U.S. Foreign Sovereign Immunities Act of 1976) Title 28 U.S. Code §§ 1602-1611

§ 1602. Findings and declarations of purpose

The Congress finds that the determination by United States courts of the claims of foreign states to immunity from the jurisdiction of such courts would serve the interest of justice and would protect the rights of both foreign states and litigants in United States courts. Under international law, states are not immune from the jurisdiction of foreign courts insofar as their commercial activities are concerned, and their commercial property may be levied upon for the satisfaction of judgments rendered against them in connection with their commercial activities. Claims of foreign states to immunity should henceforth be decided by courts of the United States and of the States in conformity with the principles set forth in this chapter.

§ 1603. Definitions

For purposes of this chapter —

(a) A "foreign state", except as used in section 1608 of this title, includes a political subdivision of a foreign state or an agency or instrumentality of a foreign state as defined in subsection (b).

(b) An "agency or instrumentality of a foreign state" means any entity —

> **(1)** which is a separate legal person, corporate or otherwise, and
>
> **(2)** which is an organ of a foreign state or political subdivision thereof, or a majority of whose shares or other ownership interest is owned by a foreign state or political subdivision thereof, and
>
> **(3)** which is neither a citizen of a State of the United States as defined in section 1332(c) and (d) of this tile, nor created under the laws of any third country.

(c) The "United States" includes all territory and waters, continental or insular, subject to the jurisdiction of the United States.

(d) A "commercial activity" means either a regular course of commercial conduct or a particular commercial transaction or act. The commercial character of an activity shall be determined by reference to the nature of the course of conduct or particular transaction or act, rather than by reference to its purpose.

(e) A "commercial activity carried on in the United States by a foreign state" means commercial activity carried on by such state and having substantial contact with the United States.

§ 1604. Immunity of a foreign state from jurisdiction

Subject to existing international agreements to which the United States is a party at the time of enactment of this Act a foreign state shall be immune from the jurisdiction of the courts of the United States and of the States except as provided in sections 1605 to 1607 of this chapter.

§ 1605. General exceptions to the jurisdictional immunity of a foreign state

(a) A foreign state shall not be immune from the jurisdiction of courts of the United States or of the States in any case —

(1) in which the foreign state has waived its immunity either explicitly or by implication, notwithstanding any withdrawal of the waiver which the foreign state may purport to effect except in accordance with the terms of the waiver;

(2) in which the action is based upon a commercial activity carried on in the United States by the foreign state; or upon an act performed in the United States in connection with a commercial activity of the foreign state elsewhere; or upon an act outside the territory of the United States in connection with a commercial activity of the foreign state elsewhere and that act causes a direct effect in the United States;

(3) in which rights in property taken in violation of international law are in issue and that property or any property exchanged for such property is present in the United States in connection with a commercial activity carried on in the United States by the foreign state; or that property or any property exchanged for such property is owned or operated by an agency or instrumentality of the foreign state and that agency or instrumentality is engaged in a commercial activity in the United States;

(4) in which rights in property in the united States acquired by succession or gift or rights in immovable property situated in the United States are in issue;

(5) not otherwise encompassed in paragraph (2) above, in which money damages are sought against a foreign state for personal injury or death, or damage to or loss of property, occurring in the United States and caused by the tortious act or omission of that foreign state or of any official or employee of that foreign state while acting within the scope of his office or employment; except this paragraph shall not apply to —

(A) any claim based upon the exercise or performance or the failure to exercise or perform a discretionary function regardless of whether the discretion be abused, or

(B) any claim arising out of malicious prosecution, abuse of process, libel, slander, misrepresentation, deceit, or interference with contract rights; or

(6) in which the action is brought, either to enforce an agreement made the foreign state with or for the benefit of a private party to submit to arbitration all or any differences which have arisen or which may arise between the parties with respect to a defined legal relationship, whether contractual or not, concerning a subject matter capable of settlement by arbitration under the laws of the United States, or to confirm an award made pursuant to such an agreement to arbitrate, if (A) the arbitration takes place or is intended to take place in the United States, (B) the agreement or award is or may be governed by a treaty or other international agreement in force for the United States calling for the recognition and enforcement of arbitral awards, (C) the underlying claim, save for the agreement to arbitrate, could have been brought in a United States court under this section or section 1607, or (D) paragraph (1) of this subsection is otherwise applicable.

(7) not otherwise covered by paragraph (2), in which money damages are sought against a foreign state for personal injury or death that was caused by an act of torture, extrajudicial killing, aircraft sabotage, hostage taking, or the provision of material support or resources (as defined in section 2339A of title (18) for such an act if such act or provision of material support is engaged in by an official, employee, or agent of such foreign state while acting within the scope of his or her office, employment, or agency, except that the court shall decline to hear a claim under this paragraph —

(A) if the foreign state was not designated as a state sponsor of terrorism under section 6(j) of the Export Administration Act of 1979 (50 U.S.C. App. 2405(j) or section 620A of the Foreign Assistance Act of 1961 (22 U.S.C. 2371) at the time the act occurred, unless later so designated as a result of such act; and

(B) even if the foreign state is or was so designated, if

(i) the act occurred in the foreign state against which the claim has been brought and the claimant has not afforded the foreign state a reasonable opportunity to arbitrate the claim in accordance with accepted international rules of arbitration; or

(ii) the claimant or victim was not a national of the United States (as that term is defined in section 101(a)(22) of the Immigration and Nationality Act) when the act upon which the claim is based occurred.

(b) A foreign state shall not be immune from the jurisdiction of the courts of the United States in any case in which a suit in admiralty is brought to enforce a maritime lien against a vessel or cargo of the foreign state, which maritime lien is based upon a commercial activity of the foreign state: *Provided*, That —

(1) notice of the suit is given by delivery of a copy of the summons and of the complaint to the person, or his agent, having possession of the vessel or cargo against which the maritime lien is asserted; and if the vessel or cargo is arrested pursuant to process obtained on behalf of the party bringing the suit, the service of process of arrest shall be deemed to constitute valid delivery of such notice, but the party bringing the suit shall be liable for any damages sustained by the foreign state as a result of the arrest if the party bringing the suit had actual or constructive knowledge that the vessel or cargo of a foreign state was involved; and

(2) notice to the foreign state of the commencement of suit as provided in section 1608 of this title is initiated within ten days either of the delivery of notice as provided in paragraph (1) of this subsection or, in the case of a party who was unaware that the vessel or cargo of a foreign state was involved, of the date such party determined the existence of the foreign state's interest.

(c) Whenever notice is delivered under subsection (b)(1), the suit to enforce a maritime lien shall thereafter proceed and shall be heard and determined according to the principles of law and rules of practice of suits in rem whenever it appears that, had the vessel been privately owned and possessed, a suit in rem might have been maintained. A decree against the foreign state may include costs of the suit and, if the decree is for a money judgment, interest as ordered by the court, except that the court may not award judgment against the foreign state in an amount greater than the value of the vessel or cargo upon which the maritime lien arose. Such value shall be determined as of the time notice is served under subsection (b)(1). Decrees shall be subject to appeal and revision as provided in other cases of admiralty and maritime jurisdiction. Nothing shall preclude the plaintiff in any proper case from seeking relief in personam in the same action brought to enforce a maritime lien as provided in this section.

(d) A foreign state shall not be immune from the jurisdiction of the courts of the United States in any action brought to foreclose a preferred mortgage, as defined in the Ship Mortgage Act, 1920 (46 U.S.C. 911 and following). Such action shall be brought, heard, and determined in accordance with the provisions of that Act and in accordance with the principles of law and rules of practice of suits in rem, whenever it appears that had the vessel been privately owned and possessed a suit in rem might have been maintained.

(e) For purposes of paragraph (7) of subsection (a)—

(1) the terms "torture" and "extrajudicial killing" have the meaning given those terms in section 3 of the Torture Victim Protection Act of 1991;

(2) the term "hostage taking" has the meaning given that term in Article 1 of the International Convention Against the Taking of Hostages; and

(3) the term "aircraft sabotage" has the meaning given that term in Article 1 of the Convention for the Suppression of Unlawful Acts Against the Safety of Civil Aviation.

(f) No action shall be maintained under subsection (a)(7) unless the action is commenced not later than 10 years after the date on which the cause of action arose. All principles of equitable tolling, including the period during which the foreign state was immune from suit, shall apply in calculating this limitation period.

(g) Limitation on discovery. —

(1) In general. —

(A) Subject to paragraph (2), if an action is filed that would otherwise be barred by section 1604, but for subsection (a)(7), the court, upon request of the Attorney General, shall stay any request, demand or order for discovery on the United States that the Attorney General certifies would significantly interfere with a criminal investigation, or prosecution, or a national security operation, related to the incident that gave rise to the cause of action, until such time as the Attorney General advises the court that such request, demand, or order will no longer so interfere.

(B) A stay under this paragraph shall be in effect during the 12-month period beginning on the date on which the court issues the order to stay discovery. The court shall renew the order to stay discovery for additional 12-month periods upon motion by the United States if the Attorney General certifies that discovery would significantly interfere with a criminal investigation or prosecution, or a national security operation, related to the incident that gave rise to the cause of action.

(2) Sunset.—

(A) Subject to subparagraph (B), no stay shall be granted or continued in effect under paragraph (1) after the date that in 10 years after the date on which the incident that gave rise to the cause of action occurred.

(B) After the period referred to in subparagraph (A), the court, upon request of the Attorney General may stay any request, demand, or order for discovery on the United States that the court finds a substantial likelihood would—

(i) create a serious threat of death or serious bodily injury to any person;

(ii) adversely affect the ability of the United States to work in cooperation with foreign and international law enforcement agencies in investigating violations of United States law; or

(iii) obstruct the criminal case related to the incident that gave rise to the cause of action or undermine the potential for a conviction in such case.

(3) Evaluation of evidence. — The court's evaluation of any request for a stay under this subsection filed by the Attorney General shall be conducted ex parte and in camera.

(4) Bar on motions to dismiss.— A stay of discovery under this subsection shall constitute a bar to the granting of a motion to dismiss under rules 12(b)(6) and 56 of the Federal Rules of Civil Procedure.

(5) Construction.— Nothing in this subsection shall prevent the United States from seeking protective orders or asserting privileges ordinarily available to the United States.

§ 1606. Extent of liability

As to any claim for relief with respect to which a foreign state is not entitled to immunity under section 1605 or 1607 of this chapter, the foreign state shall be liable in the same manner and to the same extent as a private individual under like circumstances; but a foreign state except for an agency or instrumentality thereof shall not be liable for punitive damages; if, however, in any case wherein death was caused, the law of the place where the action on omission occurred provides, or has been construed to provide, for damages only punitive in nature, the foreign state shall be liable for actual or compensatory damages measured by the pecuniary injuries resulting from such death which were incurred by the persons for whose benefit the action was brought.

§ 1607. Counterclaims

In any action brought by a foreign state, or in which a foreign state intervenes, in a court of the United States or of a State, the foreign state shall not be accorded immunity with respect to any counterclaim —

(a) for which a foreign state would not be entitled to immunity under section 1605 of this chapter had such claim been brought in a separate action against the foreign state; or

(b) arising out of the transaction or occurrence that is the subject matter of the claim of the foreign state; or

(c) to the extent that the counterclaim does not seek relief exceeding in amount or differing in kind from that sought by the foreign state.

§ 1608. Service; time to answer; default

(a) Service in the courts of the United States and of the States shall be made upon a foreign state or political subdivision of a foreign state:

> **(1)** by delivery of a copy of the summons and complaint in accordance with any special arrangement for service between the plaintiff and the foreign state or political subdivision; or
>
> **(2)** if no special arrangement exists, by delivery of a copy of the summons and complaint in accordance with an applicable international convention on service of judicial documents; or
>
> **(3)** if service cannot be made under paragraphs (1) or (2), by sending a copy of the summons and complaint and a notice of suit, together with a translation of each into the official language of the foreign state, by any form of mail requiring a signed receipt, to be addressed and dispatched by the clerk of the court to the head of the ministry of foreign affairs of the foreign state concerned, or
>
> **(4)** if service cannot be made within 30 days under paragraph (3), by sending two copies of the summons and complaint and a notice of suit, together with a translation of each into the official language of the foreign state, by any form of mail requiring a signed receipt, to be addressed and dispatched by the clerk of the court to the Secretary of State in Washington, District of Colombia, to the attention of the Director of Special Consular Services — and the Secretary shall transmit one copy of the papers through diplomatic channels to the foreign state and shall send to the clerk of the court a certified copy of the diplomatic note indicating when the papers were transmitted.

As used in this subsection, a "notice of suit" shall mean a notice addressed to a foreign state and in a form prescribed by the Secretary of State by regulation.

(b) Service in the courts of the United States and of the States shall be made upon an agency or instrumentality of a foreign state:

(1) by delivery of a copy of the summons and complaint in accordance with any special arrangement for service between the plaintiff and the agency or instrumentality; or

(2) if no special arrangement exists, by delivery of a copy of the summons and complaint either to an officer, a managing or general agent, or to any other agent authorized by appointment or by law to receive service of process in the United States; or in accordance with an applicable international convention on service of judicial documents; or

(3) if service cannot be made under paragraphs (1) or (2), and if reasonably calculated to give actual notice, by delivery of a copy of the summons and complaint, together with a translation of each into the official language of the foreign state —

(A) as directed by an authority of the foreign state or political subdivision in response to a letter rogatory or request or

(B) by any form of mail requiring a signed receipt, to be addressed an dispatched by the clerk of the court to the agency or instrumentality to be served, or

(C) as directed by order of the court consistent with the law of the place where service is to be made.

(c) Service shall be deemed to have been made —

(1) in the case of service under subsection (a)(4), as of the date of transmittal indicated in the certified copy of the diplomatic note; and

(2) in any other case under this section, as of the date of receipt indicated in the certification, signed and returned postal receipt, or other proof of service applicable to the method of service employed.

(d) In any action brought in a court of the united States or of a State, a foreign state, a political subdivision thereof, or an agency or instrumentality of a foreign state shall serve an answer or other responsive pleading to the complaint within sixty days after service has been made under this section.

(e) No judgment by default shall be entered by a court of the United States or of a State against a foreign state, a political subdivision thereof, or an agency or instrumentality of a foreign state, unless the claimant establishes his claim or right to relief by evidence satisfactory to the court. A copy of any such default judgment shall be sent to the foreign state or political subdivision in the manner prescribed for service in this section.

§ 1609. Immunity from attachment and execution of property of a foreign state

Subject to existing international agreements to which the United States is a party at the time of enactment of this Act the property in the United States of a foreign state shall be immune from attachment arrest and execution except as provided in sections 1610 and 1611 of this chapter.

§ 1610. Exceptions to the immunity from attachment or execution

(a) The property in the United States of a foreign state, as defined in section 1603(a) of this chapter, used for a commercial activity in the United States, shall not be immune from attachment in aid of execution, or from execution, upon a judgment entered by a court of the united States or of a State after the effective date of this Act, if—

(1) the foreign state has waived its immunity from attachment in aid of execution or from execution either explicitly or by implication, notwithstanding any withdrawal of the waiver the foreign state may purport to effect except in accordance with the terms of the waiver, or

(2) the property is or was used for the commercial activity upon which the claim is based, or

(3) the execution relates to a judgment establishing rights in property which has been taken in violation of international law or which has been exchanged for property taken in violation of international law, or

(4) the execution relates to a judgment establishing rights in property—

(A) which is acquired by succession or gift, or

(B) which is immovable and situated in the United States: *Provided*, That such property is not used for purposes of maintaining a diplomatic or consular mission or the residence of the Chief of such mission, or

(5) the property consists of any contractual obligation or any proceeds from such a contractual obligation to indemnify or hold harmless the foreign state or its employees under a policy of automobile or other liability or casualty insurance covering the claim which merged into the judgment, or

(6) the judgment is based on an order confirming an arbitral award rendered against the foreign state, provided that attachment in aid of execution, or execution, would not be inconsistent with any provision in the arbitral agreement; or

(7) the judgment relates to a claim for which the foreign state is not immune under section 1605(a)(7), regardless of whether the property is or was involved with the act upon which the claim is based.

(b) In addition to subsection (a), any property in the United States of an agency or instrumentality of a foreign state engaged in commercial activity in the United States shall not be immune from attachment in aid of execution, or from execution, upon a judgment entered by a court of the United States or of a State after the effective date of this Act, if —

(1) the agency or instrumentality has waived its immunity from attachment in aid of execution or from execution either explicitly or implicitly, notwithstanding any withdrawal of the waiver the agency or instrumentality may purport to effect except in accordance with the terms of the waiver, or

(2) the judgment relates to a claim for which the agency or instrumentality is not immune by virtue of section 1605(a)(2),(3),(5), or (7) or 1605(b) of this chapter, regardless of whether the property is or was used for the activity upon which the claim is based.

(c) No attachment or execution referred to in subsections (a) and (b) of this section shall be permitted until the court has ordered such attachment and execution after having determined that a reasonable period of time has elapsed following the entry of judgment and the giving of any notice required under section 1608(e) of this chapter.

(d) The property of a foreign state, as defined in section 1603(a) of this chapter, used for a commercial activity in the United States, shall not be immune from attachment prior to the entry of judgment in any action brought in a court of the United States or of a State, or prior to the elapse of the period of time provided in subsection (c) of this section, if —

(1) the foreign state has explicitly waived its immunity from attachment prior to judgment, notwithstanding any withdrawal of the waiver the foreign state may purport to effect except in accordance with the terms of the waiver, and

(2) the purpose of the attachment is to secure satisfaction of a judgment that has been or may ultimately be entered against the foreign state, and not to obtain jurisdiction.

(e) the vessels of a foreign state shall not be immune from arrest in rem, interlocutory sale, and execution in actions brought to foreclose a preferred mortgage as provided in section 1605(d).

§ 1611. Certain types of property immune from execution

(a) Notwithstanding the provisions of section 1610 of this chapter, the property of those organizations designated by the President as being entitled to enjoy the privileges, exemptions, and immunities provided by the International Organizations Immunities Act shall not be subject to attachment or any other judicial process impeding the disbursement of funds to, or on the order of, a foreign state as the result of an action brought in the courts of the United States or of the States.

(b) Notwithstanding the provisions of section 1610 of this chapter, the property of a foreign state shall be immune from attachment and from execution, if —

(1) the property is that of a foreign central bank or monetary authority held for its own account, unless such bank or authority, or its parent foreign government, has explicitly waived its immunity from attachment in aid of execution, or from execution, notwithstanding any withdrawal of the waiver which the bank, authority or government may purport to effect except in accordance with the terms of the waiver; or

(2) the property is, or is intended to be, used in connection with a military activity and

(A) is of a military character, or

(B) is under the control of a military authority of defense agency.

(c) Notwithstanding the provisions of section 1610 of this chapter, the property of a foreign state shall be immune from attachment and from execution in an action brought under section 302 of the Cuban Liberty and Democratic Solidarity (LIBERTAD) Act of 1996 to the extent that the property is a facility or installation used by an accredited diplomatic mission for official purposes.

III.
U.S. Federal Rules of Civil Procedure, Rule 4. Summons

(a) Form.

The summons shall be signed by the clerk, bear the seal of the court, identify the court and the parties, be directed to the defendant, and state the name and address of the plaintiff's attorney or, if unrepresented, of the plaintiff. It shall also state the time within which the defendant must appear and defend, and notify the defendant that failure to do so will result in a judgment by default against the defendant for the relief demanded in the complaint. The court may allow a summons to be amended.

(b) Issuance.

Upon or after filing the complaint, the plaintiff may present a summons to the clerk for signature and seal. If the summons is in proper form, the clerk shall sign, seal, and issue it to the plaintiff for service on the defendant. A summons, or a copy of the summons if addressed to multiple defendants, shall be issue for each defendant to be served.

(c) Service with Complaint, by Whom Made.

(1) A summons shall be served together with a copy of the complaint. The plaintiff is responsible for service of a summons and complaint within the time allowed under subdivision (m) and shall furnish the person effecting service with the necessary copies of the summons and complaint.

(2) Service may be effected by any person who is not a party and who is at least 18 years of age. At the request of the plaintiff, however, the court may direct that service be effected by a United States marshal, deputy United States marshal, or other person or officer specially appointed by the court for that purpose. Such an appointment must be made when the plaintiff is authorized to proceed in forma pauperis pursuant to 28 U.S.C. § 1915 or is authorized to proceed as a seaman under 28 U.S.C. § 1916.

(d) Waiver of Service; Duty to Save Costs; Request to Waive.

(1) A defendant who waives service of a summons does not thereby waive any objection to the venue or to the jurisdiction of the court over the person of the defendant.

(2) An individual, corporation, or association that is subject to service under subdivision (e), (f), or (h) and that receives notice of an action in the manner provided in this paragraph has a duty to avoid unnecessary costs of serving the summons. To avoid costs, the plaintiff may notify such a defendant of the commencement of the action and request that the defendant waiver service of a summons. The notice and request

(A) shall be in writing and shall be addressed directly to the defendant, if an individual, or else to an officer or managing or general agent (or other agent authorized by appointment or law to receive service of process) of a defendant subject to service under subdivision (h);

(B) shall be dispatched through first-class mail or other reliable means;

(C) shall be accompanied by a copy of the complaint and shall identify the court in which it has been filed;

(D) shall inform the defendant, by means of a text prescribed in an official form promulgated pursuant to Rule 84, of the consequences of compliance and of a failure to comply with the request;

(E) shall set forth the date on which the request is sent;

(F) shall allow the defendant a reasonable time to return the waiver, which shall be at least 30 days from the date on which the request is sent, or 60 days from that date if the defendant is addressed outside any judicial district of the United States; and

(G) shall provide the defendant with an extra copy of the notice and request, as well as a prepaid means on compliance in writing.

If a defendant located within the United States fails to comply with a request for waiver made by a plaintiff located within the United States, the court shall impose the costs subsequently incurred in effecting service on the defendant unless good cause for the failure be shown.

(3) A defendant that, before being served with process, timely returns a waiver so requested is not required to serve an answer to the complaint until 60 days after the date on which the request for waiver of service was sent, or 90 days after that date if the defendant was addressed outside any judicial district of the United States.

(4) When the plaintiff files a waiver of service with the court, the action shall proceed, except as provided in paragraph (3), as if a summons and complaint had been served at the time of filing the waiver, and no proof of service shall be required.

(5) The costs to be imposed on a defendant under paragraph (2) for failure to comply with a request to waive service of a summons shall include the costs subsequently incurred in effecting service under sub-division (e), (f), or (h), together with the costs, including a reasonable attorney's fee, of any motion required to collect the costs of service.

(e) Service Upon Individuals Within a Judicial District of the United States.

Unless otherwise provided by federal law, service upon an individual from whom a waiver has not been obtained and filed, other than an infant or an incompetent person, may be effected in any judicial district of the United States:

(1) pursuant to the law of the state in which the district court is located, or in which service is effected, for the service of a summons upon the defendant in an action brought in the courts of general jurisdiction of the state; or

(2) by delivering a copy of the summons and of the complaint to the individual personally or by leaving copies thereof at the individual's dwelling house or usual place of abode with some person of suitable age and discretion then residing therein or by delivering a copy of the summons and of the complaint to an agent authorized by appointment or by law to receive service of process.

(f) Service Upon Individuals in a Foreign Country.

Unless otherwise provided by federal law, service upon an individual from whom a waiver has not been obtained and filed, other than an infant or an incompetent person, may be effected in a place not within any judicial district of the United States:

(1) by an internationally agreed means reasonably calculated to give notice, such as those means authorized by the Hague Convention on the Service Abroad of Judicial and Extrajudicial Documents; or

(2) if there is no internationally agreed means of service or the applicable international agreement allows other means of service, provided that service is reasonably calculated to give notice:

(A) in the manner prescribed by the law of the foreign country for service in that country in an action in any of its courts of general jurisdiction; or

(B) as directed by the foreign authority in response to a letter rogatory or letter of request; or

(C) unless prohibit by the law of the foreign country, by

(i) delivery to the individual personally of a copy of the summons and the complaint; or

(ii) any form of mail requiring a signed receipt, to be addressed and dispatched by the clerk of the court to the party to be served; or

(3) by other means not prohibited by international agreement as may be directed by the court.

(g) Service upon Infants and Incompetent Persons

Service upon an infant or an incompetent person in a judicial district of the United States shall be effected in the manner prescribed by the law of the state in which the service is made for the service of summons or other like process upon any such defendant in an action brought in the courts of general jurisdiction of that state. Service upon an infant or an incompetent person in a place not within any judicial district of the United States shall be effected in the manner prescribed by paragraph (2)(A) or (2)(B) of subdivision (f) or by such means as the court may direct.

(h) Service Upon Corporations and Associations.

Unless otherwise provided by federal law, service upon a domestic or foreign corporation or upon a partnership or other unincorporated association that is subject to suit under a common name, and from which a waiver of service has not been obtained and filed, shall be effected:

(1) in a judicial district of the United States in the manner prescribed for individuals by subdivision (e)(1), or by delivering a copy of the summons and of the complaint to an officer, a managing or general agent, or to any other agent authorized by appointment or by law to receive service of process and, if the agent is one authorized by statute to receive service and the statute so requires, by also mailing a copy to the defendant, or

(2) in a place not within any judicial district of the United States in any manner prescribed for individuals by subdivision (f) except personal delivery as provided in paragraph (2)(C)(i) thereof.

(i) Service Upon the United States, and Its Agencies, Corporations, or Officers.

(1) Service upon the United States shall be effected

(A) by delivering a copy of the summons and of the complaint to the United States attorney for the district in which the action is brought or to an assistant United States attorney or clerical employee designated by the United States attorney in writing filed with the clerk of the court or by sending a copy of the summons and of the complaint by registered or certified mail addressed to the civil process clerk at the office of the United States attorney and

(B) by also sending a copy of the summons and of the complaint by registered or certified mail to the Attorney General of the United States at Washington, District of Colombia, and

(C) in any action attacking the validity of an order of an officer or agency of the United States not made a party, by also sending a copy of the summons and of the complaint by registered or certified mail to the officer or agency.

(2) Service upon an officer, agency, or corporation of the United States shall be effected by serving the United States in the manner prescribed by paragraph (1) of this subdivision and by also sending a copy of the summons and of the complaint by registered or certified mail to the officer, agency, or corporation.

(3) The court shall allow a reasonable time for service of process under this subdivision for the purpose of curing the failure to serve multiple officers, agencies, or corporations of the United States if the plaintiff has effected service or either the United States attorney or the Attorney General of the United States.

(j) Service Upon Foreign, State, or Local Governments.

(1) Service upon a foreign state or a political sub-division, agency, or instrumentality thereof shall be effected pursuant to 28 U.S.C. § 1608.

(2) Service upon a state, municipal corporation, or other governmental organization subject to suit shall be effected by delivering a copy of the summons and of the complaint to its chief executive officer or by serving the summons and complaint in the manner prescribed by the law of that state for the service of summons or other like process upon any such defendant.

(k) Territorial Limits of Effective Service.

(1) Service of a summons or filing a waiver of service is effective to establish jurisdiction over the person of a defendant

(A) who could be subject to the jurisdiction of a court of general jurisdiction in the state in which the district court is located, or

(B) who is a party joined under Rule 14 or Rule 19 and is served at a place within a judicial district of the United States and not more than 100 miles from the place from which the summons issues, or

(C) who is subject to the federal interpleader jurisdiction under 28 U.S.C. § 1335, or

(D) when authorized by a statute of the United States.

(2) If the exercise of jurisdiction is consistent with the Constitution and laws of the United States, serving a summons or filing a waiver of service is also effective, with respect to claims arising under federal law, to establish personal jurisdiction over the person of any defendant who is not subject to the jurisdiction of the courts of general jurisdiction of any state.

(l) Proof of Service.

If service is not waived, the person effecting service shall make proof thereof to the court. If service is made by a person other than a United States marshal or deputy United States marshal, the person shall make affidavit thereof. Proof of service in a place not within any judicial district of the United States shall, if effected under paragraph (1) of subdivision (f), be made pursuant to the applicable treaty or convention, and shall, if effected under paragraph (2) or (3) thereof, include a receipt signed by the addressee or other evidence of delivery to the addressee satisfactory to the court. Failure to make proof of service does not affect the validity of the service. The court may allow proof of service to be amended.

(m) Time Limit for Service.

If service of the summons and complaint is not made upon a defendant within 120 days after the filing of the complaint, the court, upon motion or on its own initiative after notice to the plaintiff, shall dismiss the action without prejudice as to that defendant or direct that service be effected within a specified time; provided that if the plaintiff shows good cause for the failure, the court shall extend the time for service for an appropriate period. This subdivision does not apply to service in a foreign country pursuant to subdivision (f) or (j)(1).

(n) Seizure of Property; Service of Summons Not Feasible.

(1) If a statute of the United States so provides, the court may assert jurisdiction over property. Notice to the claimants of the property shall then be sent in the manner provided by the statute or by service of a summons under this rule.

(2) Upon a showing that personal jurisdiction over a defendant cannot, in the district where the action is brought, be obtained with reasonable efforts by service of summons in any manner authorized by this rule, the court may assert jurisdiction over any of the defendant's assets found within the district by seizing the assets under the circumstances and in the manner provided by the law of the state in which the district court is located.

IV.
U. S. Federal Rules of Civil Procedure, Rule 26. General Provisions Governing Discovery; Duty of Disclosure

(a) Required Disclosures; Methods to Discover Additional Matter.

(1) Initial Disclosures. Except to the extent otherwise stipulated or directed by order or local rule, a party shall, without awaiting a discovery request, provide to other parties:

(A) the name and, if known, the address and telephone number of each individual likely to have discoverable information relevant to disputed facts alleged with particularity in the pleadings, identifying the subjects of the information;

(B) a copy of, or a description by category and location of, all documents, data compilations, and tangible things in the possession, custody, or control of the party that are relevant to disputed facts alleged with particularity in the pleadings.

(C) a computation of any category of damages claimed by the disclosing party, making available for inspection and copying as under Rule 34 the documents or other evidentiary material, not privileged or protected from disclosure, on which such computation is based, including materials bearing on the nature and extent of injuries suffered; and

(D) for inspection and copying as under Rule 34 any insurance agreement under which any person carrying on an insurance business may be liable to satisfy part or all of a judgment which may be entered in the action or to indemnify or reimburse for payments made to satisfy the judgment.

Unless otherwise stipulated or directed by the court, these disclosures shall be made at or within 10 days after the meeting of the parties under subdivision (f). A party shall make its initial disclosures based on the information then reasonably available to it and is not excused from making its disclosures because it has not fully completed its investigation of the case or because it challenges the sufficiency of another party's disclosures or because another party has not made its disclosures.

(2) Disclosure of Expert Testimony.

(A) In addition to the disclosures required by paragraph (1), a party shall disclose to other parties the identity of any person who may be used at trial to present evidence under Rules 702, 703 or 705 of the Federal Rules of Evidence.

(B) Except as otherwise stipulated or directed by the court, this disclosure shall, with respect to a witness who is retained or specially employed to provide expert testimony in the case or whose duties as an employee of the party regularly involve giving expert testimony, be accompanied by a written report prepared and signed by the witness. The report shall contain a complete statement of all opinions to be expressed and the basis and reasons therefor; the data or other information considered by the witness in forming the opinions; any exhibits to be used as a summary of or support for the opinions; the qualifications of the witness, including a list of all publications authored by the witness within the preceding ten years; the compensation to be paid for the study and testimony; and a listing of any other cases in which the witness has testified as an expert at trial or by deposition within the preceding four years.

(C) These disclosures shall be made at the times and in the sequence directed by the court. In the absence of other directions from the court or stipulation by the parties, the disclosures shall be made at least 90 days before the trial date or the date the case is to be ready for trial or, if the evidence is intended solely to contradict or rebut evidence on the same subject matter identified by another party under paragraph (2)(B), within 30 days after the disclosure made by the other party. The parties shall supplement these disclosures when required under subdivision (e)(1).

(3) Pretrial Disclosures. In addition to the disclosures required in the preceding paragraphs, a party shall provide to other parties the following information regarding the evidence that it may present at trial other than solely for impeachment purposes:

(A) the name and, if not previously provided, the address and telephone number of each witness, separately identifying those whom the party expects to present and those whom the party may call if the need arises;

(B) the designation of those witnesses whose testimony is expected to be presented by means of a deposition and, if not taken stenographically, a transcript of the pertinent portions of the disposition testimony; and

(C) an appropriate identification of each document or other exhibit, including summaries of other evidence, separately identifying those which the party expects to offer and those which the party may offer if the need arises.

Unless otherwise directed by the court, these disclosures shall be made at least 30 days before trial. Within 14 days thereafter, unless a different time is specified by the court, a party may serve and file a list disclosing (i) any objections to the use under Rule 32(a) of a deposition designated by another party under subparagraph (B) and (ii) any objection, together with the grounds therefor, that may be made to the admissibility of materials identified under subparagraph (C). Objections not so disclosed, other than objections under Rules 402 and 403 of the Federal Rules of Evidence, shall be deemed waived unless excused by the court for good cause shown.

(4) Form of Disclosure; Filing. Unless otherwise directed by order or local rule, all disclosures under paragraphs (1) through (3) shall be made in writing, signed, served, and promptly filed with the court.

(5) Methods to Discover Additional Matter. Parties may obtain discovery by one or more of the following methods: depositions upon oral examination or written questions; written interrogatories; production of documents or things or permission to enter upon land or other property under Rule 34 or 45(a)(1)(C), for inspection and other purposes; physical and mental examinations; and requests for admission.

(b) Discovery Scope and Limits. Unless otherwise limited by order of the court in accordance with these rules, the scope of discovery is as follows:

(1) In General. Parties may obtain discovery regarding any matter, not privileged, which is relevant to the subject matter involved in the pending action, whether it relates to the claim or defense of the party seeking discovery or to the claim or defense of any other party, including the existence, description, nature, custody, condition, and location of any books, documents, or other tangible things and the identity and location of persons having knowledge of any discoverable matter. The information sought need not be admissible at the trial if the information sought appears reasonably calculated to lead to the discovery of admissible evidence.

(2) Limitations. By order or by local rule, the court may alter the limits in these rules on the number of depositions and interrogatories and may also limit the length of depositions under Rule 30 and the number of request under Rule 36. The frequency or extent of use of the discovery methods otherwise permitted under these rules and by any local rule shall be limited by the court if it determines that: (i) the discovery sought is unreasonably cumulative or duplicative, or is obtainable from some other source that is more convenient, less burdensome, or less expensive; (ii) the party seeking discovery has had an ample opportunity by discovery in the action to obtain the information sought; or (iii) the burden or expense of the proposed discovery outweighs its likely benefit, taking into account the needs of the case, the amount in controversy, the parties' resources, the importance of the issues at stake in the litigation, and the importance of the proposed discovery in resolving the issues. The court may act upon its own initiative after reasonable notice or pursuant to a motion under subdivision (c).

(3) Trial Preparation: Materials. Subject to the provisions of subdivision (b)(4) of this rule, a party may obtain discovery of documents and tangible things otherwise discoverable under subdivision (b)(1) of this rule and prepared in anticipation of litigation or for trial by or for another party or by or for that other party's representative (including the other party's attorney, consultant, surety, indemnitor, insurer, or agent) only upon a showing that the party seeking discovery has substantial need of the materials in the preparation of the party's case and that the party is unable without undue hardship to obtain the substantial equivalent of the materials by other means. In ordering discovery of such materials when the required showing has been made, the court shall protect against disclosure of the mental impressions, conclusions, opinions, or legal theories of an attorney or other representative of a party concerning the litigation.

A party may obtain without the required showing a statement concerning the action or its subject matter previously made by that party. Upon request, a person not a party may obtain without the required showing a statement concerning the action or its subject matter previously made by that person. If the request is refused, the person may move for a court order. The provisions of Rule 37 (a)(4) apply to the award of expenses incurred in relation to the motion. For purposes of this paragraph, a statement previously made is (A) a written statement signed or otherwise adopted or approved by the person making it, or (B) a stenographic, mechanical, electrical, or other recording, or a transcription thereof, which is a substantial verbatim recital of an oral statement by the person making it and contemporaneously recorded.

(4) Trial Preparation: Experts.

(A) A party may depose any person who has been identified as an expert whose opinions may be presented at trial. If a report from the expert is required under subdivision (a)(2)(B), the deposition shall not be conducted until after the report is provided.

(B) A party may, through interrogatories or by deposition, discover facts known or opinions held by an expert who has been retained or specially employed by another party in anticipation of litigation or preparation for trial and who is not expected to be called as witness at trial, only as provided in Rule 35(b) or upon a showing of exceptional circumstances under which it is impracticable for the party seeking discovery to obtain facts or opinions on the same subject by other means.

(C) Unless manifest injustice would result, (i) the court shall require that the party seeking discovery pay the expert a reasonable fee for time spent in responding to discovery under this subdivision; and (ii) with respect to discovery obtained under subdivision (b)(4)(B) of this rule the court shall require the party seeking discovery to pay the other party a fair portion of the fees and expenses reasonably incurred by the latter party in obtaining facts and opinions from the expert.

(5) Claims of Privilege or Protection of Trial Preparation Materials. When a party withholds information otherwise discoverable under these rules by claiming that it is privileged or subject to protection as trial preparation material, the party shall make the claim expressly and shall describe the nature of the documents, communications, or things not produced or disclosed in a manner that, without revealing information itself privileged or protected, will enable other parties to assess the applicability of the privilege or protection.

(c) Protective Orders. Upon motion by a party or by the person from whom discovery is sought, accompanied by a certification that the movant has in good faith conferred or attempted to confer with other affected parties in an effort to resolve the dispute without court action, and for good cause shown, the court in which the action is pending or alternatively, on matters relating to a deposition, the court in the district where the deposition is to be taken may make any order which justice requires to protect a party or person from annoyance, embarrassment, oppression, or undue burden of expense, including one of more of the following:

(1) that the disclosure or discovery not be had;

(2) that the disclosure or discovery may be had only on specified terms and conditions, including a designation of the time or place;

(3) that the discovery may be had only by a method of discovery other than that selected by the party seeking discovery;

(4) that certain matters not be inquired into, or that the scope of the disclosure or discovery be limited to certain matters;

(5) that discovery be conducted with no one present except persons designated by the court;

(6) that a deposition, after being sealed, be opened only by order of the court;

(7) that a trade secret or other confidential research, development, or commercial information not be revealed or be revealed only in a designated way; and

(8) that the parties simultaneously file specified documents or information enclosed in sealed envelopes to be opened as directed by the court.

If the motion for a protective order is denied in whole or in part, the court may, on such terms and conditions as are just, order that any party or other person provide or permit discovery. The provisions of Rule 37(a)(4) apply to the award of expenses incurred in relation to the motion.

(d) Timing and Sequence of Discovery. Except when authorized under these rules or by local rule, order, or agreement of the parties, a party may not seek discovery from any source before the parties have met and conferred as required by subdivision (f). Unless the court upon motion, for the convenience of parties and witnesses and in the interests of justice, orders otherwise, methods of discovery may be used in any sequence, and the fact that a party is conducting discovery, whether by deposition or otherwise, shall not operate to delay any other party's discovery.

(e) Supplementation of Disclosures and Responses. A party who has made a disclosure under subdivision (a) or responded to a request for discovery with a disclosure or response is under a duty to supplement or correct the disclosure or response to include information thereafter acquired if ordered by the court or in the following circumstances:

(1) A party is under a duty to supplement at appropriate intervals its disclosures under subdivision (a) if the party learns that in some material respect the information disclosed is incomplete or incorrect and if the additional or corrective information has not otherwise been made known to the other parties during the discovery process or in writing. With respect to testimony of an expert from whom a report is required under subdivision (a)(2)(B) the duty extends both to information contained in the report and to information provided through a deposition of the expert, and any additions or other changes to this information shall be disclosed by the time the party's disclosures under Rule 26(a)(3) are due.

(2) A party is under a duty seasonably to amend a prior response to an interrogatory, request for production, or request for admission if the party learns that the response is in some material respect incomplete or incorrect and if the additional or corrective information has not otherwise been made known to the other parties during the discovery process or in writing.

(f) Meeting of Parties; Planning for Discovery. Except in actions exempted by local rule or when otherwise ordered, the parties shall, as soon as practicable and in any event at least 14 days before a scheduling conference is held or a scheduling order is due under Rule 16(b), meet to discuss the nature and basis of their claims and defenses and the possibilities for a prompt settlement or resolution of the case, to make or arrange for the disclosures required by subdivision (a)(1), and to develop a proposed discovery plan. The plan shall indicate the parties' views and proposals concerning:

(1) what changes should be made in the timing, form, or requirement for disclosures under subdivision (a) or local rule, including a statement as to when disclosures under subdivision (a)(1) were made or will be made;

(2) the subjects on which discovery may be needed, when discovery should be completed, and whether discovery should be conducted in phases or be limited to or focused upon particular issues;

(3) what changes should be made in the limitations on discovery imposed under these rules or by local rule, and what other limitations should be imposed; and

(4) any other orders that should be entered by the court under subdivision (c) or under Rule 16(b) and (c).

The attorneys of record and all unrepresented parties that have appeared in the case are jointly responsible for arranging and being present or represented at the meeting, for attempting in good faith to agree on the proposed discovery plan, and for submitting to the court within 10 days after the meeting a written report outlining the plan.

(g) Signing of Disclosures, Discovery Requests, Responses, and Objections

(1) Every disclosure made pursuant to subdivision (a)(1) or subdivision (a)(3) shall be signed by at least one attorney of record in the attorney's individual name, whose address shall be stated. An unrepresented party shall sign the disclosure and state the party's address. The signature of the attorney or party constitutes a certification that to the best of the signer's knowledge, information, and belief, formed after a reasonable inquiry, the disclosure is complete and correct as if the time it is made.

(2) Every discovery request, response, or objection made by a party represented by an attorney shall be signed by at least one attorney of record in the attorney's individual name, whose address shall be stated. An unrepresented party shall sign the request, response, or objection and state the party's address. The signature of the attorney or party constitutes a certification that to the best of the signer's knowledge, information, and belief, formed after a reasonable inquiry, the request, response, or objection is:

(A) consistent with these rules and warranted by existing law or a good faith argument for the extension, modification, or reversal of existing law;

(B) not interposed for any improper purpose, such as to harass or to cause unnecessary delay or needless increase in the cost of litigation; and

(C) not unreasonable or unduly burdensome or expensive, given the needs of the case, the discovery already had in the case, the amount in controversy, and the importance of the issues at stake in the litigation.

If a request, response, or objection is not signed, it shall be stricken unless it is signed promptly after the omission is called to the attention of the party making the request, response, or objection, and a party shall not be obligated to take any action with respect to it until it is signed.

(3) If without substantial justification a certification is made in violation of the rule, the court, upon motion or upon its own initiative, shall impose upon the person who made the certification, the party on whose behalf the disclosure, request, response, or objection is made, or both, an appropriate sanction, which may include an order to pay the amount of the reasonable expenses incurred because of the violation, including a reasonable attorney's fee.

V. Title 28 U.S. Code, Judiciary and Judicial Procedure.

§ 1782. Assistance to foreign and international tribunals and to litigants before such tribunals

(a) The district court of the district in which a person resides or is found may order him to give his testimony or statement or to produce a document or other thing for use in a proceeding in a foreign or international tribunal, including criminal investigations conducted before formal accusation. The order may be made pursuant to a letter rogatory issued, or request made, by a foreign or international tribunal or upon the application of any interested person and may direct that the testimony or statement be given, or the document or other thing be produced, before a person appointed by the court. By virtue of his appointment, the person appointed has power to administer any necessary oath and take the testimony or statement. The order may prescribe the practice and procedure, which may be in whole or part the practice and procedure of the foreign country or the international tribunal, for taking the testimony or statement or producing the document or other thing. To the extent that the order does not prescribe otherwise, the testimony or statement shall be taken, and the document or other thing produced, in accordance with the Federal Rules of Civil Procedure.

A person may not be compelled to give his testimony or statement or to produce a document or other thing in violation of any legally applicable privilege.

(b) This chapter does not preclude a person within the United States from voluntarily giving his testimony or statement, or producing a document or other thing for use in a proceeding in a foreign or international tribunal before any person and in any manner acceptable to him.

VI. CALIFORNIA CIVIL PROCEDURE CODE

§ 410.10 [long-arm statute] (West 1973 & Supp. 1995)

§ 410.10 Basis

A court of this state may exercise jurisdiction on any basis not inconsistent with the Constitution of this state or of the United States.

VII. ILLINOIS COMPILED STATUTES ANNOTATED ch 735, para. 5/2-209 [long-arm statute] (Michie 1997)

§ 735 ILCS 5/2-209. Act submitting to Jurisdiction —Process

Sec. 2-209. Act submitting to jurisdiction — Process.

(a) Any person, whether or not a citizen or resident of this State, who in person or through an agent does any of the acts hereinafter enumerated, thereby submits such person, and, if an individual, his or her personal representative, to the jurisdiction of the courts of this State as to any cause of action arising from the doing of any of such acts:

(1) The transaction of any business within this State;

(2) The commission of a tortious act within this State;

(3) The ownership, use, or possession of any real estate situated in this State;

(4) Contracting to insure any person, property or risk located within this State at the time of contracting;

(5) With respect to actions of dissolution of marriage, declaration of invalidity of marriage and legal separation, the maintenance in this State of a matrimonial domicile at the time this cause of action arose or the commission in this State of any act giving rise to the cause of action;

(6) With respect to actions brought under the Illinois Parentage Act of 1984, as now or hereafter amended [750 ILCS 45/1 et seq.], the performance of an act of sexual intercourse within this State during the possible period of conception;

(7) The making or performance of any contract or promise substantially connected with this State;

(8) The performance of sexual intercourse within this State which is claimed to have resulted in the conception of a child who resides in this State;

(9) The failure to support a child, spouse or former spouse who has continued to reside in this State since the person either formerly resided with them in this State or directed them to reside in this State;

(10) The acquisition of ownership, possession or control of any asset or thing of value present within this State when ownership, possession or control was acquired;

(11) The breach of any fiduciary duty within this State;

(12) The performance of duties as a director or officer of a corporation organized under the laws of this State or having its principal place of business within this State;

(13) The ownership of an interest in any trust administered within this State; or

(14) The exercise of powers granted under the authority of this State as a fiduciary.

(b) A court may exercise jurisdiction in any action arising within or without this State against any person who:

(1) Is a natural person present within this State when served;

(2) Is a natural person domiciled or resident within this State when the cause of action arose, the action was commenced, or process was served;

(3) Is a corporation organized under the laws of this State; or

(4) Is a natural person or corporation doing business within this State.

(c) A court may also exercise jurisdiction on any other basis now or hereafter permitted by the Illinois Constitution and the Constitution of the United States.

(d) Service of process upon any person who is subject to the jurisdiction of the courts of this State, as provided in this Section, may be made by personally serving the summons upon the defendant outside this State, as provided in this Act, with the same force and effect as though summons had been personally served within this State.

(e) Service of process upon any person who resides or whose business address is outside the United States and who is subject to the jurisdiction of the courts of this State, as provided in this Section, in any action based upon product liability may be made by serving a copy of the summons with a copy of the complaint attached upon the Secretary of State. The summons shall be accompanied by a $5 fee payable to the Secretary of State. The plaintiff shall forthwith mail a copy of the summons, upon which the date of service upon the Secretary is clearly shown, together with a copy of the complaint to the defendant at his or her last known place of residence or business address. Plaintiff shall file with the circuit clerk an affidavit of the plaintiff or his or her attorney stating the last known place of residence or the last known business address of the defendant and a certificate of mailing a copy of the summons and complaint to the defendant at such address as required by this subsection (e). The certificate of mailing shall be prima facie evidence that the plaintiff or his or her attorney mailed a copy of the summons and complaint to the defendant as required. Service of the summons shall be deemed to have been made upon the defendant on the date it is served upon the Secretary and shall have the same force and effect as though summons had been personally served upon the defendant within this State.

(f) Only causes of action arising from acts enumerated herein may be asserted against a defendant in an action in which jurisdiction over him or her is based upon subsection (a).

(g) Nothing herein contained limits or affects the right to serve any process in any other manner now or hereafter provided by law.

VIII. NEW YORK CIVIL PRACTICE LAW AND RULES; § 302 [long-arm statute] (Bender 1997 Redbook)

§ 302. Personal jurisdiction by acts of non-domiciliaries.

(a) Acts which are the basis of jurisdiction. As to a cause of action arising from any of the acts enumerated in this section, a court may exercise personal jurisdiction over any non-domiciliary, or his executor or administrator, who in person or through and agent:

1. transacts any business within the state or contracts anywhere to supply goods or services in the state; or

2. commits a tortious act within the state, except as to a cause of action for defamation of character arising from the act; or

3. commits a tortious act without the state causing injury to person or property within the state, except as to a cause of action for defamation of character arising from the act, if he

(i) regularly does or solicits business, or engages in any other persistent course of conduct, or derives substantial revenue from goods used or consumed or services rendered, in the state, or

(ii) expects or should reasonably expect the act to have consequences in the state and derives substantial revenue from interstate or international commerce; or

4. owns, uses or possesses any real property situated within the state.

(b) Personal jurisdiction over non-resident defendant in matrimonial actions or family court proceedings. A court in any matrimonial action or family court proceeding involving a demand for support, alimony, maintenance, distributive awards or special relief in matrimonial actions may exercise personal jurisdiction over the respondent or defendant notwithstanding the fact that he or she no longer is a resident or domiciliary of this state, or over his or her executor or administrator, if the party seeking support is a resident of or domiciled in this state at the time such demand is made, provided that this state was the matrimonial domicile of the parties before their separation, or the defendant abandoned the plaintiff in this state, or the claim for support, alimony, maintenance, distributive awards or special relief in matrimonial actions accrued under the laws of this state or under an agreement executed in this state. The family court may exercise personal jurisdiction over a non-resident respondent to the extent provided in sections one hundred fifty-four and one thousand thirty-six of the family court act.

(c) Effect of appearance. Where personal jurisdiction is based solely upon this section, an appearance does not confer such jurisdiction with respect to causes of action not arising from an act enumerated in this section.

IX. OHIO REVISED CODE ANNOTATED 2307.382 [long-arm statutes] (Anderson 1997)

§ 2307.382 Personal jurisdiction.

(A) A court may exercise personal jurisdiction over a person who acts directly or by an agent, as to a cause of action arising from the person's:

(1) Transacting any business in this state;

(2) Contracting to supply services or goods in this state;

(3) Causing tortious injury by an act or omission in this state;

(4) Causing tortious injury in this state by an act or omission outside this state if he regularly does or solicits business, or engages in any other persistent course of conduct, or derives substantial revenue from goods used or consumed or services rendered in this state;

(5) Causing injury in this state to any person by breach of warranty expressly or impliedly made in the sale of goods outside this state when he might reasonably have expected such person to use, consume, or be affected by the goods in this state, provided that he also regularly does or solicits business, or engages in any other persistent course of conduct, or derives substantial revenue from goods used or consumed or services rendered in this state;

(6) Causing tortious injury in this state to any person by an act outside this state committed with the purpose of injuring persons, when he might reasonably have expected that some person would be injured thereby in this state;

(7) Causing tortious injury to any person by a criminal act, any element of which takes place in this state, which he commits or in the commission of which he is guilty of complicity;

(8) Having an interest in, using, or possessing real property in this state;

(9) Contracting to insure any person, property, or risk located within this state at the time of contracting.

(B) For purposes of this section, a person who enters into an agreement, as a principal, with a sales representative for the solicitation of orders in this state is transacting business in this state. As used in this division, "principal" and "sales representative" have the same meanings as in section 1335.11 of the Revised Code.

(C) When jurisdiction over a person is based solely upon this section, only a cause of action arising from acts enumerated in this section may be asserted against him.

X. TEXAS CIVIL PRACTICE AND REMEDIES CODE § 17.042 (1997)[long-arm statute in suit on business transaction or tort]

§ 17.042. Acts Constituting Business in This State

In addition to other acts that may constitute doing business, a nonresident does business in this state if the nonresident:

(1) contracts by mail or otherwise with a Texas resident and either party is to perform the contract in whole or in part in this state;

(2) commits a tort in whole or in part in this state; or

(3) recruits Texas residents, directly or through an intermediary located in this state, for employment inside or outside this state.

TABLE OF CASES

TABLE OF CASES

TOPIC INDEX

A

B

C

D

E

L